PRAISE FOR *SUBVERSIVE SOUTHERNER*

"*Subversive Southerner* is filled with powerful gifts that we need in these difficult times when many Americans seem to have forgotten that the central vocation that binds us together as citizens is 'to form a more perfect union,' to expand our democracy beyond the limits of its best possibilities. Catherine Fosl's carefully researched and thoughtful story tells of Anne Braden, a remarkable representative of that courageous, unsung group of native white southerners who risked their social status and their lives to stand openly with the African American freedom movement of the post–World War II years. This book is both a reminder of important forgotten history and a source of inspiration to those of us who are committed to the continued democratic re-creation of our nation. In our time of 'war against terrorism,' it is good to be reminded that Braden had to face not only the white terrorism and bitter ostracism of her native region, but also had to stand firm with her husband, Carl Braden, against the fierce anticommunism that was often used against workers for racial democracy during the Cold War. The fact that it is Anne Braden who remains and not the anti-democratic system of southern legal segregation strongly suggests that we need not be permanently shackled by the culture of our origin."

—Vincent Harding,
Co-Chairperson, The Veterans of Hope Project
and Professor of Religion and Human Transformation,
Iliff School of Theology

"Anne Braden's life as a social activist spans more than half a century, and her story is as instructive as it is inspirational. Catherine Fosl's marvelous biography does justice to her subject, and that is high praise indeed. The old cliché certainly applies here: I could not put this book down and did not want it to end."

—John Dittmer,
Crandall Professor of History,
DePauw University

"Catherine Fosl's book is filled with insights into the lives of Anne Braden and her husband Carl, prophetic dissenters from the orthodox racism of the mid-twentieth century South. But this is no narrow-gauged biography. In vivid and moving prose, Fosl places Anne Braden in the context of a changing South and shows her readers how and why the Bradens joined with others in fighting to destroy a world in which white men ruled, white women served, and black Southerners were supposed to remain docile and subservient."

—Dan T. Carter,
Educational Foundation Professor of History,
University of South Carolina

SUBVERSIVE SOUTHERNER

ANNE BRADEN AND THE STRUGGLE FOR RACIAL JUSTICE IN THE COLD WAR SOUTH

Catherine Fosl

First published 2002 by
PALGRAVE MACMILLAN™
175 Fifth Avenue, New York, N.Y. 10010 and
Houndmills, Basingstoke, Hampshire, England RG21 6XS.
Companies and representatives throughout the world.

PALGRAVE MACMILLAN is the global academic imprint of the Palgrave
Macmillan division of St. Martin's Press, LLC and of Palgrave Macmillan Ltd.
Macmillan® is a registered trademark in the United States, United Kingdom
and other countries. Palgrave is a registered trademark in the European Union
and other countries.

ISBN 0–312–29487–5 hardback

Library of Congress Cataloging-in-Publication Data
Fosl, Catherine.
Subversive southerner : Anne Braden and the struggle for racial justice in the
Cold
War South / by Catherine Fosl.
    p. cm.
  Includes bibliographical references.
   ISBN 0–312–29487–5
   1. Braden, Anne, 1924-   2. Women civil rights workers—Southern
States—Biography.   3. Civil rights workers—Southern States—Biography.
4. White women—Southern States—Biography.   5. African Americans—
Civil rights—Southern States—History—20th Century.   6. Civil rights
movements—Southern States—History—20th century.   7. Southern
States—Race relations.   8. Louisville (Ky.)—Race relations.   9. Louisville
(Ky.)—Biography.   I. Title.

E185.98.B73 F67   2002
305.8'00973—dc21

                                                                                  2002074836

A catalogue record for this book is available from the British Library.

Design by Letra Libre, Inc.

First edition: November 2002
10 9 8 7 6 5 4 3 2 1

Printed in the United States of America.

To my sons,
Isaac and Elijah

The dark ancestral cave, the womb from which mankind emerged into the light, forever pulls one back—but . . . you can't go home again. . . . You can't go back home to your family, back home to your childhood . . . to one's youthful idea of . . . "art" and "beauty" and "love," back home to the ivory tower . . . back home to someone who can help you, save you, ease the burden for you, back home to the old forms and systems of things which once seemed everlasting but which are changing all the time—back home to the escapes of Time and Memory.

—Thomas Wolfe, *You Can't Go Home Again*
(New York: Harper & Row, 1940;
reprint 1998), 666.

When we are 80 years old, I think we will have no regrets.

—Anne Braden to Carl Braden, prison correspondence,
February 17, 1955

CONTENTS

Foreword by Angela Y. Davis   ix
Acknowledgments   xii
List of Abbreviations   xv
Chronology of Anne Braden's Life   xvii
Introduction   xx

PART ONE

Prologue   The Power of Place   3
Chapter 1   A White Southern Childhood   13
Chapter 2   Intellectual Awakening   33
Chapter 3   Alabama Newspaperwoman   57

PART TWO

Chapter 4   Political Awakening   83
Chapter 5   Marriage and Movement   103
Chapter 6   The Wade Case—No Turning Back   135
Chapter 7   Fighting Back—The 1950s Resistance Movement   175
Chapter 8   A Voice Crying in the Wilderness—
             Early SCEF Years   201

PART THREE

Chapter 9   The Mass Civil Rights Movement—
             Beginning of a New Day   245

Chapter 10 Opening Up the Southern Police State   269
Chapter 11 End of an Era   293

PART FOUR

Chapter 12 The Next Three Decades:
            The Struggle Continues   313
Epilogue   333

Notes   343
Bibliography   393
Index   407

16 pages of photos appear between pages 242 and 243

FOREWORD

Angela Y. Davis

WHEN CATHERINE FOSL AND ANNE BRADEN began collaborating on this history of Anne's radical activism during the Cold War years, they could not have predicted how dramatically it would resonate with current political conditions. This riveting account of dangerous alliances across racial boundaries can now be read as an incisive reflection on the importance of challenging the Bush administration's aggressive policies in the aftermath of the 2001 attack on the World Trade Center. The labeling of much opposition to U.S. foreign policy (and especially the war on Afghanistan) as "unpatriotic" recalls in a startling way the depiction of anti-racist activism as "un-American" during the Mc-Carthy era. If we recognize these historical parallels, then perhaps we should also be prepared to learn from those who resisted easy indifference or active co-operation with the anticommunist practices of the post–World War II period.

Subversive Southerner covers Anne Braden's life before and during the era of the civil rights movement. As Catherine Fosl reminds us, after more than 50 years of campaigns, protests, and advocacy, Anne Braden still devotes her life to the eradication of racism. She surely knows that her work has enabled vast and often spectacular social changes—changes that most of her contemporaries during the 1950s would never have been able to imagine. I hope she also recognizes how much she helped to reconfigure the very terrain on which social movements are organized. When we challenge structural racism and violence by vigorously defending immigrant rights, opposing violence against women, and protesting the prison industrial complex, we should know that we are also upholding the legacy of struggle that emerges from Anne's life story.

I consider myself extremely fortunate to have learned about Anne Braden's obsession with racial equality when I was still quite young. During my two high school years living in New York with the family of the Rev. William Howard Melish, I listened avidly to Reverend Melish's accounts of the work of Anne and her husband, Carl, and I met Carl on several occasions. They all worked together in the Southern Conference Educational Fund, and I ardently read each issue of SCEF's *Southern Patriot*, which Anne began to edit in 1957. I will never forget Carl's last visit to New York before he surrendered to federal authorities on May 1, 1961. I was so impressed by his demeanor—he did not behave like a man about to spend the next year of his life in prison—that when I myself was arrested a little less than 10 years later, I was profoundly heartened by my old memories of Carl's amazing courage at the moment of his entry into prison.

The era during which I came to know Anne as a friend and colleague—from 1972 to the present—follows the period emphasized in this book. In 1972, I had been politically active for only 10 years and considered Anne Braden—who had been working by then for more than 20—a legend. I had read *The Wall Between* while still in high school and knew about her myriad encounters with the belligerent guardians of Kentucky's white supremacy. Anne and Carl were the first white southerners I knew personally who were willing to put themselves on the line no matter what the consequences. As a small child growing up during the era of segregation in Birmingham, Alabama, literally on the border of a white neighborhood, I witnessed the bombings and burnings of homes indirectly purchased by black families (as was the case in the Braden's proxy purchase of the Wade family home and its subsequent bombing). For me, the Bradens symbolized the possibilities of a different future for the South.

After my acquittal, I had the privilege of working closely with Anne in the National Alliance Against Racist and Political Repression, the organization that succeeded the National United Committee to Free Angela Davis and All Political Prisoners. Charlene Mitchell, the central organizer of the campaign for my freedom, had insisted that we try to harness the powerful resources that had been generated in this successful effort. As I reflect on our initial organizing attempts, I remember how absolutely excited Anne was about the prospect of creating a national organization that would emphasize grassroots activism. Because I already thought of Anne as a historical figure, I was utterly impressed by her ability to sustain such a passionate engagement with struggles of the '70s. There were obvious continuities with Anne's previous work. We developed campaigns against the Ku Klux Klan in North Carolina and designed model legislation that helped pave the way for laws against hate crimes. We generated support for university professors who stood to lose their jobs because of their progressive political activities. And in an attempt to subvert prevailing assumptions regarding the perpetrators of "crime," we exposed what we called "police crimes" by inviting international jurists to conduct hearings on the conduct of police departments in some of the country's major urban centers.

But the major focus of our work was political prisoners. Among our earliest cases were the Attica prisoners charged in connection with the September 11, 1971, rebellion, Lolita LeBron and the Puerto Rican nationalists, American Indian Movement activists, and the Rev. Ben Chavis and the Wilmington Ten. While Anne used her extensive network in the South to garner support for all these political prisoners, she was especially committed to Ben Chavis and his codefendants. If North Carolina, she argued, was representative of the "New South," then it was important for people to know that the imprisonment of Ben Chavis and the Wilmington Ten was merely the most visible aspect of a deep-going pattern of racist repression in that state. At that time there were more political prisoners in North Carolina and more people on death row than in any other state.

As I came to know Anne Braden through our mutual involvement in the work of the Alliance, I realized that her deep commitment to the South was and remains the major theme around which she has forged her identity. Her work to free Ben Chavis—which consumed the better part of a decade—was indicative of an unrelenting dedication to transform the world of the South. It is precisely this dedication that *Subversive Southerner* strives to share with us. Unlike many people who measure the significance of their lives by a sense of their own prominence, Anne likes to position herself in the background. Each time I have visited Louisville, I have left inspired by the degree of solidarity among many different kinds of people there—ministers and church people, students and unionists. Anne always positions herself as only one member of such coalitions. Thanks to Anne's incorrigible optimism—and her willingness to do whatever work is necessary—the Kentucky Alliance Against Racist and Political Repression has survived and has continued to attract new members even though the national structure no longer exists. We established the Alliance in 1973. Almost 30 years later, the Alliance still has an important presence in the political life of Kentucky, taking up new issues and struggles that point to the persistence of racism in its contemporary manifestations and mutations. I attribute this continuity to Anne Braden's obstinacy as an anti-racist activist. She refuses to give up.

ACKNOWLEDGMENTS

"MOMMY, HOW MUCH LONGER WILL YOU be writing your book?" That plaintive question was one my youngest son put to me often as the new century arrived. I wish I could say I had churned this book out quickly, but everyone who knows me also knows that is not the case. As the years have mounted up, so has the list of people whose contributions were vital to the book's creation. To thank each one would take another book, but there are some whose names I must call.

First on that list is the Kentucky Foundation for Women, which made this book possible by providing generous initial research funding and then a second grant in the home stretch. Judi Jennings, the foundation's director and a good friend, gave me particular encouragement and support. Other grant providers include the Spring Foundation for Women in Contemporary Society, which awarded me a 1994 dissertation writing grant, and the Kentucky Oral History Commission, for interview stipends and transcription assistance. I owe a special thanks to the Mary Anderson Center for the Arts, a lovely writers and artists retreat in southern Indiana, and to its staff—especially Sarah Yates and Debra Carmody—for providing me with a haven for writing that allowed me to get started on this book and then, amazingly, to finish it. And many thanks to the University of Louisville's Commonwealth Center for the Humanities and Society, and to its director, Tom Byers, for providing me with my first "real" academic job—and thus the means to apply myself to getting the book out.

My editor, Debbie Gershenowitz, has been unflinchingly supportive and enthusiastic even when she delivered the sternest advice, and I surely appreciate it. When she got as excited as I had over the photo selection, I knew my instincts about her fit with me and this book had been correct. Readers of various drafts and sections strengthened the book considerably, and I thank especially Mike Honey, Mary Odem, Jacquelyn Hall, Elizabeth Keyser, Tracy

K'Meyer, Nancy Theriot, John Dittmer, and Blaine Hudson—who all took time from their own busy schedules to read, comment, and sometimes comfort. The preeminent biographer in my life for the years of this project's gestation was Dan Carter, who directed Phase One—my dissertation. I was his final student at Emory University, and to him I owe perhaps the greatest intellectual debt. Dan has been a wonderful editor, mentor, friend, and maybe even therapist who always believed in me and in the people and things I was writing about. I am also grateful to Robin Kelley and Clayborne Carson, without whose encouragement I might never have entered Emory's Department of History.

My appreciation goes out to all the wonderful librarians, archivists, and library assistants in Alabama, Georgia, Virginia, Wisconsin, Tennessee, and Kentucky who helped me uncover or access hidden bits of information, but I must at least mention the support of two. One is Harry Miller, who oversees the Braden Papers at the State Historical Society of Wisconsin and who handled all my requests with patience, efficiency, and good humor. The other is Ella Peregrine—my friend, former student, and lay-archivist-extraordinaire, who helped with nit-picking details and endless positive energy as my project wound to a close.

Biographers collect people's stories, and I thank all those who shared theirs with me through interviews or over cocktails or coffees. They helped me to understand the freedom movement emotionally and to shape an image of Anne Braden that covered her whole life and not just the period I have known her. People such as Andrew Wade, the late Lyman Johnson, Bill Allison, Suzy Post, Eric and the late Mary K. Tachau, Tom Moffett, Fred Shuttlesworth, Jane Stembridge, Connie Curry, Joan Browning, Julian Bond, Bob Moses, Bob Zellner, Gwen Patton, Carla Wallace, and Ilene Carver inspired me more than they know. So many people from Anne's youth offered reflections and relics that amplified her young life: among the most generous were Jean Willett, Elise Ayers Sanguinetti, Allen Draper, Edith Alston, Mary Evelyn Jefferson, and Dot Silver.

I couldn't have managed without my friends. Liz Natter listened and read and soothed and listened some more. Betsy Brinson kept my confidence above water and gave me a great example to follow. Gary Washington taught me about race and, when I began, helped me stay strong as a single mother. June Walker's support follows me through everything I do. Drue Barker and Ellen Spears offered unfailing encouragement. Lin Billingsley was my resource person for Louisville and more: she read my work and listened cheerfully to my moaning about it even as she rescued me from a bevy of minor technical disasters.

My grandmother, Carolyn Bohn Sullivan, who raised me, imparted to me a love of the past, of learning, and of Louisville without which this book would never have been possible. She was my muse. I also thank my Bohn family in Louisville, especially Aunt Liz Bohn; they welcomed me as their own. When I was overwhelmed by it all, my wise and wonderful sons, Isaac and Elijah, were usually sympathetic, and they always reminded me there was life past my computer and archive boxes. I look forward to spending it with them, and I appreciate the sacrifices they have made, as well as Isaac's technical assistance.

There are two others, last but never least, whose contributions to this book I find difficult to describe. One is my spouse, Peter Fosl (that's "Foster" + "Wasel"): loving, loyal, available, and indispensable with his broad knowledge of so many things, his technical wisdom, his unflagging faith in me and in this book, his wit and good humor, and his endless willingness to go to the ends of the earth if necessary to help. I would not be who I am today without him. The final thanks goes to my subject and friend, Anne McCarty Braden, who is one of the more amazing human beings I have ever known. Anne asks a lot of people, but she gives a lot in return. She walked down this long road with me even when she did not fully trust where I was going, and I have learned much from as well as about her. For that opportunity I am eternally grateful.

The best in these pages stems from all of these folks and more; the shortcomings are all my own.

LIST OF ABBREVIATIONS

ACLU	American Civil Liberties Union
ACMHR	Alabama Christian Movement for Human Rights
AFSC	American Friends Service Committee
AP	Associated Press
CCPAF	Citizens' Committee to Preserve American Freedoms
CIO	Congress of Industrial Organizations
CORE	Congress of Racial Equality
CP	Communist Party
CRC	Civil Rights Congress
ECLC	Emergency Civil Liberties Committee
ELSA	Episcopal League for Social Action
FE	Farm and Equipment Workers' Union
FEPC	Fair Employment Practices Commission
FOR	Fellowship of Reconciliation
FP	Federated Press
HUAC	House Committee on Un-American Activities
ILD	International Labor Defense
KCLU	Kentucky Civil Liberties Union
KKK	Ku Klux Klan
LUAC	Louisiana Joint Legislative Committee on Un-American Activities
NAACP	National Association for the Advancement of Colored People
NCAHUAC	National Committee to Abolish the House Un-American Activities Committee
NCC	National Council of Churches
NSA	National Student Association
NWPC	National Women's Political Caucus
R-MWC	Randolph-Macon Woman's College
SCEF	Southern Conference Educational Fund

SCHW	Southern Conference for Human Welfare
SCLC	Southern Christian Leadership Conference
SDS	Students for a Democratic Society
SISS	Senate Internal Securities Sub-Committee
SRC	Southern Regional Council
SNCC	Student Nonviolent Coordinating Committee
SNYC	Southern Negro Youth Congress
SOC	Southern Organizing Committee for Economic and Social Justice
SSOC	Southern Student Organizing Committee
UAW	United Auto Workers
UE	United Electrical Workers
VEP	Voter Education Project
WCC	White Citizens' Councils
WDC	Wade Defense Committee
WECC	West End Community Council
WILPF	Women's International League for Peace and Freedom

CHRONOLOGY OF ANNE BRADEN'S LIFE

July 28, 1924   Born Anne Gambrell McCarty, Louisville, KY
1931–1941   Anniston, AL, childhood
1941–1945   Attends Stratford College, Randolph-Macon Woman's
                    College, VA (B.A., English, 1945)
1945–1948   Reporter for *Anniston Star, Birmingham News, Louisville
                    Times*
June 21, 1948   Marries Carl James Braden in Louisville
1948–1951   Works for left-wing unions, tobacco factory, various
                    short-term jobs
September 15, 1951 Gives birth to James McCarty Braden, Louisville
February 17, 1953   Gives birth to Anita McCarty Braden, Louisville
1954   With Carl, buys home on behalf of Andrew and Char-
                    lotte Wade in segregated Louisville suburb (May);
                    house is dynamited (June); grand jury indicts Bradens,
                    five other whites for sedition (October); Carl convicted
                    of sedition, sentenced to 15 years (December)
July 1955   Carl released on bond, pending appeal
1956   After Bradens organize national protest and in wake of
                    Supreme Court decision nullifying state sedition laws,
                    Carl's conviction and indictments against Anne and
                    other defendants thrown out
1957   With Carl, joins staff of Southern Conference Educa-
                    tional Fund (SCEF) to mobilize white southern civil
                    rights support. Anne becomes editor of *Southern Patriot*
                    newspaper covering regional desegregation
1958   *The Wall Between*, Anne's memoir, is published, be-
                    comes National Book Award finalist

1958–1959	Carl refuses to answer questions of House Un-American Activities Committee southern hearings on First Amendment grounds, is convicted of contempt of Congress, sentenced to year in prison, appeals
July 30, 1959	Commonwealth's Attorney Scott Hamilton commits suicide, Louisville
February 7, 1960	Anne gives birth to Elizabeth McCarty Braden, six days after Greensboro, NC, sit-in sparks new student civil rights movement
1961	U.S. Supreme Court upholds Carl's contempt conviction; on May 1, he enters federal prison; Anne initiates clemency drive, headed by Martin Luther King, Jr.; Anne recruits Bob Zellner for Student Nonviolent Coordinating Committee white student project
1962	Carl Braden released from prison; Bradens and Fred Shuttlesworth organize first interracial mass meeting in Birmingham in 24 years; in August, Carl is red-baited in *Jackson Daily News*
June 1963	Bradens' daughter Anita diagnosed with terminal heart-and-lung disease
October 1963	SCEF's New Orleans headquarters raided; SCEF director Jim Dombrowski charged with violating Louisiana's anti-subversive law
June 9, 1964	Death of Anita McCarty Braden, Louisville
Mid-June 1964	Anne, Carl "uninvited" from Ohio training session for Mississippi Freedom Summer
1965–1967	Carl, Anne become SCEF executive, associate directors; move headquarters to Louisville (January '66); implement broadened (economic justice) program with Southern Mountain Project and Deep South GROW
September 11, 1967	Anne and Carl charged with sedition with three other SCEF staff after Pikeville, KY, raid
September 14, 1967	A federal court declares Kentucky sedition law unconstitutional
April 4, 1968	Martin Luther King assassinated, prompting mass uprisings, including one in Louisville that leaves two dead, six indicted for conspiracy
1973–1974	Bradens depart SCEF; organization splits, later disintegrates

February 18, 1975   Carl dies of heart attack, Louisville

1975–1979   Anne helps establish Southern Organizing Committee for Economic and Social Justice (SOC); spearheads biracial opposition in Louisville to white antibusing violence; Anne and SOC organize responses to southern Ku Klux Klan resurgence

1980–1989   Anne plays key role in bringing 10,000 to Greensboro in 1980 protest of Klan/Nazi murders; continues linking peace, women's, environmental crusades with antiracism; builds white support for Jesse Jackson presidential runs, serving as alternate delegate to Democratic Convention in '84 and delegate in '88

1990–2001   Anne receives ACLU's first Roger Baldwin Medal of Liberty, precipitating other honors, culminating with her own and Carl's 2001 induction into Kentucky Civil Rights Hall of Fame; *The Wall Between* is re-released in 1999; her work against white supremacy continues regionally with SOC and locally with the Kentucky Alliance

INTRODUCTION

IN MAY OF 1954 MOST SOUTHERN COMMUNITIES were reeling from the *Brown v. Board of Education* decision, in which the U.S. Supreme Court struck down school segregation. In Louisville, Kentucky, however, housing desegregation was just as much in the news after a local white couple bought a new suburban home on behalf of two African American friends, Andrew and Charlotte Wade, who were unable to buy it themselves because of racial restrictions in real estate. On Saturday, May 15, 1954, two days before the Supreme Court announcement, the Wades moved into their new house and were greeted by white neighbors who burned a cross on the lawn, threw a rock into the living room bearing the epithet "Nigger go home," and shot out the windows as they slept. With only a mild rebuke for the neighborhood's racist attack, the Louisville *Courier-Journal*, the most liberal and respected of southern newspapers, harshly criticized the white woman and her husband for "forcing an issue of race relations in [an] artificial and contrived way" by buying the house for occupancy by blacks. Threats and harassment of the Wade family continued for weeks, and on June 27 a charge of dynamite destroyed part of the house. The bombers were never brought to justice, but in September 1954 the white man and woman who originally bought the home found themselves the target of a grand jury investigation that focused not on the antiblack violence, but on their own beliefs, associations, and reading materials. The two were labeled "Communists" and their purchase of the house a Communist plot undertaken to stir up racial unrest. They, along with five other white supporters, were charged with sedition against the state of Kentucky for their role in the Wade purchase.[1]

Dramatic even by the standards of Cold War America, gripped as it was by anticommunism, the case drew national attention because of the obviously racist motives driving it, and it became something of a cause célèbrè for the beleaguered American left. Rather than retreating into crushed anonymity from political activism as so many left-wingers did during the period, the white couple used their case as a platform to speak ever more forcefully against segregation and, against incredible barriers, to deepen their involvement in the burgeoning civil rights movement of the 1950s.

The young white woman at the center of that sensationalized case was Anne McCarty Braden, and her life is the subject of this book. The word "integration" is almost obsolete today, but in the South of the mid-twentieth century it was a fire word for some and, for others, a hopeful vision of a more humane society free of racial barriers. Anne stands very nearly alone among women of her race, class, region, and generation in her single-minded dedication to that vision.

Anne Braden came of age at the end of WWII, part of the last generation of southern whites to grow up under Jim Crow segregation so blatant and static on the southern cultural and political landscape that, for Anne, it took an internal explosion to throw off the lessons of her childhood. Hers was a transitional generation, on the front lines of postwar racial, gender, and economic upheaval. She came of age after the women's rights/social reform crusaders of the early part of the century and after the more broadly based social protesters moved to action by the urgency of the Great Depression, but before the young activists who formed the ranks of the 1960s student civil rights movement and later the antiwar and women's liberation movements.[2]

During WWII, in the close-knit women's community she found at two genteel Virginia women's colleges, Anne's political transformation began as an intellectual awakening born when she met other intellectuals and New Dealers critical of segregation. It continued when she saw the ugly underbelly of racial hierarchy as a young reporter covering the Birmingham courthouse, and it matured when she met activists in the left wing of Louisville's postwar labor movement. The timing of Anne's becoming a radical (as she describes herself) is particularly provocative because her commitment to racial and social justice was nurtured in the late 1940s, when dissent was all but silenced, especially among white southerners, by equating it with disloyalty in the gathering force of what one historian has called the "anticommunist purge" of a domestic Cold War.[3]

Anne became a supporter of the African American freedom movement at a time when white southern allies were few and getting fewer, but her commitment to integration outlasted the violent opposition to it. She is one of the few slender threads tying southern protest movements of the 1930s and 1940s to

the new mass civil rights movement that sprang up in 1960 and to the continuation of racial justice campaigns in the last quarter of the twentieth century.
Through her more than 50-year immersion in racial justice activism, Anne's life
has intersected on some level with the great social movements of her lifetime.[4]

Unlike most white southerners of her generation and earlier ones who
disagreed with their politicians' desperate, unwavering embrace of white supremacy, Anne Braden did not become an exile from either her region or her
race. Instead, she concentrated her efforts on awakening the consciences of
white southerners. In doing so, she provoked the wrath of southern political
officials many times, beginning with the sedition case in 1954, which branded
her and her husband, Carl, as "red." As Carl Braden awaited trial and was then
convicted of sedition and sentenced to fifteen years' imprisonment, Anne traveled and spoke widely, fighting back against the powerful silencing of anticommunist hysteria and alerting civil liberties supporters nationwide to the
particular links being made in the South between efforts against segregation
and cries of "communist!" subversion.[5]

After a U.S. Supreme Court decision reversed Carl's conviction and all remaining charges were dropped, Anne and Carl Braden were political and social pariahs. Yet the fury unleashed on them had convinced Anne especially of
how wrongheaded the white South was, and they elected to remain in
Louisville and to remain active. Already outcasts in their hometown, they became regional field organizers in 1957 for an outcast organization—the
Southern Conference Educational Fund, or SCEF. SCEF's aim was to generate southern support for desegregation, especially among whites, but amid the
convulsive fear of communism that punctuated the era, any questioning of
segregation tainted one as "red." SCEF's program was made more controversial by its unwillingness to purge suspected communists from its own ranks, a
position that had already brought it under persistent investigation by the
House Un-American Activities Committee (HUAC).

In this hostile climate, the Bradens spent the next 16 years crisscrossing
southern highways working to counter the racism and opposition to integration so prevalent in southern white culture. They took turns with field work
and staying at home caring for their three children, and Anne edited SCEF's
Southern Patriot newspaper, which publicized southern desegregation battles
in and outside the region and to countered the isolation among the small
pockets of southern integrationists and leftists who refused to be driven out by
southern-style McCarthyism.[6]

"The Bradens," as most coworkers knew them, were working against the
grain. Yet other forces were also at work which would shortly infuse their efforts.

The Montgomery bus boycott had already taken place by the time they joined the SCEF staff. As journalists, Anne and Carl were instrumental in helping to publicize school desegregation struggles that were shaking up regional complacency. Then, when the student sit-ins started in early 1960, the couple brought their organizing and media know-how to bear on a new generation. Anne in particular impressed the young student activists with her passionate dedication to ending racism, journalistic expertise, knowledge of a network of activists nationwide, and—perhaps most important—her way of collaborating without attempting to dominate. Her stories in the *Patriot* on the sit-ins gave the students their first analytical coverage, and Anne helped to craft a compelling image of the student movement that widened both its self-consciousness and its threat to the status quo. Yet the tag "communist" also followed her through 1960s mass civil rights protest and beyond. That taint consigned her and Carl to relative invisibility, even among liberals, and won them another sedition indictment in 1967 for a SCEF campaign they spearheaded to organize Kentucky's Appalachian poor against strip mining.

When the mass civil rights movement blended and was repressed back into the larger social fabric as the 1970s arrived, Anne did not stop. For three decades since, and in spite of Carl's unexpected death in 1975, she has continued to campaign for racial and social justice, retaining close ties with African Americans but directing her voice of conscience mostly to other whites. She has carried her message of whites' joint responsibility to oppose racism to the women's, labor, peace, and environmental movements, where her activist seniority has given her a kind of authority.[7]

In the small but persistent subculture of social justice crusaders who have been an ongoing feature in American life, Anne Braden is known as one of the most enduring and reliable of white anti-racist activists, an icon for the few southern white women who, like her, rebelled wholeheartedly against their culture. Her influence has perhaps been most profound on those who experienced for a while the "beloved community" of the early 1960s southern civil rights movement, especially the first organizers of the Student Nonviolent Coordinating Committee (SNCC). The historian Sara Evans, writing on the young women in SNCC, found that Anne stood out as virtually the only southern white woman of her generation who was living a life of principles to which the young women and whites of SNCC could relate. More than three decades after the demise of SNCC, ex-members remain in awe of Anne's commitment.[8]

In her native Louisville, she has not been famous so much as infamous. The 1954 sedition case kept the Bradens' names in local headlines, and in its aftermath they remained notorious as the city's resident "common-ists" and agitators. Within a few years of Carl's death in 1975, two of Anne's cars had been torched, but she eventually found greater acceptance for her relentless anti-racist campaigning. Although her words are usually directed to whites, she has remained lodged primarily within the black community of Louisville's West End—in the same house she has lived in for 50 years, the same one segregationists marched on in 1954.[9]

While Anne has been a leader in the southern freedom movement for half a century and helped to shape SCEF's identity through her editorship of its *Southern Patriot*, she has retained the persona of a rank-and-file activist, especially in her hometown, churning out leaflets and making phone calls until late into the night. Her leadership has been of a more decentralized variety than that of more well-known movement leaders. That is partly because—like that of her friend Ella Baker (an African American organizer some years her senior whom many 1960s aficionados hail as a "mother" to the student civil rights movement)—Anne's style of leadership has been participatory, intentionally staying in the background while nudging others to take the lead. More important, however, anticommunist ideology was so potent in the wake of the 1950s McCarthy era that Anne Braden had to struggle for legitimacy even within the civil rights movement itself. Such ostracism forced her to keep a low profile in movement activities to avoid attracting a hail of criticism to any causes she championed, especially in Louisville. Yet over the years she has found it an effective strategy for cultivating new leadership. As a consequence of all of these factors, she appears only at the margins or, more commonly, in the acknowledgments of most major civil rights histories.[10]

In 1988 I discovered a copy of *The Wall Between*, Anne's then out-of-print memoir of her sedition case. The worn red volume stayed with me so much that on impulse I wrote to her, asking her to think about working with me on a book about her life. I had never met her, but through my participation in women's peace activism of the 1980s I had heard her hard-hitting words at a demonstration. She was coming to my home city, Atlanta, shortly after, and we met by the reflecting pool at the Martin Luther King memorial. I believe she was touched by my sincerity; I remember mostly her tiny frame, her candor, her steady gaze, and the ambivalence with which she agreed to consider my proposal. As a writer herself and as someone whose actions had been frequently misrepresented for public consumption, she was understandably wary of opening her life to a stranger, but hesitantly agreed to some oral history interviews and to grant me access to her manuscript collection.[11]

The approach to this book has changed in the years since Anne and I first contemplated it. The collaboratively authored autobiography we first decided upon fell by the wayside, partly because she was too consumed by activism to devote time to it. I too changed over the years, becoming an academically trained historian instead of simply a writer of history, and I grew increasingly interested in feminist biography. Finally, the fields of civil rights history and women's biography have also been transformed. Since 1988, there has been a flowering of literature that studies women's contributions to that movement in the form of community histories, oral history autobiographies, biographies, and collective memoirs, including—most recently—the particulars of white women's experiences in the movement.[12]

That fateful meeting with Anne at the reflecting pool eventually catapulted me into the emotionally and intellectually complicated world of biography with a living subject. Even the word "subject"—though I use it for lack of a better substitute—is mildly onerous and depersonalizing. Anne Braden never wanted a biography written about her, but neither was she about to take time off to write or even cowrite her own story. We thus engaged in a battle of wills that persisted for years, until I was finally able to convince her that, conceptually, what I was doing was just not that different from a "life and times" account that used her experiences to reflect on larger themes of politics and culture.

This book, written primarily in third-person narrative, is generously peppered with Anne's words, taken from a variety of oral histories done with her by me and others. Because she is such a forceful writer, I have included substantive excerpts from her published and unpublished writings. Long before the rise of identity politics, Anne laid claim, forcefully sometimes, to an identity that is white, southern, female—and radical. Each of these elements is inseparable from the person she became. This biography can capture the sources and sustenance of her identity only in part, but I have tried to include enough of her voice to convey a generous sense of who she was and is. The prose voices are thus constantly shifting, a process I have attempted to make clear by italicizing Anne's words wherever they appear.[13]

I believed and still believe in her agency, not in the rarefied pages of my text but in the real world in which she remains deeply engaged. My end product, I believed strongly, needed to be something she could live with because that is just what she, more than I, would be forced to do. That conviction sets me apart from many of my peers and immediately summons critics who fear a compromise of that holiest of the historians' crafts, "critical distance." What distance may have been lost in the process of working with a living subject, however, is more than compensated for by the insights and immediacy that derive from my direct access to Anne and to others' impressions of her less mediated through the lenses of time and sentimentality. Interpretation of the subject, after all, is only a small part of historical biography: interpretation of her times and culture is ultimately the more demanding task.

This book explores the making of a crusader, but I am also fascinated by the forces that keep one going. What has captivated me the most about Anne Braden's activist life is her absolute immersion in the struggles for racial and social equality. Anne's tenacity, I found, has come from—and in turn been reinforced by—the fusion of her social and political commitments with her life as a whole. Her biography, like those of other women activists, helps to illuminate not only how the "personal is political," as women's liberationists audaciously announced in 1968, but also how the political necessarily gets personal. In other words, a lifetime of sustained activism is enormously draining. There is a huge personal cost to trying to change power relations, especially perhaps for women who also take on the pleasures and burdens of family life.[14]

But what stands out more is Anne's remarkable resiliency—her ability to keep on struggling against racism in the face of institutional barriers and a social ostracism that was at times totalizing. A basic quality of hers, one she shares with most longtime advocates, is a real appreciation for people, whatever their politics. Anne dearly loves not just to talk but to listen, and her optimistic view of human nature has been dimmed only scantily by the opposition she has faced. What has sustained her most fully, it seems, is the camaraderie she found with fellow activists even in the repressive years of the 1950s and has continued to find throughout her life. As she wrote in 1999, *Everyone needs roots, a home. I had to separate myself from the corrupt society I was born into; I found a new home in the "other America," in its current incarnation in the social justice movements of my time, and in the sense of connection to a past and a future.*[15]

Ultimately, for Anne, the "other America" is always and profoundly personal—the major source of her resiliency—and as such has found its way into these pages thematically as a cornerstone of what gave and gives her life meaning. But it is also political, a forceful reminder of the power of culture—in this case, an oppositional culture—in any understanding of politics or social change. The creation and sustenance of a radical subculture was an integral part of the beleaguered but lively social justice movement of the 1940s. What historians know as the "Old Left" held out not only the prospect of long-term structural social change, but also a liberating alternative worldview, friendship network, music, literature, and even jargon from the stiflingly narrow provinces of mainstream U.S. and southern culture. In the other America Anne discovered in 1948, besieged as it was by the onset of anticommunist hysteria, one could cross the color line, offer scathing criticism of "male supremacy," find more relaxed attitudes about sexual expression, and hear the latest in jazz or folk music—all among friends. That other America was never entirely extinguished by Cold War anticommunism. It was reborn in new forms in the 1960s and thrives still in the new century within an American political landscape that remains, in the majority, hostile or indifferent to the idea of fundamental social changes toward social and racial justice. Culture, as Anne's story attests, is a key ingredient in keeping activists going.[16]

I have known and interviewed Anne over a period of more than a decade, but I have also had access to oral histories that were done with her nearly 30 years ago. Though all human memory tends to reinscribe its own memories, her narratives have a continuity that is almost disturbing. I attach two kinds of meaning to that static quality. First and foremost is the powerful tenacity of racism into the twenty-first century, making Anne's message still extremely— troublingly—relevant. The other is as a metaphor for the script she has developed for her life: her kind of dedication and resiliency must come at some cost, and that cost has entailed a kind of tunnel vision (her word is *compulsion*) that is not entirely inflexible but also does not allow for a great number of new stimuli outside the general rubric of social inequality and race. Anne's inquiring mind gravitates easily to whatever topic is in front of her, and she has the endearing quality of attending totally to whomever she is speaking with. Yet even the books that she seeks out to push her thinking are nearly exclusively on this topic. There are moments when even she has bemoaned the narrowing of her intellectual interests, but she is more commonly stoical on the subject. Only a commitment so total could sustain a lifetime so focused on the overwhelming task of dismantling white supremacy.[17]

This book traces Anne's life in largely chronological fashion. Part One (prologue, chapters 1–3) examines her life from birth through early adulthood, locating the roots of her southern identity in her family history and finding in the intellectual awakening of her college years and early journalism career the origins of her transformation into a lifelong spokeswoman for southern racial change. Part Two (chapters 4–8) explores her discovery of and early life in the other America from 1947 to 1960, a period when the anticommunist witch hunts largely decimated the Old Left, leaving only a committed few southern white dissenters at the 1954 juncture when legal segregation officially ended. Chapter 5, the only chapter that is more topical than chronological, examines Anne's marriage to Carl and their family life over 27 years together. Part Three, comprising chapters 9–11 and covering the period of roughly 1960–1967, discusses the passionate eruption of the mass freedom movement that the Bradens had hoped for and helped to facilitate. The final section, Part Four, is only one chapter (12), in which I summarize Anne's continued justice crusades in the nearly four decades since legal segregation was demolished and the right to dissent established in the South. Though Cold War anticommunism no longer had the crippling effect that it had in the postwar years, her struggles for racial justice were far from over. An epilogue offers a synthesis of her life that reflects on more than 50 years of unbroken white southern antiracist activism in the form of a dialogue between Anne and me that took place once this book was otherwise complete.

As the book's title suggests, my primary emphasis is on the Cold War years, from 1947 to 1967. A zest to "win" the Cold War gave the United States an imperative to enact civil rights reforms at home in order to project a democratic image abroad. But domestic anticommunism also severely narrowed the discussion of what reforms were possible and discredited those, like Anne, who might espouse wider social changes. Her experiences in that time and space form an almost perfect illustration of the powerful buttress that anticommunism provided for segregation and its proponents until the southern *police state*, as she has often referred to it, was broken and civil liberties established. Anne's unique odyssey as a white, anti-racist, activist woman in the post-WWII South began in a searingly painful process she has called *turning myself inside out* and persisted in spite of the best efforts of southern image-makers to discredit or demoralize her. Her unlikely political transformation in that crucible of the postwar South, the daring actions that sprang from it, and the torrent of anticommunist repression that rained on her for years because of it are the focal points of this book.[18]

In an era of resegregation, when many gains of the 1960s civil rights movement are under attack and even the federal courts boast of a social "colorblindness" that simply does not exist, Anne's life may seem not to have had much impact. But a focus on how unfinished remains the civil rights revolution to which her life has been dedicated misses the point of just how repressive the South was under Jim Crow segregation, particularly for African

Americans, but also for whites. Several generations of southerners who have known and worked with Anne have more to say of the hopeful symbol of a white southern conscience she has unwittingly become. That is the heart of the story contained here.

PART ONE

THE POWER OF PLACE

DURING THE MONTH OF JUNE, burnt-orange tiger lilies and purple thistle light up the fields as you drive along State Highway 55 on the edge of Kentucky's bluegrass. Every summer of her childhood, Anne McCarty would ride that road, winding past some of the state's prettiest horse country, in her father's Ford. At the end of the long day she would be delivered, along with her mother and brother, to her mother's family home in Eminence, an almost stereotypical rendition of the "sleepy little town" that abounds in southern literature. About thirty miles east of Louisville in the heart of tobacco country, Eminence was the highest point along the Louisville-to-Lexington Railroad.[1]

Anne spent long hours studying the sundial in her grandmother's flower garden or racing the length of the wraparound front porch to catch up with her brother and cousins as they left her behind to go riding on their ponies. As the youngest and the only girl cousin, she had to struggle even then against being excluded, as a little sister often must do.[2]

"Place" is a powerful concept for southerners, defensive after generations of hearing their region both extolled and reviled. Anne was born and has lived most of her adult life in Louisville, but in a way, Eminence is where her story begins. Her family connection to Eminence and its surrounding Henry

County was a constant throughout her young life, drawing her back there annually no matter where in the South the family was living that year. It was part of what drew her back to her native Kentucky as a young adult and what kept her there when many sought to drive her and her ideas away from the state.

By any measure, Anne is thoroughly a Kentuckian. Both sides of her family were among the early settlers of the land the Iroquois knew as "Kanta-ke," meaning "meadows." On her mother's side, her family history lays claim to eight generations in Kentucky, predating the birth of the republic itself. Her maternal ancestors came to Henry County six generations ago when land around Fort Harrod, Kentucky's first white settlement, became scarce at the dawn of the eighteenth century. Before that, Anne's great-great-great-great-great-grandmother—also named Anne—was one of the first few dozen pioneers to settle Kentucky with Daniel Boone in 1775.[3]

Since the antebellum era—when the idea of a uniquely southern identity took shape against a backdrop of growing outside criticism of the region's embrace of slavery—Anne's family members held firmly to their southern heritage. At the time of secession, her male forebears chose the Confederacy in a state that was deeply divided internally. At least one of her antebellum ancestors was opposed to slavery, but he and any others who might have been Unionists if not abolitionists had faded entirely from the family mythology as Anne heard it.[4]

Both of Anne's parents came from families who had held slaves and fought for the South in the Civil War, but her mother's branch was the more vehement about it, and it was that side of the family with whom Anne identified most deeply as she was growing up in the 1920s and 1930s. Like many early twentieth-century southerners who adopted the "lost cause" ideology sentimentalizing the Old South, Anne's mother, Anita Crabbe McCarty, viewed her heritage proudly, feeling that it helped to legitimize the family claim to being aristocratic, however modest their present economic circumstances. Both frontier Kentucky and the slave South became centerpieces of the family legendry, variations of the stories told in other white southern families as means of cementing youths' identities to the land and culture of their birth. The ties of place and history were impressed upon Anne repeatedly as a child, especially by her maternal great-grandmother, Mattie Owen Crabb. Anne was strongly imprinted by Mattie Crabb's stories, as she later recalled. *She lived alone in a tiny old house, and she was a cranky old lady, a demon really, who terrified the whole family. Mammy Crabb, we called her. Always on Sundays I had to go and Mammy Crabb would sit for hours and regale us with her tales of the Civil War. [She] was a very young woman during the Civil War and her husband had been in the Confederate Army . . . so she remembered it very well. There was a time when they were pretty wealthy. She was an ardent Democrat because she associated Republicans with Yankees and she hated Yankees. She always said anything was better than a Republican! Mother wanted me to hear all these stories so I could write a great American novel about it. This was before* Gone with the Wind, *you know. From me to Mammy Crabb it was just one more step back to the Revolutionary War. She remembered sitting as a child just the same way I did and listening to her great-grandmother, Mary Pogue, tell stories about growing up in Fort Harrod.*[5]

The ancestor who seemed to inspire most of the family folk tales and who sounded most fascinating to the child as she listened to them was Mary Pogue's mother, Anne Poage, one of Kentucky's earliest female pioneers. Swashbuckling tales of the pioneers' triumph over native peoples to settle Fort Harrod in 1776 were an integral part of the family lore, especially the proud claim that Anne Poage had given birth to the first white child born in Kentucky. Though the birth was in actuality the fourth, those early settlement narratives situated Anne Poage and her descendants right at the center of Kentucky history.[6]

Perhaps the fact that they shared a first name created an affinity between the two Annes, though if she was named for this ancestor, Anne McCarty's parents never told her so. But for whatever reason, the pioneer Anne—who had crossed the Cumberland Gap with four children, brought the first spinning wheel into Kentucky, and outlived four husbands—loomed larger than life in the mind of the imaginative youngster in the 1930s. Unconsciously perhaps, she began to see herself as one of a long line of commanding Kentucky women, dating back to Anne Poage, who could turn hardship into creativity. *I was fascinated by this five-times-great-grandmother of mine. I think she was a very strong woman. What I always heard—and this must have been word-of-mouth through the family—was that she sort of ran the fort. She was considered something of a tyrant by the men, even though they kept marrying her, because she insisted that they stick around the fort and till the land, whereas their inclination was to go out and fight Indians. I really think I would have liked her.*[7]

Visitors today to the Fort Harrod historic site will find Anne Poage McGinty memorialized there as the "epitome of a pioneer woman." At her grave—alongside that of the cabinetmaker William Poage, her second husband and father of all six of her children—is a historical marker. Nearby, her life is revisited in the "Ann [sic] McGinty Blockhouse," where during visitors' hours a woman in colonial dress displays quilts and demonstrates the "linsey-woolsey" cloth Anne Poage McGinty originated by weaving buffalo hair and nettle lint into what became the mainstay of pioneer clothing. No marker discusses the various legal actions taken by and against her, the land she amassed through the deaths of her husbands (at least three of whom were killed in conflicts with Native Americans), or the slave and indentured labor she used to run her various business ventures. Though the "ordinary" she established is re-created elsewhere in the fort, there is no acknowledgment of Anne McGinty as the first tavern operator in Kentucky.[8]

History has inscribed only her positive contributions to the culture of the emerging state and nation—those that affirm popular understandings of frontier womanhood. County records detailing her roles as "keeper of the public morals" in Harrodsburg suggest that she was a much more complicated presence two centuries ago, and that remains the case for her descendant Anne McCarty Braden, excoriated by many as a communist, a race traitor, a troublemaker. Well into the 1990s a few Louisvillians still winced at the name that inspired so many newspaper headlines in the 1950s, and more than a few Kentuckians would be loath to liken Anne Braden to her illustrious forebear, Anne Poage McGinty.

Yet it is impossible to make sense of Anne Braden's choices in the twentieth century without first understanding the depth of her roots in Kentucky and the origins of her steadfast claim to a southern identity. A particular vision of history played a powerful role in her upbringing, and though she was encouraged to see her place in the world through the eyes of her family's collective past, the conclusions that she reached from that history were dramatically different from those her elders hoped for.

———————

Besides the frontier conquest narrative, the other emphasis in the family mythology was on slavery and its bitter aftermath. Anne heard repeatedly as a child of the five slaves whom "Mammy" Crabb (born Mattie Owen) was to receive as a gift upon her marriage to William Crabb. But the Civil War disrupted that plan: instead, William Crabb left to fight under one of Kentucky's most dogged of Confederate generals, John Morgan. Four times the number of Kentuckians fought for the Union as for the Confederacy. Despite the numbers, however, Crabb was among a majority who disagreed with the direction of the Republican Party toward federal expansion and against slavery: in the 1860 presidential election, Abraham Lincoln received less than 1,500 votes from his home state.[9]

Although Kentucky remained in the Union and its legislature called on the Confederate Army to withdraw from the state, the Civil War itself proved pivotal in crystallizing a southern identity among many Kentuckians. Because of its strategic location at the river break of the vital Louisville & Nashville Railroad linking North and South, Louisville was designated a major staging area for troops moving southward and a supply base for western armies. The presence of Yankee troops had a grating effect on the local population, and the continuing debate over abolition put Kentuckians in an increasingly defensive posture facing south.[10]

The very gesture of the Emancipation Proclamation, viewed alongside federal debates over gradual, compensated emancipation and later recruitment of local blacks into the Union Army, made Kentucky slavemasters realize with alarm that the destruction of their way of life and the loss of a cumulative $7 million–$10 million investment were imminent. People like Mattie Owen and William Crabb clung even harder to their institutions as they crumbled. Nearly 100,000 African Americans were still enslaved in Kentucky by the end of the Civil War and only gained their freedom months later with the ratification of the Thirteenth Amendment in December 1865. Though they were never part of the stories Mammy Crabb detailed for her grandchildren, antiblack hostilities had become commonplace across the state by war's end, especially in Louisville, where black troops were stationed and into which thousands of former slaves poured as the war ceased.[11]

Mammy Crabb's reminiscences more than half a century later re-created for her great-granddaughter the post–Civil War Reconstruction era in Kentucky history in much the same way it was viewed by the majority of other white southerners of Crabb's class and time—a bad dream in which traditional race relations were turned upside down by Yankee "carpetbaggers" who profited from the proud but defeated white southerners, setting up corrupt governments kept afloat only by their manipulation of black voters eager for revenge against their former masters. In reality, there was very little real "reconstruction" in Kentucky: African Americans often faced greater discrimination there than they did farther south because the state remained so firmly under Democratic control. The state legislature defiantly refused to abolish slavery; to ratify the Thirteenth, Fourteenth, or Fifteenth amendments; or to enact legislation assisting former slaves. Black churches and the U.S. Freedmen's Bureau established some semblance of order, but hooded night riders terrorized rural blacks, and lynchings were an ever-present threat.[12]

The commonwealth's stance on race relations continued to be ambivalent, however. When the Fifteenth Amendment became law in 1870, Kentucky's legislature took no steps to prevent black voting, and blacks were never disfranchised as they were in much of the South. Louisville had a distinctly southern flavor to it, both before the war and more so after it, as ex-Confederates flocked in and garnered positions of power. Yet it was first and foremost a commercial center, and the constant flow of goods, people, and ideas made it a slightly more diverse, cosmopolitan place than major cities in other southern states.[13]

Little is known of the politics of Anne Braden's ancestors in the post–Civil War nineteenth century, but she was reminded constantly as a child of her male relatives' loyalty to the Confederacy. From 1870 well into the twentieth century, celebrations honoring the Confederate "lost cause" were a fixture of life in Louisville and its environs. In Eminence, Mattie Owen married William Crabb, and in 1867, at the age of 19, gave birth to their first and only surviving child, Lindsay Crabb, grandfather of Anne McCarty Braden. Over the next few decades, as Mattie recaptured the Old South fondly in story form, her family prospered in the New South through her husband's Blue Ribbon Whiskey distillery and, later, the fashionable Drennon Springs Hotel, a mineral-springs resort outside Eminence where the wealthy sought cures for anything from insomnia to gout.[14]

William and Mattie Crabb's son Lindsay (who for unknown reasons added an "e" to the spelling of the family name) followed his father into the distillery business and joined two prominent Henry County clans in 1888 when he married Agnes Thorne, daughter of another popular ex-Confederate politician, William P. Thorne, who later served as lieutenant governor. Anita Crabbe, who would become Anne Braden's mother, was their fourth child, born in 1896 into the shelter of two highly respected southern families.

William Crabb's hotel burned in 1909, and the arrival of Prohibition in 1919 sliced deeply into his prosperity. By the time she reached old age, Mattie Crabb had lost her husband, her son, and much of the grandeur of her midlife. Her glorious tales of earlier times were a kind of bulwark against the contrast of humbler circumstances.

While the foremothers and -fathers of Anne Braden were making fortunes and losing them, the period of the late nineteenth and early twentieth centuries was a nadir for African Americans, and Kentucky was no exception. By ruling that segregation was not discriminatory, the 1896 *Plessy v. Ferguson* Supreme Court decision demolished blacks' dreams of equal rights and became the benchmark for a host of other segregation laws passed by southern states. In Kentucky, the Jim Crow laws were patchwork, covering mental hospitals but not hospitals, schools but not libraries or parks. The state's most sweeping segregation ruling, aimed primarily at the integrated Berea College, was the 1904 Day Law, racially dividing all public and private schools.[15]

Ten years later—and ten years before Anne Braden's birth—the city of Louisville tried to pass an ordinance enforcing residential segregation, and the ensuing struggle resulted in the formation of a branch of the National Association for the Advancement of Colored People (NAACP). In 1917 the U.S. Supreme Court declared the ordinance unconstitutional and asserted the rights of property owners to sell to whomever they pleased, without restrictions according to race. The decision was a landmark for the NAACP nationally and established the Louisville branch as a vigorous defender of African American rights.[16]

With or without legal props, residential segregation patterns were remarkably fixed in practice, however, and the very idea that things should be otherwise inflamed whites. Various restrictive covenants (quasi-legal neighborhood agreements maintaining segregation in home sales) followed the defeat of the segregation ordinance. But white harassment of any blacks who dared to violate the color line in housing was the most effective form of deterrence, as Anne and Carl Braden would learn at midcentury.[17]

The hardening of Jim Crow segregation in the early twentieth century quieted but did not quell the turf battles pitting white privilege against black demands for access. Regionally, white families like Anne's contented themselves with the myth that segregation had been around forever and always would be, developing a "fortress mentality" about any kind of change. In Louisville, NAACP militancy and the numerical power of black voting strength were not sufficient to defeat Jim Crow, but black community leaders never let whites relax into it either. The association was most successful in curbing racial violence and securing black economic progress. When the Ku Klux Klan was reborn in the turbulent years preceding World War I, the NAACP won in 1920 the first statewide antilynching bill, which sought to suppress mob violence.[18]

Although race relations in Louisville were fraught with protest and negotiation, white supremacy went virtually unchallenged in rural Kentucky. In 1921 the Ku Klux Klan marched through the center of Eminence, and local whites turned out en masse to watch. Each year, whites attended the huge local Fourth of July celebrations at the Henry County fairgrounds on the edge of town without much thought to the absence of black faces.[19]

Anita Crabbe's frequent returns to Eminence throughout her childhood and as an adult brought her to the same insular community she and her mother before her had known since birth. When she left her parents' home to attend the University of Kentucky, she was the first woman in the family to attend college. There Anita became a reporter for the *Kentucky Kernel* newspaper, and she pledged Kappa Kappa Gamma, a prestigious sorority. At one of the many Greek social gatherings, she met a young Kappa Alpha man named Gambrell McCarty, who had a background very much like her own.[20]

Gambrell, the son of a pharmacist, was from Owensboro, in western Kentucky. His family too could be traced back to eighteenth-century frontier folk and had strong Confederate ties during the Civil War. Anita's and Gambrell's college romance was interrupted by U.S. entry into WWI, and he left for military service in the 801st Infantry. Anita never graduated, and the two were married in August 1918 while Gambrell, now a first lieutenant, was on leave from Camp Taylor. Fittingly, their wedding took place in the Thorne family home in Eminence. After the war the young couple settled in Louisville, and Gambrell began his career as a salesman for Allied Mills, a livestock feed company.[21]

The Kentucky in which Anita Crabbe and Gambrell McCarty began their lives together in the post-WWI era was a mixture of North and South and of racial confrontation and white complacency. But it was decisively the white southern complacency, mixed with a strong dose of family and regional pride, that had shaped Anita's consciousness, and this she tried to impart to her only daughter, Anne McCarty Braden. She was only partially successful: Anne claimed the southern identity but committed her life to undermining white complacency.

Anne Braden never lived in Eminence, but her attachment to it has gone hand in hand with a lifetime of activism that took aim at many of the values her family of origin held dear. She renounced those values but never the emotional ties of family and sense of place that were centered there. The power of Anne's rootedness to Eminence peppers any interview ever done with her, and when she lost loved ones later in life, she buried them there, alongside her ancestors. While she rarely went back to Henry County in her elder years, local history buffs followed her activities and claimed her as a native daughter even when they disagreed with the causes she espoused.[22]

Anne's family heritage, beginning with the adventurous pioneer grandmother whose name she shared, included a host of strong, independent women who left an impression on her for as far back as she could remember. Although whites in the several generations before her liked to think of themselves as highly separate from African Americans, her family also had an ongoing set of culturally characteristic experiences with race that touched Anne in a radically different manner than they had her forebears. She turned upside down the mythology of whiteness that had been imparted to her, from the tales of white frontier bravery against the so-called savagery of native peoples to those of plantation gentility as a treasured part of the family's past. From that mythology she drew a different conclusion: that having perpetrated so much injustice, it was now the task of southern whites to work with those they had disempowered to set the society right. Anne too made a claim on history, but it was a history of resistance to injustice that inspired her, and she turned the life that was expected of her inside out to join that resistance. The little girl Gambrell and Anita McCarty raised would someday be accused of trying to bring down the government of Kentucky, but her twentieth-century radicalism was nurtured from within a deep attachment to place and to a vision of that place as it might be.

CHAPTER ONE

A WHITE SOUTHERN CHILDHOOD

In Louisville, while it was understood that Negroes had a place and should be kept therein, it was also understood that Louisville was a better than average town where ugly, brutal, open racial friction was not the accepted thing.

W. E. B. DuBois once spoke of the life of the American Negro, and the limitations imposed upon it, as a life within a veil. Perhaps nowhere in America did his words ring truer than in Louisville. Through a veil I could perceive the forbidden city, the Louisville where white folks lived. . . . I knew that there were two Louisvilles, and in America, two Americas.

—Blyden Jackson, literary critic, on growing up in the 1920s, from *The Waiting Years: Essays on American Negro Literature*[1]

ANNE MCCARTY WAS BORN INTO THAT "Louisville where white folks lived" on July 28, 1924, at St. Anthony's Hospital. The benighted South around her was under sharp outside criticism for its religious fundamentalism, lagging educational and living standards, and staggering racial violence. As a border state, Kentucky managed to avoid some of that stigma, particularly by virtue of its culturally attuned largest city, which shared generously in the prosperity of the 1920s despite the blow Prohibition delivered to its liquor industry. Yet from Louisville, as from the rest of the South, African Americans fled in droves after WWI, leaving the manacles of Jim Crow with hopes of better opportunities north- and westward.[2]

Blacks' lives behind the veil were a blend of despair and the good times more popularly associated with the 1920s "jazz age." African Americans were limited mostly to laboring or domestic jobs, breaking into only the dirtiest, least secure industrial work. But on Walnut Street black-owned stores, services, and restaurants bustled with the support of all sectors of the black community. And within that community lemons became lemonade as African Americans built a lively esprit des corps from the largely separate world to which Jim Crow confined them.[3]

Still, the year of Anne McCarty's birth was one of bitter disappointment for African Americans in Louisville as they watched segregation encroach upon yet another area of their lives. As 1924 dawned, the NAACP branch was inactive and financially exhausted, but a June 13 confrontation changed that. Two black teachers were arrested after taking schoolchildren to picnic in Iroquois Park in Louisville's white South End. The group played without incident, but upon leaving, they were reprimanded by park guards. The teachers reacted by standing on their constitutional rights and resisting arrest. Indeed there was no law mandating segregated parks; yet an NAACP protest campaign yielded little, and the judge who heard the case ruled that segregation was enforceable because it was established practice. The teachers received a reprimand from the board of education, which asserted that segregation "allays friction," adding the threat that future offenders would be "enemies of the social order . . . and . . . summarily dismissed." The NAACP would fight that battle for three decades more before overturning park segregation in 1955.[4]

———

No such humiliations plagued the McCarty family in white Louisville. With a small home in the Highlands and a newborn daughter to complement their son, Lindsay, born four and a half years earlier, Gambrell and Anita McCarty were optimistic about their future. Their Louisville was the good-times setting of F. Scott Fitzgerald's best-selling *The Great Gatsby*, which the following year would immortalize the era as the Roaring Twenties. The story that most captivated local newspaper readers on the day of their daughter's birth concerned a young Maryland woman tarred and feathered in her small town as a punishment for too much partying.[5]

Not much of the family mythology surrounding Anne's birth was passed down to her. Her name came from those of both her parents. "Anita" means "Little Anne," so they called her Anne, and her middle name was Gambrell, after her father. As a child she was always referred to by both names—Anne Gambrell—in keeping with the southern predilection for "double names."[6]

The family's stay in Louisville after Anne's birth was brief—only six months—because professional success at Allied Mills demanded frequent moves of Gambrell McCarty in his early years as a salesman. The following five years were spent in Jackson and Columbus, Mississippi, where Anne completed her first year of school after excelling on a test given her to determine her readiness to enter first grade at the age of five. She surprised her mother by filling in the correct date on the test, which Anne reported afterward that she had figured out by counting forward the few days since the "Eight of May," a date she remembered—oddly, her mother thought—from their maid's absence. The woman had explained to the young Anne the day's meaning—a holiday celebrating the end of slavery in Columbus's black community—and the story remained with her.[7]

By the time Anne reached second grade, the family had moved again, this time to her father's hometown of Owensboro, Kentucky. They then relocated to Lexington, Kentucky, where she finished that school year, and then to Little Rock, Arkansas. Those constant moves made the link to Eminence that much stronger for Anita McCarty—and consequently for her children—and they spent at least a month there every summer. As the Depression hardened its grip on the South in the late 1920s, times were increasingly tight, and Gambrell was lucky to keep his job even if it did mean moving often. Little from the moving around stayed with Anne. She drew from her earliest years only a stable sense of emotional security within her family.[8]

The next move took the McCartys back to the Deep South, and it was there that Anne would spend most of her youth. In November 1931, the family settled in Anniston, a mill/industrial town in northeast Alabama in the iron ore–rich southern Appalachian foothills. Settled in 1872, Anniston was among the more prosperous of late nineteenth-century New South industrial ventures. Promoted as a "model city" by regional boosters such as Atlanta's Henry Grady, Anniston drew investors' families as well as their dollars, becoming a thriving community dotted with Victorian mansions and charming gabled cottages on one side of the railroad tracks, and two-room shotgun houses populated by blacks and working-class whites on the other. The tracks underscored race and class differences and helped to shape neighborhoods that reinforced those divisions. By the 1920s, Anniston, with a population of 22,000, was the world's largest producer of iron pipe and Alabama's third-busiest center of industry.[9]

The coming of the Great Depression did not entirely paralyze Anniston industry, but severely crippled it. Textile mills and some pipe and chemical companies continued to operate throughout the 1930s, though at reduced hours and wages, and only one bank closed. By the time the McCartys arrived in late 1931, Noble Street—the center of town activity—remained deceptively bustling, and crowds filled the Ritz Theatre nightly. Still, business declined sharply, and the agricultural economy in surrounding Calhoun County went from bad to worse as cotton prices plummeted. Every week the *Anniston Star* reported two or three mortgage foreclosures on area farms.[10]

Anne, of course, saw the Depression through the eyes of a child. Her father's employment was stable, but she comprehended the wretchedness around her and was troubled by the moral conflicts it posed between haves and have-nots. *There was a constant stream of beggars coming by [our house] asking for food, sometimes 20 a night. People would get off the trains and go looking for food. They were all white; I guess blacks would've been afraid to come into a white neighborhood like that. My father would cook egg sandwiches for them—but sometimes Mother would get tired of it and turn them away. I really took the Bible seriously, and it said, "feed the hungry." I remember lying awake at night for fear she was going to hell.*[11]

Only the very rich were able to isolate themselves from the deprivation around them. Not only was the public regaled with horribly detailed daily news accounts on the radio; hundreds of local residents were themselves homeless, hungry, and bewildered. All through the early 1930s, charities struggled with marginal success to alleviate the suffering where government would not. Lean times in Anniston, as elsewhere, set the stage for a landslide victory for Franklin Roosevelt on November 8, 1932, in the nation's most difficult year of the Great Depression. Calhoun County voters backed FDR and his promise of recovery by seven to one, even though Hoover had carried the county in 1928. The McCarty household was part of that FDR tide.[12]

Alabama had a homegrown drama unfolding in the early 1930s that easily rivaled the excitement of the presidential race. On March 25, 1931, nine young African American men were accused of raping two white women aboard a freight train near the northern Alabama town of Scottsboro as they all rode the rails in search of work. Their fates sealed by local white hysteria and inflammatory press coverage, the "Scottsboro boys" (as they became known) were tried, convicted, and sentenced to death in three days' time. The death penalty was almost standard punishment in the South for black-on-white rape or assumed rape when such cases managed to reach trial, but what set the Scottsboro case apart from others like it was the initiative of the Communist

Party (CP) in bringing the episode to the world's attention. Up to that point, the CP in the United States had been primarily located in urban industrial areas outside the South, but the Scottsboro case presented an opening wedge for the party to put into practice its theoretical commitment to an interracial working-class movement. The Depression years gave new meaning to the manifesto the CP had issued at its 1919 founding—"Capitalism is in collapse." In the first three years of the Depression, CP membership doubled.[13]

Adding sex, race, and region to its class-based social critique, the party entered the Scottsboro case, charging that the "southern ruling class" was using the issue of black-on-white rape to inflame white fears and split interracial working-class unity. The CP dispatched a legal team to take over the young men's legal defense, demanding new trials. Telegrams from all over the world flooded the office of Alabama Governor Benjamin Miller, and newspapers everywhere covered the story.[14]

Alabama journalists and politicians reacted with characteristic defensiveness, reviling the Communists and applauding themselves for having avoided a lynching. A few Alabamians, however (mostly but not exclusively blacks and sharecroppers), began to meet secretly, raise money for the case, and organize unions, assisted by CP organizers sent south. Authorities and plantation owners brutally suppressed these tiny organizing drives, especially in rural areas, but only weeks before the 1932 presidential elections, the Communist Party turned out 1,000 interested locals for a rally in Birmingham. The Alabama CP became the party's largest southern group, though it worked against daunting odds in a climate that had little tolerance for dissent and even less for any cause considered "communistic," especially when members were so blatantly contemptuous of segregation. Alabama CP activists continually faced beatings, arrests, or even death, and blacks and whites were fearful of meeting together except in secret; yet they continued organizing and met with a few successes.[15]

Once Anne reached adulthood and joined the movement for racial and social change, the Scottsboro case would become an important symbol to her of the possibility of interracial mass action in the Deep South. But as a young child, a hundred miles to the east of Scottsboro, she knew nothing of the events there. *None of those stirrings of change impinged on me,* she would muse as an adult.[16]

Despite the tense racial atmosphere surrounding the Scottsboro drama and the more general backdrop of distress crafted by the Depression, Anne's childhood in Anniston was secure, even idyllic compared to the lives of many around her. The McCartys rented a house on Quintard Street, a fashionable, tree-lined boulevard just east of downtown, and Anne entered the Woodstock School, a public elementary school a short walk away. Three years later the family bought a two-story, dark green house with a wide, low-slung front porch down the block at 502 Quintard, and it was there that Anne spent the rest of her childhood.[17]

The family's household income was modest, but the McCartys were solidly middle-class and considered themselves part of what Anne later called the *southern aristocracy. . . . We were not wealthy, but we moved in those circles. In those days social status in the South depended more on family origin than money. If anybody had told my mother she was middle-class, she would have been insulted although economically that's exactly what she was. But she thought it a mark of great distinction that she was descended from the first settlers, and in Eminence her family was recognized as being among the leading families. I picked up that same sort of attitude Mother had: I was so sure I was part of the upper class of society, I didn't even have to think about it.*[18]

Without her extended family's reputation to rely on in Anniston, Anita McCarty worked hard to ensure social standing. She sought out the most elite families and actively discouraged her daughter's friendship with a neighboring child she considered socially inferior.[19]

The world of men was somewhat remote for Anne as she was growing up. She and her elder brother, Lindsay, were never particularly close. To her, he seemed a rather distant big brother who considered her a nuisance. She also never felt entirely at ease with her father as a child because of his extended absences, though she found him sweet and indulgent. More of Anne's time was spent with her mother and sometimes her grandmothers, both of whom spent long periods in the McCarty household, especially in winter. Both were widows who impressed Anne as independent women. Agnes, or "Nana," Crabbe turned stories into theatrical performances, holding listeners spellbound by acting out the parts of each character. Agnes Crabbe was also deeply involved in Democratic Party women's clubs in Kentucky. Gambrell's mother, Mai McCarty, known to her grandchildren as "Momma Mai," was an active participant in the Young Women's Christian Association (YWCA) and a patron of Chautauqua, an eclectic summer educational center that catered to elites. Both grandmothers loved expansive conversations, which Anne, frequently sitting among the adults, drank in. Still, the closest adult in Anne's young life was her mother, who encouraged her without ever fully understanding her.[20]

Anita McCarty valued education and achievement, but she was a generally conservative woman, and her own achievements had thus been bound by her need to devote herself to what she saw as the overarching roles of wife and mother. The McCartys' tendency to *live through their children*, as Anne has put it, was exacerbated in Anita's relationship with her daughter by the fact that she herself was a frustrated journalist and aspiring intellectual. Though she had been the only girl in her family to attend college, Anita had left school to get married when WWI began and had never worked outside the home. Anita came of age in the midst of the sweeping social movement that enfranchised women after 70 years of struggle, but she was never part of it, though she did support woman's suffrage and always voted. Like many young modern women of her time, Anita felt that one could not—indeed, should not—combine marriage and motherhood with a career, yet she tentatively hoped her daughter's generation might be different with social and technological advancements. If Anita ever regretted her own choices, she adamantly refused for the rest of her life to let Anne know it.[21]

Anita harbored plenty of ambition for her little namesake, however, and as Anne's academic promise began to show, once she entered school, her mother began to nudge her toward a career as a writer. By the time the family moved to Anniston, Anne was already immersed in the world of books: she wrote long letters and kept detailed diaries, even beginning a novel during the third grade. Anne had her first story accepted for publication in *Junior Home* magazine in March of 1933. Later that year she won a bicycle by being selected as the statewide winner of a contest to elicit the best advertising jingle for Keds sneakers. (Her brother had already won the family dog, "Keds," in the same contest a few years earlier.)[22]

Anne's diaries and recollections of her childhood years reveal a fairly typical—if unusually talented—middle-class youngster. A classmate remembered Anne's first day at their elementary school because of her long brown hair and "big eyes that just stared." Anne took dancing classes, spent much of her free time with neighborhood girlfriends, and went to the "picture show" (as the movies were commonly called) at every opportunity, at least once or twice a week. Like many of her peers, she was hopelessly enamored of Shirley Temple. In the summers she swam the cold mountain waters at nearby Camp Willett for Girl Scouts, unable to afford the more expensive faraway camps some of her friends attended.[23]

Once her children were settled into school, Anita McCarty turned to the PTA and other civic activities. She became a leader of the local Daughters of the American Revolution, and she enrolled Anne in a branch of the Children of the Confederacy. An organization formed decades earlier to indoctrinate southern youth into the culture of the Confederate "lost cause," the Children of the Confederacy had by Anne's generation evolved into more of a social club that might, at most, raise money for plaques commemorating Confederate heroes. (Ironically, as Anne would laugh years later, it was as secretary of this organization that she first learned the etiquette of taking minutes and chairing meetings.) The Wednesday Study Club, a reading group of well-to-do housewives whose teas were chronicled in the *Star*'s society pages, fed Anita's intellectual interests, and Anne observed her mother's painstaking preparations when it was her turn to present a book review and her pride when clubwomen applauded her efforts.[24]

Anita pointed out leading women journalists as role models for her daughter and made sure Anne got generous exposure to the world of letters. Whenever published authors, especially women, read in Anniston, Anita and Anne were there. Emma Gelders Sterne, a well-known author of children's books with relatives in Anniston, was one such writer whom Anne had occasion to meet and hear. Sterne, a Jewish Alabamian living in New York, had vastly more liberal social and cultural views than those of most white southerners, and the lessons Anne took from her were perhaps somewhat different from the ones Anita had intended. (A quarter of a century later Sterne and Anne became good friends, and Sterne memorialized Anne's sedition case in a juvenile readers' anthology titled *They Took Their Stand*.)[25]

Anita's encouragement spurred her daughter's accomplishments, but where Anne really found herself was through religion, which she has called the *motivating force* of her young life. Anita's religious background was Episcopalian, and upon arrival in Anniston she sought out Grace Episcopal Church, where she enrolled the children in Sunday school. (Gambrell was born a Baptist and remained one until later in life.) The first church built for whites and one of only two Episcopal churches in town, Grace was a tiny but elegant stone chapel in the prestigious east end of Anniston. Grace had always attracted a mostly elite following, a quality that added to its appeal for Anita McCarty.[26]

The privileged members of Grace, however, could not easily leave their religion behind when they left for Sunday dinner after services. For its denomination and its day, the congregation had an unusually high involvement in community service. Social service efforts were stimulated partly by a traditional sense of noblesse oblige among the South's upper classes and partly by the magnifying glass the Depression held up to the needs of their poor and working-class neighbors. More than any other motivator, it seems, was the passionate conscience of the Rev. Jim Stoney, a serious-looking bespectacled man who pastored Grace from 1921 to 1942. Stoney was informed by the social gospel

strain of early twentieth-century Protestantism, which evolved nationally in response to the grinding urban poverty associated with the dramatic rise in industrialization. Proponents of the social gospel suggested that the causes of
poverty could be found not merely in personal failings but in the social environment, and they emphasized Christians' responsibility to improve society as
well as to seek personal salvation. Stoney established several "missions" to provide medical and social services and ministry to poor whites in Anniston's mill
districts and rural outskirts. By the time the McCartys found Grace, community work with poor whites was a well-established part of its ministry.[27]

For Anne, Stoney was an influential moral presence: *I adored Jim Stoney.
He was a maverick, and yet he managed to stay at this church, and people liked him,
they just thought he was a little bit cuckoo. He always let them know they weren't the
only people in the world by trying to give those wealthier people an awareness of what
poverty was like. He didn't have any kind of radical social program; he was really
just suggesting giving to the poor, but there was enough of a caring atmosphere [that]
it influenced me because I'd never been around poor people just like I'd never been
around blacks.* Stoney encouraged children from the missions to attend Grace,
and Anne sensed that *over there was a world where people didn't have as nice a
clothes as I had.*[28]

The invitation to interact meaningfully with people different from herself
was a new one for Anne, and her realization of such people as more than just
objects was *almost intuitive*, as she later characterized it. The philosophy was a
contrast to that of her parents, who never questioned the perceived wisdom of
the hierarchies in southern white culture. *There was just nobody nicer and kinder
than my father, but he was Dr. Jekyll and Mr. Hyde if anyone challenged the society
he lived in. His was a fascist mentality—and I use that term advisedly—in that it
presumes there is a superior race or group of people. I never heard this put into words,
growing up. [Years later] when Daddy would argue with me about my mistaken ways,
he would quote [scholars], the theory being that anytime you mix dark- and light-
skinned peoples, the civilization declines, and that the last bastion of that pure Anglo-
Saxon blood is in the South because the North has gotten all mixed with the
immigrants. They thought that God looked with favor on them. When you grow up
with that sort of [thinking], you have nothing to measure it by. It was such a con-
stricted world that what I got in church was the only window out. In that kind of a situation, it's at least potentially radicalizing [to realize] there is another world out there
somewhere . . . a philosophy somewhere that says everybody is equal.*[29]

Anne's dawning awareness of social injustice was heightened with the arrival of Ralph Channon and Marshall Seifert in 1936 to work with Stoney,
whose commitment to Christian service drew like-minded church workers to

him. Seifert, not yet an ordained minister, headed a service-oriented youth group at Grace. Liberal, youthful, and very vibrant, he had a knack for what Anne has called *getting young people to think.* The Young People's Service League had regular discussions of contemporary moral issues that deepened Anne's developing social consciousness. *I remember one night, I might have been 13 or 14. There must have been a discussion of the "colored problem," which is what everybody called it if they talked about it at all. I made some mild comment to the effect that people ought to be treated equally no matter what color they were. I can remember people looking a little startled and then somebody coming up to me later and saying, "You shouldn't say things like that; people will think you're a communist." I had no idea what a communist was except I knew it was something bad.*[30]

"Captain" Ralph Channon came to Anniston as part of the Church Army, a quasi-monastic Episcopal service organization. Channon was in charge of the mission known as "Redeemer," and he immersed himself in west Anniston's poor Glen Addie mill neighborhood. Once he startled Anita McCarty's Women's Auxiliary by inquiring whether the women truly valued the humanity of poor people. Anne concluded later that Channon *really didn't have much use for the people of Grace Church.*[31]

The image of Channon's solidarity with the poor stayed with Anne. Years later, she became friends with Sam Hall, a leader of the Alabama Communist Party who had grown up only one block away from her in Anniston but was known to her as a child only as a friend's older brother. Hall too had a story of Channon's political influence when, as a young man troubled by racial and income disparities in Depression-era Alabama, he had once approached Channon looking for answers. Channon gave him none but reportedly recommended George Bernard Shaw's *An Intelligent Woman's Guide to Socialism,* and the book transformed Hall's politics and his life.[32]

Anne's induction into the church youth group during her eighth-grade year and her conversations with Seifert and Channon were the highwater marks of her youthful religious yearnings. Her religiosity and high-minded inquiries set her somewhat apart from Anita, whose concerns were more practical. The child's serious-mindedness seemed to her mother to become more apparent as she matured and expressed an interest in becoming a missionary. On her thirteenth birthday, Anne wrote a prayer in the form of a poem and presented it solemnly to her mother. *Dearest Lord Jesus. . . . Today I have entered my "teens." Childhood is behind me; girlhood is before me. . . . I have had such . . . carefree, hilarious times in work and play. . . . It is, therefore, with sadness that I step from it for I do not want to go. . . . I cannot see what may come upon me in the next hour, Lord Jesus, but I pray you give me courage to meet whatever it may be. Grant me hope and optimism in trouble, faith in sorrow, strength in temptation, courage in defeat and humiliation, love when people hate me, joy with thee in happiness, and mostly give me the grace to live a selfless life—willing to serve thee and my fellow-man with no thought for myself or my safety. With Thee . . . as my support, no matter how deep my trouble or how great my joy, I shall be able to . . . always feel that ahead, no matter how dark it seems, there is light around the next bend and somewhere off down that road a palm of victory.[33]*

The prayer reflects the intense self-awareness and idealism that would stay with Anne throughout her adolescence. It is tinged with a foreboding sense of doom that became more pronounced in her later teenage writings. The struggle against that doom is also oddly prescient of the tenacity she would exhibit as an adult. For her mother, the prayer was mildly troubling, a foreshadowing of their divergent outlooks on life.

Anne's intensity was not without its flaws. As a young child, her temper was so uncontrollable that she occasionally flung herself to the floor in kicking, screaming fits. As she matured, she could still explode in unexpected rages.

During her fourteenth year, Anne also discovered a passion for poetry. Flipping through one of her brother's college textbooks, she happened upon Edna St. Vincent Millay's "Renascence." Anne had never heard of Millay, and though she had studied poetry in school, she had never before felt its transformative power as she did upon reading Millay's verse. She later wrote about the experience: *I hid the book with all of the adolescent's feelings that no one can possibly understand the things that really matter. Possibly for the same reason I told no one about the experience. I knew that . . . I had discovered another world and childishly concluded that this poem alone held the key to that world. I hurried through lessons at night so that I could go to my room, close the door, extract the heavy volume from the cedar chest, and recapture that blinding sensation of spiritual exaltation.* Anne felt a pang of conscience for keeping the book but justified it on the basis of her solitary forays into a world she felt she could not share with those around her. The poem became a lifelong favorite.[34]

Anne's idealism meshed with widespread press coverage of the specter of fascism in Europe to make her fairly attentive to world events for someone her age. In 1939, she participated in an oratorical contest with a speech titled "Preserve Our Liberties," which defended the Bill of Rights. Her presentation won an award from the local Civitan Club and took third place in statewide competition. She reflected later: *During the '30s I was aware of fascism. The general pacifist sentiment that prevailed in the country was a part of the world I lived in too. I was more aware of what was happening in the world than what was happening in Alabama. It looked like there was going to be war in Europe. I didn't know exactly*

what fascism was, except that it was not democracy like we had. And I thought com-
munism was just as bad; I didn't have any feeling that [these were] things that were
going to impinge upon my life except just to look at from a distance.[35]

In spite of her interest in world affairs, Anne—like most adolescents—was
oblivious to the local and regional struggles being played out around her about
the nature of democracy. The vast majority of white southerners, who shared
the McCartys' general political orientation, tended in those years to live in a
dream world of denial regarding threats to the southern racial order. Changes
were afoot, nevertheless, and in November 1938, a historic event took place
just over the mountains from Anniston, in nearby Birmingham. The defiant
challenge flung to segregation and southern social relations at the founding of
the Southern Conference for Human Welfare (SCHW) was a moment that
would hold great significance for Anne throughout her adult life. As a young
teenager, though, she was completely unaware of the buds of civil rights activity that were opening in the region, or of any southern reverberations of the
gathering struggle against fascism.[36]

The wretchedness of the Great Depression generated enormous grassroots
pressure on the government to take an activist role in alleviating human suffering. The boldness of Franklin Roosevelt's New Deal for curing the nation's
economic woes engendered a great deal of social experimentation. A host of
reforms were ushered in that extended the scope of the federal government
and upset traditional southern power relations. For the first time in recent history, blacks held positions of power through administrative posts in New Deal
agencies, and New Deal reformers soon clashed with conservative white
southern politicians who maintained power by limiting political participation
not just of blacks but of a huge share of southern whites too. The Roosevelt
administration also drew in a new breed of white southerners who were critical
of the prosegregationism and antiunionism that were almost universal among
southern politicians. One of that new breed was Clark Foreman, an elite, Har-
vard-educated Georgian who after witnessing a lynching became a foe of racial
discrimination and, in 1933, FDR's "special adviser on the economic status of
Negroes." Overturning white supremacy was not part of Roosevelt's platform,
and at times he bent over backwards to humor southern Democrats. Yet there
were many in his administration determined to shake up the South's
apartheid-like system, and federal New Deal programs themselves challenged
implicitly the ideology of states' rights that upheld white supremacy. Advo-

cates of greater racial parity found a sympathetic ear in First Lady Eleanor Roosevelt, whose progressive reform spirit led to ties with African American leaders such as Walter White, head of the NAACP, and Mary McCleod Bethune, a leading educator.[37]

FDR was also a strong supporter of labor's right to organize unions, a conviction that caused many southern Democrats' hair to stand on end. Regional politicians, wishing to keep their labor costs dirt cheap, had long portrayed unions as un-American and communistic, and most attempts to organize southern unions met with swift brutality by local authorities. As the 1930s wore on, despite Roosevelt's charisma and his long stays at his Warm Springs, Georgia, getaway, southern legislators developed more serious misgivings about his New Deal. It was increasingly apparent that the political tide was moving toward greater economic opportunities and greater enfranchisement for the "little guys"—black and white—who in their dire circumstances supported Roosevelt wholeheartedly.[38]

The mobs that had threatened the Scottsboro defendants had given eloquent testimony, if any was needed, of rank-and-file white southerners' violent defense of southern racial customs. But in the new spirit of urgency that characterized the New Deal era, some broke with the past and made cross-racial alliances to improve their lives. Industrial unionism was at the heart of those alliances. Established in 1935 as a committee of the craft-based American Federation of Labor (AFL), the Congress of Industrial Organizations (CIO) became independent in 1936. Encouraged by Roosevelt's runaway reelection, the CIO stepped up organizing in southern industrial cities such as Memphis and Birmingham. In mountainous east Tennessee, the radical Highlander Folk School opened in 1933 and began encouraging southern white unionists to put aside their prejudices to build biracial alliances in the CIO. Wracked as southern locals sometimes were both by internal racial tensions and by antilabor repression, they did present some piecemeal challenges to Jim Crow and portend larger struggles to come. In Arkansas, despite fierce opposition from plantation owners, the Southern Tenant Farmers' Union brought together 25,000 black and white sharecroppers, calling stark attention to the suffering of the rural poor and winning more agricultural relief.[39]

The spread of fascism in Europe energized these new labor challenges. Internationally, the Communist Party put aside its sectarian critique of liberals and non-Communist leftists and in 1935 called for a new "Popular Front" against fascism. The CP-USA began to initiate broad-based coalitions with less radical figures and groups (FDR's New Dealers, for instance) of whom it had previously been highly critical. In the South, the developing rhetoric of antifascism spurred forward a debate about the meaning of democracy in a region where huge portions of its residents were denied the vote and other more basic forms of expression. The CP cooperated with southern liberals in bringing regional inequities to light and promoted organizations like the Southern Negro Youth Congress (SNYC), a predominantly black group established in 1937 to enlist young people in fighting for racial and economic justice. The CP's interpretation of interracialism, popularized in slogans like "Negro and white, unite and fight," was a far cry from the paternalistic gradualism that characterized black-white relations among older southern organizations such as the Commission on Interracial Cooperation (CIC), but militancy grew contagious in the crisis of the Depression. New groups such as the SNYC remained highly marginalized, and their efforts met with brutal repression. Yet they invigorated regional politics and prepared a generation of young activists for confronting racial barriers even as they nurtured a "movement culture," albeit a small one, in which black and white activists could find fellowship in challenging racial separation, top-down politics, and political passivity. Theirs was a radical interracialism that held out the promise of fundamental social and economic changes.[40]

As his presidency continued, FDR's alliance with organized labor increased exponentially. So too did opposition to the New Deal among southern Democrats, whose growing unity stalled important reforms. New Deal Democrats became interested in giving political voice to a greater core of Roosevelt supporters, and those liberal and left-wing southerners among them who had helped to craft the president's programs were eager to shine a brighter light onto their region. In 1938 a group of them headed by Clark Foreman produced a *Report on the Economic Conditions of the South*. When on July 25, 1938, Roosevelt announced to a gathering of southerners that their region was "the nation's number one economic problem" and the New Deal was the solution, the effect was electric. The liberals were thrilled, but southern traditionalists, among them politicians and journalists, invoked the horrors of Reconstruction and excoriated the president's findings. The fact that FDR's announcement was piggybacked onto a tour supporting candidates to unseat long-standing southern congressmen did not help his case. When that campaign tour failed, the legislative phase of the New Deal died with it.[41]

Yet the southern activism that had been unleashed was less easily contained. Widespread publicity of the report catapulted southern problems—low wages and prices, abysmal poverty, discriminatory freight rates, and an almost inconceivable lack of civil liberties—onto the national stage. The figure around whom the response to Roosevelt's challenge crystallized—Joe

Gelders—was a perfect symbol of the unusual coalition of southern liberals and radicals that had coalesced over the New Deal years. Gelders, a native Alabamian whose comfortable upbringing could not completely erase the stigma attached to being Jewish, was a University of Alabama physics professor. What he witnessed during the Depression soured him on capitalism, and he began reading Marx, secretly joined the CP, and left his teaching post to promote southern unionism. In September 1936, Gelders was kidnapped, viciously beaten, and left for dead in retaliation for his efforts on behalf of Alabama labor organizers. The beating triggered a public outcry by everyone from Communists to the governor of Alabama. Gelders's assailants were never arrested, but they were identified as paid agents of the Tennessee Coal and Iron Company. The incident brought Robert LaFollette's U.S. Senate subcommittee south to Birmingham for a hearing investigating free speech violations, and the climate for civil liberties improved somewhat.[42]

Gelders's ties to liberals, labor, and the left placed him in a unique position for coalition-building, and FDR's report on the South became the occasion to advance an idea he had been mulling over for a while—a South-wide conference to oppose the repression that invariably greeted any organizing for change. In mid-1938, Gelders met with Eleanor Roosevelt and, at her instigation, with the president. From those meetings came a call for progressive southerners to convene in Birmingham during Thanksgiving weekend 1938 and confront the southern problems FDR's report had detailed. More than 1,200 people—black and white and of various political leanings—answered that call. Among them was Eleanor Roosevelt. The result was the formation of the SCHW and the launching of what some historians have come to know as the "southern conference movement" to combat economic and racial injustice in the region.[43]

For all its critique of the region, the *Report on Economic Conditions of the South* had strangely avoided analysis of the racial dimensions of southern socioeconomic problems. But in the rigidly segregated world of Birmingham, once blacks and whites came together en masse, such avoidance was no longer possible. The conference was raided by Birmingham police on its first full day, and Police Commissioner "Bull" Connor threatened to arrest participants unless they complied with the laws for segregated seating. Reluctantly they did so. Yet the First Lady scandalized local officials by sitting in the black section, and, when asked to move, by symbolically placing her chair on the dividing line police had made to separate the races. The episode more or less forced the organizers to take a stand on segregation, and they vowed never to hold a segregated meeting again.[44]

That stand marked a major break from the regional defensiveness and un-willingness of southern white liberals, historically, to confront segregation as unpalatable and thus close the gap between their understanding of the society they lived in and that of their black associates. In the SCHW were a group of white southerners whose concerns were more economic than racial, yet who were also now prompted by conditions around them to condemn segregation and race discrimination as key ingredients of the region's economic backward-ness. Their first campaign—at FDR's suggestion—was aimed at abolishing the poll tax, a cumulative $1 or $2 per year voting fee and one of the prime devices to keep thousands of black and poor white southerners from voting. Perhaps it was the crisis of the Depression or the menacing threat of fascism abroad, but the unity of progressive forces that characterized American politics during the Depression and World War II now took root in the South as well, bringing new challenges to Jim Crow.[45]

Intermingling with the politics of black and white was the "red" issue. To-gether, that combination proved highly threatening to the southern social fab-ric. Although the politics of the left-liberal Popular Front were much more reformist than revolutionary, the presence of a handful of CP members and sympathizers in the southern conference movement was highly controversial. Socialists and independent leftists in the conference wished to stem what they called "communist influence," and soon the newly created Special Committee on Un-American Activities of the U.S. House of Representatives, chaired by Texas Rep. Martin Dies, began investigating the new group as a "communist front." Although fears of "outside agitators" and "subversives" had some polit-ical currency in the South, they had relatively little on the national level amid the rise of fascism internationally, and the SCHW remained effective in the face of such charges. Still, throughout its existence the SCHW was constantly defending itself against charges of communist domination, and by the postwar period those accusations became a cross too heavy to bear.[46]

The same day that Eleanor Roosevelt was evicted from her seat with blacks in Birmingham, headlines in the *Anniston Star* screamed, "1,500 Bir-minghamians are facing starvation." With those kinds of conditions in their midst, even southern journalists—notorious for their racial conservatism—re-ported on the Birmingham conference favorably. What press criticism the meeting did garner centered, predictably, on the resolution deploring segrega-tion. In Anniston, *Star* editors did not even see fit to comment on that uproar and gave the conference brief but positive coverage.[47]

Like many other white southerners of what radicals knew as the "bour-geois" class, Anne McCarty's parents had increasing reservations about parts

of the New Deal that seemed to be shaking the foundations of the region's social order, but they maintained an affection for their affable, optimistic president and a condescending tolerance for his wife's peculiar social convictions.
Anne never even heard about Eleanor Roosevelt's visit to her state, much less
the valiant efforts to enact democratic ideals by people like Joe Gelders, Clark
Foreman, or Virginia Durr, the feisty Montgomerian who headed up the
SCHW anti-poll tax campaign. Later, Anne would count them among her
mentors and friends as she dedicated her life to a continued pursuit of the
racial and economic ideals the southern conference movement sought. But
during her early adolescence, she had no inkling of any social movement in
her home state. Instead, individual concerns occupied her attention.[48]

Anne had demons to contend with all through her youth, but they existed more
internally than as something others could see. She covered her sometimes
painful shyness with a flair for drama and had successes as a prolific writer and
poet, an active churchgoer, and an "A" student. Perhaps Anne's most lasting experience from high school was her introduction to journalism through the
school newspaper: *One thing I did learn was how to put a publication together, and
somehow I have been putting them together for one thing or another ever since. It's one
thing I really love, that I'd rather do than anything else in the world.*[49]

But adolescent social pressures also loomed large. They made academics
secondary and overwhelmed—for the moment—her spiritual journey. Her
freshman diary was filled with self-recriminations about not being *cute* enough
or popular enough. Anne became, as she later described it, *all mixed up. It suddenly began to bother me that I didn't have boyfriends. There were dances, and in
those days the point was to have as many boys as possible. You were a total social failure
if you danced a full dance with any one boy. This was the most important thing in life
to people: isn't that horrible? I always had some people dancing with me, but I wasn't
getting cut in on all the time so I began to worry. I figured out that I didn't have a lot
of boyfriends because I was too smart so I'd better hide the fact that I had brains. I
don't think I put it in those words but almost. That was the prevailing notion: that the
way you could get boys to like you was to make them think they were absolutely brilliant no matter how stupid they might sound. So I began that play-acting thing. I
never was the belle of the ball but I was in that crowd.*[50]

From the age of 14 on, Anne was highly engrossed in the world of her
peers. From her diaries, it seems that a large part of the attraction that world
held for her was in the close-knit friendships she had with other girls. She and

her six closest friends established a club they called the "We Are Seven" (WAS). The "WAS's" were nearly inseparable, and their exploits flavored the pages of the high school paper. Even when she visited her grandmothers in Kentucky or her aunt in New Jersey, she moved easily from one elite social whirl to another in the company of a bevy of like-minded girls at pools, movies, and parties. The girls often had boys on their minds, but Anne spent more of her time in the company of other women, staying up all night with her friends and daydreaming aloud about life's possibilities.[51]

The pinnacle of success for Anne in that period of her life was the "DD" or Double Dozen Club, an exclusive "subdebutante" club that allowed only 24 members. Such clubs groomed future debutantes and sorority sisters and were neither unusual nor uniquely southern in this era. Originally set up by Anniston High School in 1928, the now-independent DD Club made headlines on the society pages as the convener of dances, fashion shows, and bridge parties. Some of Anne's friends were invited to join after their freshman year, but she was not, and the news devastated her. When she received word during the summer of 1939 that she too had been elected, she at last felt sufficiently popular. A year later, she held office in the club, and near the end of high school she wrote that the high point of her week was the Tuesday evening DD meeting.[52]

The frivolity the DD's cultivated (the club song went "I'm a crazy, foolish DD; we play while others work") differed sharply from Anne's serious-minded streak. Her introspective qualities were not swept aside, however, and high school friends scoffed years later at the notion that Anne changed a great deal as an adult, agreeing that she always had "idealistic leanings" and the germ of a social activist in her.[53]

Jean Lloyd, one of the WAS's and Anne's best friend in high school, thought of her friend as someone out of the ordinary because Anne had introduced her to cigarettes at 14 and to Shakespeare at 17. One night Anne reportedly took Jean onto her back porch and whispered, *Do you love life? Aren't you afraid that you'll grow old and never really have any fun? Someone once said that life's sweetest joys are unsubstantial things. Let's do something unsubstantial.* They went and bought a pack of Camels and stayed up all night sitting out on Anne's roof smoking and reading poetry.[54]

As their senior year drew to a close, Allen Draper was Anne's date for one of the many dances surrounding graduation. What he remembered about the night half a lifetime later was not the dance itself but their drive in the country afterward. The couple came upon a country schoolhouse which had caught fire. They stood and watched it burn, and he comforted Anne because she was so badly upset by the idea of all the children who would be without a school.

(Later, as one of her first newspaper assignments, she would tackle in print the devastation fires brought to the education of rural children.)[55]

On her graduation day, Anne marched next to Jean Lloyd into the school auditorium to the tune of "Largo." Throughout the ceremony, she was gripped by nostalgia and a powerful sense of unreality. When she received her diploma, she merely went through the motions. Though many of her friends were crying, Anne was never one to cry easily; her eyes remained dry. The graduates danced until after midnight, went to their favorite spot for an early "breakfast," then to another friend's house for an all-night party. Just before dawn, they piled into cars and drove over to catch the sunrise over the country club golf course.[56]

That weekend, sitting on the McCartys' roof in the dark again with Jean Lloyd, Anne pointed to the stars and told her friend, *I feel so completely happy right now. [The stars] are like little ideas that are there for us to grasp and put in a book. I'll never be as completely happy as I am right now because I'm going to be something and give something to the world.*[57]

Anne wrote of graduation night in her journal: *This was one of the happiest nights of my life, and I wanted it to go on and on. Yet vaguely I knew even then that after that night it would never be the same. We had been bound by something completely intangible—there's no word for it—you could say it was a feeling we all had. It's the feeling I've been trying to recapture in the things I've written in this book. But of course I've failed utterly. You can't put a feeling on paper [or] in words. It sounds like sentimental tripe after the feeling is gone. Nevertheless, I felt it and all the other people felt it. [And we knew that] after that night it was all going to be over.*[58]

Anne's musings in her journal circled around the ephemeral quality of relationships. Yet she had no way of knowing at the time how deep the void would become between her and her high school classmates. What she would give to the world would take her across a racial and class divide her schoolmates would not follow, and by the 1950s much of Anniston stood in harsh judgment of her choices and her radical critique of southern inequalities. Although some years would pass in the shaping of that critique, Anne's brush with what she had jokingly referred to as "unsubstantial things" more or less ended when she left Anniston for college in the fall of 1941.

CHAPTER TWO

INTELLECTUAL AWAKENING

There were mountains surrounding Anniston, and I sort of had this idea that if you could get over those mountains, there was a world out there that was more interesting . . . and being a writer was a way into that world.[1]

AS ANNE STOOD ON THE PLATFORM WAITING for the Southern Railway train to carry her to Danville, Virginia, she was ready to leave Anniston behind psychologically as well as physically. The following day, on September 15, 1941, she would enroll at Stratford College, a tiny two-year women's college nestled in the northern Blue Ridge foothills in a textile-tobacco town just beyond the North Carolina border. Attached to the college was a four-year "preparatory program," a holdover from an earlier era—1897–1930—when Stratford had functioned as a women's preparatory academy for Randolph-Macon Woman's College under the name Randolph-Macon Institute. Before that it had been Danville Female College, established in 1854. Stratford College was established as such in 1930.[2]

Anne's connection with Stratford dated to her maternal grandmother, Agnes Thorne Crabbe, who after being widowed had been a housemother there briefly during the 1920s and was a friend of Stratford's dean, Mabel Kennedy. Anne's parents—her mother especially—wanted her to attend a women's college and had taken her on a tour of several Virginia women's colleges while she was in high school.[3]

Anita McCarty's preferences in this regard were consonant with her desire to help her daughter develop her mind as well as enhance her social standing. In general, southern women's colleges were derivatives of the national female academy movement of the early to mid-nineteenth century, which, while not completely unconcerned with higher learning, tended to combine it with domestic education and ornamental skills, such as French and music, that would make an entertaining wife. Though curricula had been modified over the years to conform to modern academic standards, that tendency was particularly true in the South, where the ideal of the southern belle was remarkably enduring. Throughout the late nineteenth and early twentieth centuries, small denominational schools were a popular alternative to large secular state universities as more appropriate moral and religious environments for "young ladies."[4]

Some southern women's schools established in the nineteenth century were also influenced by the ideology of southern nationalism which peaked in the 1850s after influential publications such as *DeBow's Review* editorialized on the need for regional institutions of higher learning that would protect young well-to-do southerners from such dangerous doctrines as abolition and women's rights. The tie between southern institutions and patriarchy was deliberate and full of import for white southern daughters as proslavery ideologues propagated the idea that "southern ladies," under the careful oversight of patriarchal husbands and fathers, benefited from slavery and had better be prepared to uphold it as it came under increasing outside fire. From their outset, southern women's colleges were thus imbued with a regional consciousness that took for granted black inferiority and its counterpart, white supremacy. Such ideas persisted through the mid-twentieth century, albeit on a milder level. Though they probably did not consciously do so, families like the McCartys could also hope to buttress their daughters' regional identities by sending them to the kind of southern colleges known informally as "girls' schools."[5]

It is impossible to determine to what extent Stratford endowed its students with the sort of regional and gender identity suggested here. Although neither of the first two presidents of the original Danville Female College were southerners, gender hierarchy was a firm fixture in mid-nineteenth-century women's education. By the time Anne entered Stratford, faculty members, particularly female faculty, were likely to hold more enlightened views of female autonomy than their nineteenth-century predecessors, primarily as a result of the woman's suffrage movement and of insights from the social sciences. In 1941 Stratford had a faculty of 25, of whom 22 were female.[6]

In spite of her parents' wishes or in part because of them, Anne's decision to attend a woman's college had not come without hesitation. Her popularity those last two years of high school had convinced her that dating was a higher priority than academics, and she had been leaning toward going to the University of Alabama. But after an October 1940 congressional vote enacted the first-ever peacetime draft registration, the drift toward U.S. involvement in the war raging in Europe was obvious even to high schoolers. *War was on the horizon and there weren't going to be that many boys on the Tuscaloosa campus; it was going to be like a women's college anyway, so that's when I decided to go to Stratford. . . . I've often wondered what would have happened to me if the war hadn't been going on because most of the people I knew went to college to enjoy the dances, join a sorority, and catch a man. That's the way I was headed too. Then going to women's colleges gave me a chance to find myself, to begin thinking about myself as a woman. I don't think I ever knew the excitement of an idea until I got to college. I felt like I'd wasted 16 years of my life—all of the things I hadn't read and wanted to read, that sort of thing.*[7]

On the surface, the world Stratford offered looked scarcely less confining than Anniston had been to Anne at 17. Seventy young women entered her freshman class, most of them southern, many of them "legacies" (meaning older family members had preceded them at Stratford). Only 29 of the 70 completed the two-year program: many used Stratford as a place of transition to cushion their departure from home and entry to a larger college as sophomores. Campus activities took place in one large, elegant, ivy-covered building, with dormitory rooms on the second and third floors, classrooms on the first, and a formal dining hall in the basement. There students and faculty (many of whom lived in quarters alongside the students) dressed for dinner each evening and took their places at preassigned tables. Photographs of Anne and her classmates from their 1942 yearbook show each one dressed in a pastel cashmere pullover sweater adorned by a single strand of pearls.[8]

The Excitement of an Idea

The school's form was not much of a departure from Anne's background, but its content struck her like a strong wind. She began to pursue in earnest her twin loves of writing and drama, joining the staff of the *Traveller* (the school newspaper, named after Robert E. Lee's white horse), and becoming deeply involved in acting.[9]

Anne's submersion of her intellectual abilities to ensure social success withered away early on in her tenure at Stratford, partly because the lack of men on campus made it no longer necessary to downplay her intelligence. The first student holiday of the fall occasioned the emergence of what her family has called "the McCarty drive." *This was one of the turning points in my life. My roommate had invited three or four of us to go home with her because it was too far for us to go all that way to our own homes for Thanksgiving. At the last minute I decided not to go. . . . I longed to go, but I just decided not to because I had work to do. That was the first time I made that kind of decision, to stay and work instead of having fun. I gave up something but it wasn't self-sacrificial because the truth is, what I really enjoy is working. That's the McCarty drive, this drive to keep working. The first person I ever heard refer to it like that was my mother. She always said her husband and children all have this McCarty drive, and if she'd known about it 50 years earlier, she would have run screaming in the other direction.*[10]

Anne's tendency to immerse herself in work was challenged less frequently by the offer of a date than it might have been at a different moment in history. Less than two weeks after the Thanksgiving break, December 7 dawned—a damp, cold Sunday morning—and the radio gave the news of the bombing of Pearl Harbor. The day of infamy had little immediate impact on Anne, but sank in slowly as she discussed it with her college friends and back in Anniston for her Christmas break. *There were a lot of dances. I went to one of them with Bobby Baker—the boy I'd gone with more than any other in high school. Sitting resting in between dances, I remember him looking around and saying, "Over half the boys here are going to be killed in the next few years." I hadn't really thought about that before, but I did when he said that. Then he went into the army; they all did. It was an intense time.*[11]

In the midst of such intensity, many of her peers married their sweethearts. Nationally, marriage rates began to climb from the ebb they had experienced throughout the Depression years. Between 1940 and 1943, more than a million more new families were formed than would have been expected in peacetime.[12]

The first wedding in Anne's circle occurred just after Christmas. Her brother Lindsay, about to be shipped out for Naval submarine duty in the Pacific, moved up the date of his marriage to Beverly Logan, whom he had met on one of the family's annual vacations in Eminence. In January 1942, Anne accompanied her family to Kentucky and was a bridesmaid in the wedding. Although Anne and Baker did discuss marriage, her interests were turning more toward academia and career, and she never viewed the possibility as an attractive one.[13]

Back at school, Anne's passion for work led her to a wealth of achievements. Aside from writing for the *Traveller*, she co-chaired the Poetry Club and starred in two dramatic productions during her freshman year. The biggest honor came when she became one of 40 young actors from across the nation to receive a summer scholarship from the National Association of Dramatics. On June 23, 1942, the students joined professional actors from New York for a six-week residency at the Priscilla Beach Theater on the coast near Plymouth, Massachusetts, where they rehearsed for a performing tour of New England. *That summer was when I decided not to go on with any serious effort toward a career in theater. I saw that I wasn't that good, compared to some of those people. A woman there who had been in the theater for years [told me], "Life in the theater is hard, and if you wouldn't rather be sweeping the floor in the theater than working anywhere else, don't go into it." And I decided I didn't really feel that way about the theater. But I also realized that I'd rather be sweeping the floor in a newspaper office than holding the top job somewhere else.*[14]

Anne continued to act in college plays and even to toy with the idea of professional acting. Theatrical performances gave her the first taste of developing a public persona (a skill she would later employ in her political work through speeches that moved audiences to social action). Yet journalism became her real passion. Amid a summer of intensive acting, she still found time to edit a newspaper for students at Priscilla Beach.

In the fall she returned to Stratford as editor in chief of the college newspaper, where her writings dealt almost uniformly with moral idealism or international relations. The horrors of world war and the fascist campaign jumped to life for Anne and her peers every time they went to the picture show, looked at spreads in the enormously popular *Life* or *Look* magazines, or turned on the radio, which in the war years devoted about one-third of total programming to hard news.[15]

Anne's friendships from back home continued, but she found a deeper kinship with Lucile Schoolfield, a wealthy young New Yorker with relatives in Danville. *Lucile would flit in and out of Stratford; you never knew if she was enrolled or not. She didn't like going to school or any of the normal things, [but] she liked the life of the mind. She had long blonde hair and a sort of ethereal look about her. She was the first person I'd ever met who read poetry just for the fun of it. She was a dilettante, but she also had a love of learning.*[16]

The bond between the two was forged out of the rare new thrill of feeling truly understood by the other. After she left Stratford, Anne stayed in touch with Lucile through long letters and periodic visits to Danville and New York. Once they embarked on their respective adult lives, Lucile never fully understood Anne's growing devotion to social causes, but the two remained friends until Lucile's death in 1967.[17]

Friendships like this one helped cultivate in Anne a deep devotion to Stratford, a feeling that became a persistent theme in her writings. In the flowery prose typical for a young woman of her day, she summed up her sentiments in her final *Traveller* editorial. *There are some here . . . who in the words of our alma mater "self-forgetful try by service true to gain a purpose high" to whom this word [Stratford] means a certain spirit, an intangible thing that embeds itself deep inside them and reflects itself in their lives. It is a love of beauty, a holding to traditions, a placing of first things first, a gracious way of living, a clinging to ideals, a complete absence of littleness, narrowness, and selfishness.*[18]

Part of why Anne loved Stratford so dearly was her incredible success there. The honors of her first year paled by comparison with the second, when she won nearly every award the college offered. As well as editing the paper, she was president of the student council, part of the Christmas 1942 "Queen's Court," star of the two annual plays, class valedictorian, recipient of the "Distinguished Service" award at graduation, and voted by her classmates as "Most Representative," "Most Talented," "Best Student," and "Perfect Voice."[19]

College nurtured in Anne the joie de vivre she had felt as a younger teen while broadening her sense of what that joy encompassed. Each sophomore made a comment to accompany her own picture in the yearbook, and Anne's was *O Happy Day!* Stratford affirmed her and strengthened her self-confidence. Yet Stratford was more to Anne than a mere showcase for her talents. She discovered there something that remains, according to sociological literature, extremely affirming for adolescent development, especially among women. She met older women who would act as role models, engaging her admiration and imagination.[20]

Dean Mabel Kennedy—"Miss Mabel," as she was affectionately known—had headed Stratford since its 1930 founding and had taught literature on the campus since 1901. Kennedy had the kind of dynamic presence and teaching style that left an impression on practically every student she had. Her love of literature impressed Anne deeply. *She seemed old to us, but she was just full of life. She would sail into the classroom with a great stack of books in her arms. It was sort of like a lecture, but it wasn't like any lecture I'd ever heard. She would be going from one book to another, and then the bell would ring. "Oh, no, it couldn't be! We've been here an hour? I'll just never have time to give you girls all I want to give you," she would say. She made it all come to life.*[21]

Kennedy had two traits that were not entirely new to Anne but enlarged her sense of possibility when she saw them embodied in an older, professional woman so passionately engaged in learning: *One was the excitement of learning for its own sake. She never thought that the reason to be in school was so you could get out and get a job and make money. The other was just the idea that you don't live for yourself alone, that if you were fortunate enough to have an education, you had an obligation to be of service to your fellow human beings.*[22]

Both of those qualities probably stemmed from a rather traditional view of women's education with roots in the nineteenth century. The Victorian value system stressed polarities: women were emotional, men were rational; women were passive, men were aggressive. Among the middle and upper classes of that period, the ideology of "separate spheres," as historians have termed it, groomed elite white women for success in the private sphere of marriage, home, family, and perhaps church but not the public world of commerce, workplace, or advanced studies. By 1901, when Kennedy embarked upon her career, those values had relaxed but not disappeared. Options for women had only recently expanded to encompass higher education for those who could afford it, as well as a small range of service professions (for single women, that is—paid employment continued to be frowned upon for married women of Kennedy's race and class). Acceptable outlets for women also included reform, which may have been the kind of service Kennedy, who came of age in the late nineteenth-century Progressive era, had in mind. Throughout Kennedy's youth, advocates of women's higher education had emphasized love of learning as a way to avoid the resistance inevitably provoked by arguing for education leading to employment. By the time of World War II, women's employment was becoming normalized, however, and Kennedy's emphasis on study rather than career preparation left Anne with a greater sense of options than earlier generations may have gotten from similar messages.[23]

Another faculty member whose influence on Anne left its mark was Ida Fitzgerald, dean and English teacher in the Stratford Hall secondary program. An alumna of Randolph-Macon Institute and a 1928 graduate of Randolph-Macon Woman's College (R-MWC), Ida was closer to Anne's age than other teachers and became a friend. *I never had a class from her, but she had a way of looking for students who she thought stood out intellectually, and cultivating them. She lived right across from the college; in fact, her father owned the Dan River Mills. Every once in a while she would have cookouts in what they called "the barn." She began to invite me over. I remember feeling awkward at first because it seemed like everyone was older and smarter than me, and they were talking about things I didn't know anything about. It took me a long time to feel at home in those settings.*[24]

Gatherings at the Fitzgerald "barn"—which was actually more of a studio—were a kind of rural southern counterpart to the salon movement that was popular in New York, in which intellectuals met to discuss issues of the day. Although she had chosen a life in Danville, Ida Fitzgerald's worldview was enlarged, at least in part, by her older sister, Harriet Fitzgerald, who operated an art school in Greenwich Village. Harriet, also an alumna of Randolph-Macon Institute and R-MWC, kept a studio space in Danville, used the surrounding landscapes for much of her subject matter, and staged exhibits all over Virginia.[25]

When Anne and Harriet met, probably in September of 1942, they connected instantly. Harriet was a member of the R-MWC board of trustees, and Ida enlisted her older sister in a campaign to convince Anne that she should attend R-MWC, where they agreed she would receive a classical liberal arts education that would give her the discipline to become a successful writer. Anne was vague about where to continue her studies after finishing Stratford, thinking perhaps she would return to Alabama. She was easily convinced otherwise by two women she so admired, and she could scarcely help being flattered by their encouragement. None of them probably realized at that early point in their acquaintance what a dramatic impact Harriet would have on Anne's thinking. *I would have these long conversations with her. Often I just listened while she did most of the talking. She did a lot of reading aloud and introduced me to thinkers, including Karl Marx and Freud, whom she and her generation were really influenced by. I learned a lot from her that I wasn't learning in school. I was sort of her protégée. She had been through some metamorphosis of her own while she was in college. She was a part of that generation of women in the twenties who decided to seek careers instead of marriage, and she was quite a liberal, kept coming back to Danville and trying to shake things up there, never cutting herself off from her roots. She had become very prolabor, a good friend of Lucy Randolph Mason and a supporter of the CIO. She had friends who were Communists.*[26]

The politically sophisticated Harriet was also the first person Anne had ever met who actively opposed segregation. *I kidded her later that she was the one who radicalized me, but of course, I got a lot more radical than she was.* The older friend became a profound influence on Anne, both politically and personally. *I realized later that she was the first person I was ever in love with. It was not any overt sort of homosexual relationship because that would have scared me to death, but I'm talking about being in love with her in that she was what made life exciting and interesting.*[27]

Although Anne was not prepared to experiment with lesbianism, many whom she met in college were. She knew of quite a few love affairs between female students, though few identified themselves as lesbian. Even in the realm of platonic friendships, Anne and her closest friends spoke openly of their ardent love for one another and often addressed each other as "Darling" or "Baby." The Victorian tradition of romantic female friendships persisted into the twentieth century, and some evidence suggests that such friendships may have been more prevalent in a single-sex environment.[28]

In fact, Harriet—who engaged Anne so deeply with her expansive conversations, drawing pictures in the air with her hands as she spoke—had a female lover during the period when she met Anne, although the two friends never discussed Harriet's sexual orientation directly until years afterward. *I believe she was in love with me too in a way, although we never talked very openly about what our relationship meant. She knew I was 20 years younger than she was. She knew she had this long-term relationship in New York. I know she cared about me all her life. For me it was an intellectual excitement. Before I met Harriet, I never knew that kind of excitement was possible between two human beings. Later I told her that I didn't think I would have ever been able to have the kind of relationship I had with Carl had it not been for her. Never after that have I felt any sexual interest in someone who did not excite me intellectually.*[29]

The most immediate repercussion of Anne's relationship with Harriet was her recruitment into Randolph-Macon Woman's College in 1943. Yet those last few months at Stratford also laid the groundwork for a friendship—a romantic one, in the broadest sense—between Anne and Harriet that would offer the younger friend tremendous emotional support in the years to come. By comparison, her relationships with men seemed superficial, a situation reinforced by her immersion in a single-sex community. Yet Anne continued to be successful with *the boys*, as she referred to them. All of her romances were long-distance ones, maintained without a great deal of effort. As time went along, they faded increasingly into the background of her priorities without evaporating entirely.[30]

During much of her tenure at Stratford, she was "pinned" to Bobby Baker, her Anniston sweetheart who attended Auburn University a year ahead of her until he left for the armed services. Anne began to regard their romance as more serious during her first fall away, and by Christmas she had decided she was in love with him. Yet during the theater summer in Massachusetts, she never found time to contact him even once—until she lost his fraternity pin and felt obliged to write and apologize.[31]

Before much longer the two drifted apart entirely, but Baker was soon replaced by Chuck Evart, a soldier from Fort McClellan near Anniston who taught Anne to play tennis when she came home from school. With him too, after an initial infatuation, she scarcely found time to write, and the romance soon ended. By the time she finished at Stratford, Anne had more or less made up her mind never to marry: *The women I admired most in college were women who were older than I was, who had declared their independence of men and were defining their own lives. . . . Marriage at that time seemed like a living death because it meant being an ornament and not a human being. That felt like just about the worst thing that could happen to me, to end up living this life of going to the country club on Saturday night and to bridge parties in the afternoons. I remember a good friend of mine who had said she was never going to get married. But she left school in her last year to get married. She hadn't planned to do it. She was going off to say good-bye to her boyfriend, who was going overseas. Then she sent me a telegram asking me to come to her wedding. I wrote back and said, "No, I won't come to your funeral."* Reluctance to marry on the part of a young woman immersed for the first time in a stimulating intellectual environment is not a reliable barometer for measuring feminist sensibilities or predicting life choices. What is interesting, however, is Anne's recollection that she was not alone or even one of only a few with those feelings.[32]

Anne and her peers were two generations removed from the suffrage movement, which had begun nearly a century before in other parts of the nation but had not gained any kind of groundswell in the South until after 1900. There, cultural ideals about white womanhood, black inferiority/bestiality, and the alleged need to protect white women (typically from black men) continued to highlight women's ornamental function and the importance of keeping both women and blacks "in their place." The culture itself acted as a powerful check to keep challenges to the encrusted racial and gender conventions modest, and those who did speak up met with hot criticism.[33]

After women won the vote in 1920, the women's rights movement splintered, lacking the unifying focus the struggle for suffrage had provided. Yet the women's movement remained a vibrant force in American politics throughout the 1920s. At the same time, the insights of Darwin and Freud, along with the commercialism that accompanied the post-WWI rise of mass media, injected a strong dose of individualism among "modern" young women of the 1920s, North and South. Some began claiming a feminism that included personal freedoms such as birth control and eroticism. Such changes, punctuated by disillusionment when votes for women did not bring about the widespread social changes an older generation of suffragists had hoped for, served to dilute the power of the early-twentieth-century women's movement. By the mid-1930s, a political agenda organized around women's specific concerns more or less fell by the wayside in the rush to address the more broad-based socioeconomic problems the Great Depression brought into focus.[34]

The advent of WWII saw a loosening of traditional gender roles to allow the integration of women more fully into the wartime economy and the creation of women's branches of the armed services. That shift, however, was more a response to an employment crisis than it was the result of changed ideas about gender. Feminist organizations such as the National Woman's Party managed to survive those years, but organized feminism—with its message of women's individuality, political participation, and economic independence—would not be a significant political force again until it was revived by the women's liberation movement in the 1960s.[35]

The absence of a sizable feminist movement in the 1930s and 1940s should not suggest, however, that feminist thought was ever extinguished. Ideas about women's rights were particularly likely to retain their vigor in all-female environments like women's college campuses. Anne has insisted throughout her life that in college she caught what she has called the *spillover* from an earlier generation of feminists. Much of that spillover came to Anne directly from Harriet Fitzgerald, it seems. More broadly, however, despite the conservatism of southern women's colleges, they contained an abundance of single women on their faculties, and single women—especially educated ones—have tended throughout history to act as lightning rods for social tensions about gender. The group of women who mentored Anne in college represented a collective presence who expanded her understanding of options for women. She began to perceive what she has called a *vague feeling that as women we had something special to give to the world.*[36]

The cultural climate of the war years also framed her college experiences very differently from the postwar social landscape that greeted the next wave of students who would have been only three or four years younger. As the war raged, the home front was still resounding with echoes of the social experimentation of the New Deal years, and the Cold War, which would put a lid on rebellion, did not really take shape until 1947. Ideas about gender were in flux during the war, as were ideas about race and the very nature of democracy, in the South as in the rest of the nation.

Outside the classroom, Anne and her peers saw, heard, and read a great deal of material about women in the WWII years, but probably very little of it carried any overt message of feminist rebellion. Thanks in part to the government's propaganda campaign to attract women workers, films, magazine stories, and ads frequently depicted women breaking with traditional gender conventions to take jobs now vacated by the wartime emergency. Women in popular culture always retained their glamour, however, and they typically ventured forth into new jobs and adventures for the sake of their husbands or boyfriends, their families, their country—not for their own gain or simply because they felt like it. The reward for these fictional heroines was usually marriage and/or domestic bliss when their men returned from fighting overseas. *There was a part of me that thought you were supposed to have a man at your side, so I'd form one relationship after another . . . though I found the world of work, study, and career the world where I was happiest. There was a lot of ferment in that period that was already shaking up the South, and to a certain extent I was affected by it, as were a lot of the people I was in school with. A lot of those people did go back and fade into the scenery, the old patterns, and for some reason I didn't. . . . Part of the direction your life goes in is simply an accident of whom you meet at a certain time.*[37]

Most of Anne's peers must indeed have yielded to the pull of traditional gender roles. Popular images to the contrary, women's college enrollments, never equal to those of men, declined steadily from 1940 to 1944, and many who enrolled were lured away by wartime jobs or marriage, as in the case of Anne's friend who left Stratford to marry. That trend accelerated after the war's end. The number of marriages, already on the increase since 1940, reached a record high of 2.3 million in 1946. These women would become the mothers of the baby boomers. As female age at marriage declined, birthrates also climbed after 1946, especially among young women, to reach their peak in the early 1950s.[38]

Anne's generation of white, middle-class women were on the front lines of those whom Betty Friedan chronicled 20 years later in *The Feminine Mystique*, in which she described a widespread culture of educated homemakers so focused on the needs of their families that they had lost sight of personal or career goals and, in the process, themselves. Friedan held popular cultural representations of women, and the volley of advice directed at them, largely responsible for what she called the "problem that has no name." Although WWII served to demystify and normalize married women's employment, it also injected seriously contradictory messages about women into U.S. society, provoking a postwar resurgence of domesticity that interrupted the trajectory of women's growing independence in American society, especially among white, middle-class women. The power of those messages, coupled with the domestic repression associated with the Cold War, helps to account for the reduced social ferment of the 1950s, especially concerning women's rights. It does not, however, adequately explain the choices made by women like Anne Braden.[39]

Anne was part of a transitional generation. In the short run, young women her age were seeing, probably for the first time, others like themselves portrayed in nontraditional ways—as in the now-famous wartime image of Rosie the Riveter that Norman Rockwell created for the *Saturday Evening Post*. Married or not, women portrayed in popular culture in the WWII era often looked as if they were acting outside of male control, and that in itself may have had a liberating effect on young female audiences. In Anne's case—which was probably true of female students at other campuses during WWII, especially at women's colleges—new cultural representations of women's options were reinforced by the example that female teachers presented and the messages of feminism a few of them espoused openly. Anne and young women like her left college feeling that careers were important, indeed admirable, options for themselves, and a senior poll found most of her graduating class unattached, with no impending plans to marry but on the lookout for companionable rather than financially successful mates. In contrast, later cohorts of the generation of middle-class women now associated in the popular imagination with the "feminine mystique" typically encountered a narrowing set of social and cultural norms regarding not just gender conventions but social issues generally.[40]

In June 1943, Anne received her junior college diploma and a "college certificate" in speech and dramatic arts. For the latter, she was required to give a dramatic performance in which she played all of the parts, and on June 7, as part of commencement, she performed George Bernard Shaw's *Saint Joan* in a one-woman show.[41]

At the commencement ceremony, the centrality of the war as the lens through which Anne filtered her college experiences is evident in her valedictory address to classmates: *[Are] we a lost generation, to whom has come the challenge to pick up the broken pieces of a world corrupted by selfishness and materialism? . . . a generation to whose girls has come a double challenge—to work beside the men in more useful and active service than any former crisis of the world has ever demanded of women, and yet to fill the place that women have always filled in the world, the place that only women can fill, that of a spiritual anchor, a stabilizing force in a world devastated by greed and violence. . . . No, not lost but found—lifted from the danger of selfish mediocrity to the realm of the magnificent—a generation whose voice will reach across the ages, saying, "We were youth who thought the world was made for our pleasure; but given a war to fight . . . a chaotic world to straighten out, we forgot ourselves."[42]*

Those remarks are full of typical youthful idealism, but they can also be read retrospectively as another foreshadowing of the direction Anne's life would take. Heavily tinged with altruism and the rejection of materialism that would characterize most of her adult choices, they reflect her attitude, stated more forcefully later in life, that her college years inspired a turning away from pleasure for its own sake in favor of more serious pursuits—learning, service, and hard work. Her words suggest too the flux in women's roles during the war years. She, like many others, continued to embrace a maternalist (and, as portrayed here, an essentialist) vision of woman-as-caretaker while laying claim to a broader view of women's participation in the public sphere of work and politics. With the wisdom of hindsight, she would later characterize her cohort of college women as *premature women's liberationists*.[43]

Gambrell and Anita McCarty attended their daughter's graduation and boasted to their friends of her accomplishments, which they carefully catalogued in scrapbooks. Privately, however, Anita confessed to Ida Fitzgerald that Anne really was "a big frog in a little pond" at Stratford and that she hoped Anne would meet more challenges in the slightly larger environment at Randolph-Macon. Anita wanted her daughter to succeed, but she did not want Anne's victories to come effortlessly.[44]

During the summer of 1943, before entering R-MWC, Anne faced a different sort of challenge as she embarked upon her first experience in the world of professional journalism. Like many of her generation, she found that the wartime shortage of men enhanced her employment opportunities. In many fields, especially in industry, those opportunities dwindled away when U.S. soldiers came home at war's end. Not in all, however: in journalism, wartime gains for women never entirely disappeared, and the presence of women in newsrooms, on national magazine staffs, and even on the radio increased considerably.[45]

Though the population of Anne's home county of Calhoun had swelled by more than 7,000 between 1940 and 1943, largely because of military activities at Fort McClellan, less than two miles from Anniston, the newsroom of the *Anniston Star* looked pitifully short-staffed when she walked into it in mid-June 1943 and asked the owner and publisher, Col. Harry T. Ayers, for a job. Established in 1882, the *Star* was a major Alabama daily with a reputation as one of the state's most liberal and high-quality newspapers. *Colonel Ayers, as everybody called him, was a real institution around there. He was a Roosevelt liberal, a New Dealer. Southern liberals then didn't oppose segregation, but they talked about more opportunity. He was for all the New Deal legislation, and he was against the poll tax. I remember writing editorials against the poll tax, and my father saying, "That's ridiculous!"* Ayers was an Anniston maverick who found acceptance in polite society partly because of his family roots: his father had been editor of the *Star*'s forerunner, the *Hot Blast*. The Ayers family had spent some years in China, and Harry Ayers was an avid internationalist, a sentiment Anne shared.[46]

The *Star*'s newest reporter approached her job with characteristic zeal, frequently working until after midnight to *put the paper to bed*. At least once she even climbed out a window onto the roof to elude her father, who came to the office late at night agitated because his daughter was not yet home. Anne's first assignment was a rather unglamorous feature on the local Girl Scout camp, but she squirmed at an aged typewriter, writing and rewriting drafts. The story was received without comment, and her first days in the newsroom were spent with little to do but busy work and fillers. Seeing that she would have to generate her own ideas for articles, Anne soon came up with an array of material that dealt with the war's impact on Anniston as a result of Fort McClellan. The material ranged from a look at women in local defense-related industries to coverage of entertainment programs for soldiers. She soon began covering the fort regularly and volunteering for the USO.[47]

Although even before she came to the *Star* Anne had set her sights on a larger, more important newspaper, working there strengthened her commitment to a career in journalism. She wrote, *When I got that first check for $15 for reading proof . . . it was the strangest feeling because I thought, "Here's someone giving me money to do something I just love to do. There's something wrong with that!"* The greatest challenge of the summer for the novice reporter came when her editor offered her a chance to write an editorial, partly because she had proven herself genuinely useful and partly as a result of staff shortages. Anne initially leaped at the opportunity, but soon he was soliciting an editorial from her every day. For subject matter, Anne turned to her love of international affairs rather than to regional or local issues; yet her wellspring of ideas ran dry after only a few days, convincing her that she needed more knowledge of what she extolled as *the colorful, throbbing, chaotic world* in order to be a first-rate journalist.[48]

Randolph-Macon Years

On Friday, September 17, 1943, Anne entered the stately red brick buildings of Randolph-Macon Woman's College for her first term. Intellectually, R-MWC far surpassed Stratford. Known on occasion as the "Wellesley of the South," R-MWC ranked prominently among small colleges nationwide and had since its inception aspired to the academic prestige of the "seven sisters" women's campuses of the Northeast. In 1915 it was rated as one of only six southern women's postsecondary institutions (from a total of 140) judged worthy of the term "college" by the Southern Association of College Women.[49]

Socially, however, Anne was not as comfortable as she had been in the *cocoon* Stratford had provided for her. *I just had such a tremendous feeling about Stratford, and I never loved Randolph-Macon like that. I might have if I'd gone there first, but there were about ten of us, "junior transfers," they called us, and we were all in one dormitory, away from where the other juniors lived. I made friends there, but I just never felt like I was totally a part of that class.*[50]

The element of cliquishness Anne abhorred stemmed from an exclusivity that was an integral part of the R-MWC "tradition," expressed forcefully in many of the college's social functions. "We [are] a school of fine traditions and customs which we hold dear, and we know that soon you will love and respect them as we do," a class officer admonished freshmen in the first issue of the *Sundial* student newspaper that greeted Anne and other newcomers in the fall of 1943. Not knowing these customs made them easy to violate, however, and the bounds of acceptable behavior could, from the outside, look pretty narrow. Campus culture included several "secret societies," and it was considered a social blunder, for instance, to wear red on Fridays unless one belonged to the secret society known as STAB. The R-MWC newspaper boasted in 1944 that "no other woman's college in the country has such an imposing array" of secret societies. Only on Thursdays and Mondays could "the un-elect" wear whatever colors they wished. Another equally powerful ritual centered on a rivalry in sports and dormitories between "odds" and "evens" (so designated according to graduating year).[51]

The roots of these rituals lay in the earliest days of women's colleges, when elaborate community-building exercises were designed to initiate young women into the intense all-female culture that differed sharply from their previous experiences. By the 1920s, many leading northeastern women's colleges had eliminated or curtailed such customs as they increasingly stressed a gender-neutral environment. But in the South, the rituals still flourished.[52]

Much of campus social life was organized through the Greek sororities, a practice that contributed further to cliquishness. Each fall, the first week of campus life was devoted not to classes or orientation but to the sorority rushes that thrilled some and estranged others. Other women's colleges had encountered problems with the tendency of sororities to promote social and economic hierarchies. Barnard, for instance, had eliminated them in 1915. In the South, however, that insight was still a long way off. (In 1959, over the protests of powerful alumnae and after a stormy debate among trustees, R-MWC would abolish its sororities for that same reason.)[53]

In spite of Anne's sense of alienation, she was not yet a rebel, nor was she a social misfit. She immediately pledged Alpha Omicron Pi, but although she cabled her mother that she was *happy and thrilled beyond words*, the sorority community did not make her feel more at home. *I felt like I was going to pieces that fall. Harriet came down to see me and helped me through that period. Part of it was physical: they finally put me in the infirmary and gave me a metabolism test and determined that my thyroid was real low. That can make you depressed, so they started giving me thyroid pills and I began feeling real good. In fact, I almost got myself into trouble because I felt so good taking one that I started taking about four of them.*[54]

Anne's difficulties in adjusting to the "bigger pond" of R-MWC led her to write extensively in her journal about her search for a purpose in life and about what she thought of as a tension in her personality between the material and the spiritual. Her spiritual quest resurfaced as a problem of adjustment, and she chastised herself for selfish pursuits or for not loving others fully enough. Often she felt lonely in spite of the companionship of friends. Even after she settled into life at R-MWC more comfortably, she continued to feel that her life had a purpose she had not yet found, and she vacillated between relying on her deep religious faith to move her toward that aim and questioning the presence of God in such a troubled world.[55]

Anne's anxieties were evident only to those who knew her well, however. In classes and student activities, she continued to shine. Within a month of her arrival, she had joined the staff of the *Sundial* newspaper, and when she acted the starring role in the fall play, a reviewer noted "the feeling and assurance . . . easiness and natural talent" she brought to the stage. What appeared to ease her distress most was the discovery of modern dance. To fulfil a physical education requirement, she studied modern dance under Eleanor Struppa, a former student of Martha Graham's who employed Graham's technique in a dance group at R-MWC that she had established in 1930. Anne found in dance a way to cure what she feared at her worst moments were the beginnings of mental illness: *I began to get control of my body and then I felt like I had control of my mind too.* She now had a release valve for her volatile emotions, as the Graham method emphasized mood and interpretation, encouraging full emotional expression. In the second term of her junior year Anne became an apprentice in Struppa's ensemble, and the following year was inducted as a full member.[56]

Anne left behind her initial difficulties with R-MWC as she dived into the new intellectual waters it offered and became an English major. She was not quite the same young woman who had gone off to school in the fall of 1941, having discovered a new love of the arts and tapped into inner resources she hadn't known she possessed. Even her name was different. Somehow, without particularly intending to, she lost her double name between Stratford and R-MWC. She was no longer "Anne Gambrell" but simply "Anne."[57]

Her childhood bookishness flowered into a passion for literature of all sorts. In this wider intellectual milieu, she began to appreciate literature not only for its sheer beauty but as a tool she could use to make sense of the world. Thomas Wolfe—the North Carolina writer whose works linked

Anne's treasured concepts of truth, beauty, love to a more enlightened social consciousness—became one of her favorite authors. She read with interest the latest journalistic accounts of the war, such as William Shirer's 1941 nonfiction bestseller, *Berlin War Diary*. Inspired by the Fitzgerald sisters' insistence that one couldn't be truly educated without reading Tolstoy's *War and Peace*, Anne designed an independent study in Russian literature as a means of demystifying the vast nation that seemed to raise so many demons for Americans. Her most beloved novelist in college was Dostoevski, whose work, she wrote, gave her *a spiritual exaltation worth ten years of ordinary life*. After reading a selection of Turgenev's works, she became troubled by what she saw even then as excessive American anticommunism. *When we realize how corrupt and tyrannical the old aristocracy had become, who are we—we, who have never known such an unbalanced social system—to condemn the methods necessary for its destruction?* was a question Anne posed in a class essay on Turgenev.[58]

Anne's friendship with Harriet Fitzgerald continued to grow, and her friend encouraged her interest in affairs of the day. Because the older woman came to campus regularly for board meetings and exhibits, the two had plenty of opportunities to see each other. Anne also began to visit Harriet in New York, and during one of her early stays, she had an experience that prompted her to reject some lifelong assumptions—vaguely formed as they were—about race. She described the incident in her 1958 memoir, *The Wall Between*, as one of the supporting beams upon which her later political transformation rested. *[Harriet] arranged for me to meet and have dinner with a friend of hers, a young Negro woman just about my age, who was playing a part in a Broadway play. . . . I went to the meeting with some misgivings. Never in my life had I eaten with a Negro. I was intellectually pleased at the opportunity to break this lifelong pattern, but I was somewhat ill at ease in the face of a new experience. . . . She too was from the South, and I think looking back on it that she must have realized my feelings. She undoubtedly went out of her way to put me at ease. Soon we were talking—talking, talking—discussing all the things in which we were mutually interested. To me she was a wonder, for she was a success in a field that I at that moment aspired to. Suddenly, in the midst of the conversation, the realization swept over me that I had completely forgotten that there was a difference in our color. We were no longer white and Negro—we were just two young women talking about things we liked to talk about. Somewhere inside of me a voice seemed to say: "Why, there is no race problem at all! There are only the people who have not realized it yet." It was a tremendous revelation . . . some heavy shackles seemed to fall from my feet. . . . In more recent years, I have known many friendships across the race bar, more close and certainly more last-*

ing than that one was; but never again was there the startling revelation of that first moment when the walls came tumbling down. . . . I never got over it.[59]

Dimly, during her last two years of college, Anne began to realize that segregation was, as she put it many times thereafter, *just plain wrong*. There was no one pointed moment accompanying that insight. But her encounter with Harriet's friend in New York was a pivotal moment in that odyssey.[60]

Anne spent much of her spare time in the little reading nook in a corner of the school library, her head bent over the classics. Engrossed as she was in the life of the mind, she had only a general sense of the national debate that was drumming in the background on the subject of race. Yet as the war permeated more fully the students' understanding of contemporary society, the issue began to find its way more often into the late-night discussions for which Anne and her friends were notorious. *I don't remember talking about it much at Stratford, we really were in an ivory tower there, but my recollection of some conversations at Randolph-Macon is that most of the young women I knew were opposed to segregation. We weren't doing anything about it, so it was purely theoretical [and] it didn't take any particular courage to feel that. But it didn't seem unusual either; it was fairly fashionable. It was sort of like we rejected our parents' ideas about segregation just like we rejected their "old fogey" ideas about sex. It was a reflection of the times.*[61]

Others who attended R-MWC with Anne but socialized with a less "artsy" crowd remembered the atmosphere there as more repressive. After a painful experience with sorority rush, Helen Cotton, who became Anne's freshman "little sister" when Anne was a senior, never felt that she fit in there because of the cliquishness. Shirley Strickland, another friend from Anne's year, did more than talk against segregation privately; she actively challenged racial separation through the campus Young Women's Christian Association (YWCA). In 1944, amid a hum of controversy, the YWCA group of which Strickland was a part brought a group of young African American women to sing at a vespers service. Strickland found none of the acceptance for her views that Anne recalled; on the contrary, she experienced the climate as stifling, especially in its racial conservatism. The YWCA had historically been one of the few easily available outlets through which young southern women of Anne's race and class could surmount the social barriers imposed by regional culture, and many both before her generation and after it have reported the Y as a source of personal and social liberation. Its appeal did not extend to Anne, however; she was not yet an activist in any sense, and it may have been her very lack of activism that made controversial talk seem easily tolerated or even cool.[62]

Still, Anne perceived with excitement the portents of change around her, and she felt a part of something new. *I began to sense that people were conceiving of World War II as a fight against the ideology of Hitler, which was different from the sort of patriotism I'd learned from my parents. We were aware that in fighting Hitler, we were fighting a racist ideology, though I don't think we used that word "racist." It didn't escape people I knew that those ideas about racial superiority were akin to what we had here in the South, so there was just this atmosphere that after the war things were going to be different. We had quite an image of ourselves as part of the "New South." Every generation thinks they are the New South, you know.*[63]

Race and WWII

Talk of a New South did indeed reach back for well over half a century. In 1883 *Atlanta Constitution* editor Henry Grady first popularized the phrase in a New York speech attempting to woo northern investors to a region scarcely recovered from the economic dislocations of the Civil War. Calling for the South to leave her agrarian past behind, Grady outlined a prescription for industrial development that included a heavy, if unspoken, dose of racial hierarchy. A racially segmented labor force kept wages low, but, ironically, depressed wages also hampered the very industrialization New South boosters like Grady sought by attracting mostly labor-intensive endeavors such as lumbering or textiles and by discouraging labor-saving mechanization. As a result, southern industrialization was by the dawn of the twentieth century insufficient to loosen the firm grip of insularity, widespread poverty, and remnants of a plantation economy.[64]

To a large extent, what kept the New South old was the very centrality of holding on to its plantation-based traditions, which hinged on degradation of blacks. The Civil War abolished slavery, but sectional differences of ideology and habit lingered, animated by a fierce hostility to outsiders stemming from the experience of defeat at the hands of the North and passed down by generations of southern whites with little to hold on to save the supposed glory of their forefathers in gray. The resulting social climate did not much lend itself to new ideas of any kind, and after the turn of the century, many African Americans, liberals, and intellectuals left the region. Even Roosevelt's New Deal programs of the 1930s brought only halting moves toward modernization—and always amidst a chorus intoning the importance of southern traditions.[65]

What changed all this, more than any other single event, was World War II. The war jump-started the U.S. economy, ending the Depression in a manner that New Deal programs of the '30s, for all their optimism, were never fully able to do, partially because of the political opposition they encountered in the South. Now, defense dollars flowed across the nation, and southern politicians garnered the lion's share. Those dollars uprooted long-standing social and economic patterns, mechanized southern agriculture, enhanced transportation networks, and penetrated regional insularity. Finally, there actually was a New South, and the region became fused to the nation economically and politically, once and for all.[66]

Struggles over defense jobs energized black labor and civil rights activists and yielded a federal order banning racial discrimination in the defense industry and creating a wartime Fair Employment Practices Commission (FEPC) to monitor compliance. Well over a million southern workers were unionized by 1941, yet attempts to remedy discrimination were hampered from within by southern whites' beliefs in segregation and white supremacy. Increasing black militancy seemed only to heighten white reaction, and even where interracial trade unionism did threaten the racial status quo, unionization continued to meet with brutal retaliation from business and community leaders.[67]

African Americans responded with their feet in the greatest internal migration in American history. More than two million blacks emigrated in the 1940s from the South to northern and western industrial centers, where the boom in wartime defense jobs held greater promise of inclusion.[68]

At that moment, civil rights became a national issue. Ever since the Compromise of 1877 ended the faltering experiment in colorblind democracy that was Reconstruction, American politicians had allowed the South to carry the weight of the nation's unresolved stance toward African American freedom, but the exploding numbers of blacks in cities such as Chicago and Pittsburgh changed all that. Even among African Americans who stayed in the South, there was substantial migration into industrial centers such as Atlanta and Birmingham. There blacks faced overcrowding, employment discrimination, and inadequate public services in segregated neighborhoods but fomented a lively urban culture that, as their numbers increased, could scarcely be contained by white authority.[69]

As Anne and her classmates observed, the very issues at stake in the war also helped to propel racial injustice to the forefront of Americans' consciousness. Hitler minced no words as to the racial/ethnic component of his crusade, and fairly early on in the fight against fascism, the *Pittsburgh Courier*, a popular black newspaper, launched a "Double V" campaign for victory over fascism abroad and victory over segregation at home, purposefully linking the international situation with U.S. racial disparities. After the United States entered the war, that connection grew plainer every day through the melee of discriminatory acts against African Americans in uniform, especially but not exclusively in the South, by whites who were supposed to be on their side. These assaults highlighted the contradictions between rhetoric and reality in U.S. race relations and invigorated civil rights activism and examinations of race in popular culture. NAACP membership rose during WWII to an all-time high, with a nearly tenfold increase in the South. Black participation in the CIO climbed as unionists realized that the labor movement could not progress without the support of African American workers.[70]

These wartime developments nudged the issue of race to the foreground of American politics, exposing ugly fault lines which regional insularity had previously allowed much of the nation to ignore. In matters of discrimination and segregation, the difference between the South and the rest of the country was more one of degree than of kind, but issues like voting rights and racial violence provided glaring exceptions. The war laid at the door of both the South and the nation a challenge on race which the vast majority of white southerners were quite unprepared to meet. Faced with a loosening of the region's race hierarchy, ultraconservative politicians like Georgia's Eugene Talmadge or James Eastland, then a junior senator from Mississippi, reacted with predictable hostility to the least iota of change. Southern liberals, on the other hand, were much less united in their views, mired as they were in a century's worth of regional defensiveness. Since 1938, the Southern Conference for Human Welfare had been straining against segregation and disfranchisement, cooperating with the NAACP and the CIO wherever possible. But wars also tend to foster conservatism, and despite the relative popularity of WWII, it was little different. The result was a polarization of sentiment within the small community of southern "race liberals" which left them as a group unable to seize the opportunity for regional racial changes. Even Ellis Arnall, who defeated Eugene Talmadge for the Georgia governorship in 1942—and whom Anne remembered as a kind of *New South hero* among her college friends—repeatedly defended segregation even as he prosecuted the Ku Klux Klan in Georgia and distanced himself from an opponent he denounced as a "racist."[71]

The currents of racial change were a major ingredient in the social ferment Anne remembered from her college years. Flavoring that brew was the heightened continuation of social protest from the New Deal era, when organizers from the Communist and Socialist parties had assisted poor and working-class southerners of both races to form unions to improve their lives. For generations, white southerners as a group had been too cautious and too defensive of their region to condemn racial injustices. But with the founding of the SCHW in 1938 and the spread of the CIO with its message of biracial unionism, people calling themselves "progressive" southerners finally found a voice, however small, to speak of racial reforms.[72]

As the war raged on, however, the rapidly changing social landscape prompted a massive conservative reaction. In 1944 powerful southern Democrats, long uncomfortable with Roosevelt's direction, staged a showdown over FDR's vice president, Henry Wallace, an outspoken liberal agrarian reformer. By 1940 Wallace had become the leading voice of the Democratic Party's left wing, speaking out with unusual frankness about racial injustices. As vice president, Wallace's concerns turned increasingly global, and in May 1942 he issued a popular but controversial call for a peace to WWII that would also bring greater social welfare to the world's masses. Conservatives were not amused, and the campaign to unseat Wallace became a metaphor for the competing visions at war within the Democratic Party.[73]

The meaning of that battle was not lost on Anne. By the time she was old enough to keep abreast of politics, Wallace was vice president. His idealism appealed to her, as did his internationalism. As she began to search for a context for the tremendous social upheaval around her, his message made good sense. The 1944 Democratic Party convention was the first political event about which she ever felt strongly: *I was still too young to vote, but that was the convention where Roosevelt dumped Henry Wallace and took up Truman as vice president. Wallace was seen by a lot of people as the heart and soul of the New Deal. He was one of [its] main architects, and also a great advocate of peace in the world.* The emotionally charged confrontation over Wallace's place on the 1944 presidential ticket caught her attention and remained, for her, a powerful formative moment. She read the experience through a liberal, politically attuned reporter's lens during her summertime stint at the *Anniston Star.* Though her political sensibilities had not crystallized into a fully coherent world view, Wallace's vision of world peace undergirded by racial and social justice became an almost intuitive part of how she thought things ought to be: *I felt that the Democratic Party was selling its soul the day it dumped Wallace.*[74]

During the few weeks surrounding Anne's graduation from college, the world situation shifted daily. Like so many Americans, she now cherished a deep devotion to Roosevelt, and his death on April 12, 1945, hit her hard. For young adults of her age group, FDR was the only president they could remember, and his death fueled Anne's uncertainties about the shape of the future. Revelations of Nazi genocide in Europe and the rumors of atomic weapons capability reinforced her conviction that international cooperation and an end to wars were critical in the postwar world. The primary means of institutionalizing the president's greatness, in her view, was the creation of the United Nations as an international mediating body, and her most political act of her college career was to lead a vespers prayer service at Randolph-Macon in support of the UN on the Sunday of its founding on April 26, 1945. Anne issued a call to world leaders to adopt a commitment to peace, and she had the audience pledge aloud to a faith in the power of the human spirit as correspondent with faith in God. It would be a few months yet before Americans saw the horrors their atomic weapons could wreak, but Anne's words conveyed a sense of the fear that gripped many people as they suspected that the nuclear age was at hand.[75]

Graduation from College

Less than two weeks later, on May 8, 1945, Allied victory in Europe displaced some of the excitement Anne's class felt leading up to graduation. There could be no full-fledged celebration in the wake of a popular president's death and while war in the Pacific dragged on. A sense of crisis pierced the usual exuberance of graduation activities, and sometimes Anne thought her own destiny was being linked to world events. The end of school was coming, however, no matter what else happened. Only four days after V-E Day, she danced the lead role of Clytemnestra for the college's Greek revival of *Agamemnon*.[76]

On May 27, 1945, Anne and the 140 other young R-MWC graduates gathered on the front campus to carry out the long-standing senior tradition of planting ivy as a parting gesture to the school. After graduation, Anne left to relax with Lucile Schoolfield and a couple of other friends at the Schoolfields' cottage on the Delaware coast. Then she returned to her parents' home to write full time for the *Star*. Her future plan at that moment was to stay in the South only temporarily and to enroll in Columbia University's School of Journalism in the fall of 1946. She had her mind set on becoming a great newspaperwoman.[77]

Anne's four years in college represented an intellectual awakening which she has always maintained was a necessary prerequisite for the political transformation she would undergo in the coming few years. Her father, embittered later by the ideological gap that separated him and his youngest child for most of her adult life, agreed in a fashion. He told his adult daughter repeatedly that his biggest mistake as a parent was sending her to college.[78]

Anne left school with a lot of career spunk, a cautious optimism about what the end of WWII would bring, and a vague feeling of identification with a "New South," but it was nevertheless a terribly contested future into which she and her graduating class stepped as young adults.[79]

CHAPTER THREE

ALABAMA NEWSPAPERWOMAN

You must remember that you have allies and allies even in the white South . . . white youth in the South is peculiarly frustrated. There is not a single ideal which they can express or aspire to, that does not bring them into flat contradiction with the Negro problem. The more they try to escape it, the more they land into hypocrisy, lying, and double-dealing; the more they become what they least wish to become, the oppressors and despisers of human beings. Some of them, in larger and larger numbers, are bound to turn toward the truth and to recognize you as brothers and sisters, as fellow travellers toward the dawn.

—W. E. B. DuBois, "Behold the Land" speech to the Southern Negro
Youth Congress, Columbia, South Carolina, October 20, 1946[1]

UPON HER GRADUATION FROM COLLEGE in mid-1945, Anne knew nothing of the world of the leading African American public intellectual W. E. B. DuBois, or of the Southern Negro Youth Congress (SNYC). Looking at society still through the lens of her own privilege and not an activist in any sense, she was not yet one of the allies DuBois described. But her return to the Deep South as a newspaper reporter brought with it a mounting frustration as she began to see the distance between the promise and the practice of democracy in the region.

When she returned to Alabama to write full time for the *Anniston Star*, Anne initially had great hopes for the postwar world, with the founding of the

United Nations and the war's end in sight. The alliance between the United States and the Soviet Union was fraught with tensions, but from her youthful perspective, the two looked firmly united against the evil of fascism. The terrific shock of the atomic bombings in Hiroshima and Nagasaki jerked her idealism up short, however.[2]

Anne's idea of a peaceful, economically stable world was rather general, derived from a combination of her reading interests, discussions with Harriet Fitzgerald, and the portrait Henry Wallace had sketched in his wartime speeches. Although she was not politically active, her sympathies lay to the left of center, especially in the arenas of U.S.-Soviet cooperation and social welfare. As of yet, she was scarcely cognizant of the level of opposition such views were now engendering. As early as 1941, Henry Luce wrote a charged editorial in his *Life* magazine urging Americans to go to war to create the first "American century," a vast commercial empire secured by U.S. military triumph. Relative to its allies, the United States entered the postwar world militarily and economically supreme. As business conservatives like Luce saw it, the next step was to rebuild Western nations to shore up markets for U.S. goods. And wartime imperatives made them well placed to do it: industrial and military officials had replaced New Dealers in key positions of authority in the federal government. Proponents of the "American century" view resented what they saw as the passé ideas of liberal internationalists like Henry Wallace, who wished to spread the wealth to create what Wallace called a "century of the common man" (a phrase Anne soon adopted in her writing). The American century to which Luce aspired would become more of an anathema to Anne as she grew increasingly politicized over the next several years.[3]

"The age of concrete and rayon" was Harriet Fitzgerald's glib description of the postwar era in one of the many letters the two friends exchanged after Anne's return to Alabama. Harriet's sardonic observation on the new preeminence of consumer goods was serious business to political and corporate leaders determined to extend the free market system. Such men saw Soviet communism—with its rhetoric of workers' rights and planned economies—as a threat akin to that of fascism, and they described the two ideologies in similarly dire terms. To the alarm of people like Anne, American foreign-policy makers transformed the Soviet Union from a close wartime ally into a hostile enemy in amazingly short order. There was increasing polarization between such forces in the Truman administration and others, like Wallace, who remained committed to New Deal reforms and a buoyant internationalism that stressed cooperation over confrontation.[4]

Part of the problem was that Harry Truman was simply no Roosevelt. In his first postwar speeches Truman continued to envision New Deal social prosperity, but he soon revealed himself to be much less the ally of organized labor and social reformers than his popular predecessor had been. Republicans and anti–New Deal southern Democrats in Congress began hammering away at what remained of the New Deal almost immediately, employing hyperbolic anticommunist rhetoric that would soon become an established feature of the domestic Cold War that took shape over the coming months. There was no shortage of anticommunist legislation already in place in 1945. The House committee that would play a leading role in investigating alleged subversive activities had been established in 1938 under the sponsorship of Rep. Martin Dies of Texas (who considered the New Deal a virtual treason), and it set into motion the idea of guilt by association. In 1940 the Smith Act passed with overwhelming congressional support, making it a crime to advocate overthrow of the U.S. government by force.[5]

All that was lacking under Roosevelt was the political will to employ these anticommunist initiatives in any sustained way. Conservatives seized the opportunities presented by FDR's death and the war's end to erode what was left of such restraint in the White House. For reactionary white southerners, resistance to heightened pressure from the long-subjugated black population in their midst blended easily into the nascent collective fear of communism. The word "subversive" began to echo through the chambers of Congress and of southern state houses, applied to anyone challenging the racial status quo but conjuring up visions of internal communist conspiracies.[6]

In truth, the "red" and "black" issues in southern social protests were never entirely separate. Since the Depression era, Communists had been on the front lines for racial and social change, and their direct-action tactics (marching, petitioning, and flouting segregation in mass rallies) were more galling to community leaders than the more decorous legislative and judicial approaches of groups like the NAACP, who were themselves a source of affront. The CP held a philosophical commitment to interracial cooperation on an equal basis that was inevitably put to the test when black and white workers actually met to form unions. Still, CP doctrine was more radical and the party's challenges to segregation more direct than those of less confrontational liberal organizations such as the Southern Conference or the NAACP. The party appealed to some politically active, black, working-class southerners, and CP members (black and white, southern and nonsouthern) led the way in developing within the wartime labor movement an ideology of militant, interracial unionism that combined shop-floor organizing with workers' education to encourage a politically aware membership willing to defy racial conventions. CP members and supporters of both races were disproportionately represented in the most militant trade unions, particularly those that pushed for black self-determination. Partly because they defied white supremacy, left-leaning southern unionists—even those native to the region—triggered hostility to outsiders, trade unions, and "reds," all of whom had long been seen as threats to the southern social fabric. In Alabama, CP members were always subjects of controversy and repression; yet they were prominent in unions such as Mine, Mill, and Smelter and in groups like the SNYC. Never a large number, Communists nevertheless helped to shape a radical critique of southern society by heightened protests in both CP-initiated groups and coalitions with liberals during the postwar period. Forged during the Popular Front period of the mid-1930s, these coalitions grew more militant on the one hand as postwar racial and labor violence intensified and more beleaguered on the other, as anticommunism became a more widespread cultural fear.[7]

Anne's feelings of euphoria from what she perceived as the triumph of democratic ideals over fascism faded after only a short time back in Alabama. While international concerns continued to preoccupy her writings, it was also no longer possible to ignore the turmoil closer at hand. *After the war we had this sense that things weren't going to be this great smooth sail into the future. I could sense that even in the very restricted world I was in in Alabama. . . . When I went back home to work, I began, as a newspaper reporter, to see things I really hadn't seen before, in terms of how people lived.*[8]

There was no such thing as justice for blacks in Alabama's legal system, a fact that covering the courthouse made clear to the young reporter. Anne's immersion in journalism (an individualistic field, for the most part) equipped her very little when it came to tackling social problems in any manner more direct than chronicling them. Years after leaving Alabama she learned that groups like the SNYC and the Southern Conference had been there, resisting the racial and economic inequities that increasingly depressed her the more she noticed them. Even if she had known of their efforts, Anne might not have sought them out: she was still not a joiner. Her writings up through this period reveal a strong belief in individual over collective action. Having no movement to shape and propel her discontent, she plunged more deeply into her writing as she withdrew emotionally—repulsed—from the society in her midst.[9]

Living with her parents again was an adjustment. She spent most waking hours at the newspaper, out on assignments, socializing with other newspaper people, or in her room composing letters to friends far away. She soon decided that she needed more work experience before entering graduate school in journalism. Yet the *Star* did not really square with her journalistic aspirations either. Part of why she had returned there full time was the ease of doing so. Another reason was her lifelong difficulty with saying "no" to anyone who ever told her they needed her, and Ayers had let her know long before she finished college that he would like her to return. Within three months of returning to Anniston, she felt an internal malaise settling over her and began to consider other newspapers.[10]

Gradually Anne's editorials started to link her hope for international peace with economic stability and a world free of prejudice. The state to which she returned was not the same one she had grown up in. Just as liberal and conservative visions were warring in the foreign policy realm, so too were the divisions sharpening between New Deal reformers and disgruntled Alabama conservatives. Although it was under attack, southern liberalism emerged from the war as a vibrant political voice. In the 1940s the people historians have sometimes called "race liberals" joined forces with an extremely potent ally, the trade union movement.[11]

The wartime labor movement made considerable inroads into the state's expanding industrial centers, Anniston among them. By war's end, CIO membership in the South stood at 400,000, with Birmingham as one of its strongholds. Unionism in Dixie had a long way to go, but with the support it had received from Roosevelt's presidency, organized labor was now a player in national politics. Southern labor leaders were quick to see that they would have to amass electoral power to oust conservative, antilabor politicians who had long held political sway. To do so would require greater political mobilization of unionists, both black and white; it would also involve some political education of southern whites on race.[12]

As the influence of organized labor spread during WWII, however, supporters of states' rights and an aggressive white supremacy added the evils of trade unionism to their list of regional maladies. In the postwar era, many outside the South agreed. The short-lived postwar recession was an almost inevitable outgrowth of the economy's struggle to absorb ten million ex-military personnel and convert from wartime to consumer production. Always controversial (and particularly so in the South), trade unions—whose no-strike pledge expired at war's end—took a lot of the blame for the economic sluggishness in the immediate postwar era. By the dawn of 1946, the

Star had reported strikes in the coal, telephone, steel, automotive, and electrical industries. Labor's call for a national wage and price policy to smooth the reconversion process went largely unheeded, grating as it did on the antigovernment orientation of many lawmakers, and strikes continued, with the greatest number of strikes in any one year in American history tallied in 1946. The *Star* joined other newspapers nationally in harsh criticisms of the militancy of postwar labor, proclaiming in January 1946 that "our American way of life is threatened by strikes." Months later the *Star* named John L. Lewis, former head of the CIO, a "national menace." The idea that unions were un-American was not new to American culture, but in the postwar era it developed greater potency, meshing with growing fears of communism and of social changes more broadly.[13]

Anne's contact with trade unions was minimal during her tenure at the *Star*, but the racial hierarchy that she had once tacitly accepted as part of the southern landscape now came into sharper focus for her as she followed local politics. All around her, it seemed, the issue of race was exploding as never before. Returning black veterans brought with them a new sense of entitlement, and across the region they began to confront Jim Crow. Although some whites now supported their efforts, others responded with violence, and an estimated 40 African Americans—mostly veterans—were lynched in the aftermath of the war. One of the most violent confrontations took place in Columbia, Tennessee, in February 1946, after a disagreement in which a white store owner mistreated a black woman whose son, a veteran, was then physically assaulted by a white worker in the store for his attempts to settle the matter. Whites threatened to lynch the two, and nearly 1,000 state troopers and guardsmen rampaged through the black community, killing several and arresting dozens in reaction to the community's posture of armed self-defense.[14]

Shock waves of racial violence reverberated across the South as black veterans' demands for respect met with brutal repression. In mid-1946, a young tenant farming veteran, his brother-in-law, and their wives were lined up and shot by a white mob in Monroe, Georgia. No one was charged with the crime. By mid-decade the winds of racial change were no longer beneath the surface, something average white southerners could ignore.[15]

The climate for African Americans in postwar Anniston was considerably less charged than in towns like Columbia or Monroe. The main thrust in civil rights, according to Gordon Rogers, a local black veteran who headed the Anniston NAACP in the late 1940s, was voter registration. "Black people were reluctant to identify openly with any movement," Rogers reflected. Rogers remembered no race-based confrontations after he returned from duty in 1945, but the threat of violence was there, just as it had been less than a month after the end of WWI, when antiblack rioting at Fort McClellan followed the arrest of a black soldier for the murder of a white streetcar conductor. Rogers joined other veterans in organizing a black branch of the American Legion, and in early 1946 a new group, the Calhoun County Negro Veterans Organization, announced its intent to help blacks obtain their GI benefits. "The idea of segregation wasn't quite so strong here in Anniston as in Birmingham or Tuskegee," Rogers recalled. Yet neither was the militancy of those pushing against Jim Crow, perhaps because of the mutedness of racial conflict relative to other parts of Alabama. Despite an aura of moderation and progress, many racial barriers seemed as immutable as ever.[16]

Only a few months after her return to Anniston, Anne found herself facing down one of those barriers. Throwing her energy into her writing, she continued the coverage of Fort McClellan she had begun as a student reporter and soon met Dick Linebau, an officer who edited the *Cycle*, a base-sponsored newspaper covering life at the fort. In the fall of 1945 Linebau offered Anne a second job: working part time to put out the weekly *Cycle*. Anne already worked past midnight on some days, so she had no idea how she might manage another writing job; yet she was tempted by the offer and decided to think it over. Her parents, however, became quite hysterical when she told them that the other member of Linebau's staff was a black serviceman. The idea of a white woman working in any proximity to an African American man was still a strict social taboo in the postwar South, and in the outcry that followed, Anne yielded to her parents' protests. She declined the job offer, telling herself that her presence on the staff might jeopardize her colleague's safety (earlier in the year two charges of "assault with intent to ravish" had been filed against black soldiers at Fort McClellan for alleged improprieties with white women at the fort, and throughout the region's history the charge had frequently been levied for the most minor infraction of racial decorum by black males toward white women). Not yet possessed of convictions on race strong enough to make her defy her parents' wishes, Anne came away from the incident frustrated and critical of both herself and the culture around her.[17]

The liberal editorial policies of the *Star* partially obscured the barriers that African Americans faced by allowing local whites to rest on their laurels for being what they thought of as "moderate." The *Star* did not come out openly against segregation (nor did any other southern white newspaper until after the Supreme Court's *Brown* decision in 1954). But in mid-1945 the *Star* editorialized against the poll tax, a primary tool for preventing widespread voter registration of lower-income people, black and white. In the wake of that editorial, Anne began a running argument about racial inequities with her father, who reacted to wartime changes, as did many white southerners, with increasing racial and class conservatism.[18]

When Anne wrote about that family conflict in her 1958 memoir, she told of a troubling conversation with a *Southern white man of a generation older than mine*. What she did not say was that the man was her father, a fact she did not wish to reveal during his lifetime. Their confrontation gives eloquent testimony to the beginnings of her journey far from the southern traditions of her upbringing. As Anne described it in her book, Gambrell McCarty *was infuriated that I, a Southern girl, supposedly "well-bred," could express such treason [support for a federal antilynching law]. Suddenly in the heat of the argument, he said: "We ought to have a good lynching every once in a while to keep the nigger in his place." I was speechless. I could not believe what I had heard. To the day I die I think I will hear those words ringing in my ears. . . . A moment later when he was calmer, he regretted what he had said. I still have doubts that this particular man . . . would ever himself join a lynch mob. But in a very profound sense he meant exactly what he had said. . . . A gentle, apparently civilized man, he had already committed murder in his heart and mind. I thought to myself then and have often wondered since, "What could segregation ever do to the Negro as terrible as the thing it had done to this white man?"*[19]

The clash between Anne and her father was a microcosm of conflicts being played out in state and regional politics. To the extent that the New Deal and the war had tampered with segregation, reaction came, predictably, in a higher-pitched defense of Jim Crow. One southern change that appeared most threatening to segregation—and probably to men like Gambrell McCarty—concerned the continued disfranchisement of African Americans. In the wake of the U.S. Supreme Court's 1944 *Smith v. Allwright* decision outlawing the white primary, the Alabama Democratic Party in January 1946 reluctantly declared its primary election "open to all" while legislators privately scrambled to find a way to preserve white supremacy at the ballot box. With poll taxes and other voting restrictions still in place, African Americans were not exactly flooding southern polls in the wake of *Smith*. Yet Alabama's reaction to the ruling was, like that of other southern states, to push for ever tighter state-level voting restrictions to keep blacks out while at least paying lip service to the voting rights of lower-class whites.[20]

The result was the proposed Boswell Amendment to the state Constitution, an alteration that gave local registrars virtually unlimited power to determine the fitness of any prospective voter by conducting an "understanding" test of the U.S. Constitution. The battle over the Boswell Amendment presaged the shape of things to come. Its sponsors stoked racial fears and summoned the specter of Reconstruction-era "Negro domination," portraying their opponents as either a "radical-reformer element not really of the South . . . Communistic groups," or, worse yet in a one-party state, Republicans. Local control meant white control, legislators argued, especially in the Alabama Black Belt, where any hint of a threat to the racial order inflamed the white minority. Amid such rhetoric, the Boswell Amendment passed the state legislature almost unanimously. In the increasingly defensive climate of postwar southern white culture, even Alabama's powerful delegation of New Deal defenders were loath to defend black voting rights per se. Instead they focused on the unnecessary extremism of the amendment.[21]

Still, the southern liberalism that had coalesced in 1938 Birmingham with the founding of the Southern Conference for Human Welfare (SCHW) was at an all-time high during the immediate postwar period. The SCHW—linking southern liberals and radicals, blacks and whites, labor and agricultural interests in search of regional economic progress—recorded a membership of 10,000 in the heady postwar optimism of 1946. The Southern Conference called critical attention to regional outbreaks of racial violence, circulating its *Southern Patriot* monthly newsletter to about 17,000 readers. In early 1946 the SCHW formed a sister group, the Southern Conference Educational Fund, or SCEF, as a tax-exempt arm for nonpartisan political education. At the same time, it initiated a voter registration campaign in cooperation with the CIO's newly formed political action committee to support pro–New Deal elected officials. That spring the CIO inaugurated "Operation Dixie" to build a stronger union presence in the South, citing civil rights as a secondary goal.[22]

Despite the South's renowned obsession with states' rights, no state delegation in the nation did more to expand the role of the federal government than Alabama's did in the 1940s. A writer in the *Nation* magazine called the state "the most liberal in the South" in 1947, and one of the SCHW's most active citizen committees was in Alabama. New Dealers there continued to combat the growing conservative backlash, invoking Roosevelt's vision of a democracy big enough to embrace common folk, but without much reference to race.[23]

The *Star*'s publisher, Harry Ayers, was an ardent defender of southern liberalism. In April 1946 one of his paper's editorials proclaimed the conservative South a "myth." Yet even as editors applauded what they called FDR-style "southern progressiveness," their remarks laid bare a familiar, prickly regional defensiveness, decrying northern tendencies to regard the region as a "solid reactionary bloc." That defensiveness had impeded southern liberalism earlier in the century, and still battled within it throughout the postwar era.[24]

For a young woman like Anne—financially comfortable, professionally driven, and living in a newspaper world where social criticism was respectable—the political showdown that was taking shape around her was easy to miss. The peculiar paradox of the era was that widespread social ferment over the past decade had raised the hopes and expectations of people long locked out of full social and economic participation at the same time it triggered massive conservative reaction that quickly put activists in a defensive posture. Because they were free to champion liberalism and criticize the poll tax with their pens, young professionals like Anne experienced a rather abstract sense of possibility in the aftermath of WWII that sometimes clashed with the rigid social realities in their midst. That sense of possibility imploded upon them once the Cold War began in earnest later in the decade.[25]

The southern reform movements that the New Deal had spawned generated growing opposition as liberalism became more attached to the politics of race in the atmosphere of greater black militancy the war had created. Even in the shadow of the Boswell Amendment, the gathering confrontation in Alabama politics was yet to come, however. It was staved off until 1948 mostly because of one unusual man whose political vision made a deep impression on Anne.

"Big Jim" Folsom was a Democratic dark horse gubernatorial candidate whose flamboyant appeal advanced an extremely progressive political agenda that went beyond that of most liberals. Folsom, a towering, lanky insurance salesman, had a natural affinity for the state's downtrodden. The Depression had forced him to leave college to help his family, and a job in the New Deal deepened his intellectual understanding of economic distress. After an unsuccessful bid for the governor's seat in 1942, Folsom broke with fellow Alabama delegates in 1944 and supported keeping Henry Wallace in the vice presidency. Folsom's 1946 platform included two controversial measures that had the potential to dramatically expand the state's electorate: (1) eliminating the poll tax and (2) dislocating the centers of power in the state through reapportionment of the legislature. His program also included abolition of the sales tax and greater expenditures for schools, teacher salaries, pensions, and paving rural roads.[26]

Just as Folsom's programs were aimed at the "little guy," so was his folksy personal style. Traveling country roads almost nonstop, Folsom passed a suds bucket to collect gas money to keep going. He entertained audiences with his homespun humor using everyday rural images to symbolize people's frustrations and hopes. The suds bucket and a mop became metaphors for the needed cleanup he would administer, if elected, at the state capitol. Folsom traveled with a string band, and for back-country farmers, attending one of his rallies was as much a family outing as a political act.[27]

Although his politics were molded from historical movements such as the Populists and the Jacksonians (Andrew Jackson was his lifelong hero), Folsom also believed in the common interests of black and white and in the civil liberties guaranteed in the Bill of Rights. Unlike the Populists, he refused to play to racist sentiments, relying instead on universal concepts of fairness. Many African Americans turned out to hear Folsom speak, and he shook any hand offered to him. Folsom knew that his program would appeal to blacks but that most were unable to vote. As a consequence of both principle and political savvy, he supported black voter registration but did not put it at the center of his campaign.[28]

At first the press found Folsom's campaign amusing, and it was in that context that Anne first heard of his brand of politics. But by the May 7, 1946, primaries, the campaign had developed a momentum that defied all predictions: Folsom came out without quite the needed majority but 16,000 votes ahead of his nearest opponent, Handy Ellis, forcing a runoff. One political force the press had underestimated was the CIO, which had endorsed Folsom and gotten its people to the polls. The other, perhaps, were the white rural folk who turned out to support the man even the ballot identified as "Big Jim." *Star* editors remained skeptical of the leadership capacities of the man they called a "lovable character," but the paper covered the campaign in increasing depth when Folsom's Anniston appearances, as elsewhere, drew thousands.[29]

As a general assignment reporter, Anne followed issues more closely than she did electoral races, and the local issue she cared most about was education. So did Folsom. He and Anne shared an interest in improving educational opportunities for children of all classes, and once she heard him describe his platform, she began to consider his candidacy more seriously. She met him when he spoke in Anniston after the May primary, and she traveled briefly in the campaign's press entourage, feeling optimistic that his programs might help Alabama move in a more humane direction. Anne came to consider Folsom a friend too, though she learned that his reputation as a "ladies' man" was not undeserved when he tried to seduce her.[30]

In the weeks leading to the runoff, Folsom's well-publicized weakness for women was the least of his concerns. Before the first primary, Handy Ellis had run on a fairly liberal, New Deal-esque platform, but after May 7 he seemed desperate for a way to neutralize Folsom's enormous popularity. Suddenly he became more conservative than the conservatives in his red-baiting, race-baiting, and union-bashing attacks, taking out full-page ads in newspapers across the state to blast Folsom for his association with the CIO. Ellis did not resort to all-out racial demagoguery, but he engaged in mild race-baiting, accusing the CIO of undermining southern segregation laws. More commonly he appealed to white southerners' sense of regional solidarity by portraying the group as "alien" to southerners. He repeatedly referred to CIO leaders—and, by association, Folsom—as "communistic." Though guilt by association was not yet a reliable tactic for discrediting one's opponent, the charge presaged what was to come once domestic anticommunism was in full swing later in the decade.[31]

Folsom refused to sling his own mud in reply but gently chided Ellis for the attacks. If there was one thing Folsom was not, to Alabamians, it was an outsider. When he won in a landslide victory on June 4, 1946, Anne took to Calhoun County back roads, interviewing a cross section of residents, mostly rural and working- or lower-middle-class people, in preparation for a story on the phenomenal following Folsom had developed around the state. Her informal poll found that working people took seriously Folsom's identification with their plight. Especially among farmers—usually counted as opponents of unions—Ellis's attacks appeared to have boomeranged, inspiring greater defiance toward the political status quo.[32]

Anne's experience with Folsom's democratic populism helped to shape the political perspective she adopted over the coming months and years. Yet her enthusiasm for the Folsom campaign was still no cure for her restlessness. Living at home became increasingly stifling, and the row over the *Cycle* job was only one of several conflicts between her and her parents. Anita McCarty did not approve of her daughter's drinking, and confronted her whenever Anne came in late and *tipsy* (as Anne described it in a letter to Harriet). Her mother also felt Anne worked too hard, and her constant prodding to reconnect with high school friends got on Anne's nerves. Many of those friends had married their high school sweethearts and settled into lives very much like Anita McCarty's. Anne still considered that a fate worse than death. Partially because she was gone so much of the time, her parents knew little about her social life, but they did know that she spent her free time with other *Star* employees, many of whom they considered beneath them socially. Although Anne tried to avoid open conflicts with her family, she began to feel as if her real life took place somewhere else.[33]

In 1946 the petite, dark-haired young writer had her first serious love affair—with a former *Star* reporter her parents found eminently unsuitable.

Like Anne, Marshall Johnson had grown up in Alabama but had grown past many of the region's widely accepted mores. He and Anne shared a kind of disdain for the society around them. He was 28 to her 21 years and had worked on the *Star* and other newspapers before the war. When he returned to Anniston to freelance in 1945, the two began dating. Johnson had grown up poor, and he was not much concerned with impressing people. *I was quite infatuated with him because he was talented. I could talk to him. He understood how oppressed I felt by [racism], and he was too, but he came from what my family considered the wrong side of the tracks. They didn't think he was proper for me to go with at all, but I liked him so much better than the people I met at the country club dances because he was doing the kind of work I was doing. In a way I loved him, but he couldn't get himself together. He drank a lot.*[34]

Anne drank a good bit herself—as did many of her fellow reporters—but never let it interfere with her work. Her relationship with Johnson continued to deepen despite her parents' disapproval and her own misgivings about his stability. The more she was exposed to the working-class world her parents thought of as the "wrong side of the tracks," the more vital and attractive she found it.[35]

Anne was unsure what shape her adult life would take, but she was crystal clear that she did not want a life like that of so many women around her. That impulse set her apart from many of her own social class in Anniston, who—as Anne saw it—seemed to harbor no greater aspirations than to be well-to-do wives, mothers, and hostesses. She demanded to be taken seriously as a human being, not as a *plaything*. Anne was most driven by her career ambition, and one quality she sought in a man was the ability to accept her as a working woman, a peer. Letters to friends in her college and postcollege years concentrated mostly on her career or her interior struggles of right and wrong—and sometimes on politics and literature—rarely mentioning her love interests at all. When Anne did discuss her romantic life with Harriet or other long-distance friends, she puzzled over the challenge of finding such a man. Around the nation, other career-minded women faced a similar quandary. Postwar films, books, and advertisements groomed women for professional success even as they celebrated female domesticity and prepared men to expect it of their wives and mothers.[36]

Although the next few years would see a resurgence of the domestic ideal, such messages were never again as thoroughgoing as they had been earlier in the century, but coexisted with other, less familiar prescriptions for women suggesting that female success in the public sphere was also desirable. As the war ended, Anne's generation rushed headlong into marriage:

nationally, marriage rates reached a 1946 peak and remained high throughout the postwar era, while average ages at marriage also dropped precipi-
tously for both sexes. Women's employment rates continued to climb, but
the proportion of women attending and completing college continued its
decline in proportion to men. Divorces also became much more commonplace in the postwar period, however, suggesting that many women, like
Anne, were insisting on greater personal fulfillment.[37]

Perhaps the greatest shift for Anne during this period was the loss of the
female community that had so nourished her in college and even in high
school. No longer interested in the same pastimes as her women friends in
Anniston, she kept in closer touch with Harriet and Lucile by mail, but even
that correspondence dwindled as time passed. A very immediate person, Anne
tended to become immersed in whatever situation she found herself in, and
she had a hard time staying connected across space and time. The world of
journalism was still largely a male province, and part of Anne's strategy against
being labeled a "girl reporter" covering mainly society news and features involved becoming, metaphorically speaking, "one of the boys." More and more,
Anne's focus was on her career, and she worked tirelessly at becoming a successful reporter.[38]

She was not alone in that trend. Nationally, postwar media increasingly
celebrated women's career successes and pointed women toward hard work
and public achievements even as they downplayed structural obstacles to such
successes and highlighted female achievers' traditional qualities such as glamour and domesticity. Anne was part of a growing sector of young American
women whose prime focus was on career as well as on matrimony. The young
women who left college in the postwar era entered a culture rife with tension
about proper gender roles, and as social conservatism grew with the spread of
the early Cold War, an antifeminist popular literature appeared that cautioned
women to return to the home and abandon paid employment. Those who
came on the heels of Anne's graduating class found that the widespread prescriptions for women in popular culture left them between the proverbial rock
and a hard place. Long-term career success for women required greater male
participation in domestic duties, but that was an idea whose time was yet to
come. Little wonder that middle-class women of Anne's generation—and their
daughters—responded so passionately to the idea of liberation from the confining "feminine mystique" that the journalist Betty Friedan (herself only
three years younger than Anne) presented to them later in life. Unlike many of
her peers, Anne never retreated from public life into the supposed bliss of domesticity, but like them she saw tremendous cultural reinforcement for the no-

tions of dependency and marriage as the paths to female happiness. Anne's own exacting standards for a partner did not keep her from the same fantasies of romantic fulfillment that were virtually culturally dictated.[39]

Single and ambitious, she found herself facing a medley of conflicting cultural messages about womanhood—and facing them largely alone. Lacking the female kinship she had found so comforting in college, she came to rely more on her own resources for decisions about the direction of her life. At the same time she became more driven, more focused on her work: she abandoned the detailed diaries she had kept since childhood to reflect on her interior life. Though many women from the group who had orbited around Harriet Fitzgerald remained individual supports for Anne, the sense of female community that pervaded her college years would not be replicated in her life again.

———————

Soon after the runoff that won Folsom the governor's seat, Anne concluded that she had had enough of Anniston and the *Star*. In midsummer 1946 she traveled alone to the North Carolina coast, using the first part of her vacation for reflection and the rest to interview with some of the South's most liberal newspapers in Raleigh (*News & Observer*) and Nashville (*Tennessean*). She then went home to Kentucky to visit Mark Ethridge, newspaper publisher and former chairman of Roosevelt's Fair Employment Practices Commission. Anne was not drawn to Louisville only because of her family roots there. Under the tutelage of Ethridge (and of editor in chief Barry Bingham), the *Courier-Journal* had achieved national prestige. When they offered her a position, she was tempted, but because the job was on the staff of the society section rather than in "hard" news, Anne declined, feeling that working in this traditionally female division would limit her.[40]

Her final stop was the *Birmingham News* and *Age-Herald*. The Birmingham newspapers considered themselves among the region's finest too, but that claim did not mean much outside the South. The *Age-Herald*'s prestige derived mainly from its syndicated columnist, John Temple Graves. Before WWII, Graves was one of the South's leading journalistic advocates of New Deal liberalism, but like many of his contemporaries, he embraced an ultraconservative politics of race when faced with the social upheavals of the war years. By 1946 Graves still thought of himself as "liberal," but he now proclaimed segregation worth defending at all costs, even with another Civil War if necessary. His harsh, bitter regional defensiveness flavored his columns and, by association, the tone of the *Age-Herald*. Its sister paper, the afternoon *News*, looked mild by comparison. The competition daily, the *Post*, also struggled to present more "balanced" coverage. Yet the very idea of balance was ludicrous in the context of Birmingham's extraordinary racial and labor violence, much of which was carried out under the auspices of police commissioner Eugene "Bull" Connor (whose brutality would become infamous 17 years later in the glare of television cameras). In the first six weeks of 1946 alone, five African American veterans were reportedly killed in the city by uniformed police officers.[41]

In the postwar South, state-sanctioned violence against blacks was not even news, however. Without warning, Anne stepped into this maelstrom of racial repression at the beginning of September 1946, when she moved to Alabama's industrial center and took a job on the *News*, covering the courthouse beat for both that paper and the morning *Age-Herald*. She stayed only eight months, but what she witnessed during that short time was a profound shock to her sense of fairness. Although Anne has always maintained that no singular event transformed her political outlook, she has reiterated in subsequent years that more than anything else, *what made a radical of me was covering the Birmingham courthouse.*[42]

Her 1958 memoir described it thus: *In covering the Birmingham courthouse, I soon learned that there were two kinds of justice: one for whites and one for Negroes. If a Negro killed a white man, that was a capital crime; if a white man killed a Negro, there were usually "extenuating circumstances" if not outright justification; if a Negro killed a Negro, that was "just a nigger murder"—worth at most a year or so in prison. If a white man took advantage of a Negro woman, it never reached the courts. If a Negro so much as looked at a white woman in a way she thought improper, that was "assault with intent to rape." . . . Over the door of the Birmingham courthouse are inscribed the words of Thomas Jefferson: "Equal and exact justice to all men of whatever state or persuasion." I read it every morning when I went to work until finally I began looking the other way as I entered the building.*[43]

However narrow her angle of vision may have been on race compared to what it became later, Anne could not ignore the rigid racial apartheid in Birmingham, especially the blatant miscarriages of justice she observed in court and the way most whites turned their backs on them. In that context, Jefferson's words began to make her literally sick to her stomach, and she had a hard time maintaining emotional distance from what was going on in front of her.[44]

Another disturbing sight that greeted the new reporter as she entered the courthouse one day soon after her arrival was the presence of young African American veterans, lined up all the way to the street, trying—unsuccessfully—to register to vote. She saw them return repeatedly over the next weeks. The story Anne wanted to write on their attempts was just not considered newsworthy by her editors, and Birmingham culture was so stratified and segregated that she might as well have been a world apart from African Americans in the city. Nor did she have enough contact with activists to realize that there was more struggle than met her eye.[45]

Because of people like Bull Connor, official Birmingham showed next to no tolerance for social dissenters of any kind. The surface of civility that characterized race and class relations in Anniston was almost entirely lacking there, in part because of the city's history of industrial labor struggle and its larger black population. Although the NAACP branch was among the South's largest, with more than 8,000 members in 1946, it was not very active. An annual branch report noted that blacks were "gripped with an almost paralyzing fear" in the face of brutal retaliation for any step outside the narrow confines of Jim Crow. Only the most radical would take such risks, and many middle-class NAACP members felt they had too much at stake. Admittedly a small presence, the SNYC (which was then based in Birmingham), the SCHW's Committee for Alabama, and the tiny but militant cadre of Communist Party members who formed the left wing of the CIO waged a valiant struggle for black voter registration in the postwar era. These were distinct groups, but with a lot of crossover.[46]

Repression against such organizations was so thorough that a white middle-class southerner like Anne could miss their presence altogether. White Birmingham had made denial of local racial and class struggles into an art. Since January, when 100 African American veterans marched through downtown in a voting-rights rally sponsored by the SNYC, black activists had been systematically pushing at the limits of disfranchisement, periodically turning out several dozen would-be registrants who were rejected as a matter of course. Throughout her stay there, despite being at the center of what passed for local news, Anne remained totally oblivious to the efforts of trade unionists and of groups like the SNYC and the SCHW to build interracial coalitions. Had she known of them, her experiences in Birmingham might have been less suffocating.[47]

As it was, Anne's world revolved around covering the courthouse, and that, too, limited her exposure to other happenings. She spent most of her time in the tiny courthouse pressroom, which she shared with a reporter from the *Post*.[48]

When Anne came to Birmingham, the state's political establishment was still reeling from the Folsom landslide. As veterans and a handful of radicals pressed openly against voter discrimination, conservative politicians were more focused on the Boswell Amendment as the surest way to preserve voting restrictions in Alabama and to contain Folsom's ability to unite masses of working-class southerners. Reporters wondered whether Folsom's popularity would combine with his opposition to the measure to defeat it at the polls that November, but even though Folsom made it clear he thought the plan was wrong, he did not make opposing it a central thrust of his program. When the amendment squeezed by at the polls, Anne was as disappointed as other liberals in the state, but she failed to see the ramifications of such successful race-baiting. The battle lines were being drawn in postwar southern politics, and even Folsom's enormous popularity failed to carry his political agenda very far in the mood of increasing racial conservatism that was settling in.[49]

As white southerners clung more feverishly to segregation, the national mood around them grew steadily more conservative. The term "Cold War" had not yet been coined, but U.S.-Soviet relations became increasingly strained. In March 1946 Truman and Winston Churchill stood side by side in the tiny town of Fulton, Missouri, as Churchill delivered a carefully scripted address calling for a strong Western alliance against the threat of communist expansion. From Churchill the American public learned of an "iron curtain" that had dropped over Europe, and Truman soon adopted the phrase in his speeches. On September 20, 1946—the same month Anne came to Birmingham to work—Truman ousted Henry Wallace from his cabinet. In spite of the new administration's growing hostility to the Soviets, Wallace had continued to defend the experiment that Soviet communism embodied and to espouse Popular Front collaboration with Communists at home and abroad. For that he lost his post as secretary of commerce, earning for the new president the undying scorn of Popular Front groups such as the Southern Conference.[50]

In the South such groups attracted only the enlightened few, especially among whites. Outside the region, they had broader popular appeal, but they also began to suffer sustained attacks of red-baiting. Anticommunism was not new to American culture, but—legitimized by the top echelons of power—it now began to emerge as a more mainstream ideology of the postwar social landscape. When the Republican Party declared the 1946 elections a referendum on communism and distributed 638,000 copies of a pamphlet titled "Communist Infiltration in the United States and How to Combat It," it captured both houses of Congress. Amid widespread social upheaval, a surprising cross section of U.S. society jumped on the anticommunist bandwagon. Red-baiting was no longer confined to conservative zealots. Opinion polls taken after the 1946 discovery of a Soviet spy ring in Canada showed a large majority of Americans in the psychological grip of a "Red Scare" that would only tighten as time progressed.[51]

In this climate, many liberals increasingly distanced themselves from CP members who had been their close collaborators during the Depression and WWII. Throughout FDR's presidency, most liberal organizations had at least some Communist presence, and amid the deepening crises of Depression and world war, these alliances had flourished. Such coalitions had always been fragile, however, and the cries of "Communist!" that groups like the Southern Conference had faced since their founding had made more fainthearted supporters shy away. In 1939, the progressive unity that characterized the prewar era temporarily broke down when the CP-USA revealed its uncritical loyalty to the Soviet Union by reversing its antifascist policies and adopting an isolationist posture in the wake of Stalin's nonaggression pact with Hitler. Actions like these—together with the air of secrecy that surrounded the CP (some followers routinely kept their membership secret)—fueled a distrust of cooperating with the party that both enlarged and was enlarged by the popular ideology of anticommunism. Though the foreign policy split was healed when the Nazis invaded the Soviet Union in June 1941, the idea of the Communist Party as a threatening totalitarian force gained force in American culture. The liberal-left alliance was maintained through the war years, but it grew more strained after 1945 for liberals who were themselves a waning influence in American politics. The CP inadvertently assisted in its own downfall by renunciation of its Popular Front leadership and a reinvigorated critique of what it called "class collaborationism."[52]

Conservative southern Democrats had long been fiercely anticommunist, seeing much social protest as the work of hostile outside forces. Now, amid the upsurge of racial and labor activism that was shaking the foundations of white supremacy, they suddenly found new legitimacy for their cause and were quick to unite with Republican anticommunists. Predictably, southern leaders pursued with a new vengeance those they thought of as "communistic" troublemakers—a group that included nearly all popular challenges to white supremacy.[53]

The bipartisan alliance of Republicans and southern Democrats was still congealing in the early postwar era. Its first significant act was to revive the nearly defunct House Special Committee on Un-American Activities—formerly the Dies committee, now known as HUAC—and make it the only permanent investigating committee of Congress, endowed with special subpoena powers. Over the coming years, that alliance would make possible a domestic anticommunist witch hunt unparalleled in Britain or other Western allies.

HUAC and its sister committee in the Senate, the Internal Securities Sub-Committee (SISS), toured the nation investigating any hint of Communist association. By the 1950s a subpoena from one of these legislative bodies was often the starting point for a public banishment that destroyed careers, personal lives and—most thoroughly—liberal or leftist social activism. At the grassroots level, social protest continued to thrive well into the postwar era, but after 1945 hints abounded that the fortunes of liberal and left-wing reformers were about to reverse.[54]

Focused on politics only in the narrowest sense, Anne, like most young women of her race and class, was largely ignorant of the shifting intellectual currents around her. In early 1947 she heard a rumor among reporters that seemed insignificant, silly even, at the time. Later, however, she remembered it as a harbinger of the obsessive anticommunist crusade that would soon grip the South and the nation. A *Post* reporter with whom she shared the courthouse pressroom and a friendly rivalry for getting a "scoop" came in one day with some news of his own. The Scripps-Howard newspaper chain, owners of the *Birmingham Post*, had announced a contest to *uncover a Communist*. The first reporter to do so would receive a bonus, Anne remembered her colleague telling her. *I said, "What!?" He mentioned the name of a writer, whose name I've forgotten now, on the Age-Herald. I said, "But she isn't any Communist!" He [told me], "It doesn't matter. She's been writing all these critical stories, and I think I can make a good story out of that." And he did! This boy knew nothing politically; he just wanted to win the prize [and] was bound to go find a Communist. I was so unaware myself that it didn't strike me as particularly shocking that he would do that either . . . with the sort of ethics I had at that time, I would have done anything to get a good story myself. That's the way we operated. But looking back on it, that's part of how the Red Scare was created.[55]*

Years later, once she became a committed socialist and anti-racist, Anne developed an almost obsessive interest in the radical currents of southern history that had rippled silently by her, unnoticed, as she naively began her writing career in postwar Alabama. In 1946, for example, she met and socialized with Gould Beech, an idealistic young *Southern Farmer* editor who wrote against regional inequalities, but she did not recognize him then as a kindred spirit. When Beech was forced from a Folsom appointment in 1947 after being lambasted by the legislature as a dangerous "leftist"—one of the early victims of the same anticommunist fervor that would someday rain upon Anne herself—the implications of the governing body's action made no impression on her at all. By chance Anne never even met Beech's employer and mentor, Aubrey Williams, the former New Deal administrator who had returned to his native state after a similar rebuke from the U.S. Senate in 1945. Williams, a racially enlightened white southern reformer, was a prominent figure in shaping the most visionary aspects of the New Deal, yet was refused confirmation as FDR's head of the Rural Electrification Administration in early 1945 for being "left-of-center"—that is, tainted by association with the CP. Williams expressed his opinions freely in the pages of his *Southern Farmer* magazine, but he remained controversial, and his leadership role in the much-maligned Southern Conference contributed to that controversy. In ten years' time Anne would count Aubrey Williams as a mentor of her own, but through an accident of fate, she never even made his acquaintance when she lived in his hometown.[56]

When Anne looked back later on her life in Birmingham, she could not help playing games with herself about what might have become of her if she had met people like Williams or like Hosea Hudson, an African American Communist who pushed for unionism in Birmingham from 1930 to 1947, when his party affiliation cost him both his CIO leadership post and his job. Hudson's memories of Depression-era and postwar Birmingham reveal a much more dynamic community than the stagnant cultural environment that Anne perceived. Not that Birmingham looked any less repressive for Hudson than it had for Anne. Far from it. He risked arrest even for being a CP member (an illegal act, by city ordinance). But Hudson had found a movement culture and with it a feeling of connectedness that sustained the spirits of those who worked against the grain in Birmingham. Nor were such subcultures exclusively the province of those who held party membership. Social networks that extended beyond the boundaries of Alabama also nurtured non-CP reformers like Aubrey Williams, who worked with Communists on Popular Front initiatives yet remained on cordial terms with liberal Democrats within the national political power structure. Radical and reform movements could provide a psychological home to their participants that strengthened their inner resources for challenging the larger southern culture in their midst, racist and segregated as it might be.[57]

I really should have stayed right there, Anne commented wryly when she reflected years later upon the popular upsurge that shook even such a static social environment as Birmingham's. But just as she had once felt alone in the world of poetry, Anne now felt alone in her alienation from southern culture. She dutifully wrote a weekly letter home to her parents, giving no hint of the despair that played at the edges of her days. By habit she threw herself even more fully into her work. Occasionally she discussed her disaffection in long letters to Harriet, but she found fewer and fewer opportunities to write.[58]

Most of her spare time was spent with Marshall Johnson, who had moved with her to Birmingham and also wrote for the *News*. Anne had a few college friends who were living in Birmingham, but she made no move to contact them. Her life revolved around the newspaper and Marshall. At 22, she made what was at the time her biggest break with her upbringing when she decided to move in with Marshall, a choice she thought of as bold but scandalous. She continued to maintain an apartment of her own for the sake of appearance, but she and Marshall rented a second residence under the names of Mr. and Mrs. Johnson. She hid her circumstances from her parents and from their landlady, who nevertheless discovered the deceit and forced Anne to move after an ugly confrontation.[59]

Anne was not prepared to marry Marshall; in fact, she had growing reservations about the future of their relationship. As what she called her *restless feeling* grew more persistent, she began to want to get away from both Birmingham and her lover there. *I felt like I was the strong one in the relationship [though] I didn't analyze it then or put it into words. I didn't want to be a mother to a man. My relationship with him was one of the things that got me to thinking about the whole social system because I felt that in some ways he was a victim of the society. He just never had a chance to really use his talents like he should have been able to do. But he was going to pieces because of that, and I felt a sense of tragedy about it all. I just wanted to get away—from the South and from him too. I didn't want to spend my life taking care of him, and I [felt] guilty because that seemed selfish.*[60]

Anne's memories of this period circulate mostly around her dawning awareness of the *sickness* (as she thought of it) of southern society. In any individual's life, it is the moments of epiphany or pain that bring about shifts in consciousness. For her, a casual encounter with an African American waitress became one of those moments that stood out from her months in Birmingham as a pivotal point in propelling her awareness of racial injustice. Anne has recounted the incident many times; she first wrote of it in *The Wall Between: I was meeting a friend [Marshall] for breakfast at a downtown cafeteria. I was running a little late that morning, so I asked him to get my breakfast while I made my usual calls. When I finished at the telephone, I met him at our table where a Negro waitress was taking our breakfast off the trays. "Anything doing?" my friend asked. I shook my head. "No," I said. "Everything quiet. Nothing but a colored murder." It was the reporter that I had become who was talking. Reporters soon learn to think in news values rather than human values. It was a simple fact that in Birmingham the killing of one Negro by another was not big news. . . . It was nothing to stop me from . . . taking time for breakfast before going on to work. I might never have given a further thought to the remark I had made—except that, even as I spoke, I suddenly sensed the reaction of the Negro waitress who was pouring coffee into my friend's cup. . . .*[61]

I forced myself to look up at her. Her body was stiff, and her hand on the coffee pot jerked. But her face was a stony mask, her eyes cast down. My impulse was to rush over to her and take her hand. I wanted to say: "I'm sorry for what I said. . . . It's not that I don't care if one of your people is killed . . . it's the newspaper; they say what news is—I don't. I am not a part of this thing that says that Negro life does not matter. It isn't me."[62]

But all of a sudden—like a shaft of morning sunlight over the breakfast table— the truth dawned on me . . . if what I had said had not been in my mind, I wouldn't have said it. I could not shift the blame to my newspaper; I was a part of this white world that considered a Negro life not worth bothering about. If I did not oppose it, I was a part of it—and I was responsible for its sins. There was no middle ground.[63]

The clarity of Anne's recollections, years later, of her disgust with southern society and with herself as a part of it was likely heightened with hindsight by her nearly lifelong anti-racist activism. At the time, the situation was just plain murky, and unsettling in a number of ways. She did not like what she saw around her in Alabama, nor did she feel she fit in there. She was beginning to feel trapped in relation to Marshall Johnson. Yet Anne had always been an ex- tremely driven person. She did not give up easily trying to adapt herself both to the society around her and to the needs of her romance. Ever since her "McCarty drive" had emerged in college, she had frequently burned the mid- night oil and expected unblemished achievement from herself. That exertion kept her on edge. It also fed her ambition.

But when an opportunity presented itself to advance her career and get out of Alabama at the same time, she jumped at the chance. She was conscious enough of her motives to know she was running away, yet she wasn't sure what she was running toward. Anne felt that journalistic success would lead her to New York or Chicago, and although she had declined to write for the society pages of the *Courier-Journal*, the Louisville newspapers had a national reputa- tion that drew her to accept a job offer with the *Louisville Times* in early 1947. She hoped this move would be a stepping-stone to a job in the North—away from segregation and toward a more prestigious paper.[64]

The *Louisville Times* was founded in 1884 as an afternoon paper in the shadow of its enormously successful morning companion, the *Courier-Journal*, pub- lished since 1868. Both newspapers were established by financier Walter Haldeman and editor Henry Watterson, a leading Democrat and New South industrial booster of the late nineteenth century whose pen lambasted both the Republicans and the Ku Kluxers. Housed in the most up-to-date publishing plant outside New York, the solidly pro-Democratic papers helped to craft Louisville's image as a uniquely prosperous river city that was nevertheless decidedly southern. Since 1919, the papers had been owned by the Bingham family, purchased by patriarch Robert Worth Bingham with part of a controversial $5 million inheritance he received after the untimely death of his wife, Mary Lily Flagler, heiress to the Flagler Hotels estate. Like Anne's forebears, the Binghams proudly claimed a role in the settlement of Kentucky and in the Confederacy, and Robert Bingham's fortune secured for his descendants a place at the pinnacle of elite Louisville society. The Binghams have been linked in the popular imagination with the fortunes of the city itself through most of the twentieth century, and many a cultural outlet has benefited from their philanthropic largesse.[65]

The papers were often referred to jointly as the "Ethridge papers" during the 1940s, though the *Times* was no match for the *Courier-Journal* in reputation. When the *Times* offered Anne a general assignment reporting post, she consulted with *Courier-Journal* editors as insurance that she could transfer later to the more prestigious paper. Once assured, she quickly accepted the *Times* offer, eager to escape Birmingham after less than a year. Louisville still held some sense of home for her, but it was also a way out of the Deep South, where she felt increasingly ill at ease. She was adamant, even after her editor at the *News*, Victor Townsend, offered her a raise and a promotion. Anne agreed to work out a month's rather than the customary two weeks' notice, but she left a $70-per-week paycheck for a $50 one with scarcely a backward glance.[66]

Still suffering from pangs of conscience and out of genuine respect for the bond they had shared, Anne did not make a clean break with Marshall Johnson, but she did make it clear that she was setting off on a new adventure of her own. He could visit, but their time as a couple was over. Both Birmingham and Marshall were now part of her past.

Over the following year and a half, Anne would go through a radical transformation of her values and goals. In Louisville she encountered civil rights activists for the first time and found a mentor who would introduce her to the left wing of the labor movement and to historical figures like Eugene Debs. Although the threat of communism was in the headlines nearly every day by that point in time, the flowering social movements spawned by Popular Front organizing were still wide open, and they beckoned to her as a spiritual home after she began to perceive the glaring inequalities in the culture that had produced her.[67]

PART TWO

CHAPTER FOUR

POLITICAL AWAKENING

In anybody's life there is a time that's a turning point, and this was the turning point in my life. Everything else is anticlimactic. I hope I've grown since then, but for me the real change was from being a woman of the white privileged class in the South to being what I consider a revolutionary.

—Anne Braden, 1981[1]

WHEN ANNE CAME TO LOUISVILLE, the postwar era held out a lot of promise for a young liberal-minded reporter. Newspaper journalism was still in its heyday, and so was the reform spirit. But just a week before she left Birmingham in March 1947 for her new life in Louisville, national politics shifted further to the right. President Truman dramatically aligned himself with the gathering anticommunist fever when on March 22 he established loyalty review panels for all federal employees. His executive order came only days after he had outlined a fiercely anticommunist foreign policy that became the Truman Doctrine, condemning Soviet expansionism, sending military aid to fascists in Greece and Turkey, and proclaiming American leadership in containing communism globally. The institution of loyalty oaths, as they became known, were a signal development in what amounted to a domestic Cold War against communists that denied due process to thousands and ultimately muted nearly all dissent. In spring 1947, the nation's most prominent leftists were the ones feeling the heat most: in April Henry Wallace, the actor Paul

Robeson, and a host of others were cited by HUAC as linked to Communist causes. But even at the grassroots level, reformers were no strangers to repression and to being called "communists," especially in the South, where the Southern Conference faced its most serious assault yet. That May, HUAC issued a report damning the Southern Conference as a "Communist front" advancing not human welfare but the aims of the Communist Party. The charges lacked solid evidence and were repudiated by reputable scholars, but the report gave southern critics a new weapon and dried up the group's revenues. Such actions were a mere harbinger of what was to come. Still, just what a turning point the coming year would become was something that most activists could not yet predict—let alone a young woman like Anne who was only beginning to notice the cracks in the mold of southern society.[2]

On the morning of Monday, March 31, 1947, when she reported to the *Times* newsroom for her first day's work, she had no inkling of the turbulent years ahead. But the wheels were put into motion from the moment Ed Aronson, her new editor, led her through the newsroom to meet her four colleagues on the city desk. Carl Braden—gruff, dark-haired, stocky, a decade older than Anne—was just one of a sea of faces when they were introduced that day. She was too caught up in the blur of new sensations to get much of an impression of a rather ordinary-looking fellow reporter whom she did not even know.

Carl Braden had a worldview very different from Anne's, imparted to him by a hardscrabble upbringing in the working-class neighborhood of western Louisville known as Portland. Born in 1914 in Indiana (just across the river from Louisville), Carl was named for Karl Marx by his father, a union man and railroad worker who lost his job for participation in the 1922 Louisville rail strike. James Braden was a socialist-minded follower of Eugene Debs who was inspired by the Russian Revolution and who worked such long hours, when he could find work, that he and his son were never particularly close. Carl's mother, Mary Elizabeth Braden, was a Catholic of German descent who sympathized with her husband's radicalism. She doted on Carl, her eldest, a bright boy whom the nuns at school encouraged in his studies.[3]

Carl became a voracious reader and something of an intellectual, yet was also drawn to the streets and was active in Portland's neighborhood gangs. At 13 he entered Mt. St. Francis Preparatory Seminary just a few miles from Louisville in southern Indiana. There he discovered journalism through the school's newspaper. At 16, Carl's formal education ended, though he remained a lover of learning for the rest of his life, with a habit of reading dictionaries, encyclopedias, and other compilations of facts. He left school to become a police reporter on the *Louisville Post-Herald*, where he saw considerable graft and corruption, as well as lives crushed by the Great Depression. During the 1930s he worked on papers in eastern Kentucky's Harlan County (the scene of intense coal mining labor struggles) and in Knoxville and Cincinnati, mostly covering labor news and, in the process, becoming a reformer active in CIO organizing drives. In those years Carl was also known as a prodigious drinker and fighter, but by his return to Louisville in 1945 as labor reporter for the *Times* he had renounced drinking and violence for more effective working-class activism in an atmosphere he feared might turn repressive for the left. Carl never drank or smoked again. His feisty, confrontational style, directness of speech, and quick wit endeared him to some and alienated him from others.[4]

When Anne began working alongside Carl, she saw him only as a friendly, knowledgeable veteran reporter. Because Carl was married and had been since 1937, there was no real temptation to see him as more. What camaraderie they did share was bounded by his marital status and the commitments that stemmed from it (Carl and his first wife, Virginia, had no children together, but were raising her daughter, Sonia). As a single, attractive new woman at the *Times*, Anne spent more of her spare time with other singles. Again she located herself within a primarily male domain in which her attractiveness won her acceptance while her writing and dedication won her respect. She spent that first spring trying hard to learn Louisville and the nuances of her job, and she enrolled in evening classes at the University of Louisville. She liked many things about the city, but it was also something of a disappointment. *I thought I was getting away from the South. [Then] I found that Louisville really wasn't very different from Birmingham. Louisville was completely segregated except for the buses and streetcars. That was different because people just got on and sat anywhere, but otherwise it was totally segregated—the schools, the libraries. . . . Then I found out that all along there had been some people trying to change that. . . . I just met the right people.*[5]

Post-WWII Louisville was not so terribly different from what it had been when Anne visited there as a child, but there was a feeling of possibility that had been missing in Birmingham. Louisville was both southern and not southern, and its racial conventions reflected that tension. Its ethnic blend (primarily German, Irish, and Jewish) and river-industrial base, together with its proximity to urban centers like Cincinnati, set it somewhat apart from the South, yet the city clung to its southern heritage. Crossing the Ohio River had once symbolized entry into freedom for blacks fleeing slavery, and Louisville remained a gateway to and from the South and thus a boundary of sorts: segregated seating on southbound trains, for example, began there. In most areas of life, segregation was the norm in Louisville, but in a less thoroughgoing, more contested, and—from Anne's point of view—more permeable way than in the deeper South. For African Americans, the piecemeal implementation of Jim Crow made Louisville a little more agreeable in the quality of life it offered than its more southern counterparts. The postwar black population hovered at around 15 percent of the city's total, still less than it had been at the turn of the century.[6]

Farther north and out of her parents' oversight, Anne began on her own to seek out the NAACP, which was more visible than it had been in Birmingham. Her 1947 return to Louisville coincided with a new wave of civil rights activism to desegregate public facilities, particularly parks and concerts. The *Louisville Defender*, an African American weekly newspaper, gave greater voice to the crusade against discrimination. Energized by the increased militancy of returning black veterans, the state NAACP doubled its number of branches in the decade after WWII.[7]

Because Anne was assigned to cover education shortly after coming to the *Times*, she also met African American educators fighting discrimination. Kentucky activists had won equalization of black and white teacher salaries in 1941, and continually pushed toward school equity and desegregation. In those pre-*Brown* years much of the focus was on higher education. Since 1936, Kentucky—like other southern states—had paid out-of-state tuition for African Americans to attend professional programs not open to them in their own state. In March 1948, Lyman Johnson, a high school history teacher in Louisville who was unwilling to go away for graduate training, applied for admission to the University of Kentucky. Anne was the reporter who covered the case for the *Times*, and after interviewing Johnson in his classroom at Central High School, she insisted to her editors that his campaign merited more than the assigned few paragraphs and was front-page news. Johnson's subsequent lawsuit, filed by the NAACP, became a landmark challenge to the state's infamous Day Law, which since 1904 had mandated segregated schooling. Anne had left the staff of the *Times* by the time Johnson won his suit, but in 1949 he and a handful of others desegregated the University of Kentucky and paved the way for further desegregation of the state's institutions of higher learning.[8]

In covering Louisville's African American community, Anne also became friends with Jim Crumlin, a young attorney who presided over the Kentucky conference of NAACP branches. Crumlin's office was in the heart of Louisville's "Little Harlem" black business district on what was then Walnut Street, and Anne began going by there to catch up on the latest civil rights news, frequently having a drink with him after work. *I don't know what any of those black people [during that time] thought of me because I was like a bull in a china shop. I didn't have any experience with black people at all. I [even] had a hard time pronouncing the word "Negro." Then people didn't say "black," you had to learn to pronounce "Negro." It was a great salvation for white southerners when [that changed] and they didn't have to learn that word anymore, for that was always the hardest thing for people to do. I suspect I said "Nigra" because you had a feeling you were speaking in a very affected sort of way when you said "Negro." I think Jim told me later I wasn't very good at pronouncing that word when he met me.*[9]

Like many white southerners, Anne had grown up in a household where "nigger" and "colored" were the only terms of racial identification she heard—and the two were used fairly interchangeably. She had eliminated the former term of derogatory slang from her vocabulary in college. Now her consciousness about race shifted again with greater contacts with African Americans, and she saw them more clearly, not just as a mistreated class of citizens, but as genuinely individuals, like herself, with agency and ambitions. Anne had gotten her first glimpse of that insight in college when introduced to the young African American actress. That awareness was reaffirmed now by the friendships she was forging across racial lines. But after years of seeing African Americans primarily as an unfamiliar group who were distinctly "other," she had to unlearn old habits and consequently was still not entirely at ease with interracial friendships. Long after he had met Anne, Crumlin remembered being "a little leery" of the attractive young woman who frequented his office. Although he became fond of her, he believed—self-servingly, perhaps—that she was "not quite so liberal as she thought she was" because she resisted his romantic overtures. Anne may or may not have been "liberal" enough to consider interracial romance, but she was uninterested in that sort of involvement with Crumlin, who was also married. Still, the two remained friends and many local blacks grew to think of Anne as a sympathetic resource at the *Times*.[10]

Post-WWII grassroots activism for racial equality was bolstered by an increasingly pro–civil rights climate in the federal government. As the Cold War took shape in the ashes of Hitler's fascist campaign, the status of African Americans in the South became an increasing source of international embarrassment to the United States in its emergent role as purveyor of democracy. In the wake of such outrageous antiblack violence as that which had occurred in 1946 in Columbia, Tennessee, President Truman convened a federal commission to make recommendations for federal action. The Truman commission's October 1947 report, "To Secure These Rights," criticized segregation and ultimately committed the administration to extend the freedoms available to Americans of color, but the very idea was anathema to most southern

Democrats and opinion makers. Ironically, the Popular Front labor/liberal coalition which could have built crucial public support for a national civil rights policy agenda was splintered by the widening anticommunist fear the Truman administration also cultivated. Those were fears to which liberals were also susceptible, and by mid-1947 anticommunism was becoming a sort of dividing wedge. What had once been a Popular Front was now becoming two distinct factions—one still inclusive of Communist participation in social change, and another increasingly powerful one defiantly opposed to it.[11]

Anne could not have been totally oblivious to the widening influence of anticommunism in American culture. Only weeks after she came to Louisville, local headlines informed the reading public of Attorney General Tom Clark's threat to prosecute "subversive forces." That summer, national magazines blazed charges that "Reds [are] in Our Bomb Plants." In 1947, crystallization of the phenomenon that has come to be known in retrospect as McCarthyism seemed to her regrettable, offensive even, but also minor—irrelevant to her life or to the civil rights cause she had begun to cherish. The many painful humiliations of African Americans' "life behind a veil" in Louisville (as one historian of the city has termed it) dawned on Anne when she realized that a woman very much like her but for skin color could not even try on clothing in a department store or pause for a drink at a soda fountain. Yet the freedom to protest such limitations felt abundant in postwar Louisville. And the young writer saw cultural trends that made her feel as if millions might soon share her budding racial conscience. She was no baseball fan, but no American—and certainly no Kentuckian—could stay completely aloof from sports news. When Jackie Robinson stepped up to the plate in Dodger Stadium that first spring she came to Louisville, Anne knew that a momentous racial boundary had been crossed. The future seemed to hold more of the same.[12]

When Anne was not at work, she spent the lion's share of her time with other reporters, just as she had in Alabama. She soon moved from the Highlands rooming house her father had secured for her to an apartment closer to downtown in an elegant Victorian mansion on Fourth Street. *Times* reporters had a long-standing reputation of being liberal on race, and she too found that to be the case. *I had made a good many friends among the young reporters, who liked to sit around and drink and talk and philosophize. That was the kind of world I was moving in here—these young reporters who were somewhat socially conscious, but not many of them a part of any movement.*[13]

Anne casually dated several coworkers, and through one of them, Red Vance, she got to know Carl Braden. Vance had Anne over to his apartment for dinner in the fall of 1947, and he invited Carl and Virginia Braden to join them. It was the first time Anne and Carl had ever talked seriously, and she was impressed by his ideas, knowledge, and convictions.[14]

Carl started giving Anne reading material that varied from Lenin's *State and Revolution* to biographies of Eugene Debs to Howard Fast's banned novel, *Citizen Tom Paine.* She began spending more time with Carl at work, and he often recruited her to fill in for him on weekend labor assignments because she worked Saturdays and he did not. He briefed her on Louisville's industrial labor movement, which, though very vital in the postwar era, was equally riveted with local variants of the national political disputes that would erupt in the 1949 expulsions of left-wing unions from the CIO. As deeply committed a trade unionist as his father had been, Carl had friends in both wings of the CIO and in the AFL. For the first time, through his introductions, Anne met radical trade union activists, many of whom were committed to a vision of racial equality she was beginning to embrace. Something in her responded deeply to the vigor that she felt emanated from those activists, and as 1947 wound to a close, her view of the "good life" enlarged with her dawning awareness of social change movements and the passionate commitments they inspired.[15]

Labor and the Left

The U.S. labor movement came of age with the support of FDR and the New Deal. But by 1947, a postwar swell of industrial union organizing had fallen victim to the same fragmentation of left-liberal alliance that plagued other reforms. Despite increasingly negative publicity, CIO unions continued to win elections with their message of workers' rights. Yet in a national political climate that grew steadily more obsessed with foreign policy and the perceived Soviet threat, red-baiting attacks also escalated, and leftist union leaders found themselves on the defensive as former allies became suspicious critics opposed to any supposed CP influence. This was particularly true in the South, where a long-standing hostility to unions mingled with opposition to biracial collaboration to make "red" a convenient means of discrediting union drives that held little public legitimacy in the first place. Southern politicians were paranoid about the new bent of the Democratic Party toward racial change and especially fearful of the shift in regional power relations suggested by an increasingly vital interracial industrial labor movement. Thus, they bought into the

Red Scare with particular zeal, using to their advantage the national mood of blacklisting "communistic" dissenters whether they were CP supporters or not. Unfortunately, once CIO leaders allowed their own ranks to be split by such fears and began eliminating Communists and left-wing locals from membership, they purged some of their most dedicated organizers, perhaps especially in the South. The CIO's "Operation Dixie" southern organizing drive never really got off the ground, having handicapped itself by barring Communists, socialists, and left-wingers of any persuasion—including the Southern Conference for Human Welfare.[16]

Passage of the Taft-Hartley Act in June 1947 was both a symptom and an outcome of such trends, dealing postwar union activism a blow that ultimately proved fatal. Taft-Hartley hobbled organized labor by outlawing the closed shop and placing severe limitations on strikes. Perhaps more significantly, its Section 9-H was labor's own version of loyalty oaths, requiring union officials to swear affidavits that they were not CP members, with harsh fines imposed for falsehoods. Only unions that complied were recognized by the National Labor Relations Board (NLRB). The bill deepened the CIO's ideological divisions and ignited internal uproar in many unions.[17]

Initially, however, it evoked a wave of trade union unity. In Louisville, the most active locals helped to elect Democrat Earl Clements as governor of Kentucky in the fall of 1947. Unionists mobilized partly in response to Clements's vocal opposition to Taft-Hartley, and they claimed his victory as a repudiation of the bill. It was in that context of intensified organizing that Anne had her first substantive contact with unionists during her early months at the *Times*.[18]

In 1947 and 1948, despite heightened anticommunist rhetoric within the CIO, the closing circle of anticommunism was held at bay in Louisville by the incredible solidarity that characterized several locals, enhanced by a multitude of victories that organized workers won under left-wing leadership. That kind of solidarity made the labor left more able to maintain a voice in local politics than was the case in most southern cities, where trade unions were themselves inherently suspect. The fact that the Louisville newspapers were moderate to liberal on both trade unionism and anticommunism also served to bolster labor's authority and postpone the intense ostracism that the CIO's left received elsewhere in the South. Only days before Anne joined the *Times* staff, the paper's editorial cartoon depicted a masked Klansman labeled "Intolerance" bearing a document titled "Proposed Red Witch Hunt"—a spoof that would become serious business in the coming few years.[19]

Carl's introductions brought Anne into contact with what one labor historian has called "the most perfect union" from a worker's perspective: Local 236 of the United Farm Equipment Workers, or FE. The local exhibited the kind of member solidarity and interracial unity that most union organizers only dreamed of, especially in the South, where white unionists were often unwilling to challenge racial conventions. African American workers were among the most dynamic leaders of FE Local 236, and some of them influenced Anne profoundly. One in particular, shop steward Sterling Neal, became a mentor who did not hesitate to confront her on her assumptions of white privilege, and their conversations shattered some of her paternalism.[20]

A little less than a year before Anne moved to Louisville, the International Harvester plant opened there. The preeminent maker of tractors, Harvester was riding high in the postwar wave of southern agricultural modernization, and the company had especially high hopes for its first plant in the nonunion, wage-depressed South. With more than 6,000 employees, the new Harvester plant became Kentucky's largest factory and Louisville's largest employer, with a workforce composed predominantly of WWII veterans of both races. Young men who found work in the new plant had little union experience, but they did not remain unorganized long. To the company's dismay, the militant FE followed the company south, bringing with it a tradition of aggressive shop-floor organizing and interracial solidarity nurtured by national leaders who were in or close to the Communist Party. In July 1947 FE won recognition of Local 236 at Harvester's Louisville facility, and the local quickly established its own reputation for militancy with frequent walkouts and demands for equal treatment of blacks and whites. The plant allowed African Americans unusual opportunity in work that was at least semiskilled—unlike the norm in industry, which was to relegate them to the dirtiest, unskilled jobs. Routine exchanges between blacks and whites on the job then cultivated in Local 236 a willingness to combat racial disparities out of a strongly honed sense of fairness.[21]

The struggles between FE and Harvester flavored the pages of local labor news, especially a September strike at the plant soon after enactment of Taft-Hartley. The local struck to eliminate what employees called the "southern differential," which paid lower wages in Louisville than at other Harvester shops. Local 236 prevailed with a unity welded from dramatic confrontations with the police and from fighting off sustained red-baiting attacks by the company and by conservative locals.[22]

Such working-class militancy cemented Carl Braden's affinity with the FE. He lent his journalistic skills to helping put out FE's *Cub* newsletter in his spare time. Once Anne began covering labor, she too volunteered her help. FE activists were living the kind of social criticism that Harriet Fitzgerald had only talked about, and their example appealed to Anne's sense of immediacy—particularly in their radical interracialism. Though the left wing of the labor movement was growing more embattled as anticommunism became a cultural frenzy, the local subculture of the labor left was still on the offensive in demands for workers' rights and racial equality, and CP membership—whether open or discreet—was no particular albatross. The first FE colonizer sent to organize the Louisville plant, Vernon Bailey, was a Communist, and to no ill effect. The result was that the inevitable showdown brewing in the CIO nationally over anticommunism had little immediate impact on the power of FE-236. The larger ideological disputes could not escape even a newcomer like Anne, but they remained somewhat theoretical.[23]

The announcement that summer of the Marshall Plan economic aid package for rebuilding devastated European nations took those disputes to a new level. Accompanied by even greater anticommunist rhetoric, the plan was seen by the left as a step toward eclipsing the Soviet Union and creating a world capitalist empire. The American CP, like other Communist parties internationally, vehemently opposed it, and that stance furthered the divisions smoldering between CP unionists and the rest of the CIO leadership, who backed the Marshall proposal as a boost to industry and a democratic safeguard. Foreign policy now threatened an irrevocable split in the CIO nationally, and heated discussions of these controversies were part of the union discourse to which Anne was privy. Debates in the labor movement centered on questions of CP membership and foreign policy, but equally at issue was an approach to trade unionism that emphasized greater democracy within plants and empowerment of rank-and-file workers over bureaucratic procedures and an unflinching alignment with the Democratic Party. It was that militant tradition, embodied in 236 and other locals like it, that captivated workers' loyalties but was soon to be more or less subsumed by the growing anticommunist furor.[24]

Although by fall of 1947 Anne was finding her way to the sidelines of the ideological battles that ripped through the labor movement nationally and in Louisville, local victories provided for her a more salient test of the effectiveness of the CIO's left wing. FE-236 had plenty of those in its early years. FE and three smaller allies—the Transport Workers' local, covering city bus drivers; the United Public Workers (garbage collectors); and a local of the United Furniture Workers—became known as the "Seventh Street Unions" because they shared a militant perspective, a weekly newspaper, and a bustling union hall on Seventh Street. Anne loved the fellowship and the intense political exchanges that encircled her in these new settings. She came to know CP members and their allies not as abstract menaces to society but as simply people who were outstanding organizers and role models of idealism, especially in their defense of racial equality.[25]

Turning Myself Inside Out

As the 1948 election year approached, Cold War rhetoric heated up in both major parties. After the Republicans reinvigorated HUAC in 1947, they won lavish publicity through an inquest into alleged Communist influence in Hollywood. That sensationalized press attention centered the Red Scare in the popular imagination and nudged President Truman toward greater domestic anticommunism in his policies. Truman's hawkish foreign policy, domesticated with the loyalty oaths, soured his relations with the left wing of the Democratic Party, which still had as its champion former vice president Henry Wallace. Meanwhile, a large contingent of liberal Democrats supported the Cold War wholeheartedly and condemned U.S. Communists and any who worked with them. The same conflicts needling the CIO now split the Democratic Party, and postwar liberalism became more widely gripped by anticommunism. Regional progressives from the Southern Conference needed whatever allies they could find, and they continued to espouse a Popular Front approach, as did the CIO left, becoming part of a wider coalition which opposed the interventionist, anti-Soviet drift in foreign policy. These Popular Front groups continued to achieve local victories, as the case of Local 236 illustrates, but they found their appeal increasingly narrowed with the spread of anticommunist liberalism. Since the Depression era, the Communist Party had been a centerpiece of what historians and activists have come to know as the "Old Left," a patchwork of reformers, unionists, and revolutionary activists, many of them radicalized by the social distress of the Depression, who worked for social justice and utopian aims in or alongside the party. The CP's decline in legitimacy now did not bode well for the broader currents of social change over the coming decade.[26]

What remained of the Popular Front supported Henry Wallace as he spoke out more forcefully against both segregation and Truman's escalating Cold War stance. In the fall of 1947 the Southern Conference was one sponsor of a speaking tour to test the waters for a possible Wallace presidential run. Anne attended a "mailing party" to send out flyers advertising his Louisville appearance, and she was energized by the conversations she took part in, feeling that what was said all made sense. When Wallace spoke at the Louisville armory on November 21, 1947, Anne was there amid a cheering crowd of 16,000—the largest unsegregated meeting ever held in the city. Wallace's message of racial equality and an end to the Cold War struck a deeply responsive chord with her, and the admiration she had long felt for him grew into a more informed support for the movement building around him. What congealed into the Progressive Party became a passionate outlet for those fed up with racial injustice and what they considered saber-rattling rhetoric from Democrats and Republicans alike. For young southern radicals and liberals of both races, the Progressive Party symbolized not just a breakaway from the Democratic Party but from the very tradition of racial hierarchy. Even in the rural Deep South, Wallace addressed interracial crowds and courageously denounced segregation, earning tremendous admiration from some and dodging tomatoes and rotten eggs from others. He portrayed Wall Street, the Ku Klux Klan, and the HUAC as bedfellows—a dramatic analogy that was bound to stir passions pro and con.[27]

The two policy issues that moved Anne the most and formed the strongest base for Wallace's support were peace and civil rights. Wallace was intensely critical of Truman's foreign policies and advancement of what Anne later called an *empire thrust* for the United States abroad. But he also attacked the administration for moving too slowly on racial reform. Wallace advocated an end to segregated schools, new safeguards for black voting rights, and a permanent Federal Employment Practices Commission to combat job discrimination. In nearly every speech, he discussed the urgent need for racial justice. Having waited for years to hear a politician speak so frankly against racism, many of both races in the South remembered the 1948 Progressive Party campaign as a galvanizing moment in their political activism.[28]

For Anne, the Progressive Party movement that coalesced in late 1947 became a touchstone for a political transformation already in motion. On the December night when Wallace finally announced his presidential candidacy on a third party ticket, she was visiting at the home of a family friend, an older woman physician who tried to help acclimate Anne to Louisville by introducing her to other young professionals her age. The group at the dinner party were strangers to Anne, and they found it first odd and then boring when all she wanted to do was to tune in for Wallace's radio speech. Anne's sense of utter alienation from her companions made her realize that night that her once-familiar social orbit no longer fit.[29]

It was thus a natural step for her to seek out other Wallace supporters. She attended the founding meeting of 75 or so who formed the Wallace Committee for Louisville, held at the Seventh Street Union Hall. There Anne met

Barbara Lane, a young transplanted New Yorker who headed the Louisville group. The two became friends, and when Lane needed a place to live, she became Anne's new roommate on Fourth Street. Still not quite a joiner, Anne refused her friend's invitation to serve on the group's board. Instead she stayed at the fringes of the Progressive Party movement—talking it up, giving press coverage when she could, attending rallies, but without fully joining in.[30]

The simple act of making friends with those her culture had pronounced "other"—African Americans, unionists, and Communists—set Anne far adrift from the psychic terrain her family and childhood friends occupied. She could not make such friendships without also taking stock of the political ramifications of social conventions she had more or less accepted before, and the world she had grown up in took on a new and harshly uncomfortable light. These insights produced a wellspring of inner turmoil in Anne during the closing months of 1947. What happened to her during this period is a process she has repeatedly called *turning myself inside out.* She has explained it this way: *I had to come to terms with the fact that my whole society—one that had been very good to me—my family, friends, the people I loved and never stopped loving—were just plain wrong. It's a searingly painful process, but it's not destructive, because once you do it, you are free.*[31]

It took her awhile to find that experience of freedom, however, and Anne's intensity turned in upon herself in the interim. In weekly letters to her parents, she only hinted at the conflicts bubbling inside her. Anne wanted very much for her life to be *significant,* and she saw her search for meaning as linked to the mandate she had gotten in college—especially at Stratford—for a life of service. She admitted to her parents only that she felt *the voice of a terrible conscience* and worried that failure to rise to the challenge might make her *go crazy.*[32]

By Christmastime of that year, Anne's introspection had taken her to a place of profound despair amid what was ordinarily her favorite time of year. She spent a few days in Anniston but the usual holiday celebrations only deepened her sense of alienation with that milieu. She felt utterly alone.[33]

As 1948 opened, Anne had discarded many of her old beliefs but had not yet constructed a new road map for her life. She still loved news reporting but was questioning the ambition that had suffused her since finishing college. Years later, when the internal spinning had long since quieted and the direction of her life was clear, she saw that emotionally turbulent period this way: *I think I had grown up in a totally restricted world, a world that was passé, a world that was morally wrong. In ways that I didn't analyze then, I was already questioning that world. On the other hand, everything in my life had geared me toward becoming a success in that world according to its standards. I happened to run into a catalyst in*

Carl—other people I met too, but mainly Carl. If I hadn't run into him, maybe I would have begun to question in the same way. Or maybe the moment would have passed and it would have been harder to kick over the traces. . . . But to me it [brought] a change in where I stood in the world. . . . There was no way of going back to the old values or the old ambitions. The idea of being a successful newspaperwoman didn't even appeal to me anymore. I had a feeling that I could contribute a little something; I didn't expect to contribute a great deal, but I was going to be on the side of history that represented life instead of death.[34]

Anne's painful search to recast her values was more complicated than merely being attracted to the excitement of the social movements she was treading at the edges of. If it had been simply that, she might have enjoyed a radical fling and returned to her earlier trajectory. She began to view her old life as a prison, one she desperately wanted to be free of, in order to forge a more creative future.[35]

From Anne's later perspective, the *open sesame* that allowed her to develop a social critique was race—as she believes it has been for nearly all white southerners who have participated in social change movements. *For all of us who got involved in the social justice movement, the starting point was race because that was so obvious. It was easier then to see [the corruption of white society] in the South than in other parts of the country. . . . Once you recognize the painful fact that you have benefited because African Americans have suffered, the entire structure you've identified with begins to crumble, and everything in the society comes into question.*[36]

Anne's interior wrestling with her views on race began before she ever left Alabama, and merely intensified once she met civil rights crusaders in Kentucky. But the painful change she endured from 1947 to 1948 also involved class. *In that year I think I changed sides in the class struggle. Before that I had not even known there was one. Like most people who identify with the upper class, I didn't think there were any social/economic classes. Essentially I came to identify with the oppressed instead of the oppressor, which changed my whole worldview. When I realized that I had grown up part of a privileged class that enjoyed its place in society because not only black people but because most of the rest of the population was subjugated, I really had to turn the world as I saw it and the world within myself [inside out]. It was a lot to manage all at once. . . . I had a very emotional feeling about [our country's] democratic rights, and now I was coming to terms with the fact that these things really weren't rights but were privileges I had gotten because of my class. I remember crying—and I don't cry easily—with Harriet [Fitzgerald], wondering about whether I was turning against my own people.* Those months were among the most painful yet most significant of her life.[37]

An Outlaw Movement

Ironically, just as Anne was finding her way into the social justice movement, the windows of opportunity for southern change that had opened in the New Deal years were closing with alarming speed. The positive response to Wallace's southern tour in late 1947 raised the hopes of many southern activists, but there were other, more ominous indications about the direction in which the country and the region were headed. As the nation became more obsessed with foreign policy and the Cold War, its willingness to grapple with domestic social problems declined in tandem, and nowhere was this more apparent than in the South. Just as groups ranging from the NAACP to the Southern Conference were lifting up a critique of segregation, anticommunism ignited a backlash against further social change by uniting conservatives and liberals—and, more significant perhaps, opinion makers both North and South—in what they saw as an almost holy crusade. When new charges of communist infiltration of the Southern Conference came from prominent white southern liberals such as the novelist Lillian Smith and Ralph McGill, editor of the *Atlanta Constitution*, they undermined what popular support for civil rights—especially among whites—activists had been able to amass in the region. For the average southerner (or American), communism was only a vague, foreign ideology, but definitely something to avoid. Numerous southern politicians over the years had harped on the link between communism and racial activism, and that rhetoric became increasingly shrill amid intensifying Cold War ideology and murmurs at the federal level of civil rights for blacks. Once the charge of "communist!" emanated from those who called themselves liberal on race, it added a cost to opposing segregation that was simply too great for most southerners to bear.[38]

With community repression as almost a given, the ranks of southerners who actively supported racial change had always been thin, and they had long contained Communists. CP members like Alabama's Joe Gelders and Hosea Hudson were among the most dedicated of southern activists. To purge them was unthinkable to some southern liberals; failure to do so was equally vile to others. But the issue became more of a dividing line as the Communist Party lost what small legitimacy it had once held in American culture, and endless organizational debates began on whether to exclude communists. Such polemics took their toll on social action. This was especially true in the South, where activists were fewer in number and more likely to have been affiliated with the CP in some fashion—which in turn made them more vulnerable to heightening national concern over communism as an external and an internal threat. The nation was now animated by the sort of anticommunist fears that had once been more or less confined to the South and to the extreme right wing of the political spectrum.[39]

The context for Wallace's presidential run was thus highly problematic. Mainstream Democrats put aside any reservations to back Truman and his vice-presidential candidate, a Kentucky native son, Senator Alben Barkley. Even apart from the growing influence of anticommunism, Wallace's decision to bolt the party generated controversy among liberals who were loath to leave the party of Roosevelt that had been, for years, so instrumental in reforms. The CIO had gained what clout it held through the Democratic Party, and at its postwar height, most leaders believed that leaving the party would destroy their organization. CIO head Phillip Murray had initially shared leftists' concerns about Truman's imperialistic foreign policy, but the president's July 1947 veto of Taft-Hartley (though soon overridden by Congress) returned mainstream union leaders to the Truman fold, with all of the Cold War embrace that entailed.[40]

Wallace's Progressive Party campaign was the last straw for labor's national leadership in its dealings with its troublesome left wing, and that hostility completed the isolation of the left within the CIO. Even within the SCHW, which was a staunch Wallace booster and had much less of a Cold Warrior mentality than the CIO, the leaders could not agree on what the organization's official position should be on Wallace's candidacy. In the end they agreed to disagree, but the ensuing chaos helped to bring about the group's demise (it ceased operations in November 1948). While leaders such as Clark Foreman dropped their SCHW commitments to campaign full time for Wallace, others—Alabamian Aubrey Williams, for example—simply could not abandon years of Democratic allegiance and thought it a mistake for Foreman to do so.[41]

Yet even skeptics like Williams had to acknowledge the fresh new challenge that the Progressive Party movement posed to white supremacy in the South. The third party never became a central organizing vehicle for the African American masses, but it did inject a lot of vigor into southern black activism and in some ways prefigured the mass, direct-action civil rights movement that developed after 1960. As the leftist actor-singer Paul Robeson toured the South speaking against racism and for Wallace, he observed Progressives reinvigorating black southern radicalism in spite of a larger stream of mounting conservatism. Though most black voters stayed with Truman in the election—mostly as a result of his mid-1948 desegregation of the armed forces—Progressives ran black candidates even in Deep South cities like

Macon, Georgia, where Larkin Marshall, an African American newspaper editor, campaigned for the Senate in the face of relentless white harassment. In Louisville, the African American activist lawyer Alfred Carroll ran for a seat in the Third Congressional District. Wallace's Louisville campaign nurtured an interracial coalition that included CP members, ex-GI's, small-business owners, college professors, left-wing unionists, and peace and civil rights activists of various persuasions united by a dissatisfaction with the direction of Truman's policies.[42]

When the Progressive movement began in 1947, Henry Wallace, with his message of U.S.-Soviet cooperation, had a chance to slow or even halt the pace of the Cold War. The failure of liberals across the nation to unite massively behind him might have been overcome as the campaign picked up steam. Even in March 1948, opinion polls suggested that Wallace had ten million supporters. Yet in the context of the gathering "culture of the Cold War," as one historian has phrased it, the issue of supposed Communist domination weighted down the Progressive Party more heavily as 1948 unfolded. The CP endorsement of Wallace gave the Progressives a built-in cadre of seasoned organizers many thousand strong (the CP was still a viable political organization in those years with a membership of about 60,000–80,000). Yet in the long run CP support probably cost him more votes than it won for him because it unleashed a barrage of criticism that mushroomed as the election approached. That criticism was stoked by a combination of Soviet actions and American collective response to those actions, a response that was carefully cultivated by policymakers in the Truman administration.[43]

A coup in Czechoslovakia in February 1948 that replaced a coalition government with a solidly Communist-controlled one took anticommunism in American culture to new heights. The Soviet blockade of Berlin that summer made matters worse, causing many Americans of all political persuasions to worry that war was just around the corner. But it was also the aim of the Truman administration to correlate its foreign policy of containment with the idea of an internal Communist threat that must be thwarted. In the fall of 1947, the administration adopted a strategy of portraying Wallace's supporters as Communists or Communist pawns in order to crush the Progressive challenge and ensure Truman's reelection. In a memo to the president written even before Wallace declared, adviser Clark Clifford acknowledged that the Progressive Party could not honestly be characterized as Communist driven, but he nevertheless recommended that Truman maintain a state of high tension with the Soviets in foreign affairs and make every effort "to identify Wallace in the public mind with the Communists." Prominent anticommunist writers such as

Dorothy Thompson and the historian Arthur Schlesinger joined in this effort. Wallace politely and regularly differentiated himself from CP policies. He would not, however, disavow CP support, insisting that Communists should be accorded the same legitimacy as others to participate in politics.[44]

But even that view isolated him further from the direction in which American political culture was headed. The cultural currents of anticommunism reached fever pitch in 1948 through a series of frightening, rapid-fire events abroad and on the home front. In July, 11 leaders of the CP-USA were indicted for violations of the Smith Act, the 1940 law which made it a crime to advocate violent overthrow of the U.S. government. That same month, Truman desegregated the armed forces by executive order, triggering new anxiety about racial change among segregationists who seized frantically what they saw as the stabilizing aims of anticommunism. Atomic spy cases had been a growing fear over the past year, but the explosive September 1948 accusation that former State Department official and New Dealer Alger Hiss had passed government secrets to the Soviets cast a dark shadow over social reform as no previous publicity had been able to do.[45]

Thus, what began as a fairly broad-based movement of Progressives suffered such sustained red-baiting attacks that by mid-1948 it dwindled to only the most committed Popular Front liberals—black and white—together with dedicated CP members and supporters. Anne observed the change herself when Wallace returned to Louisville for an August 1948 appearance. Only a few hundred turned out to hear him despite the campaign's prediction of an overflow audience.[46]

For those relatively few supporters, however, the Wallace campaign meant more than just a presidential run. Defying segregation again on his return to Louisville, Wallace chose to stay not at one of the downtown establishments catering only to whites, such as the Brown or Seelbach, but at a hotel in the black community. Even though his political movement was waning, actions like this won him tremendous respect from African Americans and awakened new strains of racial activism. In spite of Wallace's dismal vote count that November (660 in Louisville; only slightly above a million nationwide), the Progressives' local legacy was to get blacks "moving," as one commentator has described it. A handful of Progressive veterans (including FE organizer Jimmy Wright, lawyer Alfred Carroll, and Anne herself) continued thereafter in a lifetime of getting others to move as they had.[47]

In a Cold War climate increasingly predicated on fear, getting blacks moving was just what some white southerners feared most. The Progressives were not the only breakaway movement from the Democratic Party in 1948. At the opposite end of the political spectrum were the "Dixiecrats," reflecting a decidedly reactionary trend in southern politics. When Alabama and Mississippi delegates stalked out of the Democrats' convention in the summer of 1948 after the adoption of a strong civil rights plank, their stormy action indicated just how firmly Democratic liberalism had become attached to the politics of race in the postwar South. New Deal reform and the Second World War had brightened the region's economic prospects but had severely shaken its static racial order. Even Missourian Harry Truman (who remained something of a segregationist in his personal sympathies) appeared to be moving toward a more active pro–civil rights stance. For diehard segregationist politicians, now seemed an opportune moment to hold the line against further racial challenges by pairing them with the specter of communism hanging over the national consciousness. During the campaign, Congressman John Rankin of Mississippi, for example, charged that Truman wished to "ram the platform of the Communist Party down the throats of the people of the United States" by promoting civil rights legislation.[48]

The Dixiecrat candidacy of Strom Thurmond for president offered up a murky mixture of racism and anticommunism as a cure for national and regional ills. With their repeated references to "mongrelization" and "totalitarianism" as they waved the Confederate flag, the Dixiecrats were a frightening precursor of what was to come for southern political culture. The Dixiecrat rebellion took hold in four southern states and mobilized more voters in November than the beleaguered Wallace could mount. Still further to the right was the Christian Nationalist Crusade, running Gerald L. K. Smith for president on a platform to stop all immigration of dark-skinned peoples and to build a "strong Christian Germany to help us contain the Communist beast." Admittedly, this fascist organization was a fringe group, but it received less public scrutiny than did the Communist Party during this era.[49]

In the shifting political winds of the postwar period, Henry Wallace's Progressive Party campaign through the South represented the last gasp of Popular Front liberalism. Wallace's southern run reflected both the power that people's movements had amassed there in the previous decade and the resurgence of racism and reaction accompanying postwar conservatism and the dramatic intensification of domestic anticommunism. What the SCHW organizer Clark Foreman pronounced a "decade of hope" had wound to a close by late 1948. By the time Anne committed her life to the movement for progressive social change, she was informed enough to know that she was joining what she has called an *outlaw* movement.[50]

Anne came of age politically as divisions over the CP crystallized in the ranks of liberals and as anticommunism took center stage in the popular imagination generally. Because she had been introduced to social action first through dialogues with Harriet Fitzgerald during WWII and more directly later through her contact with left-wing unions in Louisville, she saw Communists as more heroic than demonic. More than that, however, she observed that racist and anticommunist ideologies were often espoused by the same people (with notable exceptions, as in the case of Lillian Smith, whose work Anne admired). Thus Anne sided almost instinctively with what remained of the Popular Front. As her new worldview took shape, the *mission consciousness* instilled in her during her youth in the Episcopal Church resurfaced with a zeal that looked secular but felt spiritual to her. After years of discomfort with southern race relations and a nagging sense of inner discontentment, as if she had not quite found her niche, Anne now thoroughly repudiated the Jim Crow society around her. She turned instead to the sense of possibility she found in the tiny but tenacious subculture of civil rights activists and left-wingers who failed to be silenced by the increasingly repressive larger social climate. Despite the diminishing social space available for dissenters, Anne was in impressive company in the post-WWII left—with such figures as W. E. B. DuBois, whose work she now read voraciously, and Paul Robeson, whom she had the chance to interview for a *Times* article in May 1948 when he came to Louisville on a Wallace campaign stop. She found in the milieu of the left a worldview she could identify with because of its commitment to racial and working-class justice and a camaraderie that in some ways grew more solid as the progressive moment grew more beleaguered. Having grown up an introspective individualist and something of a loner, emotionally, Anne was still at the fringes of the left as 1948 dawned, but she was now prepared to join her life to the compelling social causes that overshadowed the career ambition that had guided her for the past several years.[51]

Not surprisingly, considering the time period and the years of being unconsciously groomed to find fulfillment in a lover, the major influence in Anne's political metamorphosis was a man. Postwar ideas about women's place were in a state of flux: even as birthrates soared and ages at first marriage declined, single and professional women enjoyed greater independence. Yet family and personal relations also continued to exert a powerful claim on young women—particularly those of Anne's background. As the Cold War fastened its paranoid grip on the popular imagination, cultural notions about gendered family roles also narrowed. It was thus no surprise that Anne should look to a strong male figure like Carl Braden for some resolution of the value conflicts bedeviling her and the profound longings they evoked.[52]

CHAPTER FIVE

MARRIAGE AND MOVEMENT

Are you marrying a man or a movement?

> —Harriet Fitzgerald to Anne McCarty, 1948[1]

When I first heard of them, they were always a couple. It was always just "the Bradens."

> —Julian Bond, former SNCC activist, 1997[2]

LIKE JULIAN BOND, MANY WHO KNEW Carl and Anne Braden after 1948 (and especially after they won national notoriety in 1954) thought of them jointly, as one entity. In some fashion, the two even saw themselves that way. Their relationship fit few of the stereotypes of marriages formed at midcentury, and the family they built conformed even less to those norms. Theirs was a partnership fired in a common purpose, affirmed by personal compatibility, and sustained by something much larger than itself. In order to achieve the vision of social and racial justice they both sought, they were willing to make such sacrifices as had to be made. And the times would demand many. Because of the force of Anne's and Carl's convictions, their political lives in the besieged Old Left cultural milieu deeply influenced their familial experiences. Their shared social commitment became the ground wire for their

relations both to each other, to the world, and, invariably, to the family they
built together. Once they became targets of a modern-day witch hunt against
dissenters and leftists unleashed in the 1950s by the cultural prevalence of anticommunism, their persistent refusal to be silenced or discounted also
brought unrelenting disruption to their personal lives and those of their children. The resulting politicization of the personal impinged on every aspect of
their lives.[3]

Because domesticity has been widely viewed as a predominantly female
sphere, women have found that questions of identity relating to marriage and
parenthood historically are much more complicated than they have been for
men. Generations of women in public life have come under intense fire from
the press, from biographers, and, indeed, from themselves for their perceived
deficiencies as wives and mothers. Earlier reformers (Susan B. Anthony, for
example) sometimes chose to steer clear of marriage and children entirely because of the difficulties of balancing activism and family. By the post-WWII
period, fewer women chose such a course: certainly not Anne, who, as her
friend Ida Fitzgerald liked to say, was "a glutton for life." Unwilling to forgo
any human experience that might prove enriching, she thoroughly embraced
marriage, had three children, and wanted even more. Yet her unique journey
through marriage and motherhood can only be fully understood in relation to
her political activism.[4]

Although Anne's and Carl's identities became deeply bound up with
each other through their marital and movement collaboration, it is important in understanding Anne as a woman to abstract her experiences from
Carl's regarding matters of marriage, motherhood, and gender consciousness more broadly. His mentoring role in her political development and
their ensuing political partnership led Anne to see herself in something of a
dialectical relation to Carl. But she also lived a kind of politics that were distinct from his. Despite their bond, she was a strong presence in her own
right. She also has spent much of her adult life without him, never remarrying after his premature death in 1975. And as a parent, her experiences stand
clearly apart from his because of the cultural weight assigned to motherhood. The challenges Anne faced as a mother are no less problematic than
those of myriad women activists who have tried to "have it all," claiming for
themselves both a political life and the more individualistic pleasures of family. Her absolute engagement with social activism, and the repression that
rained on both Bradens as a result of that engagement, inhibited her ability
to be present as her children may have wished her to be and as she herself
wished to be. Partly because of Anne's choices and partly because of the

times in which she made them, the public and private arenas of her life became inextricably, sometimes painfully linked.

During her early months in Louisville, a multiplicity of influences crashed in on Anne and prompted her to question her value system, but the most profound of them was certainly Carl Braden. Those who attribute female agency to intrapsychic forces might conclude that Anne's political evolution toward an anticapitalist, anti-racist perspective grew out of falling in love with both Carl and his ideas. Anne herself has always insisted on the reverse explanation: *It was my early association with him—long before I realized I was in love with him—that introduced me to the working-class perspective. Maybe it was because I was falling in love with him that the whole thing hit me with such impact. That's probably what some people would say, especially those who think all the changes we go through come from some personal forces and the outside world has no impact. I'd say that rather it worked the other way. . . . What attracted me to him was the movement he represented, the kind of social vision he represented, and the feeling of being with somebody that I would really be in tune with, intellectually.*[5]

Carl and Anne's friendship contained a mentoring dimension from the outset, but it remained platonic for months. Carl admitted to himself that in spite of his marriage—or, perhaps, because of its stagnancy—he was falling in love with the dark-haired, intense 23-year-old (a decade younger than he) who had become his almost constant companion at work. Yet because he was someone who always felt bound to honor commitments he had made, he did not act on those feelings or even reveal them to Anne for some months. In early 1948, floundering about the direction of her life and with a fairly romanticized view of the working class, she began to consider leaving Louisville and going away somewhere to escape her background, find a new identity, and perhaps work in a factory. Carl was *gallant* about her plan, she said later, encouraging her and even bringing her a county data book of nationwide statistics to help her decide where to go. Yet privately he agonized over the prospect of losing her.[6]

The moment of truth in their future together came over a political crisis—as would many of the pressure points ahead of them. In mid-March 1948 Anne spent several days in Frankfort at the state capital, covering the legislative session and weathering a series of thunderstorms. She returned to a different kind of storm in the *Times* newsroom over Carl's having been ousted from a Louisville CIO council meeting two days before. His expulsion took place in the context of ideological differences over the national CIO's policy (set in

January 1948) opposing the Progressive Party and affirming the Marshall Plan. Specifically, the council barred Carl from covering the meeting for the *Times* on the basis of what they called his "leftist sympathies," or "following the communist line." All four Seventh Street unions walked out in protest—one in a series of escalating local CIO splits.[7]

This was Carl's first experience with being publicly accused of communism, though certainly not his last. In 1948 Louisville, such an instance of red-baiting was still a mere tempest in a teapot, but it received newspaper coverage and earned Carl an admonition from his editors for getting too involved. More significantly, perhaps, the episode provoked a showdown in his marriage. When his wife became upset about the effects of the coverage on their reputation and demanded that he curb his political activism, Carl refused, which prompted Virginia Braden to end the relationship after years of their drifting apart. Carl's feelings for Anne made him sure divorce was the right thing to do.[8]

Upon Anne's return from Frankfort, she and Carl went in the late afternoon to a cafe on Jefferson Street—a spot where they frequently met—and he relayed the shocking news to her. *We had never talked about his personal life. . . . I had just kind of assumed they were happily married like everybody else. It was never like I was the "other woman" whom he told about his bad marriage. That's when he told me he was in love with me, and all of a sudden I realized I was in love with him too. It had literally never occurred to me before. I had never thought of him as anything but a friend until that minute. Of course, I was bound to have known before, but I had been repressing it because I knew he was married. That day was March 19, and we always considered it our real anniversary.*[9]

Their coming together happened unexpectedly and very, very quickly. For Anne, her almost worshipful admiration for Carl flowed easily into the sort of infatuation that falling in love requires. The two spent that very night together, and once they proved to be sexually compatible as well, a partnership with Carl became the fulfillment of her particular kind of romantic yearnings. Having seen her relations with men in high school and college pale by comparison with her passionate attachment to Harriet Fitzgerald, Anne was truly appalled by romances that were superficial or forced a woman to submerge her intelligence. *After I knew Harriet, I think I could never have fallen in love with anyone unless there was that element of intellectual communication. It all came together with Carl, and after living with him, I was literally never even sexually attracted to anyone unless that element was there. . . . I was lucky because we were [also personally and physically] compatible, although sometimes we fought like cats and dogs. I think I probably did have an unusual marriage.*[10]

From the beginning, they were enchanted not only with each other's personal appeal but by their joint effectiveness and seemingly boundless compatibility in working together. Though both were talented journalists, her eye was for drawing out a subject fully and highlighting the human interest angle of any story, whereas his strengths were in attractive layout of a publication and in conciseness (he always shortened her writings). In their case, opposites did indeed attract, and over time it became more apparent that their personalities were very nearly polar opposites. Yet they also complemented each other, and their polarities seemed to lend greater balance to their dealings with others. Carl was abrupt and highly opinionated, given to explosive outbursts but with a streak of tenderness and an inner calm that appealed to Anne. She, on the other hand, was more diplomatic and patient, but tended to worry and have a constant, gnawing internal tension. Her explosions, when they did occur, were more likely to be directed at those she cared about (a difficult aspect of her personality that Carl simply ignored throughout their years together). He was decisive, while she moved much more carefully both in decision making and in human relations. She loved poetry and tended to be more solemn; he read the encyclopedia and always had a joke to tell. Politically, he was factional but fiercely loyal to allies and friends (his motto was "you have to protect your people"). She, meanwhile, worked tirelessly to get all disputes into the open and to resolve conflicts among disparate factions. Perhaps as a result of his streetwise upbringing, Carl had an attitude of what Anne called *when in doubt, fight*. Over the years he would joke that in interpersonal relations, he battered people up and Anne buttered them up; her counter was that she spent untold hours composing three-page letters to soothe disputes he had created in three sentences. Although both were intensely idealistic people, his blustery personality made him less effective at working in coalitions than she, but well suited for the loneliness of the battle they waged throughout much of the 1950s as adamant white supporters of integration. Eventually she would soften him somewhat, while she herself—gradually and only occasionally—would adopt his zest for a spirited disagreement.[11]

Considering Anne's class and cultural background and the context of mid-twentieth-century America, it is no surprise that she was attracted to Carl because of his personal power. Anne was an independent woman, but she lacked self-confidence and lived in a culture that did not offer much in the way of support for professional women. Also, Carl's tendency to *take the bull by the horns*, as she characterized it, was a refreshing antidote to Marshall Johnson's emotional dependency, which had become onerous to her. She acknowledged the subconscious dynamics of their attraction in later years: *One reason—in addition to all the more rational ones—that I fell in love was that I felt he was stronger than I was. I think a woman who has a strong personality is miserable with a man who is not as strong. I find myself very impatient with weak men. This is sexist, I suppose, in reverse. [But] I can put up with weakness in a woman more than I can in a man; [that] just makes my skin crawl. I think that as a strong woman, unconsciously I was looking for a man stronger than me because I did not want [another] relationship where I had to mother a man.*[12]

In looking at the impact of Anne's feelings for Carl on her political transformation, the force of his personality and social commitments cannot be ignored. But neither can the sequence of events. Anne was already in the process of reevaluating her beliefs before she and Carl became a couple. What the outcome of that process would have been had she completed it on her own is only speculative, of course. But it is a topic Anne has frequently speculated upon, wondering if she might have been better off to work through her conflicts on her own. As it was, her coming together with Carl functioned for her as a kind of *short cut*, as she has called it, into a radical life. At the time, she wrote to her friend Lucile Schoolfield that their new partnership clarified a sense of direction for her, *like a shoestring that had been knotted up, but suddenly comes clear when you pull the right string.*[13]

Though she later felt almost ashamed of what a *savior* Carl was for her in their early days together, she also doubted that her convictions would have become as clear without him: *It took something as strong as the emotional pull to him to shake me loose from my past.* Without him, she believed, she would have had a much different, more *cautious* life. There were no regrets. Rather than perceiving any particular sense of loss of her individuality, Anne deeply internalized the notion of herself and Carl as a team. Whatever power differential existed between them in their early days together leveled out considerably as she developed more confidence in their bond and in her own effectiveness as an activist.[14]

Since college, Anne had considered herself "liberal" or "modern" in her thinking about sex. She and Carl moved in together within weeks of declaring their love for each other, renting a tiny upstairs apartment on West Main. In living together without being married, they were not entirely outside the bounds of cultural acceptability, but they were definitely at its outermost margins. Although sexual conventions had relaxed considerably by the post-WWII era—especially for women—compared to what they had been earlier in the century, the number of cohabitating couples was a tiny proportion of the U.S. population amid the widespread rush to the altar during those years. Anne and Carl's decision to live together so quickly was the more unconventional step, particularly for the era. Yet that seemingly impulsive choice derived not so much from experimentation as from their absolute certainty in the relationship. *[When we] started living together, there was never any doubt in either of our minds that this was a permanent relationship. I knew that I did not want to spend my life any way except with Carl. Even through our disagreements, our lives were like two trees entwined together.*[15]

The notion of the "companionate marriage" that could provide both personal and sexual satisfaction to partners was not new to American culture in the post-WWII era: a book of that title had appeared in 1927 and psychologists frequently commented on the reshaping of marriage as a more psychologically rewarding institution. Still, the idea felt like a novelty to Anne, who had been shocked in college to realize that one of her friends had a boyfriend with whom she actually shared intellectual interests. That had not been Anne's own experience with adolescent dating partners, and she looked back on those fledgling forays into romance as unmitigated disasters. As someone who lived primarily in the world of ideas, Anne sought and found a partnership that was at least as rooted in intellect as it was in sexuality.[16]

Apart from the limerance that most lovers go through, what provided the glue for Anne and Carl's relationship was the shared political vision that they adopted from its outset. *There was a real sense when Carl and I decided to get married that we were joining our lives to bring about a new world. We often used the term "revolution" but we had no idea how this revolution was going to come about any more than most young revolutionaries do. . . . We believed in the same sort of world, and we wanted to spend our lives working for [that] world. That was the main point, not extra-curricular. Carl said it first and I picked it up, that we were more effective together than either one of us singly. He used to say that one and one make more than two, like in that Pete Seeger song.*[17]

Their compatibility was reinforced over the years by a kind of sixth sense that Carl felt he possessed, and Anne became convinced that he was right. The couple experimented, sometimes quite successfully, with telepathic communication. Their ability to sense each other's moods and needs when they were apart became a means of coping with the distances that often separated them.[18]

Once the two had committed their lives to each other—and jointly to a larger cause—getting married was, in 1948, an almost automatic next step. Many of Anne's friends from adolescence were already married, but those who were not were skeptical at first of her about-face on her vow never to marry. Once they made plans to wed, Anne made a special trip to Virginia to discuss her feelings for Carl with Harriet Fitzgerald. When Harriet asked her friend, "Are you marrying a man or a movement?" Anne realized that she was doing both.[19]

Even their wedding itself was symbolic of Anne's new allegiances taking precedence over the old. When her parents came to visit in the spring of 1948, she rode with them out to her mother's family home at Eminence. En route she tried to explain that her relationship with Carl was more than just a marriage but a metaphorical change in her priorities and life direction. *I didn't have any animosity toward my family at all. I really didn't want to hurt them because I loved them, but I felt like I really had to be straight with them. I was rejecting their whole world, and they needed to know that. So I told them some of the things I'd been going through as best I could. It did hurt them. They didn't understand what it was all about, but once they realized that this was what I was going to do, they decided, well, they might as well have a respectable wedding.*[20]

Anne had no desire to return to Anniston to marry, but agreed to have a ceremony in Eminence. She soon developed misgivings as she, like many brides, saw the wedding plans take on a momentum of their own. Her mother's well-to-do sister from New Jersey wanted to manage the flower arrangements, and tedious discussions ensued over colors and attire. *I didn't want any sort of big wedding. I could have gone through it rather than upset them. But I was [also] very fond of Carl's mother. She was very aware that my parents were in a different social class, and I began to sense that she was worried about that wedding because she would feel different. I just didn't see any use in putting her through that.*[21]

On the morning of Monday, June 21, 1948—only three months into their romance—Anne and Carl impetuously abandoned her family's elaborate plans in favor of a simpler, impromptu ceremony of marriage in Louisville. Their courtship ended as rapidly as it had begun. Anne phoned her friend Barbara Lane to ask her to accompany them, and Lane, protesting that her day was already too busy, cheerfully acquiesced, as did Herb Monsky, a lawyer and Progressive Party activist whom Carl chose as his best man. They met their witnesses after work at the Unitarian Church downtown, as Anne wished to be married in a church even though she no longer attended one. The pair took no honeymoon, but went in to work the morning after their wedding as if nothing had transpired, never even mentioning their news. Colleagues at the *Times* learned of the marriage through a daily information sheet that came in from the courthouse.[22]

Anne's parents were stung by the couple's disregard for what they saw as standard social obligations. The newlyweds held a rather casual view of marriage—particularly its economic aspects—that family members never fully understood. They glibly gave away most of their wedding presents, including, for instance, a full silver service that Pat Ansboury, president of an AFL local, presented to them, telling each other they wished to *travel in pairs, but travel light.* From the outset of their marriage, they regularly donated 10 percent of their income to left-leaning social justice organizations in much the same way some Protestants tithe to their churches. Yet Anne and Carl worried not at all over their own financial security and were unconcerned by economic planning even in the face of parental advice. (They became a little more practical in this regard once they had children, but never enough to suit Anne's parents.)[23]

The unconventionality of their relationship shaped their approach to family life in a variety of ways. Though both his own parents and his first marriage had been quite traditional, Carl realized that in marrying Anne, he was embarking on more of a working partnership than a purely economic or even romantic one. Anne—who tended to be rather oblivious to her surroundings—had never been much of a homemaker, and she did not become one despite her mother's frequent attempts to nudge her in that direction by sending recipes and household hints. Because both Bradens prioritized their writing and, later, organizing, they shared mundane household tasks like cooking and cleaning to free themselves up for what they agreed were more important matters. Luckily for Anne, however, Carl tended to be tidier and more detail oriented than she, so he fell into the habit of taking care of her and their home in little ways. In their early years together domestic labor was minimal anyway, as they had only small apartments and were constantly on the go. When Anne reflected later on their division of labor, she did not recall its having presented conflicts: *If he resented making those changes, I think he probably decided that's what he had to do in order to live and work with me.*[24]

The more significant difference, to her, was the way he encouraged her to take leadership politically and would do what it took to enable her to do so. He valued her abilities and opinions without expecting her to cater to his personal needs—an expectation that Anne had thought was near universal between men and women. Carl began to pride himself on their being "different" from the families around them in which wives guided the domestic sphere but husbands were supreme heads of household. Though he was dominant in the early days of their relationship, he was considerably less so than was the norm in that day and time.[25]

The left-wing circles in which they located themselves also had a more heightened consciousness about gender than did the larger U.S. (never mind southern) culture of the late 1940s. Since the Depression era, the CP-USA had recognized the home as a political space, and the rhetoric employed by

Communists and their allies was a language not only of class and race, but also of gender—in the sense of recognizing that women as a group have unique concerns and experiences. By the late 1940s, the ideology of eschewing "male chauvinism" had gained currency in the left generally, and both Anne and Carl were sarcastically critical of males who oppressed women.[26]

Neither they nor those around them saw relations between men and women as a compelling political issue, however. Although the Equal Rights Amendment was repeatedly raised in Congress after 1923 and some female trade unionists kept women's rights issues alive in segments of the labor movement, the postwar social landscape was distinctly lacking in a visible women's movement. Those who did identify themselves as feminists tended to be affluent and conservative, keeping at arm's length from other causes, and generally adopting an anticommmunist ideology after WWII. Neither did the American left really make gender equity a thrust in its organizing or literature. Meanwhile, women—especially middle-class women—faced advice literature from the burgeoning mass media about the glories of both domesticity and public achievement but little structural support for the double burdens of household and wage labor. The result was a period of "doldrums" when patriarchal family relations were obliquely criticized but not on explicitly feminist grounds. There were currents of what historians now call "left feminism" within and surrounding the CP, but they were a relatively small part of the postwar progressive movement—and got even smaller as the Cold War muted dissent. In the late 1940s, Anne had no close contact with women's rights-oriented trade unionists. To the extent that she ever even pondered the concept of "feminism," she saw it as something positive yet distinct from her life, harkening to an earlier era. Those surviving strands of left feminism impinged on her very little or not at all in the first year or two after her politicization.[27]

Anne had never been one to subjugate herself to a man. Yet in the realm of social activism Carl seemed so vastly wiser, more politically savvy, and more at ease than she that she virtually accepted his opinion as law. Especially during their first year or two together, she followed his lead almost without exception on how to direct their political energies and was brought up short on one occasion when she tried to tell a fellow activist, "Carl said," only to be interrupted with the curt reply: "Carl isn't always right!"[28]

Leaving Newspaper Journalism

Anne no longer felt the need to run away in search of a new identity: she felt that she had found one by marrying into the working class. The internal questioning that had plagued her for months lifted somewhat, and she was contented with work at the newspaper and on the fringes of the labor movement and Progressive Party. Carl, however, was not. He wanted to apply himself more fully to defending the CIO's left wing as it mounted an offensive amid growing anticommunism. The wider cultural climate was becoming what Carl called "more reactionary" almost daily. In Louisville, the conservative drift that had once been a joking matter among journalists was now deadly serious: in October 1948, for example, the Louisville school system banned the *Nation* magazine for its supposed communistic leanings.[29]

Carl *could easily precipitate a crisis*, Anne later observed, and he did so in the fall of 1948 as a means of provoking their exodus from the *Times*. During this politically charged election year, Anne and Carl were not the only third-party sympathizers among *Times* reporters. M. L. Sharpley, an ebullient copy editor, was an active Dixiecrat. When his presidential hopeful, Strom Thurmond, spoke in Louisville, Sharpley insisted that a group of five African Americans leave an area of the auditorium designated for whites. In editing Carl's coverage of the episode later, Sharpley changed the wording from their "removal . . . on orders from . . . Sharpley" to read that their "departure" occurred at the "request" of Sharpley. When the two locked horns on the accuracy of the changes, Carl tendered his resignation in protest of the editing, and Anne followed suit. Neither of them even considered that she might stay, so certain were they of their desire to work together. On this matter as in others, she deferred without much deliberation to what she saw as Carl's greater expertise. Although their editors entreated them to reconsider, Carl would not, and the Bradens' resignations became effective on November 6, just after the presidential election. Anne's passion for the world of newspaper journalism had been replaced with a new kind of passionate commitment, and even though the leavetaking had not been her idea, she readily embraced it. She continued to love the actual work of journalism, but concluded that she wanted to be fully engaged with social issues rather than merely chronicling them.[30]

Though the departures left the Bradens free to become more deeply involved in the labor movement, they were at a momentary loss as to where to begin. For the Christmas holidays, Anne waited tables for 25 cents an hour in the Brown Hotel tearoom and worked part time in the lamp department of Bacon's department store, while Carl drove a taxi. She then spent a brief stint filing for Belknap, a wholesale company that was notoriously nonunion. Carl hoped she would help to organize the company's workers, but Anne was not prepared to do that. Her idea was to try working with her hands as a way of proving something to herself. Even that desire was pretty short lived, as the work itself bored her to tears. Still uncertain about what sort of work to do long-term, the two knew only that they wanted to be a part of bringing about social change, and they realized they could do that best by using their journalistic skills.[31]

Working for the Left-Led Unions

In spring of 1949, in response to a proposal from Anne and Carl, the Seventh Street unions, under the leadership of FE-236, established a Labor Information Center and hired the Bradens to direct it. Thus began the couple's lifelong practice of sharing work, rank, and salary and of sacrificing monetary security for advancement of a social cause. Declaring themselves as "just one family unit," the couple offered both of their services as full-time publicists for an equivalent of the average wage earned by one union employee. Anne's brand of trade unionism affirmed her—and perhaps even more so, Carl's—working-class identification, but left entirely aside the question of equal pay for women workers. She was more concerned at that time with renouncing the class privilege that had so underpinned her young life.[32]

Carl and Anne put out the unions' local newspaper, *Labor's Voice*; generated publicity in local mainstream media; and taught publication skills to other unionists. Their commitment to working-class militancy was a welcome boost to FE, which despite its local vitality was increasingly besieged on the national level by unions that had once been allies. In metropolitan Louisville, the Seventh Street unions together represented nearly 7,000 workers, more than half of the area's industrial union workforce. Yet even with such numerical strength, it was a heated moment to be coming on board. At the same time Anne and Carl opened the center, FE faced almost certain revocation of its charter nationally if it did not follow the CIO's orders to merge with the United Auto Workers (UAW), a more conservative and anticommunist union. Early on, the couple also created quite a stir among center supporters with their coverage in *Labor's Voice* of the violent anticommunist attack on Paul Robeson fans at a scheduled Peekskill, New York, concert in mid-1949. Unity was preserved, but not without much internal debate as to whether the attack merited local labor coverage.[33]

Later that year, CIO national conflicts reached a stormy crescendo, and FE became one of the first unions to be expelled on allegations of "Communist domination" at the CIO convention. Ten other expulsions followed in short succession (among them the other unions that formed the Seventh Street alliance in Louisville), ceremoniously completing the isolation of the left wing of labor and crippling the effectiveness of the labor movement as a whole.[34]

By fall of 1949 Carl and Anne were embroiled in heading off a raid by the UAW, which attempted to replace Local 236 in Louisville's Harvester plant. Nationally, CIO leaders looked to this contest as a test case for the success of the purges they had wrought. In the December election, the militancy of Local 236 paid off despite an all-out campaign by UAW which included bringing anticommunist priests and ministers into the plant to excoriate the FE. Aided by a hasty merger with the United Electrical, Radio, and Machine Workers of America, or UE, (another of the ousted national left-led unions), FE-236 held the Harvester workers by a margin of nearly two to one and won a modicum of respect from a culture that increasingly clamped a lid on any entity alleged to be "communistic." The *Courier-Journal* pronounced the UAW tactics "heavy-handed and inept," and affirmed that Harvester employees were "ordinary Kentuckians and not Soviet agents," with a union that served "its members rather than the interests of any ideology."[35]

The atmosphere of solidarity Anne and Carl found at FE could not hold on forever against the rising tide of anticommunism, however, and the year they spent working for the Seventh Street unions was the swan song for militancy in Louisville's labor movement. Amid abundant anticommunist rhetoric emerging from the CIO, local labor leaders were soon at loggerheads over a host of minor disputes that had their roots in ideological differences but manifested themselves in personality conflicts and candidate choices. FE managed to hold the line against further raids in the Louisville plant until 1955, when the UAW finally won in its contest to represent the workers.[36]

Organizing Women

Although the Bradens' short-lived tenure with the Labor Information Center lasted only until April 1950, the experience infused Anne's working-class perspective with a new consciousness about race and gender. It was also her real introduction to grassroots organizing. Anne's primary project with Local 236, in addition to coediting its publications, was the formation of a women's auxiliary, the only one of its kind in the area.[37]

Like many women's organizations of the era, the women's auxiliary empowered women by creating a space for them to gather separately from men to address both gender-based and wider social concerns. Originally established with the intent of mobilizing family support in the event of strikes, FE Women's Auxiliary was a far cry from an independent women's movement. For one thing, it was composed primarily of wives rather than women workers (except for cleaning women, the Harvester staff was all male at that time).

Rather than tackling the issue of women's exclusion from the workforce, the auxiliary made its organizing appeal to women in their traditional roles as "wives, mothers, daughters, and sweethearts." Members more or less accepted female domesticity, and in the women's auxiliary column Anne established in *Labor's Voice*, she made recipes and shopping tips a regular feature, side by side with book reviews and more political topics. The auxiliary did, however, take tentative stabs at combating sexism. A column in the June 1949 *Labor's Voice*, for example, advised readers to "ask the men . . . if you don't believe women are as good at office work as housework" after auxiliary volunteers began assisting in office management. Meanwhile, the fact that the back page of each edition of FE's *Cub* featured voluptuous young women in swimsuits, accompanied by occasional lewd captions, was an issue the auxiliary never confronted.[38]

In adolescence, Anne had experienced the emotional sustenance of female alliances, and that point was reinforced for her now. She enjoyed working in groups of women, and she saw how life-changing the auxiliary was for some of them who had to fight with their husbands for even the right to participate in activities outside the household. It was in this context that she began to see herself as having *a mission to get women out of the kitchen and active.* The auxiliary experience was also instructive because the group circumvented the rigid social conventions of segregation once black women and white women who had never before been in a room together began cohosting children's parties and other community-building events. In fact, the women's brand of interracialism became more radical than that of their husbands, who initially balked at the idea of an unsegregated dance at the union hall. Once the dance was held without incident, racial barriers relaxed, and some of the women established friendships that went deeper than mere union collaboration.[39]

The auxiliary was Anne's first real opportunity to know African American women as individuals, and the bonds she formed with women such as Mildred Neal, wife of FE leader Sterling Neal, became important to her as she embarked on a new course of motherhood and a more aggressive civil rights activism that would land her in the headlines in the coming few years.[40]

Some of the FE women became increasingly politicized, and in 1950 a group of them, energized by their single-sex organizing, established a separate organization known as Louisville Women for Peace. Anne's peace activism during this era is a good indicator of the quickening pace of the Cold War. Once the Soviets achieved atomic capability in late 1949, an arms race became almost inevitable amid Cold War tensions. The U.S. government's announcement in the spring of 1950 that it would develop the hydrogen bomb was a particularly menacing foreign policy move, from the perspective of opponents of the Cold War. Anne was among a handful of FE Women's Auxiliary members who were troubled enough by the plan to condemn it in a cultural climate in which all criticism of U.S. foreign policy bordered on treason. They drew up a petition in June 1950 calling on Truman to outlaw atomic weapons and initiate a process for nonviolent world conflict resolution.[41]

The outbreak of the Korean War later that month further solidified the cultural consensus equating dissent with disloyalty, however, and the small organization was extremely beleaguered. As one historian of the Cold War has pointed out, the very notion of "peace" at that point in U.S. history represented "not merely the absence of war but a particular conception of world order" in line with Soviet communism. This mentality left painfully little cultural space available for antiwar protest, and activists tended to be either religious pacifists or leftists sympathetic to the Soviet Union's plight. Either way, they were subjected to intense public opprobrium.[42]

Women for Peace, of which the Louisville group was a part, was one of many initiatives informally linked to the Women's International Democratic Federation (WIDF), a post-WWII international women's organization, millions strong, that was a product of the antifascist, pro-Soviet left in Europe. In spite of ongoing criticism in the local media for taking up Communist-led initiatives—especially the Stockholm Peace Appeal—Women for Peace managed to raise a small but vigorous collective voice against the nation's increasing militarism and readiness to make war on communism. Spearheaded by Lillian Elder, an African American member, the group generated 2,000 postcards, mostly from the black community, supporting W. E. B. DuBois—who at age 83 faced indictment for failure to register his Peace Information Center as "agent of a foreign principal." Anne's memories of her anti–Korean War activism circulate mostly around the repression she received for it, at times being pelted with eggs merely for seeking petition signatures.[43]

Anne's experience in Women for Peace was obviously most colored by the repressive cultural climate in which the group took shape. Nevertheless, it exposed her to currents of left feminism to which she would often return over the coming years. Groups like Women for Peace promoted female independence and agency yet were undergirded by essentialist notions of womanhood that linked peace sentiments to women's nurturing tendencies and to motherhood. That ideology is not necessarily at odds with feminism, but it suggests a kind of quasi-essentialist maternalism that can also appeal to nonfeminist women—on the basis that women have a unique voice because of their mothering abilities and therefore at least a potential unity of gender that crosses lines of class, race, and nation. Anne has described her views thus: *I felt, and still feel, that women—if they don't suppress it—have a kind of compassion that the world needs, a caring-for-others component that some would call a maternal instinct.* A similar perspective guided groups like WIDF and the Women's International League for Peace and Freedom (WILPF). Anne worked closely with the latter group later in the 1950s, and she frequently employed the message of women's unique peacemaking capacities as she became more of a spokeswoman for racial justice causes over the coming two decades.[44]

"Five Minutes to Midnight"

In the context of the widening Red Scare, the Bradens found ever fewer local organizing outlets after the Labor Information Center closed in 1950. While the couple continued part-time publicity for FE and were labor correspondents for the Federated Press (FP), a left-oriented news reporting service, they also had to eat. The two held various short-term jobs during 1950 and '51. For Anne, these included working in a tobacco factory and on a bakery production line. In mid-1951, as they awaited the arrival of their first child, the pull of secure employment and of traditional gender roles trumped their quest for meaningful work. Carl returned to the Louisville newspapers, joining the *Courier-Journal* staff as a copyreader, while Anne sought no further paid employment for several years.[45]

Although union work had distracted them from further Progressive Party involvement after the 1948 elections, they drifted back now to what remained of it: a group of two or three dozen who espoused a program of radical interracialism and an end to the Cold War. The Progressive Party agenda, as the *Courier-Journal* pointed out, did "not differ in its essentials from the 'peace and plenty' platform of 1948." Some members were open Communists, but regardless of their relations to the CP nationally, these local activists were far more concerned with racial injustices and with the increasing repression of dissenters in their midst than they were with national policy machinations, whether they emanated from the CP or from the U.S. or Soviet governments. Galvanized by the Korean War, the anticommunist witch hunt was in full swing by 1950. Late summer of that year saw the arrests of Ethel and Julius Rosenberg, who became the most compelling symbols for the fear of internal subversion that swept the nation. Where there had been a Popular Front, those who remained now were, increasingly, the committed few amid a widespread "culture of the Cold War" that quelled social protest. The role of the "fellow travelers" (as non-Communists who refused to become anticommunists became known) had always been little understood by Americans outside the left, and such people now became almost as widely suspect as self-professed CP members.[46]

Henry Wallace's departure from the Progressives in mid-1950 after the outbreak of the Korean War cost the party what small legitimacy it possessed. The Louisville group, like others across the nation, was the subject of frequent press criticism for its inclusion of CP members and goals. Luckily, however, the "Ethridge newspapers" also continued to assail the Red Scare and to defend the free speech rights of such fringe groups even while critical of their politics. In mid-1951, the *Courier-Journal* warned that the U.S. Supreme Court's recent decision upholding the Smith Act convictions of CP leaders "set the nation's feet upon a difficult and dangerous path [that] undoubtedly restricts and modifies the First Amendment to the Constitution." The newspapers' liberal policies helped to secure in Louisville an opening for social protest long after it had been more vehemently repressed in other comparable cities, especially those farther south. Such policies became harder to sustain as the Cold War proceeded, and liberalism and anticommunism became more and more inseparable in the public mind. A hint of Communist association or even a failure to denounce the CP now branded one as "communistic" and therefore a threat to society.[47]

Anne viewed with growing alarm the increasing *de-legitimization* of social criticism. As she saw it, the cultural crusade against CP members was only the tip of the iceberg. Like other Progressives, she and Carl were supporters of the socialist experiment the Soviet Union appeared to embody. Yet she had her doubts about the cultlike following coalescing around Stalin and wrote to the Soviet Embassy in 1950 to complain of the increasing difficulty of getting information about ordinary Soviet people. She never distanced herself from domestic Communists, however. *The Communists were going to jail. By then people we knew of all over the country were going to jail. We didn't think it would ever happen to us because we weren't any major players. We didn't feel like we were doing enough, and the net result was that our contacts and the world we were operating in became much more narrow. We moved more to the left, whereas we had previously been operating in a much broader world. I think if you look at it in the long pull, we would have been better off to have had more patience and built that base, [but] I would do it again, feeling as I did then, as if World War Three [and fascism were] right around the corner.*[48]

As the 1950s opened, a siege mentality descended over the American left because of the irrational anticommunist hysteria that reached new heights daily. Virginia Durr of Alabama, an independent leftist and later Anne's close friend, had this to say of the fierce inhibitions facing socially engaged people in the early Cold War era: "It was so ridiculous. Someone would find himself in a loyalty hearing if he had a phonograph record by Paul Robeson or if he read the *New Republic*. . . . And there was always danger that they would lose their jobs . . . it was a reign of terror."[49]

That "reign of terror" brought a creeping silence across the social landscape, especially in the South, where all divergences from the racial status quo were widely viewed as deviant. Nationally, the CP had been at the center of Old Left social protest, and the anticommunist campaign generated a climate of fear. After the Smith Act trials of 11 CP leaders began in July 1949, the CP developed a frightened assessment of the onslaught of fascism (known as the "five minutes to midnight" thesis) and sent much of its leadership underground, a decision most party analysts later saw as hyperbolic. On the local level, the siege mentality manifested itself as a vibrant esprit des corps that gave Anne a sense of community strong enough to combat the oppressive climate she and other activists faced in the larger society. Psychologically, that feeling of community probably helped to propel the Bradens' leftward migration. By the early 1950s their small circle of left-wing activists had become like an extended family for her and Carl. Parties at their home drew the same crowds as the meetings they attended. She and her friends wore the label "subversive" as a badge of honor in an era in which virtually any deviation from the status quo qualified one as such. That camaraderie became a lifeline when they found themselves jailed later in the '50s: these were the people who posted their homes for bail and looked after the Bradens' children.[50]

In the decade prior to 1954, Louisville's only homegrown Red Scare centered on the 1952 suspensions of Walter Barnett and Frank Grzelak from the local U.S. Quartermaster Depot as alleged security risks. Both were friends of the Bradens, who publicized the injustices heaped on the men for their political opinions. Barnett, an African American who chaired the local Progressive Party and the Louisville Area Negro Labor Council, worked reconditioning tents and mess kits. He appealed his ouster, but an Army loyalty security board upheld firing him even though it found "not a reasonable doubt as to your loyalty to the . . . United States." Although it had a better outcome, Grzelak's case was even more blatantly unfair, as his suspension was blamed on political associations that were not his own but those of his wife, Josephine Grzelak, a Progressive Party member and petitioner of the Stockholm Peace Appeal. After disassociating himself from his wife's politics, Grzelak (who was white) was reinstated by the same review board that had fired Barnett. The *Courier-Journal* editorialized against the firings, noting that "the principle of disciplining a man because he holds opinions contrary to those in public esteem still has no sanction in our national law." In two years' time, however, the newspapers' commitment to that principle would be put to the test and found wanting.[51]

The Interracial Hospital Movement

As the newlyweds' political commitments crystallized during their early life together, the big exception to Carl's leadership was on the issue of race. Opposing segregation and racism became a *compulsion* to Anne. With an energy nudged forward by the new challenges to segregation that burst forth even in Cold War America, she pushed Carl hard on that matter. The result was that as their relationship cemented over the next several years—and Anne assumed a stronger stance in their political partnership—the couple increasingly focused their activism on campaigns against segregation. The working-class identification they shared was easily enlarged to explain the uniquely dispossessed position of African Americans in the segregated South. (That injustice had never been a priority for Carl until he met Anne, however.)[52]

The first civil rights crusade in which Anne played a major organizing role was the Interracial Hospital Movement, a local initiative that became statewide as the group raised public consciousness about the restrictions facing African Americans needing hospitalization in Kentucky. The incident that spurred the group's formation was an automobile accident that occurred in August 1950 in Breckenridge County, two hours southwest of Louisville. Three young men were seriously injured in the crash, but because a nearby hospital refused to treat blacks, one died there on the hospital waiting room floor. The two survivors lay without treatment for hours until an ambulance arrived to transport them back to Louisville, where they were treated on a segregated basis.[53]

Anne's friend Mary Agnes Barnett, a black Progressive Party activist and the wife of Walter Barnett, launched a petition drive to insist that Kentucky hospitals begin offering treatment without regard to race. Because of Anne's media skills, she was one of the first people Barnett solicited to help. Perhaps because of the fatality, the hospital campaign conveyed an urgency that overcame the leeriness some liberals had about Progressive Party involvement, and a broad coalition developed. Their efforts dovetailed with other local desegregation initiatives : in 1951, for example, the University of Louisville—facing a possible lawsuit—began admitting black students, and the following year, segregation was ended in the public libraries.[54]

In those years, the Bradens had no car, and Anne rode her bicycle almost everywhere she went. When she pedaled door-to-door in the black community delivering petitions, the novelty of her transportation mode, coupled with the poignancy of the appeal, led to a rather unusual friendship. The Rev. J. C. Olden was an elderly African American Baptist minister who headed a small but vocal group known as the Militant Church Movement. When Anne delivered him a few petitions, he cautioned her against riding the bike alone at night, but her insistence on doing so won his respect. Later Olden joked that any white woman so committed to the cause of civil rights, and so unafraid of blacks, was all right by him. He opened the door to new contacts in Louisville's activist black community; through him Anne and Carl met the Reverend M. M. D. Perdue, who would become one of their staunchest long-term allies.[55]

Olden's budding friendship with the Bradens prompted him to get more involved with the Interracial Hospital Movement. He became its co-chair, along with a white clergyman Anne also recruited, the Reverend Albert Dalton. As a lapsed Episcopalian, Anne had been particularly incensed that Louisville's Episcopal hospital refused to treat blacks. Having heard that Dalton, the rector of St. Stephen's Episcopal Church, was socially conscious, she went to visit him one day to discuss the matter. Not only did Dalton plunge into the campaign: he also convinced Anne that she should put aside her doubts about the Episcopal Church's inaction on matters of racial injustice and return to church to work at remedying that lack. She and Carl joined St. Stephen's and remained members there following Dalton's departure. Never again abandoning the Episcopal Church, Anne raised her children in that faith and became active in church causes.[56]

The Interracial Hospital Movement ended legally mandated racial restriction in Kentucky's hospitals. The petition drive penetrated about 60 communities statewide and generated more than 10,000 signatures. In January 1951, 150 Kentuckians, black and white, presented the results to Governor Lawrence Wetherby, who immediately ordered an investigation of all public hospitals. After the inequity was made public, Wetherby opened medical facilities receiving public funds to blacks on an equal basis. The coalition continued public pressure, and legislation sponsored by Rep. Thelma Stovall (a Louisville tobacco worker recently elected to the legislature) included emergency treatment without regard to race as a licensing requirement for private hospitals as well.[57]

Racial Radicalism: The Civil Rights Congress

Perhaps more than any other organization during this era, the Civil Rights Congress (CRC) captured Anne's interest because of its vigorous legal defense of African Americans it identified as facing racist treatment in southern courts. Anne had seen those courts in action in Birmingham, and the experience remained seared into her memory. Like its forerunner, the International Labor Defense (the Communist-backed legal representative in the 1930s Scottsboro case), the CRC, established in 1946, combined legal defense with mobilizing public opinion. By 1950, in the rapidly shrinking American left, participation in one initiative invariably led to contacts in others, and Anne learned of the CRC through her work with the American Peace Crusade. When she heard the dramatic plight of one CRC client, Willie McGee—an African American facing the death penalty in Laurel, Mississippi, for the alleged rape in 1945 of a white woman—she was moved to action.[58]

In May 1951, Anne traveled to Mississippi, one of only three white southerners to participate in a CRC-sponsored white women's delegation protesting the execution of McGee. Another Louisvillian among those three was Alberta Ahearn, one of Anne's friends from Women for Peace. With her broad southern accent and her comfort in public speaking, Anne found herself selected as spokeswoman for the group. Her statement vehemently rejected racial violence as a defense of southern white women: *We are here because we are determined that no more innocent men shall die in the name of southern white womanhood.* Like Women for Peace, the CRC raised gender as an issue, in this case linking it to southern racial injustice, but without an explicit agenda for women's emancipation (except insofar as *the power to protect was the power to control*, which Anne recalled later as the main point that attracted her to a women-only brigade).[59]

The group's attempts to meet with the governor were unsuccessful; instead, the women were taken into "protective custody." The irony of that phrase was not lost on Anne when she found herself, at age 26, jailed for the first time. The jails in which the women were placed were strictly segregated, but they knew that McGee was held elsewhere in the building, and they decided to make their presence known to him. As a gesture of solidarity, they began singing, "Hallelujah, I'm A-travelin' Down Freedom's Main Line" and other freedom songs a younger generation would again sing in Mississippi jails a decade later. That afternoon the women were ordered to leave the state. Three days later, after a protracted legal battle and in spite of new evidence suggesting the alleged victim had been McGee's long-time mistress, McGee was executed in front of a cheering crowd of 700.[60]

Anne's rough treatment by a Mississippi police officer, who upon discovering she was a native southerner told her she "ought to be shot," provoked a kind of awakening in her to her own independence as a woman. McGee's plight and her confrontation with southern political officials magnified for Anne the ugly underside of southern paternalism, and she realized that her racial convictions placed her now—for the first time—at odds with a power structure from which she had always previously benefited. The experience bolstered her conviction that southern whites, especially southern white women, had a unique responsibility to oppose racism. She wrote and spoke widely about the tragedy of Willie McGee, which stayed with her so vividly that she still returned to it decades later.[61]

The CRC experience taught her that her white southern female voice gave her a unique platform for critiquing segregation and racism. Anne's class privilege, enmeshed with her race, gender, regional background, and perhaps even marital status, created for her a kind of shield many other activists simply did not enjoy. Up to a point, she was freer to criticize regional conventions, and she maximized that discursive space, still benefiting in a small way from the kind of male "protectionism" toward elite southern white women that she herself decried and that the historian LeeAnn Whites has identified as shaping gender relations in the South since the Civil War. The narrow limits of that "protection" are suggested too, however, in the threats she received from the Mississippi policeman.[62]

In the early 1950s, criticism of segregation was controversial enough, particularly for whites in the South. But the CRC took "civil rights" a step further, applying it to Communists too. For that reason, the CRC took up the legal defense of CP members facing Smith Act prosecutions. That twinning of civil rights and civil liberties—or the "black" and the "red"—made the CRC a leading target of the escalating anticommunist campaign. In its first few years of existence, the CRC's Communist leadership and its support for Communists under siege had been but one aspect of its mission and had not compromised its effectiveness in other areas: it also attracted substantial non-Communist support because of its anti-racist work. By 1950, however, the CRC, like many left-wing groups of the period, was constantly distracted from the work it wished to do by the fight for mere existence. William "Pat" Patterson, CRC's African American founder/director, was first indicted that year for failure to register the group as a "Communist front" under the newly passed McCarran Internal Security Act, the most severe of 38 pieces of anticommunist legislation to be introduced before the U.S. Congress in 1950. Thus began a protracted government campaign to force the CRC to disband.[63]

Anne's association with the Progressive Party, Civil Rights Congress, and other so-called "Communist front" groups in the early 1950s left her and Carl more vulnerable to the "subversive" charge that would haunt them for years. What she gained was worth the danger, however. Such work, especially that of the CRC, affirmed her. By 1951, the CRC's Pat Patterson was a menacing figure among U.S. government officials and was shunned by liberals in the NAACP and the American Civil Liberties Union (ACLU) for his strident anticapitalist rhetoric and dedication to the CP and to Soviet Communism. For Anne, however, he was a mentor who took the time to write to her at a crucial moment in her early political journey with some advice that set a course for the rest of her life.[64]

After Anne's participation in the failed mission to save McGee's life, she wrote about the experience in the *Defender* (Louisville's black newspaper) and spoke at black churches. When she reported these activities in a letter to Patterson, he admonished her that it was white people whose minds she needed to change, not blacks'. Anne took his suggestion to heart. Over time it became her life's work.[65]

More significantly, however, the young activist sought emotional resignation to what she still experienced as a painful discrepancy between national ideals and policies. Patterson's reply heartened Anne at a critical moment in her political development. He wrote, as she recalled later, *You don't have to be a part of the world of the lynchers or a part of those who deny justice. You do have a choice. You can join the "other America."* The "other America" Patterson described offered her a historical framework for her social justice activism that included past generations of American dissidents such as abolitionists and early trade unionists. It also suggested a legacy to current struggles that would reach past the troubled times in which they were living and past her own lifetime. She took the phrase as a powerful metaphor for the social milieu of the post-WWII American left—embattled as it was—that provided her with a spiritual home. Perhaps the reason Anne needed that home more than Carl seemed to was the lack of understanding for her views in her own family. What was on the one hand an outlaw movement, as she freely admitted, was still sufficiently vital to counter the dominant anticommunist, prosegregationist culture around her. From Patterson's words, Anne shaped for herself a vision of community that would give her both tremendous personal resiliency and a commitment to building unity in whatever social movement she became a part of. That vision also reignited the senses of history and of place she had carried with her, sometimes reluctantly, since childhood—but with a new fascination for the undercurrents of social dissent that had persisted, unknown to Anne until now, throughout the region of her birth.[66]

Activist Mother

When Anne and Carl first married, they agreed there would be no room in their hectic, socially committed lives for children. In the late 1940s the decision to remain childless was a controversial one amid the postwar baby boom and a media blitz glorifying motherhood. Yet by comparison with previous generations of women, Anne was lucky even to have an option: contraceptive information had finally become widely available to middle-class women, and technology was advanced enough to be fairly effective. For young married women, however, there was tremendous cultural pressure to reproduce, with childbearing commonly put forward by the medical community and the media as their destiny. (Forty years after she became a mother, Anne would reflect that she and Carl had *waited* to have children, although at the time she said it, three years was hardly the long wait that it had seemed to her as a young bride in the late 1940s.)[67]

Most of Anne's friends in the women's auxiliary had young children, and by 1950, surrounded by a bumper crop of families as the baby boom began in earnest, she felt more inclined to have a baby. The catalyst for her journey into motherhood was a series of conversations she had with a friend, Bill Sentner, a white labor organizer who came in from St. Louis to help Local 236 withstand the UAW raid. Sentner, an open CP member, was also a family man, married to a Croatian immigrant, Toni Sentner, with whom he had three children.[68]

When in the course of working together, Anne told Sentner of her decision to forgo having children and why, he pronounced her reasoning "ridiculous" and told how his wife, informed by her upbringing in a mining family, had insisted that they would simply have their children in the course of everything else they were doing. When Anne met Toni Sentner in person, that message was reaffirmed by Toni's obvious pleasure in family life despite its travails. *I just got to thinking about that, and [it seemed] right. If you wait until everything is fine to have children, nobody would ever have any. . . . Having children is a part of life, and you should just do that while you're doing these other things. What's it all about, unless you're going to have another generation coming along? I began to really want a child, so I began to talk to Carl about it.*[69]

Carl was not enthusiastic at first, having had a son with Virginia who had died in infancy. But he went along with the idea, mainly to make Anne happy. By early 1951 Anne was pregnant. Experiencing little physical discomfort, she did not even realize her condition until three months or so into it (halfway through the pregnancy, she led the women's delegation to Mississippi). That September, at 27, she gave birth to James McCarty Braden, named after Carl's late father and nicknamed "Jimmy" and later "Jim." As Anne recalled it, Carl fell for their newborn *like a ton of bricks* and was eager to have another.[70]

When Anne first became a mother, she was quite unprepared for the sea change parenthood brought to her life. Taking the advice of friends, she had lined up plenty of baby-sitters before her son's birth in order to be able to continue her activism unabated. But even a helpful husband and all the best planning could not cushion for her the emotional impact of new motherhood. Having a baby was exhausting as she had never known exhaustion: Jim was colicky and frequently cried inconsolably. Carl's stepdaughter, Sonia, came to live with them for a while, and she helped with the baby. Yet Anne remained overwhelmed by the never-ending tasks associated with caring for a young child. The Braden family lore placed a high value on breast-feeding. Carl's mother had lost her first two infants, allegedly because of spoiled milk, and had thus nursed Carl until he was two, which Anne felt had ensured both his physical and emotional health. Anne was therefore determined to nurse Jim and did so until her milk supply dwindled almost a year later, probably due to stress. By that time she was pregnant again and doubly exhausted, yet still driving herself hard.[71]

Anita McCarty Braden arrived in February 1953, a much jollier, more easy-going baby than her brother had been. With two youngsters in diapers, Anne began to feel as if she really needed to slow the pace of her activism. Domesticity seemed in that context like a haven. She even developed a fantasy about their moving to Denver, which promised anonymity and a more congenial climate. She yearned for a day when the phone would stop ringing. Yet her fantasy remained just that: she never learned to say no to the urgency of a social cause or a friend in need.

After a mid-1954 miscarriage amid the anxieties of the sedition charges, Anne intentionally avoided further pregnancies for several years. Yet by the late 1950s, she again felt that she wanted another child. Elizabeth McCarty Braden ("Beth") was born on February 7, 1960, less than a week after the student sit-ins in Greensboro, North Carolina lit a spark that ignited the region.

Anne's children quite literally grew up with the civil rights movement. When they became parents, Anne and Carl had no way of knowing just how intricately their children's upbringing would be entwined with their own activism and with the social movements that erupted from the efforts of others like them. Anne embraced motherhood with the same exuberance she brought to all of life's challenges. Yet she developed a confidence and comfort level in her work as a writer and activist that she never entirely found as a mother. There were just too many presses on her time and too many external stresses on the Braden family. Her experiences as a parent have thus been a somewhat problematic arena of her life—through an unfortunate combination of her and

Carl's commitment to social action, the havoc wreaked on their personal lives by the anticommunist witch hunt, and the loss of their oldest daughter at age 11 to a fatal heart disease.[72]

The 1954 sedition case shattered what tranquility the Braden household possessed when the older children were babies. When Jimmy was three and Anita only one and a half, their lives were disrupted by their parents' arrests, and they lived for nearly a year with Anne's parents, who saw their daughter and son-in-law as wrongheaded at best. In Louisville, especially among whites, Anne and Carl became outcasts of almost demonic proportions. When the children returned home, the family's rhythm was interrupted repeatedly as Carl and Anne plunged more deeply into regional civil rights activism and faced constant attack for their "communistic" beliefs. Because they lived thereafter in a subculture that was predominantly African American, the children were somewhat sheltered from ostracism on a daily basis: especially in their schools, they received a great deal of positive attention. But their household contained an unspoken tension that was sometimes palpable. At times the children saw their parents berated on television, and they could sense that their maternal grandparents disapproved of the way they were being raised. It was a strain on them to feel "different" in so many ways from other families. Like other wars, the Cold War found its victims in children, and the Bradens' two surviving children paid a price for their parents' activism that has sometimes seemed to them too dear. Punctuated as it was by crises—and at times by ugly threats of violence from segregationists—their household lacked the continuity they saw in other families, and it was stressful to have one parent away so frequently, engaged in work that was obviously dangerous.[73]

There were no books for the Bradens' generation on the sociology of parenting—or, if there were, Anne did not know of them. She had only the first (1946) edition of Benjamin Spock's baby book, given to her by Jimmy's pediatrician. Anne relied heavily on Spock's manual on baby and child health. The message she drew from it concerning emotional development consisted of: *don't worry, your child will be fine if you just give him plenty of love.* Spock's peace activism and the literature on combining parenting with social activism (or even a career) were for a future generation, not hers. Later in life, Anne reflected on the disruptions her children faced, but never fully laid them to rest. *Combining children and marriage with a career was quite different from combining it with activity in the social justice movement. A career is more likely to have regular hours so people can go to work and know when they're coming home so they can plan what's called "quality time" with their children, whereas in any sort of movement you never know what's going to happen next. There's a lot of tension and strain; you can think you're going to sit down and have supper with your family, but then the phone rings and somebody is in jail. . . . We just never had the option of trying to create an ideal environment for our children—like the parents who read all these books. In the early '50s, we thought we were literally on the brink of World War III and fascism—and I still think we were. In the '60s we were in the midst of a racial revolution. In the '70s we were beset by massive repression of the black liberation movement. The ranks of whites doing what we were doing were very thin. I just don't think there were any other options to the way we lived.*[74]

At the most basic level, Anne, as a young mother, took Spock's advice to "stay home" with her babies insofar as she held no paying job for more than five years after Jim's birth. Yet neither she nor Carl was strongly imbued with the prevailing notion that she should spend all of her waking hours caring for the children. Instead, she tried to respond to the demands of her enormous social convictions with full-time activism while rearing the children as well, even if it meant sacrificing sleep or a moment to relax. Though Anne spent plenty of time helping her children with homework and shuttling them to music lessons, drama classes, and Scouts, she did not allow domestic responsibilities to divert her from social change campaigns, even if the consequences of her actions—especially in the 1950s and '60s—wreaked havoc on family harmony.[75]

It was not just the larger society that tugged at Anne regarding her parental duties. The sedition case and its aftermath clarified her convictions in the eyes of her own parents, who remained staunch segregationists sharply critical of their daughter's and son-in-law's politics. Rather than tackling head-on the vast ideological differences between them, Gambrell and Anita McCarty conducted a decades-long war of attrition over what they perceived as Anne's deficiencies as a parent. They disapproved wholeheartedly of her absences from home and worried over every detail of their grandchildren's well-being. Were the children dressed warmly enough? Was Anne watching them for signs of the flu? Anita McCarty felt she could not even trust her daughter to protect them from sunburn at the beach. Admonitions were constant, and they gnawed at Anne, providing some explanation for the *bad nerves* of which she sometimes complained and was accused. The never-ending barbs directed at her by parents who had once supported her every endeavor chipped away at her self-confidence as a mother.[76]

Anne and Carl continued sharing household and child-care tasks and—after the sedition case—wage-earning responsibilities. After 1957, when they took jobs as full-time civil rights field workers, the two took turns staying home to care for the children and traveling the South. Carl handled more of the travel for the first few years, particularly when Beth was an infant. From

May 1961 through February 1962, he was completely absent from the household, imprisoned for contempt of Congress after his testimony before the House un-American committee. During his absence, Anne had a full-time assistant to help with both the family and her work, enabling her to continue a good bit of traveling. For the following decade, one parent was regularly on the road, while the other balanced the domestic front and the never-ending mountain of paperwork their outreach generated. The Braden household was simply not governed by the same conventions that dominated the larger society. Even as toddlers, the children always addressed their mother as "Anne" (usually their father was also "Carl," but occasionally "Daddy"). They were not alone in these casual references, of course: in left-wing and bohemian circles, especially in places like New York, it was not unusual for parents to encourage children to address them by their given names. In postwar Louisville, however, it raised eyebrows.[77]

Within a few years, cultural changes of the 1960s further altered the Bradens' family dynamics as they were embraced by a new generation of activists even as they remained suspicious figures among many of their own age and race. Their once fairly isolated household became Freedom House, a temporary home for dozens of young people immersed in the student movement that emerged in 1960. Anne and Carl became role models and friends to student activists for whom they (particularly Anne) were deeply influential mentors, but whom their own children frequently saw as troublesome competitors for their attention. Youths who came to stay with the Bradens sought Anne's advice on returning to school, relations with parents or lovers, or (later) drug and alcohol problems, and her own children resented the patient attention she gave to people they sometimes regarded as interlopers.[78]

The most difficult blow to the Braden family's life came at the height of the civil rights movement in 1963–64. When their oldest daughter fainted for no reason at age ten, tests showed that the seemingly healthy Anita had a rare and fatal heart-and-lung disorder. Months of visits to specialists around the country in search of help proved useless as the child continued to weaken. Anita died in June 1964, four months after her eleventh birthday. Anne and Carl kept going, but the loss was a tragic wound that stayed with each family member in different ways. For Anne especially, Anita's death spurred a new intensity to activism as a way of muffling the relentless sorrow. That pattern replicated itself when Carl died unexpectedly in 1975, leaving Anne a single parent through most of Beth's teenage years. Anne coped, but she did so within the context of even greater intensification of her social action involvements.[79]

Their single-minded commitment to social justice activism gave form to Anne's and Carl's other commitments, and that included their family experiences. Though she did not conform to her era's stereotypical image of the mother, Anne participated actively in her children's school PTAs, took them on summertime beach vacations, weathered with them the storms of adolescence, and was with her youngest as labor coach when Beth gave birth to Anne's first grandchild. Passionately devoted to her children and, later, her grandchildren, Anne had trouble prioritizing her time in ways that lined up with that devotion. Her children felt they never had her undivided attention, and they resented it.[80]

Anne's parental experiences point to the difficult terrain that women with immense social commitments navigate in managing domestic or maternal obligations. Like so many other women activists throughout American history, Anne struggled—and not always successfully—to find a balance between the needs of society as she saw them and the needs of her own family. She made her choices, as did other activist women, mostly because there were no better options. Her fretful nature also caused her to worry more about their implications than Carl did. More than Carl, she—as the mother—would have to account for them. Anne once noted wryly that in terms of renegotiating family responsibilities between men and women, *the one thing [we] women have never been able to share is the guilt.* She rarely felt free of that guilt during her children's growing-up years and never fully so, even long after Jim and Beth had become adults and made a kind of peace with their upbringing and their mother.[81]

Inadvertently, perhaps, Anne became mother not only to a family but to a movement, and in this more collective maternal role she found less opportunity for self-recrimination or family criticism. With the emergence of the Student Nonviolent Coordinating Committee (SNCC), she and several peers such as Ella Baker and Fannie Lou Hamer were among the few adult women to whom young student activists like Joan Browning, Casey Hayden, Diane Nash, and Dorothy Miller could look in the early 1960s for elders who possessed capacities they could admire rather than reject as either too conservative or too subservient to men.[82]

Organizationally, Anne was not quite the "mother of SNCC" that Ella Baker was in terms of having direct responsibility for its growth. But, continuing with the family metaphor, she was at least an adoring aunt in her attempts to encourage the young activists without usurping their autonomy. Especially for young white women in the sit-in movement, her example of strong, enduring activism and her concern for their personal dilemmas made her into something of a mother figure—one who was both more awe-inspiring and accepting, as well as closer to their own ages, than were their own mothers. The close relationships she formed with young SNCC women in the early 1960s helped to impart both her radicalism and a nascent feminist consciousness to some of them—with whom she continued to collaborate later as they revived the women's movement.[83]

Women activists who came of age in the 1970s and '80s also credit Anne with helping to shape their consciousness. Carla Wallace, for instance, a white Louisvillian nearly 35 years Anne's junior, knew the Bradens when she was a child. By the 1990s Wallace had become a dedicated anti-racist activist, as well as a leading figure in the Kentucky Fairness Alliance for lesbian and gay rights. When she first embarked on her own course of social action in the 1970s, Wallace benefited from Anne's mentoring and saw her in a maternal light. Later, their relationship evolved to a more balanced friendship in which, as Wallace explained, "Anne's been there for me for so many years. I learned from her that [social justice activism] can be a lifetime's work."[84]

A potentially transitory relationship as a mother figure or role model to youthful devotees is vastly different from the more intensive work of actually raising children from infancy to adulthood, of course. Yet there is tremendous common ground in the qualities required for both processes. Anne's cultural training as a woman prepared her for parenting, but those same skills of compassion, patience, and careful interpersonal relations also contributed to the way she was regarded by younger activists. Parents are often judged by society for how their children "turned out." In this respect, it seems Anne's influence has stretched far beyond her impact on her own children, which from her perspective and theirs is both mixed and emotionally charged. In the *other America* she chose as her homeland, she has been an example—a "political mama," to use a phrase from her friend Ella Baker's biography—for several generations of women and regional activists.[85]

Historians have tended to portray the post-WWII era as a sort of disjuncture between the Old Left that was decimated by the Cold War and the New Left that emerged in the 1960s. Anne Braden's experiences—particularly regarding gender and family relations—defy that dichotomy, straddling both periods and blending elements from each in the life she constructed. Her political transformation, the sense of camaraderie that sustained her through the Cold War, and the radical vision of social change she adopted in 1948 were firmly rooted in the Old Left. Yet although she was shaped by the ideology of liberal-left collaboration symbolized in the Popular Front, she was more an inheritor than a full participant in that generation's social movement. By the time Anne became politicized, that movement was already being eclipsed by the repressive anticommunist crusade. As part of a transitional generation of American women, Anne became a sort of bridge between the Old and New Left in the ideology she espoused and in the example of an independent woman and seasoned social crusader she represented to younger activists.[86]

More significantly, perhaps, her marriage was atypical even among her contemporaries in the post-WWII left. Because the Bradens shared the tasks of domestic and parental labor, Anne's familial responsibilities never hobbled her immersion in social causes. Without exaggerating the egalitarianism in the Bradens' marriage—they were products of their culture and thus limited by it—they nevertheless challenged the postwar domestic ideal. Anne was perfectly capable of falling back on that ideology when it would advance her ideals to do so—as in the housewife image of "Mrs. Carl Braden" that could allow her greater freedom (or invisibility, which was sometimes equally useful) in speaking against social injustices. Marriage and motherhood framed her social engagement, but they never fundamentally altered it. She was unusual in this regard even by comparison to female activist peers of the postwar era— such as Peggy Dennis (wife of CP-USA General Secretary Eugene Dennis), whose 1979 autobiography chronicles several decades of social action which nonetheless remained decidedly secondary to her partner's involvement. Anne was considerably younger than Dennis, however, and her life has reflected those differences with regard to female agency and leadership.[87]

Also, perhaps because she was still a fairly young woman when the second-wave women's movement arose in the late 1960s, Anne was just as influenced by the new generation as they were by her example of female assertiveness and social conviction. Anne never saw women's rights as the central focus for her activism, but she lived her adult life as a feminist. The rebirth of the women's movement then gave her a theoretical and collective base for the organizing of women in which she had long engaged as well as a greater cultural reinforcement for the individual reworking of gender roles that was not new to her or to Carl.

To a great extent, Carl helped to shape Anne's politics and life direction, and their marriage gave her a kind of support and independence that few women of her generation found in their partnerships. Yet she pursued that life direction as a strikingly independent woman, especially once their 1954 sedition case thrust both Bradens into the headlines and left Anne—like it or not—in charge of publicizing the case while Carl sat in prison.

CHAPTER SIX

THE WADE CASE—NO TURNING BACK

Even our grandmothers would tell us, "You've got to turn the other cheek. You must be patient." They turned their cheeks on both sides, so to me it . . . seemed like we were expected to wait a hundred years for progress. My feeling was very deep to oppose discrimination any way I could.

I wanted to buy a house that I wanted to buy, that was the basis of the whole thing. I'd see a house that I liked and then [learn] that it was in the "forbidden area," and I said, "This doesn't make any sense." I wasn't begging. I felt justified in trying to buy what I wanted with my own money.

—Andrew Wade, 35 years after he
bought a home on Rone Court[1]

NINETEEN-FIFTY-FOUR BROUGHT A TURNING POINT in American race relations when the U.S. Supreme Court overturned half a century of legal segregation in its ruling in *Brown v. Board of Education* on May 17—a decision that invigorated a new generation of black civil rights protest and triggered a wave of massive white resistance to southern school desegregation. But if segregated schools were dear to most whites, segregated neighborhoods were more so. Anne and Carl Braden, Andrew and Charlotte Wade, and a group of their friends found out how dear. Their challenge to white supremacy in housing swept the city of Louisville into a crucible of its own in the spring of 1954— one for which it was quite unprepared—that overshadowed regional ripples from *Brown* and evoked a local Red Scare of glaring proportions. For Anne, the drama that unfolded aligned her solidly and for life with the African American freedom struggle.[2]

Segregation in Louisville was not quite as rigid as it was in cities farther south. In fact, Louisville became one of the few southern locales to accept token school desegregation without a fight in the years immediately following *Brown*. Yet throughout the twentieth century, the question of blacks living in close proximity to whites struck at the nerve center below Louisville's thin veneer of racial civility.[3]

The tide of white public sentiment leaned toward greater racial separation after 1920 in Louisville and elsewhere, North and South. Racial bias in housing thus became institutionalized through the real estate industry's use of restrictive covenants—contractual agreements signed by property owners in a given neighborhood promising not to sell or lease to blacks for a specified period. When the code of segregated housing was violated, it was not uncommon for white residents to pool their money and offer potential black neighbors a handsome sum for the house before they could ever occupy it. Purchasing proffers were made more appealing by accompanying threats and intimidation. Restrictive covenants covered 75 to 80 percent of Louisville properties at the time of the Supreme Court ruling declaring them unconstitutional in 1948, and real estate brokers neither expected nor encouraged change thereafter. Covenants continued to operate informally and with the tacit support of real estate agents. Lending institutions also red-lined poor and predominantly black communities, creating restrictive loan policies that helped sustain the color line. Thus, black housing patterns continued to be defined by white hostility. Amid Cold War anxieties and an ever shriller paranoia over accelerating legal challenges to segregation, to defy the norms of Jim Crow in housing became truly subversive—traitorous even—in the minds of many white southerners in the postwar era.[4]

Enter Andrew Wade IV. Wade was an African American WWII veteran and electrical contractor who knew Anne and Carl slightly, having worked with them peripherally in the 1948 Wallace presidential campaign. Wade and his wife, Charlotte, were close in age to Anne, and they had a toddler the same age as Jim Braden with a second baby on the way.[5]

For Anne and Carl, the point of no return in their commitment to their ideals arrived—unwittingly at first—when Wade came to them in March 1954 with a dilemma that seemed to be within their power to solve. Because of race-based restrictions, Andrew and Charlotte Wade were unable to buy the ranch-style suburban home they dreamed of for their family, and he asked the Bradens to assist them by acting as their white "fronts." This strategy—which would become known across the nation in 1960s open housing campaigns as a "dummy" purchase—would allow Wade to bypass real estate agents' unwillingness to sell to him in an all-white neighborhood.[6]

The Bradens were a last resort for Andrew Wade, who had been trying for months to purchase a suburban house after the family's apartment became too crowded. The Wades wanted a house with a large yard, away from the congestion of the city yet an easy commute. Like so many families of the postwar era, they preferred the newer ranch-style homes that proliferated in the suburbs. Wade had concluded from his own informal survey of Louisville real estate that "there was not a single ready-built stone ranch type house for sale [to blacks]" in the entire Louisville metropolitan area. Consequently, he simply did not volunteer information on his race when he looked at homes. Wade's light mocha complexion got him past the initial hurdles toward home ownership four times, only to have the deal collapse once the agent learned the family was African American.[7]

The first white acquaintances Wade approached for help told him "point blank" that they were afraid to defy community prejudices. Utter frustration prompted him to seek out the Bradens, whom he knew more by their reputation as white advocates of black freedom than personally. He asked around and got their address.[8]

After the Wade purchase exploded into a community hysteria made possible by the toxic mingling of segregationist and anticommunist fears, authorities found it unbelievable that Wade had approached Carl and Anne on his own initiative and instead saw the Wades as mere pawns in a menacing Communist plot that the Bradens had shaped. Yet Wade's father was what had been known since Emancipation as a "race man," living within the confines of Jim Crow but subscribing to black newspapers and rearing his children to be proud of black achievements. By 1954, both generations of the family were ready to push those confines, and that same spring Wade's father became a plaintiff in a suit to end segregation in Louisville swimming pools. The younger Wade's WWII experience had heightened his impatience with racial restrictions, and he had participated in various local civil rights campaigns. Both he and Carl Braden were what Anne has called *daredevil-ly types* unafraid of confrontation.[9]

In terms of the housing market for African Americans in Louisville, there were numerous reasons why the Wades would seek relief from the

housing limitations they faced. By the 1950s the national postwar trend toward suburbanization had created a new "crabgrass frontier," but one with
few opportunities for African Americans, who were heavily concentrated in
crowded, all-black urban ghettos after their recent migration northward and
into cities. Thousands of Americans, most of them white, were moving out
from cities to more spacious outlying areas. The GI Bill had made home
ownership attainable for a wider cross section of the U.S. population than
had ever been the case prior to WWII, and in the postwar era, housing demand exceeded supply. Predictably, blacks were the most frequent losers in
this equation. Nationally, housing projects for low-income blacks were on
the rise, yet stable, older, black urban neighborhoods were razed to make
room for new industrial development in the postwar economic boom.
Robert Weaver, later the first secretary of the U.S. Department of Housing
and Urban Development (HUD), observed in 1948 of federal housing
policy, "provision of more space for minorities is the most immediate
need ... accelerated by a sound national housing program which insists
upon widespread participation by all elements."[10]

Such a program never materialized. In Louisville, most African Americans
lived near the central city in neighborhoods that suffered disproportionately
from postwar commercial expansion. A 1950 Municipal Housing Commission
study found that 16 percent of Louisville's residential blocks were slums, and
nearly a quarter of its housing substandard. Virtually the only post-WWII
new home construction for blacks was housing projects, and even those generated white opposition. Segregation was strictly observed in the projects, and
African Americans endured long waits for an apartment while units designated
as "white" sometimes sat vacant for months. More than 20,000 new homes
were built locally in the five years preceding 1954, but one community study
found that in 1950 scarcely 200 privately built new houses were available for
sale to blacks.[11]

African American outmigration took place predominantly within the city
limits to the west of downtown, where older homes were being vacated by
whites. There too, considerable opposition crystallized in response to black
purchases. In 1950, 400 white residents organized the Shawnee Homeowners
Association to oppose the general westward migration of Louisville blacks and
their specific encroachment into the Parkland area in the southern West End.
The West End was also where Anne and Carl lived in a modest, two-bedroom,
red-shuttered bungalow they had purchased in 1952 after the birth of their
son. The Bradens were well aware of the patchy, contested desegregation
going on around them as blacks moved in on mostly a block-by-block basis

under the guidance of real estate agents who often sold to them at above-market prices.[12]

Once approached, Anne and Carl felt a moral imperative to agree to Andrew Wade's request for help. Their response was, as Anne characterized it, *automatic.* She wrote of their moment of decision that *any other answer would have been unthinkable.*[13]

Lulled into a false sense of optimism by the relatively liberal atmosphere that continued to thrive in Louisville and by local civil rights gains of the past decade, the Bradens were largely oblivious to the power of prosegregationist ideology in their midst and the additional boost it received from anticommunist conservatism. Because they lived in a subculture that validated interracial friendships and civil rights gains, the couple overestimated progressive trends in Louisville and vastly underestimated the hostility their act would provoke. In addition, they were too preoccupied with a local drive for school desegregation in anticipation of *Brown* to really ponder Wade's request too deeply. Only a few days before Wade first approached them, Anne had helped to coordinate a hearing at the state capitol—part of a campaign to repeal the Day Law mandating segregated schooling.[14]

Because she tended to worry more over things than Carl, Anne had a brief moment of consternation the night after Wade's visit—a premonition, she thought later—when she wondered if their plan was legal. She quickly put aside her misgivings, however.[15]

Given Anne's and Carl's passionate disdain for racial hierarchy, the subterfuge that was an inescapable feature of the Wade purchase seemed insignificant by comparison to the ongoing betrayal of blacks by the larger society. In her 1958 memoir of the sedition case, Anne acknowledged that, unconsciously, fronting for the Wades may have appealed to her desire for a radical elimination of racism. *How can I say for sure that the purchase of a house did not also fulfill a need in me: a need to fling a dramatic challenge to a community I thought was moving too slowly, to a society too satisfied with its own sins . . . to fling it like a prophecy, impractical perhaps but hopeful, of a new world that could come, a world without walls.*[16]

It took several weeks and two more foiled attempts for the Wades to settle on a location. The home they selected lay in Shively, a western suburb that had become—unknown to them—a magnet for "white flight" from the complexities of the city. Originally a haven for distilleries wishing to avoid paying

Louisville taxes, Shively incorporated as a separate town in 1938 and has in recent decades seen unbridled development of used car lots, adults-only businesses, and strip malls on its main thoroughfare, the Dixie Highway. In 1954, however, it retained a more rural, provincial character that was laced with grimmer anti-black sentiments than either couple anticipated, especially since there was at least one black neighborhood only about a quarter mile from the house Wade selected. Yet Andrew Wade had already had one bad experience in the Shively vicinity: one of the real estate ventures that fell through after the agent realized Wade was black was on nearby Kramer's Lane. Rather than making him steer clear of Shively, however, that humiliation had stiffened Wade's determination to insist on his right to a home there. It was, after all, a pastoral area convenient to his job and his relatives in town.[17]

The house the Wades chose was a two-bedroom ranch built of the limestone so prevalent in Kentucky. Situated in Jefferson County just outside the Shively town limits off Crum's Lane, the house was only the third to be constructed on a dead-end street still unpaved and surrounded by open countryside. The fledgling subdivision was the creation of James Rone, a small-scale contractor who lived in an older farmhouse at the edge of a tract he had purchased to subdivide. Rone had proudly named the cul-de-sac Rone Court and was developing it one house at a time. His son, James Junior, or "Buster," owned the lot adjacent to what became the Wade house, with plans to build also.[18]

Once Wade identified the house for them, Anne and Carl looked at it, negotiated through a real estate agent, Ben Hudson, a selling price of $11,300, and secured a mortgage through South End Federal Savings and Loan—all under the ruse that they themselves would be the occupants. They never actually stated their intention to live there, but allowed the other parties to assume it. The deal proceeded without a hitch, and on Monday, May 10, 1954, the transaction was completed. Wade accompanied the Bradens and Rone on a walk-through of the new purchase, and no questions were asked, no information volunteered.[19]

It took the Rones three days of watching Andrew Wade and members of his family work on the house and move furniture into it before they asked, and he told them, that he was indeed "colored" and was now the owner. Wade tried in vain to enlist Buster Rone's approval, assuring him of their intent to be good neighbors and reminding him of the promises of U.S. democracy. But that afternoon, a child visiting the Rone grandchildren ventured into the Wades' yard and was escorted hastily back across the property line and scolded loudly enough so the Wades could hear. Those admonitions directed at the guileless child gave Andrew and Charlotte Wade their first chill of the danger that lay in store. By evening a crowd of 20 or so had assembled on Rone's property, where they milled around for hours before getting into cars and driving into Louisville to confront Carl Braden.[20]

Anne was not at home the night the mob descended on her doorstep. She was out at a concert while Carl stayed behind to mind the children. He did not deny the accusations hurled by the Rone family members and real estate agent Ben Hudson, who did most of the talking. Nor was he moved by their demands, however, and seeing that, a few of the men mumbled threats.

"You got any children?"

"I do."

"You own this house?"

"I do."

"You better watch out."

The group soon dispersed, however. Anne did not hear those threats to her children, and later she was glad to have been spared them: there would be plenty more to face in the coming weeks. Over the next two days, she tried unsuccessfully to assuage James Rone as she and Carl lived with a barrage of telephone threats, including someone who promised to blow up the Bradens' own home at noon on Saturday, May 15, if they did not "get the Wades out."[21]

Meanwhile, Andrew and Charlotte Wade firmly declined Rone's offer to buy back their house. Despite the hostility, they prepared to spend their first night there on Saturday, minus their young daughter, Rosemary, whom they left with relatives in town. When they arrived late that afternoon to Rone Court, the front picture window lay in shards, smashed by a rock with a piece of paper encircling it bearing the words: "nigger get out." Later that evening they watched as a handful of men burned a cross on Buster Rone's lot. Andrew Wade ran out onto his lawn and lifted a pistol into the air, but dropped it to his side and watched the cross burn, shouting bitterly to the antagonists, "You're burning your own American flag!" At 2:30 Sunday morning, as he and his wife lay sleeping, half a dozen rifle shots broke the stillness, shattering more windows and barely missing their friend Carlos Lynes, who was lending them his support by sleeping over on a couch in the kitchen. Not yet having a telephone, the Wades and Lynes waited anxiously for the light of dawn. By midmorning, reporters and policemen swarmed the property, and Andrew Wade informed them that his family would not be driven out. Yet no criminal charges were filed in conjunction with the violence. Wishing to avoid further friction, Anne and Carl resisted friends' advice to take out a peace warrant against the mob.[22]

In additional to the piecemeal desegregation taking place in Louisville's public spaces, local successes in opening neighborhoods to minorities gave the Wades and the Bradens some basis for thinking that the neighborhood conflict would subside. Six months earlier, Nina Hardman, a Filipino immigrant of Spanish descent and a former member of the WWII Women's Army Corps, purchased a house in town on Fetter Street. Before she and her three children could move into their new home, neighbors—led by a Louisville alderman—circulated petitions opposing her locating there, and Hardman feared violence would erupt. Yet after the petitions were reported in the news, they were withdrawn; a few Fetter residents offered Hardman a welcome; and the *Courier-Journal* editorialized against the "malcontents," noting that "Louisville has been blessedly free of this sort of hostility among neighbors."[23]

But anti-Filipino sentiments were less savage than those against blacks in 1954, and the Wade incident met with a very different response. Initial news coverage of the violence was mixed, though the headline—"Shots, Rocks, and Burning Cross Greet Negroes in House Whites Got for Them"—set the stage for the criticism the paper (and the community) would continue to lodge of the Bradens' recklessness in the purchase. The story also recounted, however, almost word for word the statement Anne and Carl had given as explanation for their actions: *We feel that every man has a right to live where he wants to, regardless of the color of his skin. This is the test of democracy. Either you practice what you preach, or you shut up about believing in democracy.*[24]

The liberal journalistic ethos Anne had found when she first came to work for the Louisville newspapers had made them an important voice for a gradualist approach to greater African American opportunity in the postwar years. Until the *Brown* decision, the *Courier-Journal* never editorialized against segregation per se, but it portrayed local civil rights crusades sympathetically and covered African Americans' accomplishments generously. The presence of an established black newspaper, the crusading *Defender*, also nudged the mainstream media toward greater racial liberalism. The Louisville newspapers located themselves within a progressive tradition that had a commitment to "render the greatest public service" (in owner Robert Worth Bingham's words, memorialized in the newspaper's lobby). Editorials deplored inferior facilities for blacks but stopped short of a clarion call to dismantle segregated institutions. The newspapers were still far too reserved to suit most black Louisvillians chafing within the bounds of segregation, but compared to their counterparts in other southern cities, the papers were a decidedly moderating force in race relations and substantially more liberal than the majority of their white readership.[25]

They were unprepared for the direct challenge to segregation that the Rone Court purchase laid at their door, however. In the sedition case that followed, even the lukewarm support the *Courier-Journal* and *Times* had given to racial reform would be streaked with a red brush by local opponents of change. With the additional awkwardness of having Carl Braden in its employ, the newspapers' management remained more concerned with distancing themselves from any association with the whole endeavor than they were with examining critically the injustices bound up in the case. Although the newspapers' editorial policies had been generally critical of the anticommunist hysteria that had gripped the country over the previous few years, they grew more quixotic when the Red Scare located itself right there in Louisville. Where the Wade case was concerned, the papers' management bent over backwards to avoid seeming sympathetic to those supporters of the Wades later indicted for sedition, lest they too be labeled "soft" on communism.

It may be the case that the campaign against the Wades would have escalated no matter what. Unfortunately, however, those first nights of violence took place on the weekend before the announcement of "Black Monday," as segregationists came to think of it. On Monday, May 17, 1954, to no one's surprise but to the great dismay of many white southerners, the U.S. Supreme Court, in unanimous voice and at high noon, struck down school segregation.[26]

For an idealist like Anne, the decision was a welcome break in the steady drumbeat of the region's stagnant racial conventions—the beginning of the end of Jim Crow. Many young African American students across the South hoped so too. John Lewis, for example, who would in a handful of years join the student sit-ins that took the region by surprise and decades later serve in the U.S. Congress, listened to the radio newscast as a 14-year-old in rural Alabama and believed that now he and his people would have better schools, more promising lives. But social change would not come without prolonged struggle, neither in Alabama nor in Louisville. Anne's initial optimism received a swift dousing with reality. *I thought that when the Supreme Court [ruled] everybody would say, "Well, now that's the law of the land," and settle down. But the reaction was the opposite. And I always thought we got the first fury . . . people who were upset by the decision couldn't get at the Supreme Court but they could get at us. All of a sudden it wasn't just one black family but the schools were going to be integrated [too].*[27]

As Anne was about to learn, the mid-1950s were not a propitious time to welcome any kind of reform. The anticommunist purges that were the domestic counterpart of Cold War foreign relations had cast a gray pallor over social activism for nearly a decade. In light of the Chinese revolution, the Soviets' achievement of atomic capability, the Korean War, and the spy trials at home, the ethos of anticommunism had become so powerful by 1950 that some liberal groups (the NAACP, Congress of Racial Equality, and the ACLU, for example) began instituting their own internal noncommunist oaths, in effect conducting purges of their memberships. Once Senator Joseph McCarthy seized upon anticommunist demagoguery in February 1950 and elevated it to a political art form, there was little remaining national conversation on civil liberties but a virtual outpouring on the specter of Communism. In November of that year, Congress passed the McCarran Internal Security Act, which established an attorney general's list, monitored by a five-member Subversive Activities Control Board, to which groups could be compelled to register as "Communist action," "Communist front," or "Communist-infiltrated." Meanwhile, HUAC and its Senate counterpart, the Senate Internal Securities Sub-Committee (or SISS), enjoyed unique investigating and subpoena powers and the close cooperation of the FBI to enable full exposure of activities they considered "communistic." Through the actions of these two committees, more contempt of Congress citations were issued between 1950 and 1952 than in the previous 92 years. Many liberals no longer even denounced the Red Scare by the early 1950s, and most saw the excesses of anticommunism as regrettable (insofar as innocent U.S. citizens' lives were occasionally ruined) but insignificant compared to the need to expose the domestic proponents of Soviet Communism, enshrouded as they were in a secret conspiracy to subvert the country from within.[28]

The anticommunist witch hunt had been in place now for several years, and routing supposed Communists had become a national obsession, ritualized in the mid-1953 execution of Julius and Ethel Rosenberg—convicted as traitors, Communists who passed atomic secrets to the Soviets. By 1954 anticommunism was as much a defining ideology of most liberals as it was of conservatives. Anyone publicly accused of communistic sympathies was subject to a kind of social censure that effectively quashed personal and professional lives, not to mention social activism. Because the CP-USA had been at the center of the left-wing upsurge of the 1930s and '40s, few social reformers—especially in the South—could claim absolutely no association with it. As a consequence, the parameters for social criticism became very narrow indeed. Dissent translated too easily into disloyalty, and many reformers retreated—or were harassed—into silence.[29]

The cultural obsession with anticommunism found special resonance in the South, where authorities had long been quick to suppress or discredit as "red" virtually any dissent that threatened the racial or political status quo. As the years of the Cold War wore on and the challenges to white supremacy continued, what became known as "red-baiting" gained greater effectiveness as a way to muzzle any who advocated racial justice. Such charges focused primarily— though not exclusively—on whites, whose devotion to black civil rights genuinely mystified southern segregationists and seemed to indicate a kind of subversiveness that easily squared with "common-ism," as they thought of it.[30]

Southern image-makers often insisted that the campaign for social and racial equality was nothing more than a foreign conspiracy run by communists who might or might not be in the CP. Because southern anticommunist publicists in the 1950s devoted a generous share of their energies to smearing civil rights workers—and they were good at it—the *Brown* announcement could hardly have come at a less opportune moment for southern voices who would have campaigned to support school desegregation. The red-baiting assault of the past few years had rendered too marginal the work of such people, and facing now the greater threat posed by *Brown*, southern segregationists turned up the heat even further, launching a modern-day witch hunt. The long-standing association of any challenge to segregation with communism was mild compared to what it became during and after that year.[31]

In March 1954, as southerners awaited the *Brown* ruling, for example, arch-segregationist Mississippi Senator John Eastland convened Senate Internal Securities hearings in New Orleans—the first ones to be held in the South. There, he grabbed headlines by hauling in for questioning some of the region's most prominent white supporters of integration. These included Myles Horton of the Highlander Folk School, Virginia Durr, Aubrey Williams, and James Dombrowski. The latter three were leaders of the Southern Conference Educational Fund (SCEF), an offshoot of the older, now-defunct SCHW. SCEF carried on what remained of the New Deal–era southern conference movement—now a single-point program for racial integration. All of these were native southerners who had been active in regional social justice causes since the Depression, but were only now being publicly touted as "communistic" and subjected to the humiliation of a subpoena that threatened any community standing they held. It was the prevalence of these sorts of currents in southern culture that made possible the movement of massive resistance that erupted after *Brown* among white southerners opposed to school desegregation.[32]

In Louisville, no such fierce red-baiting had heretofore accompanied civil rights activities, partly because of the moderating perspective provided by the newspapers. Nevertheless, anticommunism had become a national mood, a tense awareness that the United States had to be on guard at all times against an internal threat that was only vaguely defined. In the spring of 1954, the Louisville newspapers—like their counterparts around the country—were in the habit of giving plentiful, though not uncritical, coverage to McCarthy's pronouncements, and they turned a worried eye to the fall of the French in Indochina. Following the national trend, the papers' brand of liberalism was girded with an anticommunism that in retrospect looks pronounced yet was still moderate by regional and even national norms of the times.[33]

Perhaps it was because the Wade purchase flew in the face of the moderation that Louisville opinion makers so valued. Or perhaps there was some psychological displacement at work, at least in the form of a convenient opportunity to criticize a more radical pro–civil rights action in order to cushion the reading public for the *Courier-Journal*'s support of school desegregation. It may simply have been a desire to distance the newspaper from the impetuous activism of its copyreader. Whatever the reasons, on May 18, 1954, the *Courier-Journal*'s editorial page carried a strong endorsement of the *Brown* ruling. Right next to it was an editorial that offered scarcely a frown at the Shively residents who had burned a cross and shot into a neighbor's home. Instead, the newspaper was harshly critical of Carl and Anne Braden for "forcing an issue of race relations in this artificial and contrived way" and for "agitation in the name of progress." Reaffirming the notion that black immigration would cause property devaluation, the editorial noted that whites in Shively were "entirely within their rights in protesting the purchase of property in their sub-division by Negroes," though not with violence. This time, it seemed, the malcontents were not the bigoted neighbors, but those who had created circumstances for that bigotry to reveal itself.[34]

A number of historians have written about the vacuum of moral and political leadership in the South that could have defused the massive white resistance that soon crystallized in opposition to the *Brown* decision. Just as that void of responsible leadership left an opening from which emerged a pro-segregationist movement, the *Courier-Journal*'s choice, initially, to focus on the folly of the dummy purchase rather than to champion the Wades' right to live in the house of their choice left a kind of vacuum in that community that failed to stem antiblack violence and perhaps even encouraged it. Later that week, emboldened by the extreme anticommunist hysteria of the past decade, the reactionary voices that had been murmuring beneath the surface of Louisville's "polite racism" decried the incident as Communist-inspired and spoke up in support of further white resistance to the Wades' move.[35]

On the front page of the *Shively Newsweek*, a suburban weekly, an editorial appeared on May 20, 1954, that defended the rights of whites to live in segregated neighborhoods. The words of John Hitt, owner and publisher of the small paper, conveyed a sense of urgency that was likely fueled by the racial changes *Brown* portended; Hitt's remarks mirrored what politicians farther south were saying. Alluding to *Brown* without overtly mentioning it and invoking the Bradens' press statement on democracy as their motivation, Hitt wrote that "the law does state that the colored race may live anywhere they choose, but there is no law protecting the feeling of the white race at all. . . . This . . . Democratic country . . . will not remain Democratic when the rights of the colored race surpass those of the white. That is the trend now."[36]

From Hitt's framework of a white community under siege, it was not much of a leap to see the entire purchase as subversive. Hitt's initial commentary on the desegregation of Rone Court made that jump easily, and it was he who introduced the notion that the entire purchase may have been Communist-inspired. Emphasizing the Bradens' and Wades' links to the Progressive Party (defunct though it was by 1954), Hitt theorized by posing a volley of questions to his readership: "Is Wade, with the help of Braden, really looking for happiness, or is he being a martyr to a cause? What cause? The cause of non-segregation, or is it the cause which made Stalin the lion of Russia, or could it be the cause of the Communists in this country to encourage panic, chaos, and riot?"[37]

There was considerable range of opinion on the matter, however, and it illustrated the yawning racial divide separating white complacency and black aspirations. On the same day Hitt's editorial appeared, the African American newspaper, the *Defender*, also a weekly, ran an editorial praising the Wade purchase and scarcely mentioning the Bradens' role in it other than to dismiss their pretext as merely whites and blacks "working together [to] pierce the vicious practice of not allowing a Negro freedom of purchase." The *Defender*'s early coverage of the purchase suggests just how much resentment simmered in Louisville's black community because of the racial hierarchy that underlay the river city. The paper began its coverage of the Rone Court violence with a banner headline repeating Andrew Wade's impassioned statement, "We intend to live here or die here," and its account detailed the city's history of denying adequate housing opportunities to blacks.[38]

After the violence of May 16, the Jefferson County police posted a 24-hour armed guard outside the Wade home. This gesture provided some modicum of security, but Andrew and Charlotte Wade felt none too reassured when police officers began spending much of their post in the Rones' yard. On May 22, the Bradens and the Wades began organizing an independent Wade Defense Committee (WDC) for additional oversight of the property and for material aid in the face of institutional threats to the Wades' continued ability to reside on Rone Court. One result was that someone was in the house keeping watch around the clock.[39]

After the neighborhood discontent became public on May 17, a new obstacle troubled the purchase. The mortgage holder, South End Savings and Loan, received notice that insurance on the house had been terminated, and it consequently demanded full payment of the loan within ten days. Scrambling to secure new homeowners' insurance, Wade had little success until he tapped into a network of interracial liberals through the Urban League and met Eric Tachau, vice president of the Louisville Fire and Marine Company. Tachau, a young white businessman whose principal customers were in Tennessee, stood to lose little in the arrangement, and he agreed to insure the house out of a sense of fairness, arguing that "it just didn't seem to me that whether these people should or should not be allowed to live in their house in a white neighborhood should be decided on a technicality."[40]

Even with new insurance, South End Savings and Loan demanded foreclosure of the loan, on grounds that the two couples had violated the contract by transferring the property without the bank's written consent. Neither couple had realized that the contract contained such a prohibition. South End refused to accept Wade's monthly payment and instead initiated court action against the Bradens and the Wades. The defendants argued that the bank's claim was a mere technicality through which they could deny a mortgage to blacks desegregating a neighborhood without prior approval from real estate interests. The immediate problem, however, was to secure a new mortgage or an influx of cash swiftly to pay off the loan.[41]

The next few weeks amounted to what Anne called a *war of nerves*. Telephone threats and hate mail continued. One night a volunteer guard fired his gun after he reportedly observed a man crawling on his belly through an adjacent yard toward the house, but police failed to apprehend anyone and soundly reproved the guard for his shot. The Wades met with a solid wall of white economic resistance to their move. No local dairy would deliver them milk, and Wade received a letter from the *Courier-Journal* explaining that he could not get the newspaper delivered because the independent circulation contractor in his neighborhood refused to handle his account.[42]

In the absence of new violence and despite the Wades' continued unease, the police removed the daytime guard in mid-June. The Wade Defense Committee recruited new volunteers to stay with Charlotte Wade and her daughter during the day while Andrew worked. Vernon Bown, a white truck driver and longtime left-wing activist, virtually moved into the Wades' home—along with another night shift worker, who was African American—because their work schedules allowed them a daytime availability most Wade supporters did not enjoy.[43]

In the black community, armed defense of property against white violence was nothing new. In fact, it was part of a long tradition that had grown up in response to white aggression. It had not even been a decade since mobs had virtually destroyed the black community in Columbia, Tennessee, and such offenses made Wade and others like him alert to the violence that could erupt when African Americans stepped out of the bounds whites had drawn around them. Yet the actions of the Wade Defense Committee probably struck their new neighbors as incendiary. Attempts to intimidate the newcomers lessened but did not subside.[44]

Anonymous callers also continued to warn Anne and Carl of plans to bomb their home or otherwise harm their children. Even after several warnings proved to be pranks, the harassment left Anne sleepless, edgy, and more reactive to the threats than Carl. Several weeks after the first violence and in the wake of a direct threat on her son's life, she reluctantly accepted a .32-caliber pistol that Andrew Wade offered her. During the long hours when Carl worked the night shift, she kept the gun nearby as she sat restlessly writing publicity materials on the Wades' plight and fielding phone calls after the children were asleep. Each night she and Carl moved their son's and daughter's beds into the hallway to shield them from any shots that might be fired, though none ever were.[45]

Amid the ideology of domesticity that infused 1950s popular portrayals of women, Anne Braden and Charlotte Wade were all but invisible in media coverage of the purchase and subsequent violence. Carl and Andrew were the activists, the protagonists, and the women attached to them were merely the supporting cast, rarely even identified by their given names. It was the men against whom opponents' worst fury was directed and to whom journalists turned for comment, even though nearly all of the Bradens' actions with respect to Rone Court were taken jointly. Perhaps because the women's challenge to segregation did not entirely fit with the era's stereotypical models of womanhood, not one reporter on the case saw fit even to examine the "woman's perspective" they might provide. Yet in the anxious weeks after the Wades moved into Rone Court, simply being in their respective homes brought both women unyielding duress as they squired their toddlers—who were too young to realize the danger to themselves and their families—through each day. Charlotte Wade was near delivery of her second child, and soon into the endeavor Anne became pregnant as well, so they shared that experience in the midst of the spring's tensions. Anne, Jimmy, and Anita often spent afternoon hours with Charlotte and Rosemary Wade on Rone Court, with both women maintaining a facade of normalcy though they were emotionally spent. Anne got some reprieve when she returned to the West End, where her actions were accepted if not appreciated, whereas Charlotte faced an unrelentingly hostile environment in her surroundings and the dissonance of knowing that her very presence in her new home was the source of that hostility. That awareness kept a certain distance between the two that no commonalities of gender or circumstance could surmount. For Anne, the Wade purchase was a cherished cause that became personal once she and Carl faced ruin because of it. For Charlotte, who was not by nature a crusader, it was a more personal matter that turned into a life-or-death situation and required a crusade.[46]

At that time, Louisville's African American community was more or less united in support of the Wades. Attempts to rally white support achieved fewer results. The only whites willing to get involved in the Wade Defense Committee were leftists, and probably not more than a dozen at that. Most were among those later indicted for sedition: in 1954 white southern integration activists were few enough in number that they *stuck out like sore thumbs*, as Anne later described it. These included friends of the Bradens such as Louise Gilbert, a social worker who, like Anne, had been active in the Civil Rights Congress. Gilbert and her roommate, LaRue Spiker, a writer and former union activist, were part of a local chapter of the Women's International League for Peace and Freedom (WILPF), an international organization that maintained cordial relations with the Soviet Union but also a bit more domestic respectability than the CRC. The Louisville WILPF branch was tiny but had been a voice for desegregation, leading a 1953 campaign to open the city's new amphitheater to blacks. Under WILPF auspices, Gilbert and Spiker sent letters to residents near Rone Court, calling on the league's history of peacemaking and asking for neighborhood reconciliation and acceptance of the Wades. Their efforts yielded little but personal reprisals later. Women who were activists, leftists, unmarried, and living by choice with other women were particular "sore thumbs" at midcentury.[47]

In response to pleas from Anne, who telephoned every white pastor in the vicinity asking for support, a few ministers phoned or called on the Wades, and one even visited the Rones. But none took more active steps to turn the tide of public sentiment in Shively. There were a few dissenting voices, however. On the page following Hitt's initial editorial in the May 20 *Shively Newsweek*, a contributor to the letters column expressed dismay with the Klan-like "mob violence." As the paper's editorials grew more inflammatory, one letter writer took the editor to task for inciting "violent thinking." But these were mere cries in the wilderness of the white majority's silence.[48]

The days lengthened, spring turned to summer, and the *Shively Newsweek* became more heated in its criticism of the purchase. Hitt's editorial stand got the attention of Millard Grubbs, an ultraright ideologue and former Dixiecrat once investigated for his links to KKK violence. Though he did not live in Shively or even close by, Grubbs latched onto the idea of the Wade purchase as a "Communist conspiracy" to establish "a black beach-head in every white subdivision." In early June he expressed those views in a lengthy letter to the *Shively Newsweek*, proclaiming segregation to be ordained by God and excoriating the "Marxist world plotters" who would undermine it—a group in which he included Presidents Roosevelt, Truman, and Eisenhower. Warning readers that "if you are a member of the Caucasian race this matter involves all that you hold dear whether you know it or not," Grubbs suggested that any challenge to segregation was part of a "rising red bureaucracy." He ended his fiery tract with an invitation for "loyal white people" to join his newly formed American White Brotherhood. The letter was signed "in care of *Shively Newsweek*."[49]

Grubbs's extremism seemed to propel the newspaper's publisher to the right. Editorials dwelled increasingly on the Wades and Bradens as troublemakers in a previously idyllic suburb. On June 17, Hitt proposed that perhaps the shots fired into the Wade house in May had been "self-inflicted."[50]

Anne realized later how the suburban newspaper had aroused segregationist and anticommunist anxieties in Shively, but in the context of more immediate threats to the Wades' ability to remain on Rone Court, it was easy to dismiss such rhetoric at the time as merely *the ravings of the Shively Newsweek*. The Wade Defense Committee was busy raising funds, issuing pamphlets on the family's situation, and organizing volunteer guards. It took most of June for Andrew Wade to secure a new loan that would pay off South End and, they hoped, end the impending lawsuit.[51]

During the last week of June, the loan was on its way to approval, this time through a black-owned mortgage company, and the Wade Defense Committee released a statement to the effect that financing for the house was now solvent and the Wades' claim to it entirely legal. A slight ease in tension turned out to be the calm before a storm.[52]

That weekend, shortly after midnight on Sunday, June 27, and without warning, a dynamite blast destroyed one whole side of the Wades' house on Rone Court. With it went their dream of a home—and the peace of mind of all connected to the incident for many months to come.

Remarking on how unusually dark and placid the neighborhood was for a Saturday night, Andrew and Charlotte Wade came in late on June 26 from a rare evening out. They chatted on the side porch with the two volunteers who had kept watch in their absence, learning of an odd phenomenon the guards had noticed a few minutes before: flashing lights that formed an L-shape of which the house was the center. Down the road in the Rones' front yard sat the police guard. Suddenly, an explosion ripped through the opposite end of the house. No one was injured, but the damage amounted to about $5,800, almost precisely half the value of the house. More than that, the symbolism of the bomb's having been placed under the bedroom of the Wades' daughter was chilling (the child routinely spent Saturday nights with her grandparents in town). Although the explosion was thunderous, none of the neighbors turned on lights or came out to see what was wrong. When the police guard came running from across the street, what stayed with him the most from those moments was the hollow sound of Charlotte Wade's sobs. Oddly enough, a few hours before the blast, the officer allegedly reported later, *Shively Newsweek* publisher John Hitt had driven down Rone Court and inquired if anything had happened there.[53]

In the face of such outrageous violence, the *Courier-Journal* now condemned the perpetrators and affirmed, belatedly perhaps, the Wades' "right as Americans to live anywhere they choose, even if they choose to live in an atmosphere poisoned, as theirs is now, with hate and malice." What the editorial only implied, but supporters knew only too well, was that this sort of violent intimidation to maintain residential segregation was not simply an anomaly but part of a historical pattern that was more national than it was southern. Farther south the boundaries of segregation had been maintained by Jim Crow laws and widespread acts of individual antiblack terrorism; yet residential patterns remained less fixed than did those in northern and midwestern cities with significant black populations. In the latter, battles to maintain residential segregation had been extremely intense since large-scale migration of

African Americans out of the South had begun in the WWI years. Waves of escalating neighborhood violence that culminated in a bombing—much like that which took place on Rone Court—had convulsed cities such as Detroit and Cleveland during the 1920s. Such tactics were still common in the 1950s as a means to discourage blacks from moving into white neighborhoods. That same summer, black residents who had integrated Chicago's Trumbull Park housing project faced systematic attacks of violence that had persisted for a year without effective police deterrence.[54]

Situated as "gateway to the South," Louisville straddled two worlds, neither of which was without serious travails for African Americans. The Rone Court incident brought to the surface a kind of extremism that seemed at first take southern but in fact drew from repugnant traditions that were not confined to the South. The destruction stood in stark contrast to the gradualist course of racial "progress" the *Courier-Journal* was attempting to steer. Only the sheer drama of the bombing forced the newspaper's editors into supporting the Wades' right to the house, and even then they reiterated their dismay that the purchase had ever been made. That very moderation brought them sharp criticism from the African American community. As a *Defender* editorial pointed out, "disgrace can rightfully be placed on the doorsteps of all who have not sought to protect the rights of the Wades."[55]

What had been a home turned now into a crime scene, but Andrew Wade, his frustration at a boiling point, refused to relinquish his rights to be there. Charlotte and Rosemary Wade moved back into town with relatives as Charlotte awaited the birth of her baby, a daughter who arrived August 2. But Andrew returned each evening to spend the night in what was left of their house. On June 30 county officials denied a request by the Wade Defense Committee for a court of inquiry into the violence, allowing the police to proceed instead with a standard investigation. They also refused the committee's suggestion that they hire black policemen to work on the case (the Jefferson County police force was all white in 1954). Having returned to around-the-clock observation of the house, county police continued using the Rones' yard as their watchpoint. The officers—annoyed, perhaps, at having to defend black property rights in a "white" neighborhood—were irked by what they saw as Wade's stubborn, aggressive behavior, and they had him make out a list of all persons he would allow inside the house. On July 22 they arrested and charged him with breach of the peace after an altercation in which Wade attempted to bring a friend into the house with him whose name was not on the list. When the police would not accept his verbal approval, Wade grew angry and was jailed. The charge was later dropped, but it was the kind of thing that reminded Wade and his supporters—as it was intended to—how forbidding white society could be to African Americans.[56]

The militancy of the Wade Defense Committee not only annoyed county officials; it effected a split within the black community. The heart of that dispute rested primarily with C. Ewbank Tucker, an African American attorney who was a temperamental, sometimes irascible person but a committed defender of blacks' rights. Tucker had more or less single-handedly desegregated the Louisville bus terminal the year before by staging a one-man sit-in after a client of his was arrested for sitting mistakenly in the white waiting room. Finding that no segregation laws pertained to the bus depot, Tucker vowed to return and use the "white" waiting area himself, and he did so uneventfully. Tucker's theatrical but erratic personality would provoke division as well as forward motion in the black community in the coming years. Now he publicly criticized the NAACP and rebuffed its offers of legal assistance in the case, actions that alienated more moderate activists. As Louisville NAACP President George Corderay remembered years later, between Tucker's provocative remarks and the involvement of known "leftists," the NAACP monitored the situation but kept itself at arm's length. As in Alabama's Scottsboro case of the 1930s, the NAACP wished to avoid becoming embroiled in an organizational turf battle, especially one with potentially "communistic" associations. The Red Scare that had gripped the United States for years suddenly seemed to be right here in their midst, and the Rone Court protagonists' participation in groups like the Progressive Party and the CRC, together with the *Shively Newsweek*'s relentless campaign to tar them as "red," prompted Louisvillians to back away from their cause.[57]

For Anne, the weeks following the explosion were even more nerve-wracking than those before it. Four days after the blast, she learned that her own home might be the next target. Louisville Police Chief Carl Heustis personally summoned Carl into police headquarters, even sending a patrol car to the couple's Virginia Avenue home to retrieve him. Warning that county police had obtained one confession and believed another dynamiting to be imminent, Heustis recommended preventive measures such as checking under the hood of their car before starting it. That very afternoon Carl installed floodlights outside their house, and Anne arranged for the children to spend several nights with friends. All through the sticky heat of the July Fourth weekend, the couple observed plainclothes officers keeping watch over their house from the field across the street.[58]

But no mischief materialized, the police were removed to attend to other matters, and the summer dragged on with no arrests and no real lift in the tension surrounding both the Braden and Wade households. On Rone Court, the damaged house stood, partially roped off, as a brooding reminder of the lack of resolution, with the funds needed to rescue it tied up in court proceedings.[59]

Minus police protection, Anne kept up her nightly vigil over her own house. In the unending strain and sleeplessness of those weeks, she miscarried the gestating baby she and Carl had already nicknamed "Mike." The emotional pressure seemed to have no end in sight. She and Carl had agreed that out of respect, they would not advise Andrew Wade of what to do, but Anne began to have doubts of her own, partly in reaction to Charlotte Wade's growing unwillingness to stomach the entire endeavor any longer. After Wade's mother informed Anne that she would hold the Bradens personally responsible if Andrew were harmed, Anne tentatively suggested to Wade that he give up the house. When he refused, she did not press the matter further.[60]

The Wade Defense Committee refused to let the family's plight fade into obscurity but sent regular delegations to the courthouse to demand action. The *Shively Newsweek* kept the matter alive as well. Interspersed with photos of smiling high school sports heroes and announcements of births and charity benefits, the paper ran stories suggesting secretive communist subversion and reinforcing a sense of widespread opposition to the Wades' presence.[61]

In the white community in town, Anne was aware of the largely unspoken but consistent disapproval surrounding her and Carl's actions. At the couple's St. Stephen's Episcopal Church, not one parishioner—with the exception of the minister, Rev. Irwin McKinney, who offered them consistent comfort—ever even spoke to them of the situation on Rone Court, though all must have known of it. Anne and other Wade defenders still scoffed at Hitt's exaggerated anticommunist sentiments as little more than a joke. They had no inkling yet that Hitt's seemingly paranoid notion that the violence against the Wades was an "inside job" was about to become the state's official line of reasoning.[62]

Commonwealth's Attorney A. Scott Hamilton was the man who heard the bulk of complaints from the Wade Defense Committee that summer. Hamilton, only three years in office, was a hard-driving, politically ambitious prosecutor whose trademark was his thick, prematurely gray hair, always so tousled it gave him the look of a lion. Not particularly liberal, he was nevertheless firmly aligned with the "insider" Democrats who ran Louisville—a group that also included the upper echelons of the *Courier-Journal* and *Times*.[63]

After two months of relative inactivity on the matter, Hamilton announced that he would bring the Wades' complaint before the Jefferson County Grand Jury in September. At first both families felt that the investigation was an occasion for celebration, for resolution at last. Still, rumors were flying as to what an investigation by the all-white grand jury would actually consist of, and Hamilton appeared suspicious of both the Wades and the Bradens.[64]

On the opening day of the hearings, Anne and Carl discovered that their troubles had barely begun. Having made advance arrangements with Hamilton so that Carl could be at home with their children, Anne was the second witness to be called on Wednesday morning, September 15, 1954—also, coincidentally, her son Jim's third birthday. Following the testimony of the policeman on duty the night of the explosion, she told only part of her version of the events on Rone Court. In midstream the jurors shifted to another subject: her political beliefs and associations. *I hadn't been there but a few minutes when I realized that I was in the middle of a witch hunt. I knew about HUAC and these committees. The minute they began asking me about things that had absolutely nothing to do with the Wade house bombing, it became pretty clear to me. My reaction was anger, just "how dare you!"* Almost instinctively, she refused to answer questions regarding her membership in the Civil Rights Congress or a host of other organizations listed as subversive by the U.S. attorney general. The jurors quizzed her about her friendship with Walter Barnett (the fired Quartermaster Depot worker) and wondered whether she read or subscribed to CP publications such as the *Daily Worker*. When Anne declined to answer, she was called before County Judge L. R. Curtis, who threatened her with contempt. Anne told Curtis that she was perfectly willing to answer any questions relating to the Rone Court violence and was withholding other answers not out of fear of self-incrimination but on grounds of irrelevance: *I refuse to answer because I consider it beyond the power of this grand jury or the Commonwealth's Attorney to inquire into the private opinion of any citizen, what he reads, or what organization he belongs to. We have enough McCarthys in America without the Jefferson County Commonwealth's Attorney's office turning into one. Hamilton has even asked our neighbors if we have many books in our house and what they are.*[65]

Anne listened that morning in amazement to Hamilton's first speech detailing what he called the "two theories" about the dynamiting. Either it had been set by neighbors who resented the entry of blacks into a white neighborhood or it had been an "inside job," part of a Communist plot to stir up racial friction in an otherwise contented community. Anne felt her adrenaline rushing. She was as shocked as she was angry that the notions advanced all summer by the *Shively Newsweek* had now emerged almost word for word from someone with real authority—the commonwealth's attorney. Anne was not cited for contempt despite the judge's admonitions, and, excused from further questioning, she rushed home to warn Carl of what to expect when he testified later that day. Her plans for a birthday celebration for three-year-old Jim were swept away in the frantic flurry of uncertainty that permeated the rest of that day and the days that followed.[66]

From the first, the strict secrecy normally attending grand jury proceedings was missing from this body. That afternoon, worried, Anne telephoned Mark Ethridge, publisher of the Louisville newspapers and the person originally most responsible for her return to the city of her birth. In spite of a stern warning from Assistant Commonwealth's Attorney Lawrence Higgins *not to tell anyone* about the proceedings, she explained what had gone on behind the closed doors. *I had a feeling Ethridge would be supportive. He was. I told him, "They're not investigating that bombing, they're going to investigate us. They want to know what I read and what [organizations] I belong to." I remember he interrupted me: "It's none of their business." He was very sympathetic.*[67]

After talking it over with Ethridge, Anne contacted the *Times* and *Courier-Journal* news staff, feeling that maintaining the secrecy of the proceedings would promote further injustice. The next day the papers defied judicial decorum to cover the grand jury extensively. By then, both Andrew Wade and Carl had also testified, and they too had been asked about membership in various organizations, including the CP. Refusals to reply landed them, at Hamilton's behest, in open court for the matter to be brought before Judge Curtis—a development that further nudged the proceedings into the public eye. In light of Hamilton's charges of Communist underpinnings, Curtis ruled that such questions must be answered, except the one regarding CP membership, which, he said, could be self-incriminating and therefore could be forfeited. Andrew Wade answered "no" to all questions of membership except one regarding the Progressive Party, which he declined to answer. Carl, however, held fast in his decision not to detail any political affiliations, and he exchanged hot words with an enraged Hamilton, who continued to threaten contempt citations or obstruction charges but took no immediate action.[68]

On September 17, the *Courier-Journal*—true to its steady if muted resistance to the excesses of McCarthyism—ran its strongest editorial yet, expressing "deepest disapproval" of Hamilton's questioning, dismissing his theory of Communist subversion as lacking any evidence, and affirming the witnesses' refusals to answer queries on their political beliefs, associations, and reading materials. The editors faced a problem nearly inevitable in a readership that was noticeably more conservative on race than the views expressed in the paper. They knew that some Louisvillians tended to see Carl Braden as an "agent" of the *Courier-Journal* because he was an integration activist who also happened to be in its employ. Thus, the editorial took pains to distance the paper once again from the Bradens, calling them "politically misguided" people whose subterfuge was "deplorable" and had perhaps harmed their cause "irreparably." Yet the essay also stated that Carl Braden would not be fired for the "unorthodoxy of his political views," so long as he pursued them on his own time. Decrying the anti-red "hysteria" that appeared to be descending upon Louisville, the editorial concluded, "The matter under investigation is not what the Bradens believe or read," but "the wanton destruction of a man's house in the middle of the night." With that one bold editorial, the newspaper stepped into a fray from which it could not easily disengage, and it soon found itself a secondary focus of the grand jury's probing gaze.[69]

For all of her problems with what she thought of later as the *establishment press*, Anne still had a deep attachment to the profession of journalism. She was, as she put it, *terrifically moved* by the courage that the paper's editors, presumably under Ethridge's leadership, had displayed. The morning the editorial appeared, she took time to convey her reaction to him in a personal letter, which, she stipulated, was not for publication. Ethridge wrote her a consoling personal reply a few days later but soon went abroad on a diplomatic mission and had no further dealings with the proceedings.[70]

After the editorial criticizing Hamilton appeared on the third day of the proceedings, *the situation went from bad to worse*, as Anne reflected later. Before, Hamilton's ire had turned on her and Carl's refusals to answer all of his questions; he had already vowed to punish them for that stubbornness. As well as calling attention to its racial liberalism, the newspaper's stronger new stand now put Hamilton and the grand jury he headed in a bristly, defensive posture. McCarthy-era political rivalries frequently drove local anticommunist prosecutions, and the *Courier-Journal's* September 17 editorial was the opening shot in a battle Hamilton would wage with both the "communist threat" and the newspapers for years to come. The aspersions the editorial cast on the grand jury must have given the jurors added impetus to abandon what had to have been an uncomfortable investigation into white-on-black violence in favor of a more exciting and—given the times—decidedly righteous search to eliminate communist subversion in Jefferson County. One of the grand jurors, Esther Handmaker, was the wife of Herman Handmaker, a man known for his outspoken, ardently anticommunist views. Over the course of two weeks, the grand jury called 52 additional witnesses, including neighbors and relatives of the Wades, members of the Wade Defense Committee, policemen, and reporters. Hamilton railed to the press that the body possessed "broad inquisitorial powers."[71]

The grand jury was composed of 12 white citizens (nine men, three women) whose specific opinions on segregation are not known. But their questioning of Wade and his associates makes it clear that their lives, like those of most southern whites, were so walled off—to borrow a metaphor from Anne's later memoir of the case—from those of African Americans that there was not even a crack that allowed them to peer through. Over and over jurors quizzed Andrew Wade on who had "influenced" him to buy a house in a white neighborhood. They made little mention of weapons routinely kept by the Rones or of the shots fired into the Wade house their first night there, but they had many queries about the "arsenal" Wade and his friends possessed. They simply had no clue why African Americans did not trust white law enforcement. One juror remarked that it was "far-fetched" to think that an antiblack mob might actually defy the police. Jurors' comments suggested that they found the whole notion of interracial friendships unusual, awkward, and—coupled as it was with radical pro–civil rights views—highly suspicious. Numerous questions regarding Vernon Bown (the white truck driver who moved into the Wade house as a daytime guard) indicated that the mere willingness of a white man to go to such lengths on behalf of an African American made him particularly suspect.[72]

Once local residents became alarmed by the possibility of Communist involvement—according to the perverse logic of the Red Scare—it was no more unreasonable to conclude that melee-seeking Communists had first coerced a black man into buying a house and then bombed it than it was to think that hostile white neighbors had resorted to violence. As the proceedings continued, Hamilton made just such an assertion in response to Judge Curtis's wry observation that he saw no evidence of an "inside job." More of the questioning centered on the politics of Wade's supporters, most of whom refused to answer questions on their political affiliations, further alienating the jury. Wade had provided investigators with an extensive list of suspects and the license plate numbers of cars from which threats had been made, but questioning of white Shively residents became more perfunctory. No charges were filed against Buster Rone and two friends, Lawrence Rinehardt and Stanley Wilt, even after they admitted to burning the cross on May 15. (The men insisted that what they had torched was not a cross, but merely two boards nailed together.)[73]

Meanwhile, the *Shively Newsweek* continued to publicize Hamilton's theory of Communist subversion in banner headlines and portray Wade supporters in a negative light. The coverage resurrected in vivid detail Walter Barnett's dismissal from the Quartermaster Depot and colorfully relived Anne's and Alberta Ahearn's 1951 mission to Mississippi, representing a "communist front organization" (CRC) on behalf of a "convicted Negro rapist" (Willie McGee).[74]

What is most striking in retrospect, however, is what the grand jury did not pursue. They let pass without comment the revelation that Rinehardt was a former county policeman who now worked in an Indiana explosives factory and whose own recently vacated, heavily mortgaged house on Rone Court had burned shortly after the explosion at the Wade house, with no charges lodged but arson suspected. Police Chief Carl Heustis was never called in to explain the information he had allegedly received from county officials about the culprit. Despite his history of extremist associations and his bold call for Shively whites to unite against desegregation, Millard Grubbs was never summoned as a witness either. A Shively hardware store owner who admitted under oath that he "may have" heard someone say that the home should be blown up was not queried further, and the officer who investigated the man's statement never appeared. No questions directed at Shively newspaperman John Hitt probed why or even whether he had driven to Rone Court the night of the explosion. These and other disturbing inconsistencies received less attention as the days passed and a wider assortment of associates of the Bradens were called to testify. Although jurors inspected the charred rubble at the site of the blast, they appeared more concerned about Communist solicitation for an uprising of blacks against segregation than they were with whatever tragedy had befallen the Wades. Some became openly derisive of whites who would "bend themselves over in a situation of this kind . . . to protect a colored man's family and yet not do the same thing for a white man." By their own lights, they were investigating Communism, but they formed many of their conclusions from questions about race.[75]

In the unlikely event he had not been aware of it before, Scott Hamilton must have realized by now that he was orchestrating public attention as well as an investigation. Near the end of the inquiry the prosecutor began implementing the contempt citations he had first only threatened. On September 23 he recalled Vernon Bown. The controversy surrounding Bown centered not only on his refusal to answer questions of a political nature, but on a radio belonging to him that detectives had discovered in debris from the blast. Hamilton theorized that it may have been used as a detonation device. Though it was more likely that the radio had merely fallen through the hole the explosion had blown in the floor of Rosemary Wade's bedroom, where Bown slept during his days at the house, the jurors were intrigued by Hamilton's speculations despite a sworn statement placing Bown in Milwaukee the weekend of the bombing. When Bown took the position that he was being treated as a defendant and refused to answer additional questions to avoid possible self-incrimination, the judge upheld his refusal, and the witness was excused. His seemingly uncooperative stance troubled the grand jury further. That afternoon Hamilton issued an indictment for Bown's arrest on contempt charges for failure to cite the Fifth Amendment regarding one earlier question to which he had also refused to reply: "On how many occasions during the past two weeks have you met with Mr. and Mrs. Braden?"[76]

The investigation made new headlines that day with the seizure of "Red literature" from Bown's apartment. Ostensibly to serve a bench warrant for Bown's arrest, Hamilton accompanied Louisville detectives to the apartment Bown shared with I. O. Ford, a 79-year-old retired river boat captain who had no connection to the Wades but was a self-professed former CP activist from Ohio. There, without a search warrant, officials confiscated printed matter that included the *Daily Worker*, CP pamphlets, and other Marxist and race-related publications. The raid gave Scott Hamilton the break his case had sorely needed. He told the press he had "hit the jackpot."[77]

After photos of the "red" reading matter graced the pages of the local papers, there was no turning back. What Anne has always referred to as a *community hysteria* built rapidly those final days of September. Though she and Carl continued to generate all the written materials they could on the case, they also had enough foresight to retain Robert Zollinger, a local attorney who was not particularly progressive but had a reputation as a crusader for underdogs. Zollinger was reluctant at first to risk his reputation in the Bradens' defense, though he spent hours discussing the case with Anne on the phone. When he made his first appearance with her at the grand jury, Anne quoted to him a line from her favorite Episcopal hymn, adapted from a poem written by a nineteenth-century abolitionist: *Once to every man and nation, comes the moment to decide; in the strife of Truth or Falsehood, for the good or evil side.* Zollinger—also an Episcopalian—replied with another stanza of that hymn. He never again wavered in his willingness to defend them.[78]

Hamilton's threats to punish Anne and Carl, generously reported in the media, were bound to congeal into some form of criminal indictment, and rumors abounded as to what that might be. Anne watched helplessly as she and Carl became—according to Hamilton's theory, which he now detailed daily—the point of axis linking all characters in this drama, and thus the embodiment of evil.[79]

Other arrests followed. On September 29, Louise Gilbert and LaRue Spiker, the two women who had circulated the neighborhood letter eliciting support for the Wades, were held for contempt after they too refused to either admit to CP membership or take the Fifth Amendment (a reply some judicial bodies took as admission of guilt). Lew Lubka, a young white unionist and General Electric employee who had assisted the Wades, was held on the same grounds. Like Bown's, his apartment was raided and ransacked, though Hamilton found nothing he considered significant. All maintained they knew nothing about the bombing and should therefore be excused from testifying. For Spiker, being hounded for political activism was nothing new. The newspapers revealed that in 1950 she had been fired from the Indiana Welfare Department for her association with the Civil Rights Congress.[80]

The Bradens realized with a sense of unreality that they were next. Anne went through the motions with her children and her publicity efforts, but she was so stricken with worry over what was to become of them all that she came to dread the news and the rumor mill each day. Because of the ideological gulf between them, she had shared nothing with her parents for all these months about the Wade purchase and the ensuing uproar. Now, facing arrest, she attended Sunday morning church services and, upon returning home, sat down reluctantly to write a letter preparing them for what lay ahead. Sticking to a rather general explanation, she suggested that they *stay out of this thing entirely.* Anticipating that the McCartys' primary concern would be their grandchildren, Anne countered: *I don't believe you can possibly understand what I have been going through. . . . Don't write me upbraiding me about doing things that will hurt the children. I love my children more than anything in the world and more than you could ever possibly love them. I have battled with my conscience on this whole thing and weighed all the factors. . . . It is a terrible thing for a parent to have to decide between doing something that might possibly hurt his children some and doing (or not doing) something that will help make the world a place not worth any children (including his own) growing up in.* Anne closed with the hope that her mother and father would find the strength to rise to the occasion. In preparation for what lay ahead, she also made arrangements for Jimmy and Anita to be cared for by Frank and Josephine Grzelak. The charge, when it came a few days later on October 1, was sedition, and the indicted included Anne, Carl, Louise Gilbert, LaRue Spiker, Vernon Bown, and I. O. Ford—all of whom were white. Almost as an afterthought, Bown was also charged with the dynamiting of the house.[81]

State antisubversive measures were often merely symbolic gestures that were never actually used. Passed in 1920 during an earlier Red Scare in which 21 states adopted sedition or antisyndicalism laws, Kentucky's sedition law had been just such a measure. It carried inordinately stiff penalties (up to 21 years in prison, a $10,000 fine, or both) and was enacted in the wake of Louisville's own version of the notorious Palmer Raids—in this case, a raid against the Socialist Party of Carl's father's youth—amid a sensationalized climate of fear that rivaled the one that prevailed in the 1950s. The law's constitutionality had never been tested, and it had lain largely dormant for 34 years until Hamilton, as Anne put it, *pulled it out and dusted it off* to use against a newer generation of radicals.[82]

At the time of the bill's passage, Kentucky's post-WWI Governor Edgar Morrow had been troubled enough by it to oversee repeal of a portion of it prohibiting speech or writing that would "incite ill feeling" among groups. What remained of the bill was so vaguely worded that its violation was difficult to define, a fact that should have worked in the defendants' favor. In fact, reporters covering the arrests turned to *Webster's Dictionary* for a definition more satisfactory than that offered by the commonwealth. The law's actual text identified a guilty party as:

> Any person who by word or writing advocates, suggests, or teaches the duty, necessity, propriety, or expediency of criminal syndicalism or sedition, or who prints, publishes, edits, issues, or knowingly circulates, sells, distributes, publicly displays, or has in his possession for the purpose of publication or circulation any written or printed matter in any form advocating, suggesting, or teaching criminal syndicalism or sedition, or who organizes or helps to organize, or becomes a member of, or voluntarily assembles with any society or assemblage of persons that teaches, advocates, or suggests the doctrine of criminal syndicalism or sedition.[83]

Resurrection of the sedition act triggered new legal debate on its constitutionality since it conflicted with a portion of the Kentucky Constitution guaranteeing citizens the right to "alter, reform, or abolish their Government in such a manner as they deem proper." The constitutionality of all state sedition laws was also on its way to review by the U. S. Supreme Court in *Pennsylvania v. Nelson*, in which defense attorneys contended that sedition was a federal, not a state offense, and thus was preempted by the Smith Act. The 1956 outcome of *Nelson* would carry important implications for the Wade defendants, but not at this juncture. Insisting that the two were unrelated, the judge refused to delay prosecutions pending a ruling in *Nelson*.[84]

By the time Hamilton made the arrests, he was infuriated by the articulate, unapologetic resistance of the Bradens and their friends, and perhaps even more so by the negative press coverage offered him. On the final morning of the grand jury hearings, Hamilton subpoenaed Richard Oberlin, news director of radio station WHAS (also owned by the Binghams), just moments after an early broadcast in which Oberlin had accused Hamilton of the "reprehensible techniques of Senator Joseph McCarthy." The prosecutor also tried to cite Richard Harwood, a *Louisville Times* reporter, for contempt for failure to reveal sources, but the judge ruled out that proposal. When Hamilton summoned Carl Braden to return to the courthouse later that day, he exploded when Carl reread a prepared statement in response to every question asked. Hamilton excused Anne before she could do the same, but she barely had time to get home to her children before she got a call from Carl informing her that their time had come: they were under arrest and she had best phone Zollinger and get a cab to the police station.[85]

The grand jury's final report, also issued October 1, stated that while Shively whites who might have had something to hide had testified "in a forthright and unhesitating manner," the Wades' supporters had testified "with an apparent desire to obstruct" the grand jury's search for the truth. The one characteristic shared by all of those indicted was their unwillingness to detail or deny association with any subversive organizations. Despite the testimony of every participant, including various Wade family members, that the idea for a dummy purchase had been Andrew Wade's, the report contended that the case followed a "pattern used by the Communist Party in this country to create trouble between the respective races": purchase of property for blacks in an area "normally" occupied by whites.[86]

Finally, the grand jury assailed the news media, whose reportage "border[ed] on the obstruction of justice," and it recommended that all clippings and radio scripts be forwarded to the FBI, attorney general, and chair of HUAC. In the anxious Cold War climate of 1954, this was no small threat. Although the *Courier-Journal* struck back hard in an editorial the next day, the charges placed Louisville's most prominent media outlets under a defensive cloud from which they never fully reemerged throughout the trial and its aftermath. As current and former staffers of the newspapers, Carl and Anne were caught in the crossfire.[87]

When Anne entered the grand jury room on the afternoon of Friday, October 1, she left a statement with the press in anticipation of her incarceration. It read, in part: *In my opinion, this is a test case for the white supremacists. . . . So far as I know, this is the first major case where an attempt has been made to place the blame for [anti-Negro] violence on the people fighting segregation. . . . I am convinced that there is no longer a question in the South as to whether segregation will be ended. It will be. The question now is whether it will be ended peacefully or whether many people, white and Negro, will be killed in the process. I am convinced it can come about peacefully—if the democratic-minded people in the South, who are in the majority, can control its violent minority, who would go to any length to preserve segregation. These people can be controlled—but if their hoax succeeds in Louisville their hand will be dangerously strengthened elsewhere.* She and Carl told the press they were firm believers in the U.S. and Kentucky Constitutions and *absolutely opposed to violence in any form* but supported racial integration and social changes aimed at broadening democracy. The two added that they were perfectly willing to discuss their principles on any subject with interested individuals but were suspicious of the *trap set by the misuse of words in America today. The word "communist" means something different to almost everybody. It usually means somebody we don't like or who does something we don't like. To the white supremacist in the South, it means somebody fighting segregation. To the employer trying to keep down wages, it means anybody who demands higher wages.*[88]

From their opponents' viewpoint, the Bradens were being, at best, stubborn and, more likely, devious. Among strident segregationists and anticommunists like Hitt, even the concern Anne expressed over widespread violence probably conjured up paranoid images of a "race war" that had long peppered southern whites' imaginations. Maybe Hamilton even hoped to make a "little Rosenberg" case of the Bradens: he had their jail correspondence copied and sent to him for further study of their private lives. For more public consumption, on the third day after their arrest Hamilton oversaw a raid on the couple's Virginia Avenue home in search of "communistic literature"—this time with a search warrant based on questions put to Carl's 16-year-old stepdaughter, Sonia, with no parent present. Apparently not satisfied with the proceeds, the prosecutor made headlines again when he led detectives on a second search of the Bradens' massive library three days later. Each time, large quantities of printed matter were removed—everything from Karl Marx's *Communist Manifesto* to essays on Russian literature Anne had written in college to a guide to learning German. Photos in the *Courier-Journal* revealed only the most damning of the contents with close-ups of books like *Joseph Stalin* and *The Secret of Soviet Strength.*[89]

The preceding weeks had kept Anne in a state of high tension, but no amount of mental preparation could cushion her for going to jail. To be stripped of all the privileges her race, class, and gender had created and maintained for her even after she began protesting the southern social order was emotionally daunting. In what seemed like no time, the relative harmony that had characterized her 30 years had been whisked away, and now she, Carl, and most especially their children faced an uncertain, frightening future. How had she been so unlucky as to find herself at the epicenter of local antiblack and anti-red passions? But she realized, intellectually at least, that it was not simply luck but choices that had landed her in jail. When she found herself in a cell, moreover, things suddenly did not seem quite as terrible as she had worried they would. In a sense, it was a relief.[90]

One of the first things she did that night was to write Carl a note to let him know she was all right. In her letter she invoked an image her friend Harriet Fitzgerald had once impressed upon her: *There come times in everyone's life when he must go back to the crossroads.* For Anne, the coming days—first in jail, then in Anniston to see her children and face her parent's disapproval, and finally back in Louisville alone to secure bond for Carl and continue their resistance—brought her to a crossroads during which she reexamined and ultimately reaffirmed her actions and beliefs. She would need that kind of inner sustenance in the coming months, when it seemed as if almost all of Louisville was against her.[91]

The McCartys were jolted by the news of their daughter's arrest, which they received from her friend Josephine Grzelak. Intensely loyal to Anne in spite of their political differences, Gambrell McCarty posted bond for her as quickly as he could, though Anne made clear that in doing so he could not hope to change her stance. Friends in Anniston readily lent him what he lacked of the $10,000 needed for bond, but the entire process took about a week because the court at first refused to accept any surety but Kentucky property. Meanwhile, Gambrell and Anita McCarty drove north to Louisville and retrieved from Grzelak their two grandchildren. They returned to Anniston with the children and sheltered them there for the next ten months.[92]

Soon after her release on October 8, Anne too went south to Alabama to spend several days with her children after all the upheaval they had endured. Jimmy and Anita were too young to understand what was happening to their parents, and she found them at ease in the care of their doting grandparents. She was not quite prepared for the torrent of emotions the visit would unleash, however. Passionate differences on race have divided countless southern families, and in this crucible of the sedition charge, the painful conflicts between Anne and her family had never been rawer. Her parents were *crushed* by the weight of all that had happened, as she later wrote to a friend, with neighbors and friends sympathetically surrounding them as if there had been a death in the family. And Anne's own emotions were stretched taut: pity over how badly she had *turned out* was not what she or her children needed. During one dinner-table confrontation when her parents besieged her with questions regarding her maternal responsibilities, she had to literally flee their presence, so great was the emotional pull of the world she had willingly left behind for a different sort of freedom. She wrote a friend of the *insidious attacks that stifle from within: I could stand being nagged at from the outside, but I was scared because [these] attacks were also from the inside.* Her only place of refuge in Anniston was the little stone cathedral of Grace Episcopal Church, where, as a child, she had first glimpsed a broader world. The pastor, Bill Stoney, brother of her childhood minister Jim, expressed sympathy with Anne's views and remained a supportive mediator for the families throughout the ordeal.[93]

Back in Louisville, the affirmation she had craved came only in very small doses in between what was in large measure public vitriol. During those weeks before the trial, Anne got her first taste of life as a pariah—a state she and Carl would occupy in Louisville for years to come. Hate mail and threats continued: one writer, claiming he spoke for many whites, wrote that "everyone thinks you should be tarred and feathered and run out of town." Friends and neighbors also gave her the cold shoulder, some refusing even to speak when they saw her on the street. Others, wishing to avoid guilt by association, sent word to her that she had their sympathy, but to please, please keep her distance. Among people she had known for years, she had a hard time finding anyone willing to contribute to Carl's bail. Even in the black community, the taint of Communism had a silencing effect that was underscored by the fact that all of the defendants were white. Most liberal-minded people of both races simply turned their heads and wished the whole matter would go away. Anne heard rumors from African American friends—told by women working as domestics—of prominent Louisville liberals dumping their books into the Ohio River. Hamilton kept the pressure on, calling Andrew Wade and others in for repeated questioning. For a brief while, his harassments managed to make Wade doubt Anne and Carl, though by the time of the trial those doubts had subsided. Friends like the Reverend Perdue offered some encouragement, but were uncomfortably aware that they too might become targets at any minute. At one point in the fall, Anne escaped the pressure she felt in Louisville to spend a few days in Virginia with her old friend Harriet. Harriet offered comfort, and seeing Anne's despondency, sent follow-up letters filled with encouragement even though Anne had scant time or emotional energy to reply.[94]

Among the most stalwart of Carl's and Anne's local friends were Walter and Mary Agnes Barnett, who felt they owed the Bradens a debt of gratitude for their vigorous support during Walter's fight to keep his Quartermaster Depot job and thereafter, when he was blacklisted. With a spunk that flew in the face of both sustained intimidation and long-standing barriers separating blacks and whites, the Barnetts courageously put up their house toward Carl's bond. With their assistance and that of Carl's mother, who likewise put up her house, Carl made bail on October 22.[95]

After more than a week of meetings with lawyers preparing their defense strategy, Carl and Anne headed back to Anniston to see their children. Anita had adjusted easily to her grandparents' care, but Jim was now homesick and especially missed Carl, whom he adored. The reunion was cut short, however, when Zollinger phoned on their first day in Alabama to tell them they were being indicted on a second count and must get back to Louisville the following morning for arraignment. It was an agonizing moment, but the couple felt they had no choice in the face of Zollinger's stern pronouncements. When they told their young son their time together would be cut short, he seemed to withdraw from them—his father in particular, who always thought of that moment as something from which Jim never entirely recovered.[96]

Anne had thought she could no longer be shocked in the wake of all that had transpired, yet the second charge was in some ways even more unbelievable than the events preceding it. Indicting five codefendants for "conspiracy to damage property to achieve a political end—communism" gave form to Hamilton's notion that the violence on Rone Court was an inside job. Those named included Anne and Carl, Bown, Ford, and now Lewis Lubka (the other person who had refused to answer Hamilton's questions and had seen his home raided). The very word "communism" in the indictment—and the news coverage of it—raised the emotional pitch around town further. The defendants who had jobs lost them, and Carl was placed on paid leave from the *Courier-Journal*.[97]

The defendants asked for, and were granted, separate trials. Despite the defense team's request that Bown be tried first, the state insisted that Carl, the perceived ringleader, face trial first on the initial sedition charge (*garden variety* sedition, Anne later nicknamed it to indicate the incredibly general nature of the offense). As November 29, the trial date, approached, the "Louisville Seven"—as they, half in jest, called themselves—had no shortage of legal advice from attorneys concerned about civil liberties aspects of the case. A few days before the trial, the ACLU announced that it would have Louis Lusky, a well-respected civil liberties attorney who had once clerked for Supreme Court Justice Harlan Stone, work with the defense team on the ACLU's behalf, representing Carl not directly but as a friend of the court. Once the trial began, Lusky's role expanded because of his greater familiarity with civil liberties law, and it was he who later wrote the appeals brief.[98]

On November 29, a jury of 11 men and 1 woman—all white—faced a courtroom packed with spectators and recording equipment. Outside was a town "in an uproar," as one local resident remembered it, over the excitement of supposed communism in its midst. No one present could fail to realize that what was before them was not simply a legal proceeding, but a scandal—one that had also become a modern media spectacle. Early on, Judge Curtis ruled that television and radio stations could tape in the courtroom for intensive coverage, and numerous reporters, many of them Carl's long-time colleagues, cut away from the newspaper offices as often as they could to observe the drama, whether for assignment, curiosity, or fear their names would be mentioned. In the sensationalized atmosphere that now surrounded the case, any association with the protagonists, particularly Anne and Carl, was potentially incriminating. Marjorie Yater, who with her husband, George, had participated in liberal causes and occasionally socialized with the Bradens, lived in such apprehension of receiving a subpoena that she dreaded any knock on the door and withdrew from social action for decades.[99]

Until the trial opened, defense attorneys remained uncertain—because of the ambiguity of the sedition statute—just what acts the state would attempt to base its case upon. But Hamilton made clear from his opening argument that other than the Wade purchase, it was not really specific acts that were under scrutiny, but rather ideas, reading materials, and membership in subversive organizations, particularly the CP. For background, Hamilton's opening recounted the Rone Court transaction, concluding that it was merely part of the Communists' plan to take land from whites. His assistant prosecutor, Lawrence Higgins, even interrupted the defense's opening commentary with a shout: "What about [Carl's] being a correspondent for the *Daily Worker?*" (The CP newspaper was a subscriber to the Federated Press news service for which Carl and Anne sometimes wrote.)[100]

Carl's trial was lengthy by 1950s standards—13 days, some of which stretched far into the night and included weekend sessions. It immediately became clear from his slate of witnesses that Hamilton was working closely with both HUAC and the FBI. The first week was spent on the testimony of nine former CP members, now paid FBI informants who were shuttled around the nation for similar appearances at trials and investigative committee hearings. None of these witnesses claimed to know Carl, Anne, or anyone connected to the case. Their testimonies were largely biographical, detailing the evils of Communism in their own lives and asserting that the CP-USA was an organization bent on violent overthrow of the U.S. government. Their relevance to Carl's plight hinged on their allegedly expert testimony that some of the Bradens' books were the types that only CP members would read. More threatening were their detailed descriptions of Communists' aim to take land from whites to set up separate "Negro states" in the South. Several of the witnesses, in perhaps the most immediately damning testimony in light of the Wade purchase, stated that their local CP "cells" had been instructed to "incite racial trouble whenever possible."[101]

Besides their validation of the prosecution's theory of racial destabilization, the theatrical value of these FBI witnesses was immeasurable. Several received gasps, cheers, and applause during their testimony. Some of the informers—Manning Johnson, for example—would turn such performances into lucrative careers over the next few years, testifying throughout the South on the "communistic" aims of a wide spectrum of civil rights activities.[102]

In retrospect, it is clear that the courtroom atmosphere was so rabidly anticommunist—and, among whites, so solidly prosegregationist—that once Carl, a self-proclaimed integrationist, had been linked to communist ideology, he became demonized. Hamilton and assistant prosecutor Higgins played to an audience predisposed to hate anything reeking of communism or "race mixing" by half a decade of American cultural currents and half a century of Jim Crow in the South. Carl's critique of unemployment became evidence of his belief, as the prosecution charged, that "our U.S. economic system doesn't work." So did his half-playful signature on a personal letter: "yours for the abolition of capitalism."[103]

Anne now understood infinitely well why anticommunist prosecutions were called "witch hunts" by those who opposed them. She heard whispers in the court that she and Carl should be lynched. The hostility in the courtroom was *so thick you could cut it with a knife*, Anne remembered later. Each day, she sat, composed yet tense, at the defense table, her blue-green eyes defined by the shadowy circles surrounding them. She kept up a facade of bravado but remained inwardly in shock.[104]

Both legal teams conducted excruciatingly detailed examinations of the scores of confiscated books. The Bradens' copy of the USSR Constitution could only have been in the possession of a CP member, the prosecution argued; but

Zollinger produced two witnesses—one political scientist and one English professor—who acknowledged having purchased copies. Witnesses such as these
left the court to find themselves also objects of community scorn.[105]

On the seventh day of the trial, the prosecution rested. Hamilton had produced no evidence at all linking Carl to the Rone Court violence and no proof
that he had instigated the Wade purchase. In fact, Andrew Wade had testified
to the contrary, enduring numerous insistences by the prosecution that he acknowledge "for the record" that he was "colored." Hamilton's allegations that
Carl was a Communist were all based on letters and books taken from the
Bradens' home: no local witness admitted knowledge of any CP affiliation. A
Christmas card from William Patterson—an acknowledged CP member—and
a letter addressed "Dear Comrade" but bearing no CP identification constituted the prosecution's best proof.[106]

In preparing Carl's defense strategy, his attorneys realized that his own
testimony was key. For any hope of success, they had to convey his humanity
to a community and a jury that regarded him as demonic. But then came the
thorny question of how to deal with his Marxist views and his relationship to
the Communist Party. Before the trial ever opened, the Bradens and their attorneys had discussed whether Carl should forthrightly deny that he was a
Communist. To do otherwise was problematic: refusal to answer the question
on the grounds of self-incrimination condemned one in the public mind as a
"Fifth Amendment Communist." In the 1950s South, admission even of
"communistic" sympathies would almost certainly ensure a guilty verdict. Yet
denial was also a tricky route in light of Carl's affiliations with groups like the
CRC and the Progressive Party and his obvious familiarity with the CP and
Marxism. More than the others, Anne had misgivings about the decision that
he must disavow the CP as a way of legitimizing himself to reenter the human
community.[107]

In the stress of Carl's predicament, Anne's musings on the matter were a
mere precursor of what thereafter became a cherished belief of hers—after the
sedition case gave her and Carl a sort of notoriety that preceded them
throughout the South. Afterward, people she met often seemed interested to
know, above all else, whether or not she belonged to the CP. As she explained
it some years later, *It became very important, not just as a matter of principle, but as
a matter of practical politics, not to give into that. Either you resisted it or you were a
part of it. There was no neutral ground. Whether you were a Communist or not, if
you answered the question, you were conceding to the assumption that the very question was the test of whether you could be considered a human being or not.* She would
never dignify that question with a public reply.[108]

The defense's approach was to portray Carl as a gadfly who was nonetheless an upstanding citizen and to convince jurors that such people should not be punished for their heterodoxies. On December 9, Carl testified that although he had read extensively in that field, he was not a Communist, and he opposed violence in any form. Over the next two days he explained, sometimes in painstaking detail, his views, reading materials, and reform activities—everything from opposition to the Korean War to his and Anne's decision to live in an integrated neighborhood. He displayed a consistent professionalism, keeping his calm even when the prosecutors goaded him outrageously. Current and former coworkers, friends, and neighbors took the stand to verify his good character, and it appeared that the tide in the courtroom was beginning to shift somewhat.[109]

But whatever goodwill Carl's personable, articulate testimony may have amassed was completely canceled on the afternoon of December 11. The defense had rested before the lunch recess when the prosecution announced a surprise witness—a local informer released to testify by the FBI. Anne could barely conceal her shock that afternoon when Alberta Ahearn, her friend and a long-time activist colleague of both Bradens, rose and took the stand. A slim, pale woman with dark red lipstick and dressed completely in black, Ahearn looked as if she had just stepped from the pages of Mickey Spillane's anticommunist pulp fiction, and the courtroom, filled to overflowing, fell silent as she spoke. Telling the jury that she had begun working for the FBI in 1948 at a salary of $50 per month, she quietly denounced both Carl and Anne as leaders of a local CP "cell" who had recruited her into the party in January 1951. Ahearn also named five other local members (only one, Ford, was a co-defendant) and a Lexington man as the state organizer. Both Anne and Carl simply stared at Ahearn as she painted them in the worst possible light, describing numerous CP meetings over three years' time at their home, where the group discussed what she called "peace on Russia's terms." She did not link the supposed meetings to the Rone Court purchase. Ahearn admitted that she had no proof of either her allegations or her employment with the FBI, but her work for the bureau was confirmed by testimony from FBI Special Agent Edward Boyle.[110]

The defense was stunned, and Anne's worst fears realized. Attempts to subpoena Ahearn's FBI reports were rejected on grounds of "national security," and Zollinger's only recourse was to call Carl back to the stand to rebut Ahearn's testimony. The defense rested in a state of confusion and dismay. Possessing no other avenues through which to dignify the tarnished portrait of Carl that Ahearn had sketched, Zollinger closed with his own reluctant appeal to white prejudices, noting that the only real evidence the prosecution had produced was one witness—a woman who had been discovered in the back seat of a car with an African American man and arrested on a morals charge four years after her alleged employment with the FBI began. It was merely her word against Carl's, he stressed, and even if Ahearn were to be believed, she had admitted to never having heard violence advocated nor any "plot" surrounding the Wade purchase discussed. Higgins's closing words to the jury, on the other hand, reemphasized what he called a "simple issue": that "sedition is communism, and communism is sedition." There was no further attempt to examine Carl's actions in relation to buying a house on Wade's behalf.[111]

The jury deliberated that night for only three hours, during which Anne remained seated alone at the defense table, too distraught and exhausted even to contemplate what would come next. Reporters commented later on the thin, nervous smile she gave the jury as they silently filed back into the courtroom well after nightfall. Before the verdict was read, Carl was brought to stand beside her.[112]

Juries, Lusky and Zollinger had repeatedly reminded their clients, are notoriously unpredictable. Still, the verdict of "guilty"—delivered exactly 11 days after Senator Joe McCarthy's censure by the U.S. Senate had condemned the messenger but not the message of aggressive anticommunism—was no surprise to anyone. The sentence: 15 years' imprisonment and a $5,000 fine. Carl was led away, with Anne left to listen dully to the judge wish the jurors a hearty merry Christmas before she returned to her empty house. Over the next couple of days only her next-door neighbor and one other friend, Sterling Neal, her former FE coworker, dared even to visit her.[113]

CHAPTER SEVEN

FIGHTING BACK — THE 1950s RESISTANCE MOVEMENT

It was the time of the Red Menace. The fear of Communists taking over the PTA and Community Chest affected the lives of ordinary people in ordinary towns. Anyone who knew anyone who was a Communist felt tainted. Everything that could be connected to the Communists took on taint. People who defended their civil liberties on principle. The First, Fifth, and Fourteenth Amendments to the Constitution. Pablo Picasso, because he had attended the Communists' World Peace Congress in Paris and painted doves for peace. Doves. Peace.

—E. L. Doctorow, *The Book of Daniel*[1]

WHAT BEGAN AS A DEVASTATING CRISIS ultimately propelled Anne into a lifetime of civil rights activism by introducing her to a community of so-called subversives across the nation who were fighting back against the powerful silencing of the anticommunist witch hunt. Within the beleaguered left of the period, the Bradens' case became a kind of cause célèbre, and both of them— Anne in particular—contributed a unique white southern voice to what she has called the 1950s resistance movement against the Red Scare. In that milieu she found a group of steadfast friends and an esprit des corps that helped her endure the repression the larger society heaped generously upon her and Carl in those years.[2]

In the days immediately following Carl's conviction, however, prospects for the couple's future looked pitifully bleak. The *Courier-Journal* had made his firing official the day after he was found guilty. For weeks, the newspapers' letters columns were inundated with expositions on the Bradens. Though not all writers were critical, those who were voiced a frightening racial and social extremism of the sort that was coalescing into the ideology of massive resistance across the South.[3]

Anne and Carl had become symbols of a demonic internal subversion in their hometown, a local variant of Alger Hiss or the Rosenbergs. There is still considerable historical dispute as to whether such people were actually spies and, if so, to what extent they were truly a threat to the United States. But no one was claiming that the Bradens were spies. Their crime was subverting the racial hierarchy that had traditionally characterized southern race relations. Such actions were inherently traitorous, in the minds of many white southerners of the era, and could be understood only as part of a Communist plot, never as part of legitimate social dissent. Indeed, the fear generated by the sedition investigation was not confined to Louisville or even to the South. Two weeks after Carl's conviction, a prominent feature in *U.S. News and World Report* echoed Scott Hamilton's theory of the bombing, with the disclaimer that even if the dynamiting had not been the work of Communists, its effect had demonstrated "that fomenting trouble between races in America is a Communist pattern." A smaller article in *Time* magazine lambasted Carl for "devot[ing] most of his time to Communist causes" and leveled oblique criticism at the *Courier-Journal* for its mild reaction to the anticommunist charges. Obviously, the critiques of Joe McCarthy during his censure proceedings represented no real retreat from the Red Scare ideology that had thus far characterized the 1950s. American politicians and image-makers still tended to engage in a collective denial of domestic social ills and to explain instead the dynamics of social change in terms of an international Communist conspiracy. In fact, Cold War ideology was finding fertile new ground in the prosegregationist movement in the South, the rhetoric of which neatly joined racial reform to communist subversion.[4]

Popular memories of HUAC-style investigations have tended to focus on Hollywood. Outside the South, the anticommunist crusade reached its peak in the years between 1948 and 1954. But in the wake of *Brown* and the hysterical reaction of southern segregationists to it, much of the focus of HUAC and SISS investigative hearings shifted southward as southern congressmen who had long seen civil rights agitation as communistic now began to see it as a most immediate threat to their southern "habits, customs, traditions, and way of life" (as southern congressmen noted in their 1956 anti-*Brown* "Southern Manifesto"). After 1954 at least eight southern states established or reinvigorated investigating committees that were close facsimiles of HUAC. McCarthy's histrionic public demeanor became standard fare for a generation of southern politicians in the months and years following *Brown*.[5]

This framework concealed the real injustices that the Wades and other African Americans experienced just as it concealed Anne's and Carl's genuine commitment to eradicating racial barriers. It would take years of struggle for those commitments to be viewed as they really were and not as a devious Communist attempt to "use" racial discord.

———

On January 21, 1955, Carl was transferred from the county jail to LaGrange Reformatory, 20 miles northeast of Louisville, where he spent the next six months held under what his attorneys concluded was the highest bond ever set in Kentucky—$40,000. For the first 42 days, he was kept in solitary confinement, and Judge Curtis turned a deaf ear to defense pleas that the bail for the period of his appeal was exorbitant compared to any danger Carl might have represented locally. In the first weeks after the December 1954 verdict, Anne felt, for the first time, unable to go on. She never actually slowed down, but she felt perpetually bewildered, with a heavy veil between her and the rest of the world. Only five days after Carl's conviction she appeared at a fundraiser in New York, sponsored by the Emergency Civil Liberties Committee (ECLC) for the couple's defense. Later she had absolutely no memories of the speech she gave or even with whom she had sat. A few days before Christmas, she took the train to Anniston to spend the holidays with Jimmy and Anita. There, under her parents' watchful eye, she slept a lot but was troubled by dreams. She returned to Louisville alone after New Year's Day, sad to leave the children again but knowing they would be better off with their grandparents during the coming battle she would face for her own freedom.[6]

The next few weeks were, for Anne, a blur of mimeographing briefs and legal motions—a necessity because the Bradens were without employment and wished to minimize their mounting expenses by the technical assistance Anne could provide. Although most of their attorney fees were either pro bono or paid for by assistance organizations, there were thousands of dollars of related legal costs.[7]

Just when it seemed as if things could get no worse, in early 1955 she heard a rumor that she and Carl might be indicted for the murder of Melvin

Edwards—one of Andrew Wade's two friends who had guarded his house the night of the bombing. (Edwards had turned up dead in the fall of 1954 under mysterious circumstances.) Her life in shreds, Anne felt more besieged and weary than she ever had. When Zollinger asked her to produce motel receipts proving her and Carl's whereabouts on the night of Edwards's death, the request struck her as a kind of "last straw." She became convinced that she and Carl must cease all resistance—drop his appeal, get quickly through her trial and the conviction she was sure would follow, and simply serve out their respective prison terms. With early releases for good behavior, she speculated, they could be free in five years or less. Then, her daydream continued, they could just move away—far away, retreat from activism, and raise their children in anonymity. Unable to see Carl for weeks after his imprisonment because of a technicality, Anne corresponded with him almost daily. She wrote of her idea, and Carl did not object but merely advised her to do whatever she thought best. Anne then suggested this new course of action to two of her lawyers, Lusky and Zollinger. Lusky, who knew the Bradens only as crusaders, could hardly take her seriously. He pronounced her as suffering from "post-conviction depression," which he likened to postpartum depression, advising her, "Just don't make any important decisions until it's over."[8]

It was Zollinger, ironically, not ever one to share Anne's politics, who persuaded her to keep going. Zollinger was not particularly optimistic about the couple's chances for success, but he urged her strongly to put up a fight for the sake of civil liberties. Anne retreated from the temptation to yield, somewhat ashamed of herself. Her wavering continued inwardly, but after a few weeks of toying with the idea of quitting, she put aside her doubts and applied herself more fully to the battles ahead. Nothing ever came of the reputed murder investigation.[9]

In the context of being a sedition defendant in a highly sensationalized case, Anne needed to construct a new kind of self, a more public one than she was used to, even though she had been an outspoken activist for some years. The public life she was now called upon to lead required some of the same stage presence she had developed years before as an actress. She continued to get jittery before she spoke publicly, but nervousness did not interfere with what she had to say once she began. Whereas she had once possessed a certain anonymity in her activism, all trace of that was gone now: her every move was potentially newsworthy, her every choice laden with interpretative value. Her days of being an ordinary citizen with political views and actions that, while controversial, were of no particular repute, were behind her, and they would not come again. In telling the story of the Rone Court violence, she and Carl had referred to it as the *Wade case*. Once it became the "Braden case," Anne took note of how racism had shaped that very change in the language (for the rest of her life she wondered if she could have done more to prevent the change).[10]

From the very first time Anne had heard that label—on the couple's first trip to New York after their indictment—she had recoiled from it. *All these cases we'd worked on: the McGee case, the Rosenberg case. But I'd never expected to be a case! You become a symbol, and it's a funny feeling. It has to become a way of life. Ultimately, people who had never heard our names heard about this case in Kentucky where some people got thrown in jail and sentenced to 15 years in prison because they sold a house in a segregated neighborhood.*[11]

Her attorneys tried to impress upon her that the affair could drag on for years. That realization was staggering at first. Anne wrote to Carl that spring: *Darling, I am so tired of being a "case." All I really want to do at this moment is get the children back and have you out and live just a little bit.* She wondered sometimes whether theirs would be a pyrrhic victory, but her musings on dropping the fight became more of an outlet for fantasy than a real option she wished to exercise. Although Anne occasionally gave in to anxieties about the future they faced, both Bradens tried to prepare themselves mentally for the long haul. Their prison correspondence reflects a persistent theme of trying to respond creatively to what was also a personally wrenching situation. Not surprisingly, they frequently reminded each other of the justness of their cause, as Carl's words to Anne (written Christmas Eve 1954) suggest: "You are right in thinking that returns may come on a different level. You never do wrong by doing the right thing. . . . My respect and love for you grow daily, and I look forward to the day when we can again live in peace and happiness."[12]

To cope with his confinement, Carl cultivated in himself an ascetic quality, keeping a series of prison notes that centered on lofty aims of self-improvement, some of which he relayed to Anne in correspondence. Anne relied on her absent partner as an emotional sounding board for the many personal and political decisions she faced alone and for the mood swings that sometimes overwhelmed her. She poured out to him the daily details of her life and the children's progress, interspersed with legal updates. Anne remained subject to moods of extreme depression, feeling occasionally as if they had *lost everything* and always anxious that she herself should be doing more. But she also came to realize that her plunging spirits—often linked to the dreary, rainy Kentucky winter—were only temporary setbacks, and that she would inevitably recharge, sometimes to feel more vibrant than before.[13]

In early spring 1955, she began an ambitious campaign to raise Carl's bail. At 30 years of age, operating politically without him was new to her. Although she continued to worry that she was too dependent on him, Anne was a very effective writer and speaker, and her fighting spirit slowly reasserted itself. The lesson she and Carl eventually took from the sedition case became their lifelong approach to community organizing: to use every attack as a platform through which to espouse their prointegration views more forcefully. The two employed their journalistic backgrounds to become forceful propagandists— know-how they then passed on to others as the civil rights revolution flowered later in the 1950s, '60s, and '70s. *Our approach, our whole psychology was to fight back. They gave us a platform and we used it. . . . From the very beginning, we kept saying, A man wanted a house; the house was blown up; and instead of doing anything about it, they had charged with a crime the people who were supporting his right. That's exactly true; we weren't telling any lies! . . . For many people around the country, the prosecution side never caught up with our interpretation because we got out our story first.*[14]

Inexplicably, it was the Commonwealth's Attorney's Office that gave Anne the opportunity to fight back by what looks in retrospect like retreat in the face of victory. Hamilton had determined that Anne would be tried next, and a court date of February 7, 1955, was set. But Hamilton postponed his prosecution, first to February 28, then to March, then April, then indefinitely, pending a U.S. Supreme Court ruling in *Nelson*. Nor were trial dates set for the other defendants (most of whom were also out on bond) despite defense pleas that Bown be scheduled for trial on the bombing charge. Anne continued leaving the children with her parents and began to travel and to write prolifically to promote awareness of the case. It became her platform to reach southerners of both races and to inform civil liberties advocates outside the region of the particular links being made between southern efforts against segregation and charges of communist subversion. Although back in Louisville she shared generously in the community ostracism Carl received, her status as a mere "wife" in Cold War America defined her as implicitly subsidiary in the eyes of men like Hamilton, leaving her free to agitate for justice for the seven crucial months Carl was imprisoned. Had she too been sentenced and jailed, the defendants' resistance might have been effectively quelled. As Anne put it years later, *I'm convinced that if we hadn't gotten out and organized this national campaign when we did, we would have spent 15 years in prison. They could have stifled that, but they lost their nerve between the middle of December and the middle of February.*[15]

The Bradens were probably not Hamilton's best choice for the starring roles of Communist defendants in the first place. They were too articulate not to get their viewpoints out in writing, and too stubborn to go down without a fight, as prosecutors should have known from the bevy of press releases the couple had generated in the Wades' defense even before they themselves were accused of any crime. Still, outside Louisville, the sedition case received little publicity before it was tried. What national press attention it did garner took place primarily through the efforts of Anne and Carl themselves, who spread the word as best they could under the circumstances. A starting point was the Federated Press (FP), a left-leaning labor news subscription service that had started in 1919 as an alternative to wire services like the Associated Press (AP). Although they had been FP correspondents for several years, Anne and Carl were largely local activists until the time of their arrests. Still, through associations with the FP and with such groups as the Peace Crusade, the Progressive Party, and the CRC, the two had developed a few national contacts, and there they found immediate sympathy for their current struggle. In publications of the beleaguered 1950s left, reports of red-baiting crusades abounded, but even so, the Bradens' and Wades' plight stood out as particularly poignant. Not only had the Wade family lost their home: the focus of that injustice had shifted to the wrongdoing of their staunchest white advocates in Louisville, who now faced lengthy prison terms. As Anne's statement the day of her arrest had noted, it was an unusual set of circumstances for white integrationists to be so harassed as to face criminal charges for their activism. It was, as she termed it, a *flamboyant* case that was bound to attract attention, and it became something of a rallying point for left-leaning activists nationwide who had themselves experienced anticommunist repression.[16]

The Louisville defendants had two consistent journalistic outlets that laid the groundwork for their national *fightback* campaign, as Anne always called it. One was the *National Guardian*, a weekly newspaper established in 1948 as a "non-Communist, non-anticommunist" left-wing news organ that was nonetheless "a bit too red" for the tastes of many liberals. By 1954 the *Guardian*, which had initially covered and supported Henry Wallace's ill-fated presidential campaign, had become the primary means of publicizing and organizing protest against the numerous anticommunist prosecutions stifling dissent nationwide. The *Guardian* covered the Wade incident in depth throughout 1954 and as Carl's trial and appeal proceeded.[17]

The other publication to offer the couple early, unqualified support was the *Southern Patriot*, monthly newsletter of the Southern Conference Educational Fund (SCEF), the integrationist group that was the inheritor of the 1930s southern conference movement. Anne's contact with SCEF had begun in the early 1950s during her work with the interracial hospital movement. Al Maund, a friend of Carl's from the *Courier-Journal*, assisted in laying out the *Patriot*, and he introduced Anne and Carl to the publication by covering in its pages their work for hospital desegregation. In early 1953 Carl initiated what would become a lifelong relationship with Jim Dombrowski, SCEF's executive director, when he wrote to inquire about SCEF's work. SCEF was not a membership organization, he learned, but an informal network of regional activists for whom joining the SCEF board often required a singular amount of courage.[18]

By the time of the Wade purchase, the Bradens were covering Louisville civil rights activities for the *Patriot* themselves. But in the context of the sedition case their alliance with SCEF deepened. After the 1948 demise of the economic justice-oriented Southern Conference for Human Welfare (SCHW), SCEF became a single-issue group dedicated to building southern support for integration. It was, however, under constant attack itself for its failure to exclude Communists (or former or suspected Communists or Marxists) from its slim ranks. Mississippi Senator Theodore Bilbo led the charge in 1946 with a verbal trouncing of SCEF as an "un-American, negro [*sic*] social equality, communistic, mongrel outfit." Dombrowski, a Popular Front–era southern white progressive living in New Orleans, was SCEF's only staff person, and he was intimately familiar with the stymying effect anticommunist investigations could have on integrationist efforts in the South. He knew too that southern agitation for racial equality was the quickest way to become the target of such an investigation. With Virginia Durr, Myles Horton, and Aubrey Williams, Dombrowski had faced his own inquisition in March 1954 by the investigating committee headed by Mississippi's other senator, James Eastland, an archconservative racial ideologue.[19]

Although he had never met Anne or Carl in person, Dombrowski was tremendously moved by their courage in supporting the Wades, and he gave extensive play in the monthly *Patriot* to the injustices done the Wades and, later, the white sedition defendants. The *Patriot*'s readership included leftists and liberals across the nation, and it brought the case to the attention of a network of southern-born progressives who saw it as a frightening example of what could easily happen to any one of them. Upon hearing of Carl's conviction, Dombrowski—intensely aware of the social ostracism being branded a Communist carried with it—swiftly telegrammed Anne: "Tell Carl I'm proud to be his friend." He contributed $1,000 of his own money toward Carl's bond and wrote Anne a Christmas card telling her he was "confident history will honor you both." The three soon became close friends. For the rest of her life Anne considered Dombrowski—a democratic socialist of southern Methodist background who had received a doctorate in theology from Columbia University—a significant mentor. She thought of the patient, soft-spoken activist (who was the age of her own father) as a saint.[20]

The publicity generated in the *Patriot* and the *Guardian*—although their readerships were rather small—provided the beginnings of a support campaign for the sedition defendants. Except for the elderly Ford, who remained in jail longer than the rest, unable to meet the high bond, the other defendants also had networks through which they mobilized public awareness of the case. Louise Gilbert, for example, soon moved to Philadelphia and joined the staff of the Women's International League for Peace and Freedom: through her contributions to its publications, WILPF kept its members apprised of the defendants' progress. Anne's and Carl's media skills supplemented the support their friends generated. One of many brochures they designed, *Frame-Up in Louisville*, went out to a variety of trade union contacts the defendants collectively compiled. A few unions, in particular a handful of United Packinghouse Workers and United Auto Workers locals, took strong stands in support of the Wades and their defenders.[21]

Through such coverage, a support network for the defendants sprang up in New York, Chicago, Boston, Washington, D.C., and California—all sites of the largest concentration of activists resisting inquisitorial bodies like HUAC. In November 1954, before Carl's trial, he and Anne made their first trip to New York on $50 given them by Miriam Kolkin, their contact from the Federated Press. The Bradens stayed with Barbara Lane, Anne's old roommate from the Louisville Progressive Party, now married to Walter Bernstein, a blacklisted screenwriter. They spoke, in meetings Kolkin had arranged, to a host of people who were at the center of what passed for a civil liberties movement in those years. Palmer Weber, a Virginian once active in the Southern Conference and now living in New York, introduced them to Clark Foreman (the white southern New Deal administrator who had become involved in SCHW in the 1930s) and to other southerners-in-exile who would prove important contacts.[22]

These individuals saw—and helped the Bradens to see—the sedition case as a vehicle through which to expose the sweep of the anticommunist witch hunt. This trip led to a series of 1955 speaking engagements publicizing their case. In Washington, a group who read about the incident in the *National Guardian*—many of whom had themselves been investigated as subversives—established the "Washington Committee for the Louisville Cases." These activists, whom Anne and Carl did not even know, raised money for the defendants' legal expenses, wrote letters of protest to Kentucky authorities, and held local meetings to publicize the injustice.[23]

Anne also sent updates on the case to mentors from both of her Virginia alma maters. From the Fitzgerald sisters, Mabel Kennedy, and others, she received a support that was almost familial in its warmth. That was less true among members of the Randolph-Macon alumnae group in Louisville, who ceased sending Anne notices about their meetings soon after her arrest on sedition charges; she mysteriously began to receive their mailings again in late 1958.[24]

Getting on the road to talk about the case and corresponding with interested supporters not only built a groundswell of public sentiment for the defendants. For Anne especially, separated from Carl and her children, it provided an emotional sustenance that was unavailable in the anticommunist cultural climate that hung over Louisville. That period set the stage for the regional and national networking that she pursued ever after. Her day's high point was checking her post office box, as it was so frequently stuffed with mail from sympathizers, and she got in the habit of lengthy replies to as many people as she could manage. Over the coming decades her voluminous correspondence with activists around the country charted the emotional life as well as the actual progress of the social movements of which she was a part.[25]

One source of local support, however—something Anne always appreciated as she looked back on those years—was the spirit of unity in the defendants' dealings with one another. The "Louisville Seven" never passed blame among themselves—a pattern their attorneys warned them was common in a group facing these sorts of political charges. Although all but Anne and Carl left Louisville soon after their indictments were resolved, they never turned on one another or lost touch. (In 1994, the five who were still living gathered to commemorate the forty-year anniversary of their ordeal.)[26]

Except for that short period in the fall of 1954 when, under sustained pressure from the prosecutor and investigators from HUAC and the FBI, he wondered if he had been deceived, Andrew Wade also remained a loyal friend and ally. The Wades had troubles of their own with payment for damages on the house still tied up in court amid the foreclosure suit they, together with the Bradens, faced. Yet throughout 1955 and 1956 Andrew Wade joined the defendants in travels publicizing the case.[27]

It was a source of outrage and anguish to Wade that the issue of his family's right to a home on Rone Court had been so completely obscured by the cries of "communism!" There was plenty of investigation over suspected reds yet still no resolution in sight to the troubling matter of who had actually destroyed the house. It had become, as the *Defender* remarked acidly after Carl's conviction, an "incidental issue" by virtue of the hysterical atmosphere surrounding the trial. In springtime 1955, the injustices done to Wade multiplied when a Jefferson County judge dismissed charges he had brought against

Buster Rone, Stanley Wilt, and Lawrence Rinehardt for their May 1954 cross-burning. The court left no recourse for Wade, ruling that it had no jurisdiction because the 1954 grand jury had failed to act. A subsequent grand jury refused to take up the matter again. Anticommunism defined the Bradens' experiences after the bombing, but anticommunism only compounded the unrelenting racism that defined the Wades'.[28]

Probably as much as an any one organization could, the Emergency Civil Liberties Committee (ECLC) enabled Anne and Carl to organize a broad-based fightback against the forces threatening their freedom. The ECLC was an advocacy group founded in 1951 by Corliss Lamont, Harvey O'Connor, and other former ACLU board members who had grown impatient with the older organization's liberal anticommunism. O'Connor, a crusading writer whose exposes of wealthy U.S. industrialists had won him acclaim in labor journalism, had worked closely with Communists, and he passionately rejected the post-WWII embrace of anticommunism by liberals. O'Connor publicly criticized the Soviet Union and the CP-USA, but he also believed that CP supporters were worthwhile contributors to progressive social change and as deserving as anyone else of defense against repression. More important, he thought that "red hunters," as he thought of the congressional investigating committees, were the greater danger and desperately needed to have their activities exposed and halted before they undermined all semblance of democracy. When the ACLU seemed unwilling to meet this challenge head-on, O'Connor and others established the ECLC to resurrect collapsing First Amendment rights and to protect the civil liberties of a wider assortment of people, notably those the ACLU considered too close to the CP. Unlike the ACLU, the ECLC was scathingly critical of the FBI, HUAC and its Senate counterpart, Smith Act prosecutions, and their facsimiles at the state level—of which the Kentucky sedition case was one.[29]

The ECLC also employed direct-action techniques for its legal challenges—demonstrations and letter-writing campaigns built from grassroots support. This style contrasted with the ACLU's more narrowly legalistic approach, and though critics might link the more mass-action strategy to groups like the CP-led International Labor Defense, a belief in the importance of collective action was probably the greatest single dividing line between liberals and the left in this period. Although the ECLC was a national organization, its leading constituents were radical New York intellectuals, and it lacked the liberal base and congressional contacts that characterized the ACLU. The ECLC was continually red-baited but never listed by the Subversive Activities Control Board or the attorney general: meanwhile, it provided effective legal assistance through the counsel of Leonard Boudin, its head attorney.[30]

ECLC leaders also established a "Bill of Rights Fund" that provided money to sustain anticommunist defendants. Had it not been for income allotments from that fund throughout 1955 and '56, Carl and Anne might not have remained financially able to continue their battle. The ECLC was also instrumental in raising the enormous bail necessary to get Carl out of prison.[31]

Part of what drew the ECLC to become so deeply involved in the case was the very "southern-ness" of the incident, the fact that segregation was at its base. The domestic Cold War had clamped down on civil liberties nationwide, but in the South the unique marriage of segregationist and anticommunist ideologies had a particularly crippling effect on social reform. By 1954 the executive director of the ECLC was Clark Foreman, who felt a special affinity for the issues at stake in Louisville, having seen the contracting of civil liberties reverse New Deal–era gains made in southern civil rights. Foreman's own efforts had become increasingly defensive amid the red-baiting that preceded the demise of the Southern Conference. Believing the Louisville events a perfect opportunity to raise public consciousness about the role of southern anticommunism in propping up racial hierarchy, Foreman steered ECLC toward a leading role in the sedition case.[32]

Being at the center of ECLC campaigning had its cost, however. Rivalry and political animosities between that group and the ACLU were a fixture of the 1950s social-political reform landscape, and the Braden case brought them into bold relief. Nationally, the ACLU was critical of the Louisville sedition prosecution and had offered up the legal services of Lusky, who had taken a personal interest in the case and had raised funds from ACLU supporters for greater participation in the appeal, a process to which the ACLU national office raised no objection. Anne was hugely appreciative of Lusky: she called him the *most diligent and faithful lawyer who ever worked on a case of this kind anywhere—and probably the most underpaid*. But informally, ACLU officials also attempted to dissuade the Louisville defendants from accepting ECLC assistance. Not surprisingly, the reason was its "communistic" reputation. Anne and her friends were not convinced, and her exhaustive negotiations with both organizations managed to maintain the support of them both. Although Lusky headed Carl's appeal, he worked with Boudin as co-counsel.[33]

The Bradens' alliance with ECLC affiliated them with a national network of civil libertarians who would help to shape their future political work and to sustain them on a more personal level. Foremost among these, perhaps, was Harvey O'Connor. Like Anne and Carl, O'Connor personally tangled with congressional anticommunists throughout the 1950s, starting with a 1953 clash with Joe McCarthy during a Senate subcommittee hearing on the supposedly subversive nature of his books on the Mellons and other wealthy industrialists. O'Connor's real crime, it seems in retrospect, was to challenge the authority of the red hunters. O'Connor first met Anne during a talk she gave in Boston about her case. She and Carl found in O'Connor and his equally activist wife, Jessie Lloyd O'Connor, lifelong friends.[34]

Beginning in 1956, the Bradens and their children left the South nearly every summer for a month's relaxation at Little Compton, the O'Connors' rambling coastal estate in Rhode Island. The O'Connors' wealth—inherited through the Lloyds—gave them the means to provide social and cultural sustenance for beleaguered 1950s activists. These beach retreats—which the O'Connors often insisted upon financing—gave Anne and Carl the opportunity to network with literally dozens of crusading kindred spirits, who, like them, needed their resiliency restored in a culture vastly at odds with the beliefs they all cherished in one form or another. Each evening at Little Compton, friends and family members gathered for cocktails and visionary political discussions on the porch and later for international dancing in the huge living room or for group singing, often led by Pete and Toshi Seeger.[35]

In the 1950s the parameters for social criticism were terribly narrow even within much of the left, which was nearly as diminished from within by its own debates about the threat of Communism and the need to distance oneself from all Communist associations as it was decimated from without by anticommunist ideologues. In the sedition case, this internal vacillation is evident not just from the ACLU-ECLC dispute but also from the approach-avoidance coverage given the case by the *Nation*, probably the most respected liberal-to-left U.S. journal. Jennings Perry, a Tennessee journalist, wrote the magazine's initial brief report on the events in Louisville. Perry's article, which was sympathetic to the Wades and the Bradens, met with hot criticism from Walter Millis, a self-styled civil libertarian writer who decried the conviction and harsh sentence but tagged Carl as "conniving at a piece of Communist agitation." *Nation* editors then permitted Millis to write a lengthy follow-up piece on the case which, though just as critical of its outcome, took every opportunity to castigate the sedition defendants for having, as he put it, "invited the lightning." Anne wrote a letter protesting Millis's accusations, as did her friend Al Maund, a *Nation* contributor, both of which the magazine also ran. When

Carl's conviction was overturned, the *Nation* editorially applauded the decision and pronounced the couple "victims."[36]

Even left-leaning American institutions were wary of being too supportive of activists who had been that close to the CP. The Socialist Party, for example, refused to accept Carl's membership application for several years after his identification with the CP in Louisville.[37]

I. F. Stone, on the other hand, a socialist-minded journalist who had departed mainstream newspaper work in 1952 to establish an independent, Washington-based news magazine called *I. F. Stone's Weekly*, was entirely sympathetic to the Bradens' troubles and to the Wades' right to their house. Anne did not know "Izzy" Stone then, but she came to know him through her case. As soon as Stone heard the tale through Leonard Boudin (to whom he was related by marriage), he ran a story on it, labeling the trial's outcome a "nightmare in Louisville," and contacted Anne for more information.[38]

She met with him in early 1955 during a stopover in the Washington, D.C., airport, and they hit it off immediately. Stone saw Anne's stance as "heroic," as he later wrote, while his commitment to social justice–oriented journalism and his dry wit left her similarly impressed. Their initial conversation stayed with her, and Izzy Stone always maintained a special affection for Anne. *I said, "They know who blew up the house. It's just a frame-up. Nobody will print what we really know about it." And he said, "I'll do it." I said, "Well, the Louisville papers are afraid they'll commit libel." And he answered, "I'll commit libel for you. What's the use of having your own publication if you can't commit libel to do something good?" I'll never forget that. He never did [commit libel], but he wrote several articles.*[39]

Once she recovered her bearings in early 1955, Anne began to write about her experiences as an accused seditionist. In print, she was at her best when she relied on the passion of her personal narrative rather than on polemics. Like many of her white southern dissident peers (such as Lillian Smith and Katharine Lumpkin), Anne found memoir her best means of expression through which to explain her uncompromising opposition to racial and social injustices. With so much of her attention devoted to public speaking and fundraising, interspersed with daily correspondence with Carl, weekly trips to the prison, and frequent trips to Anniston to see her children, she found precious little time to write reflectively and often resorted to staying up half the night to do so. But the notes she kept during this period formed the basis for what would become *The Wall Between,* her memoir of the case, which she completed in 1956 and got published in 1958.[40]

Because the roots of her activism had always been religious, a logical place to turn for publishing a first essay on the case lay in the direction of faith-based social action. Anne had for several years served on the board of the Department of Social Relations of her diocese, and in the course of the sedition fight she became acquainted with the Episcopal League for Social Action (ELSA), an inheritor of the social-gospel strain of Protestantism and another important new network of support. In February 1955 Anne gave her account of the events in Louisville in an article for *The Witness,* ELSA's weekly magazine.[41]

ELSA also printed and distributed thousands of copies of a pamphlet titled *When Christians Become Subversive,* the text of a sermon given in early 1955 by an Episcopal priest in Brooklyn, New York, named Howard Melish. Melish preached on the subject a few days after he read Anne's account of it in the *Witness.* With a long history of civil rights activism that had begun through his exposure to African American and CP intellectuals of the 1930s and continued through his interracial congregation, Melish (who was white) had recently come through his own brush with witch hunting, having narrowly triumphed over an attempt by his diocese to unseat him for his "subversive" activities. Melish had heard of Anne and Carl through their respective work in the controversial Council on American-Soviet Friendship, and he wrote to them to convey sympathy for their plight. Once he learned more of their story, he got involved in their resistance campaign. Melish and his wife, Mary Jane, who operated a racially diverse youth center near the family's home in the majority-black neighborhood of Bedford-Stuyvesant, were another pair of supporters during this period who became dear friends as well. (It was they, incidentally, who introduced the Bradens to a younger activist who would also become a close colleague; Angela Davis met Anne and Carl later in the 1950s as a teenager when she lived in the Melish household to escape the oppressive environment of her native Birmingham and attend a progressive private school in New York.)[42]

During Carl's seven-month imprisonment, Anne deepened her ties to that portion of the religious left in which Marxism and Christianity were seen as compatible. The ELSA activists she met and corresponded with offered her a solace that she was not privy to in her own church, where she felt coldly tolerated more than embraced. Melish took Anne's distress very seriously and contacted her former ministers James Stoney (who was living in New Mexico) and Albert Dalton (then in Missouri). Dalton shied away from reaching out to Anne, but she renewed her friendship by mail with Jim

Stoney, who remembered her fondly from Anniston and did not simply dismiss her as a Communist, as did many during this time. Stoney attempted to elicit greater support for Anne from her home parish by corresponding with Louisville's Bishop Marmion, but his efforts were rebuffed, largely on the basis of Anne's alleged Communist ties.[43]

Because her children were living in Anniston, Anne could not avoid frequent visits there, but they were awkward and left her tense. Whether out of respect for her parents' stature in the community or to preserve its own distance from her, the *Anniston Star*'s coverage of the case never identified Anne as a native daughter or former *Star* staffer. Still, her actions were no secret. Her parents' friends treated her as if she had a terminal illness, and many of her own friends avoided her altogether. Only a few, like Allen Draper and Elise Ayers, stood loyally by her, although even supportive Annistonians wondered sometimes if Anne and Carl had indeed blown up the house.[44]

Despite their differences, however, Anita and Gambrell McCarty added their voices to the growing lobby for their daughter's and son-in-law's freedom, appealing to influential Kentucky friends and family members. Anita McCarty wrote a letter that ran in the *Courier-Journal* in the spring of 1955 in which she traced her daughter's identification with the oppressed to her Christian faith and asked if Anne was to be punished because she had, "by actually practicing the beliefs to which all Christians pay lip service, trespassed upon sacrosanct man-made racial barriers?" E. L. Turner, Anne's former next-door neighbor in Anniston and a close friend of her father, contacted the prosecutor on her behalf, but Hamilton indicated that unless Anne would show a "spirit of repentance," he would show her no leniency. The McCartys had little or no sympathy for Anne's and Carl's principles (a fact they reiterated at every turn), and their interest in the matter was strictly personal. But even they became alert to the political capital Hamilton had amassed by uncovering "reds" in Louisville and how it dimmed prospects for getting the conviction overturned on appeal.[45]

The very idea of raising $40,000 in bail money was daunting, but after her initial apprehension, Anne worked at it steadily. She faced numerous setbacks, one of which was her unreliable car, which seemed to break down every couple of weeks. But by early July 1955, her efforts had paid off, with some crucial assistance from ECLC. With the exception of the home owned by Carl's mother (the Barnetts had withdrawn their property bond at Anne's insistence when she learned they were in financial distress), the majority of the bail had been raised outside Kentucky. Nationally, contributions ranged from a few hundred dollars from groups such as the Baptist Ministers' Conference of Greater New York (given in response to a talk Anne gave) to the final $10,000 donated by Danny Weitzman, a wealthy New Yorker whose own hounding by the FBI had so disgruntled him that he backed Carl just to annoy the government.[46]

On July 12, 1955, Anne and Zollinger ceremoniously passed to a circuit court clerk $28,000 in Treasury bonds, $5,000 in cash, and $7,000 worth of real estate. A few hours later, surrounded by reporters, they retrieved the prisoner from LaGrange Reformatory. To Anne's great relief, she could at last bring Carl home. On the way, the three of them stopped to get him an overflowing bowl of ice cream, his favorite treat. The very next day the couple headed to Anniston to retrieve their children. Yet once they were all together again in Louisville, the hectic pace Anne had kept did not slow a bit.[47]

Reunited, in fact, the Bradens quickened their efforts to get Carl's conviction overturned. At first, to Anne's dismay, Carl was more in demand as a speaker than she. After the months of organizing alone, however, Anne refused to sit back and play the role of supportive wife at home. She let Carl know in no uncertain terms that she would accept nothing less than an equal voice in their fight, and the two were firm with all who invited him to speak. In the coming months they established a pattern that would characterize their lives for years to come: while one parent stayed home to mind the children, the other was on the road for a week or two at a time, speaking and organizing. When they traveled together, they either left the children with their grandparents or, in a pinch, brought one or both along.[48]

Near summer's end, the 13-volume, 2,500-page transcript for *Kentucky v. Braden* was delivered to the Bradens' attorneys. Soon thereafter, Lusky completed a 330-page appeals brief. No further action was expected on the sedition case pending a ruling in Pennsylvania's *Nelson* case, which questioned the validity of state sedition laws and was now before the U.S. Supreme Court. Another noted civil liberties attorney from New York, Frank Donner (later the author of *The Un-Americans*, a critique of Red Scare investigating bodies), offered his services pro bono to Carl and entered an amicus brief on behalf of the Louisville defendants—and sedition defendants in numerous other states—to the Supreme Court for consideration in *Nelson*. The brief held that the Louisville conviction was a prime example of the capricious, abusive employment of state sedition statutes. With more than 40 states facing invalidation of their laws pending the ruling, the commonwealth of Kentucky, meanwhile, joined 41 in filing briefs seeking the preservation of state sedition laws.[49]

Living on contributions from the Bill of Rights Fund and on the generosity of friends, Anne and Carl maintained a frenetic pace throughout the remainder of 1955 and early 1956. When they were not traveling, they were writing. Even an FBI informant who allegedly observed them during this period noted that "both spend numerous hours typing." Between the two of them they covered thousands of miles.[50]

Most of their travels were in the Northeast and Midwest. But in late 1955 Anne began to feel that it was important that they talk to more southerners, given the centrality of challenging segregation to their case. Carl was less optimistic of finding much support in the South, but he went along with her lead. On New Year's Day 1956, leaving their daughter in Anniston, the two set out with their four-year-old son on a southern tour. Their itinerary was loosely coordinated by SCEF's Jim Dombrowski, who set up meetings in New Orleans and provided contacts in other southern communities. They met with the veteran radical activist Don West in Georgia, and he drove them north to the Highlander School in Tennessee to introduce them to Myles Horton, whose long-standing social justice activism Anne knew only by reputation. With the help of the couple's friends Al and Dorothy Maund, who now lived near Montgomery, this trip was also an opportunity for Anne to get to know reformers in the state in which she had grown up. After a day spent with SCEF leaders Aubrey Williams and Virginia Durr in Montgomery (whom Anne had first met, briefly, while Carl was still in prison), she initiated a correspondence with both of them that was the beginning of lifelong friendships. Anne was a generation younger than most activists she met in her travels, and the deep social commitments, especially among white southerners, that had allowed them to endure sustained repression were a source of inspiration to her during her current travails. These contacts strengthened her awareness of a history of southern social justice crusades that further heightened her sense of the *other America* of which William Patterson had spoken. *It was years later before it dawned on me what a valuable experience that was. Essentially what happened was that we were traveling around the country at a time when we were supposed to be in the midst of the "silent fifties" when [social activism] was absolutely squashed—that's the mythology. We were meeting the people who were the resistance movement of the fifties, because the people who would be interested in our case were the same ones who had fought for the Rosenbergs, against the Korean War, who had kept up the civil rights struggle. How lucky we were to have met the cream of America—the people who never quit fighting back in that period.*[51]

Later that spring the couple drove cross-country in a borrowed car to tell their story in California, where there was already considerable organizing under way against further persecution of social reformers in the name of hunting "reds." The difference in the civil liberties atmosphere there and the one they had experienced in the South was stark, to say the least. Speaking far and wide about the sedition case made it clearer to Anne and Carl that opening up civil liberties in the South was a prerequisite to more substantive civil rights reforms. Starting with their publicity campaign of self-defense in the sedition case, they worked toward creating a southern—and a national—cultural climate more tolerant of dissent. Civil libertarians nationwide also needed to realize, the Bradens felt, that African American struggles in the South were opening a path for other social reforms to follow. Connecting civil liberties and civil rights would constitute a significant part of the Bradens' contribution to the emerging racial justice movement over the coming decade, but they often found it hard to get their message heard even after the rise of the mass movement in the 1960s.[52]

In their travels now, civil rights supporters who heard about the extreme punishment meted out to Carl in Louisville tended to conclude that, as Lusky's appeal brief had eloquently pointed out, "the sentence in the present case can only have resulted from the jury's passionate disapproval of the defendants' lawful purchase of the Wade house." After all, as Lusky noted, even the organizers of the CP-USA, convicted under the Smith Act, were subjected to only five years' imprisonment and a smaller fine, not the 15 years and $5,000 Carl faced.[53]

Even if Carl had been the CP plotter the government claimed him to be, the party claimed fewer than 30,000 members among a nation of 150 million during this period. Some estimates have placed it at only 5,000 by 1956—a ghost of what it had been at its postwar peak of 75,000. Ironically, reduced CP ranks seemed to spur new heights to the anticommunist crusades as officials sought to extinguish the remaining few, who, the chairman of HUAC proclaimed hyperbolically, were "hard-core disciplined agents of the Kremlin on American soil." The government pursued multiple prosecutions throughout the 1950s against Pittsburgh CP leader Steve Nelson, whose state sedition case held import for Carl's fate as well.[54]

On April 2, 1956, nearly six years after Nelson's arrest for violation of Pennsylvania's 1919 sedition law, the U.S. Supreme Court ruled that state sedition laws were invalidated, having been superseded by the federal Smith Act. It is unclear what role other state-level prosecutions like the one Carl had endured played in the decision, but the Bradens heard rumors that the impact of the Kentucky sedition case had been substantial. *Carl heard later through his newspaper connections that the story of the Louisville case and the [amicus] brief had been influential on the Supreme Court justices because they saw it as such a horrible example of what could happen when you turned every little local prosecutor loose with a state sedition law.*[55]

Even after the anticipated ruling came down in *Nelson*, however, the Kentucky Court of Appeals did not immediately act upon Carl's appeal. There were rumors that the defendants would now be tried under a federal indictment if the current conviction was voided. Yet in spite of a plea from Kentucky congressman John Robsion that Carl be indicted under the Smith Act, the Department of Justice declined to do so.[56]

Eleven weeks after *Nelson* and after considerable posturing by state officials, the Kentucky Court of Appeals formally overturned Carl's December 1954 conviction but left the door open to a new sedition indictment more narrowly directed at his attempt to overthrow "exclusively" the state government. Further indictments never materialized, though Hamilton's office continued to block defense attempts to get remaining charges dropped against Anne and the other defendants. In the summer of 1956, Hamilton tried to rally new enthusiasm for the prosecution by reconvening the grand jury investigation of Communism in Louisville. Shortly thereafter, a contempt citation was issued to Henry Rhine, a white unionist who refused to answer questions about his friendship with the Bradens and his 1954 participation in the Wade Defense Committee.[57]

The Louisville newspapers continued to keep a low profile with respect to the sedition case. After Carl's conviction was reversed, he wrote to Barry Bingham and requested reinstatement of his job, but was met with the curt reply that "your activities were heedless of any damage you might be doing the papers . . . you did in fact damage them." Though Carl had not been accused of slanting the news before the Wade case, Bingham charged that "you do not possess and cannot exercise the objectivity which must characterize the handling of news." Bingham was unmoved by Carl's counter, in which he recalled the paper's September 17, 1954, editorial comment that "we do not think the day will ever come when a man will be fired by us because we do not like his beliefs or his friends."[58]

But the political currents in Louisville and across the South had become more polarized in those intervening 21 months. Having a writer on staff who had been publicly fingered as a Communist was a liability Bingham could not tolerate. As the region heated up under the threat of increasing desegregation, the papers' editorial position continued to counsel moderation, as it had at the time of the Wade purchase. At times, as it had in 1954, that moderation squared with an unwillingness to challenge racial barriers and meant that the paper, in effect, aligned itself with the segregationists who said "wait" (e.g., when Autherine Lucy's 1956 attempt to desegregate the University of Alabama met with violence, the Louisville newspapers editorialized for a "time out for sober thinking").[59]

The matter of the remaining sedition indictments dragged on into the fall with much bluster in the form of continued threats to restructure the case and hints by Hamilton of a perjury indictment against Carl. It also took the state courts more than a month to return Carl's bail after the reversal of his conviction. The fulminations served to keep the defendants on edge and poised to mount a new fightback, but they portended little real action. In November, Hamilton reluctantly dropped the remaining sedition charges, but announced his intent to prosecute Bown (who was by now living in California) on the bombing charge. Hamilton seemed to ignore the fact that he had no credible evidence and that Bown's defense attorneys held affidavits from witnesses who swore Bown was in Milwaukee when the blast took place. After Judge Curtis ruled that the prosecution could not introduce subversive literature as evidence of Bown's motive, Hamilton—shorn now of the ability to play to local anticommunist hysteria—read a prepared statement recommending the dismissal of all charges, flung the paper on the judge's bench, and stalked out of the courtroom. Except for his histrionics, the case that had begun in such a fury died with precious little fanfare—and Hamilton himself would be dead too in three years' time, shooting himself to death during a family argument and in the wake of a flagging political career.[60]

Scott Hamilton's doggedness in the sedition case was an early example of the right turn southern politics took in the aftermath of *Brown*. Anticommunist anxiety formed the national backdrop through which segregationist defensiveness now took center stage in the region. At least for a moment, that included a border city like Louisville, where a convulsion of anticommunist hysteria gave segregationists their day.[61]

The intermingling of segregationist and anticommunist ideologies was an even deadlier mix in terms of the possibilities for civil rights reform farther south, especially in states like Alabama and Mississippi. There, the dissenting white southern voices of those Anne called *the cream of America* were soft indeed compared to the louder chants of the archsegregationists, who built in 1955 and 1956 a movement of massive resistance to racial change that used the rhetoric and emotional charge of anticommunism to blunt civil rights support. Those fitting the description of "outside agitators," as southern racists had long referred to communists, union organizers, northern philanthropists, and most other voices who supported racial or democratic reform, now broadened dramatically to include the federal authority that threatened to desegregate regional schools as mandated by *Brown*. Southern politicians referred to the federal government in those very words in the 1956 "Southern Manifesto" opposing school desegregation that was signed almost unanimously by the region's congressmen.[62]

By 1956, about 250,000 to 300,000 southern whites had joined White Citizens' Council (WCC) groups that, in the words of sociologist Charles Payne, "pursued the agenda of the Klan with the demeanor of the Rotary." The Citizens' Councils aggressively organized whites uncommitted on the subject of race. They were openly dedicated to white supremacy and depicted all threats to it as "Communistic" and Soviet-inspired—"convinced," as one WCC observer put it, "that the 1954 decision was part of a Red conspiracy to create turmoil in the South [and] mongrelize the white people." Council organizers and their working-class counterparts, often through the KKK, took up the mantle of Joseph McCarthy throughout the South.[63]

The Citizens' Council movement never gained the absolute respectability nor the stronghold over state politics in Kentucky that it did farther south. Yet it was a visible political presence whose leader was none other than Millard Grubbs, the white militant whose call to arms in Shively perhaps raised his ambitions of a white-supremacy movement in Kentucky. In 1956 the *Courier-Journal* logged four council chapters in the state, with Louisville having been the first, established through the support of people like James Rone. Grubbs never gained either the numbers or the political clout he hoped for, however. In Henderson, one of the first rural Kentucky school districts to desegregate, Citizens' Council members attempted to organize opposition to desegregation that fall, but they did not succeed.[64]

Despite the stern warnings the Louisville newspapers had issued that the Wade purchase could impair race relations locally, the fall of 1956 saw the relatively peaceful, if token, desegregation of Louisville schools. The profound wrong done to the Wades was never undone nor properly atoned for, and the matter of housing desegregation was left for a later battle. Yet hard-core segregationists were simply not sufficiently powerful to control the city's institutions. Reflecting on their ordeal in a group letter to supporters, the Louisville defendants liked to think that they had played some role in nonviolent school desegregation. They believed that the city's prominent liberal spokesmen, who had kept their distance throughout the Wade-Braden episode, had "evidently resolved that this kind of thing would not be allowed to happen again. . . . If we have contributed to that progress—even by serving as lightning rods for some of the ancient prejudice and fury—we feel that our efforts were not in vain."[65]

When Anne and Carl picked up the gauntlet laid before them by Wade's request, the subsequent drama that culminated in the dynamiting of a house and sedition charges filed against the Bradens and five others demonstrates the limits of southern liberalism in the postwar era. It also suggests why legal segregation could be broken, finally, only by the moral authority commanded later by Martin Luther King's poignant pleas to the nation and by students whose sit-ins at lunch counters revealed their willingness to be beaten, jailed, or even killed to exercise their citizenship rights. Only that powerful strength of purpose could break through the thick buttress of reinforcement for segregation that anticommunism formed in the 1950s. Eric Tachau, one of Anne's white contemporaries who considered himself a liberal and only later became active in the civil rights movement, recalled 1950s Louisville this way: "Most people who claimed to be progressive were upset because they thought this [act] could block progress. More than anything else, they thought it was a dumb thing for the Bradens to have done. Whether they were Communists or not, that didn't really matter. I don't think many of us [whites] except for Anne and Carl Braden understood the importance of confronting the evil of segregation and bigotry and racism. [Then] Martin Luther King came along and he's the one who taught us that. Anne already knew it."[66]

A moral confrontation with segregation was a lesson Louisville was not ready to learn in 1954. The simple act of buying a home on the Wades' behalf in the white Louisville suburb of Shively wreaked unforeseen violence and brought both couples violent disapproval. It drove Andrew and Charlotte Wade from the home they had always wanted, and it brought Anne and Carl to the brink of personal disaster. The events set in motion from the moment the transfer of the house became public seem in retrospect to have been almost preordained to link prosegregationist and anticommunist ideologies in a way that, given the times, was bound to create witches. One critic, who wrote on the case for the *Nation*, called Carl and Anne "difficult, dedicated, and argumentative people with a compulsion to lofty causes—generally of a left-wing coloration." Depending on where one sat, that argumentative quality could be abrasive, part of what E. L. Doctorow's fictional child of the Rosenbergs, Daniel Isaacson, wryly called "the merciless radical temperament."[67]

Just as significantly, perhaps, both Bradens were idealists who were unapologetic on the need for a radical dismantling of racial segregation. Anne reflected later that *the feeling of people like us was that our destiny rested with the freedom movement of blacks. . . . It wasn't that we were "helping those poor blacks." It was our struggle too.* Such determination in the face of the domestic Cold War and a region clinging desperately to racial hierarchy brought a calamitous clash. The charge of dynamite that partially destroyed the Rone Court house on June 27, 1954, after weeks of threats, took Louisville society by surprise. Nationally, this kind of hyperbolic, violent white reaction to blacks' moving into "their" neighborhood was not new to American history, nor had it become obsolete even at the end of the twentieth century.[68]

But only midcentury Cold War paranoia over internal subversion, blended with the complacency of white southern customs, allowed the racist atrocity of the blast and the apartheid-like conditions that made a "front" purchase necessary to be glossed over by labeling the entire affair a "Communist plot." In very different ways, both the Bradens and the Wades felt most acutely the long-term brunt of the eruption that seized Louisville in mid-1954.

Andrew and Charlotte Wade were never able to see the culprits of the bombing prosecuted, and they continued to be legally and financially embroiled with the damaged, unlivable structure on Rone Court until 1957, when they obtained clear title to the property. Hoping to give the Wades the opportunity to return to their home, a wealthy white Chicago couple, Kay and David Simonson, lent them the money to pay off the mortgage, accumulated interest, and court costs. By that time, however, Charlotte Wade had concluded she could never feel safe surrounded by such avowed racists, and the couple sold the property that had caused them such grief and returned to the city's West End to live. Andrew Wade found new outlets for his desires for equal treatment, leading sit-ins in Louisville parks in 1956 and later participating in 1960s sit-ins. Charlotte Wade, however, declined further civil rights activism and chose to minimize her contact with whites, living a private existence within the black community. What began as the "Wade case" shifted irreversibly to obscure the terrible wrong committed against Andrew and Charlotte Wade, becoming in the public imagination the "Braden sedition case" and casting Anne and Carl as diabolical symbols of evil.[69]

The Bradens and their codefendants triumphed over the state's attempt to brand them as seditionists. But the "communist" taint followed Anne and Carl for decades, and they became pariahs in their home city. Gilbert, Spiker, Ford, Bown, and Lubka all found it necessary to leave Louisville to find either employment or a more welcoming social climate. Anne and Carl refused to be driven out, but neither were they able to really organize effectively there for many years to come. The twinning of segregationist and anticommunist ideologies that had so rocked Louisville throughout 1954 and catapulted Scott Hamilton to momentary fame was never sufficient to direct policy as it did further south, but it was as if Anne and Carl became the human placeholders in Kentucky for these savage sentiments. In effect, the pair remained all through the 1960s and '70s the same symbols of evil they had become during Carl's sedition trial. The hostility that lingered from their and the Wades' bold initiative coalesced into a lasting demonization of "the Bradens" that prevented their taking effective leadership in upcoming local civil rights battles and inflicted daily humiliations on the lives of them and their children. Anne and Carl never retreated from activism, but they found it expedient to concentrate more on regional civil rights campaigns and to play only behind-the-scenes roles in local activities. They remained the local lightning rods they had been as sedition defendants.

The person who had most confirmed them in that status, Alberta Ahearn, faded relatively quickly from public life. Although Ahearn continued to live in Louisville until her death in 1995, neither Anne nor Carl ever saw her again. Once Anne's initial sense of betrayal and amazement wore off, she could never bring herself to condemn Ahearn for her testimony. Instead, Anne developed a view of her former friend as a victim of the domestic Cold War just as she herself was a victim of it, albeit one of a different sort. After her day in court, Ahearn appeared as an informant at two subsequent anticommunist investigative hearings. Soon thereafter, she more or less *faded into the woodwork*, as Anne put it, having alienated herself from those who had been her friends and having spent her limited value to local authorities.[70]

Anne and Carl, on the other hand, were survivors, not casualties, of the domestic Cold War of the 1950s. They never stopped fighting back and—despite Scott Hamilton's best efforts—were never silenced. They jumped onboard the new civil rights movement that was blossoming farther south and hauled some of its energy back to Louisville. They also led the southern charge toward greater civil liberties, becoming regional participants in a nationwide campaign to flatten the power of inquisitional bodies such as HUAC and its southern counterparts.

The mid-1950s saw the foundations of southern segregation crack. When its defenders erupted in protest, Andrew and Charlotte Wade were among those who suffered most. As whites who backed the Wades, the Bradens' radical views made them easy targets in the anticommunist cultural climate that pervaded the country during that era. Historians such as Patricia Sullivan and John Egerton have shown in recent studies of white southern civil rights activism that the Red Scare of the post-WWII years throttled the black-white alliance that had budded during the Depression. In the South, the anticommunist discourse of what has become popularly known as the "McCarthy" period became even fiercer in the wake of the *Brown* decision. Southern anticommunist campaigns forced people like Clark Foreman, Aubrey Williams, and now the Bradens—a newer generation of race reformers—into a defensive posture, scrambling for their own legitimacy rather than focusing their energies on the racial injustices they wished to correct. The demise of the Popular Front and the rise of anticommunist red-baiting as a prop for segregation left painfully little opening in the region for civil rights activism.[71]

Yet even as white segregationists decried the "reds" and "outside agitators" in their midst, there was another movement brewing as well. While the Bradens were immersed in a local battle for their own freedom, new African American voices were being raised in Montgomery, Alabama, in support of the same general goals the Wades and they had espoused. Anne and Carl would connect with that movement soon enough, and ultimately the demand for dignity that had prompted Andrew Wade to seek out the couple in the first place would become too great to be neatly contained any longer.

CHAPTER EIGHT

A VOICE CRYING IN THE WILDERNESS — EARLY SCEF YEARS

Communism and integration are inseparable. . . . Integration is the southern expression of the communist movement.

—John Garrett, Louisiana state legislator, 1958[1]

THE MONTGOMERY BUS BOYCOTT OF 1955–1956 inaugurated an era of large-scale African American protest that ultimately spelled the end of Jim Crow segregation by launching an independent African American movement in the South that looked to whites more for support than for leadership. Yet the mood in the majority of the white South was one of massive resistance to racial change. Although *Brown* gave the force of law to school desegregation, it did so without a specific plan for implementation. The lingering national discourse of anticommunism gained new energy in the South from the federal mandate on school segregation, and segregationists worked aggressively to quell even the most moderate challenges to the racial status quo, especially among whites.

The next few years would give Anne the opportunity to enact more fully William Patterson's advice about organizing whites. She and Carl became part of what remained of the southern conference movement when they joined the Southern Conference Educational Fund (SCEF) staff in 1957 with a mandate to "find white southerners" who had the courage to support blacks in their struggle for freedom even in the face of enormous obstacles against doing so.

_____

For Anne, the mid-'50s had been something of a lost time in terms of civil rights activism except insofar as she and Carl were on the road proselytizing about their case and speaking widely about the bankruptcy of segregation. Like everyone else concerned about racism, Anne was inflamed by the 1955 Emmett Till slaying. Yet because the Bradens were *so wrapped up with trying to survive*, she was *hardly aware* of the Montgomery bus boycott that erupted near the end of that year: *People didn't realize how important this was going to be. . . . What is it that lights the spark that creates a mass movement? But this was a qualitative change. As I see it, what happened when that bus boycott started was that all of a sudden great masses of black people were out in the streets saying no.*[2]

The Bradens attended one meeting of the Montgomery Improvement Association during the early days of the boycott, but were unable to do much to support that struggle in the midst of their own. Even once the sedition case was behind them, it would be awhile before they connected with the great regional ferment brewing. First the couple had to reconstruct their shattered personal and economic lives. The two were driving a Dodge donated by Anne's parents. Reliance on relatives' and supporters' assistance had been necessary while they fought the sedition charge, and in its wake contributions continued to pour in during the 1956 Christmas season. Still, the generosity of others represented no long-term solution. Carl searched for more than a year for a job, but his reputation invariably preceded him.[3]

At the end of 1956, resorting to an employment agency, Anne managed to land a job as clerk for a wholesale supply company owned by Arthur Kling, a former candidate for mayor on the Socialist Party ticket who, coincidentally, was quite familiar with the Bradens' case. In 1955 he had been at the forefront in establishing the Kentucky Civil Liberties Union (KCLU), an affiliate of the national ACLU. The branch had been organized mainly in response to issues raised in the Braden case and to the silencing effect it had on Louisville liberals. Yet instead of inviting Anne and Carl to participate, the KCLU rebuffed their efforts to do so, and Kling in particular had presented them in a negative light at national ACLU meetings.[4]

When Anne was sent to Kling anonymously through an agency, however, he could scarcely refuse to hire her. For nearly a year she handled all phases of office work for a salary of $54 per week. Anne was stoic later when she remembered that period of their lives: *Carl couldn't get any job. We both tried, and I was able to get one first because people don't consider that the woman is as dangerous as the man: that's a male supremacist attitude. I ended up doing practically everything in the office, so they were getting me for about half the money I was worth. So then Carl stayed home and took care of the children.*[5]

In addition to their financial woes, the pair continued to be shunned by the local civil rights community. In early 1957 they battled exclusion from the Louisville NAACP after the chair, Earl Dearing, wrote Carl informing him that "your presence on the membership committee threatens to disrupt the entire campaign." Anne fired off a quick reply, reminding Dearing that they had been invited by her old friend Jim Crumlin to assist in the membership drive and adding, *I assure you that neither Carl nor I want to do anything that would hurt the NAACP. We believe too much in its aims and principles. And we have been through too much because of our belief in these principles to want to do anything now that others working for the same aims even think is going to hurt their cause—no matter how mistaken we may think they are.* Crumlin interceded; yet the Bradens found themselves forced into the background in any activist role they assumed in Louisville. They were seen, in the words of one colleague, as "the kiss of death"—a tag that would haunt Anne in Kentucky long after she achieved regional and even national prominence. Anne would joke later that for years after the Wade case she *couldn't have organized a meeting in a phone booth* in Louisville, but at the time the ostracism was profoundly hurtful to her.[6]

Nationally, however, the red hunt seemed to be lifting a bit. The battle to reestablish civil liberties picked up some steam in the wake of McCarthy's censure, as reflected in decisions of the Warren Supreme Court such as that which had freed Carl. A 1957 ruling in *Yates v. U.S.* provided more encouragement by curbing the reach of the Smith Act. Two additional decisions that year gave adversaries of the anticommunist crusades cause for hope: *Watkins* restricted the power of congressional investigating committees, and *Sweezy* applied those restrictions to state legislative inquisitions into academic freedom.[7]

From the marginal status their sedition case had left them in, both Bradens saw the creation of a social environment more tolerant of dissenters generally as a necessary step to break through the southern racial status quo. They were not alone in their desire to broaden the right to dissent. A growing national network of civil libertarian–minded leftists wished to develop a campaign against the congressional investigative committees and their counterparts at the state and local levels. Two integral figures in this process were the Bradens' friend Harvey O'Connor and the civil liberties activist Frank Wilkinson. Wilkinson, a former California Housing Authority official who had been identified in FBI secret documents as a CP member, had lost his job in 1952 when he refused to adhere to a Los Angeles City Council demand that he list his organizational affiliations. Like Anne and Carl, Wilkinson was among the heartier of 1950s crusaders, and he responded to his firing by becoming a full-time civil liberties activist, establishing a Los Angeles–based ad-hoc group he called the Citizens' Committee to Preserve American Freedoms (CCPAF). Wilkinson worked closely with the Southern California Civil Liberties Union, which was fairly outspoken in its criticism of the anticommunist repression that was a periodic feature of the state's cultural landscape after the initial HUAC hearings uncovered "reds" in Hollywood in 1947. By the mid-1950s Wilkinson wished to make his work national, partly in response to incidents like the one that had nearly engulfed the Bradens. When Anne and Carl first heard him speak boldly of a HUAC subpoena as a "badge of honor" that proclaimed the effectiveness of any activist who received one, they were impressed. Though the very idea of abolishing HUAC seemed to them at that juncture in the Cold War *like a pipedream*, the couple's collaboration with Wilkinson led to a national campaign toward that end.[8]

O'Connor and Wilkinson admired the Bradens' skill as organizers and wished to capitalize on their energy. Nonsouthern civil libertarians saw the pair—in light of their sedition case and dedication to ending segregation—as the perfect spokespersons on the perniciousness of "anticommunism southern style." In the spring of 1957, having exhausted his job search in Louisville, Carl spent a month in Chicago working with O'Connor on shaping a program to expose the inquisitional nature of the FBI and the congressional investigating committees. In April, the newly reconstructed CCPAF proposed hiring Carl to direct a Chicago-based campaign organizing leftists and liberals to oppose the HUAC and its sister Senate committee. After conferring with Anne on the offer, Carl—wishing to counter what he described to O'Connor as the "male supremacy" that often underlay even movement work—insisted that he could accept only if the position could be made a joint one for both Bradens. His reply noted, "Anne must be given an equal role with me in this organization, or we will not come . . . I feel that my effectiveness is cut by two-thirds unless Anne and I are working together as a team . . . we complement each other and I need her brains and talent very badly.[9]

Their ultimatum met no opposition. In fact, O'Connor felt that a certain "tactlessness" on Carl's part would be effectively counterbalanced by Anne's diplomacy and commitment to inclusiveness. Her appeal was partly a matter of personal style. Anne's upbringing as a woman had left her with an attention to process, a social engineering ability that enhanced interpersonal relations in any group with whom she worked. Yet it was more than that too. Anne had a certain charm because she was so obviously a southern white woman of elite background. Her femaleness was reaffirmed by her physical attractiveness; her class background, by her polished manners; her southern-ness, by her broad accent every time she opened her mouth. For northern leftists of this era, female leadership was enough of a rarity, but there was an almost exotic quality about a genteel southern white woman so passionately opposed to racism and enamored of Marxian thought. The icing on the cake was that she was eloquent enough to be able to maintain a dialogue with more moderate souls. O'Connor told her, "Your participation increases the committee's appeal 100%."[10]

These job prospects were an improvement over their current situation, but Anne continued to have misgivings about leaving Louisville and the South. She maintained a deep affection for the city of her birth. Yet it was more than just a sense of home and family connections that motivated Anne to want to remain in the South. Her experience with the Wade purchase had strengthened her view that segregation must be demolished, and she felt a sort of urgency, as a white southerner, to stand with blacks in the new struggles they waged in the aftermath of *Brown*. Numerically, white integrationist voices were sufficiently few that each one counted, in her opinion: *While we were absorbed in the case and our survival, the whole new civil rights movement burst forth in the South. Just from the little bit of traveling we had done around the case, the disturbing thing [we saw] was that there seemed to be so few white people who were openly supporting the movement. This new black movement just made it so obvious that some whites had to catch up with this history that was moving so fast. I have been the main push on this, but Carl was committed to it too. I knew white people were there somewhere, and we had to get to them. A lot of the whites who had been active earlier in the South had been caught in the witch hunts and run out.*[11]

Anne's budding friendship with Montgomerians Aubrey Williams and Virginia Durr had meant a lot to her throughout her recent troubles, and she wrote now for advice to Williams, who had faced red-baiting of his own since the final days of the New Deal. Williams was intensely sympathetic to white southerners who had been through the fire for their beliefs on race. He reinforced her determination to stay in the South when he wrote back with typical dramatic flair, urging them not to leave the place "where you have sown your blood in the streets and in the courts and in the prisons . . . under any circumstances except on a stretcher." Anne's conviction carried the day, and stay they did, not just in the South but in Louisville. They continued to participate in the CCPAF campaign but did not accept employment in it.[12]

A Job with SCEF

Anne's plight had moved Williams as more than just a friend. As the president of SCEF, he was always on the lookout for new foot soldiers for racial reform. He discussed with Jim Dombrowski, SCEF's executive director, the idea of dipping into the group's $15,000 savings fund to hire the Bradens. Having noted in the wake of the *Brown* decision that "SCEF must expand or die," Dombrowski—who had long felt the weight of being the fund's only staff person—readily agreed.[13]

As a civil rights group that consciously identified itself as southern, SCEF had come under continual heat for being "communistic," just as its predecessor, the Southern Conference for Human Welfare, had. SCEF had been sustained through 11 stormy years of existence mostly through the efforts of Williams and Dombrowski. Williams—whose ouster from the Truman administration because of his leftist leanings was probably one basis of the subsequent attacks on SCEF—was a strange blend of personal anticommunist and political civil libertarian, a former social worker of working-class Alabama origins who fervently opposed racial hierarchy and never bought into the logic of liberal anticommunism (though he privately ranted about "Communist devils").[14]

After his return to Alabama, Williams applied himself fully to building integrationist support through SCEF, and he had a few successes through some important political contacts from his days in government. The most influential was Eleanor Roosevelt, whose interest in civil rights had led her, after attending the founding meeting of the SCHW in 1938, to maintain a connection with SCEF that by 1957 was peripheral but significant for fundraising purposes.[15]

In his post as director, Dombrowski had built a fundraising base in the Northeast that kept SCEF afloat as he catalogued support for integration in the pages of its monthly *Southern Patriot*. Dombrowski also traveled the South, visiting SCEF supporters and appearing on radio talk shows. But his abilities were hampered by being just one person with limited resources in the face of ongoing opposition and, now, the surging mob spirit fomented by the White Citizens' Councils brought to life by the changes portended in *Brown*.[16]

SCEF's militancy was a carryover from that of its parent SCHW, which was rooted in the Old Left—specifically in an interracial (but white-led) Popular Front coalition with an economic reform agenda and composed of trade unionists, liberals, New Dealers, Socialists, and a handful of CP members. After the 1948 demise of SCHW, Dombrowski turned SCEF's focus solely on segregation, an issue that, its predecessor had found, undermined any program of economic reform. Although SCEF sought to end segregation, its leaders never abandoned the vision of broader economic and social reform that had launched the southern conference movement. Like SCHW, SCEF retained a Popular Front style of politics, which is probably what kept it going in the post-*Brown* era.[17]

Still white-led but with direction now from blacks on the board, SCEF had more in common with the moral idealism of the new civil rights movement that would emerge in the 1960s than it did with the "pragmatic, self-consciously anticommunist liberalism" of its closest southern counterpart in those years, the Southern Regional Council (SRC). Just as SCEF was descended from SCHW, SRC was a derivative of the older Commission on Interracial Cooperation, whose program had emphasized limited social contacts between the races. Based in Atlanta, SRC was a regional think tank that considered itself "liberal" on race but floundered internally for five years after its 1944 founding because of an unwillingness to denounce segregation head-on. When it finally went on record against segregation—timidly in 1949, more forcefully in 1951—many white supporters who had once thought of themselves as liberal fled the group, unwilling to break so drastically with racial conventions. An important role SRC played in regional reform was to sponsor biracial human relations committees in southern states to overcome the long-standing racial divide. In practical terms, although a few individuals worked with both groups, SRC had always been more "gradualist," as Aubrey William phrased it, than either SCHW or SCEF, which emphasized a more grassroots model of social change. Because both organizations sought to generate white southern support for racial realignment, most SRC members viewed SCEF as a rival that was too radical. They were not above joining or even initiating attacks upon it. In the 1950s, SRC issued publications critical of segregation, often using liberal anticommunism as the rationale for the enactment of greater racial democracy even as it, like other civil rights groups, fought the widely applied "red" label from southern society at large.[18]

By the time Anne first heard of SCEF in the early 1950s, the organization's resources were severely strained by the increasing assaults on it, which were given greater legitimacy than they had been a decade earlier. Although there were no known members of the CP in SCEF by the mid-'50s, its failure to outlaw communists from its ranks made it an ongoing target of controversy. The 1954 anticommunist investigation by Senator Eastland's committee in New Orleans had a ripple effect that was enhanced by the kind of rhetoric emerging from a medley of new segregationist publications that sprang up after 1955. If anything, opposition to SCEF's work was even fiercer in post-*Brown* years, although, ironically, the attacks on SCEF also gave it a kind of visibility in the press that made it seem to threaten segregation. Out of necessity, SCEF had become an organization that connected civil rights and civil liberties. It was never listed in any federal government reports as a "Communist front," or even as "subversive." All subsequent charges stemmed from the HUAC report on the Southern Conference that had been issued earlier—and from innuendo, speculation, and highly publicized inquiries like the one in New Orleans. Yet in the collective southern mind, the taint lingered.[19]

The citizen support SCEF had hoped to build for the *Brown* decision never crystallized amid the rise of segregationist sentiment. In the late 1950s, Aubrey Williams's Alabama publishing business foundered and failed when contracts pulled out in the increasingly polarized atmosphere on race. Integration activism was not for the faint of heart. By 1957, *Patriot* subscriptions had dropped from a 1943 peak of 29,000 to 2,200, though major universities and libraries continued to subscribe.[20]

Anne and Carl possessed the same sort of idealism that motivated SCEF, and they had demonstrated the pluck to withstand repression. After securing support from the organization's biracial board, Williams and Dombrowski offered the Bradens jobs. In June 1957 Anne and Carl took the train to Birmingham, where they met with the two men to discuss the matter. *Aubrey said to us, "What we need is people. I know there are more white people around the South that think like we do, but you have to get out and find them. They are not going to come to us. We need to go out and beat the bushes and find people, and that's what we want you and Carl to do."* . . . *And so we became traveling agitators.*[21]

In Birmingham the Bradens also had the opportunity to meet Fred Shuttlesworth, Birmingham's powerhouse civil rights leader whom they knew only by his reputation for unflinching courage. The group met at the Gaston Hotel, where Shuttlesworth and his family were living while their house was being rebuilt after a Christmas 1956 racist bombing. *We got in a cab and went out to see his church. I remember riding along, and he said, "You know this is illegal? We aren't supposed to be riding in a cab together."*[22]

Anne saw the twinkle in Shuttlesworth's eye when he remarked on their cab ride together. She liked him immediately, and he would be a close ally and friend for the rest of her life. Shuttlesworth would also become SCEF's most important link to the emerging black movement. He joined the SCEF board in 1958 and made frequent appearances on its behalf thereafter, becoming its president in 1963. He raised funds which were shared by SCEF and his Alabama Christian Movement for Human Rights (ACMHR), the organization

he created to get around the statewide ban on the NAACP. (ACMHR ultimately became the Alabama arm of the Southern Christian Leadership Conference.) The ongoing repression Shuttlesworth faced in Birmingham made
him well situated to make the connections between civil rights and civil liberties that Anne and Carl felt were a prerequisite to real change in the South.
Impressed by what he knew of the Bradens' sedition case, Shuttlesworth was
drawn to the them partly because of his strong belief that "white people were
the missing link" in achieving civil rights. He sensed that the couple's dedication to racial justice came close to matching his own and was struck by their
humility: they never even mentioned the Rone Court incident. From his observation in Birmingham that "anybody who believed in integration was a
communist," the Bradens' reputation in southern white political culture was of
little consequence to him.[23]

Continuing to be based in Louisville, the couple began their SCEF work
on a part-time basis right after the meeting. Full-time employment started in
September 1957. Their titles were "field secretaries," and as was their prefer-
ence, they shared equally the job and a joint salary of $80 per week plus travel
expenses, office supplies, and telephone costs. The first order of business was
to obtain a reliable used car to use for fieldwork, an initial outlay borne by
SCEF. That fall the couple took possession of a black 1953 Ford sedan.[24]

The Bradens' informal plan was for Carl to do the bulk of travel while
Anne stayed at home more often with the children, doing what limited travel
she could manage and taking over the editorship of the *Southern Patriot*, which
she hoped to transform into more of an actual newspaper dedicated to racial
progress. Anne had more projects than she did time, a pattern that was becoming habitual. In addition to helping Carl set up the SCEF field operation from
their house in mid-1957, Anne spent the next few months putting the finishing
touches on the manuscript that was to become *The Wall Between*. To deal with
the couple's backlogged finances, she continued to work part time at the Kling
Company for several months after the SCEF job began. With young children
also needing her, what was most often sacrificed was sleep. The result was that
Anne was perpetually keyed up, running on her "McCarty drive."[25]

Upon starting work for SCEF, what the couple found was *a small operation, very beleaguered, very much under attack, but it was like a voice crying in the
wilderness in the South in those days.* That was a voice Anne was committed to
keeping alive. She considered it vital to sustain some white support, however
limited it might be, for the African American freedom movement that had
broken through what she thought of later as *the pall of the '50s.* SCEF had the
perfect blend of militancy and idealism to suit her, and its inclusion of civil

liberties in a civil rights agenda echoed the emphasis she and Carl saw as essential. Once she became more familiar with the organization's past, she also identified closely with its history, reading all she could find about the early days of the Southern Conference and soaking up stories told by people like Dombrowski and Virginia Durr, whose work had bridged both SCHW and SCEF. Anne's "other America," the spiritual home she had first heard of from William Patterson, came to be lodged in SCEF as the current incarnation of what she (and later historians of it) called the "southern conference movement." The vision of both SCEF and SCHW, as Anne saw it, was informed by a radical interracialism, rooted in the Old Left, with race as the fulcrum toward a broader economic and social justice. Her own politics were also a product of that vision. It had been at the very heart of the painful political transformation she had gone through only a decade before.[26]

Involving southern whites in an interracial action group was a tall order, particularly at a time when dissenters from the existing racial order risked, at best, social ostracism and, at worst, violence or legal and economic reprisals. Leaders of the new segregationist movement believed (as Anne did, with different conclusions) that there was no middle ground in relation to civil rights, and White Citizens' Councils had rushed to recruit the uncommitted southern whites who were in the majority in those years. Their aggressive campaigning—which coupled any questioning of southern racial norms with a kind of regional disloyalty—attempted to line up white southerners in a unified defense of segregation. In many communities this strategy found success for a time.

That much was already apparent to the Bradens when they joined the SCEF staff. They got more details about the job they faced when they visited SCEF supporters in 13 southern states in mid-1958. Carl and Anne met with about 200 integrationists, black and white, as well as with a few segregationists who were willing to discuss their beliefs. While they found encouragement in the black and white *stirrings* favoring integration in nearly every community they visited, with a *potential for a really meaningful interracial integrationist movement*, they also documented a lack of *common outlook* and alarming levels of isolation and feelings of *futility*. SCEF's attempt to build integrationist support was complicated, of course, by the fact that it was not even a membership organization and by its being one of the most heavily red-baited entities in the 1950s South.[27]

Another obstacle—a more surprising one to Carl and Anne—to organizing antisegregationist white southerners lay in the paternalism that had traditionally governed white liberals' working relations with African American activists. Longtime southern white supporters of a gradual "racial progress" such as that espoused by Mark Ethridge and the *Courier-Journal* had a hard time adjusting to the impatient upsurge of black leaders in the post-WWII era who by the mid-1950s were, as Anne noted in a report, *militant . . . people who have fully committed themselves to ending segregation and who will not be swayed by threats or intimidation or violence.* At a time that called for a corresponding militancy by white integrationists, few at the grassroots level were able both to withstand the red-baiting assaults and to take what seemed a further risk of meeting the new black leadership on an equal footing. The SCEF supporters Anne and Carl met were mostly older people who had been active in New Deal–era Southern Conference activity. More recently, many had been cowed by the fury of segregationist discourse into a moderation that pushed the limits of possibility among whites yet was hard for blacks to take.[28]

Anne and Carl welcomed the death of what they called the *pattern of paternalism.* But they realized that its collapse was a process that, for southerners of both races but especially whites, required a complete social and psychological reorientation after a lifetime of being indoctrinated with the notion that blacks were inferior. During this period Anne came to place great value on the emergence of an independent black freedom movement, which the 1957 founding of the Southern Christian Leadership Conference (SCLC)—with Martin Luther King, Jr. as its head—seemed to foretell.[29]

Under these conditions, the most that SCEF could hope was to provide a *rallying point for the most forward-looking people in the South.* The most immediate need was to strengthen communication among blacks and whites within localities. Those strong enough to resist were subjected to tremendous social isolation, often feeling that they were alone in their views—a sentiment Anne remembered only too well from her Birmingham days and intended to counter by providing a more visible, sustained regional support network for like-minded whites. This meant additional contacts by mail and in person, as well as more regional opportunities to gather.[30]

The isolation experienced by civil rights supporters was not limited to whites either. Although they were more likely to get support from their families and community institutions, African Americans also sometimes felt alone in their efforts. Plus, they faced sustained repression from segregationists, and most knew no other kind of whites. The opportunity to meet with such obviously committed integrationists as Anne, Carl, and Dombrowski went a long way toward generating confidence in SCEF among African Americans. The majority of blacks and whites inhabited largely separate worlds, especially in the Deep South, as they had throughout southern history. There were exceptions, but even there, interracial socializing was kept tightly concealed from the majority culture. Anne and Carl resolved to build more of the kind of cross-racial alliances in SCEF that they had been part of in their days with the FE union. *We had a very clear concept that although our outreach was to whites, we were an interracial organization. Those first years when Carl and I were going to SCEF board meetings, one of our main jobs was to guarantee that there would be enough white people there so that it wasn't overwhelmingly black. So usually they were about half and half.*[31]

Yet all the white encouragement in the world was of limited value without some political realignment. Seeing greater enfranchisement as key to changing the shape of southern politics, the SCEF board hoped to get more deeply involved in black voter registration. To do so would require strengthening the working relationships between black civil rights workers and white supporters. The Bradens wanted to see more public events like the SCEF Conference on Voting Restrictions, which Anne coordinated in Washington in April 1958. It was a milestone for her: the biggest organizing task she had ever faced. That event, which drew nearly 1,000 concerned citizens from around the region to hear firsthand of the horrific obstacles faced by blacks attempting to register, put the couple in touch with increasing numbers of African Americans working in the face of incredible odds.[32]

Above all, money was needed to support new black voter registration campaigns. Consequently, Anne and Carl agreed to assist in SCEF fundraising, which would unavoidably be concentrated outside the region. They would continue to tap contacts they had established in the sedition case and others that Dombrowski had cultivated for years.[33]

When Anne and Carl met with Dombrowski and Williams in Birmingham and agreed to work for SCEF, Aubrey Williams sounded a warning to Anne. *He said, "This whole question of how you can get white people in the South to really deal with the issue of segregation has broken the hearts of most people who have tried. I just hope it doesn't break yours."*[34]

Far from breaking her heart, the struggle against racism became Anne's lifeblood. It did break the hearts of her parents, however. One of the greatest sorrows of Anne's life was the deep divide that separated her from her family of origin because her convictions and choices were at such odds with theirs. Her parents were horrified to learn of their daughter's new job. As Anne wrote later to Virginia Durr, with whom she shared the emotional turbulence of being a white southern woman dedicated to racial equality, *Mother and Daddy bore up pretty well through [the sedition case]. . . . They hoped against hope that [afterward] Carl and I would leave the South and start life over in some "respectable" channels. When instead we not only stayed but plunged deeper than ever into the integration struggle, it was just too much.*[35]

Throughout the mid-1950s and thereafter, Anne was as embattled from within her own family as she ever was by southern politicians. After she and Carl made news in Louisville, her brother Lindsay, then a career Naval officer, severed all ties with her, and they had no further contact for nearly 25 years. Family rumor had it that his advancement in the Navy was impeded by Anne's radicalism: though Anne never found proof of that, she did find out later from her FBI file that the Navy had indeed investigated him because he was her brother but had vindicated him when investigators concluded that the two no longer had contact.[36]

Anne's allegiance to social and racial change was solid, but so was her devotion to the McCartys. The unbridgeable divide between her and her parents was a source of unrelenting sadness and tension to her: *I felt only and always this terrible pain that I had to hurt them. There was no way I could avoid it without changing the whole direction of my life, which I could not do. But they had been so proud of me, and they had been good parents, always encouraging me to develop my talents—and to be independent of them too, because it never occurred to them that I would move into such a different world.* The McCartys would never think of disowning Anne, but they were full of vitriol on the subject of her politics and lifestyle, matters which they could hardly fail to take intensely personally. *I don't see how they could have been different,* Anne reflected years later. *They were born in the 1890s and grew up in a cocoon that told them this world they knew was forever . . . then racial tumult impinged on them—because of me—to an extent that few of their place in society ever experienced.*[37]

When *The Wall Between,* her memoir of the sedition case, appeared in 1958, Anne's mother begged her never to send copies to Anniston and assured her daughter that there was absolutely no support for her radical ideas there. The divide was more than just generational: few other white southerners of Anne's generation so thoroughly threw off the ideology of segregation with which they had been raised. The McCartys viewed the zeal with which their daughter and son-in-law pursued their convictions as a pathology, and reminded Anne often how hurtful her life course was to them.[38]

Anita and Gambrell McCarty would not—or could not—accept Anne's choices, particularly as they related to Jim and little Anita. Letters from one or the other of her parents arrived regularly, and they were full of innuendoes couched in a language of concern for the children and, secondarily, for Anne's health. The sedition case had first put Anne on the defensive in the larger society, but she now settled into a long-term lifestyle in which she had to develop a kind of inner steel with which to defend herself in the ongoing emotional war with her own parents. These battles were sometimes overt, more often subterranean, but they were never-ending and enormously draining for Anne. She rarely exposed the depth of that wound even to her closest friends. Because she also tried hard to avoid open conflict with her parents, there were a lot of silences between them, especially on the issues Anne cared most about. Confrontations occasionally erupted, however, as indicated in a 1959 letter to her mother—who often blamed Anne's political acts on an inflated sense of self-importance. *I do not feel that what I do alone is going to make a great deal of difference in the world. . . . I do have some unconquerable drive that tells me I must do my part . . . stand up for what I think is right, regardless of what anybody else does. And I know that if I don't live up to the demands of this drive, if I back down from what I feel is an important principle . . . I would not be able to get up in the morning and face the light of day. I would be no good to anybody, to my children or anybody else. . . . Better to be destroyed from without than within.*[39]

Rather than cutting or even diminishing her ties with her parents, Anne continued to leave her children with them regularly. Even with one grandparent (Carl's mother) nearby in Louisville, leaving Jimmy and Anita with the McCartys was essential in freeing Anne to do the field work both she and Carl loved, but it also kept a little more common ground between her and the McCartys. Anne acknowledged her reliance on her parents for child care, but she also held fast to the belief that her children's frequent stays in Anniston kept her parents from sinking into self-pity over what they saw as their daughter's tragic outcome. She wrote to a friend in the late 1950s, *My children are the one thing I can give my parents now, and I believe if they didn't have [the children] coming to visit occasionally, they really would decide life is useless. So I make every effort to get the children there as often as possible.* Perhaps she needed to feel that way to make the separations more palatable or to try and make up for the hurts the McCartys so often accused her of inflicting on them. Or maybe some part of her took to heart her parents' lack of faith in her ability to care for her children: if so, she never acknowledged it openly.[40]

Anita and Jim were four and six, respectively, when their parents took jobs as full-time regional organizers, and the family sacrifices required by such a lifestyle were not new to them. Though they had various other familial supports (their paternal grandmother, uncles and aunts nearby, and their Alabama grandparents only too glad to have them for vacations), the children continued to live in a household from which one parent was routinely missing for a week or two at a time and the other highly engrossed in public affairs as well as in caring for them. From the Braden children's perspectives as they grew older, their mother was just not the domestic figure that other mothers were, and though their household was loving, it was also full of disruptions.

When Jim and Anita first went to live temporarily with their grandparents in 1954, Anne's father had vowed to her that he would not try to indoctrinate them with his views on race. Although the McCartys tried to keep that promise throughout subsequent decades, their stint as stand-in parents for the Braden children gave rise to a protectiveness that constantly challenged Anne's authority to make her own decisions when they failed to square with what her parents understood the children's best interests to be. One such battle took place when Anne put Anita in their predominantly black neighborhood kindergarten, an action that drew a stream of protest from her parents but about which she stood firm. Anne realized that her parents used the children as a lever to try to make her change her life course, but she could not bring herself to put a stop to it. She acknowledged then and later on the subject of her children that *it could make their life very difficult*, as she wrote to her parents in the late '50s, to be *pulled between two worlds*. With such deep disagreements and pointed silences, that dynamic was virtually unavoidable, even amid the best of intentions.[41]

Strengthening Interracial Alliances

In spite of the criticism that hung over them like a cloud, the Bradens jumped into their new jobs of building southern support for the civil rights movement. They turned first to strengthening alliances with African Americans already working in the movement. Carl contacted E. D. Nixon, chair of the Montgomery NAACP, longtime unionist, and friend of Aubrey Williams. The Bradens had never met Nixon but knew him by reputation as a galvanizing figure in the bus boycott, the movement's most visible victory at that time. In fall 1957 Nixon accompanied Carl on a speaking trip to Chicago, which the Bradens had chosen as a fundraising base because of their preexisting contacts there. Carl continued the technique he and Anne had found successful in building support for their case: speaking at house parties organized by local contacts. The gatherings pulled in crowds of 60–100 each night, and with them needed dollars for both SCEF and the Montgomery movement. Nixon returned to Montgomery full of praise for Carl's organizing abilities, and he took on a larger advisory role on SCEF's board.[42]

On that tour, Carl and Nixon established the model "Friends of SCEF" group—the first of what would become a series of similar groups across the Northeast, Midwest, and West Coast. Their primary purpose was to raise funds for southern civil rights activities. In the South, the Bradens and Dombrowski expanded SCEF's grassroots network by creating an interracial "advisory committee" of 50–80 people who never "joined" SCEF (it never became a membership organization) but became like a second tier to the board.[43]

The Bradens' skills, together with their obvious dedication, made other southern activists sit up and take notice. When Anne visited the Highlander Folk School in September 1957 for its twenty-fifth anniversary celebration, she had her first opportunity to meet Martin Luther King, Jr. As the weekend ended, King needed a lift to a Baptist convention in Louisville, and his long car ride with Anne through the winding mountains of east Tennessee and Kentucky gave him the opportunity to hear not only about the Wade case but about her transformation to what would be called today an anti-racist. The two also reflected on the haunting quality of the song that the folksinger Pete Seeger had taught the gathering: "We Shall Overcome." It was the first time either of them had heard it. King later told his wife that he could not believe such a white woman existed, a response echoed by many African American leaders with whom Anne established close ties during this period. Anne's friendship with Martin and Coretta King solidified during the next few years as they became more convinced of her commitment and more critical of the sustained assaults on her intentions as "communistic." She and Carl sometimes stayed at their home when they passed through Atlanta.[44]

King shared Anne's commitment to interracialism: he once wrote to her that "the tension in the South is between justice and injustice rather than white people or Negro people." In 1959 he expressed the hope that the Bradens would become "permanently associated" with his organization, the Southern Christian Leadership Conference (SCLC). As King became a more recognized national and international figure in the 1960s, he fell under harsh criticism for associating with allegedly "communistic" activists like the Bradens, but he never disassociated from them and on occasion went out of his way to include them in spite of persistent opposition from other voices within SCLC.[45]

A few contacts led to others. Anne had met the African American reformer Ella Baker in 1955 in New York as she publicized her sedition charge, but had fallen out of touch. Around 1958 the two were reunited in Fred Shuttlesworth's kitchen in Birmingham. Baker, a longtime organizer who during this period was in the anomalous position of being the female director of a group of male ministers (SCLC), became a revered rights leader in the '60s. She was more than a decade older than Anne (as were most movement friends in those years). Yet the two both labeled themselves proudly as "radicals," and their shared political vision led to a close friendship. Baker was not worried about SCEF's subversiveness, and she found in the three SCEF staffers an informal yet respectful style that felt comfortable. For a time, in the 1960s, she even joined the SCEF staff. The first major project together came in January 1960 when Baker, on behalf of SCLC, and Carl, representing SCEF, coordinated public hearings with a "Voluntary Civil Rights Commission" in Washington as a way of publicizing the inadequacies of the U.S. Civil Rights Commission in the face of continued harassment of African Americans across the South who were attempting to register to vote. Cosponsored by SCEF, SCLC, and more than a dozen black-led southern civic groups, the hearings drew national media attention and affirmed SCEF's relevance to African American activists in spite of its size and beleaguered status.[46]

In the fall of 1957, at Dombrowski's request, Anne took over editing the *Patriot*. She began subscribing to the nation's most influential African American newspapers and supplementing the media list she and Carl had generated in their sedition fight. In January 1959 she doubled the publication's size, making it a tabloid, and began to offer a broader array of coverage of each month's most pressing civil rights and race-related developments. By this time, the Bradens had more or less divided up the region between the two of them in terms of responsibility for fieldwork. Carl took the majority of states, and Anne's major role was putting out the *Patriot*.

Once she was in the position of shaping editorial perspective and covering topics about which she cared passionately, all of Anne's misgivings about the supposed objectivity of journalism evaporated, and her love of putting out a newspaper reasserted itself. *I had to get out of the concept of running a daily paper. We weren't reporting the news but were trying to say what was significant. [Our readership consisted mainly of] people who were already in some way either interested in or committed to what the civil rights movement was about, whether they were doing anything or not.*[47]

When the Bradens came into SCEF, Dombrowski used the *Patriot* primarily as an organizing tool, and Anne expanded upon his approach. She added profiles of African American leaders such as Shuttlesworth and Nixon and solicited contributions from white supporters for regular features like

"Why I Believe in Integration." By the late 1950s she had just about tripled the paper's circulation. *You could write a story about somebody, and that gave you an excuse to go talk to people. So you got to know them, they began to come into your orbit, and then you could call on them to do other things. We built up what we called an action list. I believed in networking. I still do.*[48]

Anne used the power of the printed word as effectively as her small venue would allow. Whenever she featured a community action in the *Patriot*, she sent multiple copies of that issue to the locals. *Somebody's struggle is more real if they see it in print. An idea is real too if you see it in print. We probably overplayed when whites spoke up and did something, but we wanted to point that out. We wrote a lot, obviously, about black struggles. But if whites were doing anything, we said so. Once they saw something in print [and realized] it was significant enough for somebody to notice it, that made it more likely they could keep struggling.*[49]

Gradually the *Patriot* evolved into more of a real newspaper of the civil rights movement, fulfilling a dream Anne cherished of using journalism in service of southern social justice. After the sit-ins began in 1960, the *Patriot* followed each development closely, becoming for a time possibly the only media outlet in the region that was analytical yet supportive, reflecting the perspectives of activists themselves.[50]

In the late 1950s the South was not the headline news it became five years later when civil rights confrontations escalated into mass protests, jailings, and blatant violence that drew national television cameras. The Bradens' media skills were among the most valuable assets they brought to the developing movement. Not only did the *Patriot* assuage the isolation southern dissenters felt; it became a conduit of news on race for a variety of other small publications, especially for African American newspapers that were short-staffed and dependent on news services for stories. The Bradens' press contacts enabled them to get news out more widely even within the mainstream media. *One of the by-products that SCEF was able to develop was a . . . publicity machinery because in the '50s it was quite hard to get [press] attention, and a lot of times it was a matter of life and death to get the word out.*[51]

One such case was that of Shuttlesworth, who was the target of repeated violent repression by Birmingham whites. One of the worst instances took place when he and his wife attempted to enroll their children in all-white schools: Shuttlesworth was badly beaten, and Ruby Shuttlesworth was stabbed in the hip, but they refused to curtail their crusades against segregation. He reflected later that "if it had not been for Carl and Anne Braden, I'm sure I would have been dead already. We couldn't get the news out many times." Those were instances in which the Bradens' newspaper experience proved critical: *They couldn't put him in jail and beat him up under cover of darkness. He could always call us up and we'd get it on the wire services that Fred [had been] arrested. What we found out was that you couldn't get the local Associated Press or UPI to send out news about the black movement, but we could call people we knew on papers in other parts of the country and they would request that the AP or UPI do a story on Fred Shuttlesworth being in jail in Birmingham, for example. And that would break it loose.*[52]

From Shuttlesworth's travails and her own hellish memories of the place activists thought of as the "Johannesburg of North America," Anne believed that *if you could crack segregation in Birmingham, you could crack it anywhere.* The Bradens carried on a steady campaign, including a major 1959 pamphlet (titled "They Challenge Segregation at its Core") and mass media contacts that brought the Birmingham movement its first national attention—a pattern they then replicated in other locales. The couple typically did not use their bylines or even claim SCEF responsibility for publications such as these. Instead they worked quietly so as not to attract the negative publicity tag of "Communist-backed" that association with them might bring. Even Dombrowski, they felt on occasion, was too easygoing in printing the names of civil rights participants in SCEF mailings. Friends like Shuttlesworth did not necessarily need such protection, but not everyone was as vocal as he in standing up to those who would silence him.[53]

"How Can You Do This to Us?"

In the face of widespread repression and an abundance of popular stereotypes of southern white racists, the Bradens labored under no illusion as to the numerical strength of whites who felt as they did. They were determined, however, to increase the visibility of those white southerners who supported integration. Even in the left press, where racist incidents received more in-depth coverage, the couple found painfully little encouragement offered to southern integrationists, who all but disappeared in the gallons of ink devoted to massive resistance. That invisibility frustrated Anne and Carl and unwittingly placed them in a stance of regional defensiveness not totally dissimilar to that experienced by earlier generations of southern white liberals—though unlike them, the Bradens were quick to distance themselves from regional social conventions. Soon after they began working for SCEF, the couple chastised I. F. Stone for *lumping all southern whites into one big mass of white supremacy* in an October 1957 issue of *I. F. Stone's Weekly.* Anne explained her feelings in more detail in a 1958 letter to the *National Guardian* after the weekly ran an editorial deploring the lack of a modern-day "abolitionist movement." She wrote: *There is an abolitionist movement in the South today, among whites as well as Negroes. Certainly it is not as strong . . . unified and cohesive as we hope it will someday be. . . . [It is] almost an underground in a sense, many people working quietly . . . who are steadily eroding the soil that has nourished the roots of segregation while all around them the White Citizens' Councils are shouting that it's eternal.* The issue was not one of publicity, she felt, but of acknowledgment. In the 1950s, southern political culture glorified conformity to racial conventions to such an extent that it demanded a kind of racist solidarity among whites. Given the larger backdrop of the Cold War, those who resisted were subject to community censure and continual red-baiting. From her friend Virginia Durr, Anne learned in 1958 of a group of white Montgomery churchwomen who had arranged just one interracial meeting. The women's tentative outreach was nipped in the bud by segregationists who tailed them, copied down their license plate numbers, taunted them with obscene phone calls, and published the names and businesses of their husbands in a local Baptist newsletter affiliated with the Citizens' Council. The women were denounced as part of a "Communist-Jewish conspiracy," and many were harangued by their own family members to the point that they distanced themselves from the cause altogether.[54]

The Bradens understood the importance of instilling greater confidence in those few who went against the grain of white racism, themselves included. As Anne reflected years later, *The attacks were so constant, you began to wonder sometimes about your own motivations.* The couple's own inner doubts were only occasional because they were sufficiently countered by the network of supporters they had across the nation. Yet their first regional field trip in 1958 had convinced Carl and Anne that integrationists in rural southern towns often had no external affirmation. As Anne explained of her generation and those who had come before her, *There was a certain amount of physical terror and economic pressure, but one of the greatest pressures that was brought on white people in the South was, "How can you do this to us?"* Her observations derived in part from her own family conflicts. She sometimes felt that she wrote the same letter to her parents over and over for decades, and she knew in her bones that community ostracism could whittle away one's resiliency when there was no counterbalancing support for going against the grain of white supremacy.[55]

She saw a tragic outcome of such alienation in 1959. From Virginia Durr, Anne learned of a white Montgomery librarian named Juliette Morgan who had taken her own life under such pressures. Morgan, Anne learned, was a devout Episcopalian who had throughout the post-WWII era found segregation hopelessly at odds with her religious principles, and had heard of SCEF and corresponded briefly with Dombrowski in the early 1950s. Virtually the only local white to write to the daily newspaper in support of the 1955 bus boycott, Morgan had been the first to draw a parallel between that action and Gandhi's nonviolent movement in India. Her letter drew threats and harassment, and she yielded to the public library's request that she desist from further displays of pro-integration sentiment. But after the violence against Autherine Lucy at the University of Alabama, Morgan wrote a private letter to the publisher of the *Tuskegee News*, praising his courage in publicly criticizing the university. That letter, reproduced as a flyer by the Montgomery Citizens' Council, brought her into the public eye again. In the resulting controversy, Morgan got little support even from those who admired her positions, and she committed suicide at the age of 43 in 1957, unable to face relentless family and community disapproval.[56]

Morgan's story held particular poignancy for Anne because the two had grown up with similarities of race, class, and value systems, both strongly imbued with a sense of southern identity. Like Anne, Juliette Morgan had forged a critique of southern racial practices which had burst forth under the energy of new African American challenges to segregation. Unlike Anne, however, Morgan had been alone in her dissent, at least among those about whom she cared most. In a letter to Virginia Durr, Anne explained why she found Morgan's case *haunting*. She felt that *I could so easily have been Juliette Morgan. . . . There was so much in her early life that was just like mine: the same intellectual bent in a society that puts little premium on these things for women, and yet approves of and helps her as long as she stays within certain bounds. . . . If I had gone back to Anniston to live . . . it is highly likely my life would have developed in much the same way hers did. I would have identified myself with liberal efforts, as she did, while there was still a respectable liberal movement to identify with. And then in this recent period, when pseudo-liberalism folded its tent and stole away, there would undoubtedly have come a time when, alone perhaps, I would have had to take some stand, as she did. I would have been subjected to the same pressures she was—a family that would have made me feel I was ruining their lives, vicious attacks from people I had known all my life. . . . Like her, I would have been unequipped to meet it.*[57]

Anne wrote an article for the *Patriot* on Morgan that never actually ran until after the student sit-ins had begun, bringing with them a sort of vindication of Morgan's support for nonviolent resistance. For months Anne contemplated writing a longer piece on Morgan, either in fiction or as part of what she described to Durr as *a collection . . . on some of the personalities being thrown into dramatic focus by the present crisis in the South.* That idea appealed to the

strong sense of history that captivated Anne once she gave her life over to social justice activism. She considered the experiences of many she encountered
in this crucible of race in the South to be either extraordinarily heroic or
equally tragic, and she wished to document them. Her idea for the collection
never found form, though the pathos of Morgan's life continued to carry an
emotional resonance for her. Instead Anne's immediacy led her to more direct
organizing work, through which she chronicled as many of these stories as she
could in the *Patriot*.[58]

School Desegregation

Across the South, the *Brown* decision had crystallized white opposition to
school desegregation, but it had also generated some limited community support. Because of sustained resistance mobilized through entities like the White
Citizens' Councils, progress toward southern school integration was minus-
cule in 1956. Several school districts in the upper and border South attempted
to comply, and by 1957 the number grew, even as the opposition flamed and
other southern districts closed their doors rather than desegregate.[59]

One of those struggles took place not far from Louisville, in the western
Kentucky towns of Clay, Sturgis, and Henderson. In 1956, before starting
work for SCEF and still caught up in the sedition fight, Anne heard of the
achievements of two white ministers in Henderson, where the White Citizens'
Council was organizing a boycott of newly desegregated schools. Sumpter
Logan, a Presbyterian pastor and president of the local Ministerial Association, and Theodore Braun, a United Church of Christ minister, were supporters of desegregation who realized their views were way out in front of most of
their community. The two were unable to convince the Ministerial Association to actually affirm school integration, but they persuaded it to go on
record as opposing the boycott. Within a week the boycott collapsed.[60]

Anne managed to write stories for the *Patriot* and the *National Guardian*
on Braun's and Logan's success. The dissolution of the white boycott—and the
subsequent decision by state government to uphold school desegregation
there (contrary to the outcomes in Clay and Sturgis)—convinced Anne of the
frailty of massive resistance. *Jim [Dombrowski] asked me to go down there [to western Kentucky] and see what was happening. You have to remember that our names
were fire words in Kentucky. But when I met Ted Braun, he was so delighted to talk to
someone who was sympathetic, he wasn't bothered about being scared.* Braun, a longtime member of the Fellowship of Reconciliation, a pacifist group, was a kindred spirit. When he saw Anne's story, he was bolstered by the positive

meaning she had attached to what he and Logan had thought of as a renegade act. Anne and Braun corresponded often after she joined the SCEF staff, and he soon was contributing to the *Patriot* himself.[61]

After her 1957 visit to Highlander School, Anne developed a working relationship with Septima Clark, an African American educator from South Carolina who worked in Highlander's civil rights program. Clark was organizing a support group—a Thanksgiving 1957 weekend workshop at Highlander—to draw together black families from across the South with children in desegregated schools. Careful to stay in a background capacity so as not to arouse opposition, Anne put Clark in touch with Jim Crumlin of the Kentucky NAACP and identified families from Louisville, Henderson, and Clay to attend the workshop. Clark later came to Louisville at Anne's invitation to give a talk. She never forgot Anne and Carl's insistence that their guest take their bed—a simple gesture of courtesy but one few whites would make, in Clark's experience.[62]

SCEF's position of unqualified support for integration not as a necessary evil but as a positive good was more progressive than that of most southern civic organizations of the mid-1950s. Movements supporting public education drew in significant numbers of whites in Virginia, Georgia, and other southern states, but that was as far as most would go. The Bradens saw the moderate path as highly problematic, even in areas like Louisville where school desegregation proceeded relatively uneventfully. Anne first remarked on the subject in a 1957 letter to Clark: *We've got a limited sort of desegregation in the schools—but we don't have integration, if you see what I mean. There's too much of an attitude of people just putting up with something, and mighty few taking a more creative approach . . . for real democratic living.* Her conclusion anticipated conversations that still resonate in the twenty-first century. Anne worried that unless southern society truly embraced integration, *we are going to end up with something too much like what many of the northern cities have—no segregation by law but segregation in fact.*[63]

In addition to her SCEF work on school desegregation, Anne had a more personal stake in the issue after her son Jim started attending Virginia Avenue Elementary in 1957. In most cases in Louisville's system, it was African American children who attended majority-white schools, but in the quickly changing residential composition of the West End, Anne and Carl enrolled Jim and later Anita in their neighborhood school, only to find they were the only white children. The couple never even considered making a transfer request, as all other whites in their neighborhood had done. Determined that her family would benefit from the experience of interracialism, Anne worked with some success to prevent white flight in her neighborhood. Starting in 1958, she also became a leader in the Parent-Teacher Association, hoping to promote a positive interracial environment in the children's school.[64]

Movement Halfway House

The contributions SCEF was able to make to the cause of racial equality were limited by its reputation as "subversive" and by its lack of people and money. There were precious few white southerners who would embrace the cause of civil rights in the Cold War years and fewer still who would risk association with an organization so surrounded by controversy. Yet SCEF became a "movement halfway house" (as the sociologist Aldon Morris has described it) that formed a crucial pillar of support for the movement's development by providing various forms of assistance.[65]

One form of that aid was the greater media attention that Anne and Carl were able to direct to African American protest. Another was in shoring up financially, morally, or both the brave few who spoke out in the face of enormous pressure against doing so. In the Mississippi Delta, where there were not many people fearless enough to ride out the persistent violence and intimidation that invariably accompanied black civil rights agitation, SCEF support in the 1950s proved essential in sustaining Amzie Moore, an activist Anne and others saw as a *spark plug*.[66]

Igniting the black freedom movement took more than money. It took courage. Amzie Moore had plenty of the latter but too little of the former to sustain his small business in Cleveland, Mississippi, once he took over the presidency of the local NAACP and began defying white supremacy directly. Returning to the Delta after WWII service, Moore had spent several years saving for his own business, convinced that black economic progress would shake loose long-standing racial restrictions. In 1954 he opened a small shopping center containing a service station, cafe, and beauty shop. But by early 1958, when he met the Bradens at the SCEF Conference on Voting Restrictions, Moore's business—and thus his organizing base—were on the verge of collapse. His recruitment for voter education classes and refusal to place "Colored Only" signs on his property had earned him white reprisals: a boycott of his gas pumps, denial of loans, and curtailment of his part-time employment at the Cleveland Post Office.[67]

A visit to the Delta in 1958 further convinced the Bradens of the significance of Moore's work and of the voter education school he had helped to initiate. Any alliance with Moore, Carl wrote, "will mean a big step forward" for black progress in the Delta—and for SCEF. Accordingly, Amzie Moore was placed on the SCEF payroll at the salary of $100 per month for four months, providing him with a means to remain in Cleveland and a mandate to "increase registration and voting in Mississippi and to cooperate with others working in the field." As a longer range cure for Moore's precarious finances, Jim Dombrowski raised nearly $19,000 to refinance Moore's business and secure him some professional management training.[68]

These were contributions that might seem indirect or even insignificant. Moore never became a SCEF representative in any real sense. His primary affiliation had been and remained the NAACP (Moore had built NAACP membership in Cleveland to 439, making it the second largest chapter in the state in 1956 despite its being a bad year for the association nationally and a growth year for Citizens' Councils). Yet keeping Amzie Moore in the Delta proved pivotal in bringing about long-term change in Mississippi. Moore was a key player who made possible what became a civil rights revolution with the arrival of student civil rights workers in the 1960s.[69]

There were others like Moore with whom Anne and Carl crossed paths in their SCEF organizing. In January 1960, the Voluntary Civil Rights Commission hearings that Carl organized with Ella Baker in Washington introduced the Bradens to John McFerren and the struggle he and others were waging in two west Tennessee counties bordering Mississippi. With 7,000 voting-age blacks in the area, not one was registered to vote; in fact, no black had successfully registered in 75 years. In 1959 McFerren—who ran a combination grocery store/gas station—and a handful of others set up an organization and won through the courts the right to register. Yet by the time they approached SCEF for help, an economic boycott had caused them to lose their homes and farms, and local whites had enlisted national oil companies in squeezing McFerren out by refusing to sell him fuel. Through SCEF, Anne and Carl bought tents for the "Tent City" the evictees set up and alerted SCEF supporters to send protest letters to the oil companies. Dombrowski directed information about the crisis to Eleanor Roosevelt, who wrote about it in her syndicated column.[70]

When the farmers faced an eviction hearing in Cincinnati (two hours from Louisville) that December, Anne phoned her friend Maurice McCrackin, a Presbyterian minister active in the radical pacifist group Peacemakers. McCrackin mobilized a large turnout for the hearing, and—moved by what he heard there—visited the Tennessee community. His visit and consultations with the Bradens led to the establishment of "Operation Freedom," a long-term program of material and spiritual aid for the struggling west Tennessee organizers and another small "movement halfway house." During the 1960s and beyond, Operation Freedom provided funds to sustain beleaguered civil rights workers in trouble spots across the region. As Operation Freedom and other groups moved in to offer support to west Tennessee blacks, Anne and Carl moved on to lesser-known crises, but they stayed in touch with McFerren and continued to advise Operation Freedom.[71]

Logging nearly 30,000 miles per year from 1957 to 1959, Anne and Carl worked tirelessly to strengthen what small pockets of white integrationist activity they could find, and their passionate commitment to interracialism led them to intensify cooperative projects with African American leaders that grew more ambitious as the civil rights movement blossomed. They possessed an exuberance that tended to, as Anne admitted, *remake SCEF in our own image*. To many in communities across the South—for better or for worse—the Bradens were SCEF.[72]

Their determination and steeliness brought new internal divisions to the organization, however. Conflicts soon emerged between Aubrey Williams and the new field organizers, especially Carl. Williams never renounced capitalism to the extent that the Bradens did, but the differences were more personality clashes than they were political. Carl and Williams were both brash, impatient, and what Anne called *rugged individualists* at heart.[73]

The biggest tension, predictably, was financial. Anne and Carl—frustrated by having to do so much fundraising outside the South that it impaired their fieldwork—pushed the organization to establish a permanent fundraising committee in New York (the geographic source of most of their revenue) and to hire a full-time fundraiser. Williams, whose idea of fundraising involved personally tapping a few wealthy promoters annually, objected, but Dombrowski and the board agreed. When the Bradens' friend Howard Melish emerged as the only candidate willing to work for such a small salary, Williams objected again, this time to Melish's identification with left-wing causes. Though Williams had once embraced the Bradens in similar circumstances, the intervening two years had taken their toll on his resiliency: now, for the first time, he argued that SCEF should adopt an anticommunist plank.[74]

Because of Dombrowski's support, Melish was hired anyway, but it left Williams bitter. Unfortunately, it also cost SCEF Eleanor Roosevelt, the single most important figurehead in its funding operation. Roosevelt sided with Williams: she wrote that SCEF "had a hard enough time without employing such a controversial figure." Although she attended two more SCEF receptions in New York, she officially severed her connection with the group in 1960 after a former CP member whom she despised appeared at that year's reception. Melish was vindicated too, after a fashion, however, when he demonstrated himself highly capable, generating $20,000 in less than six months on the payroll.[75]

Ironically, perhaps, considering his stand on Melish, what probably defined Williams's difficulties, more than anything else, by 1959 was his increasing despondency over the many personal losses he had sustained for the cause of racial reform. His sense of betrayal grew so deep that at times it was ill placed—as with the disdain he voiced for Martin Luther King, Jr.'s emerging leadership. Anne and Carl thought highly of King, and they could see that alliance with him was a virtual necessity to be relevant to the cause of civil rights. They argued with Williams about inviting King to join the SCEF board, but the disagreement continued until Williams retired from SCEF.[76]

Anne respected Williams enormously, and her careful mediation managed to keep an uneasy peace between him and Carl. After years of harassment and with the prodding of people like Dombrowski and Anne, Williams left Alabama to pursue a new and fresher outlet for his activism as the 1960s opened: back in Washington with the Capitol Hill networks he loved as a leader of the newly established National Committee to Abolish HUAC (NCAHUAC). He resigned the SCEF presidency in late 1961 on cordial terms with Anne and, to a lesser extent, Carl.[77]

Cold War against Southern Dissenters

The Montgomery bus boycott broke through the pall of the 1950s to reassert the power of collective social action, but the anticommunist and prosegregationist campaigns that swept the South with a vengeance during that period left southern black activists with painfully few white supporters. As Anne's friend Al Maund quipped with more than a touch of bitterness after he was virtually run out of Montgomery for having written an article for the Federated Press that showed up in the CP's *Daily Worker,* "there ain't no room for positive action in these parts. It's all defensive."[78]

Civil rights activism frequently earned one a "blacklisting" like the one that sent Maund packing from the region. Those who stayed faced employment problems, social isolation, or, on occasion, violence. Claudia Sanders's home in South Carolina was dynamited in 1958, for example, after she condemned segregation in an essay for an anthology on race titled *South Carolinians Speak.* Sustained harassment most often prompted a kind of exile that was not unlike that which had driven out nineteenth-century abolitionists and racial critics such as Angelina Grimke and, after the Civil War, George Washington Cable. The difference in the 1950s and '60s was the "communist" label.[79]

It took stalwart souls to keep going against the grain because the punishment appeared never-ending. One attack typically provided the basis for subsequent ones—a cycle that could go on for years, as Anne and Carl were finding. The point of origin for smearing an individual or organization was often nothing more than a report generated by one of the congressional investigating committees and based on the testimonies of paid ex-CP witnesses. Impeding integrationists' work by Communist smears which then necessitated a campaign of self-defense rather than an offensive for civil rights was a widely used stalling tactic of segregationist-minded politicians and editors in the 1950s, particularly against whites. The age-old strategy of violent intimidation remained popular as a deterrent to black activists, who were nevertheless increasingly adamant in their demands for change. Whether opinion-makers acted out of a genuine fear of suspected Communists or merely to discredit any civil rights efforts by local whites, their actions had the latter effect, and the attacks intensified as pro–civil rights activity by both African Americans and the federal government escalated throughout the 1950s.[80]

Carl and Anne soon discovered that SCEF's notoriety or their own reputations as seditionists preceded them around the South, especially in small towns. The couple had to get used to a kind of "thanks but no thanks" from white liberals seeking to avoid suspect associations. More than once, Anne found herself asked not to cover a local development for the *Patriot* because of the negative publicity even that distant a relation with SCEF might carry. It was not uncommon for her to find herself derided in the southern or even national press. An October 1958 piece by David Lawrence, an archconservative syndicated columnist, resurrected Hamilton's theory of the Shively bombing as a possible explanation for the outbreak of dynamitings ripping apart southern synagogues and black churches, and Anne and Carl found themselves touted nationally as violent Communist hatemongers.[81]

The shadow of the sedition charge stayed with them most acutely in Louisville. Scott Hamilton harangued them publicly at every opportunity, but in mid-1957 Carl appealed personally to the Kentucky Court of Appeals and secured the release of a portion of their hundreds of books taken as evidence in the fall of 1954. In September, as the court debated returning the remaining mountain of books, Hamilton called a news conference to announce a possible perjury indictment against Carl. Nothing came of it, however, and the remainder of the books were released that fall, along with some unfamiliar volumes the Bradens believed the government had planted for evidence against them. All were *properly marked "government's exhibit" and signed by the court reporter,* Anne jokingly wrote to a friend. The couple proudly displayed the returned books on a bookshelf in their living room and dispensed souvenir copies of the more obscure ones to visitors.[82]

Although local interest had long since subsided for the sedition drama, Hamilton's zeal for rooting out communists continued to guide his actions. In October 1957 he and Alberta Ahearn testified at regional hearings on subversive activities—"Communism in the Mid-South"—called by Eastland's Senate subcommittee. For these sessions, held in Memphis and chaired by Indiana Republican Senator Jenner in Eastland's absence, the subcommittee had subpoenaed a number of southern civil rights sympathizers who were connected in one way or another to causes thought to be "communistic" or to figures previously identified as CP members. Some of these connections were to SCEF, Anne, and Carl.[83]

Already outcasts in Louisville, when the Bradens went to work for an outcast organization, it was a decision more or less guaranteed to rain down on them further stigmatization by the larger society. Although Carl was not subpoenaed to Memphis, "his presence overshadowed the hearings," according to the historian Sarah Brown, and Anne did not escape mention either. Hamilton replayed his Louisville performance, emphasizing the threat that SCEF posed to southern security. Ahearn echoed those themes by detailing the litany of racial justice causes she had allegedly embraced during her days as a paid FBI Communist.[84]

From the Memphis hearings, Hamilton grabbed hometown headlines again when he cited a "void" in domestic security as a result of *Nelson.* His words were echoed by the National Association of State Attorney Generals, meeting that same week in the nation's capital, a majority of whom were not from the South. Despite a slight ebb in its fortunes, anticommunism still held enormous political currency throughout the country, and the slightest hint of association with "communistic" causes brought widespread ostracism.[85]

Why, then, did SCEF leaders adamantly refuse throughout the 1940s, '50s, and beyond, to exclude or condemn Communists? To some extent, their position was a carryover from 1940s Popular Front liberalism, when CP membership or participation in wider reform coalitions was simply part of the social landscape, not the albatross it became through the hardening of Cold War foreign relations and a corresponding anticommunist cultural hysteria. In the 1950s South, Popular Front politics had a pragmatic component as well. The muting of dissent that had been the domestic harvest of the Cold War had left so few white southerners willing to speak in support of racial change that further polarization among anticommunists, non-Communists, and former Communists was truly disabling. It was understandable—in the context of how wide the sweep of anticommunist repression had become—to want to keep quiet about having had any form of association with the CP.

Occasionally a proposal came up for SCEF to adopt a ban on communists. At one board meeting in Atlanta, the matter consumed an entire afternoon, but it was put to rest once and for all. *We debated it for hours until Jim Dombrowski pointed out very quietly—as was his way—that we had wasted all afternoon on this question while the violence of the segregationists was rising all around us. He said one thing that stayed with me: "I'm not sure it's important whether SCEF survives, but I think it's important that American democracy survive. If we adopt this policy, we will be supporting the witch hunts that threaten any hope of democracy."* Rather than exorcise people for their affiliations or even submit its supporters to some form of loyalty test, SCEF sought to shift the focus of popular opinion away from the fantasy of "Communist subversion" and onto what its director and staff saw as the real issues bound up in integration. Until that shift was accomplished, anticommunism would continue to deify segregation.[86]

The more the federal government advanced the pace of racial changes, the more moderate anticommunist liberals such as those in the ACLU or the SRC were subject to the same vicious southern red-baiting that trailed SCEF. In 1956 the state of Alabama even began legal proceedings to outlaw the NAACP: the group's numerous anticommunist resolutions and internal purges failed miserably to dignify it in the eyes of southern white political culture.[87]

Once Anne and Carl became regional organizers for racial integration, it was only a matter of time until they felt the heat from the probing gaze of HUAC, SISS, or both. That moment arrived in summer 1958, on the heels of the couple's regional SCEF organizing tour and 12 weeks after SCEF's Conference on Voting Restrictions had exposed the depth of southern repression against prospective black voters. When HUAC announced that it would hold hearings in Atlanta to investigate "Communist Party propaganda activities in the South," the very news spurred SCEF leaders into action. Modjeska Simkins—an African American activist from Columbia, South Carolina, and a vice president of SCEF—had already discussed with Dombrowski the need for a public rebuke of HUAC for harassing civil rights workers. Now she, along with other black SCEF activists, initiated a petition letter to the U.S. Congress suggesting that HUAC change its focus and instead investigate the pernicious violence against black voter registrants, synagogues, and black churches in the Deep South. The letter read in part: "It is . . . increasingly difficult to find white people who are willing to support our efforts toward full citizenship. It is unthinkable that they should . . . be harassed by committees of the U.S. Congress." Dombrowski circulated the letter—which was ultimately signed by 200 African American clergy, college presidents, and other dignitaries—and mailed a copy to each member of Congress. SCEF then sponsored its placement as a full-page ad in the *Washington Post* (the *Atlanta Constitution* refused the ad, claiming it might provoke a libel suit from segregationist Georgia politicians). This drive—the strongest public anti-HUAC stand to date—got the attention of the African American press, from which came new voices calling for abolition of the congressional investigating committees.[88]

Actions like this would flow into a larger collective critique of southern anticommunist prosecutions in the coming years. At the moment, however, it was a little like blowing in the face of a mad bull. On July 27, 1958, HUAC issued subpoenas to more than 20 southern white labor and civil rights organizers. Among them were Anne and Carl. By the time a federal marshal located the pair at the O'Connors' beachfront estate in Rhode Island, Carl had less than 24 hours to get to Atlanta to testify.[89]

Anne was saved from the same fate by the presence of her children, though it was unclear whether they played into HUAC's sentimentalized cultural views about motherhood or mere stinginess. *[The marshal said that] Representative Walter would send us airplane tickets. I told him, "You just call Representative Walter right back and tell him to send two more because I've got two children, and I'm not going to leave them here on this beach."* As with the sedition case, Anne's gender gave her a little leeway for dissent that her husband simply did not possess. Instead of meeting her request, committee officials postponed Anne's testimony, and she was never recalled. She, Jimmy, and Anita remained at Little Compton, and Anne spent her time on the telephone mobilizing opposition while Carl flew south. While southern political officials were quick to call her a "communist" or worse, they reserved the most extreme forms of repression for her husband. It was during this period that Carl developed his joking observation that it was always he who went to jail while Anne wrote the pamphlets about it. As Anne saw it, at least that arrangement allowed her to keep the household afloat and continue their work.[90]

The Bradens always felt that the immediate reasons they were subpoenaed were twofold. First and foremost were their organizing efforts against the revival of state sedition laws, a matter now before Congress. In the couple's southern tour earlier that summer, they had urged local activists to write against the bills. It also seems likely that Scott Hamilton, still stinging from *Nelson*, urged federal HUAC officials forward in their pursuit of Kentucky's notorious pair. The final rub for him, perhaps, was the release of Anne's novel-like account of their sedition case, *The Wall Between*. It was only eight days later that they received subpoenas. As the Bradens' press statement issued in conjunction with the subpoenas noted, Anne's book portrayed HUAC (and, to a lesser extent, Scott Hamilton) in a "somewhat less than honorable" role. Hamilton, the couple knew, had received an advance copy.[91]

The HUAC hearings, like the SISS ones the previous summer, gave the government a fresh opportunity to reprosecute the sedition case in the press. Officials probably would not have seized that opportunity, however, had the Bradens seemed inclined to back down in their assault on segregation. Quite the reverse was true, however; they now appeared poised to mount a campaign against HUAC too. The congressional investigating committees routinely monitored every attack made on them, and investigators in Atlanta asked Carl almost as many questions about his efforts for ECLC as about SCEF. In the committee's interpretation, the Bradens' beach vacation with the O'Connors became a kind of leftists' summit. Plus, when Frank Wilkinson—whose work was increasingly centered on the abolition of HUAC—arrived in Atlanta at Dombrowski's invitation to observe the hearings, he too was slapped with a subpoena.[92]

Anne's and Carl's political sophistication, particularly relating to civil liberties, had come a long way since the 1954 trial. This time Carl was prepared for the intensity of the assault upon his intentions (HUAC's lead counsel called him a Communist "masquerading behind a facade of humanitarianism"). Again he and Anne used the attack as a platform to showcase the repression integrationists faced. Experience had taught him that it was useless to deny identification with the CP, especially since the government had Alberta Ahearn as a ready witness to substantiate it. On July 30, Carl faced the committee, flanked by attorneys John Coe of Florida and C. Ewbank Tucker, a co-counsel from the sedition case. One was black, the other white. Both men were SCEF board members who were willing to take risks: they knew that even their presence at the hearings made them HUAC targets now or in the future.[93]

Giving only his name, residence, and a brief description of his work, Carl refused to answer additional questions. Like other southern activists who testified, he also repeatedly insisted that "integration is what you are investigating." Instead of invoking Fifth Amendment privileges against self-incrimination, he stated that, "My beliefs and associations are none of the business of this committee," and relied on First Amendment rights of speech and assembly. Wilkinson did the same. This strategy aligned the two men with more than three dozen other "First Amendment Defendants" nationwide, and like most of them Carl and Wilkinson were cited for contempt of Congress.[94]

Carl was cited on six counts of contempt, corresponding to six of a total of fourteen questions he refused to answer. Rather than pressing on the issue of Carl's relationship to communism and the CP, questioners more or less accepted his affiliation as a given and instead focused on his work with SCEF and ECLC, especially with Harvey O'Connor. The probe of SCEF activities concentrated on a recent board meeting in Atlanta (the only item connecting SCEF with Georgia, scene of the hearing), as well as on the July 1958 SCEF letter the Bradens had distributed opposing state sedition laws. Richard Arens, HUAC lead counsel, also seemed convinced that Carl had "secretly" authored the anti-HUAC petition SCEF had recently circulated among black leaders.[95]

On all these points, Carl stood on the First Amendment but sparred jauntily with his inquisitors. He was silent on the origins of the controversial anti-HUAC letter but insisted on reading its contents into the record. As a consequence, the press conveyed not only the petition's supposed "Communist-initiated" origins but its alarmed message of the irrelevancy of anticommunist investigations in the face of racist violence so blatantly "un-American." Carl also explained his silences to the press: "Every question that was asked has been answered in court proceedings, in public reports of meetings, and in the forum of public opinion. . . . The point is that this committee has no right to ask the questions." Questioning the committee's relevancy was more than just political posturing. Even the *Atlanta Constitution*, whose liberal anticommunist editor Ralph McGill was always on the alert for Communist infiltration of integrationism, reported that the inquiry uncovered no "Georgia reds" and only perhaps half a dozen in other southern states. The only so-called Communist organization that HUAC located was SCEF.[96]

Yet the resulting charges against Carl turned out to mean a lot more than the nuisance value Anne had first anticipated of them. On August 13, the U.S. Congress was only one vote away from unanimous in citing Carl for contempt. He was convicted in January 1959 by a jury that deliberated only 40 minutes, and one month later was sentenced to a year in federal prison and a continuance of his $1,000 bond.[97]

The SCEF policy for responding to anticommunist attacks had traditionally been to downplay the charges and continue its civil rights crusades in as unimpeded a manner as possible. This was Aubrey Williams's approach, which Anne and Carl respected but could not agree with. As Anne wrote to Williams soon after the hearings, *If nothing were at issue but our personal welfare, our own reaction would be that it would be simpler for Carl to spend six months or a year in jail than to spend three or four years—plus the time and money of a lot of people—trying to stay out of jail. . . . However, this is not the answer. . . . You can't just let the Un-American Committee ride over you . . . somebody has got to make a fight.* The Bradens advocated a head-on campaign of exposing the moral corruption expressed in HUAC. They offered to leave the SCEF staff for the duration of Carl's battle with *the un-Americans* (a reference to HUAC they borrowed from Frank Donner's book of that name, which skewered the committee). But Jim Dombrowski was impressed by the argument that Carl's civil liberties case was integral to the southern civil rights struggle SCEF must wage. Under Dombrowski's leadership, SCEF took an offensive stance in Carl's defensive campaign. Rather than leaving the legal representation to ECLC, SCEF employed its own attorney, the Floridian John Coe, to co-lead Carl's legal team with Leonard Boudin, who ostensibly worked as an individual and not in an ECLC capacity. Dombrowski was sensitive to the fact that SCEF and, before it, the Southern Conference had long battled opponents' claims that it was New York–financed and thus "Yankee-controlled." In that context, association with ECLC could only add to SCEF's troubles. This time, the Bradens' fight would remain a southern one to the extent that SCEF could make it thus. Though John Coe was largely unknown to them, Anne and Carl yielded to Dombrowski's judgment.[98]

The resulting *Braden v. United States of America* case went on for two more years and was ultimately argued before the Supreme Court, consuming—as Anne had predicted—considerable monetary and human resources. One of several test cases attempting to reinvigorate First Amendment rights, it illuminated the southern variant of anticommunist excess, providing a tangible link between civil rights and civil liberties. As they had done in the sedition case, Anne and Carl used the HUAC attack as an organizing vehicle through which to publicize this link. The networks they had tapped into over the previous four years had reinforced their view that only the freedoms guaranteed in the Bill of Rights held any hope of breaking through the *police state,* as Anne subsequently referred to it, that was the South in those years. In a manner prescient of the interest she would take months later in the tragedy of Juliette Morgan, Anne wrote at the end of 1958 that *the real victims of the witch hunt . . . in my opinion, are those who . . . have been quietly driven out of their professions, out of useful work—and more especially, those who simply lapsed into si-*

lence . . . quit expressing any ideas that might be controversial, because of fear the witch hunt would strike them.[99]

Not all SCEF leaders agreed with the decision to make Carl's defense a central part of its program, or with his stance of total noncooperation with HUAC. Shortly after the arraignment, Albert Barnett, dean of Emory University's Candler School of Theology and a SCEF board member of long standing, wrote the Bradens to that effect. Barnett would not leave SCEF over this matter, but he would have preferred that Carl register a protest to HUAC's investigation but nevertheless answer the questions posed, so as to "get on with the business [of] integration." Anne wrote Barnett a lengthy reply, reiterating that they would not *cooperate with evil. . . . When a governmental committee begins to ask such questions, the freedom we have in theory has already been proscribed in practice. . . . People begin to accept the notion that certain associations are forbidden. . . . If you answer the committee's questions, even under protest, you are admitting their right to [ask].* She also pointed out that denying one's "communistic" ties appeared to have little practical effect. Of all the southerners she and Carl had met in their travels for SCEF, many knew that its leaders were accused of communism in the 1954 New Orleans SISS hearings. Yet, she wrote, *Not one had ever heard that Aubrey and Jim both testified they were not communists. The answer just never catches up with the question.*[100]

Anne reiterated their willingness to leave SCEF if their stance was too divisive. Because they had Dombrowski's full support, that never became necessary. Yet both Coe and Boudin found Carl a difficult client on occasion because of his unwillingness to yield beyond an absolute First Amendment defense and his insistence on rewriting portions of Coe's briefs to more accurately reflect that stance. But Carl's position was backed totally by Anne, who vowed that had she been called upon to testify, she would have mimicked Virginia Durr's performance in New Orleans and stood mute. In early 1959, she wrote these words to her mother in a vain attempt to explain their position: *The most important difference [between the United States and Russia] is that in Moscow the average citizen must be . . . constantly careful what he says, [knowing] he can't criticize his government. In America the average citizen at least theoretically has these rights. . . . I feel in recent years they have been abridged and that is exactly what our fight with the un-American committee is all about. . . . I know the value of civil libertarian concepts. I don't ever intend to be party to giving them up.*[101]

A second-tier but nevertheless significant issue, from the couple's perspective, was the demonization with which American culture had so thoroughly suffused the CP by the late 1950s. Both Bradens casually referred to themselves as socialists, and in conversations of any depth they soon revealed themselves to be Marxist thinkers. Most of all, they believed strongly in a unified left which did not repudiate the CP, and they were deeply opposed to the decimation of the left that anticommunist persecutions had made possible. Because 1950s red-baiting tended to label everyone on the left as "Communists"—when in fact there was a wide spectrum of Marxists that included independent socialists, Trotskyists, Maoists, as well as CP members—the Bradens felt that all leftists should stand opposed to the "witch hunting." Carl and Anne did not identify wholly with the CP, but neither did they reject it. The CP's brand of radical interracialism had shaped their commitments, and they were sufficiently close to people in the party to be unwilling to build a legal defense that relied on differentiating Carl from Communists. After Carl threatened to tear up a draft of the legal brief, Anne argued with Leonard Boudin about this matter: *My feeling is that we wouldn't want to win this case on the basis that Carl is not a Communist and therefore should be immune to Congressional inquisitions. Our position is that the inquisitions are evil—period. All inquisitions, of Communists, non-Communists, and screwballs. I surely wouldn't want his case to establish a principle that it's all right for the un-Americans to investigate Communists if they'll leave the non-Communists alone. I think we'd all feel guilty as hell if that happened.* The Bradens' uncompromising idealism set them apart even from many of their own activist peers, who tended to be more pragmatic or more skeptical of the CP, even in its increasingly diminished form after the onslaught of the domestic Cold War and in the wake of the Khrushchev revelations.[102]

Yet in mid-1958 the couple were not being entirely unrealistic in their initial optimistic assessment that Carl had a chance at winning a pure First Amendment victory at the U.S. Supreme Court level. Chief Justice Earl Warren had won everlasting enmity from southern segregationists in *Brown*, but his Court's judicial activism did not stop with issues of race. Starting with *Nelson* in 1956, the Supreme Court had begun to stem the tide of the domestic Cold War with decisions that promised to curtail the reach of the congressional investigating committees and their state counterparts. But the committees were not without their allies, many of whom were powerful southern politicians. In mid-1959, as Carl's case wound its way through the lower courts, the U.S. Supreme Court's fling with judicial liberalism ended abruptly when it handed down the *Barenblatt* and *Uphaus* decisions, which effectively gutted the restrictions it had placed on anticommunist prosecutions almost exactly two years before. These decisions were taken in a 5–4 majority with biting dissents written by the liberal Alabamian Hugo Black. For opponents of segregation and anticommunism, it was a bleak day at the Supreme Court.[103]

Despite the changed legal climate with relation to congressional investigations of dissent, the Bradens were committed to sticking with their original legal course. In fact, Anne became the idea person for a short-lived campaign called the "Committee of First Amendment Defendants" to give such resisters a visibility they presently lacked. Alert as usual to the issue of press attention, she and Carl were alarmed by the lack of publicity the two Supreme Court decisions had generated. The one good thing about Joe McCarthy had been that, as Anne wrote that summer, *the witch hunt was front-page news . . . people either hated McCarthy or they loved him, but at least they cared.*[104]

As the 1950s drew to a close, the phenomenon known as "McCarthyism" was supposedly in eclipse, yet popular anticommunism continued to encroach upon civil liberties—and, in the South, civil rights—not only of CP sympathizers but of dissenters of many stripes. It was during this period that the Highlander Folk School in Monteagle, Tennessee—long hounded by the FBI, Internal Revenue Service, and the congressional anticommunist committees—was shut down during an interracial voting rights workshop in what became another expensive court battle that dragged on for years. Throughout the South, the power of anticommunism would not be spent for a long while to come.[105]

The Wall Between

Dovetailing as it did with the HUAC subpoenas, the release of Anne's memoir of the sedition case may have made Hamilton and southern segregationists "see red," but her book also developed a small following that enhanced the couple's regional organizing. The Bradens excerpted it in the *Patriot* and liberally dispensed copies in their travels, finding that its personal tone could sometimes reach people more effectively than any pamphlet.

Writing the book was cathartic for Anne: she had begun it like a woman possessed during the frantic days before the sedition case was resolved, when she and Carl faced the possibility of lengthy prison terms. Anne's self-consciously southern voice went way beyond simply documenting the events surrounding the Wade purchase, though that was the narrative frame for the plot. Her title, *The Wall Between*, was a metaphor for the starkly separate psychic, social, and economic worlds inhabited by blacks and whites, and her book evoked those divisions for those in the region familiar with them and explained the psychological and political dynamics of southern race and class relations in a way that outsiders could understand. As Lillian Smith had done in her 1949 memoir, *Killers of the Dream*, Anne personalized the dilemma of the white southerner opposed to segregation and racism. Anne went further than Smith, however, in bringing to life nonfictional black protagonists, and exploration of the Wades' dilemmas became part of her indictment of southern segregated life.

The genre of memoir gave Anne the opportunity for a range of emotional expression not always appropriate in her job as an organizer. Her narrative reexamined the lessons of her childhood on race, religion, and community and found within them painful disparities that formed the seeds of her political transformation to a radical anti-racist (though she did not refer to herself in those terms in 1958). She also devoted considerable attention to development of her drama's other characters, including Carl, Andrew and Charlotte Wade, and even Scott Hamilton, of whom she drew a rather even-handed portrait. The book was allegorical insofar as each of the protagonists stood in for a larger cast: description of Andrew Wade's life, for instance, became an opportunity to explain the many humiliations African Americans experienced in Louisville under segregation, while Anne's own experiences became a framework for examining the psychic costs of racial and class privileges.

Like any autobiographer, Anne constructed a self to whom the reading public could relate. The result was a voice that was dispassionate without being passionless, objective but not uncritical of segregationist and anticommunist ideologies. She wrote in the preface that *there are no heroes in this story . . . no villains . . . only people, the product of their environment, urged on by forces of history they often do not understand.* Anne's was perhaps the only book of its time to suggest a link between segregationist and anticommunist ideologies, and in 1958 she had to tread carefully in doing so. She also located herself within a language of female domesticity that was familiar to readers of that era. Frequently seen preparing dinner or swinging her child in the yard, the Anne in her portrayal is an extraordinarily independent thinker whose character was nevertheless drawn in close relation to her roles as wife, mother, and daughter. Though she genuinely saw herself in these roles, she also depicted herself in a somewhat more conventional fashion in order to appeal to general readers, particularly women. (When at 75 she resurrected *The Wall Between* for a revised edition, Anne commented in an author's note, *I had not remembered . . . the sexist nature of the terminology of the 1950s.*)[106]

As always, Anne wrote mainly as an activist. In revealing her political and psychological odyssey, she did so with an eye toward collective action. She unpacked the white collective psyche from which she had emerged in a conscious attempt to rouse other southern white consciences. When that process worked, the effect was electrifying. She received numerous personal notes from rural white southerners, who found the book spoke to them as few had. A prominent white South Carolina liberal, James MacBride Dabbs, wrote to Anne, "You and Carl are the awakened conscience of the South. And people don't like it when their consciences begin to awake[n]. But they turn; however slowly, they turn."[107]

If Anne had published *The Wall Between* a decade later—when Americans had become more sensitized to the poisoning effects of racism—it might have gotten wider critical attention as a poignant firsthand account of white southern racial transformation. At the time, however, anticommunism was still powerful enough to narrow its exposure. Even outside the South, the fact that the book had been issued by the left-leaning Monthly Review Press (the only kind of publisher that would touch it) limited its circulation and its credibility. Some Cold War liberal reviewers dismissed the Wade incident as "ill-advised" and branded Anne "naive."[108]

The book was of sufficient literary stature, however, to qualify as a finalist for the 1958 National Book Award for nonfiction. Within the civil rights movement, it won hearty praise from the likes of Martin Luther King, Jr. and Eleanor Roosevelt, who called it "one of the most remarkable stories" and expressed the hope that it would be widely read. It also drew attention from religious and left-leaning social action journals and from the African American press: P. L. Prattis, for instance, publisher of the *Pittsburgh Courier*, urged his African American readers to put a copy into the hands of every white person they knew. A few reviewers in the mainstream press grudgingly praised Anne's talent as a writer, and even the *Courier-Journal*—still among the region's most enlightened newspapers, even if it was the "scene of the crime," so to speak—acknowledged the book's nomination for the National Book Award.[109]

Anne barely had time even to think about her book's reception, so immersed were she and Carl in the two-pronged battle of dismantling segregation and fighting for their right to do so. The book's opening was highly indicative of the lives they lived: on the couple's very first day at Little Compton in the summer of 1958, the O'Connors threw a big party to celebrate its publication. But in less than a week Carl was whisked off to Atlanta for the HUAC hearing and the three-year battle that followed.[110]

Anne's career as an activist always took precedence over that as a writer, and she never wrote another book, though she harbored strong desires to do so. Yet both literarily and politically, the book struck a chord within the relatively small number of readers it managed to reach. Who can know what her path might have been had her activism not been so hounded by those who would silence her? The fight against marginalization was constant, and though it was never so consuming as to derail her organizing work, it did take energy that might have gone into other literary ventures. Anne saw and still sees herself as a journalist, a chronicler of the human condition. For her, writing has been primarily a tool for mobilizing people into greater awareness of social conditions, and into social action. Because the whole tenor of the civil rights movement increased immeasurably less than two years after the publication of *The Wall Between*, Anne's immediacy led her into a very direct form of propagandizing, and her media skills were fully focused on the mass mobilization of which she was a part. Her interpretive writing was confined to the *Patriot*, contributions to left-leaning periodicals, and the legions of pamphlets she authored through SCEF.

Civil Rights and Civil Liberties

Anne and Carl tried as best they could to keep the HUAC case from, as she had worried at its outset, *hamper[ing] the positive program of SCEF for integration*. Dombrowski set up a separate fundraising apparatus for the HUAC defense fund, and both Bradens continued to log in countless hours for the cause they had been hired to promote. Carl simply worked his various court appearances in Georgia into his field travel schedule. It was also during this period that Anne doubled the *Patriot*'s size. Because of the overwhelming odds against which they worked, Anne found considerable cause for optimism in the fact that the SCEF board consisted of more than 80 members now, and the advisory committee had surpassed 100.[111]

Yet the very nature of the political stand that Carl made with his HUAC case forced SCEF to denote even more sharply the tie between civil rights and civil liberties. The legislation to revitalize state sedition laws was defeated in committee in the 1958 Congress, but it was reborn in 1959, and Anne and Carl knew only too well that they could easily become its *first victims*, as Anne wrote that spring. The bills never became law, but harassment continued. In North Carolina, Anne and Carl had mobilized civil rights activism among whites and publicized numerous atrocities. Most glaring, perhaps, was the 1958 Monroe "kissing case" in which kisses exchanged by a 10-year-old African American boy and an 8-year-old white girl wreaked intense antiblack violence and landed the boy and his friend (also African American) in a "reform school" for years. Soon after, at a meeting in Charlotte of the liberal National Conference of Christians and Jews in early 1959, North Carolina Attorney General Malcolm Seawell excoriated SCEF as "communistic" and more dangerous than the KKK or Nazis. His source? Congressional investigations of the previous year. W. W. Finlator, a Baptist minister and SCEF board member from Raleigh, wrote a letter of protest to his local newspaper, but he recalled later that the smear eventually caused him to drift away from SCEF, not from fear but from harassment. The HUAC inquiry also led to spin-off investigations by state legislative committees that plagued Carl in Mississippi and Florida.[112]

There was still plenty of *emotional fire in the subversive charge*, Anne knew, and the HUAC citations placed new millstones on the already uphill job of opposing southern racism. Anticommunist crusaders were increasingly on the defensive as the pace of racial change quickened, but they had a field day with the HUAC charges. In January 1960, when Ella Baker and Carl jointly coordinated the Voluntary Civil Rights Commission hearings, the conservative commentator Fulton Lewis devoted four radio programs to attacking the project's validity because its leading organizer (Carl) was "red." Lewis hauled out the Louisville case and the HUAC citations. In the resulting fray, Methodist Bishop Bromley Oxnam resisted tremendous pressure from the anticommunist Methodist "Circuit Rider" group to disassociate from SCEF and the hearings. Oxnam stood firm, but the Washington, D.C., Baptist church that had offered to host the hearings pulled out at the last minute. Other sponsors followed. The hearings went off as planned, however, and succeeded in publicizing the utter failure of the U.S. Civil Rights Commission to rein in voting rights violations.[113]

The legal machinations that caused Carl's HUAC case to linger for nearly three years before it was ruled upon by the highest court in the land were fortunate insofar as the timing left him free—and Anne, therefore, freer—to proselytize for civil rights during the critical years of 1959–1961. By the time he was actually imprisoned in May 1961, students were in the streets and Jim Crow segregation was collapsing all around them. Only 13 days later, segregationist thugs burned the freedom riders' bus on Mother's Day in Anne's childhood home of Anniston, Alabama—an action that failed to stop the riders from continuing south. Those young people would not be easily scared away from the Bradens by their notoriety.

———————

In the late '50s, Anne and Carl were working "against the grain" of southern racism, as the historian Anthony Dunbar has pointed out. But they did the important, sometimes gut-wrenching work Anne described in a 1959 letter to a friend as *plowing ground* for the mass movement that would burst forth in early

1960. The Bradens found and encouraged as many integration-minded whites as they could, while directing media attention to civil rights pressure points. At the same time, they built alliances with African American leaders who in time would become both the sung and unsung heroes of the civil rights movement. The couple began a long and personally disruptive process of consciousness-raising about the restricted right to dissent in the region—civil liberties work that eventually helped to break the police state mentality that so permeated southern culture. Ultimately, it also gave the force of the southern civil rights movement to the national campaign to end the power of HUAC and its counterparts.[114]

Years later, Anne summarized their work of the late 1950s in this way: *We certainly never made any mass breakthroughs with the white South in that period, but we were able to guarantee that in some places at least, it wasn't just black against white. A few white people on a picket line do make a difference—you set an example and you raise the issue, and we provided a way for people to do that.*[115]

Only the kind of inner fire that Anne and Carl possessed allowed them to persist through the repression that hounded all of their organizing work. For sustenance, they had each other and a small but vigorous community of kindred spirits across the nation. In their persistence, they became a bridge between the Old Left that was so devastated during the Cold War years and the New Left that emerged after 1960. As the Supreme Court's rejection of Carl's HUAC appeal indicated, the country was not ready for their radicalism. But in 1960 it was getting ready to be ready. Anne in particular found that her collective-mindedness would endear her to the young generation that would bring Jim Crow down at last in the 1960s. As history would show over the coming decade, the Bradens' ground-plowing work was not in vain.

(left) Anne Gambrel McCarty as a child with her parents, Gambrell and Anita McCarty, Columbus, Mississippi, circa 1929–1930 (courtesy of Anne Braden)

(below) Brother Lindsay McCarty, Cousin Joe Brady, and Anne Gambrell McCarty on their grandmother's front steps, Eminence, Kentucky, with Agnes Thorne Crabbe (Nana) in background, n.d. (courtesy of Anne Braden)

May Court, Stratford College, 1943: Anne McCarty is third from left (courtesy of Anne Braden)

Anne and Carl Braden in the living room of their Louisville apartment, circa 1950 (courtesy of Anne Braden)

Anne Braden confers with Rosalie McGee, widow of Willie McGee, who spoke in Louisville at a Civil Rights Congress rally in December 1951 (Daily Worker)

May 16, 1954: On the day before the U.S. Supreme Court rules school segregation unconstitutional, Charlotte and Andrew Wade and their two-year-old daughter Rosemary stand in front of their damaged house on Rone Court near Shively, Kentucky. The night before, vandals shot out windows and burned a cross to protest the Wades' move into the neighborhood. (Courier-Journal)

Carl and Anne Braden with their children, Jim (age 3) and Anita (age 1½), seated in the McCartys' living room in Anniston, Alabama, as they await trial on sedition charges in the fall of 1954 (courtesy of Anne Braden)

Braden sedition trial, Louisville, December 1954: Carl and Anne Braden look over documents during a recess from Carl's testimony (courtesy of Anne Braden)

Spring 1959: Arkansas Attorney General Bruce Bennett outlines for the Tennessee legislature the links between SCEF leaders and the Highlander Folk School, thought to be communistic enemies of the social and racial order. This testimony triggered the attack that closed Highlander in 1959 and forced its relocation. (courtesy of Anne Braden)

(above) The Braden family: (l-r) Anita, Anne, Beth, Carl, and Jim on the occasion of Beth's christening, spring 1960 (courtesy of Anne Braden)

(below) Anne Braden interviewing Rosa Parks in Bradens' living room, May 1960 (courtesy of Anne Braden)

September 14, 1967: Former sedition defendants pose in front of federal courthouse, Lexington, Kentucky, with family and friends after learning that sedition law has finally been declared unconstitutional. (l-r) Al McSurely, Margaret McSurely, Carl Braden, Beth Braden, Anne Braden, Karen Mulloy, and Joe Mulloy (Wisconsin Historical Society, image #WHi-2479)

Anne Braden at SCEF's annual New York fundraiser, 1962, pictured with Chuck McDew (center), chairman of SNCC, and Bob Zellner, SNCC's white southern student organizer (Photo by Jack Lessinger, courtesy of Anne Braden)

April 29, 1961: SCEF send-off reception just before Carl Braden and Frank Wilkinson surrender to Atlanta authorities to begin one-year federal prison sentences for contempt of Congress. (l-r) Jim Dombrowski, Carl Braden, Anne Braden, Frank Wilkinson, Martin Luther King, Jr., and Coretta Scott King. (Wisconsin Historical Society, image #WHi-2480)

Beth Braden at 15 with her mother, pictured in front of O'Connors' beachfront estate, Little Comptin, Rhode Island, in the summer of 1975, a few months after Carl's death (courtesy of Anne Braden)

Anne Braden joins Fred Shuttlesworth at podium at SOC conference celebrating the southern conference movement's 50th anniversary, Birmingham, 1989 (courtesy of Anne Braden)

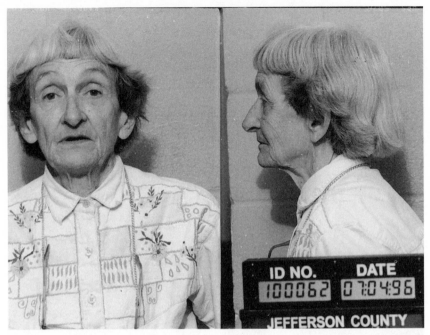

Police mug shots document Anne's 1996 arrest with nine others demonstrating to protest lack of minority hiring for Professional Golfers' Association tournament in Louisville. When the PGA returns to Louisville in 2000, one third of the vending contracts go to minority firms. (courtesy of Anne Braden)

Anne Braden addresses a rally against racially motivated prosecution at Jefferson County Hall of Justice, Louisville, circa 1997 (courtesy of Tom Moffett)

Anne sits on the front steps of her Louisville home with daughter Beth Braden (front) and grandchildren Alice Braden (l) and Henry Owens IV with friend Denise Link (rear), circa 1997. (courtesy of Beth Braden)

Anne Braden reminisces with son Jim Braden at her 75th birthday celebration at the Carl Braden Memorial Center in Louisville, December 1999. Portraits of Anne and Carl are in the background. (courtesy of Anne Braden)

(above) March for Jobs, Peace, and Justice, Louisville, 1984, sponsored by the Kentucky Coalition of Conscience. Left to right are Betty Payne, Anne, John Johnson, and Carla Wallace. (courtesy Anne Braden)

(below) Ann Braden (l) and Catherine Fosl, Louisville, November 1994 (Courtesy Michael Honey)

PART THREE

CHAPTER NINE

THE MASS CIVIL RIGHTS MOVEMENT— BEGINNING OF A NEW DAY

Traveling about the South today, distributing the doctrine of totalitarian government, is a husband-wife team by name of Carl and Ann [sic] Braden.

—Dale Alford, United States congressman (D-Arkansas), 1959[1]

THE SIT-IN MOVEMENT THAT TOOK THE SOUTH by storm in early 1960 altered forever both the region's social order and the interior lives of all participants and many observers. Young people who became swept up by the prospect of social change at that historical moment often found their consciousness transformed far more swiftly than the process that Anne had undergone more than a decade before. Student activism seemed to burst forth from nowhere, launching a mass civil rights rebellion that spawned other protest movements and ultimately defined the decade of the 1960s. Although student activists were warned away from Anne and Carl by many of their elders, they rebelled against that advice too and began to reclaim the Bradens, Anne in particular, as coworkers and mentors. That process of reclamation would take considerable time: it stretched well beyond the 1960s and even past the 1970s, but it was born in the upheaval of early 1960.

Like most adult civil rights organizers, Anne was completely startled by the rash of student sit-ins that started on Monday, February 1, in Greensboro, North Carolina. Within 60 days after four students sat down at Woolworth's lunch counter, the "sit-downs" (as they were initially called) had spread to 80 communities in 12 southern and border states, involving thousands of high school and college students who were predominantly but not exclusively African American.[2]

In those initial weeks, Anne could only follow the events through second-hand reports: she was homebound with her new daughter, Beth, born February 7. But she kept up-to-date on the inspiring new developments through the extensive correspondence she maintained even amid the chaos a new baby lends to any household. She wrote to Fred Shuttlesworth in early March that the students' discipline and courage surely heralded *the beginning of a new day*.[3]

Anne's offhand commentary became more prophetic for the new decade than she could ever have guessed. Throughout the late 1950s, there were signs of growing restlessness under segregation, but only with hindsight did they indicate a clear new direction and thrust. The use of nonviolent resistance to racial injustice, for instance, had been the subject of much debate in the African American press and within the civil rights community. In January 1960, Anne moved to correct what she worried was a *glaring omission* of that discussion in the pages of the *Patriot*. She editorially welcomed the new decade with an article reprinted from the pacifist *Liberation* magazine. "Is Violence Necessary to Combat Injustice?" posed Martin Luther King's views against those of Robert Williams, the Monroe, North Carolina, NAACP leader who encouraged blacks to stand up for themselves with weapons if need be.[4]

As the new decade opened, SCEF's heavily red-baited hearings for the voteless in January 1960 were as much a tribute to the courage of would-be black voters in the Deep South as they were an exposé of the reprisals against them. Yet all that came out of Congress in the wake of debate on civil rights legislation was a new bill that was basically "toothless" (as Carl referred to it) when it came to deterring segregationist harassment. Clearly, stronger medicine was needed, and members of the younger generation suddenly showed themselves ready to administer it.[5]

Few if any adult activists could foresee how forcefully the young would emerge as the real protagonists in the unfolding drama of the 1960s. Not even the "Greensboro Four" realized at that early juncture that their actions would trigger a mass movement. The first weeks of sit-downs left older activists basically shaking their heads in a combination of perplexity, admiration, and—not in Anne, but in some—even a touch of stolen thunder. Anne remarked on the unexpected turn of events to a friend that April: *I remember the discussions at Highlander's college workshop last year—just about a year ago this weekend—when the students from the various Negro colleges represented were all swapping complaints because their fellow students "weren't interested in anything" and "would never do a thing." You just never know.*[6]

Anne's confinement by domestic duties for the first three months of the new wave of student activism fueled her need to reach out in writing and trade impressions with friends closer to the hub of protest activity. By the time the baby reached six weeks of age, she often managed to eke out six-hour workdays, but she was still homebound amid Carl's frequent road trips and the icy weather that plagued Louisville throughout March. By spring she still had not attended any sit-ins or talked directly to the participants, but was keeping a close tally on the cities to which they had spread—and thinking a lot about the young folks who sat down. The students' willingness to endure unremitting aggression in service of their ideals took discussion of Gandhian nonviolent resistance to new heights. Anne's exchanges with her friend Virginia Durr during the early days of the sit-ins were among those that enlivened conversations among liberals and leftists, black and white, across the nation.[7]

The two friends' correspondence in 1960 prefigured the sort of tension that would run through the civil rights movement in the coming few years on whether nonviolence was a tactic or a philosophy of life. Both women were passionate supporters of the peace movement that was also brewing in those years. Though both the Women for Peace group she had helped to establish and the Louisville WILPF branch were long defunct, Anne continued to be in touch with activists nationally in WILPF, in which Durr also held membership. In keeping with her religious convictions, Anne had always been something of a pacifist at heart, and her ties in recent years with people from the radically pacifist Peacemaker group had deepened those convictions. From her perspective, the students' "passive resistance" (as Durr referred to it) was anything but passive, signifying instead a commitment of faith more thoroughgoing than her own. Anne would never condemn blacks who felt forced to pick up guns—she and Carl were fiercely supportive of Robert Williams, whose rhetoric and actions called on a long tradition of armed self-defense as integral to achieving black equality. But she found greater emotional attunement with nonviolent resistance and considered it a *practical impossibility* for African Americans to win civil rights with weapons because they would be swiftly outnumbered and overpowered.[8]

Nonviolence notwithstanding, the directness of the students' actions also squared with Anne's vision of social change as a response to collective demands. She saw the rise of nonviolent direct action as a qualitative, positive move away from the more legalistic approach of the NAACP, for example, which had achieved important victories that nonetheless left the bulk of segregation standing. Anne objected to Durr's observation that court action, not mass protest, had put an end to segregation on Montgomery buses: *Do you really think the court decision would have been what it was if the Negroes' movement had not dramatized the struggle to public opinion and the nation? . . . I just do not believe that court cases are won in a vacuum or that they are won primarily on the law. . . . Don't gather from this that I don't think lawyers and courts are important— I do. . . . My point is that I don't think the court decision won the Montgomery bus boycott—I think the boycott won the court decision.*[9]

Durr's perspective was shaped in part by being the wife of a reform-minded attorney. The two women agreed to disagree on matters, like this one, where they differed. Being southern white women of privilege who had rejected major pieces of their upbringing, each brought to the friendship her own brand of social alienation and found in their bond a unique freedom to theorize and to personalize issues of race and politics as well as those of gender, class, and region. As the elder of the two by 21 years, Durr had a kind of seniority in Anne's eyes that made her on occasion an almost maternal figure, replacing in part the emotional closeness Anne no longer had with her own mother. Durr pronounced Anne a brilliant writer with courage and boundless energy, though she also admonished Anne that "you work too hard and you take things too hard." During this period the two provided a sort of stand-in familial relation for each other that became difficult to maintain as the pace and scope of Anne's activism expanded later in the 1960s.[10]

Even for civil rights supporters more jaded than Anne, there was plenty of cause for encouragement in the spring of 1960. Campuses that had been politically inactive for twenty years now sprang to life in support of the sit-ins, with expulsions and white reaction seeming only to spur protesters forward. These young people were not the sort of radicals Anne might have wished them to be insofar as they sought to extend rather than subvert dominant sociopolitical values. But she would have been the last to offer any criticism of them. Instead, the risks they took were deeply moving to her, as they seem to have been to Americans of varying persuasions.[11]

Anne was determined to stay close to home for at least a few months so as not to interrupt her newest daughter's nursing schedule. Her maternal responsibilities thus kept her from attending what turned out to be the major event of the spring: the founding conference of the Student Nonviolent Coordinating Committee (SNCC), which took place in mid-April in Raleigh, North Carolina. The meeting was organized by Ella Baker, who was executive director of SCLC at this time. Baker's experience working for a group of male ministers had made her impatient with the rigidity and hierarchy of existing civil rights groups, and she wrote Anne of her high hopes for the conference. This development, Baker believed, was the most important of her lifetime, and she did not care to see the youthful initiative absorbed by any of the established organizations. Under the sponsorship of SCLC, she brought together 200 student activists from 12 southern states and from 11 border and nonsouthern states, as well as representatives of various social action groups. To keep the conference focus strictly regional, nonsoutherners participated but did not vote. About a dozen of all who attended were white.[12]

With Baker's support—and her willingness to defy King's and the other ministers' desire to organize the conference into a youth wing of SCLC—the students opted to form their own independent group. What had been a series of purely local actions sparking almost spontaneously from one southern town to another now coalesced into SNCC, an autonomous, though decentralized and loosely structured, organization. Like Anne, Baker had a vision of social reform that was more radical and well defined than was that of most of the students, but she believed (correctly) that they would grow into more expansive views. Initially, however, she won the students' admiration by being mindful of the boundary between encouragement and control. Baker gently nudged the gathering toward a broader reform agenda with her address, "Bigger Than a Hamburger," a title Anne carried over in the coverage of the event Baker submitted for the next *Patriot*. That phrase would resound through the civil rights movement for years to come.[13]

Anne was introduced to the sit-ins on her home turf later in April when Len Holt, a young Virginia attorney who had known the Bradens for several years, came to Louisville as field representative for the Congress of Racial Equality (CORE). CORE, a national organization founded in 1942 that had espoused the philosophy of nonviolent direct action well before the sit-ins popularized it, expended considerable effort in aiding the early student movement. At the request of the militant but irascible Bishop Tucker, CORE dispatched Holt to Louisville to conduct workshops on nonviolence. Not realizing how truly scandalous Anne and Carl were seen as in their hometown,

Holt invited, controversy upon his arrival by staying at their home, and the couple's "subversive" reputation quickly spilled over onto CORE in Louisville.[14]

Holt's fledgling workshops with high school and college students produced some results, however. Some in the student group had already been galvanized by their recent activities in nearby Frankfort, where a CORE group at the historically black Kentucky State College (KSC) had led demonstrations to demand equitable facilities and better treatment. In April the college administration withdrew recognition of CORE, and 12 KSC students were expelled. Undaunted, several moved on to new protests in Louisville.[15]

Although the city saw no widescale desegregation until more than a year later, its first "test" sit-in took place on April 30, with students joined by African American adults such as Tucker and the Reverend M.M.D. Perdue, both of whom were SCEF board members. Stands like the one taken by Perdue and Tucker put them at odds with other adult leaders. Practically speaking, organizational and generational infighting in Louisville may have been as dampening to effective activism as was red-baiting. Having sworn off demonstrations during negotiations with city business leaders that had been under way all spring, the local NAACP did not take kindly to the radical interlopers. Also, as Anne lamented in a follow-up note to Holt, the generational conflicts that would become more pronounced as the decade unfolded were already becoming evident. *Your kids are really moving . . . only problem is that Perdue et al. are getting their feelings hurt because they feel students are not taking them into their confidence but are going it alone. This is true—obviously they don't want adult interference. I didn't go to the meeting today as I sensed they didn't want adults there. . . . I think their independent spirit is healthy myself—although probably with a little tact they could maintain some important contacts with adults.*[16]

Although Anne and Carl continued to carry a taint even among other activists, the resurrection of their reputation began in the admiration they won from young people they met during this period. Anne's instinctive respect for the autonomy of the Louisville youth mirrored the treatment Baker had given and continued to give the SNCC students. That stance—together with an approachability and a level of commitment to ending racism that seemed to be more a matter of character than of politics—won both women a stature among students that continually eluded many civil rights elders in their dealings with the "younger generation." These were not consciously planned strategies but simply extensions of each woman's way of being in the world. Anne was never one to attempt to impose her views on colleagues, but she did try in a variety of small ways to get other adult activists to agree—as she wrote that year to

Clark Foreman—that *it's not up to us [adults] to try to tell them what is the "best" way to do things. Generally speaking, the young people feel that the older generations have failed in this whole battle so they are not looking to us for advice. But if we can go easy on the advice and heavy on the assistance where they take the initiative, they are glad to have our help.* Those sentiments became her guiding principle for interactions with the students.[17]

To Emphasize White Voices

On the one hand, Anne was wholly enthused by the new stage SNCC represented in the development of an independent black movement *unwilling to poke along on an adjustment process.* SNCC always contained a few whites, and that number grew as did its popularity among reform-minded youth. It was organized and led, however, by African American young people, and that quality was unique, new, and, as Anne saw it, pivotal in ushering in real racial change.[18]

On the other hand, her strong commitment to interracialism made her wary of diluting SCEF's focus on what whites were or should be doing to support the emerging movement. She could see how easy it was to get caught up in the new energy African Americans were injecting into southern culture, and she wrote in mid-1960: *It seems to me that in past years the SCEF emphasis on white voices has been greater than it has within the last year. Our plan has always been to emphasize white voices and interracial activity. But lately I notice that we tend to have more and more news of what Negroes alone are doing. The explanation is simple enough. It's mainly the Negroes who are doing things and it comes easy and natural to report what they are doing.* Yet because Anne also believed that acknowledging white support tended to supplement it, she wished to guard against such a drift, preferring to regard the new momentum in terms of its challenge to white supporters.[19]

After she began to meet and correspond with the new generation of activists—white and black—she became increasingly eager to nurture what small white presence there was in SNCC. Doing so became one of her major contributions to the development of the student civil rights movement. She reflected later: *The problem as we saw it was, here was this tremendous thing happening in the black community, and how could [we] get more white people to see that this was their struggle too and join in it?* Too often, even the few whites who did act remained cut off from sources of support, and Anne saw the passionate moral eruption of SNCC as an opportunity to bring black and white youth closer together than most of their adult peers had ever been.[20]

She remembered well the blossoming of ideas she had experienced in her own college years and soon began to wonder how to involve white southern students in the exciting new ideas now in the air. For the September 1960 *Patriot*, she wrote an essay titled "What Is White Person's Place in Current Struggle?" which suggested that the time had come for white southerners to move beyond simply soul-searching or participating in interracial social gatherings and to take a more active role in civil rights causes. As the African American freedom movement expanded throughout the '60s, she and Carl focused more and more on building a white presence that was equal in commitment if not in numbers.

A prime opportunity to boost white involvement became evident in October of 1960, when she met SNCC leaders en masse at their second conference. Carl had for some months been getting to know student activists in Nashville—which had perhaps the most active, radical contingent—and in Florida, where he concentrated most of his organizing in 1960. But Anne had met only a few of the students, briefly, at a workshop at Highlander in May, her first time away from three-month-old Beth. During a stopover in Atlanta en route to Anniston that summer, she was also introduced to Jane Stembridge, a young, white, former seminary student who staffed the SNCC headquarters on Atlanta's Sweet Auburn Avenue. As usual, Anne's reputation preceded her, but in this case the response to it was favorable: Stembridge looked forward to meeting someone whose dedication to justice was "so total." Anne and Stembridge hit it off at once, and they corresponded warmly in the weeks leading up to the fall conference. At Stembridge's urging, Anne hired a baby-sitter and made arrangements to get back to Atlanta for the meeting.[21]

Anne was to attend on behalf of SCEF as an "invited observer"—a role that was made ongoing thereafter. She learned later that a debate had waged within SNCC for months leading up to the fall conference on the advisability of associating with SCEF because of its "communistic" reputation. For many students, decisions regarding this gathering constituted their first real grappling with questions of civil liberties. The connections most eventually made between civil rights and civil liberties remained inchoate at this early stage in their activist careers. The coordinating committee, for example, rescinded its invitation to Bayard Rustin to address the conference when faced with the withdrawal of foundation funding. Rustin was a close associate of King but also a socialist, one-time CP member, and (most damning, perhaps) a homosexual. Stembridge was not alone among the students in feeling uncomfortable with the treatment of Rustin, and she had little or no hesitation about including Anne, particularly once the two had met.[22]

From the beginning of their work together, the depth of Anne's dedication to social change impressed Stembridge, and she saw Anne as "a person beside whom I have always measured my own commitment." The blonde, blue-eyed daughter of a Baptist minister who claimed Georgia as home, Stembridge was ultimately more of a poet, philosopher, and moralist—as one of her movement friends later wrote—than a political activist, and in the coming years she would find herself alternately attracted by the movement's promise and repelled by its stark revelations about human weakness. In August 1960, Anne wrote to Stembridge from Little Compton of her and Carl's participation in pacifist protests against the Polaris military submarine, and of walking picket lines opposing the jailing of civil libertarian Willard Uphaus. Activities of this sort were music to Stembridge's ears after the staid social landscape of the 1950s South in which she had grown up. For the group of young people of which she was a part, so many things that had once seemed static had begun to "burst loose" since February 1960. Anne's and Carl's lives had a kind of drama that derived from their absolute immersion in the civil rights movement, and that willingness to make sacrifices appealed terrifically to some of the young activists who had adopted or would soon adopt similar stances.[23]

Heralded by some of its most energetic participants as tantamount to the U.S. Continental Congress, the October 1960 SNCC conference may not have been quite that historic. But it was, as one historian of the organization has pointed out, a "turning point in the development of the student protest movement," with SNCC leaders charting an increasingly ambitious course for the movement's future.[24]

Anne traveled back and forth each day to the sessions from the home of Martin and Coretta King. More than she had anticipated, she found the students' ardor contagious. She counted 12 white southerners at the meeting—all students—and she was pleased to take note that two of the young women came from Virginia. One, Jane Meredith, hailed from Randolph-Macon Woman's College, and Anne made it a point to seek her and the other Virginian out. *I said, "I'm a Randolph-Macon alumna, and I'm so glad that you're here." They said that for the first time since they had been in college, the students were really asking questions and wanting to talk about the issue.* Though Meredith appeared tentative about being identified with the civil rights cause, only weeks afterward she and other Randolph-Macon students sought out black students from nearby Lynchburg College, sat in together, and were arrested.[25]

The impassioned statements against racial prejudice and for human community that Anne heard at the SNCC conference gave form to her thinking on white southern involvement in the new movement. If only one of these young white southerners could impart that kind of energy to a cross section of southern white campuses, surely more whites would be seized by the new crusading spirit so apparent in Atlanta. In whatever moments they could carve out together from the full agenda of the weekend, Anne discussed the idea with Jane Stembridge, then asked Jane if she would consider taking such a job under the auspices of SCEF.[26]

Stembridge confided to Anne her decision to leave the SNCC staff, both because of the Rustin incident and because she believed that as long as the group could only afford one staff person, the job should go to someone who was black. Yet neither was she certain that she wished to work for another organization. She did not say no, however, and Anne immediately advanced a proposal—first to Carl and Dombrowski, and then to the SCEF board—for a white "student project" that would subsidize Stembridge to organize white southern students to join blacks in civil rights campaigns. Her work would stimulate activity not on behalf of SCEF but rather to build autonomous local groups that might then feed into SNCC—or not, as they saw fit.[27]

The SCEF board readily approved the project, and Anne wrote of it to Marion Barry, a young Fisk University student who chaired SNCC. SNCC's African American leaders were not averse to the idea, nor were they as wary of SCEF as some of the more established civil rights leaders. But white organizing remained peripheral to them, partly because it seemed so bleak in its potential. *They never were terribly enthusiastic about it, but it was okay if we wanted to do it. They really had very little hope that we were going to get any white students involved.* With Anne handling the bulk of negotiations, SCEF and SNCC reached an agreement that the white student project would be funded by a SCEF grant, but that the person selected would join the SNCC staff and work in tandem with African American organizers.[28]

Yet Stembridge continued to hesitate about the project and soon opted out altogether. Like many young activists of the era, she was, as Anne explained to Dombrowski, *in a state of flux,* having left after her first year at New York's Union Theological Seminary and uncertain now about a direction for her life in the new movement. The younger woman concluded that she would prefer freelance writing to the SCEF project, and she remained firm despite pleas from Anne to reconsider. Though Stembridge never said so, Anne always felt that fear of SCEF's reputation had played at least some role in her friend's decision. As Stembridge herself reflected later of that year, "We were very brave, very committed, but not terribly discerning and wise in terms of thinking through" the meaning of red-baiting.[29]

Throughout the rest of 1960, Anne's brainchild was dormant for lack of a staff person. Sandra Cason (later Casey Hayden), a young Texas activist who ultimately became one of the most dedicated of white SNCC leaders, was another of several who were tempted by the job but turned it down. Anne wrote to Ella Baker of her frustration over these *stumbling block[s]*, but continued to put out word of the search.[30]

Anne's exchanges with Stembridge—as well as the general tenor of the October SNCC conference—gave her greater insight into the collective suspicion with which student activists regarded what they thought of as "adult organizations," and even organizations in general, insofar as they bespoke hierarchy, centralized power, and a lack of local or individual control. Race later became more of a dividing line among young SNCC activists, but at this early juncture in the life of the student civil rights movement, age was a more sensitive division, and Anne understood that she must tread lightly in her efforts toward greater cooperation with SNCC. *They [SNCC workers] were very anxious to be independent, and we bent over backwards in SCEF to make it clear that we didn't want to dominate . . . and the reason was that we felt that what they were doing was the yeast in the loaf of what was going to make a difference. Ultimately I think we had the best relationship with SNCC of any of the so-called adult organizations for that very reason.* The force of Anne's opinion on honoring the youths' self-determination was able to more or less direct SCEF policy on this matter.[31]

As Anne worked more closely with student organizers to develop the white student project, she was increasingly able to dignify, if not shed, the "subversive" label and to gain their trust and respect. Casey Hayden pointed out years later that most young SNCC idealists felt sure that SNCC was simply not capable of being subverted anyway, and that to think of someone as "subversive" "fell in with red-baiting as a way of thinking which contributed to fear," and was thus something to be avoided. When Jane Stembridge left the SNCC staff later in 1960, she was replaced with Ed King, one of the students who had been expelled from Kentucky State that spring. Anne knew King fairly well, and running drafts by the SNCC staff for checks of letter and spirit became part of her routine in preparing *Patriot* copy.[32]

Covering the Movement

SNCC students were introduced to Anne the journalist when she interviewed several of them in Atlanta. That image, for many, made quite an impression.

Part of what attracted Stembridge to Anne was her feeling—maintained long after the 1960s—that Anne was "one of the great all-time journalists," both because of her prose style and her choice of subject matter. Joan Browning, another white southern student who came into SNCC, remembered "being greatly impressed at the time with writers. [Anne] always seemed to have a notepad on her lap, a pen or pencil poised. So I was predisposed to think of her as a fascinating person." Julian Bond, one of the early Atlanta sit-in leaders who later became SNCC's communications director, first met Anne at the October 1960 meeting. Bond was one for whom her journalistic skills made all the difference. He thought of her as a professional, someone worthy of respect, and it would be several years into knowing her before he would drop the formality of calling her "Mrs. Braden." Decades after they had become friends, Bond recalled that "because of the *Patriot*, which I admired not only because of its content but because of its design, Anne became a role model for me as a propagandist. I mean that in the good sense of the word, as someone who could get this movement out there in the public eye."[33]

The *Patriot* offered early student activists a level of coverage not available through the more mainstream press, which tended to print only the more sensational news of arrests or brutality. Anne, on the other hand, was not constrained by socially established concepts of what constituted news: she offered plenty of firsthand reflections, which she often solicited from students themselves, and observations that were analytical but clearly sympathetic. During that first year of sit-ins Anne worried occasionally that she was *romanticizing* the excitement of the new movement, but concluded that *the things I've said are true.*[34]

Despite the limitations of the *Patriot*'s four-page format, she devoted generous amounts of space to this significant new outbreak of activism. Bond later reflected that "Anne helped to define who we were to the *Patriot* audience and to a broader audience as well. That was very helpful to us because it was the definition we held of ourselves as this vanguard challenging not just the segregation system but older organizations too, like the NAACP, for instance." With a few exceptions, not even the African American press so accurately reflected the perspectives of the students themselves.[35]

Anne's and Carl's help to SNCC went far beyond the coverage given in the *Patriot*. In late 1960 they shared their press list with the young organizers and put together a "how-to" packet in media skills for Ed King, who was new to the business of getting press attention. The list contained 320 news outlets not confined to the South and included African American, religious, labor, farm, liberal, student, and left publications. By the early 1960s the Bradens were able to help civil rights youth reach a wider "market": they operated a fledgling press service of their own—under *Patriot* auspices—that filled the void left when Federated Press went under. With the help of their contacts at other newspapers, they got out stories concentrating on southern social change-related news, especially on the actions of SNCC.[36]

The new student upsurge seemed to vindicate the past decade of Anne and Carl's hard work, and the couple were quick to introduce the SNCC activists to sympathetic long-standing networks on the left. As these new alliances congealed, however, it was Anne that the students more often turned to. A combination of Carl's brusque individualism and his yearlong imprisonment from 1961–1962 kept students from having as much contact with him as with Anne, whom some perceived as more approachable. She may also have appeared, on a political level, less threatening. Stembridge reflected later that "when people's fears surfaced, they were [thinking] more about Carl than Anne because Carl's activities were more known and he was in prison. . . . There was a lot of fear—should SNCC 'risk' the Bradens?—which was ridiculous." Julian Bond also remembered that he had been warned away by civil rights elders from the Bradens because they were "leftists, maybe Communists, who—regardless of whether they were good people or not—were probably not [people] we wanted to associate with." Later, Bond had only the vaguest recollections of early SNCC associations with Carl, but recalled Anne's presence in the early student movement vividly: "[She] widened our list of political and fundraising contacts and exposed us to journalists and writers whom we didn't know about."[37]

These included people like I. F. Stone and writers for the *National Guardian*. Anne wrote occasionally for the *Guardian* herself and directed its editors toward greater contacts with the southern movement. Also, she and Carl had the support of James Higgins, editor of the *Gazette and Daily* in York, Pennsylvania. The *Gazette and Daily* was probably the nation's most left-leaning daily newspaper throughout the post-WWII era, and both Bradens acted as occasional stringers for the paper, having met Higgins through mutual friends. Prodded by a tip from Anne or Carl, Higgins would sometimes request Associated Press coverage of a protest or act of racial violence. Once such news went out over the wire, public exposure to it increased many times over.[38]

The kinds of contacts the Bradens were able to provide were not only journalistic. Throughout 1960 and thereafter, a number of students demonstrated their commitment to the new movement by leaving school—as Stembridge had done—to plunge into the work more fully, not only on college campuses but in grassroots communities. By early 1961, however, the organization was floundering, partially because of its leaders' unfamiliarity with organizational fundraising. It was during this period that Anne and, through her, SCEF, began to augment SNCC's efforts to raise money. In April 1961 Ed King sent a poignant plea to SCEF via James Dombrowski, whom he had contacted at Anne's suggestion, asking for a sizable contribution to SNCC that could go toward staff salaries. Though funds had already been allocated to SNCC for the unfilled white student project, Dombrowski obliged with a $1,000 SCEF donation. Less than a month later Ed King was back with a new request for a thousand dollars more.[39]

Put Your Body into the Struggle

The outbreak of the freedom rides in the spring of 1961 brought a new, sharper edge to the youth civil rights brigades and a solidifying of the alliance between Anne and the most militant leaders of them. The young riders were determined at all costs to make the country live up to its democratic promises. Anne remembered later that the freedom rides popularized a new slogan: *The temper of the times was that it wasn't enough to go to a meeting; [you had to] "put your body into the struggle."*[40]

The violence the freedom rides triggered in Deep South segregationist culture gave SNCC organizers a new dynamism. The ensuing brutality and imprisonments tremendously expanded public awareness that social forces were in motion that could not—perhaps should not—be stopped. Although the rides directly involved relatively small numbers of protesters, they mesmerized the nation and had a dramatic effect on the riders themselves, who—as one historian of SNCC has observed—"suddenly became aware of their collective ability to provoke a crisis that would attract international publicity and compel federal intervention."[41]

The range of SNCC activities and the corresponding need for funds to administer them grew exponentially at this juncture, but young leaders—most of whom were jailed, facing jail time, or trying to get a coworker out of jail—had precious little energy to devote to matters as mundane as fundraising. That summer SCEF underwrote the cost of a funding appeal sent out on behalf of SNCC to the *Patriot* mailing list. Soon such assistance became standard procedure. Despite in-house grousing over a few instances in which donations to SNCC meant fewer dollars to SCEF, Anne and Carl shared with the SNCC staff the names of their large donors in cities like Chicago and Detroit, and Melish and the New York fundraising committee were mobilized. Soon after that, of course, the militancy and idealism of SNCC led it to become a sort of icon for youthful revolutionary activism on a variety of social issues. As a consequence, SNCC's reputation grew to the point that its fundraising apparatus became many times over what that of SCEF had been. But in the first two years of the existence of the student group, the Bradens opened new funding vistas as SNCC struggled to maintain its initial momentum.[42]

As the uprisings of early 1960 settled into a more sustained—though ever more intense—student movement, the fact that the Bradens were so deeply dedicated and so helpful to early SNCC organizers reinforced the determination of some of them to collaborate more closely with Anne and Carl. In order to do so, however, they had to resist the taint attached to the couple. Years later, veterans of SNCC found it impossible to pinpoint the sources of the disinformation they received about Anne and Carl. Rumors about the two seemed to be simply "in the air."[43]

Even though McCarthyism was becoming a thing of the past, particularly since the 1957 death of its standard-bearer Joe McCarthy, anticommunism was still such an integral part of southern culture that it was virtually invisible. Coming from a generation weaned on the anticommunist witch hunts, young southerners of both races were a sort of "southern-naive," as one SNCC supporter later joked. Connie Curry, a young white North Carolinian employed by the National Student Association (NSA), became an early adult adviser to SNCC even though less than five years of age separated her from most students. Curry recalled the response of southern youth to the assortment of people attracted to the widening movement: "I remember being so undone by [people who] talked fast, didn't shave their legs, wore sandals, or were from New York. They must be communists because they were so 'other-worldly.' Back then, if anybody was strange, the first thing you would say was that they were a communist."[44]

By Curry's lights, Anne was not at all strange. In fact, she struck some students who met her as a kind of renegade southern lady: soft-spoken, well-mannered, "ladylike" even—yet driven by some inner flame to bring down segregation. As Joan Browning later observed, Anne was "one of the small group of [older] women who showed me that one could be a loyal Southerner and a respectable woman while fighting for social justice. The fact that Anne was Southern to the bone and had that wonderful slow Southern speech helped me redefine myself." Although Anne rejected the lion's share of southern white ideology, her personal style was one that expanded rather than defied popular notions about southern "ladies." She had not yet adopted the attire of blue jeans and T-shirts that would characterize her later years, but was usually clad in dresses that were casual but well put together. (Unknown to young activists for whom she held a kind of mystique, Anne paid scant attention to her wardrobe choices.) She also possessed a gender consciousness that in 1960 far exceeded that of most SNCC students, and few of the younger women probably realized at the time what an unconscious model of female opposition she functioned as for them. Sue Thrasher, another white southern activist, recalled later that Anne had strong opinions and was unafraid to voice them at meetings or argue with opponents—all qualities Thrasher found unusual in a woman, but captivating.[45]

Even among adults in the movement, Anne felt a kinship with other women and tried to draw them more deeply into activism. She once confounded Martin Luther King with the request that his wife, Coretta, be included in a strategy discussion under way at his Atlanta home. King seemed taken aback, but he complied and invited Coretta to join them (which she did). Anne also made it her business to direct attention to women's accomplishments—as when she cowrote and organized a dramatic reading, "Tribute to the Heroines of the South," at SCEF's 1961 New York fundraiser.[46]

To Connie Curry, Anne seemed more serious than most adult activists in the SNCC circle: it was clear that the cause of racial justice was more to her than just the job it appeared to be for some employed civil rights workers, such as those from the Southern Regional Council. Like Ella Baker, however, Anne could, and often did, lean back—cigarette smoke swirling in the air above her—and tell a good story over a fifth of bourbon at the end of a long day and night's work.[47]

Both Bradens also appeared to have the trust and friendship of respected civil rights elders such as Baker, Shuttlesworth, and even Martin Luther King Jr. Yet senior members of Curry's NSA advisory committee and staffers of the SRC, with whom she worked closely, were always leery of the couple, not openly criticizing their "communistic" politics, but possessing, Curry remembered, "a kind of unspoken distrust. The one thing ever articulated was that you needed to be careful of the Bradens because you couldn't trust them to use information in the most responsible way. . . . [It was said that they might] put the cause ahead of relationships."[48]

In the lingering Cold War culture of the early 1960s, even coverage in the *Patriot* might seem to anticommunist liberals to be sacrificing relationships insofar as it was a somewhat controversial news organ, but Anne refused to relinquish her prerogative to print civil rights news. In reality, except for family ties, nearly all of the Bradens' closest relationships were intimately linked to "the cause." Their friendships with Baker and other movement leaders grew out of a shared belief system reinforced by a history of cooperative work that had proven the couple's mettle over time. Not all of Anne's and Carl's friends in the African American community shared their anticapitalist views, but the pair also possessed a zeal about activism that was too genuine to be ignored. In practice, at least among the most committed supporters, ideology was a lower order of business in the civil rights movement than was the kind of steely reliability that Anne and Carl possessed.[49]

King and the Ambivalence of SCLC

Anne's embrace of nonviolence endeared her to people like King, who with his wife, Coretta, maintained a friendship with the Bradens even after he realized they were a political liability. The autobiographical odyssey that she had described to King the night they met in 1957 remained, for him, a defining feature of Anne Braden, and in the early years of the movement she never let him forget it—or her. Anne often wrote long letters to King throughout the late 1950s and early '60s, as she did to all her friends—such lengthy missives that they became a joke between her and almost everyone who knew her. Whenever King was jailed, she and Carl sent telegrams of support, and Anne was one of the handful of white southern supporters King later referred to with admiration in his now-famous April 1963 "Letter from Birmingham Jail." The Bradens also proposed numerous cooperative projects between SCLC and SCEF, only some of which SCLC embraced. The successes were usually through King's influence, as in the case of the voteless hearings of January 1960, with which SCLC proceeded despite opposition from a few vocal board members. King frequently appeared receptive to closer cooperation with SCEF but claimed he was hamstrung by other SCLC leaders who were wary of SCEF.[50]

Anne felt that King, more than most clergymen with whom he worked (except for Shuttlesworth, whom Anne saw as a most kindred political spirit), genuinely understood how the politics of southern red-baiting served only to reify segregation and racial hierarchy. She tried to persuade him to use his growing influence in American culture to criticize what remained of the anticommunist witch hunt. In mid-1960 she wrote him a 13-page, single-spaced, typed letter on the subject—a "book," she joked to Coretta, through whom she sheepishly delivered the letter. Although Anne emphasized to King that he need not take time to reply, he told her later that he had read "every word" of it in an airplane 40,000 feet over South America. King never took the major step forward on this issue that Anne wished he would, but he displayed great courage in diffusing red-baiting sentiment when a particular moment called for it. Despite considerable pressure to do so, he never repudiated SCEF.[51]

Anne found it hard to get to the heart of the SCLC coolness toward SCEF, however, because King himself wanted to have it both ways. With Anne and with other leftist associates, he was torn—as one of his biographers has written—by the "painful conflicts of pragmatism, belief, and personal loyalty." King felt a genuine bond with Anne and Carl. Yet he also felt he had to keep his movement work as free as possible from the red smear that constantly threatened southern social change efforts, and such pressures only mounted as his stature in civil rights leadership rose. When he first spoke with Anne and Carl directly concerning the rumors about SCEF, he suggested—perhaps out of tactfulness—that the ill feelings in SCLC were mostly a carryover from the New Deal-era Southern Conference and that the most questionable figure in SCEF seemed to be Dombrowski, whom King had never met. But on at least one occasion during 1960 King himself warned Bob Moses, a young SNCC recruit, away from associating with SCEF not because he perceived any real misguidedness or even ideological division but because—as he allegedly told Moses—"some people think it's Communist and that's what matters." And when Anne, with the help of Jim Wood, SCLC public relations director, and Wyatt Tee Walker, Baker's replacement as SCLC executive director, arranged a December 1960 meeting for leaders of the two groups to discuss their differences, she learned at the last minute that she and Carl, not Dombrowski or SCEF's history, were the central sticking points. Wood and Walker thought it best the couple not attend the meeting in order to allow freer expression of sentiments, and they did not go.[52]

On paper, however, Anne marshaled plenty of arguments for greater co-operation between the two organizations. She wrote these thoughts to Wood a few days before the meeting: *Our objective is to stimulate white Southerners to act openly and unequivocatingly [sic] for integration. We work at this task constantly—night and day, contacting them, helping them think of things they can do and how to do it, putting them in touch with others of like mind. We run into many roadblocks, as you can imagine . . . but there is one obstacle which it is almost impossible to fight. This is when the potentially liberal white person you are trying to move can say to you: "But the Negroes must not want what you are working for, because they won't work with you." Of course they can't ever say this with complete accuracy because we do have the support of Negroes. But it seems to me SCLC is key: if people can say the SCLC refuses to work with us, we are crippled from the start. . . . It is inconceivable to me that they [SCLC] could not see that this is precisely what the segregationists are trying to do when they call us "red."*[53]

Although everyone at the meeting agreed to closer working relations, the process effectively ended in stalemate. With advocates like Shuttlesworth,

Walker, and, on occasion, King, SCLC would work with SCEF on occasion, but there remained significant internal opposition to "the Bradens." SCLC would continue to be unwilling to go to the wall on their behalf.[54]

The Burden of Other Battles

This was not the first and it was far from the last time Anne would have to fight for acceptance by the civil rights community. By now, being "subversive"—as supporters and opponents alike referred to her and Carl—simply came with the territory. That label meant having to prove their sincerity again and again. Anne and Carl had to choose their battles carefully, and even so, the process was time-consuming and tiresome but also necessary if they were to be effective at all. Only Anne's stick-to-it-iveness kept her self-confidence from being whittled to a nub by the never-ending innuendoes and snubs from a variety of corners, but the whole business distressed her more than it did Carl.

In addition to the suspicions hovering around them, there were genuine divisions of political outlook that put the Bradens at odds with a few coworkers. Ellen Roberts, a longtime SCEF board member from Florida, was alienated by Carl's fiery anticapitalist rhetoric. After hearing him exclaim repeatedly of the frustrations of "the capitalist system," Roberts resigned her membership on the SCEF board and refused to reconsider despite Dombrowski's attempts to mollify her.[55]

Yet few of the conflicts of those years were as clear-cut as that one. Along with the flowering of the civil rights movement throughout 1960 came a new outpouring of concern among southern adult activists over the danger represented by associating with "known subversives" like Anne and Carl. These concerns had more to do with the couple's reputation than they did with any inclination they had ever shown toward trying to subvert any organization of which they were a part. In the summer of 1960, for instance, Anne wrote to John Morris, executive director of the recently established Episcopal Society for Racial and Cultural Unity, to express her enthusiasm for the organization's agenda and to ask if he had plans to organize a group in Louisville. She had never met Morris: he had been introduced to Carl during one of Carl's stops through Atlanta, and the two had talked about Episcopalianism and race. Carl had left Morris a copy of Anne's book with the suggestion that he might enjoy talking to her. Morris's reply to Anne was gentle but firm: "I do not think it would be wise for you or your husband to be initiators or, if a [Louisville] group were formed, to take any leading role in it. . . . Your identification with the Society would frighten off prospective members." Morris acknowledged that

Anne had never volunteered to lead a local organizing drive and added that "perhaps after such persons got to know you better, they would not have any such reticence." He maintained, however, that his group was unwilling "to bear the additional burden of fighting other battles" that would come as a result of the Bradens' involvement. Anne usually took the time to reply to such letters, and she thanked him for the spirit in which he had written and reassured him that she and Carl had no intention of forcing themselves on any group.[56]

Such exchanges had to be draining, but as long as anticommunism had the power to inspire such fear among reformers, the couple's reputation would feed on itself. Because not many people in the early 1960s were willing to stand up for inclusiveness but there were always a few who—like Stembridge—could not stomach the idea of excluding anyone who supported the cause of civil rights, the Bradens' presence did in fact generate "other battles" for the organizations to which they gravitated, as Morris had suggested it would. They remained particularly controversial in Louisville, and the battles surfaced more frequently as civil rights activism intensified there throughout 1960 and thereafter. Once Louisville's CORE group got under way in the wake of Len Holt's organizing tour, the national CORE office attempted to distance itself from further relations with the Bradens. Yet a handful of local participants refused to cease turning to Anne even after she and Carl agreed not to have any "formal association with the chapter." Despite her attempts to mitigate ill feelings, the group lodged a formal protest with the national office and subsequently nearly split over the question of her participation in it— mainly because a contingent of them so passionately wanted her to stay. Resolution of this conflict remained uneasy in spite of her insistence on settling it with her complete withdrawal.[57]

Within organizations that embraced a more Popular Front, inclusive approach, Anne sometimes still found herself marginalized. In the fall of 1960, she appealed to the national headquarters of WILPF—an organization that included a few CP members and had often fended off red-baiting attacks—to send her news of the group's southern affiliates for inclusion in the *Patriot*. Months later, receiving no reply, she heard from Virginia Durr that WILPF feared its southern contacts might become "prejudiced against" the league if it supplied news to the *Patriot*. These sorts of exchanges were not in the least exceptional in the Bradens' southern organizing work.[58]

In general both Anne and Carl simply grinned and bore it, masking or minimizing to themselves the wounding effects of coworkers' words. Their southern experiences were not without affirmations, and trips to New York, Chicago, and northern California reunited them with thriving left networks that provided an antidote to the criticism. Yet with cultural anticommunism on the wane as a national frenzy and with the promise of expansive new reforms across the South, Anne's and Carl's experiences in this regard were stinging, constant reminders to them of the need for more southern activists to take on the cause of civil liberties as inseparable from that of civil rights.

In the absence of such an assault, southern political authorities continued to rely heavily on anticommunism as a weapon against civil rights advances. In early 1961, as the Bradens awaited the Supreme Court's ruling on Carl's HUAC case (which John Coe and Leonard Boudin had argued before the Court in November 1960), Carl received a new subpoena, this time to appear on February 6 before the Florida Legislative Investigation Commission, a state investigating body modeled on HUAC. This group was one of eight committees of this nature set up in southern states since *Brown*, and over time most of them turned their attention to the Bradens.[59]

In Tallahassee, after six hours of testimony by "secret witnesses," some of whom had attended meetings he had organized throughout 1960, Carl refused to testify and was freed from subpoena. No further steps were taken toward prosecuting him, but the commission put him on record as "a member of a Communist-front organization [SCEF]." The dismal outcome was made no better by the critical headlines it generated anew in Louisville.[60]

Broadening the Southern Movement

Throughout 1960 and 1961 Anne continued to move at the periphery of SNCC activities, forging close personal and political ties with some young southerners but held at bay by others because of the innuendoes that tailed her and Carl. To the extent that any single individual could be credited, the one most responsible for bringing Anne more fully within the SNCC fold was Jim Forman, an African American writer and organizer who became SNCC's executive secretary in September 1961. Born in 1928, Forman was closer in age to Anne than he was to his fellow SNCC staffers, and he was more politically experienced than most in SNCC. Forman considered himself a revolutionary, not a liberal, and he did not share the wholehearted commitment to nonviolence that animated some student protesters. To some, his sophistication was suspect; to others, like Julian Bond, it was appealing. Bond remembered that "it was not until Forman came along" that SNCC organizers became conscious of how much anticommunism was limiting the movement.[61]

Forman had first met the Bradens and established a correspondence with Anne in 1958 in his hometown of Chicago, where he was then writing for the black *Chicago Defender* newspaper. The Bradens had run into Forman again in the context of support work they all carried on in Fayette County, Tennessee, where the plight of rural African American farmer-activists worsened as 1961 dawned.[62]

That year, inspired by the radicalism emanating from the freedom rides, Forman appeared at the door of Atlanta's cluttered, one-room SNCC headquarters just as Ed King left to return to school. At that chaotic moment in SNCC's organizational life, Forman's maturity and experience transcended the perceptual divide that prompted the students to see themselves, often, in contradistinction to adults. Assuming the executive post, he provided much-needed organizational skills such as fundraising and directing a staff, as well as a more focused political mission. Forman was visionary but also highly pragmatic: he appreciated the Bradens' political experience and their wider contacts with the left and with potential donors. Readily dismissing the rumors about them, he established regular contacts with Anne and Dombrowski. Forman understood the divisive nature of red-baiting, and he worked actively at moving the students toward greater inclusiveness.[63]

Other forces were at work that would help propel SNCC workers in that direction. From the earliest sit-ins, southern black student protesters had energized small groups of white college students across the country who saw them as heroic and worthy of emulation. Half a continent away from the Jim Crow South, the earliest student crusaders at the University of California-Berkeley that spring of 1960 protested not racial segregation but the inquisitorial powers of the House Committee on Un-American Activities. A group of UC students attempting a peaceful protest of HUAC hearings found themselves clubbed and sprayed with high-intensity fire hoses that sent them hurtling down the rotunda steps of San Francisco City Hall. The experience politicized many and became a catalyst for the Berkeley student movement and its organizational vehicle, the campus-based political party SLATE.[64]

On a fundraising trip to California in early 1961, Anne spent an evening with some of the Berkeley student leaders whose campus activism had been spurred by the protest at City Hall, which they had initially undertaken as something of a lark. She experienced almost a sense of déjà vu when she compared their stories to those she had heard from southern SNCC activists. *They [told me their picket] developed because "we read about what the students were doing in the South, and we thought we oughtn't to just sit here." From there they grew and the Berkeley movement [became] a very powerful sort of [force] on that campus. Before that, nobody had heard of Berkeley except it was one branch of University of California. For years after that, I ran into people in one place or another who had gotten radicalized that day, being washed down those [City Hall] steps.*[65]

As numerous histories of twentieth-century social change have observed, the domestic Cold War all but destroyed the small but energetic left-wing stream in American politics that had bubbled up during the Great Depression. In practical terms, what that meant was that the broad socioeconomic reform agenda advanced by the Old Left lay in shreds by 1960, and when a new generation of students took it up, they did so in piecemeal fashion—through the emergence of what the historian Todd Gitlin has called "single-issue movements: civil rights, civil liberties, campus reform, peace."[66]

Anne was both a survivor of and an inheritor to the Old Left, however, and she was one of a small number of adults who kept its ideas alive to a new generation of activists. She took up the task of attempting to knit the new issue-based crusades together, in practical as well as theoretical terms, into a wider critique of social and economic injustice. It was second nature for her to put the West Coast students in touch with SNCC, and she wrote to Ed King soon after returning from California with contacts that included Berkeley's SLATE as well as campus activist groups at San Jose State, Stanford University, San Diego State, and even at a San Francisco high school. Wherever she spoke in California, it seemed that young people wanted to hear more about SNCC and wondered what they could do to help. Anne readily passed on information about SNCC and was full of praise for its dynamism. Some of these young Californians had already had limited contacts with southern students but had fallen out of touch as SNCC work intensified in the first year of protests. For others, it was their first opportunity to hear from someone who was actually a part of the southern civil rights movement and to establish communications with people in SNCC.[67]

For her own part, Anne saw the Berkeley anti-HUAC protests as the *beginning of the end* of the witch hunts that had bedeviled her and Carl's lives for so long. Yet even there, young people had to fight for the right to hear Anne's words. When a student group at San Jose State invited her to speak on February 23, 1961, her planned appearance generated a storm of protest from a second campus organization, "Students Against Communism." In a dispute the local newspaper later pronounced a "teapot tempest," the anticommunist group insisted (wrongly) that Anne had invoked in federal hearings the First and Fifth Amendments to the Constitution with regard to CP membership and should not be allowed on campus. Civil liberties held greater sway on California campuses, however, than they did on southern ones, and the university president, John Wahlquist, declared that as long as Anne held "intact" citizenship rights, her talk would proceed as scheduled. Wahlquist's public statement added that "our students are sufficiently mature to hear all sides of such questions." A threatened "mothers' march" of protest amounted to only three parents and two students. Instead, the furor over free speech turned what might have been a few dozen listeners into a standing-room-only crowd of 400. After her talk on southern civil rights, Anne took questions. *Someone got up and "Mrs. Braden, are you a member of the Communist Party?" And this is what I always [answered]: "Well, I'm not going to answer that question and I'm going to tell you why." [And I explained that] the whole setting up of membership in the Communist Party as the test of whether a person can be considered a human being in this country has stifled any real discussion of the issues that face the country and it's stifling the discussion of the civil rights movement in the South. The only [solution] to that is for Communists to be considered human beings like everybody else, so I'm not going to be a part of this process. When the day comes that a person can be a member of the Communist Party and say so and continue to work and function in this society, I'll answer that question, but until that day comes I will not.* Anne was gratified and a little surprised when the crowd broke into spontaneous applause. She concluded that *there was an instinctive reaction on their part that this was an important battle.* Domestic anticommunist fears were by this time subsiding outside the South. In the region, however, escalating challenges to Jim Crow had given anticommunist hysteria new energy that was still insufficient to stop the collapse of segregation.[68]

Back home in Louisville, new mass protests erupted at almost exactly that moment. On the day following Anne's speech at San Jose State, vanloads of young African Americans—a total of 58, mostly high school students—were carted away from downtown Louisville, where they picketed against discriminatory treatment in department stores. The demonstrations, which continued for weeks, were nonviolent, though those arrested faced disorderly conduct charges for blocking entrances. Judge Henry Triplett's comment that the youthful protesters were being "exploited" by adult activists sprang from the same paranoia about internal subversion that had dominated American culture throughout the postwar era and kept Anne and Carl marginal figures in local civil rights campaigns. But such innuendoes failed to defuse the "creative extremism" (as Martin Luther King, Jr. later described it) of the new generation now demanding an end to segregation.[69]

CHAPTER TEN

OPENING UP THE SOUTHERN POLICE STATE

The very passion for "Americanism" in the South was at least in great part the passion that the South should remain fundamentally unchanged.

—W. J. Cash, *Mind of the South*, 1941[1]

So much of our problem is one of ignorance. In high school in about 1950 to 1954 I first heard of "Reds," Communists. I was still afraid when I got to college. Then somehow I began to see how they use "Red" to keep down the liberal movement. I was so ignorant when CORE invited me to take a job with them: I was afraid [since] CORE had "socialists," "Communists," all that "foreign stuff." Then I met Carl and Anne Braden and SCEF. Then the headlines came about them, but she [Anne] was a sweet lady, not a red monster coming down on me. . . . I came to feel that whether a person is a Communist or anything else, I will relate to him as a human being. . . . I will accept any person who will stand side by side and fight against discrimination and for civil rights. . . . I just don't care anymore. I want to work for the movement.

—Charles Sherrod, SNCC activist, 1963 speech[2]

ALTHOUGH NEW STREET PROTESTS IN Louisville could not fail to capture Anne's and Carl's attention, they remained caught up in difficult circumstances of their own that prevented them from focusing solely on the movement in bloom around them. In late February 1961—while Anne was still out West—the U.S. Supreme Court rejected Carl's appeal, and Frank

Wilkinson's, on the HUAC contempt citations. Alabamian Justice Hugo Black wrote a strongly worded dissent, warning of consequences that "may well strip the Negro of the aid of the many white people that have been willing to speak up on his behalf," if the committee maintained "the power to interrogate anyone who is called a Communist." Publications ranging from *I. F. Stone's Weekly* to the *Norfolk Journal and Guide* editorialized against the decision. Yet southern anticommunism flourished through the state investigating committees that Anne called "little HUAC's" and at the grassroots level through groups like the Minutemen and the John Birch Society, while events like the U.S.-Soviet standoff over the Bay of Pigs that spring drove the Cold War forward.[3]

The Bradens began to make preparations for Carl's impending year in prison. Without the help of her partner and besieged by pleas from her parents concerning the couple's choices, it looked like a difficult year ahead for Anne and her children. Both she and Carl were resigned to the fact: as he put it, "This is the price we were prepared to pay."[4]

Luckily, Anne did have household help. In their fieldwork, the Bradens confronted plenty of opposition but they also met individuals who—inspired by their obvious dedication—would ask, "What can I do for the cause?" During Carl's Florida organizing that year he had met Dorothy Johnson, a committed white pacifist who presented herself with this request. This time, Carl had a real need, and he proposed to Johnson that she move to Louisville to help Anne with SCEF work and the children during his imprisonment. Not only would Anne have to manage her usual obligations: the Bradens were in the midst of finishing their attic to create an additional bedroom and an office for their mushrooming paperwork. Anne's arrangement with Johnson was not without its pitfalls. Johnson did not get along smoothly with Jim Braden, and she appeared nervous in the Bradens' predominantly black neighborhood. Yet her help allowed Anne to maintain a level of social action that the pitch of the movement seemed to call for in 1961.[5]

Carl's Imprisonment

On May Day, 1961, Carl—flanked by Anne and nine-year-old Jim—and Frank Wilkinson presented themselves to federal authorities in Atlanta to begin their terms. The event followed SCEF's board meeting, and a contingent of regional activists turned out to see the two men off. The prisoners were held for ten days in Atlanta's Fulton County Jail, then transferred in hand and ankle cuffs to a federal minimum-security prison camp at Donaldson Air Force Base in South Carolina. They spent mornings in office work and devoted afternoons to helping less literate prisoners fill out parole applications and write letters home.[6]

In the days immediately following Carl's incarceration, the stakes of the movement heightened considerably with the unfolding drama of the freedom rides, especially the violence of the Mother's Day Massacre in Anniston and Birmingham on May 14. It comforted Carl to feel that, as he wrote to Anne, "the world moves forward through the jails." In general, he approached the coming months with a calm confidence about the stand he was making that was distinctly different from the uncertainty that had characterized his 1954–55 jailings. Despite tight restrictions (only family members were allowed to visit) and extremes of treatment, Carl had determined to make the best of the situation. After consulting King and other movement leaders, he and Anne concluded that even accepting parole would be an ethical mistake, as it would prohibit him from doing field organizing for civil rights. Instead they decided to launch a clemency campaign as a means of organizing protest.[7]

Anne's life grew enormously more complicated with his imprisonment, however. Days after the rides began, homebound with the children in Louisville, she fielded phone calls from Shuttlesworth, who was trying to round up fresh recruits from across the country. Anne spoke with various people but found no one willing to replace the fallen riders. Troubled especially by the brutality in Anniston, she wrote of the grim events to Carl: *When nobody else would go from here, I was tempted to go myself—in fact, I still am. I keep telling myself that with half the family already in jail, it would only be quixotic at this point. But if it goes on much longer I don't know what I'll do. I'm sure if you hadn't been in jail I would have had to go.* Instead of giving in to what in her situation would have felt like *false heroics*, she contented herself with publicity and fundraising for the rides, as well as what support she could offer the young resisters via telephone.[8]

Despite her constraints, Anne was determined to keep up her work in the movement, and that required some travel. She made it a priority to visit Carl whenever she was on the road, even though it frequently meant a detour of hundreds of miles. She brought their son, Jim, along as often as she could manage and usually hauled in pints of ice cream to brighten Carl's day. Those first few months of operating alone proved extremely wearing, however, and though she attempted to match her stoicism to his, she felt herself stretched thin. The notes she managed to jot to him almost daily were written in airports or bus stations or in the wee hours of the morning. In spite of how busy she remained, being on her own gave her time to reflect with some sadness on the tension that permeated their lives. She wrote him in mid-1961 that *you and I both seem to have changed so over the years. A long time ago we used to have a more relaxed interest in life, an interest in all the little things around us, the interesting people and their complex lives, the exciting new ideas. Of late years, there's the press of things that must be done and sometimes you wonder just a little why, and we no longer seem to have time to look around us and to savor life.* Frustration about not having enough time had nagged at Anne periodically for years and would continue to do so. But she also noticed on prison visits that Carl seemed more relaxed than he had in years, and she encouraged him to use his time there as a rest cure.[9]

Far from abating, the tension accompanying her own hectic schedule grew more intense as she scrambled to ensure that her children were cared for without sacrificing all her other work. There were times when she felt nagged at too by Carl when he—knowing that Anne had a hard time saying "no" to any requests for help—expressed concerns lest she neglect the children. Such expressions, while well intended, were painful reminders of ongoing conflicts with her parents. She wrote him that *our lives have become too complicated,* and insisted that he *at least acknowledge that this confusion [is] a joint responsibility.* Complicating her management of the home front without him was the knowledge that their older children endured cruelties at school for his imprisonment for "communistic" beliefs. The taunts troubled Anne, but she felt that Jim and Anita bore up relatively well under the strain. She wrote to Carl that they were *pretty remarkable people,* allaying her worries with the conclusion that *I don't know that we are any worse parents than most people and probably better than lots . . . most children who turn out well probably do it in spite of their parents.* She talked the children through the conflicts and countered them by soliciting for Jim a scholarship to spend the summer in Vermont at the left-leaning Timberlake Farm and Wilderness Camp, where his parents' politics were more appreciated. The girls spent most of their summer vacation with the McCartys, leaving Anne several weeks' relative freedom to travel. Except for intimations of her household stresses to Carl in small doses—and a kind of edginess that became a fixture of her personality—she tried to draw satisfaction from what work she was able to accomplish and to let go of what she could not. She continued to juggle as best she could the competing demands on her time from children, household expansion, parents, in-laws, and—unceasingly—the movement.[10]

The Clemency Campaign

Because their work focused on the South, the Bradens—on the advice of King—chose to separate the issue of Carl's clemency from Wilkinson's even though the two men's cases had proceeded together and had been considered jointly by the Supreme Court. In Carl's case, however, subjection to HUAC prosecution seemed to be retaliation, clear and simple, for civil rights activism. This correlation made the case uniquely southern, and a device through which to fight back against the segregationist use of latter-day McCathyism. Thus, two separate but related campaigns took shape. The one for Carl's clemency was led by Anne and directed at southern civil rights supporters. The second was organized by civil libertarians through the newly established National Committee to Abolish HUAC (NCAHUAC)—which Wilkinson had been organizing at the time of his subpoena—and aimed at freeing both men on civil liberties grounds. Anne worked with the new committee but kept her emphasis largely southern.[11]

The first step in the Bradens' fightback strategy was to mount support for Carl's clemency petition, which Anne had undertaken even before he went into prison. On her way back from California, she stopped in Atlanta to ask King to initiate the petition. Anne knew that King's leadership would bring more signers onboard than she could otherwise hope for. *[Martin] had heard about the decision because it had been in the news and he was commiserating with me. He said, "What can I do for you?" And I said, "I want you to initiate a clemency petition for Carl." When I say that now, it doesn't sound like much to ask, but I knew when I said it—and he did too—that it was a big request. People were afraid of HUAC and afraid of people who had been condemned by HUAC. He looked at me and kind of laughed, and he said, "Well."*[12]

Alluding to the now-famous billboards that read "Martin Luther King at Communist Training School," erected across the South by the Georgia Education Commission (Georgia's "little HUAC"), King pointed out that he too was called a Communist. Anne did not back away from her request, however, arguing that only he held sufficient stature to get away with such an initiative. She left without a reply and did not contact King for several weeks. During that time, Wyatt Walker and Shuttlesworth committed their leadership, and the campaign developed some momentum. *Finally I began calling him back. And it was the only time that I tried to reach Martin—before or after that—when I had a hard time getting him. He was pretty good about returning calls. I really began to feel he was avoiding me.* After numerous attempts, Anne phoned King's home late one Saturday night and was told that he was not in. She had the gnawing feeling that he really was there, however, and called Shuttlesworth in a quandary. The erstwhile Alabamian pronounced King mired in indecision and recommended that she forget about his reply and simply get on with their campaign. Anne reluctantly agreed, knowing that to do so would lessen its effectiveness.[13]

Very early the next morning, however, the phone rang, and King told Anne to put his name on the petition. He told her he had prayed all night about the matter and knew it was the right thing to do. *And so, of course, [we] got a lot of publicity, and he was attacked for it too. I always thought about that later, in about the middle '60s, when people on our side would attack Martin. People forget that before he died, he was terribly under attack too, because of his stand against the Vietnam War, from some of the established black leadership. I think Martin did compromise on occasions when he thought it was the best tactic, but I don't think he was ever doing those things for personal aggrandizement. In our case, there was absolutely nothing he was going to get out of signing our petition except a lot of trouble.* Anne never forgot King's courage, and her vision of him has always focused on the revolutionary ideas he embraced as the movement went on.[14]

King's name on the petition came with the proviso that he be one of a group rather than the sole initiator. The remainder consisted of tried-and-true allies—aside from Shuttlesworth and Walker, there were Bishop Tucker, Aubrey Williams, and the like. Soon after Carl's imprisonment, the document was circulated under the sponsorship of 17 white and black civil rights leaders. It was Anne, of course, who did most of the actual footwork of getting signatures and publicity. By August, more than 1,000 people from more than 40 states had signed. The heart of their position, the petition stated, was that "we are witnessing today a revival of McCarthyism in the South, because all the other weapons of the segregationists are failing. The success of the House Un-American Activities Committee in jailing Carl Braden will create fear and thin the ranks of the white people who would join with the Negro in the struggle for a democratic South."[15]

On August 17, 1961, Anne joined a delegation to Washington headed by Ralph Abernathy, with nearly all of the initiators (but not King) present. The group presented their petitions to Harris Wofford, President Kennedy's special adviser on civil rights. The problem with White House intervention, Wofford explained, was the apparent contradiction between asking the public to support the Supreme Court's *Brown* decision and then going against the Court on another civil rights issue. On these grounds (and perhaps others), the White House declined to act, unpersuaded even after a second delegation headed by Clarence Pickett of the American Friends Service Committee delivered 3,000 new signatures that November in support of freeing Carl and Wilkinson. The Kennedy administration was not entirely unsympathetic to the goals of the civil rights movement, but in 1961 any hint of communism remained highly inflammatory amid international Cold War tensions and pressure from insiders like FBI Director J. Edgar Hoover, an avid anticommunist. Both Carl and Wilkinson would remain in prison for nine months.[16]

The SNCC White Student Project

The other matter that Anne felt required her attention during Carl's absence was the white student project for SNCC. For months she had continued to search for the right young southerner for the job. By early 1961 she was thoroughly frustrated with having to *beat the bushes* for such a person. She explained later that *we had [a lot] to overcome to find a white student who could stand up to the red-baiting and fear around that issue to have [such a close] association with SCEF.* Other SCEF leaders did not fully understand her insistence that the person hired be placed on the SNCC rather than the SCEF staff—one result of her painstaking negotiations with SNCC leaders who were determined not to be beholden to adult organizations. But part of Anne's stubbornness was also a practical consideration: the closer the affiliation with SCEF, the more leery the candidates became.[17]

While on another assignment, she finally found the perfect person, courtesy of Reverend Ralph Abernathy, a Montgomery movement leader now facing economic ruin. Abernathy, along with three other black ministers and the *New York Times*, had been slapped with a $5 million libel suit by Alabama officials who claimed their reputations had been tarnished by a newspaper ad the ministers had placed asking support for King and student protesters. Abernathy detailed the case for Anne, and in response to her query as to whether he had found any local white sympathizers, he pulled from his briefcase a crumpled letter of encouragement signed by Robert Zellner and 13 other white students from Huntingdon College, a Methodist institution outside Montgomery. Abernathy told Anne the letter—sent in with a small contribution—had meant so much to him that he had read and reread it. He suggested she consult Zellner before quoting from it in the *Patriot*. Anne soon fired off a note, sent in care of Huntingdon College, asking Zellner to phone her collect to discuss the matter.[18]

Zellner did not tell Anne during their initial conversation that he had already been asked to leave Huntingdon because of his dissent. A senior and the son of a Methodist minister from Mobile, he had been "tremendously affected" by the student sit-ins, as he later recalled: "I remember thinking, 'They're so well-dressed!' I was fairly poor myself, and they had trenchcoats and suits and ties, and they were doing something about [an issue] they felt strongly about. I was intrigued and also excited because they were going against authority. I thought, these people have guts, they don't care if they get in trouble or not." Zellner and several other students had attended a few mass meetings of the Montgomery Improvement Association—initially as research for a class—where he had learned of Abernathy's plight and initiated the letter. The youths found they had been followed by Montgomery police, who reported their activities to college officials.[19]

By the time he received Anne's note, Zellner and four others had been restricted to campus and confronted by Huntingdon's president with the request to withdraw from school. Zellner, whose father supported his actions, was the only one to refuse. The elder Zellner, a Bob Jones University graduate and former Klansman who had undergone a racial conversion of his own, filed a complaint with Alabama Methodist officials asking that the college "set [students] free to follow a Christian conscience." A cross was burned in front of Bob Zellner's dormitory, and he was soon called into the state Attorney General's Office and warned of Communist infiltrators to civil rights causes. That meeting introduced Zellner to names that would soon become familiar to him, as he later reflected: "I said, you mean there are Communists in Alabama? He said, 'Well, they come through here and you've fallen under their influence.' He took out a big stack of cards and started giving me the names of people to look out for. The first name was Anne Braden, the next name was Carl Braden, and then there was Clifford Durr, Virginia Durr, Aubrey Williams, and a couple more."[20]

It was only about a week later that Zellner received Anne's note, but by that time he was so disillusioned with Alabama's white culture that the warning served only to pique his interest in phoning her. He would later reflect that "she was a godsend to me because it was Montgomery, Alabama, 1961, and it was bitter days then."[21]

Anne continued to talk and correspond with Zellner, and they agreed to meet at a weekend gathering of student activists at Highlander in late spring 1961. When he encountered Anne in person, she came across as "deceptively soft and gentle"; he did not yet fathom the extent of her dedication. When she mentioned in passing that she assumed he was a socialist, he was truly shocked. The more he learned of Anne and other dissidents, however, the greater became his enthusiasm for the challenges civil rights activism brought to the culture of his upbringing. During that summer Anne recruited Zellner, who took little or no convincing, to apply for what she had begun calling the *campus traveler* project.[22]

Even at that late date, however—nearly a year after she had proposed the project to SNCC officials—Anne found considerable opposition within SNCC to actually accepting the SCEF grant. When SNCC's executive committee met at Highlander that August, Ella Baker sensed such internal dispute over the matter that she telephoned Anne and urged her to make the appeal in person. Anne rushed south to comply. Face-to-face with her enthusiasm, the executive committee accepted the new staffer, and in September 1961 Zellner reported to SNCC headquarters in Atlanta, employed under a $5,000 renewable annual grant from SCEF. Amid a never-ending funding crunch, the grant money earmarked for Zellner's salary soon became simply a part of the general pool of SNCC funds. To do otherwise would have created a salary hierarchy that neither Zellner nor other staffers were comfortable with. He and all of the rest simply made do and lived on next to nothing.[23]

Zellner brought a great deal of exuberance to his new post, but the job also caught him between a rock and a hard place. The project thus evolved somewhat differently than Anne had envisioned it. Zellner faced an uphill task in trying to convey the virtue of integration to a white student population who possessed not only internal psychological resistance to it but also serious institutional obstacles to hearing his message. Over the following nine months he visited 28 southern campuses, more than half of them white, and found an absolute lack of academic freedom, which put strict limits on what he could accomplish. Zellner succeeded in linking up small groups of African American students with their white counterparts in a few Deep South communities, but on white campuses—and on some black ones as well—he often had to operate in secret or face administrative removal or mob violence from white-supremacist students. At his alma mater, he had to contend with both.[24]

Zellner characterized his reaction in a staff report as a sense of estrangement from other white southern students, a feeling he explained with a question: "How do you relate to the white southern moderate or liberal and at the same time relate to a group of people who are as militant and as activist as students in the SNCC?" In addition to fielding violence from the very people he wished to mobilize, Zellner was finding his way as a minority for the first time both in terms of his beliefs in relation to majority white southern culture and as the only white field secretary on the SNCC staff, with the additional burden of being somewhat identified with SCEF, a group consisting of adults—and possibly "red" ones at that. He had to prove himself, and that dynamic resulted in a digression from the job he had been hired to do. In early October 1961, Zellner became the only white to stand with black high school picketers in McComb, Mississippi. His appearance at a prayer meeting in front of City

Hall enraged local whites, and he was badly beaten and arrested along with 119 students and two other SNCC staffers. The incident gave Zellner a noto-riety among segregationists and occasioned much harassment in the months to come, embroiling SCEF in a number of situations in which bail money had to be produced for Zellner. Within a year, bail costs that had begun with Mc-Comb had eaten up enormous resources: SCEF had paid out more than $39,000 to get young protesters released. Anne remembered that McComb *was his baptism by fire. But then I began to notice that every time you picked up the telephone Bob was in jail somewhere, having taken part in some demonstration with black people.* This trend worried her mostly because it kept Zellner from white campus organizing, which he confessed he found "boring." But when she con-sulted Jim Forman about it, he reassured her that Zellner was "influencing people by example."[25]

She accepted that analysis, though privately she continued to wonder if Zellner might have been able to do more if he had stuck with campus traveling as planned. The truth was that she had more of the kind of slow, long-term ap-proach to organizing than did Zellner and many SNCC youths, who were more conditioned by their experiences to see political radicalization itself as something that arose quickly as if from nowhere. Anne puzzled often, alone and to others, over the problem of how to motivate white southerners. She knew too well, as she once wrote to Forman, that they tended to be *buried, I mean buried, under layers of isolation from ideas that might stimulate them. . . . [I know] how hard this movement is for the buried white Southerner to find—even though it is geographically all around him. Everything is pulling at him to continue his life in its old ditches and ruts . . . something has to open the way.*[26]

It took boundless patience and perseverance to find that opening, but Anne never stopped being willing to listen to people or argue gently with them. Her friend Fred Shuttlesworth has observed that she possessed what he called a "disposition to overexplain" that derived from a "belief in absolute democracy." That absolute democracy appealed most to young recruits to the movement, who appreciated her willingness to engage in lengthy discussions about any impending decision, action, or social issue. Such dialogues also slowed some strategy meetings in ways that frustrated more seasoned cru-saders, and Anne admitted to coworkers that she found it *impossible to be brief.*[27]

Anne also believed that, as she has said many times since, *it takes an explo-sion* both internally and societally to get white people to act against racism. That belief, ironically, lent optimism to situations that looked bleak to less hopeful souls. Where others saw only brutality, she saw possibility—as in the taut, battlelike atmosphere that permeated Oxford, Mississippi, in the fall of

1962 when James Meredith desegregated Ole Miss. During those tense days, Anne wanted to *borrow* Zellner from the SNCC staff to go in and talk with white students as a *Patriot* reporter or even to go herself, believing that segregationists would be less likely to direct violence at a woman. Even in such a powder keg, she held out hope of finding racial converts such as she had found in Zellner.[28]

Those two shared a deep affection through her having been the one to introduce him to the movement. Over the next months and years, Anne spent hours on the phone reassuring Dottie Miller, a staff member in the Atlanta SNCC headquarters who became Zellner's lover and later his wife, when he was in rural southern jails. The couple became like family to her. Zellner stayed with the white student project for two years, during which he continued to intersperse campus organizing with direct action that resulted in more than 20 arrests and charges that followed him for years. The lanky young Alabamian made limited inroads into southern white colleges and functioned as a symbol of SNCC's early emphasis on interracialism and the "beloved community."[29]

When Zellner left, Anne—who habitually recruited young women to get more involved—corresponded with Joan Browning and Dorothy Dawson about taking his place. A year earlier, she had taken SNCC Chairman Chuck McDew to task for an unwillingness to consider a woman for the job, telling him, *When you get ready to fight for the whole human race, let me know.* Anne wrote to Browning that her *feminist blood was boiling.* She was disappointed too because SNCC, which had other women on staff, was much less sexist than the society at large. But the conversation with McDew took place in a Mississippi courthouse where, *surrounded by the enemy*, Anne chose not to argue. As it turned out, no woman applied.[30]

Instead Zellner was replaced with Sam Shirah, another former Huntingdon student who had been part of the spring 1961 ruckus. Because he had seen the ordeals his friend had endured and because his personal style was different from Zellner's, Shirah was more committed to campus organizing among white southerners, and he had more successes there. Although he reported finding "the strongest apathy I have ever seen" among students and "a strong anticommunist feeling" on the part of some colleges' administrations, he helped organize groups like Students for Peace at the University of Louisville that allied with SNCC. He also established relations between SNCC and other groups already active at Florida State, the University of Florida, and Tulane. He had some success at all-white Birmingham Southern, where he began organizing in 1963, only days after four little girls had died in the racist bombing of Sixteenth Street Baptist Church. There, Shirah was thrown off campus but managed to arrange some meetings between white students and African Americans at nearby Miles College.[31]

Anne's cultivating work in 1960–61 to get the white student project off the ground paid off over the following three years. The efforts of Zellner, Shirah, and later Ed Hamlett (who joined the project as co-organizer with Shirah in February 1964) contributed to an enormous growth in white interest in the civil rights movement as it sparked wider social protests against the Vietnam War and other social ills. Not all or even most of the young whites inspired to action by the African American freedom struggle were southern, of course, but by 1963 white southerners had become a visible presence among young civil rights protesters, having surmounted profound psychological and institutional barriers to get there. That year Shirah reported more than 1,000 contacts on southern campuses. *Ella Baker [used to say], "The problem in the South is not radical thought or conservative thought. It's lack of thought." It was such a closed society. People who ran the South, in order to maintain that system of segregation, had to instill a police state for everybody. What the '60s was really about, in a way, was establishing the right to organize in the South.*[32]

Anne's efforts to ensure that at least one white southern student would be on hand to transcend that *lack of thought* grew from a largely symbolic gesture to an endeavor that generated broader participation by southern whites in bringing greater democracy into the region. Within three years of launching the SNCC white student project, white southern students would be engaged enough, and numerous enough, to form their own organization—the Southern Student Organizing Committee (SSOC)—with the aim of rallying southern whites for wider social changes.[33]

Linking Civil Rights and Civil Liberties

Perhaps the one bright spot in Carl's imprisonment, from Anne's perspective, was that it gave her a forceful, immediate basis upon which to strengthen ties between the ballooning southern civil rights movement and the smaller civil liberties movement located mostly outside the region. Zellner's experiences at Huntingdon and later as SNCC field secretary provided a powerful example— if any were needed—of the police state mentality so prevalent across the South. For her generation, the battle for "civil liberties"—as it was known by liberals and leftists of that era—meant, in practical terms, confronting anticommunism. She and Carl became during the early 1960s virtual civil libertarian missionaries into the southern states, where the whole concept of free speech had received very little play in recent years. The eruption of the sit-ins changed all that, and the Bradens wanted to change it more, but doing so extracted a high price of them.

The clemency petition occupied most of the attention Anne was able to devote to civil liberties without her partner's support, but she also organized an October 1961 SCEF conference in North Carolina on "Freedom and the First Amendment." The meeting represented SCEF's first opportunity to draw together publicly the causes of civil rights and civil liberties in the South, and it aimed to give southern impetus to the new national campaign to abolish the government investigating committees. Traveling back and forth from Louisville frequently, Anne was careful to involve various segments of the regional and local civil rights community to serve on panels. She united SCLC's Wyatt Tee Walker and youthful crusaders such as Casey Hayden with long-time civil libertarians like Clifford Durr and Frank Donner to discuss with about 250 attenders the lack of free speech that routinely hampered southern organizing. Reverend Theodore Gibson, president of the Miami NAACP, described in a keynote address his prosecution by the Florida Legislative Commission (the same body that had subpoenaed Carl months before) for refusal to turn over NAACP membership lists.[34]

The conference was a victory of sorts for Anne, who labored to bring it off under the hardship not only of widespread lack of awareness concerning civil liberties but of acting without the usual camaraderie and support of Carl. Early on in planning the event, she simply resigned herself, in light of her familial commitments, to modest goals in relation to the greater effectiveness an organizer freer to travel would have brought. As it was, the increased traveling wearied her and blunted her usual optimism.[35]

The speech Anne delivered in Chapel Hill alluded to what she later called *the silencing of a generation*, which she believed was the greatest harm done by the domestic anticommunist purges of the 1950s. She spoke passionately: *Each time one of us takes a stand, it becomes easier for the next person. . . . I think perhaps our greatest job in the matter of educating the public is to give the American people confidence again that a citizen can fight this committee, that he can take a stand on controversial issues and survive. . . . It is not only facts and faith that people need—it is also the confidence to take action.* Anne saw that confidence as most pronounced in the young SNCC crusaders, and she tried hard to attract students to the meeting. With ten campuses represented, she viewed the event as the first step in a consciousness-raising process that she and fellow activists such as Baker and Shuttlesworth carried on through increasing cooperation with SNCC. Throughout 1961 they saw SNCC leaders and fieldworkers become increasingly radicalized and impatient with the violence that characterized southern protest amid continuing unwillingness by the federal government to stand forcefully behind African Americans' rights. Those frustrations were problematic in terms of the prospects for racial change, but they also led to greater willingness to confront the remaining cultural currents of anticommunism that marginalized people like the Bradens.[36]

Anne and Carl remained intimately acquainted with questions of civil liberties throughout his imprisonment, both in their social interactions and in the prison experience they shared from opposite sides of the bars: In November 1961 Carl and Wilkinson were moved without warning from South Carolina to Allenwood, part of the federal penitentiary complex in Lewisburg, Pennsylvania—the same prison to which Alger Hiss had been sent in 1950. Anne was not immediately notified but learned of the shift from a frantic late-night phone call from Frank Wilkinson's wife, Jean. She then telephoned the prison parole officer in South Carolina to demand an explanation, whereupon a sleepy respondent gave her the new address and the news that a notification letter was in the mail. She later learned from Carl a reason for the move: federal authorities had become disgruntled by the men's attempts to politicize other prisoners—which they accomplished through meetings of Alcoholics Anonymous—and had deemed them a security risk to nearby Donaldson Air Force Base.[37]

Not only from the government and the larger southern culture but from segments of the civil rights movement itself, public reaction to both Bradens remained, at best, tinged with criticism. Such dynamics weighed heavily on Anne in Carl's absence. In her loneliness, she wrote to him of the *dangers to our personalities and to our integrity . . . [that] arise from the fact that we live in a predominantly hostile atmosphere . . . rejected and condemned by much of society . . . cut off from certain community relationships that the average person has as a matter of course.* Anne saw no solution in the kind of hero status the two sometimes found among progressives in New York and California, nor in bitterness toward their southern critics (Carl's temptation, as she saw it) or (her own) emotional reliance on movement allies. Instead she believed that they should cultivate a very few friendships with sufficient depth to counter what at times threatened to become an *emotional vacuum.*[38]

The challenge, as always, was time. On the one hand Anne believed that, as she wrote to him, *even when they separate us, they have not touched the essential bonds of spirit that unite us.* Yet she had not even been able to clear her schedule to visit him for more than a month before his abrupt move. That situation was a bitter reminder of how little time they managed to spend together even when he was free. By November, she was thoroughly worn down by the endless juggling of priorities and all the travel—especially in Alabama, where ties of family made segregationist violence particularly troubling to her. Because for her Carl was a *rock* when *the rest is sand*, her usual optimism was traced with streaks of depression that could not always be contained and an exhaustion that was more extreme even than the level of fatigue to which she had become accustomed over the years.[39]

Reprieve came when Carl was freed on February 1, 1962. He and Wilkinson were still three months shy of a year in prison but received early releases for good behavior. Federal authorities were highly capricious, however, in how they regarded the men. Days before their release, the prisoners were informed that they would be set free early on February 1 and furnished with transportation to New York City. Officials' last-minute change of plans reluctantly landed the two on an afternoon bus headed west toward California. Luckily, however, having gotten wind of the switch through the prison grapevine, the men had arranged to have a car waiting to intercept them and speed Wilkinson back east to greet the crowd of 600 who were gathered for his homecoming. On Anne's advice, Carl skipped the welcome reception and headed straight home to reunite with her and the children, who—she felt—needed *to feel nothing is more important to you than they are at that moment.*[40]

The Bradens' lives resumed their usual hectic pace, but it was a great relief to Anne not to be managing it alone any longer. She still worried about her dependency on Carl, but in truth, the relationship had long ago settled into a pattern of interdependence that seemed to work for them both.[41]

Two Steps Forward, One Step Back

Anne's meticulous efforts on the clemency campaign succeeded in widening student support for southern civil liberties. Signs of encouragement included invitations the Bradens received for SCEF to conduct workshops on the topic at two movement gatherings in the spring of 1962: one a SNCC conference held in Atlanta and another sponsored by the Students for a Democratic Society (SDS).[42]

The action that set into motion these smaller breakthroughs came in April in the form of an event spearheaded by Fred Shuttlesworth. Despite muted criticism from voices within mainstream civil rights organizations, Shuttlesworth had effected increasingly strong ties to SCEF as the 1960s unfolded (a year later he would accept the SCEF presidency). "I never heard one word from anyone in SCEF even remotely un-American," he later recalled. Instead, he considered the Bradens and Dombrowski among "the greatest Americans," possessing a zeal for racial justice that could match the segregationists' ardor step for step. By 1962, Shuttlesworth had concluded, it was time to have an integrated mass meeting in Birmingham—the first in nearly a quarter century—and he more or less dared the SCEF board into braving the repressive environment of the so-called magic city for a board meeting with a conference piggybacked onto it. The resulting event, cosponsored by SCEF, SNCC, and ACMHR, brought in nearly 500 people, including SNCC organizers from all around the South. The atmosphere was thick with tension, with policemen on motorcycles surrounding the host church, snapping photos, and buttonholing white participants to demand identification. At the black-owned Gaston Hotel, where conference guests were housed, the management was poised for a raid that never came, and no arrests or outright violence marred the conference. Anne remembered later, *We got by with it because there were so many people, but I never will forget, when we all got down there that Friday and we were sitting in the Gaston eating lunch. Fred came in and said, "I'm glad to see y'all are not scared to come to Birmingham," and I said, "We're scared to death but we're here!"*[43]

The weekend's success gave Shuttlesworth and the local movement some much-needed outside encouragement, but the situation would have to get a lot worse in Birmingham before it got better. Southern segregationists possessed the power of the state, and they were equal parts determined and desperate. Only days after the Birmingham conference ended on a high note, the very visibility of the Alabama movement may have triggered the inclusion of Carl and other attenders in an injunction filed by the Talladega, Alabama, circuit court as a kind of last-ditch effort to stop mass demonstrations that had been going on there for weeks. Such displays were little more than posturing, but they consumed precious time and resources.[44]

By 1962 there was enough of a groundswell of white southern activism for SCEF to host and participate in more public regional events. Such gatherings provided both a think-tank function and a psychological respite for those on the front lines either in incremental community work or in direct-action hot spots such as Birmingham or Albany, Georgia. Yet progress on southern civil liberties in those years—in the larger society and even in the movement—was still a case of *two steps forward, one step back*, as Anne wryly observed. Only a few months after their triumphant gathering in Birmingham and on the heels of successful follow-up efforts in Atlanta, Chapel Hill, and Norfolk, the couple experienced a new fall from grace that illustrates just how tenuous was their status among fellow activists—and how divisive were the anticommunist tensions within the movement that mirrored those in larger southern culture.[45]

———————

Carl and through him Anne became embroiled in a controversy in Jackson, Mississippi, that brought out into the open at last the innuendoes that were circulated about the two by fellow activists. The trouble began in summertime 1962 when Bob Moses, who headed SNCC work in Mississippi, invited the Bradens to conduct civil liberties workshops across the state, where massive repression was a given. Carl obliged, and over six days that July, he covered Mississippi exhaustively, traveling 900 miles in the company of Moses to talk with local groups about civil liberties as Moses conducted nonviolence training for a forthcoming voter registration workshop. A week after Carl's return, he wrote a routine staff report of the trip, marked it "confidential—not for publication" (as was the Bradens' practice), and sent it to Dombrowski, who duplicated and distributed it to the SCEF board and advisory committee. On August 31, 1962, the report mysteriously appeared in full on page 1 of the archsegregationist *Jackson Daily News*, along with an inflammatory headline, "Red Crusader Active in Jackson Mix Drive," and accompanying articles that resurrected the sedition and HUAC contempt cases. The naming of names "created a state of terror among many in the movement," Carl pointed out shortly after learning of it. The director of the church-based center hosting the voter workshop was threatened with firing. Segregationist activists also delivered bundles of the newspapers to Mississippi civil rights leaders with handbills attached labeling as "Communists" Moses, Zellner, and others named in the articles.[46]

Dombrowski and both Bradens regretted the incident and suspected a "leak" (the newspaper indicated it had "intercepted a highly confidential report," and documents years later revealed a plethora of informants in the Mississippi movement). Yet they could scarcely anticipate the tenor of the accusations that were leveled at Carl, Anne, and SCEF a few weeks later. Without consulting anyone in SCEF, Wiley Branton, director of the Voter Education Project—a Southern Regional Council initiative that sponsored the Mississippi drive now so under fire—presented the tale at an Atlanta meeting of the Southern Interagency group, a coalition of civil rights organizations that had never included SCEF. In the resulting fray, the "subversive" label came back to haunt Carl when someone suggested that he had gone to Mississippi only to make trouble. Some attenders were left with the impression that Carl had intentionally released the report to the press. Shortly thereafter,

Branton wrote Carl that he was a "liability" to the movement and that "growing numbers" of people felt that SCEF should discontinue its participation in southern voting rights efforts.[47]

Carl's brusqueness served him well in these circumstances. He pronounced further dispute a "waste of time" and went on about his work. But Anne simply could not bear to let Branton's hurtful words go at that. Aghast at this confirmation that movement insiders would dismiss all their hard work and cast them aside without even hearing their side of the story, she fired off a 13-page letter of explanation to Branton and demanded that it be circulated to each participating member. She even sent out 50 copies needed for distribution. In correspondence, she maintained a tone that was even and reasonable, if frustrated, but a note of hysteria crept into her voice every time she discussed the latest ostracism.[48]

Anne pleaded with Bob Moses, whom the Bradens considered a friend, to clarify the matter. She could not even be sure he was receiving her letters, however. Moses was too consumed with surviving the day-to-day violence amid the desegregation of Ole Miss that fall to participate in what he saw as armchair conflicts that threatened to distract from the task at hand. The best he could offer was a note later in the fall that let her know he found the matter dispiriting. Moses said of her pleas to Branton for understanding, "You did a beautiful job, I'm just sorry we had to be so cruddy about it all."[49]

Taking place amid yet a new wave of Cold War anxiety generated by the Cuban Missile Crisis, Anne's negotiations were only partially successful. Several of the participants, including Branton, affected a more conciliatory stance with her when they saw her next, but there was no formal hand of goodwill extended, and SCEF was rejected by the Southern Interagency Group when it applied for admission in 1963.[50]

To call either Anne or Carl outcasts, however, is too extreme. Through these discussions, they had the active support of people like Forman, Shuttlesworth, and Ella Baker. Even the Mississippi journalist Charles Butts, whose photo appeared, damningly, in the *Daily News* spread, cheerfully claimed association with Carl. King also continued to be instrumental in shielding Anne, Carl, and Dombrowski from utter marginalization even as he shied away from them on occasion. On September 27, 1962, only days after Anne penned her first complaint to Wiley Branton, she gave one of the keynote addresses, at King's request, at the annual SCLC convention in Birmingham. Her topic was nonviolent direct action, and Anne always felt that SCLC could easily have found someone more expert on that subject than she: *I think it was his way of spitting in the eye of the people who said "don't associate with SCEF."* Anne's speech emphasized that the effectiveness of nonviolent direct action depended on the presence of at least some civil liberties.[51]

Afterward, King joined her at the podium, and Carl and Dombrowski were called to the stage to be recognized for their long-standing work for southern change. The gesture must have been heartfelt, for it certainly earned King nothing but opprobrium (this on top of the conference's melodramatic climax, when a member of the American Nazi Party attacked him onstage). The photo snapped of King that day with the SCEF staff found its way into the files of the Louisiana Un-American Activities Committee (LUAC), onto an anticommunist pamphlet that circulated the region, and even into the hands of Alabama Governor George Wallace, who waved it and derided the Bradens in a frenzied defense of Alabama segregationists on the *Today* show in late September 1963. These were only a few of the myriad ways that smears against Anne, Carl, and SCEF were given new life to constrain or discredit the entire civil rights movement.[52]

Despite setbacks like the one in Jackson, Anne's and Carl's hard work and relentlessness won them more allies in the southern movement as civil rights crusades intensified to a fever pitch throughout 1962 and 1963. Even in Louisville, where they remained virtual pariahs long after their contributions to civil rights had won them acclaim elsewhere in the region, it seemed that *slowly some of the ice surrounding us break[s]*, as Anne wrote to a friend. She firmly believed that it was important to stay involved in organizing one's home community, and by the early 1960s she and Carl had become fixtures who were accepted—if sometimes grudgingly—by other reformers.[53]

There were initiatives in Louisville such as the West End Community Council, which Anne and an African American coworker, Gladys Carter, established to stem "white flight" from that section of Louisville in an attempt to keep their neighborhoods diverse. Experiences like these, in which Anne put aside her SCEF duties to campaign door-to-door for the goals of the WECC, reinforced her commitment to interracialism. It was the group's practice always to work in pairs of blacks and whites, and she found again and again that whites confronted personally by African American faces responded sympathetically to the notion of integration. Especially in regional work outside Louisville, it began to seem to the Bradens as if greater cooperation were possible, and their very inclusion symbolic of a more actively pro–civil libertarian bent within the civil rights movement.[54]

After the successes of Anne's civil liberties speeches in 1962, she felt sufficiently empowered to begin planning for an ambitious 1963 conference on civil liberties that would unite all of the southern civil rights groups in calling for wider freedoms of speech and association that the region so grotesquely lacked. By this time, Ella Baker had joined the SCEF staff as a consultant, and she assisted in planning the event, along with Eliza Paschall, a white Atlantan who headed that city's Human Relations Council.[55]

Yet the list of supporting organizations shrank as the planning continued. The NAACP and CORE refused to participate in any joint endeavor with SCEF, and despite the enthusiastic efforts of Paschall, the SRC (coordinator of the Human Relations Councils) refused to get onboard. Wyatt Tee Walker was dramatically unsuccessful at even broaching the matter with the American Civil Liberties Union, and as supporters dwindled, King himself finally decided to withdraw SCLC's sponsorship. Though Anne pleaded with him that *SCLC's very soul* was at stake, he refused to reconsider and would agree only to encourage participation by SCLC local affiliates.[56]

Anne felt a not-unfamiliar roaring inside her head over the defections but made the best of the situation in spite of her despair. The event that took shape was a rousing but much smaller-scale workshop of 75, cosponsored by SCEF and SNCC, whose young organizers had become increasingly opposed to red-baiting and infighting within the movement. By 1963 activists who had begun only three years before as hopeful idealists had faced too many savage beatings and jailings, had realized grimly how little black lives counted in the South. They were moving steadily, as Bob Moses quietly commented later in 1963, toward "an absolute stand on the right to associate with whom we please." Moses pronounced that position "the next frontier" for SNCC. The Atlanta civil liberties workshop fueled a process of radicalization that had begun for student activists in the unspeakable violence and denunciation their idealistic moral protests had evoked from segregationists and in the gaping silences of the federal government in response to southern white intransigence.[57]

Part of what kept anticommunism alive in the movement had to do with social action organizations' relationships to authority. Groups such as SRC, NAACP, CORE, SCLC, and even SNCC sought increasing support for voter registration drives from the Democratic Party and the Kennedy administration, which might court the black vote and occasionally criticize segregationists' repressive tactics but remained beholden to archsegregationist southern senators and congressmen. By 1963, the mainstream civil rights groups also relied heavily on grant money from foundations that were part of what Anne has called the *liberal establishment*, which since the McCarthy years had been leery of any revolutionary ideas—Communist or not—and would remain so. (The Ford Foundation had by this time eliminated its subsidiary Fund for the Republic when it allegedly became "too liberal.") Funding needs combined with closer alliance with the Kennedy administration thus gave the civil rights groups competing for monies and influence a vested interest in demonstrating themselves to be "safe"—that is, not too radical. Especially after the gruesome violence perpetrated against the 1961 freedom riders took civil disorder to new levels and the resulting publicity threatened the U.S. image abroad, government pressure increased on prominent figures like Martin King to keep mass actions in check.[58]

The dynamics of the Cold War thus gave government image-makers some impetus to achieve better race relations insofar as to do otherwise left the United States open to international criticism that undercut its image as leader of the free world. But ironically, those same Cold War dynamics also tended to reinforce attitudes about alleged "subversion" that had been prominent in American culture since World War II. Fueled by controversies provoked by segregationist voices like that of the *Jackson Daily News*, the marginalization of the Bradens and SCEF developed a kind of self-perpetuating circularity that made rank-and-file activists increasingly skeptical of the validity of the charges but nevertheless kept the rumors in motion.[59]

By 1963 SCEF had been attacked for so long that its leaders had no really prominent alliances left to lose: donors willing to sponsor SCEF had long before proven their mettle. Yet as SNCC crusaders widened their critique of southern society, espoused more radical views, and claimed the Bradens as friends, they too were dismayed to see their sources of revenue dry up. James and Diane Nash Bevel, two SNCC leaders seeking funds for a 1963 Mississippi organizing center, were cautioned by SCLC aide Andrew Young against even getting help from Anne with their proposal because to do so would taint it. Young told them, "You need some institutions within the 'establishment' or some so-called respectable organization to get a grant. . . . I am questioning SCEF's role in the process for purely practical reasons. I don't believe there is anything wrong with SCEF, but neither was there anything wrong with Highlander yet it was closed down."[60]

Comments like Young's were never very successful in keeping southern youth of the 1960s away from Anne and Carl. But Anne abhorred that kind of pragmatism and told Young so. She wrote to Diane Bevel, *I admire Andy—but I do believe he should stop and give a long look at the forces he is giving in to. . . . Frankly, I don't think I'd care much to live in the society people with this attitude would build—can't see that it would be much better than what we have now.*[61]

It sometimes felt *self-serving* to Anne to keep struggling with others in the movement for her and Carl's right to participate, but she held firmly to the conviction that American and especially southern culture had repudiated the excesses of McCarthy the man but not the techniques of anticommunist investigations or marginalization of those considered too far to the left. A whole generation of so-cial reformers—only a fraction of whom had been CP members or followers—had already been lost to McCarthyism in the 1950s, a process that had created an impediment to the emergence of greater white southern support for integration surrounding the *Brown* decision.[62]

A Bridge to the Leftist Past

With the American and especially the southern left so decimated by postwar anticommunist drives, most young SNCC workers who built the new mass movement knew virtually nothing of southern freedom campaigns that pre-ceded their own by a mere dozen years. Anne was one of a few elders who took up the task of helping the more daring young recruits to rediscover the forgot-ten currents of their history, enlightening them about, for example, the earlier "Snick" (as most referred to SNCC) that had been the Southern Negro Youth Congress (SNYC). Sue Thrasher, a young Nashville activist who went on to found the white-led Southern Student Organizing Committee (SSOC), wrote later that it was Anne who "reminded me, not so gently, that ours was not the first generation of Southerners to talk about creating a 'new South.'" These history lessons were reinforced by Anne's activist agenda and her example of strong female leadership.[63]

Anne found compelling evidence of the remaining power of anticommu-nist ideology in the current movement's evident willingness to sacrifice the Bradens and SCEF rather than defy head-on the segregationists' defensive re-liance on anticommunist witch hunting. Attacks like the one Wiley Branton had made on SCEF, she believed, divided the movement and aligned its more conservative voices with prosegregationist anticommunist critics, wreaking far more serious damage than that done by the *Jackson Daily News* or the miscella-neous anticommunist outcries that were daily fare among segregationists. She reflected later that *a major part of our fight was in getting people in the movement to deal with their fear of SCEF . . . because SCEF wasn't that radical . . . the South-ern Conference wasn't that radical. They were reformist, New Deal organizations.*[64]

But therein, perhaps, lay the threat. SCEF was among the only remaining civil rights groups with origins in the leftist economic critique that had charac-terized New Deal social upheaval. (Highlander was another, and it too was under constant attack.) Despite SCEF's singular focus on ending segregation, its leaders—particularly Anne and Carl—embraced a kind of anticapitalist, anti-imperialist, pro–trade union ideology that implicitly advocated wider reforms over time. By 1960, partly as a result of the Cold War *social silencing* Anne often decried, the focus of southern social change had become much narrower, concentrating on lunch counters and seating arrangements—only the most blatant symbols of a system of racial injustice. Anne and Carl applauded the youthful campaigns that brought down Jim Crow, but they saw its destruction as only part of what it would take to usher in a better society.[65]

Anne's and Carl's Old Left vision of a radical interracialism that was also anticapitalist and anti-imperialist—unafraid to link domestic and foreign policy issues—was a consistent feature of their message to the SNCC generation and beyond. SCEF's single-point program of recruiting white southerners to join with African Americans in civil rights campaigns may have been modest in its successes, but it was also, in Anne's words, *a concept that was filled with dynamite* for those at the helm of southern society because it held such potential for more sweeping social changes. As Anthony Dunbar has argued elsewhere, it was that very urge to unite blacks and whites around common economic interests that southern politicians sought so desperately to exorcise from the civil rights movement through anticommunist smear tactics. The cultural currents inspired by the Cold War gave those campaigns some legitimacy even within the movement, especially those branches of it closest to the Democratic Party and the liberal establishment.[66]

But by 1963, southern youth—whose rallying point was SNCC—had begun to reject the demonization of the Bradens and to contemplate the revolutionary ideas the couple espoused. The new generation of activists did not adopt the Bradens' particulars wholesale. Instead, they built a mass movement with revolutionary new visions of their own and turned to figures like Anne and Carl more for counsel than for leadership. Twenty-five years after blacks and whites had defied segregated Birmingham to sit together and plan a new, more democratic South at the founding meeting of the Southern Conference for Human Welfare, yet another New South was struggling to be born. The upsurges of the Depression and postwar era were not animated by the very same impetus as that which ignited the 1960s civil rights movement, but Anne, Carl, and a few others like them were important bridges linking the two movements and eras. The notorious pair would remain pariahs for many more years in the eyes of mainstream society, especially in their native state. Yet at least by 1963 there was a critical mass of youth—black and white—willing to take up their call for southern racial and social justice, if only for a time.

CHAPTER ELEVEN

END OF AN ERA

Until the killing of Black mothers' sons becomes as important to the rest of the country as the killing of white mothers' sons, we who believe in freedom cannot rest.

—Ella Baker, August 1964[1]

NINETEEN-SIXTY-THREE SAW VIOLENCE SWELL in the struggle for African American freedom in the South. Mississippi NAACP chief Medgar Evers was gunned down in Jackson that June, and in September a ruthless segregationist church bombing in Birmingham killed four little girls. The Civil Rights and Voting Rights acts were still, respectively, one and two years away, and it would take the highly publicized murders of three young civil rights workers in the opening days of the 1964 Mississippi Freedom Summer for the nation to enact meaningful civil rights legislation. But essentially the battle for public accommodations had been won by the fall of 1963. There was a new consciousness among youth activists that it was their own collective struggle—not any benign edict of government—that would bring about more change. An affinity with disenfranchised people similar to that which guided the Bradens' lives was increasingly evident in the ranks of SNCC. The adoption by young field organizers of overalls as their primary attire symbolized greater identification with the African American rural poor and a self-conscious respect for local knowledge the larger society had discounted for so long.[2]

The concerns were no longer just access but jobs and economic justice. *I just date it from 1963 that you began to hear [movement] people everywhere saying, "Well, what good is it to be able to sit at a lunch counter if I don't have money to buy a hamburger?."* . . . *These were people in Texas, Virginia, all over—who hadn't even talked with one another?*[3]

On June 11, 1963—the very night of Medgar Evers's murder—Anne, Carl, Jim Dombrowski, and Ella Baker (now a part of the staff) had met with SCEF's newly elected president, Shuttlesworth, in New Orleans to discuss widening SCEF's program to include economic as well as racial reforms. The plan represented a return, really, to the original mission of its parent, the Southern Conference. The students appeared headed in that direction, and the SCEF staff—invigorated by Shuttlesworth's new leadership—hoped to nudge the most radical of them along. What had begun in 1960 as a sit-in movement focused on the most appalling symbols of segregation was subtly broadening its perspective as a result of being repeatedly confronted with the unyielding repression of the southern police state. Already, SNCC was the southern vanguard for a "New Left" campus activism that had spread far beyond the region, institutionalized in 1962 with the formation of Students for a Democratic Society (SDS), which looked southward to SNCC for inspiration and direction. In the coming years, Anne and Carl would continue to be controversial, but their vision of economic justice would take on new relevance to a cadre of young activists who came south and into SCEF.[4]

The years 1963–64 were dramatic, pivotal ones for the civil rights revolution. For Anne and her family, they were also shot through with personal calamity that did not halt her activism but constrained it and forever changed her. In June of 1963—only days after she and Carl returned from the SCEF staff meeting in New Orleans—Anita, ten, fainted while playing in a neighbor's yard. The Bradens' pediatrician hospitalized Anita for tests that day, and informed Anne a few days later that her daughter had primary pulmonary hypertension and could not live longer than several more years. Few cases of the illness had been diagnosed at that time: those that had, Anne learned, were mostly in preadolescent girls. Anita's condition was designated "primary" insofar as her heart contained no apparent flaw that had caused the onset of the disease—and thus her case suggested no surgical means of correction.

The prognosis sent the Bradens reeling. It was hard to believe because Anita appeared so healthy, but a heart specialist at the University of Alabama confirmed the dismal findings a few weeks later. The couple did not tell any of their children all that they had learned, but Anne did tell Anita that she had a heart-and-lung condition and would need to be less active: *But, I told her, this will give you the opportunity to develop your other talents. I told her she could work at becoming truly accomplished at the piano, and she could learn to play the guitar and take art lessons. And that is exactly what she did.*[5]

At summer's end Anita returned to school. Although she remained cheerful and devoted to her new hobbies, she looked pale, and her skin had a bluish cast. She grew weaker and fainted again, this time breaking a few teeth as she fell. Seeing her parents' agony, Jim Dombrowski raised money for the Bradens to take her to the Mayo Clinic, and Anne and Anita spent a week there in early 1964. After a series of tests that themselves seemed to bring the child to the brink of death, the attending physician informed Anne that Anita's condition was quite advanced. The only cure for her would be a new lung, he said, but such procedures were still in the distant future. No lung transplants were available in 1964 to save the little girl.[6]

During the last winter of Anita's life, Anne could not bring herself to believe her daughter was dying. She had long conversations with their minister, Thomas Kelley, and with several movement friends who held that with enough faith, a miracle might still occur. *I became convinced that if I could just believe profoundly enough that Anita would live and get well, it would happen.* She even went so far as to have braces put on Anita's teeth the very week before she died. *Making and keeping that appointment was—I knew even at the time—another way I was expressing faith that she could live to grow up.*[7]

Anne stayed at home with her children throughout most of the last months of Anita's life, but the freedom movement was at fever pitch, and she remained highly involved in it. Putting out the *Patriot* and maintaining SCEF contacts were taxing enough, but a new campaign was brewing in Louisville that vied with her child's decline for Anne's attention. Since spring, a local desegregation campaign had developed under the leadership of 19-year-old Bill Dady, a white SDS organizer who had come from Atlanta as part of that group's program to move off campuses into poor communities.

Dady had organized an interracial group of local teens, the Gandhi Corps, that protested continued segregation of the pool at Fontaine Ferry amusement park, the city's most popular warm-weather youth attraction. Because Dady (and several other young activists) lived in the Bradens' home that year, the local campaign he headed impinged on Anne more than she intended. Dady's connection to the infamous pair increased the controversy his organizing generated, and Anne found herself drawn into his negotiations with the recently established Kentucky Human Rights Commission and into press coverage of the ensuing demonstrations, in which the protesters were labeled "outsiders" (though most were native Louisvillians). During this same difficult period, she and Carl also found themselves excluded from a thousands-strong civil rights march that Kentucky activists planned on the state capitol that spring.[8]

Anne had no idea that the end might come so quickly for her daughter. On Sunday, June 7, 1964, wearing a formal white dress and veil, Anita was confirmed at Calvary Episcopal Church. That afternoon, after complaining of not feeling good, she began coughing up blood and had to be hospitalized. Carl was out of town, but Anne reached him by phone and he drove all night to get home. The two took turns staying with Anita in the hospital and dealing with the problems their son also faced. Not quite 13 years old and not really aware of the seriousness of his sister's illness, Jim had been arrested for the first time on the very day Anita was hospitalized. Along with six other juveniles, Dady, and three other young adults, Jim had sat in to desegregate Hasenour's restaurant. When he phoned his mother and asked, "Did I do the right thing?" she did not have the heart to say no. Nothing ever came of the charges, but they became one more matter the Bradens had to fight that year.[9]

Anita McCarty Braden died two days later, on June 9, 1964. When Anne called her parents to inform them of their granddaughter's death, her mother told her they would leave for Louisville immediately. The McCartys had not visited Anne in her home in several years, not since the neighborhood had become predominantly black—though as with so many other issues, they never explained why. They usually met elsewhere—in Eminence or halfway between Louisville and Anniston. Anne typically tried to shield her parents from the consequences of the two families' value differences, but this time she could not restrain the cruelty in her reply: *You never came when she was alive: why would you come now?* But, this time, Gambrell and Anita McCarty did come. Little Anita was cremated and her remains placed in the Eminence cemetery alongside a tree planted in her name.[10]

In spite of Anne's protestations that it was too much to ask, Ella Baker also left her movement work in Atlanta to come to Louisville to be with her friends in their grief. At one point, Baker scolded Anne: "You are trying to keep going as if nothing has happened—but something *has* happened." But Anne could not stop. She kept her outward focus on social action, while inwardly she tormented herself (and has continued to, on occasion) with wondering if maybe her faith had simply not been strong enough. She had many questions to brood over in the aftermath of Anita's death. When she saw Jim's stricken reaction to the loss of Anita, she thought perhaps she had done wrong not to warn him of what to expect. And somewhere deep inside, she remained haunted by the painful notion that maybe the tension in their family life—though it seemed unavoidable, given the times and their commitments—had led to her daughter's illness and premature death. *Anita had some great core of calm deep within herself. . . . An irrational part of me wondered if this life, and this world, just seemed too noisy and confusing to her—so unconsciously, she decided to go somewhere else.* In Louisville and in the South of those years, despite the positive changes in motion, there was no tranquility to be had for the Bradens. Their unyielding challenges to the status quo left them stigmatized as "outsiders" in this land of their ancestors, their own births, and now their daughter's death.[11]

"They're desperate!" Jim Dombrowski muttered. "They're going back to the weapons of the 1950s." It was late at night on October 4, 1963, when the 66-year-old SCEF director—so arthritic he needed crutches to walk—was finally allowed to consult a lawyer and make bail. Earlier that day he had watched helplessly as 13 uniformed New Orleans police officers, their guns drawn, took a sledgehammer to the door of SCEF headquarters and ransacked the office for four hours before escorting him to jail. By midnight Anne and Carl, 600 miles to the north, had heard the jolting news: the office had been pillaged, its contents removed, and Dombrowski, along with two white civil rights lawyers, was charged with violating Louisiana's anti-subversive law. Louisiana Rep. James Pfister, head of that state's un-American investigating committee (LUAC) and a candidate for reelection, accused the men of being members of subversive groups—SCEF and the National Lawyers Guild—without registering as such. Yet their immediate crime, it seemed, was to coordinate a national training (in progress in New Orleans that weekend) for 50 attorneys willing to provide legal assistance to the hundreds of volunteers who would descend on Mississippi the following summer.[12]

For Anne and Carl, and for Dombrowski, the case occasioned a new though not unfamiliar crisis: they needed money to reconstruct SCEF's records and resume operations, and they needed outlets through which the outrage of this assault could be conveyed throughout the movement and the country. This time, at least, they could count on more allies. As soon as she learned of Dombrowski's arrest, Anne phoned Mary King, SNCC's publicity director, and received assurances that SNCC would publicize the latest attack. SCLC did the same, and Bill Kunstler, Martin Luther King's attorney, assisted partner Arthur Kinoy in Dombrowski's defense. Pfister rapidly turned over proceeds of the raid to Mississippi's archsegregationist head of the SISS, Senator James Eastland, revealing that the senator had helped orchestrate the raid. Kinoy mounted a counterattack, resurrecting a federal civil rights statute that had lain inert since Reconstruction and appealing to federal courts for relief from such obvious harassment. The ensuing civil and criminal suits consumed thousands of dollars and nearly two years of effort to reclaim the SCEF records. *Dombrowski v. Pfister* wound its way to the U.S. Supreme Court, however, and the resulting 1965 ruling established an important social reform precedent: when a capricious state or local prosecution threatened to have a "chilling effect upon the exercise of First Amendment rights," a federal court could issue an injunction to stop it.[13]

The New Orleans prosecutions slowed but did not halt SCEF. Nor did they halt SNCC's preparations to bring 1,000 northern student volunteers (90 percent of whom were white) into nearby Mississippi in mid-1964. But the desperation Dombrowski had attributed to segregationists combined with antiblack violence endemic to the Magnolia State to create the most explosive situation the movement had faced yet—as SNCC organizers had believed and feared it would. Out of the very first wave of volunteers, three young men— James Chaney, Andrew Goodman, and Michael Schwerner (one black, two white and Jewish)—were missing after barely 24 hours in the state, and the national media spotlight turned on Mississippi. It stayed there for the rest of the summer as freedom volunteers continued to pour in and assist more seasoned activists working in an atmosphere of terror to register voters, run literacy classes, and build an alternative party, the Mississippi Freedom Democrats (MFDP). By the time the recovery of three mutilated bodies from an earthen dam confirmed what movement veterans already knew—nearly seven weeks after the disappearances—Mississippi had seen its most violent summer since Reconstruction: 1,000 arrests, 80 reported beatings of activists, 65 buildings bombed or burned, 35 shootings, and at least three additional murders.[14]

Anne never set foot in Mississippi during the summer of 1964. Neither did Carl. They knew that to do so would only heighten the critical scrutiny already directed at Freedom Summer by everyone from the most ardent segregationists to liberals in government. Concerns for Anita kept Anne close to home that spring, but she raised money for the summer project, promoted it, and stayed in touch by phone. By the time orientation sessions began for the volunteers in mid-June at Miami University in Oxford, Ohio, Anita was gone. Anne's first road trip after her daughter's death was to accompany Carl on a drive to Oxford. They planned to conduct a civil liberties training session for white volunteers who would focus their summer's work on white Mississippians, a project SCEF had funded. Arriving just as the first buses prepared to depart south, the Bradens never even made it out of their car. They were hastily intercepted by Ed Hamlett, who reluctantly informed them that they had been barred from attending by the National Council of Churches (NCC), which was underwriting the entire orientation. Hamlett spirited them away to a nearby professor's house, where the workshop proceeded outside the sanctioned curriculum. When Anne ran into Bob Moses later that afternoon, he apologized, "We fought for the Lawyers' Guild, and we fought for Highlander, but you and Carl were just more than we could win." They agreed to talk later, but there was really nothing more to say. Anne understood. It was the kind of thing that had happened many times before.[15]

To add insult to injury, even the box of literature they had sent at Jim Forman's request disappeared. The box, which never was recovered, contained not promotional literature for SCEF, but, ironically, copies of a newly published educational booklet Anne had authored, *HUAC: Bulwark of Segregation*, which outlined how southern anticommunists were hobbling civil rights advances. When Bob Zellner asked an NCC official where the pamphlets were, he received the reply: "I took them up." Anticommunism was on the wane, but it was nowhere near spent, even among those who advocated racial reforms.[16]

The deaths a few days later in the Delta of Chaney, Goodman, and Schwerner succeeded in getting the nation's attention mainly because two of them were white. The realization that only white lives lost could attract a national outcry had been part of the thinking that went into the Freedom Summer concept. Yet once it actually came to pass, that bitter reality was difficult for black SNCC organizers to take, especially on top of the daily humiliations and dangers heaped on movement lives in Mississippi. After such sustained degradation, SNCC organizers needed the Freedom Democratic Party's challenge to the 1964 Democratic Convention in Atlantic City at summer's end to be a culminating moment. Instead they saw the moral high ground crumble beneath their feet during their abortive attempt to unseat the mainstream, prosegregation delegates. For many, revelation of the national party's unwillingness to take on the southern segregationist Democratic machine was a kind of last straw.[17]

Though Atlantic City proved to be a turning point in the southern student movement, neither Anne nor most other grassroots organizers could see it at the time. They were too immersed in day-to-day campaigns. She remembered later that *the attack on SNCC in the liberal press started then. Before Atlantic City they were depicted as starry-eyed children walking the dirt roads of Mississippi. After Atlantic City, they became villains who appeared suddenly from the "outside." Actually, it was the same people.* But many of them had changed. Even from its early "beloved community" emphasis, most SNCC insiders had never imagined themselves "integrated" into society as it was. Though they did not have the details well formulated, they envisioned building a new, more just and humane society free of racial hierarchy. After Atlantic City, most differentiated themselves more explicitly from what had revealed itself as a corrupt system. The young people of SNCC set the tone for the '60s generation and for radicals of an earlier generation, like Anne, who welcomed their increasingly revolutionary thrust.[18]

The idea of whites organizing whites had been rumbling around in the civil rights movement for some time, partly through Anne's initiative on the white student project. Well before Freedom Summer, there was a growing belief, recorded later by Jim Forman, that "whites in SNCC simply had to begin organizing white communities if we were serious about revolutionary change." Suggestions like Forman's reiterated the same basic message that William Patterson had imparted to Anne back in 1951, the same force that had drawn Shuttlesworth to the Bradens in 1958. For too long, white people had been "the missing link."[19]

Three months before the summer project opened, white students with these ideas in mind formed the Southern Student Organizing Committee (SSOC) with the aim of organizing on white campuses against racism. Two of SSOC's leading organizers were Sam Shirah and Ed Hamlett (who now shared the position of white campus traveler for SNCC), plus Sue Thrasher of Nashville. Anne applauded the new upsurge of white students. She felt a little maternal about it, having been the one to provide the group with a regional contact list after Thrasher had learned from the *Patriot* of whites' activities in several southern states. The Bradens' emphasis on white organizing had profoundly influenced the group that became SSOC. Anne became a close adviser as SSOC took shape, even taking her older daughter (who, although frail, still seemed fit) with her to Nashville so both she and Carl could attend the founding meeting in April 1964.[20]

But she was also troubled by the separation of whites and blacks within the movement. Sensing a danger of resurgent racism in whites segregating themselves—as they had done for much of her lifetime—she cautioned white southern youth against any *white consciousness* that separated them from inter-racialism. Anne dismissed SSOC founders' claims that they needed an au-tonomous organization because SNCC was perceived as "too radical" on white southern campuses: *I thought, that is just not so. How did you all get in-volved? You were inspired by SNCC!* Instead, Anne agreed with Jim Forman, who privately observed that young whites wanted to be freer to exert their own leadership than they had felt in SNCC. Believing that *white people never get to-gether* as white people *except for a bad purpose*, she attempted to persuade the white activists to remain part of SNCC. When that failed, she pushed an agenda of close cooperation with SNCC in their new organization, now the inheritor of SNCC's white student project.[21]

The 1964 influx of white volunteers into Mississippi, many of whom stayed on with SNCC after the summer ended, unmistakably altered the orga-nizational dynamics of what had once been a small band of close-knit idealists with only a handful of whites among them. A tour of Africa by 11 SNCC lead-ers in the fall of 1964 further propelled the group's Pan-African consciousness. By 1966 SNCC elected an all-black slate of leaders and a year later withdrew its sponsorship from the few remaining initiatives staffed by whites. As the decade unfolded, SNCC heightened its critique of capitalism and imperialism even as it turned its own attention more exclusively onto race rather than class inequities through greater identification with African anticolonial struggles and the growing Black Consciousness movement in the United States. Black nationalism did not spring full-grown in the 1960s—as the historian Tim Tyson has pointed out—but developed from a long tradition of armed struggle and black militancy, the same one that had prompted Andrew Wade to carry a pistol and insist on a house in 1954.[22]

All of these currents—but especially its embrace of the slogan "Black Power" in 1966—demonized SNCC in the eyes of mainstream liberals, black and white. Offering a swift, supportive interpretation of SNCC's shift toward an exclusively black-led organizing strategy, Anne became one of a few white journalists who attempted to "translate" it to white civil rights supporters and to others on the left. She preferred to view Black Consciousness pragmatically, as a prerequisite to the truly egalitarian interracial vision she still cherished, and her espousal of it left the way open for continued alliances. In a 1966 *Pa-triot* series devoted to this topic, she wrote: *White people who really believe in a united human race should not be frightened when SNCC and other groups talk about "black power." Our society has lived by white power. Unless black people create their own power, there can never be a meeting ground . . . by forcing [white people] out of black communities [and into organizing whites, SNCC] may be providing this generation with the last chance white people will ever have to overcome the racism and white supremacy by which western man has come close to destroying this planet.*[23]

Her and Carl's unyielding support for integration and interracialism all these years had presupposed a more profound social transformation than the assimilationist impulse that was taking place in 1960s southern politics, which, on some level, simply mirrored preexisting power hierarchies, but without legal segregation. She wrote later of that period that *I was frustrated, and certainly African Americans were, by the slow pace of change. To me, the Black Power movement became the new thrust that was going to move the country in a good direction.* Anne saw no contradiction between the rise of Black Power and the sort of holistic vision she had always held of "integration." She echoed King's words from 1955 Montgomery, the night he emerged as a leader: "When the history books are written in future generations, the historians will have to pause and say, 'There lived a great people, a black people, who injected new meaning and dignity into the veins of civilization.'" To her, Black Power was *just a further development of that vision, made sharper because this generation of African Americans had experienced firsthand that there was no real support for their goals in mainstream America and its institutions.*[24]

When Democrats convened in Atlantic City in August 1964 to nominate Lyndon Johnson for the presidency, American warplanes were already bombing North Vietnamese villages. A few weeks before, the Johnson administration had engaged in a deceitful (it was later revealed) series of military exchanges off the North Vietnamese coast in order to secure a congressional resolution authorizing direct U.S. military involvement there. Bombings escalated, and ground troops soon followed, all in the name of halting the march of communism in Southeast Asia. For those on the front lines of racial protests in the rural South, however, anticommunism no longer provided an adequate rationale for enmity. It required only a small leap of imagination to see the parallels between Mississippi's antiblack aggression and U.S. chauvinism against a tiny, impoverished nation halfway around the world.[25]

By 1965, peace protests galvanized college campuses in much the same way southern sit-ins had half a decade before. Though the antiwar movement was initially centered in nonsouthern cities and college towns, it drew its earliest inspiration from the southern movement. Leading antiwar organizers had cut their political teeth in civil rights campaigns, and SNCC's Bob Moses—who held almost mythic status for those in the New Left—departed Mississippi after the MFDP challenge and soon led protests against the Vietnam War, which he consciously linked to southern liberation struggles. *People forget,* Anne recalled later, *that the first demonstration against an induction center was led by SNCC activists in Atlanta in 1966. The student antiwar movement really took off after Stokely Carmichael began traveling the South, shouting, "Hell, no, we won't go."*[26]

Anne's anti-imperialist politics and her connections to groups like WILPF and Peacemakers predisposed her to object to U.S. policy in Vietnam almost as soon as she learned of it, just as she had done when the Korean War erupted. From her days as a Henry Wallace supporter, she had always viewed peace and freedom as inseparable. When she and Carl saw in 1965 that SCEF lacked consensus for going on record against the war, they initiated "Operation Open Debate," a series of regional workshops to explore the topic. The atmosphere for antiwar dissent was markedly more open this time, and the southern freedom movement had provided that opening.[27]

The majority culture was in a state of high tension by the mid-1960s. The mass civil rights movement sparked wider social protests as it succeeded in heightening public awareness of the gap between the promise and practice of American freedoms. While southern white moderates and business leaders hesitantly acknowledged that their region's way of life was going to have to change, all around Anne were younger southerners experiencing the same kind of painful turning inside out she had endured as a youth in the postwar South. Even in Louisville, where Carl's name and hers remained *fire words,* especially to whites their own age or older, they acquired a new following among reform-minded young people who defied their elders to work more closely with the Bradens. Anne and Carl mentored and participated in public accommodations protests, and the West End Community Council—in which Anne remained active—was an important progenitor to the city's open housing movement of the later '60s, in which the Bradens also took part.[28]

With the passage of civil and voting rights laws in 1964 and 1965, the southern freedom movement wielded some real power. In early 1965 Carl and Anne attempted to put SCEF's economic justice vision into practice through a new outreach program in Appalachia, initiated with a consortium of other organizations that included SNCC, SCLC, SDS, Highlander, and SSOC. SCEF was its driving force, however. *Once there was this powerful black movement, it was realistic to start talking about poverty, economic injustice, building unions. Not that racism was eradicated, but there was a real change in the attitudes of white people in the South who had never been near the movement. We felt the African American movement was key to changing society, but we felt its logical allies were working-class whites, and that coalition has never existed very long or viably because of racism.* The Appalachian South had recently become site of the nation's most public poverty, examined in TV news specials and designated as a target area in President Lyndon Johnson's speech in early 1964 announcing the War on Poverty. That publicity, together with the region's history of economic exploitation and union battles, made it a seemingly logical starting place. SCEF's interest in Appalachia coincided with that of various other social reformers ranging from trade unionists to SDS.[29]

The flowering of the civil rights movement had also brought new people into SCEF to make such ambitious new projects seem possible. SNCC's turn toward Black Power provided SCEF with dozens of new recruits: young whites with varying levels of movement experience who took seriously the suggestion that they organize their own color. Many came to Anne and Carl, still committed to social change but unsure what to do next without the mooring SNCC had provided. That stream of young whites started in 1965 and continued for several years (even Bob and Dottie Zellner joined the SCEF staff in 1967, the last whites to depart SNCC). Some lived with the Bradens for a time, and one, Liz Krohne, even came there to have her baby.[30]

Yet SCEF's new Southern Mountain Project ran into more obstacles than anticipated. A few KKK confrontations notwithstanding, the barriers were connected less to race than they were to culture—and to lingering anticommunism. Even without Anne and Carl present (they worked only in an advisory capacity), a hail of local press criticism assailed SCEF's radical reputation, this time coupled with an antagonism toward shaggy-haired young staffers whose casual styles and group housing arrangements offended local sensibilities. Living on subsistence wages in conditions one reported as "communal, crowded, and crude," staffers often did not last long. Troubled by the rapid turnover, Anne observed in their young colleagues what she began calling a *reentry problem. This happened to whites who'd been in Mississippi, where every white face was an enemy. They just didn't like white people! You can't organize people if you don't like them.* She also found that many of the youth coming out of SNCC were shell-shocked and not entirely functional (to the point that she questioned Jim Forman as to why he was sending her his *crazy folks*). The mountain project started off with interracial teams, but as time went on and black nationalism held increasing appeal for African American youth, only a handful of whites had the patience to stay with the Appalachian organizing.[31]

The Bradens' base in Louisville expanded tremendously, however, as 1966 opened. Jim Dombrowski had served SCEF for 23 years, and he was tired now, his health failing. When he announced his wish to retire, the board nominated Carl and Anne as his replacements. They accepted, on the condition that they move its headquarters to Louisville. Though in practice they co-directed, their designated titles followed gender conventions: Carl was appointed executive director, and Anne, associate executive director. (The titles may also have reflected Anne's greater ambivalence about increasing her administrative duties when she preferred writing and working more directly with people. The board meeting minutes report that upon accepting, she added that although this was not the job she truly wished to do, she felt "history was calling her to do it.")[32]

With the help of a sizable bequest, the Bradens purchased a white frame two-story apartment building at 3210 W. Broadway in the city's West End. They transported the contents of Dombrowski's office there in a rented truck in January 1966. The hefty expense of the move seemed worth it: given their local reputations, they knew that renting a space would be tenuous if not impossible. Initially, the building also generated income: two of the four apartments remained rented for a while, with one designated for office space and another for housing volunteers. They used the backyard and wide front porch for gatherings.[33]

The couple's Virginia Avenue residence had been a stopping-off place for young activists for some time, but moving the entire SCEF operation to Louisville rooted Anne and Carl more firmly in their home community than they had been in years. Like the rest of the region and nation, Kentucky's largest city was brimming with youth activism in 1966. Younger black and white militants self-consciously styled themselves in contrast to the Old Left with which Anne and Carl were largely identified, but in practical terms, the Bradens were close to almost all of the southern organizing efforts that blossomed as the 1960s unfolded, frequently acting as mentors to younger colleagues in Louisville and the South.[34]

Their headquarters also brought to Louisville's social action community a valuable resource that was hard to come by at the time: a printing press. Anne deliberately avoided learning to operate the press because to do so would have eaten up her time assisting in the many newsletters and leaflets for local groups that now sought out the Bradens. Within months of their locating there, the SCEF office had become a vibrant gathering spot for those interested in social change, whether it be civil rights, black nationalism, welfare rights, or antiwar campaigns. SCEF staff even provided a haven for antiwar servicemen attempting to organize at nearby Fort Knox. The Bradens remained excoriated by what Anne now thought of as *the establishment* and controversial even within the local movement, but they possessed a growing base of supporters who provided a spirited counterbalance.[35]

The SCEF office also drew new activists to Louisville from as far away as Canada, Boston, and Mississippi—much to the chagrin of local authorities. By 1967—the same year that Louisville's open housing movement drew huge rallies, national publicity, and new crusaders to the city—the staff surpassed a dozen. SCEF's resources were limited: staffers received a bare subsistence, at most about $100 a month. Some worked for room and board, or for nothing at all. Yet they kept coming, fighting off disillusionment or depression but drawn still by the fire for social change that never burned low at the Bradens' house.[36]

Anne focused most of her work on the *Patriot* and on local crusades against racism, while Carl oversaw SCEF's various regional programs. Their efforts in Appalachian east Tennessee had proven fruitless, but a new SCEF project opened in the spring of 1967 in Pikeville, Kentucky, to bring economic reform to isolated eastern Kentucky. Its staffers were Al and Margaret McSurely, a pair of idealistic newlyweds who were new to Kentucky, Appalachia, and SCEF: Al had worked with the poverty program in Washington, and Margaret had been with SNCC in Mississippi. The McSurelys had assistance from Joe Mulloy, a dark-haired, stocky young Louisvillian who had moved to the mountains with his activist wife, Karen, to work with the Appalachian Volunteers, a federally funded regional initiative to bring in young antipoverty workers from surrounding colleges for community uplift projects. The Mulloys and the McSurelys forged an alliance with fledgling anti–strip mining activists native to the area who were making local headlines by standing in front of bulldozers to block their entry. The reforms the SCEF staff sought were modest, but their rhetoric was not, and any receptivity to their ideas by locals was enough to arouse the ire of coal companies that controlled the sluggish, insular local economy.[37]

When Anne got the call about their young staffers' arrests in August 1967, she was not entirely shocked: *there was always somebody getting locked up.* But when she heard the charge, she thought she must be dreaming: it was like a déjà-vu from 1954 Louisville. Al and Margaret McSurely's house had been raided, as had the Mulloys'. Sheriff's deputies had carted away two truckloads of books, and Al, Margaret, and Joe were pronounced "communists" and charged with sedition under the same law with which Anne and Carl had been charged 13 years before. The Bradens had assumed all these years—wrongly, they now learned—that the law was dead after Carl's conviction had been voided. Instead, the sedition statute had merely lain inoperative. Leading the raid was another commonwealth's attorney—Pike County's Thomas Ratliff, who was running that fall for lieutenant governor on the Republican Party ticket. Ratliff railed over what he called a "white paper" Al McSurely had authored, outlining how to "take over Pike County from the power structure and put it in the hands of the poor."[38]

Anne and Carl enlisted the New York attorney Bill Kunstler (who was becoming nationally known for his defense of 1960s radicals) to work with Dan Jack Combs, the liberal Pikeville maverick whom the McSurelys retained as local counsel. Over the next few weeks, Carl assailed the sedition charges as "pure harassment" and traded jibes with Ratliff, who continued to warn of radical outsiders taking over the mountains (rumor had it that Russian tanks were headed for Pikeville). The defense, meanwhile, hoped to halt the prosecution by invoking the precedent for federal intervention set two years before in *Dombrowski v. Pfister*—the "chilling effect" principle.[39]

On September 11, 1967, Carl drove five hours to Pikeville to meet with the McSurelys and their attorney in preparation for the upcoming federal hearing. When he phoned home later and asked, "How would you like to be indicted for sedition?" Anne took his question as a joke. She had never even been to Pike County. But Carl was not kidding: upon his arrival, he learned that the grand jury Ratliff had convened to investigate the sedition allegations had added both Bradens to the indictment. They must now present themselves for arraignment. Political posturing was probably the underlying cause: Ratliff's running mate—Republican gubernatorial candidate Louie Nunn—had been lambasting the state's most notorious couple for months. If elected, Nunn said, he would use his executive office "to run [SCEF and the Bradens] out of Kentucky." (Another candidate, Lester Burns, running for attorney general that year, printed up bumper stickers that read, "Burns In, Bradens Out.")[40]

Anne and Carl were arrested the next day as they walked along the sidewalk in Pikeville to surrender. The two made no effort to meet their $10,000 bond, the same amount that had accompanied their 1954 indictments: *It was so obvious we'd been thrown in as window-dressing. We told the judge we were tired of having to raise bond money every time some ambitious prosecutor wanted to get elected.* They asked instead to be released on their own recognizance. Unimpressed, the local judge refused, and the Bradens spent the next two nights in jail.[41]

On the third morning, a three-judge federal hearing began in Lexington, 100 miles away. Its purpose was to determine the constitutionality of the charges facing Anne, Carl, and their codefendants. Just before noon, the couple found themselves piled into the patrol car of two Pike County deputies, who *raced at 90 miles an hour up the Mountain Parkway to get to Lexington.* They soon learned that the judges had demanded their presence before the hearing could proceed.[42]

Anne could not help the feeling of dread that crept over her as she remembered Carl's first sedition trial, but the minute she walked into the large courtroom gallery, she knew this one would be different. Instead of cold stares, she and Carl were greeted by a boisterous crowd of youthful well-wishers. Robert Sedler, a University of Kentucky constitutional law professor (who would become active in both SCEF and the KCLU thereafter), had written a friend-of-the-court brief in support of Kunstler's motion for this federal hearing. Now Sedler had filled the courtroom with law students, many of whom were incensed by the legal maneuverings that had created this case. In addition, a dozen or more SCEF supporters had come from Louisville and brought along Jim and Beth Braden to watch. The main floor was overflowing, with more young people peering curiously over the balcony.[43]

Bill Kunstler assured his clients they could win that day. He put Anne on the stand, and she outlined the SCEF vision and program. Then Ratliff rose to cross-examine her. *He swelled up like a toad and began slowly, "Mrs. Braden, are you now, or have you ever been . . ." In my theater work, I had learned how an actor has to wait for the laughs. That's what Ratliff had to do then. After it subsided, Ratliff continued, "a communist—by which I mean, do you subscribe to Stalin, Lenin, Mao Tse-Tung, Trotsky, Castro, and Guevara?"* Now it was Anne's turn to wait. Ratliff mispronounced the names, prompting what seemed to her like the entire courtroom to erupt in laughter again. *After it quieted down, I said, "Mr. Ratliff, you have covered a wide spectrum of political and economic thought in that question, and I don't see how anyone could answer it intelligently." At which point Judge [Bert] Combs said, "I don't either, Mr. Ratliff. Ask her something else."*[44]

I thought about how that question, "are you now . . ." had once struck terror into the hearts of those who faced it. I realized at that moment that the 1950s were finally over.[45]

After Anne's testimony, the judges retired to consider what they had heard. After what seemed to her like a short while, they returned. As the decision was being read, Anne reached over and pressed her foot to Carl's. This had been a long time coming. The judges announced their 2-1 ruling that the Kentucky sedition law was unconstitutional because it "put a damper on plaintiffs' freedom of speech as well as on others who might be in sympathy with their objectives."[46]

———————

Anne's assessment that *the 1950s were finally over* was not entirely accurate. Those in power did not simply give up using Cold War anticommunism to attack people working for southern social change. In a deeper sense, however, she was correct. What had changed by 1967 was the audience. It was an incremental change, not the cataclysmic one that film clips of demonstrations from the 1960s suggest. But the momentum of 1960s idealism had swept away the terror that anticommunist rhetoric had previously engendered, and the sources of anticommunist repression became less monolithic. With masses of people, especially the young, no longer frightened of the inquisitors, their power evaporated.[47]

Repression, however, did not. It simply arose in different—and perhaps more virulent—forms, its target now the black liberation movement that had shaken the country for more than a decade.

PART FOUR

CHAPTER TWELVE

THE NEXT THREE DECADES: THE STRUGGLE CONTINUES

Freedom is a constant struggle.

—traditional[1]

WHEN ANNE STEPPED OUT OF THE federal courthouse in Lexington into the blinding sunlight with her family and friends that September afternoon in 1967, the moment held sweet vindication for her and for the region, the promise of redemption. Never again would she and Carl, or SCEF, face legal attack for their activism. Cold War anticommunism had lost its sting as an instrument to immobilize southern social and racial change.

It was the end of an era, but it was by no means the end of the struggle for racial justice. After the murder of Martin Luther King, Jr. in 1968, the national spotlight turned away from the South. Perhaps because of this turn, historians and popular commentators have tended to place the end of the civil rights movement at approximately this same time. But to those like Anne—immersed as she was in struggles that animated the post–Voting Rights South—the movement, as she defined it, never really stopped. In fact, people on the front lines of struggle felt in the late 1960s that they had—as she has put it—*scarcely begun to dismantle the racist infrastructure of the region.*[2]

Repression of the Black Liberation Movement

In the wake of victory in the sedition case, Anne, now 43, and Carl, 53, concentrated on moving ahead on SCEF's positive organizing program. They reinstituted the Southern Mountain Project—this time in West Virginia—and oversaw a similar drive, Grassroots Organizing Work, or GROW, staffed by Bob and Dottie Zellner in New Orleans, to organize black and white woodcutters (and other workers, including former Klansmen) in parts of the Gulf Coast Deep South.[3]

But they soon found themselves embroiled in battles against dramatic new forms of repression that became characteristic of the late '60s. Government harassment now turned to the black liberation movement, whose militancy and macho rhetoric stoked century-old cultural fears of what one historian has called the "black beast-rapist." The Pike County sedition charges coincided with a 1967 surge in the visibility of radical black nationalism, and even more mainstream leaders such as King acknowledged the need for a heightened race consciousness and condemned U.S. policy in Vietnam.[4]

This new repression was qualitatively different from the attacks on the freedom movement of the 1950s and earlier 1960s. Earlier assaults, though often violent and sometimes involving mass arrests, were almost entirely engineered by local segregationist officials, and jail sentences were usually relatively brief. The later prosecutions involved charges that carried years of imprisonment, and local police and prosecutors had the support of policymakers at the highest levels of government. The FBI initiated a new effort to "disrupt" or otherwise "neutralize" black nationalist organizations through a program known as COINTELPRO. FBI counterintelligence (originally established in 1956 to monitor the CP) now turned its full gaze to outspoken black radicals, with older white leftists like Anne and Carl scrutinized primarily as foils. Increasingly, the Bradens turned the lessons they had learned in their efforts against Cold War silencing into defenses of the increasingly beleaguered black liberation movement.[5]

In part,1960s radicalism fell prey in the end to its own disillusionments and excesses, but especially in the case of the African American freedom movement, government repression propelled its decline. *The movement of the sixties was crushed. I was traveling around the South in those years, and in just about every community, the black organizers were either in jail, on their way there, or just out because of a huge struggle.* Harsh sentences imposed on SNCC and Black Panther activists all but paralyzed the groups they served. Minor weapons violations and numerous instances of draft resistance carried inordinately stiff penalties, but more egregious injustices were also rampant. One SNCC leader in Houston—Lee Otis Johnson—fought off 16 charges in the course of 1968, only to receive a 30-year sentence for allegedly offering one marijuana cigarette to an undercover agent, whose testimony was the only incriminating evidence. Similar cases targeted rights leaders in virtually every southern state. In Wilmington, North Carolina, the Rev. Ben Chavis and nine others (who became the "Wilmington Ten," some of the more than 40 black activists imprisoned in that state) faced a total of 242 years in prison on charges of firebombing a grocery in the midst of violent attacks on the black community by white supremacist groups. In Orangeburg, South Carolina, state police violence against African American college students protesting racial discrimination left three dead and 37 injured (though this incident preceded the shootings of four white students at Ohio's Kent State University by two years, it never received the public attention the Kent State violence did). Amid widespread anger surrounding Martin Luther King's assassination, 1968 also brought to the Bradens' hometown the case of the "Black Six," in which six African American activists—ranging from radicals to respected middle-class civil rights campaigners—were charged with conspiring to blow up an oil refinery in the wake of mass civil disorders in the predominantly black West End.[6]

To Anne and Carl, the stakes seemed to heighten as the 1970s dawned. *The African American movement had activated a whole generation of blacks, whites, Latinos, and Native Americans. I believe that those who ran the society realized that if they could behead that movement, the rest of us wouldn't have a snowball's chance in hell.* Because most of the new targets were black, the Bradens tried to sound the alarm to whites around the South, but again they soon felt like voices crying in the wilderness. By that time, the "beloved community" vision of the early '60s had splintered, and social movements themselves were nearly as segregated as the larger society they had first criticized. Black activists—though they frequently opposed the Vietnam War and other injustices—kept their sights on racial freedom in any social movement of which they became a part, while whites flocked into campus organizing and new causes like the anti-Vietnam and women's liberation movements, with many leaving behind the anti-racist impulse that had first ignited 1960s social action.[7]

In some instances, however, the Bradens' use of strategies they had employed since 1954 turned defenses into counteroffensives. After a huge public outcry and a barrage of literature the couple helped to generate, Louisville's Black Six were acquitted in 1970 because of an absolute lack of evidence of any conspiracy or crime (the refinery was never harmed). The case of Walter Collins, an African American draft resister who worked with SCEF in New

Orleans, occasioned a drive that called white peace activists' attention to the disproportionately harsh measures against blacks who resisted induction. In 1970 Collins lost all appeals and began a five-year federal prison sentence—in contrast to the more positive outcome in a very similar case SCEF had also championed, that of Joe Mulloy (the Bradens' 1967 codefendant), a white resister who won his freedom at the Supreme Court level. SCEF also worked with other organizations to develop a fightback around the Wilmington Ten case that sparked into a national crusade that lasted throughout the 1970s. Chavis—identified by Amnesty International as a political prisoner—was finally freed in 1979 and went on to lead the NAACP briefly in the 1990s.[8]

Support campaigns like the ones for Chavis and Collins (among others) dovetailed with prisoners' rights movements that were coalescing all over the country at the end of the 1960s as inmates whose ranks were increasingly populated by black community organizers adopted tactics from the southern civil rights movement to protest institutionalized racism and demand internal reforms. The case that most poignantly linked those two causes was that of Angela Davis, a native Alabamian and youthful CP member and Black Panther who went underground in 1970 after being charged with murder, conspiracy, and kidnapping in California for her championing of political prisoners there. Davis's case was not uniquely southern (and neither was the antiblack repression of that era), but the protest it generated produced the most powerful southern antirepression campaign of that period and stirred a broader spectrum of southerners—black and white. Anne and Carl became some of Davis's leading southern publicists after Ella Baker invited Sallye Davis, Angela's mother, to address a SCEF board meeting in Birmingham about the situation her daughter faced. The couple coordinated a southern speaking tour on behalf of Angela—a striking young woman whose Afro hairstyle and raised fist, as well as her appearance on the FBI's "Ten Most Wanted" list, symbolized African American defiance.[9]

The "Free Angela Davis" campaign and Davis's 1972 jury acquittal suggested that the new repression held the promise of a more positive outcome than the one the Bradens had lived through in the 1950s. Anne wrote soon after the verdict that *the two major fear techniques that have long been used to cripple people's movements—the fear of the black movement and the fear of communism—were joined in Angela's case, but people didn't buy it.* Davis emerged from the courtroom determined that the momentum developed around her defense would be mobilized to help the scores of other activists behind bars. She, Ben Chavis, and Charlene Mitchell (an African American CP leader) enlisted Carl's help in a nationwide organizing effort that led to the 1973 formation of the

National Alliance Against Racist and Political Repression, which offered support primarily to blacks, Latinos, and Native Americans it identified as political prisoners. Carl Braden and Davis were among the four initial co-chairs, and over the following decades the Kentucky branch of the alliance became Anne's central outlet for local activism.[10]

In spite of the new drives to blunt social change and the Bradens' limited success in conveying to other whites the urgent need to respond to the attacks, Anne and Carl were experiencing their own kind of renascence in Louisville, where SCEF headquarters continued to attract more and more new crusaders. The organization experienced a lot of growing pains with respect to both its generational and its racial makeup. SCEF still had leadership from Shuttlesworth, Dombrowski, and the longtime South Carolina organizer Modjeska Simkins (among other elders), but most of its newest recruits were under 30. Though SCEF's historic emphasis on interracialism and the cause of black freedom kept it less segregated than many other social change organizations active during this period, the vast majority of newcomers were also white.

By 1970, SCEF had outgrown the building purchased four years before. Its staff functions were like small mass meetings, drawing 50 people. The Bradens secured a major donation to buy a second property next door, another two-story white clapboard house that had long sat vacant. That purchase increased their visibility further—as did the racial and political diversity of the crowd that was drawn to the new SCEF house. Scenes like two white women hanging a "Black Power" banner from an upstairs window or a draft resister fleeing out the back door to evade military police knocking at the front were bound to capture public attention. Soon Anne and Carl found themselves profiled in campus newspapers and even in the *Courier-Journal* more as curiosities than as pariahs.[11]

Rise of the New Women's Movement

The emergence of women's liberation—or what historians know as "second-wave feminism"—was a positive development in the late 1960s social landscape, one that blossomed just when the black liberation movement was under the severest attack. Young white feminist leaders like Carol Hanisch, who worked for a time on the SCEF staff, and Kathie Amatniek (later Kathie Sarachild) had gotten their start in southern civil rights campaigns: in fact, they held the first meetings of New York Radical Women in SCEF's New York headquarters. Anne attended their early conferences and tried to be support-ive. But because her own experience coming into social justice campaigns had been largely affirming—as had her marriage—it took her several years to fully understand the impetus for women's liberation, as she reflected much later. *By the time I got active in things, I had already decided I wanted an independent course in life. In the late '40s, I honestly never felt "put down" because I was a woman. The stories about that happening in the left were not my experience at all. Then when Carl and I began directing SCEF in 1966, it soon became a place where any number of women took leadership.* Though both Bradens recommended to the SCEF board in late 1968 that Carol Hanisch be funded in a six-month exploratory project to galvanize women's liberation groups around the South, the funding was not renewed after a meeting of SCEF women recommended against it. Hanisch left the staff embittered and feeling that neither Anne nor SCEF held any real commitment to women's emancipation.[12]

Part of Anne's resistance and that of some other SCEF women came from concern that feminists' hostility toward men would derail SCEF work with poor people in the mountains and in the GROW Deep South project. (As one historian of the women's movement has pointed out, feminist anger at men "initially created an impassable gulf between male and female activists.") From her interactions with Hanisch and others in the new women's movement, Anne had observed what she saw as a too-singular focus on women's oppres-sion, to the exclusion of race, class, and violence. *The war was raging at that point in Vietnam. I remember sitting in someone's apartment in San Francisco and hearing a woman say, "I'll never take part in another antiwar action, the men are all so terrible." I asked her how she could say that when our government was napalming children in Vietnam. She couldn't understand me, and I could not fathom her.*[13]

Anne continued to feel at odds with the new feminists until the early 1970s, when a chance meeting at a women's conference with a young former SCEF staffer whom she had not seen in several years made her realize she had been, as she admitted later, *pretty insensitive.* When Anne asked her friend what she thought about women's liberation, she was struck by the tale of her friend's disastrous marriage and comment that "I just wish I had known about it five years ago!" Generational differences had blinded Anne to what a lifeline the feminist movement offered some women: *I realized then that [SCEF's] providing women a place where they could be active and become leaders was not enough. These women had come into the movement with their own baggage. They had grown up in the fifties during that "back-to-the-kitchen" period which was part and parcel of the prevailing repression then. They had come into the civil rights movement committed to it but also still imprisoned by internal voices that told them the main object in life was to "catch a man."*[14]

Though she remained troubled by how narrow the orientation and composition of the largely white, middle-class women's movement was, Anne became more encouraging in her attempts to broaden it from within. Hers became a voice for a feminist vision that was more inclusive, anti-racist, anti-war, and socialistic in its aim. At the first statewide meeting of Kentucky feminists, Anne made a poignant plea not to exclude men who might be sympathetic. In Louisville, she encouraged a group of feminists to attend the founding conference of the National Women's Political Caucus (NWPC), which under the leadership of Bella Abzug was organizing women against sexism, racism, poverty, and institutional violence. Then in late 1971, Anne became a local leader in the formation of a Socialist Women's Caucus that projected a broader feminist agenda of peace and economic change before an early mass meeting which went on to become an affiliate of the NWPC.[15]

It was also during this time that Anne wrote her *Letter to White Southern Women*, which recalled her jarring sojourn to Mississippi to plead for the life of Willie McGee more than 20 years before. Published in 1972 as a public conversation with the women's liberation movement, the "letter" was actually a SCEF booklet aimed at feminists active in antirape crusades. It related the story of McGee and that of Thomas Wansley, a prisoner SCEF was currently championing who had been wrongly convicted at 17 of raping a 59-year-old woman in a racially troubled part of Virginia. Cautioning women to remember the history of black-male-on-white-female rape in the South, Anne suggested that they challenge rape cases in which there was racial injustice and make sure their sisterhood extended to black women too. She wrote, *I am aware that my appeal to you . . . comes at a time when the women's movement . . . is struggling to make our society . . . deal with the crime of rape. My position is not at odds with this struggle; it is simply another dimension. For the fact is that rape has traditionally been considered a crime in the South—if the woman was white and the accused black. But it has not been seen as a crime—and is not now—if the woman is black. . . . We who are white will overcome our oppression as women only when we reject once and for all the privileges conferred on us by our white skin.*[16]

In 1977 she wrote a second letter that appeared in a special women's issue of *Southern Exposure* magazine. This time she included a critique of Susan Brownmiller's scathing 1975 attack on rape, *Against Our Will*, and reiterated in stronger terms the need for white feminists to confront the *racist use of the rape charge*. Through appeals like these, Anne became one of a relatively few white women whose impassioned, sometimes uncomfortable reminders echoed the calls of radical women of color to the women's liberation movement to embrace a more multicultural feminism that was not—as the second letter noted—*at odds with the black liberation struggle.* Anne remained at the fringes of the women's movement, but though she identified herself for the rest of her life as a feminist—and bristled at anyone's suggestion that she was not one—she saw her life's course quite differently from that of most second-wave feminist activists.[17]

Tragedy, Both Personal and Political

In the 1970s, Anne encountered two crises that were both profoundly personal and profoundly political.

One of the most painful disappointments of early in the decade was a series of internecine battles among disillusioned young leftists of varying political persuasions that caused an irreparable split in SCEF and soon brought about its demise. She still despaired over that outcome years afterward: *I had spent 16 years of my life building that organization and saw it destroyed in six months.* Though she tried to preserve the SCEF spirit of unity that had been so important to her, her best efforts at conciliation were just not enough. The repression that accompanied especially black activism and the slow pace of social change brought increasing frustrations that younger radicals turned upon themselves. While African American activists became increasingly drawn to the Black Panthers or other less publicized black liberation groups, many young whites who had once rejected anything that smacked of ideological dogma now became extremely doctrinaire and joined a variety of Marxist-Leninist groups that proliferated as the decade proceeded. In this environment, SCEF—already overwhelmingly white—became a battleground for competing ideologies among self-styled white revolutionaries. Complicating these internal tensions was the group's increasingly strained relations with black radicals in Louisville who resented SCEF's resources and for a time commandeered its equipment and threatened staffers at gunpoint.[18]

The internal dissension all but immobilized SCEF. The discord finally pushed first Carl and later Anne (plus other longtime supporters, including Shuttlesworth, Dombrowski, and Modjeska Simkins, who was then the president) to end, reluctantly, their association with the organization they had nurtured for so long. Characteristically, Carl cut his losses and walked away from SCEF once he saw the direction in which relations were headed, resigning from the board in October 1973 (he had already left the directorship in 1971 before the real trouble started in order to devote his time to offering media and organizing trainings around the country). But Anne could not let go so easily. Having taken the directorship alone for a year after Carl's resignation, she stayed on as *Patriot* editor until late 1973 and remained on the board for several months longer, during which she penned lengthy correspondences and spent countless sleepless nights in debate in order to avoid a split. By the time she cut herself off from SCEF in 1974, the organization had been more or less taken over by young supporters of the October League, one of many sectarian political parties of those years, a breakaway group from SDS who were inclined toward Mao's cultural revolution. Ironically, they believed the current SCEF orientation to be too reformist, partially because some of its policies and personnel matched those of the Communist Party, which some New Leftists regarded as passé.[19]

What three decades of attacks had failed to do was accomplished from within. After learning later of the extent of FBI spying through COINTEL-PRO, Anne became convinced that the internal battles weakened SCEF and left it ripe for government infiltrators who brought about its downfall. Though she was never able to substantiate those suspicions, she suspected that *they had an agent in every faction.* Anne also concluded that the fatal flaw that had left SCEF vulnerable was the fact that it had become overwhelmingly white. *I made up my mind then that I would never spend another minute of my life building something all-white or predominantly white. That is just not what's going to change things in this country.* And she never did.[20]

When Anne and Carl departed, some of their funding sources went with them. SCEF never regained its former stature within progressive circles, but grew smaller and more marginalized. Its disintegration devastated supporters around the nation who had seen it as a rare example of unity among social change forces. Its ending took an incredible emotional toll on Anne, one she had scarcely had time to recover from when life dealt her a much more staggering blow.[21]

On February 18, 1975, Anne was on her way to Anniston to help her mother recover from surgery. At home in Louisville, Carl took a break from writing in his office to take a bath, then lay down on a couch and, without warning, died at the age of 60. Fifteen-year-old Beth Braden discovered him there that afternoon when she came home from school. Doctors concluded that he had suffered a series of undetected heart attacks over time that brought about heart failure, which probably took him quickly and relatively painlessly.[22]

Anne was stunned to find herself without the familiar mooring she had known most of her adult life. She went through the motions of having Carl's body cremated and its remains placed in a box he had used for stamps and buried beside their elder daughter in the small Eminence cemetery that marked seven generations of her family. With the help of Jim, Beth, and their family minister, she planned what began as a simple memorial service but turned into a major commemoration, held at the Bradens' St. George Episcopal Church, that drew longtime allies and friends to Louisville to speak—Shuttlesworth, Dombrowski, Frank Wilkinson, and Angela Davis, among others. Anne also spoke, feeling Carl would have wanted her to. She echoed the words of revolutionary musician Joe Hill with sentiments she knew Carl shared: *don't mourn; organize.* Later she wrote an irate letter to FBI agents who had been brazen, she felt, in attending what should have been a private affair.[23]

Anne felt as if a part of herself had been torn away. Carl and she had been, as she put it, *totally intertwined, like the trunks of two trees grown together.* She was also painfully aware of what the loss meant to her children. Both—she knew by now—had been affected more than she had anticipated by the constant attacks on their parents and by their unusual lifestyle. Jim seemed on the surface to have achieved many of his goals, having won a 1971 Rhodes Scholarship to England (soon he would attend Harvard law school). But he was going through a lot of inner turmoil trying to *find himself,* as his mother put it. Beth was in the throes of adolescence—already a trying period—and the loss of her father hit her hard. Anne tried to help them cope with the crisis: *not very successfully,* she thought later.[24]

Carl's death posed a political crisis for Anne as well. *How,* she wondered at age 50, *could one part of a two-person team . . . function alone?* She told herself and others she would need a *process of reconstructing* her life.[25]

New Vehicles for Organizing

Partly because of her extreme immediacy, however, Anne's immersion in activism never faltered, and she never allowed herself the luxury of stopping to consider the shape of the rest of her life. More than anything, the press of social changes as yet undone kept her going in the period following Carl's death. She and Beth drove cross-country in the summer of 1976 to visit Jim, who was by then living in northern California, and as usual they spent time each summer with the O'Connors at Little Compton, but otherwise Anne was hard at work.

Ilene Carver, a 19-year-old whom Carl had met a year earlier in Boston, came to live with Anne and Beth, ostensibly to get Carl's papers in order. But Carver turned out to be what Anne has called *a natural-born political organizer,* the two women became close friends, and Carver stayed for four years. Other young people also spent stretches of time with Anne and Beth in those years. What had once been casual household disarray became chaos, but it was a welcoming kind of disorder, and Anne was never one to turn anyone away.[26]

The impetus for Anne's greater intensity in her work was strong insofar as Carl's death coincided with a turbulent turning point in local race relations. Louisville was poised to begin widescale busing in the 1975 school year, and opponents—including the KKK—had been organizing for two years, leading up to a rally of 10,000 the night before schools opened, rioting the next few days, and a monthlong school boycott that was partially successful. After such overt shows of racism, Anne and others in the Kentucky Alliance Against Racist and Political Repression became instrumental in founding Progress in Education (PIE), a predominantly white coalition formed with the single purpose of opposing racism in the schools and working in alliance with the United Black Protective Parents, another grassroots group. Anne believed that, as she wrote that fall, *the lines are clearly drawn now. One cannot be against busing at this point in history and also be for equal rights.* PIE offered neighborhood workshops, culminating with a rally of 1,000 featuring the folk singer Pete Seeger, who came at Anne's invitation. Her tirelessness in PIE and its success in uniting Louisville liberals and the left offset the resurrection of slurs on her motives that accompanied the very heated tensions surrounding the start of busing. In the aftermath of that campaign, she won new criticism from a local judge, received an onslaught of hate mail, and lost two cars to arson in less than a year's time, but the paroxysm of opposition seemed to fade more rapidly, and she received plenty of local support as a counter.[27]

In the year of Carl's death, Anne also worked with other refugees from SCEF's demise to create a new vehicle for regional organizing. She believed that *the legacy of the southern conference movement was too important to let die.* The backlash against the black liberation movement and especially the breakup of SCEF had confirmed her belief in race as the fulcrum for social change in the South. Experience had also taught her that *local movements dry up on the vine unless such an entity exists. You've got to know what cathedral you're building when you lift your heavy stone; otherwise, people burn out.*[28]

They titled the new southern network the Southern Organizing Committee for Economic and Social Justice (SOC). With the lessons of the SCEF breakup in mind, they built it consciously as a biracial entity (it later reached out to Latino, Asian American, and Native American groups to become multiracial). Ben Chavis and Anne became its first co-chairs, and Shuttlesworth took a leading role as well. The general fragmentation of social justice groups during that period led SOC's founders to define their mission carefully: they saw themselves not as "the movement," but as a committee of organizers to build the movement, united by the common belief that anti-racism was the essential element in southern social change.

By then, the revelations of the Watergate scandal had created a more open atmosphere in the country than had existed in the 1960s. Watergate also produced an increasing skepticism toward government that—though it prompted some to retreat from social action and become more introspective—yielded in other circles a willingness to seek alternative paths to social progress. Thus, the "economic and social justice" phraseology in SOC's title harkened back to the original Southern Conference program—southern economic and social justice for all, but based now on a heightened understanding of the need for black leadership and the centrality of opposing white supremacy. SOC became the catalyst for broad coalitions addressing a range of race- and class-related issues—defending black elected officials under attack, for example, and mounting a "Housing Not Bombs" campaign linking the nation's bloated military spending to unmet human needs regionally.[29]

Despite an upsurge in women's and antinuclear organizing in both South and nation during this era, too many whites, Anne knew, still ignored the glaring boil of racial injustice on the body politic. She continued in the uphill task of appealing to white progressives to act against racism. In the aftermath of SCEF's demise and amid ongoing antiblack repression, she began to consider more seriously the psychological dynamics of whites confronting racism, and it was during this period that she developed what thereafter became an essential component of her philosophy and approach to organizing: *Even when I was the object of vicious attack, there were certain advantages that came to me because I was white. . . . No white people in a society founded on racism can ever totally free themselves from this prison.*[30]

A New Offensive against Racism

During one of the many argumentative, emotionally wrenching meetings that foretold the breakup of SCEF, Anne leaned over to Lenore Hogan, a New York staffer, and predicted that even the most deeply conflicted among them would find themselves reunited in a few years' time. *Because if you live and work in the South,* Anne told her, *whether you're black or white, race is the most important thing. The rest of these disputes are peripheral.*[31]

Those words turned out to be a prophecy. The Ku Klux Klan experienced a revival in the mid-1970s, and organizations like SOC and SCLC, as well as a number of Marxist-Leninist groups, began organizing actions to counter it.

The new Klan had updated the same message that had found success for a time in the 1950s White Citizens' Council movement: the idea that whites were the ones discriminated against. When robed Klansmen shot into a crowd at an SCLC anti-racist march in Decatur, Alabama, in mid-1979, it prompted the Reverend C. T. Vivian (once an aide to Martin Luther King and now working again with SCLC), Anne, and an assortment of other longtime activists to begin planning a national anti-Klan network that would hold a major conference in Atlanta later that year.[32]

But before the event could even take place, a violent atrocity left five dead and seven seriously wounded in the central North Carolina city of Greensboro on November 3, 1979. In broad daylight and in front of TV cameras, an armed caravan of Klan and Nazi Party supporters sped alongside an anti-Klan march through a public housing project, jumped from their cars wielding knives and pistols, then sprayed gunfire at participants and drove off. All five casualties (one black, one Latino, three white; four male, one female) were veterans of antiwar and black liberation campaigns who had turned to Marxist-Leninism in the 1970s and were members of the post–New Left Communist Workers Party (CWP), sponsor of the march.[33]

Though many on the left viewed the CWP with suspicion, all were stunned by the acts of blatant brutality committed against the demonstrators. Anne drove all night to attend a funeral march in their honor, which took place in spite of a cold pouring rain and a palpable tension pervading the streets, lined by National Guardsmen with their rifles drawn. The Greensboro massacre shocked the nation and gave a new sense of urgency to the anti-Klan conference held only weeks later. The Atlanta gathering reunited most of the leading figures from SCEF's final days who put aside their differences amid the enormity of the threat. *A new sense of unity filled the air. The church people weren't looking fearfully at the left-wingers. The left-wingers weren't looking down their noses at the church people. We called it "the spirit of Atlanta."* The conference ended with a call for a major anti-Klan march in Greensboro on February 2, 1980—weekend of the twentieth anniversary of the first sit-in there.[34]

The road to Greensboro was rocky, however. Fearing their presence might drive broader forces away and evoke further violence, some of the rally's organizers wanted to ask the CWP not to take part. The dispute reminded Anne vividly of her own experience in 1950s Louisville, when ACLU organizers driven to establish a branch by the Bradens' sedition case wanted nothing to do with the couple themselves. She became an outspoken, dogged defender—sometimes the lone one—of including CWP members in the march. Ultimately, the CWP did participate, and the march drew 10,000 attenders without violence, providing an impetus for invigorated southern anti-racist campaigns over the coming decade. The new National Anti-Klan Network was directed—at Anne's urging—by Lyn Wells, once one of the most strident of Anne's critics in SCEF's October League faction.[35]

The Jesse Jackson Campaign

One of the slogans of the Greensboro march was "Lay claim to the 1980s." If the measure of that claim was in elected officials and enactment of policies that benefited all Americans, it would ring hollow, even cruel, in the wake of Ronald Reagan's election. In those years, a conservative tide swept George Wallace's southern-originated, antigovernment "politics of rage"—brewing since the late 1960s—into the dominant national political discourse. But if one judges a period of history, as Anne has, on the basis of people moving and organizing for peace and justice, *we really did lay claim to the '80s. We did it through the two Jesse Jackson campaigns, especially.*[36]

In her sixties, Anne jumped into both the 1984 and 1988 Jackson campaigns, working day and night in Louisville and regionally. She was drawn to Jackson's candidacy by an article of his she read in 1983. *He said words to this effect: "we're not talking about a black agenda. We're talking about an agenda for America from the black perspective. This country looks very different if you are black or brown, or if you are white and unemployed, or if you are a woman." This, I said to myself, is what many of us have been waiting for!* As always, she saw her role as that of recruiting whites. Jackson carried Kentucky's Third Congressional District (which was two thirds white) in both campaigns. White support for Jackson's run also more than doubled between 1984 and 1988, when his ticket carried five Deep South states and Virginia, generating more than two million southern votes.[37]

Jackson's first presidential run generated enormous grassroots momentum; Anne observed this in Kentucky and especially in San Francisco at the 1984 Democratic Convention, where she served as an alternate delegate (after some initial shock and consternation among Kentucky Democrats still fearful of her reputation). Once that momentum coalesced into the Rainbow Coalition in 1986, she became a member of its national board and saw more clearly the shape of something she had long dreamed of: a mass movement, multiethnic now, and led by African Americans. It was brief, however, lasting only through the 1988 campaign. *There have been many debates as to why*, she has lamented. *But regardless of the reasons, [its collapse] was the American political tragedy of the twentieth century.*[38]

With the resiliency that had become her trademark, Anne bounced back in the 1990s, focusing much of her energy on anti-racist crusades in Louisville through the Kentucky Alliance. Regionally, she saw SOC evolve into a staffed, Atlanta-based organization that became the springboard for a new environmental justice movement of local battles against southern toxic waste dumps and polluting industries located disproportionately in communities of color and of poor whites. As the twenty-first century arrived, Anne was proudest of the fact that SOC was now clearly led by people of color: its director now was Connie Tucker (a former target of 1960s antiblack repression in Florida whose case SCEF had once championed), and she drew other nonwhites into leadership. *SCHW was always interracial, but it was dominated by whites. SCEF was very interracial, but Jim Dombrowski ran it, and later Carl and I did, because staff usually does. Even the early SOC was often kept going by my persistence. Now SOC has made this transition, and I think it's one very few "interracial" groups have made.* Anne liked to remind people: *Building a truly viable multiracial organization in a racist society is impossible. But the impossible just takes a little longer.*[39]

From Pariah to Heroine

Carl never lived to see his reputation rehabilitated in the couple's hometown. At his death, his accomplishments were heralded in the left press, while a *Courier-Journal* editorial headlined him a "zealous reformer" and concluded condescendingly—with no reference to his softhearted streak or his boundless sense of humor—that "one doesn't have to subscribe to his dark view of society, his professional martyrdom, his sometimes misguided methods or even his lack of patience to concede that a world too complacent and smug to tolerate such crusaders would be a sorry place." Only Anne studiously kept the memory of his work alive in tandem with the continuation of her own. She commemorated what had once housed SCEF's educational center in Louisville's West End as the Carl Braden Memorial Center, and it became a meeting and resource space for a medley of community groups promoting social change.[40]

Remarrying never even crossed Anne's mind: she simply assumed she could not find such an intellectual, spiritual, and sexual connection again. Those instincts proved correct. She had one brief affair in the 1980s which she first thought contained all those elements—but which turned out to be *disastrous*, as she remembered it later. Thereafter, she sublimated all her romantic energies into her work. By the 1990s, many of her closest friends and coworkers had known her only in her own right, as a widow, an independent woman attached to nothing so much as to her own enormous social conscience. In

Carl's absence, her collaborative tendencies dispersed more widely where they had once been more focused on her marriage, and slowly—even in Louisville, where animosity lasted longest—she began to evolve from a pariah into a heroine of sorts.[41]

Fifteen years after Carl's death, in 1990, Anne finally stepped out of the shadow cast on her by the "subversive" label to accept the American Civil Liberties Union's prestigious first Roger Baldwin Medal of Liberty. She was selected over more celebrated names like Ramsey Clark, former U.S. attorney general, and the historian Henry Steele Commager. Two years later the Southern Regional Council officially laid to rest old animosities by awarding her its highest honor (she called it *apologizing for 50 years of history*). In 1994 Randolph-Macon Woman's College called home its most controversial alumna to receive an Alumnae Achievement Award. That same year, Trinity College in Connecticut awarded her an honorary doctorate in humane letters. Three years later, Northern Kentucky University did the same, and Anne began teaching an honors course in social justice history there. In the final days of the twentieth century, the *Courier-Journal* paid tribute to its once-scorned resident activist with a front-page article marking her seventy-fifth birthday. She found all these honors disconcerting, muttering often that she was *used to brickbats but not awards* and drawing a line from her favorite Kahlil Gibran poem to insist that she would not be trapped by *withering laurels* into slowing down. The granting institutions might have at one time questioned her methods, but none could any longer doubt her sincerity, repeatedly proven through more than half a century of uninterrupted racial justice activism.[42]

Things had changed in that half century. Through the efforts of Anne and thousands of others, Jim Crow segregation had been overturned. African Americans held voting rights, and some were in positions of prestige and power. Civil rights legislation passed in the 1960s and a renewed women's movement that had its roots in the southern freedom movement had helped to multiply women's options in U.S. society. The demography of the American South had grown immensely more complex: Anne's call for interracialism had now become multiracialism. It had become respectable—admirable even—to speak out against racism and sexism.

One recognition of that change most gratifying to Anne personally was what she observed in her own parents. The McCartys lived to advanced ages, and after they moved to the Virginia tidewater to be nearer Anne's brother and sister-in-law, she made the long drive to see them often. *No matter what has gone before, parents always want to see their children as they grow old. I think Mother actually became proud of me. And Daddy, at a feeble 91, came to Louisville alone on an airplane to meet his great-grandchild—Beth's daughter—knowing she was biracial. Knowing the life he came from, to me that was a miracle.*[43]

Still, the dream of a just society that Anne had pursued for so long seemed as abstract as it ever had, and sweeping social movements to advance what she has called a *more humane agenda* lay nearly as dormant at the dawn of the twenty-first century as they had seemed in the pre-Montgomery "silent '50s." In the absence of such movements, 1960s voting-rights gains faced piecemeal dismantling, and the vast majority of African Americans who had not made it into the middle class experienced the "American dream" as an unending nightmare, with a whole generation filling prisons and jails. Anne's persistent message of whites' responsibility to oppose racism remained (and remains) a troublingly unmet challenge.

Three weeks before the end of the twentieth century, Anne's friend C. T. Vivian took the stage to make a speech in her honor at a reception celebrating her seventy-fifth birthday (an event she consented to only if it were paired with a fundraising campaign that ultimately raised more than $80,000 for the Braden Center). He joked gently about her drivenness by pointing out her love for the freedom song "I've Got To Do It Now."[44]

That lyric is an apt metaphor for Anne's persistence with regard to social change. Her life has not been without its vices: a lifetime of chain smoking and drinking "coffee so strong it would stain the side of a cup," as her friend Fred Shuttlesworth once chuckled. For years, her coworkers always expected at least one outburst of temper from her in every meeting (akin to her occasional explosions directed at Carl). *But I quit that after Carl died; I knew other people just wouldn't put up with it.* Her list of vices also once included bourbon-drinking talk-fests with friends, but she swore off bourbon in the 1990s, insisting that *it kept me from working half the night.* For the most part, she has been fairly ascetic in her single-minded dedication to social and racial justice.[45]

There have been sacrifices. Anne's modest frame house is in disrepair, and she has little in the way of material possessions or financial security. Though she does yoga regularly and takes daily walks, she does not eat or sleep enough. She has expressed real regrets at having allowed relationships with old friends and family members whom she deeply loves to erode due to the press of work obligations, and a Louisville news weekly affectionately referred to her in 1999 as a "rebel without a pause." She has never been able to reconcile herself to the idea that she has done her part, but remains haunted by the thought of all that remains undone. In fact, the advance of age seems only to have caused her to push herself harder and to grow impatient sometimes with others less willing to act—becoming, as one friend remarked semi-jokingly, both a "mentor and a tormentor" to younger activists through her hard-to-match stamina for social action. Yet her "McCarty drive" has never stopped her from taking time to listen or discuss patiently an idea or a project—or someone's personal dilemma—for as many hours as it takes, often sitting cross-legged in the floor into the wee hours.[46]

In the final analysis, Anne's greatest pleasures are and have long been organizing for social change and putting words to paper. A wordsmith since childhood, she chose to devote her considerable talents of writing and speaking to the movement for southern social justice, and her service to progressive social movements of the past half century has been prodigious. Perhaps her greatest contribution is in her very keeping on.

Anne's was the last generation of white southerners to come of age in a region so rigidly segregated that its own children could imagine it no other way, and she had to travel an enormous psychic distance—turning upside down the messages of her childhood—to become a part of the movement that brought Jim Crow down. Profoundly influenced by the militantly interracial, internationalist, working-class ideology of southern postwar labor and civil rights upsurges, she made a commitment to bettering society and has never swerved from it. Yet Anne has proven to be more flexible than many of her predecessors in what historians call the Old Left, and her commitment has been more to the ideals of racial and economic justice than to any ideology. In keeping at it for so long, always emphasizing the value of collective action, coalition building, and bridging racial divides, Anne has mentored (some say "mothered") several generations of young white southern radicals and inspired African American allies to believe that a white woman could be a real sister in spirit to them.

Anne's tenacious dedication to the causes she has held dear was fired, quite likely, by a combination of internal personality traits and external supports such as her partnership with Carl and the left networks of which they were a part. An additional factor may also have been—paradoxically—the circumstances in which she became politicized. It was, as she has said, an outlaw movement to which she committed herself in 1948. Half a century later, the ferocity of the repression against left-wing activism in the early years of her activist career still seems horrendous. The era has been characterized by various interpreters as the "haunted '50s," a "scoundrel time," "the great fear," and even "the dark ages." In the wake of the anticommunist hysteria that permeated the post-WWII American social landscape, the CP was all but destroyed, the lively cultural and political spin-offs that surrounded the Popular Front were reduced to mere shadows of their former selves, and political choices were severely narrowed in both the foreign and domestic arenas. Especially, especially, in the South, where repression was the most relentless, only those activists with extraordinary stamina and resiliency could survive.[47]

Yet even in the repressive years of the early Cold War, Anne found an "other America" and helped to create an "other South" sufficiently vital to sustain her own and Carl's social justice activism despite repeated attempts to quash it. She refused to relinquish the region of her birth to the racism that seemed at that juncture to be its destiny, and her sheer tenacity helped her to become a survivor rather than a casualty of the repressive postwar South, where white dissenters, especially those unwilling to "wait," were seen as traitors and ostracized. Luckily, a new generational ferment born in 1960 brought new allies who forced the region toward greater openness with their nonviolent direct actions.

Because of the controversy that surrounded Anne for so long in Louisville, she has often spoken of living as a symbol. But if Anne's life has meaning as a symbol, it is as a symbol of racial unity and the utter repudiation of white supremacy. Into the twenty-first century, her message remains: *Just as it was racism that has shaped our history as a region and as a country, so it was the struggle against racism that has moved our country in a more humane direction. Because they are at the bottom of this society, when people of color move, the foundation shifts. . . . In a sense the battle is and always has been a battle for the hearts and minds of white people in this country. The fight against racism is our issue. It's not something that we're called on to help people of color with. We need to become involved with it as if our lives depended on it because really, in truth, they do.*[48]

EPILOGUE

A biography ends with a death; the history of a war with an armistice; a scientific article with a call for more research; a balance sheet with a bottom line; a cautionary tale with a moral.

—Todd Gitlin, *The Sixties*[1]

MOST BIOGRAPHERS WRESTLE WITH THE GHOSTS of their subjects; I have wrestled with the very real human demands of mine. Though this book is the better for it (I hope), along the way I found Anne an exceedingly challenging subject and colleague. On a practical level, though she dearly loves to talk, she remained frustratingly unavailable because of her total immersion in racial justice activism. In the first year I knew her, we did one marathon set of interviews that stretched over a week I spent in her home. Thereafter, she became less willing to commit her time, and I was reduced to pestering her. For one of our later sessions, I simply accompanied her on errands, squeezing in questions as best as I could. The resulting tape was nearly inaudible because of road noise. Yet in all those years Anne rarely failed to return a phone call if my question had to do with some other civil rights leader, a wider social issue, or even a personal dilemma, as when I was considering a move to Kentucky. More recently, despite her great reservations about this book, she and I have made an easier peace. After years of eluding me, she generously put aside her own work in the final days of the book's creation and spent huge chunks of time with me to clarify details, emotional tenor, and—on occasion—prose.

Although several historians have also asked me how I could possibly extricate Anne's life from that of Carl, her husband/collaborator of 27 years, I regard the two as deeply entwined but distinct. A portrait of an activist marriage such as theirs is fascinating, and this book explores it somewhat, but that was not what I set out to do. There is a book out there on Carl, but it has yet to be written. My decisions about sources and approach have directed me toward keeping the focus, for the most part, on Anne.

I wrote from a multicultural feminist perspective that roots her experiences fully in her being a woman (more fully than she herself has ever conceded, by the way). This work is not solely a study of her public life—I delve into her upbringing, her friendships, her marital and parenting experiences, and her widowhood—but its focus is on Anne as an activist more than as a wife, mother, daughter, friend. Though I consider Anne's public and private lives inextricable, one of the consequences of my determination to be mindful of her agency as a living subject was that I chose to comment on and conclude from family dynamics rather than fully unpacking them. Out of respect for the lives her adult children have to lead and for Anne's desire to protect their privacy, this work explores those relationships less than fully.

The reader may also have noticed that I chose not to dwell on the matter of Anne's relationship to the Communist Party. I did so partially as an act of resistance against the historians who, upon learning of my work, were quick to ask what they obviously felt was a pivotal question, "Was she or wasn't she in the CP?"—as if this one answer could provide a summary understanding of Anne's life. Naively, perhaps, I was taken aback by the frequency of that question and the import it held for its askers (who were mostly closer to Anne's age than my own). One journalist teaching at a prominent university even intimated to me that the *Southern Patriot* could never be considered a reliable source in civil rights historiography because of its "communistic" associations. Such statements are rarer than they once were, but the fact that they linger at all bolsters Anne's view—held much of her adult life—that questions as to one's CP membership are used to legitimate or de-legitimate political activism. Although she has freely claimed CP leaders as mentors and in 1972 served as an elector to get the party on the Kentucky ballot, Anne has resolutely declined to respond publicly to questions concerning her own membership. As she told a *Courier-Journal* reporter in 1999, *No matter how you answer it, you're conceding that [CP membership is] the measuring stick and there's this group of people who are beyond the pale.*[2]

My own perspective is that even though Stalinist atrocities are more glaring than the dispersed suffering produced in the name of U.S. economic and "security" interests, allegiance to either nation should not be grounds for dismissal of anyone's discrete political actions. Any evaluation of CP contributions in the U.S. political sphere depends on the issue, time period, and, to some extent, locality, under discussion. Particularly in Depression-to-postwar southern history, for instance, the party made a crucial contribution to the struggle for social justice.[3]

Anne's relationship to Marxism—the value of what she calls her *working-class perspective*—has received precious little examination in the civil rights movement itself or in representations of it. Her relationship to the CP, on the other hand, has been too often misrepresented and used as a club upon her with violence of spirit if not always action. I chose to resist such a simplistic explanation or judgment. What historians know as the Old Left was in actuality an extended left network that existed in the 1930s, '40s, and even '50s, of which CP members and supporters were a vital part, surrounded by "fellow travelers" that included former Communists and liberal-to-left activists of varying persuasions with varying degrees of sympathy or distaste for the CP's style of capital-C Communism. Communist or not, the Old Left in the South was most deeply influenced by the social gospel strain of Protestantism, by African American stirrings of resistance to terror, and by the liberalism that coalesced in support of the New Deal.

Anne came of age politically into the Old Left when it was in eclipse and on the defensive. By the time she aligned herself with movements for social change, the CP had become the subject of high-profile government investigations, rendering it an illegitimate political entity, leaving the left as a whole suspiciously subversive, and *fatally stifling* (her words) social-political experimentation. For Anne—as for many left-wingers of the Cold War era (at least those who did not themselves become anticommunists)—it became of vital importance not to be part of anything that smacked of the red-baiting that almost consumed her in 1954 Louisville. More than that, she believed that restoring the CP and its ideas to legitimacy was a necessary precondition for fundamental economic change. I have chosen to explore her life in this context, having concluded that Anne's politics and choices are never, never reducible to her relationship to the CP or lack thereof. Though I examine her politics and her encounters at important junctures with CP initiatives and ideas, I leave it to the reader to consider it further as she may.[4]

Anne is not so one-dimensional as to be utterly heroic, of course. My relationship with her has not been smooth or unproblematic. I learned, as a group of theorists on feminist biography have written, "how hard it was for any of our subjects to lead lives that we would have considered totally admirable, for they . . . could never fully escape the culture in which they lived." It was a never-ending challenge for me to balance the biographer's need for a thorough life study with the subject's right to self-determination and her own strong interpretations of her life's course, filtered through the complex exchanges of an evolving relationship between us.[5]

January 6, 2002:
How to Finish an Unfinished Life?

This biography, contrary to Gitlin's dictum, does not end with a death. Therefore, I chose to conclude it by giving Anne an opportunity to respond, to fill in, perhaps, gaps that remain in my rendering of her life. What follows is a structured dialogue that took place at the Mary Anderson Center, a writer's retreat center in the southern Indiana knolls. Soon after she had read my final draft, late into the night, she sat facing me with her legs curled up around her in an easy chair and a notepad and pen in front of her—the same classic image of her I had seen so many times before and of which so many had spoken to me over the years. Here she and I reflect on the experience of being on either side of a biography.

———————

CF: I'm so familiar with the rhythms of your life, but as I read back through the manuscript one last time, I'm still struck by two things: the relentlessness of the attacks on you and the causes you championed, and the relentlessness with which you just kept on keeping on. And still do.

AB: *Yes, your unspoken question was "how could you stand it?" Well, it just wasn't that bad. Often people say to me nowadays, "Oh, you gave up so much," referring to the fact that I left a life of privilege and became an outcast. But I think I was lucky because I was able to escape from the prisons I'd grown up in and join the human race. What more can you ask of life than that?*

Also, just think about the experience of living and working in the South in the period in which we were privileged to be here. The 1950s were a bad time, but even that had its productive side because we had the opportunity to help build the resistance movement of that decade. And then the '60s! I think it was one of the two most important decades in our country's history—the other one being the 1860s, and for the same reason. Those were the times when this country was forced to deal directly with the issue of race, which has always been the cancer that threatens the soul of the nation. Both times, the process of removing the cancer was cut short. But what a privilege it was to be here when this issue was laid bare for us all to see, face to face.

But when you ask about the hard times we went through, maybe you mean how constant the battering was. But even that I look back on as very joyful. Living and working with Carl was what made it that way. Carl enjoyed a good fight, and in the most dire situations he always had a funny story to tell. His spirit was conta-

gious and I caught it. It pumped a sort of adrenaline into you that was strongest when the battles were most intense. Of course I had my low moments. But mostly it was an exuberant life. Since Carl has been gone, that exuberance is missing and I do think sometimes I've become too grim. And that's a long time. But fortunately, when the attacks were most intense we were in it together.

CF: One thing I know you've struggled with has to do with the very idea of having someone write about you. Now that we're virtually at the end of this journey, I wonder if having your life committed to paper this way—and by someone besides yourself—has made you reflect on your experiences any differently.

AB: *Since you're doing this, I've had to look at my life as a whole instead of just what is right in front of me (which is how you describe me). But you know that I didn't see any reason to have a book about me. It would seem pretty egotistical to think my life was worth a book since my notoriety is mainly not because of anything I did but because of what some people tried to do to me.*

But you were determined, and you just plowed ahead and you did get to be a nuisance to me. I got to feeling sorry for you, but I didn't have time for you. But you are pretty persuasive and you did sort of convince me. If there's something in my experience that can illuminate this whole question of race and white southerners, that's what I've been struggling to do. I want to ask you what you think is the purpose or the value of biography, to you.

CF: I have always felt that one person's story seems to offer a way into history. Also, I think I wanted to focus on one person in hopes of understanding that one person deeply. And you know I have always been interested in what keeps social change activists going. Why you? I love women's stories; I didn't want a subject who wasn't female; and I was probably looking for a white southern past I could respect.

AB: *I do want to make the point that this is your book, not mine. You don't claim to be totally objective about me. You say that you think I've had a positive effect on the world. Somebody could take those same facts you used and conclude that I'm a nut. But at some points you have a less overt lack of objectivity that I think you don't even realize. Your attitude toward my parents and the kinds of pressure they exerted on me, for example, was very different from mine. It was more judgmental, even though you thought of it as "objectivity." Whether you know it or not, when you looked at my life, you looked at it from the point of view of the time you live in. I don't know if any biographer can really look at people from the viewpoint of the time they lived in rather than the writer's. That's one thing that struck me as I read what you'd written. You've tried to include my point of view and I appreciate that. But I think this book would have been very different if we'd written it together.*

CF: And now that it's too late, you've set me straight on a few things I may
have gotten wrong. In these past few weeks, when I finally got your attention after all these years, you've filled in so many shades where before I'd
gotten only the bold strokes.

AB: *You've asked me more about what I did than what I thought. In a few places in
your book, you refer to me as a Marxist. I don't think that's entirely accurate. I
think my view of the world and society has been informed by Marxism, [which], as
I understand it, just tells us that human history is shaped by the class struggle. It
seems perfectly obvious to me that this is so. The have-nots always challenge the
haves for their place in the sun. To me, changing sides in the class struggle—decid-
ing to be on the side of oppressed people instead of the oppressors—was the key to all
the changes in my life. If I had not done that, I don't think I could have changed
sides in the racial struggle. I would have just been a white liberal.*

*But I think a "pure" Marxist believes that everything in life is shaped by mate-
rial conditions. Lots of things are: if a person is hungry, she thinks quite differently
from someone who is not. But I am more of a dualist. I see a distinct separation in
our physical beings and our spirit. And I think that often in human history, the
spirit of human beings has changed material conditions. That's why I thought that
if I just believed strongly enough, Anita would live. Some people would say that
was just "denial." But it's what I believed—and I still wonder.*

*On a lighter note, bodies are often a nuisance. They have to eat and sleep, and
I'd rather spend time doing other things. I'd rather live in a world of the spirit.
This has to do with my religious beliefs. I don't believe in a God that is like a person
and can reach out and fix things up in my life if I pray. Rather, I believe in a God
that is a spiritual force in the universe—the life force, perhaps—that I must reach
out and tap into. I have been told that my views are not that different from those of
many people who fill the pews of churches. The great thing about the Episcopal
Church is that it's full of beautiful symbolism. You can be a part of the service,
thinking something entirely different from the person next to you. That's why I've
been able to continue to find a spiritual home there long after I left my childhood
interpretations behind.*

*All this bears on another element you touch on lightly in your manuscript: the so-
cial gospel movement of my youth. I believe you consider it a part of what you call the
Old Left, and it was. It was a very important impetus for so many who struggled in
those decades in the South—Jim Dombrowski, Myles Horton—they became my
mentors and a source of great strength to me. But I don't see anything that really
parallels the social gospel movement in our churches today, and we surely need it.*

CF: You've sort of picked up my phraseology of the "Old Left," but I learned
from you that those are more scholars' words than they are yours.

AB: Yes, no one ever knew of any "Old Left" until the 1960s, when there was a "New Left." Even vocabulary is shaped by the times. Like in the way we used the word "integration." I don't use that word anymore; it's totally changed its meaning. But when we talked about integration in the '40s, '50s, even early '60s, it was in the context of building a whole new society. That's what the early students meant by the "beloved community" too—their vision was vague in its outlines, but it was never the idea that blacks are simply going to be integrated into this society. But over the years integration has come to mean that African Americans will be brought into this society that whites will still run. That's part of black disillusionment with school in-tegration: what they got integrated into was so white dominated they want no part of it. Although I was able to articulate this more clearly later, I felt at the time that the black movement was the thrust that was going to change things. That's why we never saw a contradiction between integration and black power.

CF: Yes, speaking of vocabulary, it was striking to me when you once told me you never even heard the words "Popular Front" back in the 1940s. And I had never quite thought about how the concept of civil liberties is histori-cally constructed until you mentioned it to me last night.

AB: Yes, that's what we always said [in the Cold War South]: you couldn't have civil rights without civil liberties. That seemed to be the best way to put it at the time, and it became a critical issue then, as your manuscript makes clear.

But it was something of a misnomer, and I have an uneasy feeling that to most people today, the phrase "civil liberties" doesn't have much meaning. Throughout our history those freedoms in the First Amendment have come to life only as people fought for them. In the South, the absence of those freedoms was always a major problem. The South was a "closed society," as James Silver wrote about Mississippi. The powerful few, in their determination to keep African Americans crushed, had closed off the avenues of debate that are essential to change. The particular weapon through which that was done in the '50s and beyond was the demonization of com-munism. Thus, our battles in those years were really against anticommunism—that is a more accurate description of the struggles we were waging in those years when we said "civil liberties."[6]

In the South of the 1930s, "civil liberties" meant the right of workers to organ-ize. Those people said "civil liberties" too, but what they meant was that union or-ganizers were being beaten up and run out of town. Who knows what may happen by the time your book comes out, with the fear of terrorism after September 11? But in general, in recent years, if you say "civil liberties," it doesn't mean much. Free speech? Yes, it's a good thing, but why get so upset about it? You can get in trouble if you say the wrong thing at the wrong period of time, but otherwise the Bill of Rights just sits there.

CF: You and I both have been taken by that phrase in my title: "The Cold War South." And that's ultimately what this book is about, in relation to your life. But what about the Cold War's impact more generally, more long term?

AB: *I think the thing that hit me most sharply as I read your manuscript and then had to look back over my life as you reported it is how much time Carl and I spent fighting for a right to be a part of the movement in the South because of the irrational fears engendered by the Cold War. I was always uneasy about fighting for that right because obviously, all these battles were going to get along fine without us. But my more rational self told me we had to make those battles as a matter of principle, because of what the divisiveness was doing not to us, but to the movement.*

The same syndrome applies in a larger sphere. The real damage of the Cold War was what it did to the country because social problems festered—things we could have done something about. Just contemplate the depth of the racial, social, and economic inequalities that beset us now. It will take massive movements in the twenty-first century to repair the damage.

So the reality is that there was a battle to be fought and we fought it where the barricades—for us—were, in the South. The unique thing about the Cold War in the South, of course, was that it was inextricably tied to the battle against white supremacy. That was the reason for all the fury against us in Louisville. It was the anti-red and the antiblack hysteria wrapped up together and flung at us. You could not fight the Cold War in the South without taking on white supremacy, and you couldn't adequately fight white supremacy unless you were willing to take on the Cold War.

CF: You addressed my point about the relentlessness of the attacks, but what do you think has made you able to stick with social change so fiercely and for so long?

AB: *You've discussed how important the other America has been to me, and that's a big part of what's kept me going. But—did all the people I've worked with and I accomplish anything? I'm not sure that's the right question. The meaning of our life and work was in the battles we fought. This is a very practical organizing question. People get immobilized because they've been told so often that nothing can really change—and even if they created a new society, the new would become just as bad as the old.*

I've never believed we can have a perfect society, simply because people are not perfect. We are all a bundle of good and evil. That's why I never became bewitched, as some people did, by countries that were trying to build socialism. I never thought they could be perfect, so I was not devastated when it developed they were not.

In college my friend Lucile Schoolfield and I read Thomas Wolfe, and—as you point out—he became one of my favorite authors. In speeches and presentations I still quote from that wonderful passage of his at the end of You Can't Go Home Again.

CF: Yes, that was one of those details that managed to escape me until very recently. Somehow the references to Wolfe never came up in your speeches that got recorded, or anywhere in the written record, so I had to actually hear you speak of him to know about that connection. Although you couldn't have known it would be so when you first were captivated by his prose, it does seem that Wolfe's philosophy has turned out to be instructive to your life in some pretty profound ways.

AB: *That's true. He says so eloquently the core of what I believe: that the meaning in human life lies not in what one individual or one generation can achieve, but in the fact that human beings are constantly envisioning and reaching out toward something better. I know the passage by heart. It says:*

> *Man was born to live, to suffer, and to die, and what befalls him is a tragic lot. There is no denying this in the final end. But we must . . . deny it all along the way. . . . [T]he essence of religion for people of my belief is that man's life can be, and will be, better; that man's greatest enemies, in the forms in which they now exist—the forms we see on every hand of fear, hatred, slavery, cruelty, poverty, and need—can be conquered and destroyed. But to conquer and destroy them will mean nothing less than the complete revision of the structure of society as we know it. They cannot be conquered by the sorrowful acquiescence of resigned fatality . . . by the tragic hypothesis that things as they are . . . are as good and as bad as, under any form, they will ever be. . . . [I]t is for now, and for us the living, that we must speak, and speak the truth, as much of it as we can see and know. With the courage of the truth within us, we shall meet the enemy as they come to us, and they shall be ours. And if, once having conquered them, new enemies approach, we shall meet them from that point, from there proceed. In the affirmation of that fact, the continuance of that unceasing war, is man's religion and his living faith.*[7]

NOTES

Introduction

1. *Brown v. Board of Education*, 347 U.S. 483 (1954); "A Forced Issue Can Foil Progress," Louisville *Courier-Journal* editorial, 18 May 1954.
2. I have borrowed the phrase "transitional generation" from Susan Hartmann, "Women's Employment and the Domestic Ideal in the Early Cold War Years," in *Not June Cleaver: Women and Gender in the Post-War America, 1945–1960*, ed. Joanne Meyerowitz (Philadelphia: Temple University Press, 1994), 84.
3. David Caute, *The Great Fear: The Anti-Communist Purge under Truman and Eisenhower* (New York: Simon & Schuster, 1978).
4. Aware that scholars have often diminished women's standing in history by inappropriate use of their first names, I have nevertheless chosen to refer to Anne Braden as "Anne" throughout this narrative. This decision was not made solely on the basis of ties between the two of us, but also to honor the casual, informal quality she emanates to all who know her even slightly, as well as to distinguish more easily between her and her husband (note that I also refer to him in the text as "Carl"). The couple were widely known in the movement as "Anne and Carl," and were referred to as such by their own children.
5. Throughout this book, I capitalize the words "communism" and "communist" only if they refer specifically and clearly to members of the Communist Party (CP), or if they appear that way in whatever source I'm quoting from. I have done so in recognition of the widespread use of those words to disparage civil rights activists during this period, many of whom had little or no connection to the CP.
6. A number of studies have addressed southern white integrationists in the immediate pre-*Brown* years. The most notable among them, perhaps, are Anthony Dunbar's *Against the Grain: Southern Radicals and Prophets, 1929–1959* (Charlottesville: University Press of Virginia, 1981) and John Egerton's more recent survey, *Speak Now against the Day: The Generation before the Civil Rights Movement in the South* (New York: Alfred A. Knopf, 1994). Neither of these books, however, deals much with the admittedly small southern white grassroots activism that persisted throughout the 1950s. Egerton's study focuses more on writers, image-makers, and nationally known southern liberals such as Ralph McGill, virtually ignoring leftists and what remained of southern labor activism in this period. Dunbar's book deals with the post–WWII era in a cursory way, emphasizing only the devastating impact anticommunism had on southern reform efforts.
7. As will become clear, mass civil rights protest declined not simply as part of a social movement's "natural" ebb and flow. Its descent was provoked by a well-orchestrated campaign of government harassment that meshed with widespread disillusionment brought on by, first, the movement's abortive challenge to the 1964 Democratic Convention and, later, the assassination of Martin Luther King Jr. amid intransigent institutional racism. See, for instance, Kenneth O'Reilly, *"Racial Matters": The FBI's Secret File on Black America* (New York: Free Press, 1989).

8. Sara Evans, *Personal Politics: The Roots of Women's Liberation in the Civil Rights Movement and the New Left* (New York: Vintage, 1979), 48–49. One former SNCC staffer whom I interviewed for this project told me somberly, "You're doing God's work" (Robert Zellner, interview with author, New Orleans, Louisiana, 5 November 1990).

9. I have borrowed that colloquial southern usage of "common-ist" from Michael Honey, *Southern Labor and Black Civil Rights: Organizing Memphis Workers* (Urbana: University of Illinois Press, 1993), 54.

10. The number of studies in which Anne is noted is too extensive to enumerate here, but two of the many that name her in the acknowledgments are Linda Reed, *Simple Decency and Common Sense: The Southern Conference Movement, 1938–1963* (Bloomington: Indiana University Press, 1991), xvii; and Joanne Grant, *Ella Baker Freedom Bound* (New York: John Wiley & Sons, Inc., 1998), xi. In Taylor Branch's *Parting the Waters: America in the King Years, 1955–63* (New York: Simon & Schuster, 1988), possibly the most popular history of the civil rights era, Anne receives one brief mention, on p. 328, as a red-baited (and therefore, for King, problematic) leader of SCEF. *Carry Me Home Birmingham, Alabama: The Climactic Battle of the Civil Rights Revolution*, by Diane McWhorter (New York: Simon & Schuster, 2001) does a better job, locating Anne (pp. 121–23) as a somewhat significant character in the shaping of the civil rights revolution.

11. Anne Braden, *The Wall Between*, was first published in 1958 (New York: Monthly Review Press). Out of print for some years, it was reissued in 1999 by University of Tennessee Press (Knoxville) with a new epilogue.

12. This outpouring on women in the movement began with Jo Ann Gibson Robinson's memoir, *The Montgomery Bus Boycott and the Women Who Started It* (Knoxville: University of Tennessee Press, 1987). The following year saw the first critical anthology, *Women in the Civil Rights Movement: Trailblazers and Torchbearers*, ed. Vikki Crawford, Jacqueline Rouse, and Barbara Woods (Brooklyn: Carlson, 1988), a volume that grew out of the Atlanta conference of the same name. In recent years have come more books with a greater variety of approaches, from Charles Payne's *I've Got the Light of Freedom: The Organizing Tradition and the Mississippi Freedom Struggle* (Berkeley: University of California Press, 1995)—a study of the Mississippi movement which devotes considerable attention to women's participation—to Belinda Robnett's sociology-oriented *How Long? How Long? African American Women in the Civil Rights Movement* (New York: Oxford University Press, 1997) and Chana Kai Lee's acclaimed biography of the activist Fannie Lou Hamer, *For Freedom's Sake* (Urbana: University of Illinois Press, 1999), as well as a journalist's overview of women in the movement—Lynne Olson, *Freedom's Daughters: The Unsung Heroines of the Civil Rights Movement from 1830 to 1970* (New York: Scribner, 2001). Among recent works on white women in the movement are (among others) Kathryn Nasstrom's blend of biography and oral history memoir, *Everybody's Grandmother and Nobody's Fool: Frances Freeborn Pauley and the Struggle for Social Justice* (Ithaca: Cornel University Press, 2000); a collective memoir authored by early student activists—*Deep in Our Hearts: Nine White Women in the Freedom Movement*, ed. Constance Curry (Athens: University of Georgia Press, 2000); and an anthology, *Throwing Off the Cloak of Privilege: White Southern Women Activists in the Civil Rights Era*, ed. Gail Murray (Tallahassee: University Press of Florida, forthcoming), which analyzes the influence of whiteness on southern women's civil rights activism. The reissuing of Anne Braden's 1958 memoir in 1999 is also a part of the upsurge of interest in women of the southern freedom movement.

13. Both the 1958 and 1999 editions of Anne's memoir, *The Wall Between*, are used here. Please note too that I have taken the liberty of "cleaning up" the oral histories somewhat, eliminating the repetitious use of words such as "kind of " and "and" while remaining true to the subject's style of speech. Some oral history programs do not condone my editing practice but have generously allowed me to use their interviews nonetheless.

14. My thinking on this matter was influenced by Annelise Orleck's *Common Sense and a Little Fire: Women and Working-Class Politics in the United States, 1900–1965* (Chapel

Hill: University of North Carolina Press, 1995) and by Kate Weigand's introduction to *Red Feminism: American Communism and the Making of Women's Liberation* (Baltimore: Johns Hopkins University Press, 2000), 1–14. The phrase "the personal is political" was coined by Carol Hanisch, a feminist who first became active in the civil rights movement (see Ruth Rosen's *The World Split Open: How the Modern Women's Movement Changed America* [New York: Penguin, 2000], 196).

15. Braden, *The Wall Between* (1999), 347–48.
16. These ideas are explored further in Weigand, *Red Feminism*, introduction.
17. See Bibliography for a complete listing of the oral histories.
18. Recent studies—such as Mary L. Dudziak's *Cold War Civil Rights: Race and the Image of American Democracy* (Princeton, N.J.: Princeton University Press, 2000)—focus on the pro-civil rights climate and rhetoric created by the Cold War, but my emphasis is on the repressive features of Cold War southern culture with respect to social and racial change. Anne Braden, personal correspondence with author, 11 June 1997, in author's possession.

Prologue

1. Robert Rennick, *Kentucky Place Names* (Lexington: University Press of Kentucky, 1984), 93.
2. Anne Braden, interview with author, Louisville, Kentucky, 11 June 1996.
3. Lida Scott Edwards and Robert Harrison Edwards, "The McCarty and Smith Family History," unpublished genealogical typescript manuscript, Christmas 1962, in author's possession.
4. Andrew Woods Williamson et al., *Descendants of Robert and John Poage, Vol. 1* (Staunton, Va.: McClure Printing, 1954), 931–91; Anne Braden, interview with author, Louisville, Kentucky, 10 March 1989 (Tape 5); that ancestor was Morris Thomas, a Pennsylvania Quaker who was Anne's maternal great-great-great-grandfather.
5. Anne Braden, interview with Sue Thrasher, Louisville, Kentucky, 18 April 1981, Tape 1, Side 1, 15–16 of transcript (tapes and transcripts held in Highlander Center library, New Market, Tennessee; hereinafter referred to as Braden interview with Thrasher); Braden interview with author, 10 March 1989 (Tape 5).
6. The spelling of the name "Poage" is inconsistent in the historical record. It appears in sources variously as "Poage," "Poague," "Poag," and "Pogue." One family historian has explained that in Virginia the family spelled its name "Poage," but that some confusion surrounded the will of William Poage in Kentucky in 1778, resulting in a change of spelling by all his heirs to "Pogue." Other spellings were simply mistakes, according to this source. Kentucky Papers of the Lyman T. Draper Manuscript Collection (Madison: State Historical Society of Wisconsin, 1925), Calendar series, Vol. 2 (hereinafter referred to as Draper Papers), 4CC, 113–14.
7. Braden interview with Thrasher, Tape 1, Side 1, 15–16. Interestingly, Anne recalled in relatively recent years (1990s) during a workshop on racialized memories that her first recognition of color prejudice had nothing to do with African Americans. It was evoked by the frontier tales her family told her as a child; she repeatedly inquired of her mother why the settlers killed the Indians.
8. "Old Fort Harrod State Park," Kentucky Department of Parks brochure, 1995, in author's possession. For a more complete understanding of Anne Poage McGinty's contributions to Kentucky history, see various documents in "Anne Pogue McGinty" folder at Harrodsburg Historical Society, Harrodsburg, Kentucky; and S.V. Nuckols, "History of William Poage and His Wife, Ann Kennedy Wilson Poage Lindsay McGinty," *Register of the Kentucky Historical Society* 11, no. 1 (January 1913): 101–102.
9. Robert McDowell, *City of Conflict: Louisville in the Civil War, 1861–1865* (Louisville: Louisville Civil War Roundtable Publishers, 1962), 2, 8; Thomas Clark, *A History of Kentucky* (New York: Prentice-Hall, 1937), 445.

10. George H. Yater, *Two Hundred Years at the Falls of the Ohio: A History of Louisville and Jefferson County* (Louisville: Heritage Corporation, 1979), 82; McDowell, *City of Conflict*, 123.

11. George C. Wright, *Life behind a Veil: Blacks in Louisville, Kentucky, 1865–1930* (Baton Rouge: LSU Press, 1985), 17–20; Lowell Harrison, *The Anti-Slavery Movement in Kentucky* (Lexington: University Press of Kentucky, 1978), 107.

12. Braden interview with author, 10 March 1989 (Tape 5); Wright, *Life behind a Veil*, 21; Ross A. Webb, *Kentucky in the Reconstruction Era* (Lexington: University Press of Kentucky, 1979), 25, 59.

13. Wright, *Life behind a Veil*, 27–28, 177–78; Kentucky Commission on Human Rights, *Kentucky's Black Heritage* (Frankfort: Commonwealth of Kentucky, 1971), 45–46, 50–53; Yater, *Falls of the Ohio*, 80–82, 95–96.

14. Braden interview with author, 10 March 1989 (Tape 5); Wright, *Life behind a Veil*, 21–22; "Drennon Springs Hotel" advertising circular, 1903, on file at Henry County Public Library, Eminence, Kentucky; Linda M. Roberts, "History Drennon Springs" pamphlet, n.d., on file at the Henry County Public Library; Williamson et al., *Descendants of Poage*, Vol. 1, 991; *Biographical Cyclopedia of the Commonwealth of Kentucky* (Chicago: compiled and published by John M. Gresham Co., 1896), 304–305, 437–38.

15. This characterization was coined by Rayford Logan, *The Negro in American Life and Thought: The Nadir, 1877–1901* (New York: Dial, 1954); *Kentucky's Black Heritage*, 59–63.

16. *Kentucky's Black Heritage*, 65–66.

17. Wright, *Life behind a Veil*, 236–38; the U.S. Supreme Court declared restrictive covenants unconstitutional in 1948; this thesis of violence is confirmed by Stephen Meyer in his detailed examination of residential segregation in American history, *As Long as They Don't Move Next Door: Segregation and Racial Conflict in American Neighborhoods* (Lanham, Md.: Rowman & Littlefield, 2000).

18. For an elegant discussion of the mythology surrounding segregation, see Egerton, *Speak Now*, 29–33; I borrowed the phrase "fortress mentality" from William J. Cooper Jr. and Thomas E. Terrill, *The American South: A History*, Vol. 2 (New York: McGraw-Hill, 1996), 600; Wright, *Life behind a Veil*, 240–42, 202.

19. Wright, *Life behind a Veil*, 241; Lynn Allen, conversation with author, Eminence, Kentucky, 23 June 1995.

20. Braden interview with author, 10 March 1989 (Tape 6).

21. Edwards and Edwards, "McCarty and Smith Family History"; *Descendants of Poage*, Vol. 1, 991; *Courier-Journal*, n.d., clipping in Anne Gambrell McCarty scrapbook, in author's possession.

22. Anne Braden, Thrasher interview and various interviews with author; Lynn Allen to author, personal correspondence, n.d., ca. fall 1995, in author's possession.

Chapter 1

1. The epigraph is taken from pp. 3–4 of Jackson, ed., *The Waiting Years* (Baton Rouge: LSU Press, 1976).

2. Record of birth, State Department of Health, Commonwealth of Kentucky, Record No. 14222, 28 July 1924 (available in Louisville Free Public Library); Yater, *Falls of the Ohio*, 147; Wright, *Life behind a Veil*, 197–98.

3. Wright, *Life behind a Veil*, 213–21; Jackson, *Waiting Years*, 7–8; what was then Walnut Street is now Muhammad Ali Boulevard.

4. Wright, *Life behind a Veil*, 274–75; "Two Negro Teachers Draw Reprimand," Louisville *Courier-Journal*, 2 July 1924; *Kentucky's Black Heritage*, 97.

5. Louisville *Courier-Journal*, 28 July 1924.

6. Braden interview with Thrasher, Tape 3, Side 2, 84.

7. Ibid., 73.

8. Anne Braden, interview with author, Louisville, Kentucky, 8–9 March 1989 (Tape 3).

9. Grace Hooten Gates, "Anniston: Transition from Company Town to Mill Town," *Alabama Review* 37, no. 1 (January 1984): 36–38; for more on Anniston's class and racial divisions, see also Kathryn Henry, "Life and Sojourn of a Southern Liberal," M.A. thesis, Auburn University, 1986; City Directory, Anniston, Alabama, 1931; William Warren Rogers et al., eds., *Alabama: History of a Deep South State* (Tuscaloosa: University of Alabama Press, 1994), 452.

10. *Anniston Star*, 28 October 1979, "Tried by Fire: Personal Character Was a Byproduct of Depression," and "Anniston Rallied in Depression"; for more on the collapse of the plantation economy, see Rogers et al., *Alabama*, ch. 27, especially p. 489.

11. Anne Braden, interview with author, Louisville, Kentucky, 11 March 1989 (Tape 7).

12. *Anniston Star*, 9 November 1932 and 26 November 1932; Braden interview with author, 10 March 1989 (Tape 5).

13. Dan T. Carter, *Scottsboro: A Tragedy of the American South* (Baton Rouge: LSU Press, 1969), 49; Robin D. G. Kelley, *Hammer and Hoe: Alabama Communists during the Great Depression* (Chapel Hill: University of North Carolina Press, 1990), 79–81; Harvey Klehr, *The Heyday of American Communism: The Depression Decade* (New York: Basic Books, 1984), 3; Joseph Starobin, *American Communism in Crisis: 1943–1957* (Cambridge: Harvard University Press, 1972), 108–11.

14. Carter, *Scottsboro*, 49, 145–46.

15. Kelley, *Hammer and Hoe*, 78–79 (quotation from p. 14); see also Nell Irwin Painter with Hosea Hudson, *Narrative of Hosea Hudson: His Life as a Negro Communist in the South* (Cambridge: Harvard University Press, 1979), 83–89; Carter, *Scottsboro*, 151–53.

16. Anne Braden, interview with author, Louisville, Kentucky, 9 March 1989 (Tape 4).

17. Braden interview with Thrasher, Tape 1, Side 2, 30–69.

18. References to the "southern aristocracy" can be found in "Reminiscences of Anne Braden," told to Lenore Hogan, 23 June 1972, on p. 2, in the Columbia University Oral History Research Office Collection (CUOHROC), New York City (hereinafter referred to as Braden interview with Hogan, CUOHROC); Braden interview with author, 9 March 1989 (Tape 4). Please note that marks of ellipses in Anne's voice indicate change in oral history source material here; throughout the book, changes in oral history sources within a particular excerpt of Anne's voice are indicated in this manner. Where marks of ellipses occur in an excerpt that contains only one source, they indicate material omitted from original.

19. Braden interview with author, 9 March 1989 (Tape 4).

20. Culled from Braden interviews with Thrasher and with author on 9 March 1989 (Tape 4).

21. Braden interview with author, 8–9 March 1989 (Tape 3); for more on the dilemma faced by women of Anita's generation, see Elaine Showalter, ed., *These Modern Women: Autobiographical Essays from the Twenties* rev. ed. (New York: Feminist Press, 1989).

22. Anne Gambrell McCarty, 1934 diary, 1935 diary, scrapbook, in author's possession.

23. Anne McCarty, diaries, 1934 and 1935; Elise Ayers Sanguinetti, conversation with author, Anniston, Alabama, 14 June 1989; Braden interview with Thrasher, Tape 1, Side 1, 24.

24. Braden interview with author, 10 March 1989 (Tape 5); see also "Miss Anne Poland and Miss Anne McCarty Will Attend State Convention of Children of Confederacy," newspaper clipping, probably *Anniston Star*, n.d., in Anne Braden, personal clippings, in author's possession.

25. Braden interview with author, 9 March 1989 (Tape 4); Emma Gelders Sterne, "A House to Live In: Anne Braden," in her collection, *They Took Their Stand* (New York: Crowell-Collier, 1968), 155–75.

26. Braden interview with Thrasher, Tape 1, Side 1, 26. The first church in Anniston was built by and for blacks, but that congregation was defunct by the 1930s, according to "Grace Episcopal Church Oldest in Anniston," *Anniston Star*, 10 January 1932.

27. Louisa Nonnenmacher and Carleton Lentz, "Years of Grace" (Anniston: Grace Church Publications, 1948), pamphlet, 28–29; for more on the social gospel, see Egerton, *Speak Now*, 44.

28. Braden interview with Thrasher, Tape 2, Side 1, 44–46; Braden interview with author, 9 March 1989 (Tape 4).

29. Braden interview with Thrasher, Tape 3, Side 2, 55, 91–97.

30. Louisa Nonnenmacher, "History of Grace Church, Anniston, Alabama," 1942, typescript, Vertical Files, Church Records Section, Alabama Room, Anniston-Calhoun County Public Library, p. 18; Braden interview with author, 9 March 1989 (Tape 4).

31. Nonnenmacher, "History of Grace," 16–17; Braden interview with author, 9 March 1989 (Tape 4).

32. This story comes from Braden interview with author, 9 March 1989 (Tape 4).

33. Anne Gambrell McCarty, "A Prayer on My Thirteenth Birthday," n.d., ca. July 1937, original in author's possession.

34. Anne McCarty, "Discovery," *Tattler* 30 (Christmas 1944): 9–12.

35. "Miss M'Carty Wins in Speech Contest," newspaper clipping, untitled, 2 April 1939, from Anne Braden, personal clippings, in author's possession; *Birmingham News*, n.d., p. 14, from Anne Braden, personal clippings, in author's possession; see also Braden, *Wall Between* (1958), 216; Braden reflections from interview with author, 10 March 1989 (Tape 6).

36. For more on white southerners' views of segregation, see Egerton, *Speak Now*, 18–47.

37. Patricia Sullivan, *Days of Hope: Race and Democracy in the New Deal Era* (Chapel Hill: University of North Carolina Press, 1996), 40–43; Irwin Klibaner, *Conscience of a Troubled South: The Southern Conference Educational Fund, 1946–1966* (Brooklyn: Carlson, 1989), 5.

38. Sullivan, *Days of Hope*, 64, 92–93; Honey, *Southern Labor*, 91–92.

39. Honey, *Southern Labor*, 79–80; Kelley, *Hammer and Hoe*, chap. 7; Mark Naison, "The Southern Tenant Farmers' Union" entry and Frank Adams, "Highlander Research and Education Center" entry in Mary Jo Buhle, Paul Buhle, and Dan Georgakas, eds., *Encyclopedia of the American Left* (Urbana: University of Illinois Press, 1992), 739–40 and 309–10, respectively.

40. For a more complete discussion of the Popular Front left-liberal alliance in U.S. politics, see Klehr, *Heyday of American Communism*. In *Hammer and Hoe*, Part 2, Robin Kelley explores in depth the influence of the Popular Front on the Alabama CP. On the SNYC, see C. Alvin Hughes, "We Demand Our Rights: The Southern Negro Youth Congress, 1937–1949," *Phylon* 48, no. 1 (1987): 38–50. I have borrowed the phrase "movement culture" from Robin Kelley: see Kelley's preface to *Hammer and Hoe*, xi–xv, for a fuller explanation of it.

41. Sullivan, *Days of Hope*, 63–65, 6 (her book examines this period in more depth).

42. Kelley, *Hammer and Hoe*, 128–31; Klibaner, *Conscience of Troubled South*, 8.

43. Sullivan, *Days of Hope*, 67; on the southern conference movement, see especially Reed, *Simple Decency*.

44. Sullivan, *Days of Hope*, 99–100.

45. Ibid.

46. Thomas A. Krueger, *And Promises to Keep: The Southern Conference for Human Welfare, 1938–1948* (Nashville: Vanderbilt University Press, 1967), 65–66; Walter Gellhorn examines the truth behind the anticommunist tirade against the Southern Conference in the postwar era in his "Report on the Report of the Committee on Un-American Activities," *Harvard Law Review* 60 (1947): 1193–234.

47. *Anniston Star*, 21 November 1938; for more on the racial conservatism of southern journalists, see John Kneebone, *Southern Liberal Journalists and the Issue of Race: 1920–1944* (Chapel Hill: University of North Carolina Press, 1985); on press coverage of the conference, see Krueger, *And Promises to Keep*, 33; see, for example, *Anniston Star*, 22 November 1938.

48. Braden interview with author, 10 March 1989 (Tape 6).

49. Ibid.; Braden interview with Thrasher, Tape 4, Side 1, 98.

50. Anne Gambrell McCarty, diary, 1938, in author's possession; Braden interview with author, 10 March 1989 (Tape 6).

51. Anne Gambrell McCarty, diary, 1939, in author's possession; Braden interview with author, 10 March 1989 (Tape 6); Anne Gambrell McCarty, scrapbook, 1940–1941, in author's possession; Jean Lloyd Willett, conversation with author, Anniston, Alabama, 14 June 1989.

52. Braden interview with author, 10 March 1989 (Tape 6); various clippings, n.d., summer 1940, in Anne Gambrell McCarty, scrapbook, 1940–1941, in author's possession; July 25 entry, Anne Gambrell McCarty, diary, 1939, in author's possession; Anne Gambrell McCarty, "School Silhouettes" scrapbook, n.d., ca. 1941, in author's possession.

53. Jean Lloyd Willett, correspondence with author, n.d., ca. March 1995; Sanguinetti conversation with author; Allen Draper, conversation with author, Anniston, Alabama, 14 June 1989.

54. Jean Lloyd, unpublished college paper, n.d., in author's possession; Anne Gambrell McCarty, diary, 1939.

55. Draper conversation with author; Anne McCarty scrapbook of *Anniston Star* clippings, n.d., in author's possession.

56. Anne Gambrell McCarty, "School Silhouettes," n.d., and "Senior Silhouettes," n.d., ca. 1941, personal writing in author's possession.

57. Ibid.; Jean Lloyd, unpublished college paper. As a college freshman, Willett wrote of this encounter for an assignment on someone who had left an impression on her.

58. Anne Gambrell McCarty, "Senior Silhouettes."

Chapter 2

1. Epigraph comes from Braden interview with author, 9 March 1989 (Tape 4).

2. Alvin Hall, *The History of Stratford College* (Danville, Va.: Womack Press, 1974).

3. Braden interview with author, 10 March 1989 (Tape 6).

4. This history is explored in Christie Anne Farnham, *The Education of the Southern Belle: Higher Education and Student Socialization in the Antebellum South* (New York: NYU Press, 1994); A. Hall, *History of Stratford*, 2.

5. Avery Craven, *The Growth of Southern Nationalism, 1848–1861* (Baton Rouge: LSU Press, 1953), 254–74.

6. A. Hall, *History of Stratford*, 2; *The Iris* (Stratford yearbook, in author's possession), 1942, n.p.

7. Braden interview with author, 10 March 1989 (Tape 6).

8. *Iris*, 1942; Braden interview with author, 10 March 1989 (Tape 6).

9. Braden interview with Thrasher, Tape 4, Side 2, 107.

10. Braden interview with author, 10 March 1989 (Tape 6); Braden interview with Thrasher, Tape 4, Side 2, 109.

11. Braden interview with author, 10 March 1989 (Tape 6).

12. Susan Hartmann, *The Home Front and Beyond* (Boston: Twayne, 1982), 164; Karen Anderson, *Wartime Women: Sex Roles, Family Relations, and the Status of Women during World War II* (Westport, Conn.: Greenwood, 1981), 76.

13. Braden interview with author, 10 March 1989 (Tape 6).

14. Stratford College Class Book, 1943, in Averitt College Library, Danville, Virginia; Braden interview with author, 10 March 1989 (Tape 6).

15. Priscilla Beach folder, 1942, Anne Braden personal files, in author's possession; *Stratford Traveller*, 1942–1943, Averitt College Library; this information is drawn from a CBS estimate in Michael Renov, *Hollywood's Wartime Woman: Representation and Ideology* (Ann Arbor: UMI Research Press, 1988), 28.

16. Braden interview with Thrasher, Tape 4, Side 2, 121–23; Braden interview with author, 11 March 1989 (Tape 7).

17. Lucile Schoolfield alumna file, Stratford College files, Averitt College.

18. *Stratford Traveller*, 15 May 1942.
19. *Iris*, 1943.
20. Ibid.; M. Elizabeth Tidball, "Women's Colleges and Women Achievers Revisited," in *Reconstructing the Academy: Women's Education and Women's Studies*, ed. Elizabeth Minnich, Jean O'Barr, and Rachel Rosenfeld (Chicago: University of Chicago Press, 1988), 210–11; see also Berenice Fisher, "Wandering in the Wilderness: The Search for Women Role Models," in *Reconstructing the Academy*, 234–56.
21. A. Hall, *History of Stratford*, 35; impressions of Kennedy are drawn from conversations with Anne and with Evelyn Jefferson and Lee Robertson (two alumnae), Danville, Virginia, 21 May 1996; Braden interview with author, 10 March 1989 (Tape 6).
22. Braden interview with author, 10 March 1989 (Tape 6).
23. Farnham, *Education of the Southern Belle*, 136; Linda Kerber, "Separate Spheres, Female Worlds, Woman's Place: The Rhetoric of Women's History," *Journal of American History* 75 (June 1988): 9–39; Rosalind Rosenberg, *Beyond Separate Spheres: Intellectual Roots of Modern Feminism* (New Haven, Conn.: Yale University Press, 1982). Barbara Solomon, *In the Company of Educated Women: A History of Women and Higher Education in America* (New Haven, Conn.: Yale University Press, 1985), examines developments in the twentieth century; on women in reform, see, for example, Sara Evans, *Born for Liberty: A History of Women in America* (New York: Free Press, 1989), 209–10.
24. Braden interview with author, 10 March 1989 (Tape 6).
25. Harriet Fitzgerald alumna file, Alumnae Affairs Office, R-MWC, Lynchburg, Virginia.
26. Braden interview with author, 11 March 1989 (Tape 7); Braden interview with Thrasher, Tape 4, Side 2, 124–25.
27. Braden interview with Ruth Pfisterer, Oral History Center, University Archives and Records, University of Louisville, 5 January 1981, Interview 2, 17–18 of transcript.
28. Samples of Braden's correspondence include Lucile Schoolfield file, letters to Anne McCarty, 1943–1945, in author's possession; Braden interview with author, 11 March 1989 (Tape 7). The seminal work on women's romantic friendships is Carroll Smith-Rosenberg, "The Female World of Love and Ritual: Relations between Women in Nineteenth-Century America," *Signs: A Journal of Women in Culture and Society* 1 (1975): 1–30. In *Educating the Southern Belle*, Farnham also finds female romantic friendships to have been commonplace in the antebellum South; the historian Joe Leedom, looking at Hollins College, Virginia, between 1900 and the 1920s, found that the tradition still thrived there in a popular campus society called "the Darlings," which paired young women for exchanging romantic tokens (Joe Leedom, lecture, Hollins College, Virginia, faculty luncheon, 18 January 1992).
29. The description of Fitzgerald is from her cousin Lee Robertson, conversation with author, 21 May 1996; Braden interview with author, 11 March 1989 (Tape 7).
30. Braden interview with author, 11 March 1989 (Tape 7).
31. Anne McCarty, unbound journal writings, 1941–1942, in author's possession; Braden interview with author, 10 March 1989 (Tape 6); Braden interview with Thrasher, Tape 4, Side 2, 129.
32. Anne Braden to author, "Feminism and My Relation to It," 3 January 2002, typescript manuscript in author's possession; Braden interview with author, 10 March 1989 (Tape 6); Braden interview with author, 11 June 1996; a very similar version of this story is told in Braden interview with Hogan, 23 June 1972, 8–9, CUOHROC.
33. On the southern women's suffrage movement, see Marjorie Spruill Wheeler, *New Women of the New South: The Leaders of the Woman Suffrage Movement in the Southern States* (New York: Oxford University Press, 1993). On continuities and disjunctures between the Old South and the New, see Anne Firor Scott, *The Southern Lady: From Pedestal to Politics, 1830–1930* (Chicago: University of Chicago Press, 1970). For a first-person account of the emotional costs of southern social protest, see Virginia Durr, *Outside the Magic Circle: The Autobiography of Virginia Foster Durr*, ed. Hollinger Barnard (Tuscaloosa: University of Alabama Press, 1985). LeeAnn Whites explores the term

"protectionism" in her essay "Rebecca Latimer Felton and the Problem of 'Protection' in the New South," in *Visible Women: New Essays on American Activism*, ed. Nancy Hewitt and Suzanne Lebsock (Urbana: University of Illinois Press, 1993), 41–61.

34. Nancy F. Cott, *The Grounding of Modern Feminism* (New Haven, Conn.: Yale University Press, 1987); Evans, *Born for Liberty*, 152–217.

35. Cott, *Grounding of Feminism*, esp. 271–82; Evans, *Born for Liberty*, 219–41.

36. As Cott points out in *Grounding of Feminism* (pp. 3–10), the word "feminism" was not coined in the United States until after the turn of the century, and is linked to modernity, just as the early "woman suffrage" movement was linked to Victorianism and a more singular understanding of women's nature. Cott's definition of feminism is threefold: (1) opposition to sex hierarchy; (2) understanding that women's condition is historically shaped and therefore subject to change under differing historical conditions; and (3) a group identity among women. From that standpoint, it is easy to see how such ideas continued to thrive among postsuffrage women, even those who might not necessarily identify themselves as "feminists" but who were teaching in single-sex environments. Anne Braden's use of the word "spillover" can be found in many interviews with her; see, especially the Hogan interview, 23 June 1972, 7, CUOHROC. Karen Anderson examines single women as a social threat in *Wartime Women*, 104–10; also see Joanne Meyerowitz, *Women Adrift: Independent Wage Earners in Chicago, 1880–1930* (Chicago: University of Chicago Press, 1988); Braden to author, "Feminism and My Relation."

37. Richard Polenberg, "The Good War? A Reappraisal of How WWII Affected American Society," *Virginia Magazine of History and Biography* 100, no. 3 (July 1992): 299–300; *Sundial*, 11 November 1943; Thrasher interview with Braden, Tape 5, Side 1, 131.

38. Hartmann, *Home Front and Beyond*, 103, 165.

39. Betty Friedan, *The Feminine Mystique* (New York: Dell, 1963), 7–11; William Chafe discusses both the postwar normalization of employment for married women and the contradictory host of messages glorifying domesticity in *The American Woman: Her Changing Social, Economic, and Political Roles, 1920–1970* (New York: Oxford University Press, 1972), esp. 182; Karen Anderson summarizes those messages in *Wartime Women*, 8. In a recent reinterpretation of Friedan titled "Beyond the Feminine Mystique," Joanne Meyerowitz questions Friedan's conclusions that the culture frowned on women's professionalism and political participation. The matter of how pervasive the feminine mystique was is still a matter of historical debate. For more on women whose political and social struggles were not stilled by the 1950s cultural climate, see, for example, Susan Lynn, "Gender and Progressive Politics: A Bridge to Social Activism of the 1960s" or Dorothy Sue Cobble, "Recapturing Working-Class Feminism: Union Women in the Postwar Era." All three aforementioned essays are in *Not June Cleaver*, ed. Meyerowitz.

40. Susan Hartmann characterizes women of this era as transitional in her essay, "Women's Employment," in *Not June Cleaver*, 84; Polenberg explores the mixed messages for women emanating from popular culture in the WWII years; Meyerowitz examines those messages in the postwar era; *Sundial*, 22 March 1945; *Sundial*, 15 March 1945; for more on the social conformity of the late '40s and '50s, see, for example, Marty Jetzer, *The Dark Ages: Life in the United States, 1945–1960* (Boston: South End Press, 1982), and Ellen Schrecker, *No Ivory Tower: McCarthyism and the Universities* (New York: Oxford University Press, 1986).

41. Stratford did not confer the standard associate of arts degree, a practice which may have stemmed from its lack of participation in the Southern Association of Colleges and Secondary Schools because of inadequate endowment (see A. Hall, *History of Stratford*, 50); news clipping, n.d., in Stratford College Class of '43 Book, Averitt College Library.

42. Anne McCarty, valedictory, Stratford Class of '43 Book.

43. I am using Molly Ladd-Taylor's concept of maternalist ideology, outlined in her essay "Toward Defining Maternalism in U.S. History," *Journal of Women's History* 5, no. 2 (Fall 1993): 110–13; Anne Braden, speech to Randolph-Macon Alumnae Awards Dinner, Lynchburg, Virginia, 1 October 1994.

44. Braden interview with author, 10 March 1989 (Tape 6). This conversation apparently took place with Ida Fitzgerald, who told it to Anne some years later.

45. Hartmann, *Home Front and Beyond*, 114.

46. U. S. Bureau of the Census, *County Data Book: Supplement to the Statistical Abstract of the United States* (Washington, D.C.: U.S. Government Printing Office, 1947); Anne McCarty, "From an Ivory Tower and Back Again," unpublished college paper, 1943, in Box 12, Folder 9, Carl and Anne Braden Papers, Manuscript 6, Civil Rights Collection, State Historical Society of Wisconsin (hereafter referred to as Branden Papers SHSW); Wayne Flynt, "Growing Up Baptist in Anniston, Alabama: The Legacy of the Rev. Charles R. Bell, Jr." in *Clearings in the Thicket: An Alabama Humanities Reader*, ed. Jerry Elijah Brown (Macon: Mercer University Press, 1985), 15 (biographical information on Ayers also comes from p. 156); Anne McCarty, "From an Ivory Tower"; Braden interview with Thrasher, Tape 4, Side 2, 115–16.

47. Braden interview with author, 10 March 1989 (Tape 6); the story of Anne's father is from Elise Ayers Sanguinetti, conversation with author, 14 June 1989; McCarty, "From an Ivory Tower."

48. McCarty, "From an Ivory Tower."

49. Carolyn Bell, "Learning the Contradictions: A History of Randolph-Macon Woman's College, 1950–1993," (working title), manuscript-in-progress, n.d., in author's possession; Farnham, *Education of the Southern Belle*, 185.

50. Braden interview with author, 10 March 1989 (Tape 6).

51. *Sundial*, 24 September 1943; *Sundial*, 13 September 1944.

52. Helen Lefkowitz Horowitz, *Alma Mater: Design and Experience in the Women's Colleges from Their Nineteenth-Century Beginnings to the 1930s* (New York: Knopf, 1984), 172, 287; *Sundial*, 13 September 1944.

53. Horowitz, *Alma Mater*, 153, 256; Bell, "Learning the Contradictions," 135–36.

54. Western Union, Anne McCarty to Mrs. G. N. McCarty, 23 September 1943, in author's possession; Braden interview with author, 10 March 1989 (Tape 6); Braden interview with Thrasher, Tape 4, Side 2, 119.

55. Anne Gambrell McCarty, "Diary of Thoughts," ca. January 1944, in author's possession.

56. *Sundial*, masthead, 21 October 1943; *Sundial*, 11 November 1943; *Sundial*, 13 September 1944; Braden interview with Thrasher, Tape 4, Side 2, 119; *Sundial*, 6 December 1944.

57. Braden interview with author, 10 March 1989 (Tape 6).

58. *Sundial*, 8 February 1945; Renov, *Hollywood's Wartime Women*, 27; Braden interview with author, 11 March 1989 (Tape 7); Anne McCarty, miscellaneous college papers, 1943–1945, Box 12, Folder 9, Braden Papers, SHSW.

59. Braden interview with author, 9 March 1989 (Tape 4); Braden, *Wall Between* (1958), 27–28.

60. Anne Braden, speech, Clergy and Laity Concerned, Atlanta, Georgia, 9 January 1990 (copy in author's possession); Braden, *Wall Between* (1958), 26.

61. Braden conversation with author, 1 October 1994; Braden interview with Thrasher, Tape 6, Side 1, 165–66.

62. Dot Silver, telephone interview with author, 26 May 1996; Helen Cotton, telephone interview with author, 18 July 1996; Anne Braden, conversation with author, 4 October 1994; *Sundial*, various issues, spring 1944; for more on the YWCA, see Evans, *Personal Politics*, 27–30, and Marion W. Roydhouse, "Bridging Chasms: Community and the Southern YWCA," in *Visible Women*, ed. Hewitt and Lebsock, 270–95.

63. Braden interview with author, 10 March 1989 (Tape 6); Braden interview with Pfisterer, Interview 1.

64. Jack Temple Kirby, *Rural Worlds Lost: The American South, 1920–1960* (Baton Rouge: LSU Press, 1987), prologue and chap. 1.

65. Ibid.; see also C. Vann Woodward, *Origins of the New South* (Baton Rouge: LSU Press, 1951).

66. David Goldfield, *Promised Land: The South since 1945* (Arlington Heights, Ill.: Harlan Davidson, 1987), 5.

67. Ibid., 77–80, 212–13.

68. Robert Kortstad and Nelson Lichtenstein, "Opportunities Found and Lost: Labor, Radicals and the Early Civil Rights Movement," *Journal of American History* 75, no. 3 (December 1988): 786; Sullivan, *Days of Hope*, 134.

69. Ibid.

70. Sullivan, *Days of Hope*, 135–41; Polenberg, "The Good War?": 306; August Meier and John Bracey Jr., "The NAACP as a Reform Movement, 1909–1965: To Reach the Conscience of America," *Journal of Southern History* 59, no. 1 (February 1993): 21; Honey, *Southern Labor*, 209.

71. Sullivan, *Days of Hope*, 156–58; Kneebone, *Southern Liberal Journalists*, 198. I have borrowed the term "race liberal" from Morton Sosna, *In Search of the Silent South: Southern Liberals and the Race Issue* (New York: Columbia University Press, 1977). Braden interview with Pfisterer, Interview 1, 22; Egerton, *Speak Now*, 226–27.

72. See Reed, *Simple Decency* for a history of the SCHW; on southern unions and race, see Honey, *Southern Labor*.

73. Sullivan, *Days of Hope*, 174–85. For a more thorough examination of Wallace's political vision, see John Judis, "Henry Wallace and the Common Man," in *Grand Illusion: Critics and Champions of the American Century* (New York: Farrar, Strauss, & Giroux, 1992), 59–61.

74. Braden interview with Pfisterer, Interview 1, 23.

75. *Sundial*, 26 April 1945.

76. *Sundial*, 10 May 1945.

77. Ibid.; Harriet Fitzgerald to Anne McCarty, n.d., ca. June 1945, in author's possession; Senior Class 1945 Files, Alumnae Affairs Office, R-MWC, Lynchburg, Virginia.

78. Anne's views at the time are expressed in Anne McCarty, "A Student Views the College," *Alumnae Bulletin of R-MWC* 38, no. 3 (April 1945): 39–40. A similar sentiment was expressed more recently: see Anne Braden, speech to R-MWC Alumnae Achievement Awards Banquet, 1 October 1994, copy in author's possession.

79. Braden interview with author, 11 March 1989 (Tape 7).

Chapter 3

1. Epigraph is from a speech W. E. B. DuBois delivered in 1946. "Behold the Land" is reprinted in *Freedomways* 4, no. 1 (winter 1964): 9.

2. Anne McCarty, "Annistonians Display Joy over Peace," *Anniston Star*, 15 August 1945; see, for example, Box 12, Folder 9, Braden Papers, SHSW, for a sampling of Anne's editorials.

3. Judis, "Henry Wallace and the Common Man," 64–65; Sullivan, *Days of Hope*, 222; on Anne's writing, see, for example, "Jacksonianism Alive Today," n.d., in Box 12, Folder 9, Braden Papers, SHSW.

4. Harriet Fitzgerald to Anne McCarty, n.d., postmarked 21 October 1945, in author's possession.

5. Albert Fried, *McCarthyism: The Great American Red Scare* (New York: Oxford University Press, 1997), 22–23; Caute, *Great Fear*, 25; David Oshinsky, *A Conspiracy So Immense: The World of Joe McCarthy* (New York: Free Press, 1983), 92–93.

6. Caute, *Great Fear*, 25; Egerton elaborates on "anticommunism, southern-style" in *Speak Now*, 448–60. For more on the fear of internal subversion as a theme in U.S. history, see M. J. Heale, *American Anticommunism: Combating the Enemy Within* (Baltimore: Johns Hopkins University Press, 1991).

7. Starobin, *Communism in Crisis*, 108–11; Korstad and Lichtenstein, "Opportunities Lost and Found": 786–811; Painter with Hudson, *Narrative of Hosea Hudson*, 16–20, 338–40.

8. That "euphoria" is discussed in some detail in Anne Braden, interview with Anthony Omer, Louisville, Kentucky, 1 April 1975, Oral History Center, University of Louisville Archives and Records; Braden interview with Pfisterer, Interview 1, 25; Braden interview with Hogan, 23 June 1972, 9–10, CUOHRC (please note that, as elsewhere in the book, the marks of ellipses within passages quoting Anne may indicate shift from one oral history source to another—in this case from Pfisterer to Hogan).

9. Braden interview with author, 9 March 1989 (Tape 4); see, for example, Anne McCarty, unsigned editorial, "The Decline of Individualism," n.d., ca. October 1945, in Box 12, Folder 9, Braden Papers, SHSW.

10. Harriet Fitzgerald to Anne McCarty, 23 September 1945, in author's possession.

11. For a sampling of Anne McCarty's editorials see Box 12, Folder 9, Braden Papers, SHSW, especially "Transplanting Democracy," n.d., clipping. For more on the showdown in Alabama politics, see Wayne Flynt, "The Flowering of Alabama Liberalism: Politics and Society During the 1940s and 1950s," chap. 30 in Rogers et al., *Alabama*, 524–44. The phrase "race liberals" was coined in Sosna, *In Search of the Silent South*.

12. Anne McCarty, "Against Group Prejudice," and "The Need for a Creed," in *Anniston Star*, n.d., ca. October 1945, Box 12, Folder 9, Braden Papers, SHSW; Honey, *Southern Labor*, 214; this point is illustrated in Korstad and Lichtenstein, "Opportunities Found and Lost."

13. *Anniston Star*, 7 April 1946 editorial; *Anniston Star*, 5 May 1946 editorial; for more on anticommunism and challenges to unionism in the postwar era, see Heale, *American Anticommunism*, esp. 134–37.

14. For a comprehensive study of the Columbia violence, see Gail Williams O'Brien, *The Color of the Law: Race, Violence, and Justice in the Post–World War Two South* (Chapel Hill: University of North Carolina Press, 1999).

15. Honey, *Southern Labor*, 216; Egerton, *Speak Now*, 366–69.

16. Gordon Rogers, telephone interview with author, 5 December 1997; Dorothy Autry, "The NAACP in Alabama: 1913–1952" (Ph.D. diss., University of Notre Dame, 1985), 20; *Anniston Star*, 5 September 1945; *Anniston Star*, 6 January 1946.

17. Harriet Fitzgerald to Anne McCarty, n.d., fall 1945, in author's possession; *Anniston Star*, 10 September 1945.

18. Egerton, *Speak Now*, 354; *Anniston Star*, 1 June 1945.

19. Braden, *Wall Between* (1958), 24–25.

20. *Anniston Star*, 14 January 1946; for more on black voter registration in 1946, see *Anniston Star*, 6 May 1946; William Barnard, *Dixiecrats and Democrats: Alabama Politics, 1942–1950* (Tuscaloosa: University of Alabama Press, 1974), 61–62.

21. Barnard, *Dixiecrats and Democrats*, 65–66.

22. Ibid., 4; Sosna, *In Search of the Silent South*, 145; Klibaner, *Conscience of a Troubled South*, 16–17; Honey, *Southern Labor*, 216; Barbara Griffith's *Crisis of American Labor: Operation Dixie and the Defeat of the CIO* (Philadelphia: Temple University Press, 1988) is a thorough study of Operation Dixie.

23. Rogers et al., *Alabama*, 524; Krueger, *And Promises to Keep*, 129; Barnard, *Dixiecrats and Democrats*, 4.

24. *Anniston Star*, 7 April 1946; *Anniston Star*, 16 April 1946; for more on regional defensiveness as a component of southern liberalism see Sosna, *In Search of the Silent South*, esp. 198–211.

25. Griffith, *Crisis of American Labor*, 12–15.

26. Rogers et al., *Alabama*, 526–27; Barnard, *Dixiecrats and Democrats*, 3–5; Carl Grafton, "James E. Folsom's 1946 Campaign," *Alabama Review* 35, no. 3 (1982): 172–99.

27. Grafton, "Folsom's 1946 Campaign": 176–81; see also Carl Grafton and Anne Permaloff, *Big Mules and Branchheads: James E. Folsom and Political Power in Alabama* (Athens: University of Georgia Press, 1985).

28. Barnard, *Dixiecrats and Democrats*, 13–14, 32–33; Grafton, "Folsom's 1946 campaign": 191.

29. Barnard, *Dixiecrats and Democrats*, 24–47; *Anniston Star*, 12 May 1946; Anne McCarty, "People Convinced Folsom Was the Man of the Hour," *Anniston Star*, 9 June 1946; *Anniston Star*, 12, 13, 14, 19, 29, 30 May 1946 and 2 June 1946.

30. Braden interview with author, 9 March 1989 (Tape 4); Anne Braden to Governor James A. Folsom, 13 July 1950, Box 54, Folder 3, Braden Papers, SHSW.

31. Grafton and Permaloff, *Big Mules and Branchheads*, 22; see, for example, *Anniston Star*, 19 May 1946; Barnard, *Dixiecrats and Democrats*, 39–42.

32. Grafton, "Folsom's 1946 Campaign": 189–92; McCarty, "People Convinced Folsom Was the Man"; Braden interview with Thrasher, Tape 5, Side 2.

33. Anne Braden, interview with Pfisterer, Interview 1; see *Anniston Star*, 18 October 1945, for one such engagement announcement; Harriet Fitzgerald to Anne McCarty, n.d., ca. 1946, in author's possession; Braden interview with Thrasher, Tape 6, Side 1.

34. Braden interview with Thrasher, Tape 5, Side 1, 138.

35. Ibid.

36. For one discussion of women as "playthings," see Anne Braden interview with Robert Mosby, 8 September 1968, Civil Rights Documentation Project, Moorland-Spingarn Collection, Howard University, Washington, D.C. Anne's letters to her friends are extant, but this assumption can be supported by reading the collection of several dozen letters from Harriet Fitzgerald to Anne McCarty, n.d., 1943–1946, in author's possession; see also Lucile Schoolfield to Anne McCarty, 1943–45, in author's possession.

37. Meyerowitz, "Beyond the Feminine Mystique," 229–232; Hartmann, *Home Front and Beyond*, 164–65.

38. On the stereotyping of women journalists as "girl reporters," see Vivian Van Der Veer Hamilton, *Looking for Clark Gable and Other Twentieth-Century Pursuits* (Tuscaloosa: University of Alabama Press, 1996), 47.

39. Meyerowitz, "Beyond the Feminine Mystique," 229–32; Ferdinand Lundberg and Marynia Farnham, *Modern Woman: The Lost Sex* (New York: Harper & Bros., 1947) was probably the most influential antifeminist tract; Friedan, *The Feminine Mystique*; Hartmann, *Home Front and Beyond*, 169–180. As a onetime labor journalist and leftist, Friedan herself apparently never retreated as fully into the feminine mystique as her public statements on the matter suggest; for a full examination of Friedan's politics and the leftist roots of the women's liberation movement that her book fueled in the 1960s, see Daniel Horowitz, *Betty Friedan and the Making of the Feminine Mystique: The American Left, the Cold War, and Modern Feminism* (Amherst: University of Massachusetts Press, 1998).

40. Braden interview with Thrasher, Tape 5, Side 1; Egerton, *Speak Now*, 365, 249–51; on liberals' view of the *Courier-Journal*, see also Harriet Fitzgerald to Anne McCarty, 25 September 1945, in author's possession; Braden interview with Thrasher, Tape 5, Side 1, 143–45.

41. Egerton, *Speak Now*, 251, 362.

42. Anne McCarty to James Pope, 13 September 1946, in author's possession; one such speech, for example, is Anne Braden to Randolph-Macon Alumnae Awards Dinner, 1 October 1994.

43. Braden, *Wall Between* (1958), 28–29.

44. Braden, interview with Thrasher, Tape 7, Side 1, 201.

45. This information on Anne's observations comes from Braden interview with Hogan, 23 June 1972, 4–11, CUOHROC.

46. Kelley, *Hammer and Hoe*, 224–27; Autrey, "The NAACP in Alabama," 204. Diane McWhorter's *Carry Me Home* does what I consider the best job of outlining local officials' sanctioning of racial violence. It should also be noted that the predominantly black SNYC inspired a corresponding youth group known as the League of Young Southerners—a development that repeated itself in the 1960s when young whites inspired by SNCC formed their own group for racial change: the Southern Student Organizing Committee, or SSOC.

47. Braden interview with Thrasher, Tape 5, Side 1; *Southern Patriot*, February 1946; *Southern Patriot*, March 1946, 5, 6; for a more thorough understanding of SNYC activities in Birmingham, see Hughes, "We Demand our Rights," 38–50.

48. Braden interview with Pfisterer, Interview 1.

49. Barnard, *Dixiecrats and Democrats*, 66–67; James E. Folsom, *Speeches of Gov. James E. Folsom.* (Wetumpka, Ala.: n.p., n.d.); Braden interview with the author, Louisville, Kentucky, 12 December 1997.

50. Fried, *McCarthyism*, 23; Randall Patton, "The CIO and the Search for a Silent South," *Maryland Historian* 19, no. 2 (1988): 8–13; Egerton, *Speak Now*, 448–49.

51. Ilene Philipson, *Ethel Rosenberg: Beyond the Myths* (New Brunswick, N.J.: Rutgers University Press, 1988), 196. For more on the history of anticommunism in U.S. culture prior to the postwar period, see Heale, *American Anticommunism* (esp. Part 1) or Egerton, *Speak Now*, 451–52; poll data are from Heale, *American Anticommunism*, 136.

52. Klehr, *Heyday of American Communism*, 386; Kelley, *Hammer and Hoe*, 186; Heale, *American Anticommunism*, 124–25, 134–35; Ellen Schrecker, *Many Are the Crimes: McCarthyism in America* (Boston: Little, Brown, and Co., 1998), 83–97.

53. Egerton, *Speak Now*, 455–56.

54. Caute, *Great Fear*, 88–89; Stephen J. Whitfield, *Culture of the Cold War* (Baltimore: Johns Hopkins University Press, 1991), 4; for perhaps the most thorough explanation of the anticommunist witch hunt, see, for example, Schrecker, *Many are the Crimes*; Egerton, *Speak Now*, 455–56.

55. Braden interview with Pfisterer, Interview 1, 27.

56. Braden interview with author, 12 December 1997; Barnard, *Dixiecrats and Democrats*, 81–91; John Salmond, *A Southern Rebel: The Life and Times of Aubrey Willis Williams, 1890–1965* (Chapel Hill: University of North Carolina Press, 1983), 182–94.

57. Painter with Hudson, *Narrative of Hosea Hudson*, 20–25; Kelley, *Hammer and Hoe*, xi–xiii; Braden interview with Bud and Ruth Schultz, 2 September 1984, Interview 2.

58. Braden interview with Bud and Ruth Schultz, 2 September 1984, Interview 2; Anne McCarty to Anita McCarty, n.d., ca. March 1947, in author's possession; Harriet Fitzgerald to Anne McCarty, various letters, n.d., ca. 1946, in author's possession.

59. Braden interview with Thrasher, Interview 5, Side 1, 138–40 and Interview 6, Side 1, 170; Braden interview with author, 11 June 1996.

60. Anne McCarty to Anita McCarty, n.d., ca. March 1947, in author's possession; Braden interview with Thrasher, Tape 5, Side 1, 139.

61. Braden, *Wall Between* (1958), 30–31.

62. Ibid.

63. Ibid.

64. Braden to author, 11 June 1997, in author's possession; Braden interview with Pfisterer, Interview 1.

65. Ralph Shoemaker, ed., *Chronological List of Events in the Courier-Journal and Times History* (Louisville: Louisville Free Public Library, 1947). One rather sensationalized account of the Bingham family fortunes is David Leon Chandler with Mary Voelz Chandler, *The Binghams of Louisville: The Dark History Behind One of America's Great Fortunes* (New York: Crown, 1987), 51, 130–76; an insider's account of the Bingham family story is Sallie Bingham's *Passion and Prejudice: A Family Memoir* (New York: Alfred A. Knopf, 1989).

66. John Ed Pearce, *Memoirs: Fifty Years at the Courier-Journal and Other Places* (Louisville: Sulgrave, 1997), 68; Anne McCarty to Anita McCarty, n.d., ca. March 1947, in author's possession.

67. Braden to author, 11 June 1997, in author's possession.

Chapter 4

1. Epigraph that begins the chapter is from Braden interview with Thrasher, Tape 6, Side 1, 161.

2. Fried, *McCarthyism*, 24; Wayne Addison Clark, "An Analysis of the Relationship Between Anti-Communism and Segregationist Thought in the Deep South, 1948–1954" (Ph.D. dissertation, University of North Carolina, 1976), 45; Harvey A. Levenstein, *Communism, Anticommunism, and the CIO* (Westport, Conn.: Greenwood, 1981), 220–48; Martin Bauml Duberman, *Paul Robeson* (New York: Alfred A. Knopf, 1988), 317; Sullivan, *Days of Hope*, 243; Dunbar, *Against the Grain*, 226–27.

3. James Braden, "The Life of a Reformer," unpublished paper, 21 September 1967, in Box 16, Folder 3, Braden Papers, SHSW.

4. Ibid.; Anne Braden, interview with author, Louisville, Kentucky, 8 March 1989 (Tape 2); Sue Thrasher, "In Memoriam—Carl Braden," *The Great Speckled Bird*, 27 February 1975.

5. Braden interview with Hogan, 23 June 1972, 12, CUOHROC; Braden interview with Pfisterer, Interview 1, 22; Braden interview with Thrasher, Tape 5, Side 2, 151.

6. Wade Hall, ed., *The Rest of the Dream: The Black Odyssey of Lyman Johnson* (Lexington: University Press of Kentucky, 1988), esp. 127; Toni Gilpin, "Left by Themselves: A History of the United Farm Equipment and Metal Workers Union, 1935–1955" (Ph.D. diss., Yale University, 1992), 483–86; Meyer, *As Long as They Don't Move*, 233.

7. Patrick McElhone, "The Civil Rights Activities of the Louisville Branch of the NAACP, 1914–1960" (M.A. thesis, University of Louisville, 1976), iii; *Kentucky's Black Heritage*, 92–93.

8. Ibid.; Braden interview with author, 8–9 March 1989 (Tape 3); Col. John Benjamin Horton, *Not without Struggle* (New York: Vantage, 1979), esp. chap. 2; Lyman Johnson, interview with author, Louisville, Kentucky, 24 June 1991; see also "Negro Teacher Applies for UK," *Louisville Times*, 24 March 1948, A1.

9. Braden interview with author, 8–9 March 1989 (Tape 3).

10. Ibid.; James Crumlin, interview with author, Louisville, Kentucky, 7 November 1989; Lyman Johnson interview.

11. Reed, *Simple Decency*, 113–14; see Sullivan, *Days of Hope*, esp. chap. 8 and epilogue, for a fuller explanation of the breakup of the Popular Front in the growing Cold War climate; the significant role liberal anticommunism played in the development of what became known as McCarthyism is also emphasized in Kenneth O'Reilly, *Hoover and the Un-Americans: The FBI, HUAC, and the Red Menace* (Philadelphia: Temple University Press, 1983), 193.

12. Louisville *Courier-Journal*, 25 May 1947; Philipson, *Ethel Rosenberg*, 214; Braden, *Wall Between* (1958), 41–42 ; Egerton, *Speak Now*, 420–22.

13. Jackson, *Waiting Years*, 19; Braden interview with author, 8–9 March 1989 (Tapes 2 and 3).

14. Braden interview with Thrasher, Tape 5, Side 2, 159.

15. Ibid.; Anne McCarty to Gambrell and Anita McCarty, n.d., ca. December 1947, in author's possession; Curtis D. MacDougall, *Gideon's Army, Vol. 1* (New York: Marzani & Munsell, 1965), 152.

16. Sullivan, *Days of Hope*, 92–93; Honey, *Southern Labor*, 236–37; for more on the purged unionists, see Steve Rosswurm's introduction to his edited volume, *The CIO's Left-Led Unions* (New Brunswick, N.J.: Rutgers University Press, 1992), 1–17; Patricia Sullivan, "Gideon's Southern Soldiers: New Deal Politics and Civil Rights Reform, 1933–1948" (Ph.D. dissertation, Emory University, 1983), 207–208; Griffith, *Crisis of American Labor*, esp. chap. 8, explores the failure of Operation Dixie along these lines; see also Philip Foner, "Operation Dixie," in *The Cold War against Labor, Vol. 1*, ed. Anne Fagan Ginger and David Christiano (Berkeley, Calif.: Meiklejohn Civil Liberties Institute, 1987), 164–71.

17. Caute, *Great Fear*, 354–59.

18. John Ed Pearce, *Divide and Dissent: Kentucky Politics, 1930–1963* (Lexington: University Press of Kentucky, 1987), 48; Gilpin, "Left by Themselves," 507.

19. See, for example, Toni Gilpin, "Left by Themselves," esp. chap. 5; *Louisville Times*, 28 March 1947.

20. Gilpin, "Left by Themselves," 417–21; Braden to author, 18 May 2002, copy in author's possession.

21. Gilpin, "Left by Themselves," 421–30 and 497–98; Chris Gastinger, interview with author, Louisville, Kentucky, 25 June 1991.

22. Gilpin, "Left by Themselves," 432–37; "The Louisville Story," FE pamphlet, n.d. (ca. 1951), in author's possession. Although FE Local 236 did win significant wage gains as a result of the strike and subsequent negotiations, the differential was entirely eliminated only for some grades of labor, and merely reduced for others.

23. Gilpin, "Left by Themselves," 424–25; Braden interview with author, 8 March 1989 (Tape 2); Braden interview with Thrasher, Tape 6, Side 2, 179–80.

24. Levenstein, *Communism, Anticommunism, and the CIO*, 220–21; this point on union priorities is drawn from Toni Gilpin, "United Farm Equipment and Metal Workers," in *Encyclopedia of the American Left* (1992 edition), 807.

25. Braden correspondence with author, 11 June 1997, in author's possession; Braden interview with Thrasher, Tape 6, Side 2, 179.

26. Fried, *McCarthyism*, 25–26; Sullivan, *Days of Hope*, 243–44; for more description of the Old Left, see, for example, Ellen Kay Trimberger, "Women in the Old and New Left: The Evolution of a Politics of Personal Life," *Feminist Studies* 5, no. 3 (fall 1979): 432–50.

27. Louisville *Courier-Journal*, 22 November 1947; Braden correspondence with author, 11 June 1997.

28. Braden interview with author, 8 March 1989 (Tape 2); Sullivan, "Gideon's Southern Soldiers," 242–47; see also Durr, *Outside the Magic Circle*, ed. Barnard, 201, and Gilpin, "Left by Themselves," 511–13.

29. Braden interview with author, 8 March 1989 (Tape 2).

30. Gilpin, "Left by Themselves," 508; Braden interview with author, 8 March 1989 (Tape 2).

31. Braden correspondence with author, 11 June 1997.

32. Anne McCarty to Gambrell and Anita McCarty, n.d., ca. early December 1947, in author's possession.

33. Anne Braden to Carl Braden, 21 December 1961, in Box 11, Folder 9, Braden Papers, SHSW.

34. Braden interview with Pfisterer, Interview 1; Braden interview with Thrasher, Tape 7, Side 1, 184–85.

35. Braden correspondence to author, 11 June 1997; see, for example, Braden speech at Randolph-Macon Woman's College Alumnae Achievement Awards dinner, 10 October 1994.

36. Braden interview with Bud and Ruth Schultz, Louisville, Kentucky, 2 September 1984, Interview 1, 43; Braden correspondence to author, 11 June 1997, in author's possession.

37. Braden to author, 11 June 1997; Braden interview with author, 8–9 March 1989 (Tape 3).

38. Clark, "Anticommunism and Segregationist Thought," 18–43; Duberman, *Paul Robeson*, 323; Sullivan, *Days of Hope*, 236–47; MacDougall, *Gideon's Army*, 280.

39. Ibid. These exclusions often included not just CP members themselves but also former Communists and people known to be sympathetic to Communists.

40. Egerton, *Speak Now*, 472; Levenstein, *Communism, Anticommunism, and the CIO*, 220–28.

41. Ibid.; Krueger, *And Promises to Keep*, 182–87; Klibaner, *Conscience of a Troubled South*, 37–38; Salmond, *Southern Rebel*, 202–204.

42. Klibaner, *Conscience of a Troubled South*, 37–38; Duberman, *Paul Robeson*, 325–28; Braden interview with author, 8–9 March 1989 (Tape 2); Herb Monsky to Curtis Mac-Dougall, 18 November 1953, in Progressive Party Records, Special Collections, University of Iowa Libraries, Iowa City.

43. Richard J. Walton, *Henry Wallace, Harry Truman, and the Cold War* (New York: Viking Press, 1976), 249; poll results are drawn from Cedric Belfrage and James Aronson, *Something to Guard: The Stormy Life of the National Guardian, 1948–1964* (New York: Columbia University Press, 1978), 10; Whitfield, *The Culture of the Cold War*; Wilson Record, *The Negro and the Communist Party* (Chapel Hill: University of North Carolina Press, 1951), 278–79; Starobin, *American Communism in Crisis*, 113; Philipson, *Ethel Rosenberg*, 198; Duberman, *Paul Robeson*, 324–25.

44. Robert A. Divine, "The Cold War and the Election of 1948," *Journal of American History* 59, no. 1 (June 1972): 90–110; Duberman, *Paul Robeson*, 324–25; MacDougall, *Gideon's Army*, 274–76. For an interesting sidebar on the contested meanings of political currents during this era, see Duberman on historians' widely varied interpretations of the issue of Communist influence in the Progressive Party, *Paul Robeson*, 682 n. 22.

45. Philipson, *Ethel Rosenberg*, 198; Clark, "Anticommunism and Segregationist Thought," 28–29; Whitfield, *Culture of the Cold War*, 27–28.

46. Braden interview with author, 8 March 1989 (Tape 2); Louisville *Courier-Journal*, 22 August 1948.

47. Gilpin, "Left by Themselves," 512–16; Duberman, *Paul Robeson*, 335.

48. Egerton, *Speak Now*, 476–77; Barnard, *Dixiecrats and Democrats*, 113–16.
49. Ibid.; "G.L.K. Smith Gets Party Bid for President," Louisville *Courier-Journal*, 22 August 1948.
50. The term "Popular Front" was originally coined by the Communist Party to define a strategy of left-liberal alliance that began with the Seventh Congress of the Comintern International in 1935. That strategy officially ended in 1939 with the Hitler-Stalin Pact. I refer here to the informal Popular Front that was renewed after the United States entered the war, continuing in some form even after the anticommunist purges were in full swing (see Klehr, *The Heyday of American Communism*, especially chaps. 10 and 12). Sullivan makes a strong case for the dimming of Popular Front liberalism with the rise of anticommunism in *Days of Hope* (see p. 273 on Foreman's characterization); Joel Kovel provides a view of the psychological dimensions of anticommunism in his *Red Hunting in the Promised Land: Anti-Communism and the Making of America* (New York: Basic Books, 1994); Braden interview with author, 8 March 1989 (Tape 2).
51. Braden interviews with author, 8–9 March 1989 (Tapes 2 and 3); Braden to author, 11 June 1997; Anne's interview with Paul Robeson appeared in *Louisville Times*, 18 May 1948.
52. Hartmann, *Home Front and Beyond*, 176–81. Elaine Tyler May, for example, argues this correlation between the Cold War and gender roles in *Homeward Bound: American Families in the Cold War Era* (New York: Basic Books, 1982). A somewhat different take on gender and anticommunism—one I found influential in shaping my analysis of Anne Braden—can be found in Kate Weigand, "The Red Menace, the Feminine Mystique, and the Ohio Un-American Activities Commission: Gender and Anticommunism in Ohio, 1951–1954," *Journal of Women's History* 3, no. 3 (1992): 70–94.

Chapter 5

1. Fitzgerald's question in the opening epigraph is taken from Braden interview with author, 8–9 March 1989 (Tape 3).
2. Bond's remarks in the epigraph come from his interview with author, Charlottesville, Virginia, 17 September 1997.
3. For more on Anne's and Carl's self-consciousness about their relationship, see, for example, Carl and Anne Braden, joint interview with Robert Mosby, 8 September 1968, esp. 22–24 of transcript. For more on family relations in the CP, see Paul Lyons, *Philadelphia Communists, 1936–56* (Philadelphia: Temple University Press, 1982), esp. 87.
4. See miscellaneous essays in Sara Alpern, Joyce Antler, Elisabeth Israels Perry, and Ingrid Winther Scobie, *The Challenge of Feminist Biography: Writing the Lives of Modern American Women* (Urbana: University of Illinois Press, 1992); see also Blanche Wiesen Cook, *Eleanor Roosevelt, Volume 1, 1884–1933* (New York: Viking, 1992); Anne Braden, telephone conversation with author, 16 December 1998.
5. Anne Braden to author, 11 June 1997; Braden interview with Pfisterer, Interview 2, 17 of transcript.
6. Braden interview with author, 8–9 March 1989 (Tape 3); the characterization of Carl as gallant is from Braden interview with Thrasher, Tape 6, Side 2, 178.
7. Louisville *Courier-Journal*, 17 March 1948.
8. Braden interview with author, 8–9 March 1989 (Tape 3).
9. Braden interview with Thrasher, Tape 6, Side 2, 180; Braden interview with author, 8–9 March 1989 (Tape 3).
10. Braden telephone conversation with author, 16 December 1998; Braden to author, 21 January 2002, copy in author's possession.
11. Anne and Carl Braden, joint interview with Robert Mosby, 8 September 1968; Braden interview with Pfisterer, Interview 2; see also Braden interview with author, 12 December 1997, for a discussion of her later views on the couple's political disagreements.
12. Braden interview with Pfisterer, Interview 2, 18.
13. Braden interview with author, 8–9 March 1989 (Tape 3).

14. Braden interview with Thrasher, Tape 6, Side 2, 182; Braden interview with author, 17 June 1999.

15. John D'Emilio and Estelle Freedman, *Intimate Matters: A History of Sexuality in America* (New York: Harper & Row, 1988), 261–62, 331–32; Anne Braden, telephone conversation with author, 1 November 1998; Braden interview with Thrasher, Tape 5, Side 1, 134.

16. D'Emilio and Freedman, *Intimate Matters*, 265–66; Braden interview with author, 11 June 1996.

17. Braden interview with author, 8–9 March 1989 (Tape 3); Braden interview with Pfisterer, Interview 2, 17.

18. Braden, miscellaneous interviews with author.

19. Braden to author, 11 June 1997; see also Braden interview with Pfisterer, Interview 2, 17.

20. Braden interview with Thrasher, Tape 6, Side 2, 187–88.

21. Ibid., 189.

22. Braden interview with author, 11 June 1996.

23. Braden interview with author, 8–9 March 1989 (Tape 3).

24. Braden interview with author, 11 June 1996; Braden interview with author, 8–9 March 1989 (Tape 3); Braden to author, "Feminism and My Relation."

25. Braden telephone conversation with author, 16 December 1998.

26. Van Gosse, "'To Organize in Every Neighborhood, in Every Home': The Gender Politics of American Communists between the Wars," *Radical History Review* 50 (spring 1991): 109–41, (esp. 110, 134). For a complete discussion on gender and the roles of women in the CP-USA, see Robert Shaffer, "Women and the Communist Party, U.S.A., 1930–1940," *Socialist Review* 9, no. 3 (May-June 1979): 73–118.

27. The CP's relationship to gender politics and activism is explored most fully in Weigand, *Red Feminism;* see Leila Rupp and Verda Taylor, *Survival in the Doldrums: The American Women's Rights Movement, 1945 to the 1960s* (New York: Oxford University Press, 1987), esp. 187–206; Hartmann, "Women's Employment," in *Not June Cleaver,* 84–100; Amy Swerdlow, "The Congress of American Women: Left-Feminist Peace Politics in the Cold War" in *U.S. History as Women's History: New Feminist Essays,* ed. Linda Kerber, Alice Kessler-Harris, and Kathryn Kish Sklar (Chapel Hill: University of North Carolina Press, 1995), 299. "Left feminism" is a loose concept, but connotes women's groups that typically spin off larger left-wing organizations and organize as women around issues that may include or gesture toward greater gender equality and female independence using a variety of rationales.

28. Braden interview with author, 8–9 March 1989 (Tape 3); Braden telephone conversation with author, 16 December 1998.

29. Ibid.; George Yater, interview with author, Louisville, Kentucky, 11 December 1997; *Courier-Journal,* 11 October 1948.

30. The description of Sharpley is taken from Fletcher Martin, "Times Copyreader Lands Punch for States' Rights," *Louisville Defender,* 23 October 1948, copy in Box 12, Folder 2, Braden Papers, SHSW; "Times Reporter Quits to Protest Changes in Thurmond Story" Louisville *Courier-Journal,* 23 October 1948; Braden interview with Thrasher, Tape 7, Side 1, 201.

31. Braden interview with author, 8–9 March 1989 (Tape 3).

32. *FE News,* June 1949, in Box 12, Folder 2, Braden Papers, SHSW; Anne and Carl Braden to Executive Board, Local 236, 8 October 1949, in Box 54, Folder 2, Braden Papers, SHSW.

33. Levenstein, *Communism, Anticommunism, and the CIO,* 291–92; Braden interview with author, 8–9 March 1989 (Tape 3).

34. Levenstein, *Communism, Anticommunism, and the CIO,* 291–301; Gilpin, "United FE" in *Encyclopedia of the American Left,* 807. The expulsions actually included all but one of the other locals comprising the Seventh Street alliance. The United Furniture Workers was threatened with expulsion but avoided it by holding new national elections to replace its leadership with anticommunists.

35. Gilpin, "Left by Themselves," 536–37; Louisville *Courier-Journal*, 23 December 1949.
36. See, for example, "PAC Official Stalks Away from Meeting," Louisville *Courier-Journal*, 17 July 1949; memo, 20 June 1949, Box 2, in Carl and Anne Braden Papers, Mss. 425, Special Collections, Hoskins Library, University of Tennessee (hereinafter referred to as Braden Papers, UT).
37. *FE News*, June 1949, in Box 10, Folder 2, Braden Papers, SHSW.
38. Swerdlow, "Left-Feminist Peace Politics," 300; *Labor's Voice*, June 1949, in Box 3, "Labor's Voice" folder in Braden Papers, UT; that same folder contains an assortment of issues of *FE Cub* that illustrate the swimsuit feature.
39. Braden interview with author, Louisville, Kentucky, 7 March 1989 (Tape 1); Box 2, "Forum on Peace, Women's Chapter" Folder in Braden Papers, UT, contains clippings and other references to these events; Mildred Neal, interview with author, Louisville, Kentucky, 25 June 1991.
40. Braden, *Wall Between* (1958), 50–51.
41. Lucille Elliott, "Women Take Lead in Louisville Peace Activities," typescript manuscript, n.d., in Box 54, Folder 6, Braden Papers, SHSW; for more on Anne's work with Women for Peace, see her interview with author, Louisville, Kentucky, 11 November 1989.
42. Caute, *Great Fear*, 176.
43. Claudia Jones, "Women Crusade for Peace," *Worker Magazine*, 12 March 1950, Section 2, n.p., in Box 54, Folder 6, Braden Papers, SHSW; Swerdlow, "Left-Feminist Peace Politics," 297; L. Elliott, "Women Take Lead," typescript; "Peace Petition 2nd Recently Circulated," Louisville *Courier-Journal*, 13 August 1950; Schrecker argues the irrelevance of such groups in *Many Are the Crimes*, 378. The charges against DuBois were thrown out for lack of evidence. For more on the DuBois case, see Schrecker, *Many Are the Crimes*, 378–79; "Forum on Peace, Women's Chapter" folder, Braden Papers, UT; Braden interview with author, 7 March 1989 (Tape 1).
44. Swerdlow, "Left-Feminist Peace Politics," 299. I am using the historian Nancy Cott's definition of feminism here, which stresses women's individuality, political participation, economic autonomy, and group consciousness. Both Cott's definition of feminism and the ideology of maternalism are discussed more fully in Ladd-Tylor, "Toward Defining Maternalism," 110–13; Braden to author, "Feminism and My Relation."
45. Braden interview with author, 11 June 1996.
46. "Progressive Party—Local Adversary of U.S.—Is Merely A Handful of Militant Reformers," *Louisville Times*, 13 June 1952; Braden interview with author, 8–9 March 1989 (Tape 3); Philipson, *Ethel Rosenberg*, 250–54; the phrase was taken from Whitfield, *Culture of the Cold War*; Belfrage and Aronson, *Something to Guard*, 8.
47. Norman Markowitz, *The Rise and Fall of the People's Century: Henry A. Wallace and American Liberalism, 1941–1948* (New York: Free Press, 1973), 304–10; "Is a Clear and Present Danger Conquered by This Decision?" Louisville *Courier-Journal*, 7 June 1951. On additional newspaper coverage, see, for example, "Progressive Party—Local Adversary of U.S.—Is Merely a Handful of Militant Reformers," *Louisville Times*, 13 June 1952, or "The Problem of Grzelak Is Solved, but That of Barnett Remains," Louisville *Courier-Journal*, 23 January 1953.
48. Anne Braden to U.S.S.R. Information Bulletin, 25 January 1950, Box 54, Folder 3, Braden Papers, SHSW; Braden interview with author, 8–9 March 1989 (Tape 3).
49. Durr, *Outside the Magic Circle*, 206.
50. For more on the CP's reaction to the escalating repression, see, for example, Dorothy Healey and Maurice Isserman, *California Red: A Life in the Communist Party* (Urbana: University of Illinois Press, 1993), 104–32; Braden interview with author, 8–9 March 1989 (Tape 3).
51. Louisville *Courier-Journal*, 21 April 1952, 21 June 1952, and 21 January 1953; George Yater interview.
52. Braden interview with author, 8–9 March 1989 (Tape 3).

53. "The Fight to Break Down Segregation and Discrimination in Kentucky Hospitals," typescript manuscript, n.a., n.d., ca. August 1951, in Box 48, Folder 12, Braden Papers, SHSW.

54. Braden interview with author, 8–9 March 1989 (Tape 3); *Kentucky's Black Heritage*, 97.

55. Braden interview with author, 8–9 March 1989 (Tape 3).

56. Ibid.

57. "The Fight to Break Down Segregation"; Anne Braden, telephone conversation with author, 2 February 1998.

58. Gerald Horne, *Communist Front? The Civil Rights Congress, 1946–1956* (Rutherford, N.J.: Fairleigh Dickinson University Press, 1988); Braden interview with author, 8–9 March 1989 (Tape 3).

59. Ibid.; "City White Woman Told She Should Be Shot for Attempting to Defend Negro Man's Life in Mississippi," *Louisville Defender*, 12 May 1951.

60. Anne Braden, interview with author and Michael Honey, Louisville, Kentucky, 10 November 1994; *Jackson Daily News*, 6 May 1951; "City White Woman Told She Should Be Shot"; Braden interview with Hogan, 7 December 1978, Interview 2, 108–14, CUOHROC; John Dittmer, *Local People: The Struggle for Civil Rights in Mississippi* (Urbana: University of Illinois Press, 1994), 21–22.

61. *Louisville Defender*, 12 May 1951; see, for example, Anne Braden, *Free Thomas Wansley: A Letter to White Southern Women* (Louisville: SCEF Publications, 1972), pamphlet in author's possession.

62. For Braden's writing on the perils of southern white males' protectionism toward white women, see her *Letter to White Southern Women*, 7–9; Whites, "Rebecca Latimer Felton," 41–61.

63. Gerald Horne, "Civil Rights Congress" entry in *Encyclopedia of the American Left*, ed. Buhle et al. (1992 edition), 134–35; Caute, *Great Fear*, 38.

64. Horne, *Communist Front*, 132–44; Braden interview with author, 8–9 March 1989 (Tape 3).

65. Anne Braden, interview with author, 8–9 March 1989 (Tape 3).

66. Patterson comment quoted in Braden, epilogue, *Wall Between* (1999), 347.

67. Braden interview with Pfisterer, Interview 2, 19; Hartmann, *Home Front and Beyond*, 170–74; Anne Braden, telephone conversation with author, 14 December 1998.

68. Braden interview with Pfisterer, Interview 2; Caute, *Great Fear*, 232. Note: Sentner's activism would soon be reduced to a self-defense campaign against the domestic repression of Communists.

69. Braden interview with Pfisterer, Interview 2, 20–21.

70. Ibid.; Anne Braden to Ruth Aschbacher, n.d., ca. April 1951, Box 54, Braden Papers, SHSW.

71. Braden interview with author, 7 March 1989 (Tape 1).

72. Braden telephone conversation with author, 16 December 1998.

73. For a particularly moving account of a child's suffering because of Cold War repression of Communists, see Anne Kimmage, *An Un-American Childhood* (Athens: University of Georgia Press, 1996); a more wide-ranging collective account of growing up with parents in or close to the CP is Judy Kaplan and Linn Shapiro, eds., *Red Diapers: Growing Up in the Communist Left* (Urbana: University of Illinois Press, 1998). Note: In accordance with Anne's wishes, I elected not to interview Jim or Beth Braden, but I did speak with them at length informally, and this section is informed by those conversations and by impressions offered by Anne and various family friends.

74. Braden interview with author, Mt. St. Francis, Indiana, 28 December 2001; Braden to author, 21 January 2002, copy in author's possession.

75. Spock's influence on cultural notions of child rearing is discussed by Ruth Rosen (whose conclusions differ markedly from Anne's recollections of Spock) in *World Split Open*, 14–15; Braden telephone conversation with author, 16 December 1998.

76. Intermittent correspondence in Boxes 27–30, Braden Papers, SHSW; see, for example, Gambrell McCarty to Anne Braden, 19 May 1957, Box 27, Folder 5, Braden Papers,

SHSW; for an example of comments on her nerves, see Anne Braden to Virginia Durr, 30 January 1959, Box 30, Folder 1, Braden Papers, SHSW.

77. Ibid.

78. Ibid. Sara Evans discusses Anne's influence as a role model on young women of the Student Nonviolent Coordinating Committee in *Personal Politics*, 48–50.

79. A brief discussion of Anita's death can be found in the epilogue Anne wrote for the 1999 revised edition of *The Wall Between*, in which she refers to her pain as *relentless* (p. 329).

80. Braden to author, handwritten correspondence, 30 December 2001, in author's possession.

81. Braden interview with Thrasher, Tape 7, Side 2, 211. Anne believes that her comment about women not sharing the guilt came from an Ellen Goodman column she once read.

82. Evans makes this point in *Personal Politics*, 50.

83. For more on this analysis of Baker, see Grant, *Ella Baker Freedom Bound*, 125–46.

84. Carla Wallace, interview with author, Louisville, Kentucky, 9 December 1997.

85. Grant, *Ella Baker Freedom Bound*, 125.

86. Trimberger, "Women in the Old and New Left," 433–50; Maurice Isserman, *If I Had a Hammer: The Death of the Old Left and the Birth of the New Left* (New York: Basic Books, 1987), esp. xi-xx; Evans, *Personal Politics*, 49–50; Hartmann, "Women's Employment," 84; my metaphor of Anne as a "bridge" is not to be confused with the sort of "bridge leader" Belinda Robnett describes in her *How Long? How Long? African American Women in the Civil Rights Movement* (New York: Oxford University Press, 1997). I believe that a claim can be made about Anne with respect to the typology of women leaders that Robnett outlines, but to do so is not my intent here.

87. Peggy Dennis, *Autobiography of an American Communist: A Personal View of a Political Life, 1925–75* (Berkeley, Calif.: Lawrence Hall, 1975).

Chapter 6

1. Epigraph is taken from Andrew Wade, interview with author, Louisville, Kentucky, 8 November 1989.

2. Two works that discuss the widespread acceptance of *Brown* as a watershed moment in civil rights history are John Egerton, *Speak Now*, and Patricia Sullivan, "Southern Reformers, the New Deal, and the Movement's Foundation," in *New Directions in Civil Rights Studies*, ed. Armstead Robinson and Patricia Sullivan (Charlottesville: University Press of Virginia, 1991), 81–104.

3. McElhone, "Civil Rights Activities,"18–42.

4. Scott Cummings and Michael Price, "Race Relations and Public Policy in Louisville: Historical Development of an Urban Underclass," *Journal of Black Studies* 27, no. 5 (May 1997): 621; Douglas Massey and Nancy Denton, *American Apartheid: Segregation and the Making of the Underclass* (Cambridge: Harvard University Press, 1993), 36, 188; Louisville *Courier-Journal*, 4 May 1948; Arnold Hirsch, *Making the Second Ghetto: Race and Housing in Chicago, 1940–1960* (Cambridge: Cambridge University Press, 1983), 9. Lorraine Hansberry's 1959 Broadway hit play, *A Raisin in the Sun*, poignantly highlighted the pressure on blacks to sell their houses back to whites before they could even move in.

5. Andrew E. Wade IV, "Dream House," typescript manuscript, June 1954, in Box 9, Folder 6, Braden Papers, SHSW.

6. Wade interview with author.

7. Wade, "Dream House," p. 3.

8. Ibid.; Wade interview with author.

9. Wade, "Dream House," p. 1; Louisville *Courier-Journal*, 17 May 17 1954; Braden interview with Pfisterer, Interview 3, p. 7.

10. Kenneth T. Jackson, *Crabgrass Frontier: The Suburbanization of the United States* (New York: Oxford University Press, 1985); Hirsch, *Making the Second Ghetto*, 9.

11. "Sixteen Pct. of City's Blocks Mostly Slums," news clipping, no name (probably the Louisville *Courier-Journal*), 23 February 1950, found in Box 7, Folder 1, Braden Papers,

SHSW; Louis Redding, "Louisville Travesty," pamphlet in author's possession (New York: Emergency Civil Liberties Committee, n.d.), 4–5; McElhone, "Civil Rights Activities," 119; reprint from the Louisville *Courier-Journal*, 20 February 1949, found in Box 12, Folder 10, Braden Papers, SHSW.

12. For details on the Shawnee Homeowners' Association, see Louisville *Courier-Journal*, 3 May 1950, and *Louisville Defender*, 6 May 1950; on the widespread use of "block-busting," see, for example, Chester W. Hartman, *Housing and Social Policy* (Englewood Cliffs, N.J.: Prentice-Hall, 1975), 14.

13. Anne Braden, "Church Leader in Kentucky Indicted for Sedition," *Witness* 42, no. 12 (17 February 1955): 1; Braden, *Wall Between* (1958), 3.

14. Braden interview with author, 7 March 1989 (Tape 1); "Segregated Schools Are Deplored by All Speakers at Public Hearing," Louisville *Courier-Journal*, 25 February 1954; Anne Braden to Louisville *Courier-Journal*, typescript, n.d., ca. March 1954, in Box 48, Folder 11, Braden Papers, SHSW.

15. Braden interview with Pfisterer, Interview 3, 6–7.

16. Braden, *Wall Between* (1958), 35.

17. James Nold Jr. and Julie Segal, *The Insiders' Guide to Greater Louisville* (Lexington: Lexington Herald-Leader Publications, 1985), 303; "Whites, Negroes Have Lived Together Happily in Shively Area for Years," *Louisville Defender*, 27 May 1954, in Box 10, Folder 1, Braden Papers, SHSW; Wade interview with author.

18. Braden, *Wall Between* (1958), 52–55.

19. Ibid.

20. Wade interview with author; Braden, *Wall Between* (1958), 58–59.

21. Braden, *Wall Between* (1958), 59–65; quotations drawn from Jefferson County Grand Jury Proceedings, Vol. 1, 15 to 22 September 1954, in Box 2, Folder 2, Braden Papers, SHSW.

22. Braden, *Wall Between* (1958), 62–69; "Shots, Rocks, and Burning Cross," Louisville *Courier-Journal*, 17 May 1954; Redding, *Louisville Travesty*, 9.

23. Miscellaneous articles, Louisville *Courier-Journal*, 21–22 November 1953; "The Slight Inspired a Quick Upsurge of Good Will," Louisville *Courier-Journal* editorial, 24 November 1953.

24. Louisville *Courier-Journal*, 17 May 1954.

25. Egerton, *Speak Now*, 250–51; Braden interview with the author, 7 March 1989 (Tape 1).

26. Egerton, *Speak Now*, 586–89, 606.

27. See John Lewis interview in Howell Raines, *My Soul Is Rested: Movement Days in the Deep South Remembered* (New York: Penguin, 1977), 71–73; Braden interview with Thrasher, Tape 7, Side 2, 218–19; Braden interview with Pfisterer, Interview 3, 8.

28. Fried, *McCarthyism*, 49–55; internal subversion as a theme in American history is examined in Heale, *American Anticommunism*; Caute, *Great Fear*, 38, 96; Richard Freeland, *The Truman Doctrine and the Origins of McCarthyism* (New York: Alfred A. Knopf, 1972), 359–60. As Freeland's book points out, what became known as "McCarthyism" had its origins in the early Truman administration: loyalty oaths; the association of dissent, disloyalty, and communism; and the principle of guilt by association. For a thorough study of anticommunism in popular culture, see Whitfield, *Culture of the Cold War*.

29. Clark, "Anticommunism and Segregationist Thought," 45; James Aronson, *The Press and the Cold War* (New York: Monthly Review Press, 1970), 58. On the psychological dimensions of the CP in the United States, see, for example, Vivian Gornick, *The Romance of American Communism* (New York: Basic, 1977).

30. Egerton, *Speak Now*, 603–604; the idiom "common-ism" is from Honey, *Southern Labor*, 54.

31. Numan Bartley, *The Rise of Massive Resistance: Race and Politics in the South During the 1950s* (Baton Rouge: LSU Press, 1969). Although Bartley gives only passing attention to the relationship between segregationism and anticommunism, he notes on p. 185 of his study of 1950s southern white reaction that "southern publicists blatantly asserted that the quest

for social justice and human dignity was nothing more than a foreign plot, a conspiracy dominated and directed by 'Communist' subversives"; Egerton, *Speak Now*, 614.

32. Durr, *Outside the Magic Circle*, 254–73.

33. Egerton, *Speak Now*, 613–14. A poll the *Courier-Journal* conducted that year of a dozen local children (all white) on their view of U.S. policies suggests how fully anticommunism had permeated the culture. Replies from the young respondents, who ranged in age from 5 to 14, showed an imprecise but acute awareness of Communists, spies, "reds," and the need to combat them. The report's headline read: "Statesmen Would Stop Reds by Teaming God and Annie Oakley" (see Louisville *Courier-Journal*, 12 July 1954).

34. For a fascinating summary of popular beliefs about the role of the Louisville *Courier-Journal* in the Wade incident, see George Yater, interview with author, Louisville, Kentucky, 11 December 1997; "Separate Schools Are Not Equal Schools" and "A Forced Issue Can Foil Progress," Louisville *Courier-Journal*, 18 May 1954.

35. Egerton, *Speak Now*, 615–18; Bartley, *Rise of Massive Resistance*, esp. chapters 4 and 5; Louisville's "polite racism" is discussed in Wright, *Life behind a Veil*, 4–5, 48–49.

36. "Has the Wade's *[sic]* Shively 'Dream House' Turned Out to Be a Nightmare?" *Shively Newsweek*, 20 May 1954, in Box 10, Braden Papers, SHSW; for a sampling of southern politicians' reactions to *Brown*, see, for example, Louisville *Courier-Journal*, 18 May 1954, entire front section.

37. Ibid.

38. "The Test of Democracy," *Louisville Defender*, 20 May 1954; "'We Intend to Live Here or Die Here'" *Louisville Defender*, 27 May 1954. All of these clippings are from Box 10, Braden Papers, SHSW.

39. *Louisville Defender*, 27 May 1954.

40. Braden, *Wall Between* (1958), 104–105; Eric Tachau, interview with author, Louisville, Kentucky, 12 November 1989.

41. News release, authored by "Braden," 16 June 1954, in Box 9. Folder 6, Braden Papers, SHSW; Braden, *Wall Between* (1958), 105–107; Andrew Wade to Roy Wilkins, 8 September 1956, from the personal files of Andrew Wade (hereinafter referred to as Andrew Wade files), in author's possession.

42. Typescript manuscript, n.a., no title, 25 January 1955, Andrew Wade files; the encounter between the guard and police is recounted in the *Shively Newsweek*, 8 September 1954; Edward Harding to Andrew Wade, 26 June 1954, Andrew Wade files. Note: The *Courier-Journal* letter canceling Wade's subscription was sent on the very day his house was bombed.

43. *Louisville Defender*, 20 May 1954 and 27 May 1954; Redding, *Louisville Travesty*, 9.

44. On the history of armed self-defense in African American communities, see, for example, Timothy B. Tyson, "Robert Williams, Black Power, and the Roots of the African American Freedom Struggle," *Journal of American History* 85, no. 2 (September 1998): esp. 544–46; on weaponry as discussed in the sedition trial, see, for example, Louisville *Courier-Journal*, 1 December 1954.

45. Braden, *Wall Between* (1958), 130–33.

46. Box 10, Braden Papers, SHSW, contains a wide array of clippings from all of the newspapers mentioned previously, and all of them focus on Carl Braden, Andrew Wade, or mention the wives only in relation to their husbands; Braden, *Wall Between* (1958), 73–74, 156–61.

47. Braden, *Wall Between* (1958), 116–27; Braden's comment about white integrationists can be found in her epilogue to the 1999 edition of *Wall Between*, 335; for more on the WILPF, see, for example, Catherine Foster, *Women for All Seasons: The Story of the Women's International League for Peace and Freedom* (Athens: University of Georgia Press, 1989); Anne Braden, 13 April 1955, speech on the Wade case, Madison, Wisconsin, found on Reel 1, Tape 443A, Braden Papers, SHSW.

48. Braden, *Wall Between* (1958), 73–75, 116–27; *Shively Newsweek*, 20 May 1954 and 2 June 1954, in Box 10, Braden Papers, SHSW.

49. Braden interview with Pfisterer, Interview 3, 12; "Wade Purchase a Premeditated Fraud," *Shively Newsweek*, 3 June 1954.
50. Braden, *Wall Between* (1958), 96–97.
51. Braden interview with Pfisterer, Interview 3, 12 of transcript.
52. Braden, *Wall Between* (1958), 134–36.
53. 25 January 1955 typescript, Andrew Wade files, 3–4; "Wade Case Began May 10, Moved Quickly Into Court," Louisville *Courier-Journal*, 3 October 1954; "Jurors Inspect Wade-House Damage during Silent Sight-seeing Trip," Louisville *Courier-Journal*, n.d., ca. 6 December 1954, in Wade Family Folder of Kentucky clippings file, First Floor Reference Area, Louisville Free Public Library.
54. "Do Dynamite, Hatred Make Good Neighbors?" Louisville *Courier-Journal*, 29 June 1954; more on violence to sustain residential segregation can be found in Massey and Denton, *American Apartheid*, 34–42; Hirsch, *Making the Second Ghetto*, 97–98.
55. My thinking on Louisville as a gateway was informed by Houston A. Baker Jr., "Being Framed: Afro-Modernity and Booker T. Washington in Southern Drag," paper presented at Author-Meets-Readers Workshop, University of Kentucky, 8 March 1999, Commonwealth Humanities Initiative; Louisville *Courier-Journal*, 29 June 1954; for one of the most powerful statements by the *Courier-Journal* on the value of moderate approaches to social change, see, for example, "A Forced Issue Can Foil Progress," 18 May 1954; *Louisville Defender*, 1 July 1954, in Box 12, Folder 11, Braden Papers, SHSW.
56. Braden, *Wall Between* (1958), 148–66; *Shively Newsweek*, 1 July 1954; Louisville *Courier-Journal*, 3 October 1954; "Wade Breach of Peace Charge Dropped," *Louisville Times* clipping, n.d., in Andrew Wade file.
57. Harry S. McAlpin to the Wade Defense Committee, 2 July 1954, in Box 9, Folder 6, Braden Papers, SHSW; *Shively Newsweek*, 7 July 7 1954; Louisville *Courier-Journal*, 13 December 1953; George Corderay (president of Louisville NAACP) to the Wade Defense Committee, 13 July 1954, in Box 9, Folder 6, Braden Papers, SHSW; Corderay quoted in McElhone, "Civil Rights Activities," 119. For more on the NAACP's role in the Scottsboro case, see Carter, *Scottsboro*, 53–68.
58. Braden, *Wall Between* (1958), 142–52; Heustis quoted in *Shively Newsweek*, 23 September 1954, in Box 10, Braden Papers, SHSW; Braden interview with Pfisterer, Interview 3, 14.
59. Braden, *Wall Between* (1958), 146–59.
60. Ibid., 142–65.
61. Anne Braden to Jim Dombrowski, 12 August 1954, Box 26, Folder 1, Braden Papers, SHSW; see, for example, *Shively Newsweek*, 8 July 1954 (Box 10, Braden Papers, SHSW) and 9 September 1954 (Andrew Wade files).
62. Anne Braden to Blanche Scharre, 19 September 1954, Box 26, Folder 1, Braden Papers, SHSW; Jim Stoney to Anne Braden, 5 February 1955, Box 26, Folder 2, Braden Papers, SHSW.
63. Louisville *Courier-Journal*, 31 July 1959.
64. Braden, *Wall Between* (1958), 168, 183–84.
65. Ibid., 183–84; Braden interview with Pfisterer, Interview 3, 17–19; Anne Braden's statement to the judge quoted in "Bradens Say Bomb Probe Turned Into Witch Hunt," Louisville *Courier-Journal*, 16 September 1954.
66. Braden, *Wall Between* (1958), 183–87; Hamilton quoted in *Shively Newsweek*, 23 September 1954.
67. Braden interview with Pfisterer, Interview 3, 19.
68. Ibid.; Braden, *Wall Between* (1958), 188; Louisville *Courier-Journal*, 16 September 1954; "Repercussions of Wade Case Affect the Whole Community," Louisville *Courier-Journal*, 3 October 1954.
69. "The Crime Was Bombing, Not Beliefs," Louisville *Courier-Journal* editorial, 17 September 1954.
70. Anne Braden to Mark Ethridge, 17 September 1954, in Box 11, Folder 5, Braden Papers, SHSW; Mark Ethridge to Anne Braden, 21 September 1954, Box 11, Folder 5,

Braden Papers, SHSW. Note: Anne always felt that perhaps if Ethridge had stayed, the role of the newspapers might have been different: see Braden interview with author, 7 March 1989 (Tape 1).

71. Braden interview with Pfisterer, Interview 3, 19; "Hamilton Will Try to Punish Bradens," Louisville *Courier-Journal*, 17 September 1954; Caute, *Great Fear*, 73; for details see grand jury transcript, Box 2, Folder 2, Braden Papers, SHSW; this view of Esther Handmaker was expressed by Louis Lusky in telephone interview with author; Hamilton quoted in Ione Kramer, "The Louisville Bombing," *National Guardian*, 18 October 1954

72. "Grand Jury Tells Its Story of Blast Probe," Louisville *Courier-Journal*, 2 October 1954; Braden, *Wall Between* (1958), 198–207.

73. Braden, *Wall Between* (1958), 207–208.

74. *Shively Newsweek*, 23 September 1954.

75. Untitled typescript document, summary of events in case, n.a., dated 25 January 1955, p. 11, in Box 9, Folder 6, Braden Papers, SHSW; Braden, *Wall Between* (1958), 195–98, 206; "'I'm No Red,' Magazine Publisher Tells Grand Jury in Wade Case," Louisville *Courier-Journal*, 23 September 1954.

76. Braden interview with Pfisterer, Interview 3, 19; "FBI 'May' Get Red Books Seized from Wade Witness," *Louisville Times*, 24 September 1954.

77. Louisville *Courier-Journal*, 25 September 1954, in Box 12, Folder 11, Braden Papers, SHSW; Braden, *Wall Between* (1958), 208–209.

78. Braden, *Wall Between* (1958), hymn quoted 240–41.

79. Braden interview with Pfisterer, Interview 3, 19–21.

80. "Three Witnesses in Wade Case Sent to Jail for Contempt," Louisville *Courier-Journal*, 30 September 1954.

81. Anne Braden to Anita McCarty (improperly postdated October 1954), ca. 26 September 1954, in Box 9, Folder 5, Braden Papers, SHSW; Josephine Grzelak to Anne Braden, 8 October 1954, Box 26, Folder 1, Braden Papers, SHSW.

82. Caute, *Great Fear*, 73; "At Least We Shall Soon Learn What the Evidence Is," Louisville *Courier-Journal*, 4 October 1954; " 'Bolshevik Scare' Led to Sedition Act," Louisville *Courier-Journal*, 8 October 1954; Braden interview with author, 7 March 1989 (Tape 1).

83. *Braden v. Commonwealth of Kentucky*, Brief of Appellant, Court of Appeals of Kentucky, 1955, pp. 88–89, copy in the Carl and Anne Braden Papers, #66M38, Special Collections and Archive, M. I. King Library, University of Kentucky, Lexington; "Bown Indicted in Wade Blast; He and Five Others Are Charged with Advocating Sedition," Louisville *Courier-Journal*, 2 October 1954; " 'Bolshevik Scare' Led," Louisville *Courier-Journal*, 8 October 1954.

84. "Attorneys at Frankfort Are Divided on Validity of Kentucky Sedition Law," Louisville *Courier-Journal*, 9 October 1954; Caute, *Great Fear*, 73, 217–19; "Judge Upholds Sedition Counts in Wade Case," *Louisville Times*, 22 October 1954.

85. Louisville *Courier-Journal*, 2 October 1954; Braden, *Wall Between* (1958), 211–15.

86. "Bown Indicted" and "Grand Jury Tells Its Story of Its Wade Blast Probe," Louisville *Courier-Journal*, 2 October 1954.

87. Ibid.; see also editorials of 3 October 1954, "Repercussions of Wade Case Affect Whole Community," and 4 October 1954, "At Least We Shall Soon Learn What the Evidence Is."

88. Anne Braden, press statement, 1 October 1954, in Box 9, Folder 6, Braden Papers, SHSW.

89. Anne Braden to Carl Braden, 1 October 1954, prosecutor's copy in Box 9, Folder 6, Braden Papers, SHSW; "Bradens' Home Raided; Books, Letters Seized," *Louisville Times*, 6 October 1954; "Braden Home Raided Second Time in Three Days," Louisville *Courier-Journal*, 8 October 1954; for government exhibits, see Box 2, Folder 8, Braden Papers, SHSW; see, for example, "Raiders Seize Literature at Home of Bradens," Louisville *Courier-Journal*, 6 October 1954.

90. Braden, *Wall Between* (1958), 215–30.

91. Ibid.; Anne Braden to Carl Braden, 1 October 1954, original in Box 12, Folder 11, Braden Papers, SHSW; Anne Braden explores her philosophy of life after the case in *Wall Between* (1999), 307–48.

92. Braden interview with author, 10 March 1989 (Tape 6).

93. Some of this material is taken from Braden, *Wall Between* (1958), 224–30; Anne Braden to Virginia Durr, 19 April 1959, Box 30, Folder 5, Braden Papers, SHSW; Braden interview with author, 8 March 1989 (Tape 2).

94. "You God Damn Nigger Lover," handwritten correspondence to Carl Braden, n.a., n.d., government's exhibit, in Box 7, Folder 3, Braden Papers, SHSW; Braden interview with Thrasher, Tape 8, Side 1, 228; Wade interview with author; Eric Tachau interview; Mrs. Carey Robertson, quoted in Louis Lusky, "The First Cases: Sedition and Shuffling Sam," in *The ACLU of Kentucky: 1955–1995: A Celebration*, n.a. (Madison, Wisc.: Digital Printing, 1995), 8–15; see Box 26, Folder 1, for Harriet Fitzgerald's correspondence.

95. Braden interview with author, 8 March 1989 (Tape 2).

96. Braden interview with Thrasher, Tape 8, Side 1, 230.

97. "Four Defendants in Wade Case Indicted Again," Louisville *Courier-Journal*, 5 November 1954 (it is important to note that the charges used a lowercase "c" in "communism"); see, for example, "It Takes a Trial to Acquit or Convict," Louisville *Courier-Journal*, n.d. (original clipping in author's possession); see also "Union Drops Protest of Lubka Suspension," Louisville *Courier-Journal*, 20 November 1954.

98. Braden interview with Pfisterer, Interview 3, 28; "Judge Upholds Sedition Counts in Wade Case," *Louisville Times*, 22 October 1954; "Braden Jury Chosen in 4 ½ Hours; State Starts Giving Testimony Today," Louisville *Courier-Journal*, 30 November 1954. Note: As well as defending Louise Gilbert, Zollinger was head attorney for Anne and Carl, assisted by co-counsel George Ambro, who also represented LaRue Spiker, along with Grover Sales of the American Civil Liberties Union (ACLU). The African American attorney Harry McAlpin was co-counsel for Anne, and C. Ewbank Tucker was legal counsel for Bown and Ford.

99. Ibid.; Ruth Lusky, telephone conversation with author, 19 April 1999; George Yater interview; Marjorie Yater, interview with author, Louisville, Kentucky, 11 December 1997.

100. "Hamilton Outlines Prosecution Case" and "Zollinger Makes Opening Statement in Defense of Carl Braden," both in Louisville *Courier-Journal*, 1 December 1954.

101. Braden, *Wall Between* (1958), 247–79; see also, for example, "Undercover Agent Tells Braden Jury of Joining Reds," Louisville *Courier-Journal*, 1 December 1954.

102. Ibid. Manning Johnson's indictments of groups like the Southern Regional Council and NAACP are enumerated in M. J. Heale, *McCarthy's Americans: Red Scare Politics in State and Nation, 1935–1965* (Athens: University of Georgia Press, 1998), 261.

103. "Braden Asserts He's Studied Communists but Never Was One," Louisville *Courier-Journal*, 10 December 1954; Braden interview with author, 8–9 March 1989 (Tape 3).

104. Braden, *Wall Between* (1958), 244; Braden interview with author, 7 March 1989 (Tape 1).

105. "3 Witnesses Tell of Openly Buying Red Constitutions," Louisville *Courier-Journal*, 11 December 1954.

106. Miscellaneous articles, especially "Letter Put Into Evidence," Louisville *Courier-Journal*, 3 December 1954.

107. Louis Lusky telephone interview.

108. Braden interview with author, 8 March 1989 (Tape 2).

109. Louisville *Courier-Journal*, 8–11 December 1954.

110. "Undercover Woman for FBI Says Carl and Anne Braden in Communist Cells Here" and "Braden's Counsel Sums Up Defense's Case," both in Louisville *Courier-Journal*, 14 December 1954. (Mickey Spillane's enormously popular novels of this era often featured the detective Mike Hammer tracking and killing Communist spies: see Whitfield, *Culture of the Cold War*, 34–37.)

111. Ibid.

112. Ibid.
113. Louis Lusky telephone interview; Fried, *McCarthyism*, 188–90; "Braden Gets 15 Years, Fine of $5000 in Sedition Case: Lawyer to Seek New Trial," Louisville *Courier-Journal*, 14 December 1954; Anne Braden to Bill of Rights Fund, n.d., ca. 1954, Box 9, Folder 5, Braden Papers, SHSW; Braden, *Wall Between* (1958), 271.

Chapter 7

1. The epigraph is taken from E. L. Doctorow, *The Book of Daniel* (New York: Random House, 1971), 118.
2. Braden interview with Thrasher, Tape 8, Side 1, 237–41.
3. Braden, speech to State Historical Society of Wisconsin, 13 April 1955; various clippings, in Wade Case "Letters to the Editor" Folder, Anne Braden's personal files, in author's possession.
4. On the threat of Communist spies, see, for a more left-leaning analysis, Kenneth O'Reilly, "Liberal Values, the Cold War, and American Intellectuals: The Trauma of the Alger Hiss Case, 1950–1978," in *Beyond the Hiss Case: The FBI, the Congress, and the Cold War*, ed. Athan G. Theoharis (Philadelphia: Temple University Press, 1982), 309–40, and Ellen Schrecker, "Before the Rosenbergs: Espionage Scenarios in the Early Cold War," in *Secret Agents: The Rosenberg Case, McCarthyism, and Fifties America*, ed. Marjorie Garber and Rebecca L. Walkowitz (New York: Routledge, 1995), 126–41. A more conservative view of these types of cases can be found in Harvey Klehr, John Earl Haynes, and F. I. Firsov, *The Secret World of American Communism* (New Haven, Conn.: Yale University Press, 1995) and in Harvey Klehr, John E. Hayes, and K. M. Anderson, *The Soviet World of American Communism* (New Haven, Conn.: Yale University Press, 1998); "Incident That Shook a City," *U.S. News and World Report*, 31 December 1954, 37–40; "Sedition on the Copy Desk," *Time*, 27 December 1954, n.p., in Anne McCarty alumna file, Randolph-Macon Woman's College. Wayne Clark's dissertation, "Anticommunism and Segregationist Thought" (especially pp. 14–20), remains, from my perspective, the most penetrating analysis of the twinning of segregationist and anticommunist ideologies in mid-twentieth-century southern intellectual history.
5. Fried's documentary history of the era, *McCathyism*, is an example of a text that focuses on Hollywood as the primary site for the investigative committee hearings; quotation from the "Southern Manifesto" is taken from the *Congressional Record*, 84th Congress, 2nd session, 1956, 4460; Anne Braden, *House Un-American Activities Committee: Bulwark of Segregation* (Los Angeles: National Committee to Abolish the House Un-American Activities Committee, 1963), 25–30. Wayne Clark makes a compelling argument for the adoption by southern politicians of a McCarthyist approach to curbing southern integrationists in his "Anticommunism and Segregationist Thought," especially chap. 2. These state committees had a variety of titles, ranging from the Committee on Offenses against the Administration of Justice in Virginia to what became known as the Sovereignty Commission in Mississippi.
6. Louisville *Courier-Journal*, 18 January 1955, and 22 January 1955; Louis Lusky telephone interview; Louisville *Courier-Journal*, 9 February 1955; Braden interview with author, 7 March 1989 (Tape 1).
7. Louisville *Courier-Journal*, 21 January 1955, 17 February 1955, and 23 February 1955.
8. Braden interview with Thrasher, Tape 8, Side 1, 237–45 (includes Lusky's words to her).
9. Braden, *Wall Between* (1958), 272–77.
10. Anne Braden to Wilfred Myll, 4 April 1955, in Box 26, Folder 3, Braden Papers, SHSW.
11. Braden interview with Pfisterer, Interview 3, 22–23.
12. Anne Braden to Carl Braden, 14 April 1955, and miscellaneous correspondence in Box 11, Folder 5, Braden Papers, SHSW; Carl Braden to Anne Braden, 24 December 1954, Box 11, Folder 4, Braden Papers, SHSW.

13. Anne's reflections on her mood swings can be found in Anne Braden to Carl Braden, 17 June 1955, in Box 11, Folder 5, Braden Papers, SHSW.

14. This statement is referred to in Al Maund to Anne Braden, 14 October 1954, Box 26, Folder 1, Braden Papers, SHSW; more on their strategy is found in Braden interview with Thrasher, Tape 8, Side 1, 238; Anne Braden to Howard Melish, 23 February 1955, in Box 26, Folder 3, Braden Papers, SHSW; Anne's words are from Braden interview with Pfisterer, Interview 3, 24–25, 30, and from Braden to author, 30 December 2001, in author's possession.

15. For the various trial delays, see Louisville *Courier-Journal*, 5 January 1955; 7 January 1955, 12 March 1955, 15 March 1955, 7 April 1955, on Hamilton and the postponements, see also Braden interview with Thrasher, Tape 8, Side 1, 233; Anne's remarks are from her interview with Pfisterer, Interview 3, 28–29.

16. Braden interview with Thrasher, Tape 8, Side 1, 24.

17. Belfrage and Aronson, *Something to Guard*, 8; the "bit too red" quip was made by Josiah Gitt, publisher of the *Gazette and Daily News*, quoted in Belfrage and Aronson, *Something to Guard*, 16; see, for example, *National Guardian*, 28 October 1954; 29 November 1954; 13 December 1954; 27 December 1954; 24 January 1955.

18. Carl Braden to James Dombrowski, February 1953, in Box 48, Folder 11, Braden Papers, SHSW.

19. On SCEF, see Klibaner, *Conscience of a Troubled South*, especially 79–84, on 1954 Eastland hearings; quote is from Sarah Hart Brown, *Standing against Dragons: Three Southern Lawyers in an Era of Fear* (Baton Rouge: LSU Press, 1998), 14.

20. *Southern Patriot*, June–December 1954; Braden interview with author, 8 March 1989 (Tape 2); Jim Dombrowski to Anne Braden, 20 December 1954, in Box 26, Folder 1, Braden Papers, SHSW; for more on Dombrowski, see Frank T. Adams, *James A. Dombrowski, An American Heretic, 1897–1983* (Knoxville: University of Tennessee Press, 1992); descriptions of Dombrowski as a "saint" are found in Brown, *Standing against Dragons*, 67 n. 20.

21. See, for example, Louise Gilbert to Fellow Social Workers, 18 May 1955, in Box 9, Folder 7, Braden Papers, SHSW, and Louise Gilbert to "Dear Friends," 15 January 1957, in Box 27, Folder 4, Braden Papers, SHSW; for more on union supporters, see various documents in Box 26, Folder 4, Braden Papers, SHSW.

22. Anne Braden, interview with author, Louisville, Kentucky, 17 June 1999.

23. Ibid.; see, for example, Gov. Lawrence Wetherby to William Nixon, 13 April 1955, in Box 26, Folder 4, Braden Papers, SHSW; more on this group is also found in Braden interview with Pfisterer, Interview 3, 30.

24. See, for example, Anne McCarty, '45, R-MWC Alumnae File; for more on reactions to Anne among those at R-MWC, see, for example, Anne Braden to Dot Silver, 9 January 1960, in Box 32, Folder 4, Braden Papers, SHSW; Anne's last sedition-era contact with the group appears to have been in Anne Braden to Blanche Scharre, 19 September 1954, in Box 26, Folder 1, Braden Papers, SHSW; on her reconciliation with the R-MWC group in Louisville, see Anne Braden to Mrs. Wilson Wyatt, 19 November 1958, in Box 29, Folder 4, Braden Papers, SHSW.

25. Braden interview with author, 17 June 1999.

26. See, for example, Louisville Defendants to "Dear Friend," 24 September 1956, in Box 9, Folder 7, Braden Papers, SHSW; Braden telephone conversation with author, 14 December 1998.

27. See Box 27, Folder 1, for various references to Wade's and the defendants' travels throughout early 1956.

28. *Louisville Defender*, 16 December 1954, and 13 January 1955; "Cross Burners in Wade Case," Louisville *Courier-Journal*, 10 March 1955.

29. Brown, *Standing against Dragons*, 24 n. 41; Jessie Lloyd O'Connor, Harvey O'Connor, and Susan M. Bowles, *Harvey and Jessie: A Couple of Radicals* (Philadelphia: Temple University Press, 1988), 244–51; Jerold Simmons, "The Origins of the Campaign to Abol-

ish HUAC, 1956–1961, the California Connection," *Southern California Quarterly* 64, no. 2 (1982): 141–59.

30. Simmons, "Origins of the Campaign to Abolish HUAC": 144; Brown, *Standing against Dragons*, 24 n.41.

31. On Bill of Rights Fund allotments to the Bradens, see, for example, various correspondences, Box 26, Folder 5, Braden Papers, SHSW.

32. See Box 26, various folders, for correspondence between Anne Braden and Clark Foreman throughout 1955; for more detail on Foreman, see Sullivan, *Days of Hope*, 25–26, 273–74; see Redding, *Louisville Travesty.*

33. For more on this dispute in the sedition case and on Anne's role in soothing it, see, for example, Anne Braden to Clark Foreman, 1 July 1955, in Box 9, Folder 3, and Anne Braden to Arthur Kling, 14 March 1956, both in Box 26, Folder 6, Braden Papers, SHSW (Anne Braden quoted comment is in the letter to Kling).

34. Beth Taylor, "Little Compton's Gentle Radicals," *Providence [R. I.] Sunday Journal,* 8 February 1981, 8–13.

35. Ibid.

36. Jennings Perry, "Sedition in Louisville: The Braden Affair," *Nation,* 15 January 1955: n.p., clipping in Andrew Wade files, in author's possession; Millis, "Louisville's Braden Case," 393–98 (quote on 397); see also Anne Braden, letter to the editor, *Nation,* n.d., copy in Box 26, Folder 3, Braden Papers, SHSW; Al Maund to editors, *Nation,* 4 May 1955, typescript copy in Box 26, Folder 3, Braden Papers, SHSW; "The Dynamite Was Fear," editorial, *Nation,* 8 December 1956: 490.

37. For more on Carl's application to the SP, see Dave McReynolds to Carl Braden, 25 March 1956, in Box 26, Folder 6, Braden Papers, SHSW.

38. I. F. Stone, "Carl Braden Convicted—Nightmare in Louisville," *I. F. Stone's Weekly,* 20 December 1954.

39. Braden interview with Thrasher, Tape 8, Side 2, 240–41; see, for example, I. F. Stone, *The Haunted Fifties* (New York: Random House, 1963), 235–38 (his quote on 238).

40. Smith, *Killers of the Dream;* Katharine DuPre Lumpkin, *The Making of a Southerner* (New York: Alfred A. Knopf, 1947); also Will Campbell, *Brother to a Dragonfly* (New York: Seabury, 1977). A thorough examination of southern white autobiography on race is Fred Hobson's *But Now I See: The White Southern Racial Conversion Narrative* (Baton Rouge: LSU Press, 1999).

41. Anne Braden, "Church Leader," copy in Box 12, Folder 10, Braden Papers, SHSW.

42. William Howard Melish, *When Christians Become Subversive* (New York: Episcopal League for Social Action, 1955); Klibaner, *Conscience of a Troubled South,* 153–54; Angela Davis, *Angela Davis: An Autobiography* (New York: Bantam, 1974), 104–15.

43. Albert Dalton to W. H. Melish, 17 February 1955, Box 9, Folder 1, Braden Papers, SHSW; reference to Marmion's position can be found in James Stoney to Anne Braden, 5 February 1955, in Box 26, Folder 6, Braden Papers, SHSW.

44. See, for example, *Anniston Star,* 19 November 1956 and 21 November 1956, clippings in Box 10, Folder 1, Braden Papers, SHSW; Allen Draper and Elise Ayers Sanguinetti, conversations with author, 14 June 1989.

45. Anita Crabbe McCarty to the editor, Louisville *Courier-Journal,* 27 March 1955; Anita McCarty to "Elizabeth and Gracean," n.d., ca. August 1955, Box 26, Folder 4, Braden Papers, SHSW; E. L. Turner to A. Scott Hamilton, 22 February 1955, and Scott Hamilton to E. L. Turner, n.d., both in Box 9, Folder 6, Braden Papers, SHSW.

46. For more details on the bond, see Clark Foreman to Anne Braden, 18 May 1955, in Box 26, Folder 3, Braden Papers, SHSW; on the Barnetts, see Anne Braden to Clark Foreman, 5 July 1955, in Box 26, Folder 3, Braden Papers, SHSW; Anne Braden, "Dear Friend" letter, 1 June 1955, Box 8, Folder 7, Braden Papers, SHSW; Walter Offutt Jr. to Anne Braden, 13 July 1955, Box 26, Folder 3, Braden Papers, SHSW; Braden interview with Thrasher, Tape 8, Side 1, 237–38.

47. "Requested Portion of Narration on Braden Film from WHAS-TV," n.a., 12 July 1955, in Box 26, Folder 3, Braden Papers, SHSW; "Braden out of Prison on $40,000 Bond," *Louisville Times*, 13 July 1955; Braden telephone conversation with author, 14 December 1998.

48. Braden interview with author, 17 June 1999; on one instance when they brought their eldest child along, see, for example, Anne Braden to Clark Foreman, 19 March 1956, in Box 26, Folder 6, Braden Papers, SHSW.

49. "Trial Transcript of Carl Braden Given to Counsel," Louisville *Courier-Journal*, 6 August 1955; on fundraising to send out the brief, see, for example, Anne Braden to Arthur Kling, 14 March 1956, in Box 26, Folder 6, Braden Papers, SHSW; *American Civil Liberties Union Weekly Bulletin* 1731, 2 January 1956, 1, in Box 26, Folder 6, Braden Papers, SHSW; "Braden Joins Pennsylvania Red Attacking State Anti-sedition Laws," Louisville *Courier-Journal*, 5 November 1955; press release, n.a., n.d., on Donner brief in Box 26, Folder 4, Braden Papers, SHSW; "Carl Braden Is Likely to Gain Freedom," Louisville *Courier-Journal*, 3 April 1956; Klibaner, *Conscience of a Troubled South*, 142.

50. Federal Bureau of Investigation, Anne Braden subject file, Louisville field report, "Anne Braden, was," 13 February–20 February 1956, p. 4, in author's possession.

51. For more on this trip, see Braden interview with Thrasher, Tape 8, Side 2, 242–44 (quoted material also from this interview).

52. For more on Californians' work against anticommunist prosecutions, see, for example, Simmons, "Origins of the Campaign": 141–59; for more on Anne's comments about civil liberties in the civil rights movement, see Anne Braden, "A View from the Fringes," *Southern Exposure* 9, no. 1 (spring 1981): 68–73.

53. See, for example, Anne Braden to Clark Foreman, 19 March 1956; appeals brief quoted in "Braden Appeals, Calls Law Unconstitutional," *Louisville Times*, 10 December 1955.

54. The figure of 30,000 represents an internal estimate given for the early 1950s in Steve Nelson, James R. Barrett, and Rob Ruck, *Steve Nelson, American Radical* (Pittsburgh: University of Pittsburgh Press, 1981), 319; the number 5,000 for 1956 is from Stephen J. Whitfield, "Civil Liberties and the Culture of the Cold War," in *Crucible of Liberty: Two Hundred Years of the Bill of Rights* (New York: Free Press, 1991), 60; the earlier peak figure is found in Schrecker, *Many Are the Crimes* (the quote is taken from p. 144); for more on Nelson and his multiple prosecutions, see Schrecker, *Many Are the Crimes*, 126–27.

55. Anne Braden, interview with Bud and Ruth Schultz, 2 September 1984, 23–24 of transcript.

56. "Braden May Go Free as High Court Voids State Sedition Laws," Louisville *Courier-Journal*, 3 April 1956; "Robsion Asks Indictment of Braden Under U.S. Act," Louisville *Courier-Journal*, 4 April 1956. (Note: Smith Act indictments could be entered only by action from the U.S. Department of Justice.)

57. "Carl Braden's Conviction Is Reversed," Louisville *Courier-Journal*, 23 June 1956; "Court Refuses to Free Six in Braden Case," *Louisville Times*, 28 August 1956. Rhine was fired from his job as representative of the United Furniture Workers and was later called for questioning by HUAC in Washington and by the FBI in Louisville; for more on Rhine's case, see "The Ordeal of Henry Rhine in Louisville, KY," n.a., *The Southern Newsletter* 2, no. 2 (February 1957), 4–6, in Box 5, Braden Papers, UT.

58. Carl Braden to Barry Bingham, 22 June 1956; Barry Bingham to Carl Braden, 26 June 1956; Carl Braden to Barry Bingham, 4 July 1956; Barry Bingham to Carl Braden, 21 July 1956; all in Box 9, Folder 3, Braden Papers, SHSW; "The Crime was Bombing, Not Beliefs," Louisville *Courier-Journal*, 17 September 1954.

59. *Louisville Times* editorial, 3 March 1956, in Box 12, Folder 10, Braden Papers, SHSW.

60. Charlotte Wade to Anne and Carl Braden, 16 July 1956, in Box 27, Folder 2, Braden Papers, SHSW; Louisville Defendants to "Dear Friend," 24 September 1956, in Box 9, Folder 7, Braden Papers, SHSW; Louisville Defendants, news release, 20 November 1956, in Box 5, Braden Papers, UT; "All Counts Dismissed against Braden and Six Others on Motion by State," Louisville *Courier-Journal*, 21 November 1956; on Hamilton's death, see "Hamilton Called Man of Bulldog Tenacity," Louisville *Courier-Journal*, 31 July 1959.

61. For more on this subject, see, for example, Phillip Jenkins, *The Cold War at Home* (Chapel Hill: University of North Carolina Press, 1999).
62. "Southern Manifesto" is taken from the *Congressional Record*, 84th Congress, 2nd session, 1956, 4460.
63. Membership figures are drawn from Numan Bartley, *Rise of Massive Resistance*, 84 n. 4; Payne, *I've Got the Light of Freedom*, 34–35; James Graham Cook, *The Segregationists: A Penetrating Study of the Men and the Organizations Active in the South's Fight against Integration* (New York: Appleton-Century-Crofts, 1962), 18.
64. "Prosegregation Council Formed in Jessamine," Louisville *Courier-Journal*, 19 September 1956.
65. For an insider's sentimentalized treatment of school desegregation in Louisville that nevertheless verifies its relative success, see Omer Carmichael and Weldon James, *The Louisville Story* (New York: Simon & Schuster, 1957); Louisville Defendants to "Dear Friend," 24 September 1956.
66. Eric Tachau interview.
67. Walter Millis, "Louisville's Braden Case: A Test of Basic Rights," *Nation*, 7 May 1955: 393; Doctorow, *Book of Daniel*, 154.
68. Braden interview with Hogan, 7 December 1978, Interview 2, 105, CUOHROC. On racial violence in this context, see Meyer, *As Long As They Don't Move*, or Massey and Denton, *American Apartheid*.
69. News release, Wade Defense Committee, 15 November 1957, in Box 5, Braden Papers, UT; Louisville Defendants to "Dear Friend," 24 September 1956. For discussion of being a "case," see Anne Braden to Wilfred Myll, 4 April 1955, in Box 26, Folder 3, Braden Papers, SHSW.
70. Anne Braden, interview with author, Louisville, Kentucky, 3 June 1997. On Ahearn, see "Mrs. Ahearn Testifies at Capital Hearing," Louisville *Courier-Journal*, 8 April 1956; "Kentuckians See Void in U.S. Security," *Louisville Times*, 28 October 1957; "Star of Braden Sedition Trial Ended Life as Recluse," Louisville *Courier-Journal*, 15 April 1995.
71. Sullivan, *Days of Hope*, especially 249–75; Egerton, *Speak Now*, 448–60, 553–72.

Chapter 8

1. The epigraph is taken from Jack Peebles, "Subversion and the Southern Conference Educational Fund" (M.A. thesis, Louisiana State University at New Orleans, 1970), 33.
2. Braden interview with Hogan, 7 December 1978, Interview 2, 59, CUOHROC (Hogan material rearranged somewhat from original).
3. Braden telephone conversation with author, 16 December 1998; for more on the Bradens' finances at the end of the sedition case, see, for example, Carl and Anne Braden to "Dear _____," 19 January 1957, in Box 9, Folder 3, Braden Papers, SHSW; Braden interview with author, 17 June 1999.
4. "American Civil Liberties Union Opens Campaign to Form Ky. Chapter," Louisville *Courier-Journal*, 23 May 1955; for more on Braden case as basis for KCLU, see, for example, "For Saints or Sinners," *Louisville Times*, 31 March 1960; Braden interview with author, 11 March 1989 (Tape 7); on Kling's portrayal of the Bradens, see, for example, Anne Braden to Arthur Kling, 14 March 1956, and Kling's reply, 15 March 1956, as well as Arthur Kling to Alan Reitman, 6 March 1956, all in Box 26, Folder 6, Braden Papers, SHSW.
5. Pay stub, Swango Services, n.d., in Box 27, Folder 4, Braden Papers, SHSW; Braden interview with Hogan, 23 June 1972, Interview 1, 39–40, CUOHROC.
6. Earl Dearing to Carl Braden, 19 March 1957, Box 27 Folder 6, Braden Papers, SHSW; Anne Braden to Earl Dearing, 20 March 1957, Box 27, Folder 6, Braden Papers, SHSW; Suzanne Post, interview with author, Louisville, Kentucky, 27 June 1991; Braden interview with author, 3 June 1997.

7. Whitfield, "Civil Liberties and Culture of Cold War," 61; Klibaner, *Conscience of a Troubled South*, 142. A more thorough account of the Supreme Court's actions in this period can be found in Arthur Sabin, *In Calmer Times: The Supreme Court and Red Monday* (Philadelphia: University of Pennsylvania Press, 1999).

8. O'Reilly, *Hoover and the Un-Americans*, 262; Jerold Simmons, "Origins of Campaign to Abolish HUAC": 142–45; on Anne's impressions of Wilkinson, see her interview with Schultz, 2 September 1984, Interview 2, 48.

9. This description of southern anticommunism was borrowed from Egerton, *Speak Now*, 441; Carl's comment on male supremacy is referred to in Harvey O'Connor to Carl Braden, 6 April 1957, in Box 49, Folder 13, Braden Papers, SHSW; Carl's comments are quoted in Harvey O'Connor to Anne Braden, 14 April 1957, Box 49, Folder 4, Braden Papers, SHSW.

10. Harvey O'Connor to Anne Braden, 12 April 1957, in Box 49, Folder 4, Braden Papers, SHSW; Braden to author, "Feminism and My Relation."

11. On her feelings about Louisville, see Anne Braden to Carl Braden, 23 June 1955, in Box 11, Folder 5, Braden Papers, SHSW; Braden interview with Thrasher, Tape 9, Side 1, 268–69, and Tape 10, Side 1, 287.

12. Williams quoted in Klibaner, *Conscience of a Troubled South*, 149.

13. Ibid., 120, for more on SCEF and hiring; Dombrowski quoted in Al Maund to Anne and Carl Braden, August 1957, Box 27, Folder 6, Braden Papers, SHSW.

14. On SCEF and charges of communism, see, for example, Reed, *Simple Decency*, esp. 163–84; Salmond, *Southern Rebel*, 223; for more on Aubrey Williams's anticommunism, see Virginia Durr to Anne Braden, 12 August 1959, in Box 31, Folder 4, Braden Papers, SHSW; Sosna, *In Search of the Silent South*, 169–70.

15. Salmond, *Southern Rebel*, 264–65.

16. For more on Dombrowski, see Adams, *American Heretic*.

17. For more history on both SCHW and SCEF, see Reed, *Simple Decency*; also see Anne's comments in her interview with Hogan, 7 December 1978, Interview 2, 99–100, CUOHROC.

18. The description of liberalism here is taken from Randall Patton, "The CIO and the Search for a Silent South," *Maryland Historian* 19, no. 2 (1988): 13; Sosna's *In Search of the Silent South*, especially pp. 140–71, offers a comparison of the SRC with both of the southern conference groups (Aubrey Williams's remark is taken from 169); on the SRC with regard to segregation and anticommunism, see also Egerton, *Speak Now*, 564–65, 571–72.

19. Aldon Morris, *The Origins of the Civil Rights Movement: Black Communities Organizing for Change* (New York: Free Press, 1984), 169; on Communists in SCEF, see Anne Braden to Virginia Durr, 9 August 1959, in Box 31, Folder 9, Braden Papers, SHSW; for more on segregationist publications, see Cook, *Segregationists*; on SCEF visibility, see Anne Braden's comments in Morris, *Origins*, 171, as well as Reed, *Simple Decency*, 240 n. 36; for more history of SCEF and subversion, see Klibaner, *Conscience of a Troubled South*, esp. chaps. 5, 8.

20. Salmond, *Southern Rebel*, 248; Reed, *Simple Decency*, 240 n. 36.

21. Braden interview with Thrasher, Tape 9, Side 2, 273; a similar version of this story is in Braden interview with Hogan, 23 September 1972, 48, CUOHROC.

22. Braden interview with Thrasher, Tape 9, Side 2, 273.

23. For more on Shuttlesworth, see, for instance, Raines, *My Soul Is Rested*, 139–61; see also Andrew Manis, *A Fire You Can't Put Out: The Civil Rights Life of Birmingham's Reverend Fred Shuttlesworth* (Tuscaloosa: University of Alabama Press, 1999); Reed, *Simple Decency*, 176–77; Fred Shuttlesworth, interview with author, Cincinnati, Ohio, 6 December 1997.

24. Memo, n.d., Carl and Anne Braden to Jim Dombrowski and Aubrey Williams, Box 27, Folder 5, Braden Papers, SHSW; insurance policy, 17 October 1957, in Box 2, Braden Papers, UT.

25. Braden interview with author, 3 June 1997.

26. Anne's comments are from Morris, *Origins*, 171; the "pall" comment can be found in Braden interview with Thrasher, Tape 11, Side 2, 374; for one historical treatment of the southern conference movement, see Reed, *Simple Decency;* for more on Anne's vision, see, especially, Braden interview with Thrasher, Tape 11, Side 1, 326–27.

27. Carl and Anne Braden, "Field Secretaries' Report to Officers, Board, and Advisory Committee of the Southern Conference Educational Fund on Partial Survey of Situation in the Southern States and D.C.—August 1958," n.d., in Anne Braden personal files, in author's possession; quotes are from memo, Carl and Anne Braden to Jim Dombrowski and Aubrey Williams, n.d., p. 1, in Box 22, Folder 4, Braden Papers, SHSW.

28. Carl and Anne Braden, "Field Secretaries' Report," pp. 3, 9–10.

29. Anne Braden, "Race Relations in the Southern United States," typescript manuscript to *Race Relations Journal*, 25 February 1959, in Box 30, Folder 3, Braden Papers, SHSW; Anne Braden to Edith [Tyra], 22 June 1958, in Box 28, Folder 7, Braden Papers, SHSW; for more of Anne's views on an independent black movement, see interview with Thrasher, Tape 10, Side 1, 291.

30. Memo, Carl and Anne Braden to Jim Dombrowski and Aubrey Williams, n.d., p. 6, in Box 22, Folder 4, Braden Papers, SHSW; for more on Anne's views on this subject, see Braden, *Wall Between* (1958), 29–30.

31. Those exceptions are examined in Kelley, *Hammer and Hoe;* Braden interview with Thrasher, Tape 10, Side 1, 290.

32. For more on the conference, see Klibaner, *Conscience of a Troubled South*, 130–31.

33. Memo, n.d., Carl and Anne Braden to Jim Dombrowski and Aubrey Williams, in Box 27, Folder 5, Braden Papers, SHSW.

34. Braden interview with Thrasher, Tape 11, Side 1, 336–37.

35. Anne Braden to Virginia Durr, 19 April 1959, Box 30, Folder 5, Braden Papers, SHSW.

36. U.S. Naval Intelligence, Investigative Report #32E-6: JMC:GY, 24 October 1955; see also A. B. Caruso, U.S. Navy captain, to William Allison, 16 February 1977. Copies of both of these documents are in folder marked "Anne's FBI Files," in Anne Braden personal files, in author's possession.

37. Anne Braden to author, 30 December 2001, in author's possession.

38. Anne Braden to Anita and Gambrell McCarty, n.d. except "Thursday" and hand marked (incorrectly) "1955," in Box 21, Folder 10, Braden Papers, SHSW; Anita McCarty to Anne Braden, n.d., ca. April 1958, in Box 28, Folder 2, Braden Papers, SHSW.

39. For more on the conflicts between Anne and the McCartys, see intermittent correspondence, Boxes 27–30, Braden Papers, SHSW; Anne Braden to Anita McCarty, 8 January 1959, in Box 30, Folder 1, Braden Papers, SHSW.

40. Anne Braden to Sarah Otto, 5 May 1959, Box 31, Folder 1, Braden Papers, SHSW.

41. On Gambrell McCarty's vow, see Braden, *Wall Between* (1958), 227; Anne Braden to Anita and Gambrell McCarty, n.d., "Thursday," in Box 21, Folder 10, Braden Papers, SHSW.

42. Carl Braden to E. D. Nixon, 29 August 1957, Box 27, Folder 6, Braden Papers, SHSW; Aubrey Williams to Carl Braden, 31 October 1957, Box 27, Folder 7, Braden Papers, SHSW; Carl Braden to Aubrey Williams and Jim Dombrowski, 12 January 1958, Box 28, Folder 1, Braden Papers, SHSW.

43. Klibaner, *Conscience of a Troubled South*, 122.

44. Braden interview with Thrasher, Tape 11, Side 1, 345–48.

45. King quoted in Klibaner, *Conscience of a Troubled South*, 167; for more on King's travails with the Kennedy administration over the left-wing affiliations of some of his closest associates, see Branch, *Parting the Waters*, esp. 208–12 and 850–51.

46. Braden interview with Thrasher, Tape 10, Side 2, 303, Grant, *Ella Baker Freedom Bound*, 105–106, 155–56; for more on the hearing, see, for example, SCEF news release, 14 January 1960, in Box 32, Folder 4, Braden Papers, SHSW; Klibaner, *Conscience of a Troubled South*, 168.

47. Braden interview with author, 3 June 1997.
48. Braden telephone conversation with author, 13 June 1999; Braden interview with author, 3 June 1997.
49. Braden interview with author, 3 June 1997.
50. Jim Dombrowski to Anne Braden, 22 July 1957, Box 27, Folder 6, Braden Papers, SHSW; see also Morris, *Origins*, 171; the analytical role of the *Patriot* was suggested to me by Julian Bond.
51. For more on SCEF's relations with black newspapers in this era, see, for example, Carl Braden to Jim Dombrowski, 26 April 1959, in Box 30, Folder 5, Braden Papers, SHSW. Quote is from Braden interview with Hogan, 7 December 1978, Interview 2, 126, CUOHROC.
52. Adams, *James Dombrowski*, 242; Fred Shuttlesworth quoted in Morris, *Origins*, 171; Braden interview with Hogan, 7 December 1978, Interview 2, 126, CUOHROC.
53. Braden interview with Thrasher, Tape 10, Side 2, 301; for more on the Birmingham pamphlet, see Anne Braden to Fred Shuttlesworth, 18 July 1959, in Box 47, Folder 14, Braden Papers, SHSW.
54. Carl Braden to I. F. Stone, 7 October 1957, in Box 27, Folder 7, Braden Papers, SHSW; Anne Braden to the editors, *National Guardian*, 3 September 1958, in Box 28, Folder 9, Braden Papers, SHSW; Virginia Durr to Anne Braden, 11 December 1958, in Box 29, Folder 5, Braden Papers, SHSW. More on Montgomery white women's interracialism can be found in miscellaneous correspondence between Anne Braden and Olive Andrews in Olive Andrews Papers, Alabama Department of Archives and History, Montgomery.
55. Braden interview with author, 17 June 1999; Braden interview with Thrasher, Tape 11, Side 2, 365.
56. Juliette Morgan to James Dombrowski, 8 July 1952, in Box 56, Folder 7, Braden Papers, SHSW; *Southern Patriot*, May 1960.
57. Anne Braden to Virginia Durr, 19 April 1959, in Box 30, Folder 5, Braden Papers, SHSW.
58. Ibid.; see also miscellaneous correspondence on this subject in Boxes 30, 31, and 56, Braden Papers, SHSW.
59. Bartley's *Rise of Massive Resistance* examines these developments; a thorough treatment of events surrounding the *Brown* decision and subsequent school desegregation battles can be found in Richard Kluger, *Simple Justice: The History of* Brown v. Board of Education *and Black America's Struggle for Equality* (New York: Vintage, 1975).
60. Anne Braden, typescript article, no title, in Box 27, Folder 3, Braden Papers, SHSW.
61. *Southern Patriot*, December 1956; "How Whites in One Town Defeated a School Boycott," *National Guardian*, 17 December 1956, 3; Braden interview with author, 3 June 1997; see, for example, *Southern Patriot*, December 1957.
62. See Anne Braden to Septima Clark, 25 October 1957, and Septima Clark to Anne Braden, 30 October 1957, both in Box 27, Folder 7, Braden Papers, SHSW; Septima Clark to Anne Braden, July 1984, in "Braden's 60th Birthday" Folder, Anne Braden personal files, in author's possession.
63. Anne Braden to Septima Clark, 25 October 1957, in Box 27, Folder 7, Braden Papers, SHSW; Anne's views on teacher integration are detailed in Anne Braden to Jim Dombrowski, 23 November 1958, in Box 29, Folder 4, Braden Papers, SHSW.
64. See miscellaneous materials on the Virginia Avenue PTA in Box 12, Folder 6, Braden Papers, SHSW; see also Carl Braden, "Little Jimmy Braden Gets a Lesson on Rights," *National Guardian*, 24 March 1958, 6.
65. Both historians of SCEF, while lauding the group for its "idealism" and campaigns of "public awareness," have concluded that it was of limited effectiveness in the 1940s through the 1960s. Klibaner, in *Conscience of a Troubled South*, focuses on SCEF's idealism and militancy but concludes (p. 240) that the organization was "marginal"; in *Simple Decency*, Linda Reed emphasizes SCEF idealism and its work promoting public awareness, concluding (pp. 188–89) that SCEF played "major supportive roles" to the emerging African American movement, which deserves the bulk of the credit for civil rights breakthroughs of the 1960s; see Morris, *Origins*, chap. 7.

66. Braden interview with author, 3 June 1997.

67. Jerry Thornbery, "Amzie Moore and His Civil Rights Allies, 1951–1960," paper read at the Southern Historical Association, Orlando, Florida, 12 November 1993 (copy in author's possession).

68. Ibid., 11–12.

69. Moore's importance is explained in Payne, *I've Got the Light of Freedom*, 29–33.

70. Klibaner, *Conscience of a Troubled South*, 171, 194–95.

71. Jerry Thornbery, "Operation Freedom and the Mississippi Movement," paper read at the Organization of American Historians, Chicago, Illinois, 29 March 1996 (copy in author's possession); n.a., "Carl Braden—Operation Freedom Founder," newsletter supplement, n.d., ca. 1975, in Anne Braden personal files, in author's possession; see miscellaneous correspondence on west Tennessee in Boxes 33 and 34, Braden Papers, SHSW.

72. Anne quoted in letter to Jim Dombrowski, 28 May 1959, in Box 31, Folder 2, Braden Papers, SHSW (she indicated the "image" phrase had first been employed as an accusation made to her by Williams, but she herself then adopted it, first in jest and later as an admission of what happened). The observation that the Bradens were SCEF was offered in Julian Bond interview.

73. Salmond, *Southern Rebel*, 263–64; Braden interview with author, 17 June 1999.

74. Braden interview with author, 17 June 1999; Klibaner, *Conscience of a Troubled South*, 152–53.

75. Klibaner, *Conscience of a Troubled South*, 152–55.

76. Salmond, *Southern Rebel*, 253, 264–65; Klibaner, *Conscience of a Troubled South*, 174–75; Braden interview with author, 17 June 1999.

77. Salmond, *Southern Rebel*, 269–73.

78. Maund quoted in Al and Dorothy Maund to Carl and Anne Braden, 15 June 1957, in Box 27, Folder 5, Braden Papers, SHSW; on the *Worker* incident, see *Montgomery Advertiser*, n.d., ca. March 1956, in Box 26, Folder 6, Braden Papers, SHSW.

79. On Sanders, see Carl Braden to Jim Dombrowski, 29 May 1958, in Box 28, Folder 5, Braden Papers, SHSW.

80. *Arkansas Gazette*, 11 August 1958, in Box 28, Folder 9, Braden Papers, SHSW.

81. See, for example, J. L. Blair Buck to Mr. and Mrs. Carl Braden, 19 February 1959 (and Anne's reply, 23 February 1959), in Box 30, Folder 2, Braden Papers, SHSW; see also Roy DeLamotte to Carl Braden, 26 February 1960, in Box 32, Braden Papers, SHSW; various clippings and items relating to the Lawrence column are in Box 29, Folder 1, Braden Papers, SHSW; "Tuskegee Group Makes Mistake," *Birmingham News*, 26 November 1959, in Box 6, Braden Papers, UT.

82. Louisville *Courier-Journal*, 21 September 1957; Braden interview with Thrasher, Tape 8, Side 2, 248; Anne Braden to Elinor Ferry, 2 November 1957, in Box 27, Folder 7, Braden Papers, SHSW.

83. "Kentuckians See Void in U.S.Security," *Louisville Times*, 28 October 1957.

84. Brown, *Standing against Dragons*, 164–66. Brown argues that the testimony of Grace Lorch (the lone white woman to shield Elizabeth Eckford from the mob when she desegregated Little Rock's Central High School in the fall of 1957) as well as that of Don West and other southern activists in Memphis, were mere window dressings—personally disastrous ones though they may have been—for the true objectives of the hearings. The first of these aims was to resurrect the Louisville sedition case as a first step toward a federal prosecution against Carl after his reentry into southern political life as the new SCEF field secretary. The other purpose of the hearings seems to have been to breathe new life into state sedition laws in the aftermath of the *Nelson* ruling. By 1958, legislative measures to neutralize *Nelson* and reinstate sedition statutes were before Congress.

85. "Kentuckians See Void in U.S. Security," *Louisville Times*, 28 October 1957.

86. Braden interview with author, 30 December 2001, Mt. St. Francis, Indiana; Anne Braden, "A View from the Fringes," *Southern Exposure* 9, no. 1, (spring 1981): 70.

87. For more discussion on SCEF's approach to anticommunist red-baiting, see, for example, Anne Braden, memo, n.d., in "Dombrowski" folder, Box 2, Braden Papers, UT; on the NAACP in Alabama, see Raines, *My Soul Is Rested*, 134–35.

88. *Carl Braden v. United States of America*, Brief on Behalf of Appellant, 11 August 1959, copy in author's possession, p. 9; more details on this incident are in Braden interview with Hogan, 7 December 1978, Interview 2, CUOHROC, and in Braden interview with Thrasher, Tape 9, Side 1, 261–62; Klibaner, *Conscience of a Troubled South*, 135–37.

89. Braden interview with author, 17 June 1999; the only African American subpoenaed to the HUAC hearings in Atlanta was Jack O'Dell, whose work with King in the 1960s would again hoist the tag of "communist" and cost him his job with SCLC. For more on O'Dell, see Branch, *Parting the Waters*, 850–51.

90. Braden interview with author, 17 June 1999.

91. Press statement quoted in Klibaner, *Conscience of a Troubled South*, 137; Carl Braden to Charles Pemberton, 19 September 1959, in Box 31, Folder 2, Braden Papers, SHSW.

92. For more on this, see Anne Braden to Aubrey Williams, 14 January 1960, in Box 32, Braden Papers, SHSW; O'Reilly, *Hoover and the Un-Americans*, 260; Adams, *James Dombrowski*, 247.

93. Brown, *Standing against Dragons*, 164–69.

94. Carl's statement on integration quoted in Brown, *Standing against Dragons*, 169; n.a. (authored by Anne Braden), "My Beliefs and Associations Are None of the Business of This Committee," SCEF pamphlet, n.d., copy in author's possession; n.a., "Behind the Bars for the First Amendment," SCEF pamphlet, March 1960, copy in author's possession.

95. Brown, *Standing against Dragons*, 169; appellate brief, *Carl Braden v. United States of America*, 4–6, 14–16.

96. Ibid.; United Press International story, 30 July 1958, reprinted in the *Nashville Banner*, 6 October 1958, clipping in Box 29, Folder 2, Braden Papers, SHSW; Carl's statement quoted in Anne Braden to Aubrey Williams and Jim Dombrowski, 16 August 1958, in Box 20, Braden Papers, SHSW; *Atlanta Constitution* quoted in *Southern Newsletter*, August-September 1958, in Box 5, Braden Papers, UT.

97. Anne Braden to Bill and Mary Jane Melish, 8 August 1958, in Box 28, Folder 8, Braden Papers, SHSW; Anne Braden to Aubrey Williams and Jim Dombrowski, 16 August 1958, in Box 20, Braden Papers, SHSW.

98. Frank J. Donner, *The Un-Americans* (New York: Ballantine, 1961); Klibaner, *Conscience of a Troubled South*, 139–41; Brown, *Standing against Dragons*, 172.

99. Anne Braden to Albert Barnett, 29 December 1958, in Anne Braden personal files, copy in author's possession.

100. Ibid. (A copy of Barnett's memo to Carl and Anne is also in Box 3, Braden Papers, UT.)

101. Brown, *Standing against Dragons*, 169; Anne Braden to Anita McCarty, 8 January 1959, in Box 30, Folder 1, Braden Papers, SHSW.

102. Anne Braden to Leonard Boudin, 14 October 1959, in Box 31, Braden Papers, SHSW.

103. See I. F. Stone, "A Black Day at the U.S. Supreme Court," *I. F. Stone's Weekly*, 15 June 1959, 1, copy in Box 49, Folder 2, Braden Papers, SHSW.

104. Anne Braden to Frank Wilkinson and Clark Foreman, 15 June 1959, in Box 3, Braden Papers, UT; for more on the First Amendment group, see, for example, "Committee of First Amendment Defendants" Folder in Box 2, Braden Papers, UT; Anne Braden to Frank Wilkinson, 14 August 1959, in Box 49, Folder 2, Braden Papers, SHSW.

105. More on the Highlander case can be found in Frank Adams, "Highlander Research and Education Center" entry, *Encyclopedia of the American Left* (1992 edition), ed. Buhle et al., 309–10.

106. Braden, *Wall Between* (1958), xii; Braden, *Wall Between* (1999), xv.

107. James Dabbs to Anne Braden, 6 May 1959, in Box 15, Folder 6, Braden Papers, SHSW.

108. The quotation is from Harry Golden, "Perseverance against Violence," *Nation*, 16 May 1959, n.p.

109. King and Roosevelt statements are in Box 15, Folder 6, Braden Papers, SHSW; this folder also contains various reviews; Prattis's column is in Box 15, Folder 4; other reviews can be found in Box 5 of Braden Papers, UT; "Another Nomination for Book Award: *The Wall Between*," Louisville *Courier-Journal*, 1 March 1959.

110. Braden interview with author, 17 June 1999.
111. On SCEF fieldwork, see Anne Braden to Aubrey Williams, 4 May 1959, and Anne Braden to Harvey and Jessie [O'Connor], 5 May 1959, both in Box 31, Folder 1, Braden Papers, SHSW.
112. Anne Braden to Frank Wilkinson, 14 May 1959, in Box 31, Folder 1, Braden Papers, SHSW; for a thorough study of the kissing case, see Patrick Jones, "'Communist Front Shouts Kissing Case to the World': The Committee to Combat Racial Injustice and the Politics of Race and Gender during the Cold War" (M.A. thesis, University of Wisconsin-Madison, 1996); "Seawell Raps Southern Educational Fund," *Raleigh News and Observer*, 17 February 1959; W. W. Finlator, interview with author, Raleigh, North Carolina, 18 September 1997; on the Mississippi investigation, see Carl Braden to Richard Criley, 30 November 1958, in Box 48, Folder 19, Braden Papers, SHSW; on Florida, see Carl Braden to William O'Neill, 26 January 1961, in Box 51, Folder 8, Braden Papers, SHSW (see also *St. Petersburg Times*, 12 February 1961, partial clipping in author's possession).
113. Klibaner, *Conscience of a Troubled South*, 168; see also Jim Dombrowski to Eleanor Roosevelt, 26 January 1960, in Box 20, Braden Papers, SHSW.
114. Dunbar, *Against the Grain;* Anne Braden to Harvey and Jessie O'Connor, 5 May 1959; Braden interview with Hogan, 7 December 1978, Interview 2, 63, CUOHROC.
115. Braden interview with Schultz, 2 September 1984, Interview 2, 21.

Chapter 9

1. The quote for the epigraph that opens the chapter can be found in the *Congressional Record*, 17 February 1959, 2319.
2. Numbers are drawn from Martin Oppenheimer, *The Sit-In Movement of 1960* (Brooklyn: Carlson, 1989), 42–43.
3. On Anne's correspondence, see Boxes 32 and 33, Braden Papers, SHSW; quotation is from Anne Braden to Fred Shuttlesworth, 6 March 1960, in Box 32, Folder 6, Braden Papers, SHSW.
4. Anne Braden to Jim Dombrowski, 27 October 1959, in Box 31, Folder 6, Braden Papers, SHSW; see *Southern Patriot*, January 1960, 3.
5. See summary of hearings in *Congressional Record*, U.S. House of Representatives, 8 February 1960, 2076–81; Carl quoted in Klibaner, *Conscience of a Troubled South*, 169.
6. The Greensboro Four were Ezell Blair, Jr., Franklin McCain, Joseph McNeil, and David Richmond; more on their story is available in Raines, *My Soul Is Rested*, 75–82; Anne Braden to Jim Aronson, 5 April 1960, in Box 33, Folder 1, Braden Papers, SHSW.
7. On her schedule, see Anne Braden to Russ Nixon, 12 March 1960, in Box 32, Braden Papers, SHSW; see miscellaneous correspondence, Anne Braden and Virginia Durr, in Box 33, Braden Papers, SHSW.
8. Miscellaneous correspondence, Anne Braden and Virginia Durr, in Boxes 32 and 33, Braden Papers, SHSW; Durr's phrase is from Virginia Durr to Anne Braden, 12 April 1960, in Box 33, Folder 1, Braden Papers, SHSW; various documents in Box 49, Braden Papers, SHSW, detail the Bradens' relationship with Williams; for a thorough discussion of Williams's views, see Tyson, "Robert Williams, Black Power, " 540–70; see also Tyson's *Radio Free Dixie: Robert F. Williams and the Roots of Black Power* (Chapel Hill: University of North Carolina Press, 1999); quotation is from Anne Braden to Virginia Durr, 16 April 1960, in Box 33, Folder 1, Braden Papers, SHSW.
9. For more on her view of the sit-ins, see Anne Braden, "Defense of Sit-ins," Louisville *Courier-Journal*, 20 October 1960, in Box 6, Braden Papers, UT; Anne Braden to Virginia Durr, 16 April 1960.
10. See especially Virginia Durr to Anne Braden, dated "Thursday" (ca. spring 1960) in Box 34, Folder 4, Braden Papers, SHSW, and Virginia Durr to Anne Braden, dated only April 1960, in Box 33, Folder 1, Braden Papers, SHSW; for more on the women's friendship, see Anne Braden, interview with author, 7 March 1989 (Tape 1).

11. For more on student activism in the 1930s and thereafter, see Robert Cohen, *When the Old Left Was Young* (New York: Oxford University Press, 1993), esp. 220–24, on the SNYC; Clayborne Carson explores motivations of early sit-in participants more thoroughly in his *In Struggle: SNCC and the Black Political Awakening of the 1960s* (Cambridge: Harvard University Press, 1981), 12–15; no critiques of the sit-ins were located in Anne Braden's correspondence from the era.

12. Grant, *Ella Baker Freedom Bound*, 125–27; Carson, *In Struggle*, 19–21.

13. Grant, *Ella Baker Freedom Bound*, 127–31; *Southern Patriot*, May 1960.

14. Braden interview with Thrasher, Tape 10, Side 2, 305; August Meier and Elliot Rudwick, *CORE: A Study in the Civil Rights Movement, 1942–1968* (New York: Oxford University Press, 1973), 105–20; George C. Wright, "Desegregation of Public Accommodations in Louisville," in *Southern Businessmen and Desegregation*, ed. Elizabeth Jacoway and David Colburn (Baton Rouge: LSU Press, 1982), 199.

15. Rufus B. Atwood and the Executive Council of Kentucky State College to Alumni and Friends of Kentucky State College, 5 May 1960, in Box 33, Folder 2, Braden Papers, SHSW. (Kentucky State College is now Kentucky State University.)

16. Wright, "Desegregation of Public Accommodations," 199; Anne Braden to Len Holt, 5 May 1960, in Box 33, Folder 2, Braden Papers, SHSW.

17. Bob Boyd to Anne Braden, 20 May 1960, in Box 33, Folder 2, Braden Papers, SHSW; some observations on Anne here stem from conversations with various figures from SNCC and other movement groups; Anne Braden to Clark Foreman, 14 June 1960, in Box 33, Folder 3, Braden Papers, SHSW.

18. Anne Braden to Jim Dombrowski, 17 April 1960, in Box 33, Folder 1, Braden Papers, SHSW.

19. Anne Braden, "Memo on Proposed Projects for 1960," n.d., in Box 33, Folder 3, Braden Papers, SHSW.

20. Braden interview with Hogan, 7 December 1978, Interview 2, 93, CUOHROC. For examples, see *Southern Patriot*, November 1960, and SCEF news release, 6 October 1960, in Subgroup B: Series I: Box 116, Folder 24, Student Nonviolent Coordinating Committee Papers (hereinafter referred to as SNCC Papers), Martin Luther King, Jr. Center for Nonviolent Social Change, Atlanta.

21. For more on the Nashville student movement, see David Halberstam, *The Children* (New York: Random House, 1998); Jane Stembridge, telephone interview with author, 12 October 1997; Anne Braden to Jim Dombrowski, 29 August 1960, in Box 33, Folder 5, Braden Papers, SHSW.

22. Carson, *In Struggle*, 29; Stembridge telephone interview; on Rustin incident, see also Jane Stembridge to Anne Braden, 22 September 1960, in Box 33, Folder 6, Braden Papers, SHSW.

23. Stembridge telephone interview; some of the description is drawn from Mary King, *Freedom Song: A Personal Story of the 1960s Civil Rights Movement* (New York: William Morrow and Company, 1987), 123–24; Anne Braden to Jane Stembridge, 2 August 1960, in Box 9, Folder 14, SNCC Papers.

24. Braden interview with Hogan, 7 December 1978, Interview 2, 134, CUOHROC; Carson, *In Struggle*, 29.

25. Anne Braden to Alice Cobb, 26 October 1960, in Box 34, Braden Papers, SHSW; Braden interview with Thrasher, Tape 10, Side 2, 307–308; Anne Braden to Harriet Fitzgerald, 31 January 1961, in Box 34, Braden Papers, SHSW.

26. Anne Braden to Jim Dombrowski, 17 October 1960, in Box 34, Braden Papers, SHSW.

27. Ibid.

28. Anne Braden to Marion Barry, 22 November 1960, in B: I: Box 9, Folder 14, SNCC Papers; Braden interview with Hogan, 7 December 1978, Interview 2, 137, CUOHROC; Carson, *In Struggle*, 52.

29. Anne Braden to Jim Dombrowski, 17 October 1960; Stembridge, in her telephone interview with author, maintained that, contrary to Anne's belief, uneasiness with SCEF played no role in her own decision not to take on the project.

30. Carl Braden to Jim Dombrowski, 5 December 1960; Anne Braden to Ella Baker, 8 December 1960, both in Box 34, Braden Papers, SHSW; for more on the search for a white student, see miscellaneous correspondence, Box 34, Folders 3 and 4, and Box 62, Braden Papers, SHSW.

31. See Anne Braden to Jim Dombrowski, 17 October 1960, for more of her musings on the issue of SNCC suspicions about adult organizations; Braden interview with Hogan, 7 December 1978, Interview 2, 137–38, CUOHROC; for more on Anne's relations with SNCC leaders, see Anne Braden to "Friends," 23 October 1960, in A: IV: Box 9, Folder 15/16, SNCC Papers.

32. Carson makes the point that Anne gained SNCC workers' trust in *In Struggle*, 52; Casey Hayden, e-mail correspondence with author, 1 November 1999, copy in author's possession; see, for example, Anne Braden to Ed King, 15 March 1961, in Box 9, Folder 15/16, SNCC Papers.

33. Stembridge telephone interview with author; Joan Browning, e-mail correspondence with author, 26 September 1999, copy in author's possession; on that formality, see, for example, Julian Bond to Mrs. Braden, 22 March 1963, in Box 20, Folder 13, SNCC Papers; Bond interview with author. For more on Joan Browning, see her essay, "Invisible Revolutionaries: White Women in Civil Rights Historiography," *Journal of Women's History* 8, no. 3 (fall 1996): 186–204. Julian Bond later became a representative to the Georgia legislature and in the 1990s was named national president of the NAACP.

34. Anne Braden to Jane Stembridge, 25 October 1960, in Box 34, Folder 1, Braden Papers, SHSW.

35. Bond interview with author.

36. *Student Voice*, November 1960, in Box 34, Braden Papers, SHSW; "Some Hints on Issuing News Releases," n.d., ca. early 1961, in Box 9, Folder 15/16, SNCC Papers.

37. Stembridge telephone interview; Bond interview.

38. See, for example, Anne Braden to Jim Aronson, 5 April 1960; on the politics of the York newspaper, see, for example, Belfrage and Aronson, *Something to Guard*, 13; Anne Braden, telephone conversation with author, 9 November 1999.

39. On early SNCC work, see Braden interview with Hogan, 11 June 1980, Interview 3, 162–63, CUOHROC; Ed King to Jim Dombrowski, 15 April 1961, 12 May 1961, and 27 May 1961, all in Box 9, Folder 15/16, SNCC Papers.

40. Braden interview with Hogan, 7 December 1978, Interview 2, 78, CUOHROC.

41. Carson, *In Struggle*, 37.

42. Anne Braden to Ed King, 14 June 1961, in Box 9, Folder 15/16, SNCC Papers; Jim Dombrowski to Howard Melish, 15 January 1963, in Box 20, Folder 13, SNCC Papers; for some specific figures on SNCC funds, see Carson, *In Struggle*, 71 (see also 176 and 178).

43. Stembridge telephone interview; Bond interview; Constance Curry, interview with author, Atlanta, Georgia, 8 August 1997.

44. Curry interview; the phrase is from Bond interview. For more on Connie Curry, see her first book, *Silver Rights* (New York: Algonquin Books, 1994).

45. Curry interview; Browning e-mail correspondence; Sue Thrasher, telephone interview with author, 16 November 1999. Note: Sue Thrasher became a co-founder in 1964 of the Southern Student Organizing Committee and, later, an originator of the magazine *Southern Exposure*, as well as an important contributor to the popularization of oral history.

46. Evans, *Personal Politics*, 50; Braden interview with author, 17 June 1999; Anne Braden and Alice Childress, "A Tribute to the Heroines of the South," 20 March 1961, in Box 47, Folder 15, Braden Papers, SHSW.

47. Curry interview.

48. Ibid.

49. Shuttlesworth interview.

50. See Anne Braden to Aubrey Williams, 21 June 1960, in Box 20, Braden Papers, SHSW; see, for example, copy, telegram, Anne and Carl Braden to Dr. Martin Luther King Junior, 24 October 1960, in Box 34, Braden Papers, SHSW; King's letter is reprinted in

full in *The Autobiography of Martin Luther King, Jr.*, ed. Clayborne Carson (New York: Warner Books, 1998), 187–204.

51. Anne Braden to Martin Luther King, 19 June 1960, in Box 33, Folder 3, Braden Papers, SHSW; Anne Braden to Coretta King, 19 June 1960, in Box 33, Folder 4, Braden Papers, SHSW; King's comments are from Anne Braden [to Jim Dombrowski], "Memo on possible meeting with King," n.d., ca. July 1960, in Box 33, Folder 4, Braden Papers, SHSW; for more on this topic, see Braden, "View from the Fringes": 68–74.

52. Branch, *Parting the Waters*, 328–29; Anne Braden [to Jim Dombrowski], memo, ca. July 1960; see also Anne Braden to Jim [Wood], 23 November 1960, in Box 34, Braden Papers, SHSW.

53. Anne Braden to Jim [Wood], 12 December 1960, in Box 34, Braden Papers, SHSW.

54. For more on SCEF-SCLC relations, see Braden, "View from the Fringes."

55. Ellen Fetter Roberts to Jim [Dombrowski], 15 April 1961, in Box 20, Braden Papers, SHSW.

56. See John Morris to Anne Braden, 7 July 1960, and Anne Braden to John Morris, 18 July 1960, both in Box 33, Folder 4, Braden Papers, SHSW.

57. See Henry Thomas to Jim McCain, "Report on Louisville CORE Chapter," 9 April 1962, in Box 49, Folder 5, Braden Papers, SHSW; Meier and Rudwick, *CORE*, 120.

58. On the WILPF matter, see Anne Braden to Louise [Gilbert], 5 November 1960, in Box 34, Braden Papers, SHSW; and Eleanor Fowler to Virginia Durr, 16 December 1960, in Box 34, Braden Papers, SHSW.

59. "Chapel Hill Conferees Map Civil Liberties Fight," *National Guardian*, 13 November 1961, clipping in Box 10, Braden Papers, SHSW.

60. Carl Braden to William O'Neill, 26 January 1961, in Box 1, Folder 8, Braden Papers, SHSW; Brown, *Standing against Dragons*, 195; "Probers Charge Braden's Interest Is Communism," Louisville *Courier-Journal*, 10 February 1961.

61. John Lewis expresses suspicions of Forman in his memoir with Michael D'Orso, *Walking with the Wind: A Memoir of the Movement* (New York: Simon & Schuster, 1998), 179; Bond interview; for more on Forman, see his memoir, *The Making of Black Revolutionaries* (Washington, D.C.: Open Hand Publishing, 1985).

62. See, for example, Anne Braden to Jim Forman, 9 December 1958, and Jim Forman to Anne Braden, 21 December 1958, both in Box 29, Folder 5, Braden Papers, SHSW.

63. Carson, *In Struggle*, 43; Bond interview.

64. For more on this topic, see David Farber, *The Age of Great Dreams: America in the 1960s* (New York: Hill & Wang, 1994), 77–78; and Todd Gitlin, *The Sixties: Years of Hope, Days of Rage* (New York: Bantam, 1987), 82–83; Braden interview with author, 8 March 1989 (Tape 2).

65. Braden interview with Hogan, 7 December 1978, Interview 2, 84, CUOHROC.

66. There are too many authors of this thesis to enumerate here, but a few who influence this work are Dunbar, *Against the Grain*, esp. 225–60; Gitlin, *The Sixties* (quoted material is from p. 83); Kelley, *Hammer and Hoe*; and Sullivan, *Days of Hope*, esp. 249–75.

67. Anne Braden to Ed King, 15 March 1961, and Anne Braden to Elizabeth Eisenberg, 15 March 1961, both in A: IV: Box 9, Folder 15/16, SNCC Papers.

68. Braden interview with author, 8 March 1989 (Tape 2); "Racial Talk Cleared at SJ State," *San Francisco Chronicle*, 22 February 1961; quoted editorial material is from "Dr. Wahlquist Displays Faith, Moral Courage," *San Jose Mercury*, 1 March 1961; "Protests Fizzle; SJS Students Hear Braden Integration Plea," *San Jose Mercury*, 24 February 1961 (all above clips are from Box 6, Braden Papers, UT); Braden interview with author, 8 March 1989 (Tape 2). For a fine study of free speech on a southern campus during this same era, reflecting a very different outcome, see William J. Billingsley, *Communists on Campus: Race, Politics, and the Public University in Sixties North Carolina* (Athens: University of Georgia Press, 1999).

69. "Fifty-eight Demonstrators Arrested on Fourth," Louisville *Courier-Journal*, 25 February 1961; "Twenty-Six Negro Youths Arrested in New Demonstrations against Segre-

gated Shows," Louisville *Courier-Journal*, 12 March 1961; "Judge Triplett's Statement Did Not Help the Situation," Louisville *Courier-Journal*, 14 March 1961 (all clips from Box 6, Braden Papers, UT); the phrase "creative extremism" is borrowed from King's April 1963 "Letter from Birmingham Jail."

Chapter 10

1. The first epigraph preceding the text of this chapter is from W. J. Cash, *The Mind of the South* (New York: Vintage, 1941), 303.
2. This epigraph is from Sherrod quoted in Frank Wilkinson, "Civil Liberties–Civil Rights Conference," 28–30 June 1963, typescript notes, pp. 7–8, in Box 47, Folder 9, Braden Papers, SHSW.
3. Black quoted in Klibaner, *Conscience of a Troubled South*, 178; miscellaneous clips, "Carl Braden" clippings file, Louisville Free Public Library; Brown, *Standing against Dragons*, 177.
4. On the McCartys, see for instance, William Howard Melish to Anita McCarty, 18 June 1961, in "Carl's HUAC Case" folder, Anne Braden personal files, in author's possession; Carl quoted in "Excerpts from Letters from Carl Braden to Anne Braden—May 1–August 1, 1961," in Box 11, Folder 8, Braden Papers, SHSW; Richard Criley, *The FBI v. the First Amendment* (Los Angeles: First Amendment Foundation, 1990), 53.
5. Braden telephone conversation with author, 14 December 1998.
6. Anne Braden to "Friend," 1 August 1961, in Box 20, Braden Papers, SHSW; "Excerpts from Letters," Box 11, Folder 8, Braden Papers, SHSW.
7. "Excerpts from Letters," Box 11, Folder 8, Braden Papers, SHSW.
8. Anne Braden to Carl Braden, 21 May 1961, in Box 11, Folder 6, Braden Papers, SHSW; Anne Braden to "Friend," 1 August 1961; see Bradens' miscellaneous prison correspondence, Box 11, Braden Papers, SHSW.
9. Anne Braden to Carl Braden, 21 June 1961, in Box 11, Folder 7, Braden Papers, SHSW.
10. Anne Braden to Carl Braden, 31 July 1961, in Box 11, Folder 7, Braden Papers, SHSW; Anne Braden to Carl Braden, 8 October 1961, in Box 11, Folder 9, Braden Papers, SHSW; Anne Braden to "Friend," 1 August 1961.
11. Klibaner, *Conscience of a Troubled South*, 179–80.
12. Braden interview with Schultz, 2 September 1984, Interview 3, 17–18.
13. Ibid., 19–20; a reprint of the infamous photo of King can be found in Braden, "View from the Fringes," 68.
14. Braden interview with Schultz, 2 September 1984, Interview 3, 20–22.
15. Anne Braden to Jim [Dombrowski], 20 April 1961, in "Carl Clemency Petition" Folder, Anne Braden personal files, in author's possession. The entire list of signers can be found in SCEF news release, 7 May 1961, in that same folder. Signers not named in text are as follows: William Abbot of Norfolk; the Rev. Ralph Abernathy of Montgomery; Carl Brannin, Dallas; James McBride Dabbs, South Carolina; the Rev. W. W. Finlator, Raleigh; the Rev. Clarence Jordan, Americus; the Rev. James Lawson, Tennessee; Bishop Edgar Love, Baltimore; Dorcas Ruthenburg, Louisville; the Rev. C. K. Steele, Tallahassee; Marion Wright, North Carolina; see Anne Braden to Dotty [Zellner], 24 April 1963, in Box 2, Braden Papers, UT; Anne Braden to Carl Braden, 20 July 1961, in Box 11, Folder 7, Braden Papers, SHSW.
16. James Dombrowski to Carl Braden, 18 August 1961, in Box 11, Folder 8, Braden Papers, SHSW; on second delegation, see Sylvia Crane to Carl Braden, 9 November 1961, in Box 11, Folder 9, Braden Papers, SHSW; "A Petition for Clemency," n.d., in "Carl Clemency Petition, 1961" folder, Anne Braden personal files; for a more thorough examination of Hoover and anticommunism, see Curt Gentry, *J. Edgar Hoover: The Man and the Secrets* (New York: Plume, 1991), esp. 347–528.
17. Braden interview with Hogan, 7 December 1978, Interview 2, 140 of transcript, CUOHROC; Klibaner, *Conscience of a Troubled South*, 186.

18. Braden interview with Hogan, 7 December 1978, Interview 2, 140–42, CUOHROC; *Southern Patriot*, May 1961.
19. Zellner interview.
20. Ibid.; *Southern Patriot*, June 1961.
21. Zellner interview.
22. Ibid.
23. Anne Braden to Dotty [Zellner], 24 April 1963; Klibaner, *Conscience of a Troubled South*, 187; on salaries, see, for example, Jim Dombrowski to James Forman, 19 September 1962, and Jim Forman to Jim Dombrowski, 20 September 1962, both in Box 20, Folder 13 (1), SNCC Papers.
24. John Robert Zellner, "Report on White Southern Student Project," 19 May 1962, in Box 5, Braden Papers, UT.
25. Ibid.; Carson, *In Struggle*, 49; SCEF board minutes, 26–27 October 1962, p. 2, in Box 4, Braden Papers, UT; Braden interview with Hogan, 11 June 1980, Interview 3, 165, CUOHROC.
26. Anne Braden to Jim [Forman], 11 October 1962, in Box 20, Folder 13 (1), SNCC Papers.
27. Shuttlesworth interview; Anne's comment is from Anne Braden to Frank Wilkinson, 22 August 1959, in Box 49, Folder 2, Braden Papers, SHSW.
28. Anne Braden to Jim Forman, 11 October 1962; Braden interview with author, 3 June 1997.
29. The most complete story of Anne's association with Zellner is found in Braden interview with Hogan, 7 December 1978, Interview 2, 141–44 of transcript, CUOHROC; Zellner interview; *Southern Patriot*, January 1964.
30. Anne Braden to Dorothy Dawson, 3 April 1963, copy in author's possession. Anne's comments are from her letter to Joan Browning, 13 March 1963, in Box 40, Folder 4, Braden Papers, SHSW. For more on attitudes toward women in SNCC, see various memoirs in Constance Curry et al., *Deep in Our Hearts*.
31. Sam C. Shirah Jr., "Campus Visit Report," 26 September–1 October (no year, probably 1963); also Sam Shirah, "Field Report," Birmingham, n.d., ca. September 1963; both in Box 20, Folder 6, SNCC Papers; also see Klibaner, *Conscience of a Troubled South*, 210; Braden interview with Schultz, 2 September 1984, Interview 2, 43.
32. Sam Shirah, "Report to SCEF and SNCC," 16 May 1964, in Box 4, Braden Papers, UT; Braden interview with Schultz, 2 September 1984, Interview 2, 43.
33. See Klibaner, *Conscience of a Troubled South*, especially 209–35; Braden interview with Schultz, 2 September 1984, Interview 2, 43.
34. Tentative Program of Conference on Freedom and the First Amendment, 9 October 1961, in Box 34, Folder 9, Southern Christian Leadership Conference Papers (hereinafter referred to as SCLC Papers), Martin Luther King, Jr. Center for Nonviolent Social Change, Atlanta, Georgia; "Chapel Hill Conferees Map Civil Liberties Fight," clipping, *National Guardian*, n.d., in Box 10, Braden Papers, SHSW; on the conference, see also miscellaneous documents in Box 2, Braden Papers, UT.
35. Anne Braden to Carl Braden, 17 October 1961, in Box 11, Folder 9, Braden Papers, SHSW.
36. Braden interview with author, 8 March 1989, (Tape 2); Anne quoted from transcript, "Freedom and the First Amendment" Conference Proceedings, n.a., in Box 2, Braden Papers, UT; "Chapel Hill Conferees Map Civil Liberties Fight"; more discussion of this topic can be found in Grant, *Ella Baker Freedom Bound*, 158–60.
37. Anne Braden, typescript, untitled speech marked "LA—1961, Dec., Anti-HUAC," in Box 3, Braden Papers, UT; Criley, *The FBI*, 55–56.
38. Anne Braden to Carl Braden, 29 November 1961, in Box 11, Folder 9, Braden Papers, SHSW; Anne Braden to Carl Braden, 17 October 1961.
39. Anne Braden to Carl Braden, 20 July 1961, in Box 11, Folder 7, Braden Papers, SHSW; Anne Braden to Carl Braden, 29 November 1961.
40. Criley, *The FBI*, 58–59; Anne Braden to Carl Braden, 1 November 1961, in Box 11, Folder 9, Braden Papers, SHSW.

41. For more on her emotional concerns, see various prison correspondence in Box 11, Braden Papers, SHSW; she describes their "interdependency" at some length in a letter to Jim [Braden], dated only September 1969, in Box 15, Folder 10, Braden Papers, SHSW; *Southern Patriot*, March 1962.

42. *Southern Patriot*, June 1962; Braden interview with author, 17 June 1999.

43. Braden interview with Thrasher, Tape 11, Side 1, 325; Joanne Grant, "Birmingham Reluctant Host to Interracial Conference," *National Guardian*, 30 April 1962, clipping in Box 10, Braden Papers, SHSW.

44. SCEF Board Minutes, 26–27 October 1962, in Box 22, Folder 6, Braden Papers, SHSW; see, for example, Carl Braden to John Coe, 31 May 1962, and John Coe to Carl [Braden] and Ben [Smith], 4 June 1962, both in Box 5, Braden Papers, UT; Brown, *Standing against Dragons*, 196–97.

45. Braden interview with author, 17 June 1999.

46. See Anne Braden to Wiley Branton, 25 September 1962; *Jackson Daily News* clippings, 31 August 1962; Carl Braden to Jim Dombrowski and John Coe, 2 September 1962; "Report by Carl Braden on Field Trip through Mississippi," 23 July 1962 (all the preceding are in Anne Braden personal files, "Jackson Daily News—VEP, Interagency, 1962" folder, in author's possession); "Indianola Leader Gets Anon. Note," *Mississippi Free Press* clipping, 8 September 1962, in Box 3, Braden Papers, UT.

47. Ibid.; Anne Braden subject file, Mississippi State Sovereignty Commission Papers, Jackson, Mississippi (copies in author's possession); Wiley Branton to Carl Braden, 21 September 1962, in "Jackson Daily News" folder.

48. Anne Braden to Wiley Branton, 24 September 1962; Carl quoted in Anne Braden to Jim [Dombrowski], 24 December 1962, and Cornelius Tarplee to Anne Braden, 12 December 1962. All are in "Jackson Daily News" folder.

49. Bob Moses to Anne Braden, n.d., typed script on bottom of Anne Braden to Bob Moses, 24 October 1962, in "Jackson Daily News" folder; for the evolution of Moses's views on civil liberties, see his comments in "Civil Liberties–Civil Rights Conference" typescript in Box 47, Folder 9, Braden Papers, SHSW.

50. See Wiley Branton to Anne Braden, 24 October 1962; Paul Anthony to James Dombrowski, 1 May 1963. Both are in "Jackson Daily News" folder.

51. "Butts Admits Touring State with Braden," *Jackson Daily News*, 31 August 1962, in "Jackson Daily News" folder; Braden interview with author, 17 June 1999; for more on her address, see Anne Braden to Martin King, 6 October 1962, in Box 34, Folder 15, SCLC Papers; Anne Braden, "Address," 27 September 1962, in Box 129, Folder 23, SCLC Papers.

52. Ibid.; see Jim Dombrowski to Eleanor Roosevelt, 2 October 1962, in Box 20, Folder 11, Braden Papers, SHSW; *Today* television program transcript, 27 September 1963, in Box 56, Folder 10, Braden Papers, SHSW.

53. See Braden interview with Thrasher, Tape 11, Side 1, 320–25, for elaboration on this topic; Anne Braden to Louise Gilbert, 20 March 1959, in Box 30, Folder 4, Braden Papers, SHSW.

54. Anne Braden, telephone interview with author, 14 December 1998; for more on the WECC, see Braden interview with Pfisterer, oral history tape #162, n.d., not transcribed.

55. See Klibaner's discussion of this conference in *Conscience of a Troubled South*, 182–83.

56. Ibid.; Braden interview with author, 17 June 1999; Anne Braden to Martin Luther King, 1 December 1962, in Box 47, Folder 9, Braden Papers, SHSW.

57. Miscellaneous documents, Box 47, Folder 9, Braden Papers, SHSW; Moses quoted in Pat Watters, *Down to Now: Reflections on the Southern Civil Rights Movement* (New York: Pantheon, 1971), 308.

58. See Ella Baker comments, "Civil Liberties–Civil Rights" transcript, p. 6; see also Branch, *Parting the Waters*, for his allusion to the funding matter (481) and discussion of pressures on King from the Kennedys surrounding the freedom rides (464–89); Andrew Young to "Bevel and Diane," 18 February 1963, in Box 141, Folder 5, SCLC Papers.

59. In *Radio Free Dixie*, the historian Tim Tyson discusses on pp. 103–104 the opportunities for greater civil rights reform provided by the Cold War.
60. Grant, *Ella Baker Freedom Bound*, 158–60; Andrew Young to "Bevel and Diane," 18 February 1963.
61. Anne Braden to "Diane and Bevel," 1 March 1963, in Box 49, Folder 7, Braden Papers, SHSW.
62. Braden, "View from the Fringes": 72; Braden interview with Thrasher, Tape 10, Side 2, 314; see also Anne Braden comments, typescript of "Civil Liberties–Civil Rights Conference," p. 6.
63. Sue Thrasher, "Oral History," in *Southern Exposure* 12, no. 6 (November/December 1984): 80–81.
64. Braden interview with author, 17 June 1999.
65. The ideas for this section were inspired by a speech by C. T. Vivian, Anne Braden Diamond Birthday Celebration, Louisville, Kentucky, 12 December 1999.
66. Braden interview with Hogan, 7 December 1978, Interview 2, 97, CUOHROC; Dunbar, *Against the Grain*, 247–58.

Chapter 11

1. The epigraph is from Grant, *Ella Baker Freedom Bound*, 163.
2. Some of these ideas are shaped from Anne Braden's "The Southern Freedom Movement in Perspective," Special Issue, *Monthly Review* 17, no. 3 (July-August 1965).
3. Braden interview with Thrasher, Tape 11, Side 1, 321; Anne Braden, interview with author, Mt. St. Francis, Indiana, 30 December 2001.
4. Anne Braden, interview with author, Louisville, Kentucky, 21 October 2001; Carson, *In Struggle*, 175.
5. Anne Braden to author, 2 January 2002, in author's possession.
6. Ibid.; see also Anita Braden to James Zellner, n.d., ca. early 1964, in Box 15, Folder 10, Braden Papers, SHSW.
7. Ibid.
8. "Rights Demonstrators File Discrimination Complaint," Louisville *Courier-Journal*, 9 June 1964; "Notes on Sequence of Events before and during Recent Demonstrations in Louisville," n.a., June 10, 1964, in Box 43, Folder 2, Braden Papers, SHSW.
9. Ibid.; "Five Rights Workers Guilty of Aiding in Delinquency," Louisville *Courier-Journal*, 17 July 1964.
10. Braden to author, 2 January 2002.
11. Ibid.
12. Adams, *James Dombrowski*, 276–78, 332 n. 22; Arthur Kinoy, *Rights on Trial: Odyssey of a People's Lawyer* (Cambridge: Harvard University Press, 1983), 215–84, 380. Note: The National Lawyers Guild, like Highlander and SCEF, was more connected to the Old Left than were many pro-civil rights organizations in the 1960s; like them, it became the thrust of a number of anticommunist attacks.
13. Anne Braden, interview with author, Mt. St. Francis, Indiana, 28 December 2001; Martin Luther King's condemnation of the raids can be found in *The Churchman*, November 1963, p. 15 (copy in Box 25, Folder 2, Braden Papers, SHSW); Adams, *James Dombrowski*, 275 (a fuller examination of this case can be found in Adams's book). Adams argues (p. 284) that Dombrowski saw this victory as his most meaningful political accomplishment; unfortunately, subsequent Supreme Court decisions have effectively gutted its strength in the years since 1965.
14. Freedom Summer was the brainchild of SNCC, but organizing for it was accomplished through a coalition composed of SNCC, CORE, SCLC, and the NAACP. The proportion of volunteers who were white varies according to account: in *Local People*, Dittmer estimates it at 90 percent (p. 244), whereas Becky Thompson places it at 99 percent in her 2001 study, *A Promise and a Way of Life: White Antiracist Activism* (Minneapolis:

University of Minnesota Press), 52. See Dittmer, *Local People*, 247–51 (violence statistics on p. 251); two of the three victims were CORE staff members who had previously worked in Mississippi, but all three had just arrived from the Freedom Summer's national training in Oxford, Ohio, on the evening before their disappearance.

15. Anne Braden, interview with author, Louisville, Kentucky, 2 November 2001; Anne Braden to author, 30 December 2001, in author's possession; Anne also recounts this incident in "View from the Fringes": 70–71.

16. Braden to author, 30 December 2001.

17. Carson, *In Struggle*, 146.

18. Braden to author, 30 December 2001.

19. Forman, *The Making of Black Revolutionaries*, 452.

20. Braden interview with author, 30 December 2001. Note: Thrasher and other SSOC founders admired Anne and often sought her advice, but remained wary of appearing "too radical" and thus behaved erratically in their stance toward SCEF, especially after they were specifically told by SRC officials to stay away from SCEF if they wanted SRC help in fundraising; in her interview with author, 2 November 2001, Anne discusses at length SSOC founders' hesitancy about radicalism, including Sue Thrasher's April 1965 withdrawal from the SCEF board on this basis.

21. Klibaner, *Conscience of a Troubled South*, 228–32; some of this analysis—including Anne's comments on SSOC/SNCC relations—is taken from Thompson's fuller exploration of these events in *Promise and a Way of Life*, 52–55, 69–71 (quoted material on p. 54). Anne attributes her remark on whites as whites to a point originally made by Rob Burlage. For more on SSOC, see Gregg Michel, "'We'll Take Our Stand': The Southern Student Organizing Committee and the Radicalization of White Southern Students, 1964–1969" (Ph.D. dissertation, University of Virginia, 1999).

22. Carson, *In Struggle*; 136, 241–42; Tyson, "Robert Williams, Black Power."

23. Carson, *In Struggle*, 206; Anne Braden, "The SNCC Trends: Challenge to White America," *Southern Patriot*, May 1966, 1–3 (for more of Anne's views on integration in the 1960s, see entirety of this article). It should also be noted that Anne took a good deal of heat for what was seen by some radicals at the time as a reformist view of black nationalism as a mere stage rather than as an end in itself: see, for example, Carol Hanisch, "Blacks, Women, and the Movement in SCEF," in *Feminist Revolution*, ed. Redstockings (New York: Random House, 1975), 188–91, and miscellaneous documents in "SCEF Split" folders, Anne Braden personal files, in author's possession.

24. Martin Luther King Jr., *Stride toward Freedom* (New York: Harper & Row, Perennial edition, 1958), 48; Braden to author, "Integration and Black Power," typescript manuscript, 3 January 2002, in author's possession.

25. Howard Zinn, *A People's History of the United States* (New York: Harper Perennial, 1990), 466–76.

26. Carson, *In Struggle*, 184–85; Braden to author, 4 January 2002.

27. Anne Braden, interview with author, Mt. St. Francis, Indiana, 30 December 2001; SCEF news release, 19 October 1965; SCEF minutes, Board of Directors' Meeting, 14–16 April 1966. Latter two items are in "SCEF Minutes" notebook, Anne Braden personal files, in author's possession (all subsequent SCEF minutes taken from this notebook unless otherwise indicated). In spring of 1966 both SCLC and SNCC condemned the war, and SCEF did the same.

28. For changes in mainstream southern culture, see, for example, essays in Elizabeth Jacoway and David Colburn, eds., *Southern Businessmen and Desegregation* (Baton Rouge: LSU Press, 1982); any survey of the "Carl Braden" or "Anne Braden" card files for the Louisville *Courier-Journal* (in Louisville Free Public Library) reveals a plethora of citations taking critical note of the Bradens' participation in 1960s protests; Braden interview with author, 17 June 1999.

29. Braden interview with author, 17 June 1999.

30. Ibid.; Carson, *In Struggle*, 241–42. Note: Not every youth who came into SCEF out of SNCC was white: Henry Hampton, for example, was a black Alabamian who worked successfully on the Mountain Project staff with both white and black local people (see *Southern Patriot*, December 1965, p. 4).

31. Various documents in "Southern Mountain Project" folder, Anne Braden personal papers, in author's possession; quoted material from Frank Fletcher, "Plan for Organizing in the Southern Mountains," n.d., in "Southern Mountain Project" folder; Braden interview with author, 21 October 2001.

32. SCEF minutes, Board of Directors Meeting, 16 April 1965, 2; Anne's remark recorded in SCEF minutes, Board of Directors Meeting, 14–15 October 1965, 8.

33. SCEF minutes, Board of Directors Meeting, 14–16 April 1966, 1. The donor was Emily Longstreth of Philadelphia.

34. For more on the relationship between the Old and New Lefts, see, for example, Isserman, *If I Had a Hammer*, 173–219.

35. Braden interview with author, 23 November 2001.

36. SCEF minutes, Board of Directors Meeting, 6–8 April 1966, 1.

37. Thomas J. Kiffmeyer, "From Self-Help to Sedition: The Appalachian Volunteers in Eastern Kentucky, 1964–1970," *Journal of Southern History* 64, no. 1 (February 1998): 65–94, esp. 68; for more on strip mining opposition drives, see also "Violence Grows over Strip Mining in Kentucky," *New York Times*, 16 July 1967.

38. Braden interview with author, 2 November 2001; quoted material from enclosure 105–164714, dated 14 August 1967, p. 5, from Alan McSurely file, Federal Bureau of Investigation: copies in "McSurely FBI Materials" folder, Anne Braden personal files, in author's possession. According to p. 2 of this document, Ratliff allegedly stated that he realized that a Pike County conviction would be overturned on appeal.

39. Various documents in "McSurely FBI Materials" folder. An Office of Economic Opportunity (OEO) internal investigation of the Pike County charges concurred with Carl, pronouncing them as motivated primarily by "obvious political interests": see "Poverty Aide Sedition Arrests Viewed as Inspired by Politics," *Washington Evening Star*, 1 September 1967. Because the leaked report contained FBI findings that sustained the idea of a frame-up, FBI Director J. Edgar Hoover apparently retaliated by threatening the OEO with cutting off the bureau's investigative services to it if it could not prevent further leaks: see U.S. government memorandum, D. J. Brennan to W. C. Sullivan, dated 6 September 1967, in "McSurely FBI Materials" folder. For more on Kunstler, see David Langum, *William M. Kunstler: The Most Hated Lawyer in America* (New York: NYU Press, 1999).

40. "Pike Jury Indicts Five, Including Braden, Wife," Louisville *Courier-Journal*, 12 September 1967; "Nunn Asserts Cook 'Coddles' Agitators," Louisville *Courier-Journal*, 7 May 1967; Braden interview with author, 30 December 2001.

41. Braden interview with author, 2 November 2001; "Bradens Arrested on Way to Face Sedition Charge," Louisville *Courier-Journal*, 13 September 1967; Anne Braden, "American Inquisition Part Two: The McSurely Case and Repression in the 1960s," *Southern Exposure* 11, no. 5 (September-October 1983): 20–27.

42. Braden interview with author, 2 November 2001. The panel was composed of Bert Combs (later governor of Kentucky) of the Sixth U.S. Circuit Court of Appeals, Cincinnati, Ohio; James F. Gordon, U.S. District Court, Louisville; and Bernard Moynahan, U.S. District Court, Lexington. See "Statute on Sedition in Kentucky Voided by Federal Court," *New York Times*, 16 September 1967.

43. Braden interview with author, 2 November 2001. Anne recounts a slightly different version of these events in *Wall Between* (1999), 325.

44. Ibid.

45. Ibid.

46. "Kentucky Sedition Case Is Being Kept Alive by Senate Panel's Actions," *St. Louis Post-Dispatch*, 25 November 1967.

47. This thesis is borne out by Billingsley's *Communists on Campus*, which demonstrates both the continuing state-sanctioned limits on free speech at the University of North Carolina in the 1960s and the growth of student protests against such limits.

Chapter 12

1. The epigraph, a traditional slogan of the civil rights movement, became the title of a freedom song copyrighted by Roberta Slavitt in 1965.
2. In *Personal Politics*, for instance, Sara Evans suggests that the civil rights movement had become disparate and was being eclipsed by the move to Black Power by 1967 (see p. 195); Dittmer ends *Local People* with the 1968 Democratic Party Convention in Chicago; Carson's *In Struggle* chronicles a sort of trickling away of SNCC through the second half of the 1960s; Howell Raines ends *My Soul Is Rested* with King's assassination in April 1968, as do most King biographies, with the exception of Taylor Branch's work, which (at this writing) covers only through 1965: see his *Pillar of Fire: America in the King Years, 1963–65* (New York: Touchstone, 1999); Braden to author, personal communication, 28 January 2002, copy in author's possession.
3. See *Southern Patriot*, miscellaneous issues, 1967–1971.
4. Joel Williamson explores this white conceptualization of black men in *A Rage for Order: Black-White Relations in the American South since Emancipation* (New York: Oxford University Press, 1986); Carson, *In Struggle*, 262–63, 246. Al and Margaret McSurely were exceptions to the government's late-1960s turn toward people of color for campaigns of repression: after the hearing in Lexington, their printed matter confiscated in Pikeville was turned over to the U.S. Senate Permanent Sub-Committee on Investigations, chaired by Arkansas Senator John McClellan (successor to Joseph McCarthy). The couple were convicted of contempt of Congress and sentenced to one year in prison. The conviction was overturned in 1972, but the McSurelys filed a civil damages suit that was not settled until 1983, when they were awarded $1.6 million. See Charles Young, "The Trial of Alan and Margaret McSurely," *Southern Exposure* 11, no. 5 (September-October 1983): 15–19].
5. For more on COINTELPRO, see, for example, O'Reilly, *"Racial Matters."*
6. Anne Braden to author, 4 January 2002, in author's possession; on Johnson, see *Southern Patriot*, October 1968; on this North Carolina case and others like it, see Carl Braden, "The Right to Organize: How North Carolina Tries to Wreck People's Movements," SCEF pamphlet, October 1972, copy in author's possession; on the South Carolina shootings and the antiblack prosecutions that followed them, see Cleveland Sellers, "The Orangeburg Massacre, 1968," in Bud Schultz and Ruth Schultz, *It Did Happen Here: Recollections of Political Repression in America* (Berkeley: University of California Press, 1989), 249–62; for more on the Black Six, see *Southern Patriot*, September 1970. It would be truly mind-numbing to read a complete litany of antiblack incidents of this nature during this period, but it must be noted that less than two weeks after the shootings at Kent State, two African American demonstrators were killed and nine wounded in violence at Jackson State University in Mississippi (see Gitlin, *Sixties*, 410).
7. Braden to author, 4 January 2002.
8. On the Black Six, see various pamphlets in "Miscellaneous Historic Pamphlets" folder, Anne Braden personal files, in author's possession. For more on the Collins case, see *Southern Patriot*, December 1970, as well as various follow-up issues, 1970–1972; *Protest the Jailing of Walter Collins*, SCEF flyer, n.d., ca. 1971, in author's possession; on Mulloy's case, see documents in "Joe Mulloy" folder, Anne Braden personal files, in author's possession. The Bradens published Collins's prison notes, put out leaflets, and sponsored his mother on a speaking tour to arouse mostly white peace activists to the racial disparities in his case. Collins was paroled in late 1972. For more on the Wilmington Ten, see Ben Chavis, "The Wilmington Ten: Prisoners of Conscience—Ben Chavis," in Schultz and Schultz, *It Did Happen Here*, 195–211.

9. Zinn's *People's History of the United States* offers a fuller discussion of the prison movement of the late '60s and '70s; minutes, SCEF Board of Directors Meeting, 13–14 November 1970, 3; Angela Davis's case is chronicled fully in her *Autobiography*. Her indictment stemmed from her involvement with George Jackson, one of the Soledad Brothers, prison inmates accused of killing a guard. George Jackson's brother Jonathan and a judge were killed during a courtroom uprising in which Jonathan Jackson took hostages in a failed effort to free his brother. It was that incident to which Angela Davis's charges were linked.

10. Ibid.; Anne quoted in *Southern Patriot*, June 1972, 7; various documents, in "National Alliance" folder, Anne Braden personal files, in author's possession.

11. The donors were Fred and Bertie Blossom; Braden interview with author, 2 November 2001; see, for example, Tom Lyons, "Braden Library Is Kentucky History," *University of Louisville Cardinal*, n.d., ca. 1968; and "The Bradens and SCEF 20 Years Later: 'People Have Had to Learn to Live with Us,'" Louisville *Courier-Journal*, 2 April 1972.

12. Braden to author, "Feminism and My Relation," 3 January 2002; Anne and Carl Braden, Report to SCEF Board of Directors, 14 November 1968, 2, in Box 97, Folder 2, Braden Papers, SHSW; Hanisch, "Blacks, Women, and the Movement in SCEF," 187.

13. Braden to author, "Feminism and My Relation," 3 January 2002.

14. Braden to author, "Feminism and My Relation," 3 January 2002; Rosen, *World Split Open*, 336.

15. Braden to author, "Feminism and My Relation," 3 January 2002; Braden to author, 4 January 2002; Suzanne Post, interview with author, Louisville, 27 June 1991; Braden interview with author, 17 June 1999; see "Statement from a Group of Socialist Women," n.a., presented by Anne Braden, typescript copy, 18 September 1971, Anne Braden personal files, in author's possession; *Southern Patriot*, November 1971, 3.

16. Anne Braden, "Free Thomas Wansley: A Letter to White Southern Women" (Louisville: SCEF Publications, 1972), pamphlet in author's possession.

17. Anne Braden, "A Second Open Letter to Southern White Women," *Southern Exposure* 4, no. 4 (July 1977): 50–53 (quoted material from 50). This section benefits from the insights in Becky Thompson's *Promise and a Way of Life*: I was never aware of the second letter until reading her book (see pp. 127–28). Also, Anne won everlasting enmity from Brownmiller for this review, as evidenced in the tone of her references to Anne in her memoir, *In Our Time: Memoir of a Revolution* (New York: Dial, 1999).

18. Braden to author, 4 January 2002; for more on SCEF's demise, see "SCEF Split" folders, Anne Braden personal files, in author's possession.

19. In late 1973 a SCEF vote ousted three of the organization's relatively new staff members who were open members of the CP, and more or less browbeat its executive director, Helen Greever, who was at least very close to the CP, into resigning. These events followed an unfortunate series of Louisville incidents in which violent clashes with the Black Panther Party resulted in the institutionalization of a Panther (in a mental health facility) and the subsequent kidnapping by Panther supporters of Greever and her husband, who then secured the kidnappers' arrest. From Anne's perspective, though she disagreed with some of the tactics used by all of the camps involved, the attacks on the CP faction—even though they emanated from the left instead of from right-wingers—amounted to the same stereotyping and dehumanization of Communists she had seen for 25 years. This information is detailed in "SCEF Split" folders, especially in Anne Braden to SCEF Board, Staff, and Advisory Committee, 13 November 1973.

20. Braden interview with author, 2 November 2001.

21. Braden to author, 4 January 2002.

22. Anne Braden to "Friends of Carl," 9 April 1975, "Braden, Carl's Death" folder, Anne Braden personal files, in author's possession.

23. Ibid.; Anne Braden to Carl Braden, 21 June 1961; Braden interview with author, 11 November 1989.

24. Anne Braden, personal correspondence to author, 23 January 2002, in author's possession; Braden, *Wall Between* (1999), 328.

25. Braden, *Wall Between* (1999), 328; Anne Braden to "Friends of Carl," 9 April 1975.

26. Ilene Carver, interview with author, Boston, Massachusetts, 2 August 2001; Braden to author, 28 January 2002; Stembridge telephone interview.

27. Ibid.; Anne Braden, "Report to Friends RE: The Louisville School Situation," unpublished paper in "SCEF Split" folder, 26 October 1975; "For the Cause: Pete Seeger Sings for Nothing to Keep His Hearers from Getting Discouraged," Louisville *Courier-Journal*, 12 October 1975; Anne Braden, "A Year-End Report to My Stockholders," 4 December 1977, Anne Braden personal files, in author's possession.

28. Braden to author, 4 January 2002.

29. Ibid.

30. Braden interview with author, 23 November 2001; Braden quoted in *Wall Between* (1999), 339. When Anne recapped this passage to me later, she added the word "totally."

31. Braden interview with author, 23 November 2001.

32. Anne Braden, "Lessons from a History of Struggle," *Southern Exposure* 8, no. 2 (summer 1980): 56–61.

33. James Wrenn, "Greensboro Massacre" entry in *Encyclopedia of the American Left*, ed. Buhle et al. (1992 edition), 279–80; some information is drawn from various documents in "Greensboro" folder, Anne Braden personal files, in author's possession.

34. Braden interview with author, 23 November 2001; Braden to author, 23 January 2002.

35. Braden to author, 23 January 2002; Braden to author, 28 January 2002. Despite two trials, criminal convictions were never obtained in the CWP murders, but a federal jury found three Klansmen, three Nazis, and two police officers liable in a 1985 wrongful death suit (see "8 Assessed $355,100 in anti-Klan Rally Death," *Courier-Journal*, 9 June 1985, clipping in author's possession). This outcome followed an effective national campaign led by survivors and victims' widows, enhanced by participation from the Racial Justice Working Group of the National Council of Churches, in which Anne also became active. The National Anti-Klan Network later became the Center for Democratic Renewal.

36. Dan T. Carter, *The Politics of Rage: George Wallace, the Origins of the New Conservatism, and the Transformation of American Politics* (New York: Simon & Schuster, 1995); Braden interview with author, 23 November 2001.

37. Braden to author, 23 January 2002; for more detail and statistics on Jackson's victories, see *Keep Hope Alive: Jesse Jackson's 1988 Presidential Campaign*, ed. Frank Clemente with Frank Watkins (Washington, D.C., and Boston: Keep Hope Alive PAC and South End Press, 1989), 221–32 and charts following; *Southern Fight-Back* (SOC newsletter), summer 1988.

38. Braden interview with author, 23 November 2001.

39. Braden to author, 23 January 2001.

40. For clippings related to Carl's death, see "Carl, Death" folder, Anne Braden personal files; the quoted material is from an editorial titled, "Carl Braden, Zealous Reformer," Louisville *Courier-Journal*, 21 February 1975, clipping in author's possession. In late 2001, only a few months before this book went to press, both Carl and Anne Braden were nominated and elected to the Kentucky Civil Rights Hall of Fame in a ceremony hosted by the Kentucky Human Rights Commission.

41. Anne Braden, telephone conversation with author, 1 February 2001.

42. Clarence Matthews, "Champion of Rights: Louisville Woman Chosen to receive new ACLU Award," Louisville *Courier-Journal*, 14 January 1990; for details on the other awards, see "Awards—Anne Braden," clip file in author's possession; Louisville *Courier-Journal*, 12 December 1999; quotations are from Anne Braden, various conversations with the author.

43. Braden to author, 23 January 2001.

44. Taken from author's notes made during C. T. Vivian speech, 12 December 1999, Anne Braden Diamond Birthday Celebration, Louisville.

45. Shuttlesworth interview; Braden to author, 22 January 2002, copy in author's possession.
46. Cover, *Louisville Eccentric Observer*, 24 November 1999; Post interview; Braden to author, 4 January 2002.
47. I borrowed some of these characterizations from a comment by Isserman, *If I Had a Hammer*, xii; I. F. Stone, *The Haunted Fifties*; Lillian Hellman, *Scoundrel Time* (Boston: Little, Brown, and Co., 1976); Caute, *Great Fear*; Jetzer, *Dark Ages*.
48. Anne Braden, Clergy and Laity Concerned speech, Ebenezer Baptist Church, Atlanta, Georgia, 9 January 1990, transcript in author's possession.

Epilogue

1. Todd Gitlin, *Sixties*, 433.
2. Anne Braden quoted in Mark Schaver, "Louisville Activist to be Honored for Decades of Battling Racism," Louisville *Courier-Journal*, 12 December 1999.
3. This analysis is consonant with that of Honey in *Southern Labor*; Kelley in *Hammer and Hoe*; Charlotte Nekola and Paula Rabinowitz, eds., *Writing Red: An Anthology of American Women Writers, 1930–1940* (New York: Feminist Press, 1987); and Gilpin in "Left by Themselves," among others.
4. Braden interview with author, 8 March 1989; for an interesting discussion of post-WWII leftists' relations with the CP—one that influenced my approach—see Alan Wald, "Communist Writers Fight Back in Cold War Amerika," in *Styles of Cultural Activism: From Theory and Pedagogy to Women, Indians, and Communism*, ed. Philip Goldstein (Newark: University of Delaware Press, 1994), 219.
5. Alpern et al., introduction to *Challenge of Feminist Biography*, 12.
6. James W. Silver, *Mississippi: The Closed Society* (New York: Harcourt, Brace, & World, 1963).
7. Thomas Wolfe, *You Can't Go Home Again* (1998 ed.), 698–99.

BIBLIOGRAPHY

Manuscript and Other Document Collections

Alabama Room Archives. Anniston-Calhoun County Public Library. Anniston, Alabama.
Archives. Henry County Public Library. Eminence, Kentucky.
Olive Andrews Papers. Alabama Department of Archives and History. Montgomery.
Anne Braden Personal Papers. Louisville, Kentucky. In author's possession.
Carl and Anne Braden Papers. Special Collections and Archives. M. I. King Library. University
   of Kentucky. Lexington.
Carl and Anne Braden Papers. State Historical Society of Wisconsin. Madison.
Carl and Anne Braden Papers. Special Collections. Hoskins Library. University of Tennessee.
   Knoxville.
Federal Bureau of Investigation. Anne Braden Subject File. Copies in author's possession.
Kentucky Clippings Files (and Miscellaneous Holdings). Louisville Free Public Library.
Kentucky Papers of the Lyman T. Draper Manuscript Collection. Calendar Series, Volume 2.
   State Historical Society of Wisconsin. Madison.
Ann [sic] McGinty Folder. Harrodsburg Historical Society. Harrodsburg, Kentucky.
Mississippi State Sovereignty Commission Papers. Anne Braden subject file. Copies in author's
   possession.
Progressive Party Records. Special Collections. University of Iowa Libraries. Iowa City.
Randolph-Macon Woman's College Alumnae Files. Alumnae Affairs Office. Randolph-Macon
   Woman's College. Lynchburg, Virginia.
Seventh Census of the United States, 1850. Kentucky. Slave Schedules. Kentucky Department for
   Libraries and Archives. Frankfort.
Southern Christian Leadership Conference Papers. Martin Luther King Jr. Center for Nonvio-
   lent Social Change. Atlanta.
Stratford College Archives. Averitt College Library. Danville, Virginia.
Student Nonviolent Coordinating Committee Papers. Martin Luther King Jr. Center for Non-
   violent Social Change. Atlanta.
Vertical Files. Kentucky Department for Libraries and Archives. Frankfort, Kentucky.
Andrew Wade Personal Papers. In author's possession.

Interviews
(with author and privately held by author, unless otherwise noted)

Allison, William. Louisville, Kentucky. 23 June 1991.
Alston, Edith. Anniston, Alabama. 14 June 1989.
Bond, Julian. Charlottesville, Virginia. 17 September 1997.
Braden, Anne. Interviewed by Lenore Hogan. 23 June 1972; 7 December 1978; and 11 June
   1980. The Oral History Collection of Columbia University. Oral History Research Office.
   Columbia University. New York City.

————. Interviewed by Anthony Omer. 1 April 1975. Oral History Center. University Archives and Records Center. University of Louisville. Louisville, Kentucky.

————. Interviewed by Ruthe Pfisterer. 5 January 1981. Oral History Center. University Archives and Records Center. University of Louisville.

————. Interviewed by Sue Thrasher. 18 April 1981. Louisville, Kentucky. Held by Highlander Center. New Market, Tennessee.

————. Interviewed by Bud and Ruth Schultz. 2 September 1984. Elmwood, Connecticut. (Transcript in author's possession.)

————. Louisville, Kentucky. 7 March 1989.

————. Louisville, Kentucky. 8 March 1989.

————. Louisville, Kentucky. 9 March 1989.

————. Louisville, Kentucky. 10 March 1989.

————. Louisville, Kentucky. 11 March 1989.

————. Louisville, Kentucky. 11 November 1989.

————. Interviewed by author and Michael K. Honey. Louisville, Kentucky. 10 November 1994.

————. Louisville, Kentucky. 11 June 1996.

————. Louisville, Kentucky. 3 June 1997.

————. Louisville, Kentucky. 11 December 1997.

————. Louisville, Kentucky. 17 June 1999.

————. Louisville, Kentucky. 21 October 2001.

————. Louisville, Kentucky. 2 November 2001.

————. Louisville, Kentucky. 23 November 2001.

————. Mt. St. Francis, Indiana. 28 December 2001.

————. Mt. St. Francis, Indiana. 30 December 2001.

Braden, Carl and Anne. Interviewed by Robert Mosby. 8 September 1968. Civil Rights Documentation Project. Moorland-Spingarn Research Center. Howard University. Washington, D.C.

Browning, Joan. E-mail Interview. 26 September 1999.

Carver, Ilene. Boston, Massachusetts. 2 August 2001.

Cotton, Helen. Telephone Interview. 18 July 1996.

Crumlin, James. Louisville, Kentucky. 7 November 1989.

Curry, Constance. Atlanta, Georgia. 8 August 1997.

Finlator, W.W. Raleigh, North Carolina. 18 September 1997.

Hayden, Casey. E-mail Interview. 1 November 1999.

Johnson, Lyman T. Louisville, Kentucky. 24 June 1991.

Jones, Mattie. Louisville, Kentucky. 26 June 1991.

Lusky, Louis. Telephone Interview. 20 April 1999.

Minshall, Janet. Atlanta, Georgia. 9 August 1989.

Moffett, Tom. Louisville, Kentucky. 7 November 1989.

Moses, Robert. Cambridge, Massachusetts. 1 August 2001.

Neal, Mildred. Louisville, Kentucky. 25 June 1991.

Phillips, Jan. Louisville, Kentucky. 24 June 1991.

Post, Suzanne. Louisville, Kentucky. 24 June 1991.

Rogers, Gordon. Telephone Interview. 5 December 1997.

Shuttlesworth, Fred. Cincinnati, Ohio. 6 December 1997.

Silver, Dot Berea. Telephone Interview. 26 May 1996.

Stembridge, Jane. Telephone Interview. 12 October 1997.

Tachau, Eric. Louisville, Kentucky. 12 November 1989.

Thrasher, Sue. Telephone Interview. 16 November 1999.

Wade, Andrew. Louisville, Kentucky. 8 November 1989.

Wallace, Carla. Prospect, Kentucky. 9 December 1997.

Wallace, Henry. Prospect, Kentucky. 9 December 1997.

Yater, George. Louisville, Kentucky. 11 December 1997.

Yater, Marjorie. Louisville, Kentucky. 11 December 1997.
Zellner, Robert. New Orleans, Louisiana. 3 November 1990.

News Periodicals

Anniston Star
Antioch Record
Arkansas Gazette
Atlanta Constitution
Augusta Chronicle-Herald (Georgia)
Birmingham News
Courier-Journal (Louisville)
Daily Worker
Freedomways
Gazette & Daily (York, PA)
Great Speckled Bird
I. F. Stone's Weekly
Jackson Daily News
Labor's Voice
Louisville Defender
Louisville Eccentric Observer
Louisville Times
Mississippi Free Press
Montgomery Advertiser
Nashville Banner
Nation

National Guardian
Pittsburgh Courier
Raleigh News & Observer
San Francisco Chronicle
San Jose Mercury
Shively Newsweek
Southern Changes
Southern Fight-Back
Southern Newsletter
Southern Patriot
St. Louis Post-Dispatch
St. Petersburg Times
Student Voice
Sundial (Randolph-Macon Woman's College newspaper)
Time Magazine
Traveller (Stratford College newspaper)
University of Louisville Cardinal
U.S. News & World Report
Washington Evening Star

Books, Articles, Theses, Dissertations, and Other Works

Adams, Frank T. *James A. Dombrowski: An American Heretic, 1897–1983.* Knoxville: University of Tennessee Press, 1992.

Alpern, Sara, Joyce Antler, Elisabeth Israels Perry, and Ingrid Winther Scobie, editors. *The Challenge of Feminist Biography: Writing the Lives of Modern American Women.* Urbana: University of Illinois Press, 1992.

Anderson, Karen. *Wartime Women: Sex Roles, Family Relations, and the Status of Women during World War II.* Westport, Conn.: Greenwood, 1981.

Aronson, James. *The Press and the Cold War.* New York: Monthly Review Press, 1970.

Arsenault, Raymond, editor. *Crucible of Liberty: Two Hundred Years of the Bill of Rights.* New York: Free Press, 1991.

Autry, Dorothy. "The NAACP in Alabama: 1913–1952." Ph. D. dissertation, University of Notre Dame, 1985.

Baker, Houston A. "Being Framed: Afro-Modernity and Booker T. Washington in Southern Drag." Unpublished paper. Author-Meets-Reader workshop. University of Kentucky Commonwealth Humanities Initiative. Copy in author's possession.

Barnard, William D. *Dixiecrats and Democrats: Alabama Politics, 1942–1950.* Tuscaloosa, Ala.: University of Alabama Press, 1974.

Bartley, Numan V. *The Rise of Massive Resistance: Race and Politics in the South During the 1950s.* Baton Rouge: Louisiana State University Press, 1969.

"Behind the Bars for the First Amendment." Southern Conference Educational Fund publications. March 1960 pamphlet.

Belfrage, Cedric, and James Aronson. *Something to Guard: The Stormy Life and Death of The National Guardian, 1948–64.* New York: Columbia University Press, 1978.

Bell, Carolyn. "Learning the Contradictions: A History of Randolph-Macon Woman's College: 1950–1993." Unpublished manuscript in-progress. n.d.

Billingsley, William J. *Communists on Campus: Race, Politics, and the Public University in Sixties North Carolina*. Athens: University of Georgia Press, 1999.

Bingham, Sallie. *Passion and Prejudice: A Family Memoir*. New York: Alfred A. Knopf, 1989.

Braden, Anne. "Church Leader in Kentucky Indicted for Sedition." *The Witness* 42, no. 12 (17 February 1955).

———. *The Wall Between*. New York: Monthly Review Press, 1958; reprint, Knoxville: University of Tennessee, 1999.

———. *House Un-American Activities Committee: Bulwark of Segregation*. Los Angeles: National Committee to Abolish the House Un-American Activities Committee, 1963.

———. "The Southern Freedom Movement in Perspective." *Monthly Review* 17, no. 3 (July–August 1965). Special Issue.

———. *Free Thomas Wansley: A Letter to White Southern Women*. Louisville: SCEF Publications, 1972.

———. "A Second Open Letter to Southern White Women." *Southern Exposure* 4, no. 4 (July 1977): 50–53.

———. "Lessons from a History of Struggle." *Southern Exposure* 8, no. 2 (summer 1980): 56–61.

———. "A View from the Fringes." *Southern Exposure* 9, no. 2 (spring 1981): 68–73.

———. "American Inquisition Part Two: Political Repression in the 1960s." *Southern Exposure* 11, no. 5 (September–October 1983): 20–27.

Braden, Carl. "The Right to Organize: How North Carolina Wrecks People's Movements." Louisville: SCEF Publications. 1972 pamphlet.

Branch, Taylor. *Parting the Waters: America in the King Years, 1954–1963*. New York: Simon & Schuster, 1988.

———. *Pillar of Fire: America in the King Years, 1963–1965*. New York: Touchstone, 1999.

Brown, Sarah Hart. *Standing against Dragons: Three Southern Lawyers in an Era of Fear*. Baton Rouge: Louisiana State University Press, 1998.

Browning, Joan C. "Invisible Revolutionaries: White Women in Civil Rights Historiography." *Journal of Women's History* 8, no. 3 (fall 1996): 186–204.

Brownmiller, Susan. *In Our Time: Memoir of a Revolution*. New York: Dial, 1999.

Buhle, Mary Jo, Paul Buhle, and Dan Georgakas, editors. *Encyclopedia of the American Left*. Urbana: University of Illinois, 1992. Illini Books edition.

Campbell, Will. *Brother to a Dragonfly*. New York: Seabury, 1977.

Carmichael, Omar, and Weldon James. *The Louisville Story*. New York: Simon & Schuster, 1957.

Carson, Clayborne, ed. *The Autobiography of Martin Luther King, Jr*. New York: Warner Books, 1998.

———. *In Struggle: SNCC and the Black Awakening of the 1960s*. Cambridge: Harvard University Press, 1981.

Carter, Dan T. *Scottsboro: A Tragedy of the American South*. Baton Rouge: Louisiana State University Press, 1969.

———. *The Politics of Rage: George Wallace, the Origins of the New Conservatism, and the Transformation of American Politics*. New York: Simon & Schuster, 1995.

Cash, W. J. *The Mind of the South*. New York: Vintage, 1941.

Caute, David. *The Great Fear: The Anti-Communist Purge under Truman and Eisenhower*. New York: Simon & Schuster, 1978.

Chafe, William H. *The American Woman: Her Changing Social, Economic, and Political Roles, 1920–1970*. New York: Oxford University Press, 1972.

Chamberlain, Mariam, editor. *Women in Academe: Progress and Prospects*. New York: Russell Sage Foundation, 1988.

Chandler, David Leon with Mary Voelz Chandler. *The Binghams of Louisville: The Dark History behind One of America's Great Fortunes*. New York: Crown Publishers, 1987.

Clark, Thomas. *A History of Kentucky*. New York: Prentice-Hall, 1937.

Clark, Wayne Addison. "An Analysis of the Relationship Between Anti-Communism and Segregationist Thought in the Deep South, 1948–1954." Ph.D. dissertation, University of North Carolina, 1976.

Clemente, Frank, with Frank Watkins. *Keep Hope Alive: Jesse Jackson's 1988 Presidential Campaign*. Washington, D.C., and Boston: Keep Hope Alive PAC and South End Press, 1989.

Cobble, Dorothy Sue. "Recapturing Working-Class Feminism: Union Women in the Postwar Era." In *Not June Cleaver: Women and Gender in the Post-War America, 1945–1960*, edited by Joanne Meyerowitz. Philadelphia: Temple University Press, 1994.

Cohen, Robert. *When the Old Left Was Young*. New York: Oxford University Press, 1993.

Congressional Record. U.S. House of Representatives. 84th Congress, 2nd session, 1956.

Congressional Record. U.S. House of Representatives. 85th Congress, 17 February 1959.

Congressional Record. U.S. House of Representatives. 86th Congress, 8 February 1960.

Cook, Blanche Wiesen. *Eleanor Roosevelt: Volume 1, 1884–1933*. New York: Viking Penguin, 1992.

Cook, James Graham. *The Segregationists: A Penetrating Study of the Men and the Organizations Active in the South's Fight against Integration*. New York: Appleton-Century-Crofts, 1962.

Cooper, William J., Jr., and Thomas E. Terrill. *The American South: A History*. Volume 2. New York: McGraw-Hill, 1996.

Cott, Nancy F. *The Grounding of Modern Feminism*. New Haven, Conn.: Yale University Press, 1987.

Craven, Avery. *The Growth of Southern Nationalism: 1848–1861*. Baton Rouge: Louisiana State University Press, 1953.

Crawford, Vikki, Jacqueline Rouse, and Barbara Woods, editors. *Women in the Civil Rights Movement: Trailblazers and Torchbearers*. Brooklyn: Carlson, 1988.

Criley, Richard. *The F. B. I. v. the First Amendment*. Los Angeles: First Amendment Foundation, 1990.

Cummings, Scott, and Michael Price. "Race Relations and Public Policy in Louisville: Historical Development of an Urban Underclass." *Journal of Black Studies* 27, no. 5 (May 1997): 615–49.

Curry, Constance. *Silver Rights*. New York: Algonquin, 1994.

Curry, Constance, Joan C. Browning, Dorothy Dawson Burlage, Penny Patch, Theresa Del Pozzo, Sue Thrasher, Elaine DeLott Baker, Emmie Schrader Adams, and Casey Hayden. *Deep in Our Hearts: Nine White Women in the Southern Freedom Movement*. Athens: University of Georgia Press, 2000.

Davis, Angela. *Angela Davis: An Autobiography*. New York: Bantam, 1974.

D'Emilio, John, and Estelle Freedman. *Intimate Matters: A History of Sexuality in America*. New York: Harper & Row, 1988.

Dennis, Peggy. *Autobiography of an American Communist: A Personal View of a Political Life, 1925–75*. Berkeley, Calif.: Lawrence Hall, 1975.

Dittmer, John. *Local People: The Struggle for Civil Rights in Mississippi*. Urbana: University of Illinois Press, 1994.

Divine, Robert A. "The Cold War and the Election of 1948." *Journal of American History* 59, no. 1 (June 1972): 90–110.

Doctorow, E. L. *The Book of Daniel*. New York: Random House, 1971.

Donner, Frank J. *The Un-Americans*. New York: Ballantine, 1961.

Duberman, Martin Bauml. *Paul Robeson*. New York: Alfred A. Knopf, 1988.

DuBois, W. E. B. "Behold the Land." Reprinted in *Freedomways* 4, no. 1 (winter 1964): 9.

Dudziak, Mary L. *Cold War Civil Rights: Race and the Image of American Democracy*. Princeton, N.J.: Princeton University Press, 2000.

Dunbar, Anthony. *Against the Grain: Southern Radicals and Prophets, 1929–1959*. Charlottesville: University Press of Virginia, 1981.

Durr, Virginia. *Outside the Magic Circle: The Autobiography of Virginia Foster Durr*, edited by Hollinger Barnard. Tuscaloosa: University of Alabama Press, 1985.

Egerton, John. *Speak Now against the Day: The Generation before the Civil Rights Movement*. New York: Alfred A. Knopf, 1994.

Evans, Sara. *Personal Politics: The Roots of Women's Liberation in the Civil Rights Movement and the New Left*. New York: Vintage, 1979.

———. *Born for Liberty: A History of Women in America*. New York: Free Press, 1989.

Farber, David. *The Age of Great Dreams: America in the 1960s*. New York: Hill & Wang, 1994.

Farnham, Christie Anne. *The Education of the Southern Belle: Higher Education and Student Socialization in the Antebellum South*. New York: New York University Press, 1994.

Fisher, Berenice. "Wandering in the Wilderness: The Search for Women Role Models." In *Reconstructing the Academy: Women's Education and Women's Studies*, edited by Elizabeth Minnich, Jean O'Barr, and Rachel Rosenfeld. Chicago: University of Chicago Press, 1988.

Flynt, Wayne. "Growing Up Baptist in Anniston, Alabama: The Legacy of the Reverend Charles R. Bell, Jr." In *Clearings in the Thicket: An Alabama Humanities Reader*, edited by Jerry Elijah Brown. Macon, Ga.: Mercer University Press, 1985.

Folsom, James E. *Speeches of Governor James E. Folsom*. Wetumpka, Ala.: n.d.

Foner, Philip. "Operation Dixie." In *The Cold War against Labor, Volume 1*, edited by Anne Fagan Ginger and David Christiano. Berkeley, Calif.: Meiklejohn Civil Liberties Institute, 1987.

Forman, James. *The Making of Black Revolutionaries*. Washington, D.C.: Open Hand, 1985.

Foster, Catherine (now "Fosl, Catherine"). *Women for All Seasons: The Story of the Women's International League for Peace and Freedom*. Athens: University of Georgia Press, 1989.

Freeland, Richard M. *The Truman Doctrine and the Origins of McCarthyism: Foreign Policy, Domestic Policy, and Internal Security, 1946–1948*. New York: Alfred A. Knopf, 1972.

Fried, Albert. *McCarthyism: The Great American Red Scare*. New York: Oxford University Press, 1997.

Friedan, Betty. *The Feminine Mystique*. New York: Dell, 1963.

Garber, Marjorie, and Rebecca L. Walkowitz, editors. *Secret Agents: The Rosenberg Case, McCarthyism, and Fifties America*. New York: Routledge, 1995.

Gates, Grace Hooten. "Anniston: Transition from Company Town to Mill Town." *Alabama Review* 37, no. 1 (January 1984): 34–44.

Gellhorn, Walter. "Report on the Report of the Committee on Un-American Activities." *Harvard Law Review* 60 (1947): 1193–234.

Gentry, Curt. *J. Edgar Hoover: The Man and the Secrets*. New York: Plume, 1991.

Gilpin, Toni. "Left by Themselves: A History of the United Farm Equipment and Metal Workers Union, 1935–1955." Ph.D. dissertation, Yale University, 1992.

Gitlin, Todd. *The Sixties: Years of Hope, Days of Rage*. New York: Bantam, 1987.

Goldfield, David. *Promised Land: The South since 1945*. Arlington Heights, Ill.: Harlan Davidson, 1987.

Gornick, Vivian. *The Romance of American Communism*. New York: Basic Books, 1977.

Gosse, Van. "'To Organize in Every Neighborhood, in Every Home': The Gender Politics of American Communists between the Wars." *Radical History Review* 50 (spring 1991): 109–41.

Grafton, Carl. "James E. Folsom's 1946 Campaign." *Alabama Review* 35, no. 3 (1982): 172–99.

Grafton, Carl, and Anne Permaloff. *Big Mules and Branchheads: James E. Folsom and Political Power in Alabama*. Athens: University of Georgia Press, 1985.

Grant, Joanne. *Ella Baker Freedom Bound*. New York: John Wiley & Sons, 1998.

Gresham, John M., Company, compilers. *Biographical Cyclopedia of the Commonwealth of Kentucky*. Chicago: Gresham, 1896.

Griffith, Barbara. *Crisis of American Labor: Operation Dixie and the Defeat of the CIO*. Philadelphia: Temple University Press, 1988.

Halbertstam, David. *The Children*. New York: Random House, 1998.

Hall, Alvin. *The History of Stratford College*. Danville, Va.: Womack Press, 1974.

Hall, Wade. *The Rest of the Dream: The Black Odyssey of Lyman Johnson*. Lexington: University Press of Kentucky, 1988.

Hansberry, Lorraine. *A Raisin in the Sun*. Signet, 1988 revised edition. New York.

Hanisch, Carol. "Blacks, Women, and the Movement in SCEF." In *Feminist Revolution*, edited by Redstockings. New York: Random House, 1975.

Harrison, Lowell. *The Anti-Slavery Movement in Kentucky*. Lexington: University Press of Kentucky, 1978.

Hartman, Chester W. *Housing and Social Policy*. Englewood Cliffs, N.J.: Prentice-Hall, 1975.

Hartmann, Susan. *The Home Front and Beyond: American Women in the 1940s*. Boston: Twayne, 1982.

———. "Women's Employment and the Domestic Ideal in the Early Cold War Years." In *Not June Cleaver: Women and Gender in Post-War America, 1945–1960*, edited by Joanne Meyerowitz. Philadelphia: Temple University Press, 1994.

Hayden, Tom. *Reunion: A Memoir*. New York: Random House, 1988.

Heale, M. J. *American Anticommunism: Combating the Enemy Within*. Baltimore: Johns Hopkins University Press, 1991.

———. *McCarthy's Americans: Red Scare Politics in State and Nation, 1935–1965*. Athens: University of Georgia Press, 1998.

Healey, Dorothy, and Maurice Isserman. *California Red: A Life in the Communist Party*. Urbana: University of Illinois, 1993.

Hellman, Lillian. *Scoundrel Time*. Boston: Little, Brown, and Co., 1976.

Henry, Kathryn. "Life and Sojourn of a Southern Liberal." M.A. thesis, Auburn University, 1986.

Hewitt, Nancy, and Suzanne Lebsock, editors. *Visible Women: New Essays on American Activism*. Urbana: University of Illinois Press, 1993.

Hirsch, Arnold. *Making the Second Ghetto: Race and Housing in Chicago, 1940–1960*. Cambridge: Cambridge University Press, 1983.

Hobson, Fred. *But Now I See: The White Southern Racial Conversion Narrative*. Baton Rouge: Louisiana State University Press, 1999.

Honey, Michael K. *Southern Labor and Black Civil Rights: Organizing Memphis Workers*. Urbana: University of Illinois Press, 1993.

Horne, Gerald. *Communist Front? The Civil Rights Congress, 1946–1956*. Rutherford, N.J.: Fairleigh Dickinson University Press, 1988.

Horowitz, Daniel. *Betty Friedan and the Making of the Feminine Mystique: The American Left, the Cold War, and Modern Feminism*. Amherst: University of Massachusetts Press, 1998.

Horowitz, Helen Lefkowitz. *Alma Mater: Design and Experience in the Women's Colleges from their Nineteenth-Century Beginnings to the 1930s*. New York: Alfred A. Knopf, 1984.

Horton, Colonel John Benjamin. *Not without Struggle*. New York: Vantage, 1979.

Hughes, C. Alvin. "We Demand Our Rights: The Southern Negro Youth Congress, 1937–1949." *Phylon* 48, no. 1 (1987): 38–50.

Irvin, Helen Deiss. *Women in Kentucky*. Lexington: University Press of Kentucky, 1979.

Isserman, Maurice. *If I Had A Hammer: The Death of the Old Left and the Birth of the New Left*. New York: Basic Books, 1987.

Jackson, Blyden, editor. *The Waiting Years: Essays on American Negro Literature*. Baton Rouge: Louisiana State University Press, 1976.

Jackson, Kenneth T. *Crabgrass Frontier: The Suburbanization of the United States*. New York: Oxford University Press, 1985.

Jacoway, Elizabeth, and David R. Colburn, editors. *Southern Businessmen and Desegregation*. Baton Rouge: Louisiana State University Press, 1982.

Jenkins, Phillip. *The Cold War at Home*. Chapel Hill: University of North Carolina Press, 1999.

Jetzer, Marty. *The Dark Ages: Life in the United States, 1945–1960*. Boston: South End Press, 1982.

Jones, Patrick. "'Communist Front Shouts Kissing Case to the World': The Committee to Combat Racial Injustice and the Politics of Race and Gender during the Cold War." M.A. thesis, University of Wisconsin-Madison, 1996.

Judis, John. "Henry Wallace and the Common Man." In his *Grand Illusions: Critics and Champions of the American Century*. New York: Farrar, Straus, & Giroux, 1992.

Kaplan, Judy, and Linn Shapiro. *Red Diapers: Growing Up in the Communist Left*. Urbana: University of Illinois Press, 1998.

Kelley, Robin D. G. *Hammer and Hoe: Alabama Communists during the Great Depression*. Chapel Hill: University of North Carolina Press, 1990.

Kentucky Commission on Human Rights. *Kentucky's Black Heritage*. Frankfort: Commonwealth of Kentucky, 1971.

Kerber, Linda. "Separate Spheres, Female Worlds, Woman's Place: The Rhetoric of Women's History." *Journal of American History* 75 (June 1988): 9–39.

Kerber, Linda, Alice Kessler-Harris, and Kathryn Kish Sklar, editors. *U.S. History as Women's History: New Feminist Essays*. Chapel Hill: University of North Carolina Press, 1995.

Kiffmeyer, Thomas J. "From Self-Help to Sedition: The Appalachian Volunteers in Eastern Kentucky, 1964–1970." *Journal of Southern History* 64, no. 1 (February 1998): 65–94.

Kimmage, Anne. *An Un-American Childhood*. Athens: University of Georgia Press, 1996.

King, Martin Luther, Jr. *Stride toward Freedom*. New York: Harper & Row, Perennial edition, 1958.

King, Mary. *Freedom Song: A Personal Story of the 1960s Civil Rights Movement*. New York: William Morrow, 1987.

Kinoy, Arthur. *Rights on Trial: Odyssey of a People's Lawyer*. Cambridge: Harvard University Press, 1983.

Kirby, Jack Temple. *Rural Worlds Lost: The American South, 1920–1960*. Baton Rouge: Louisiana State University Press, 1987.

Klehr, Harvey. *The Heyday of American Communism: The Depression Decade*. New York: Basic Books, 1984.

Klehr, Harvey, John Earl Haynes, and K. M. Anderson. *The Soviet World of American Communism*. New Haven, Conn.: Yale University Press, 1998.

Klehr, Harvey, John Earl Haynes, and F. I. Firsov. *The Secret World of American Communism*. New Haven, Conn.: Yale University Press, 1995.

Klibaner, Irwin. *Conscience of a Troubled South: The Southern Conference Educational Fund, 1946–1966*. Brooklyn: Carlson, 1989.

Kluger, Richard. *Simple Justice: The History of* Brown v. Board of Education *and Black America's Struggle for Equality*. New York: Vintage, 1975.

Kneebone, John T. *Southern Liberal Journalists and the Issue of Race, 1920–1944*. Chapel Hill: University of North Carolina Press, 1985.

Korstad, Robert, and Nelson Lichtenstein. "Opportunities Lost and Found: Labor, Radicals, and the Early Civil Rights Movement." *Journal of American History* 75, no. 3 (December 1988): 786–811.

Kovel, Joel. *Red Hunting in the Promised Land: Anti-Communism and the Making of America*. New York: Basic Books, 1994.

Krueger, Thomas A. *And Promises to Keep: The Southern Conference for Human Welfare*. Nashville: Vanderbilt University Press, 1967.

Ladd-Taylor, Molly, "Toward Defining Maternalism in U.S. History." *Journal of Women's History* 5, no. 2 (Fall 1993): 110–13.

Langum, David. *William M. Kunstler: The Most Hated Lawyer in America*. New York: NYU Press, 1999.

Lee, Chana Kai. *For Freedom's Sake*. Urbana: University of Illinois Press, 1999.

Levenstein, Harvey A. *Communism, Anticommunism, and the C. I. O.* Westport, Conn.: Greenwood, 1981.

Lewis, John, and Michael D'Orso. *Walking with the Wind: A Memoir of the Movement*. New York: Simon & Schuster, 1998.

"Lillian Smith: A Struggle for Wholeness." n.a. *Southern Changes* 21, no. 3 (fall 1999): 16.

Logan, Rayford. *The Negro in American Life and Thought: The Nadir, 1877–1901*. New York: Dial, 1954.

Lumpkin, Katharine DuPre. *The Making of a Southerner*. New York: Alfred A. Knopf, 1947.

Lundberg, Ferdinand, and Marynia Farnham. *Modern Woman: The Lost Sex*. New York: Harper & Brothers, 1947.

Lusky, Louis. "The First Cases: Sedition and Shuffling Sam." In *The ACLU of Kentucky, 1955–1995: A Celebration*. n.a. Madison, Wis.: Digital Printing, 1995.

Lynn, Susan. "Gender and Progressive Politics: A Bridge to Social Activism of the 1960s." In *Not June Cleaver: Women and Gender in the Post-War America, 1945–1960*, edited by Joanne Meyerowitz. Philadelphia: Temple University Press, 1994.

Lyons, Paul. *Philadelphia Communists, 1936–56*. Philadelphia: Temple University Press, 1982.

MacDougall, Curtis. *Gideon's Army*. 3 vols. New York: Marzani & Munsell, 1965.

Manis, Andrew. *A Fire You Can't Put Out: The Civil Rights Life of Birmingham's Reverend Fred Shuttlesworth*. Tuscaloosa: University of Alabama Press, 1999.

Markowitz, Norman. *The Rise and Fall of the People's Century: Henry A. Wallace and American Liberalism, 1941–1948*. New York: Free Press, 1973.

Massey, Douglas, and Nancy Denton. *American Apartheid: Segregation and the Making of the Underclass*. Cambridge: Harvard University Press, 1993.

May, Elaine Tyler. *Homeward Bound: American Families in the Cold War Era*. New York: Basic Books, 1982.

McCarty, Anne. "Discovery." *The Tattler* (literary magazine of Randolph-Macon Woman's College) 30 (Christmas 1944), 9–12.

———. "A Student Views the College." *Alumnae Bulletin of R-MWC* 38, no. 3 (April 1945), 39–40.

McCarty, Anne Gambrell. "Activities in a Southern School." *Student Life* 7, no. 6 (March 1942): 11 (copy in author's possession).

McDowell, Robert. *City of Conflict: Louisville in the Civil War, 1861–1865*. Louisville: Louisville Civil War Roundtable Publishers, 1962.

McElhone, Patrick. "The Civil Rights Activities of the Louisville Branch of the NAACP, 1914–1960." M. A. thesis, University of Louisville, 1976.

McWhorter, Diane. *Carry Me Home: Birmingham, Alabama: The Climactic Battle of the Civil Rights Revolution*. New York: Simon & Schuster, 2001.

Meier, August, and John Bracey Jr. "The NAACP as a Reform Movement, 1909–1965: To Reach the Conscience of America." *Journal of Southern History* 59, no. 1 (February 1993): 3–30.

Meier, August, and Elliot Rudwick. *CORE: A Study in the Civil Rights Movement, 1942–1968*. New York: Oxford University Press, 1973.

Melish, William Howard. *When Christians Become Subversive*. New York: Episcopal League for Social Action, 1955.

Meyer, Stephen Grant. *As Long as They Don't Move Next Door: Segregation and Racial Conflict in American Neighborhoods*. Lanham, Md.: Rowman & Littlefield, 2000.

Meyerowitz, Joanne. *Women Adrift: Independent Wage Earners in Chicago, 1880–1930*. Chicago: University of Chicago Press, 1988.

———. "Beyond the Feminine Mystique: A Reassessment of Postwar Mass Culture, 1946–1958." In *Not June Cleaver: Women and Gender in the Post-War America, 1945–1960*, edited by Joanne Meyerowitz. Philadelphia: Temple University Press, 1994.

Michel, Gregg. "'We'll Take Our Stand': The Southern Student Organizing Committee and the Radicalization of White Southern Students, 1964–1969." Ph.D. dissertation, University of Virginia, 1999.

Millis, Walter. "Louisville's Braden Case: A Test of Basic Rights." *Nation*, 7 May 1955: 393–98.

Minnich, Elizabeth, with Jean O'Barr, and Rachel Rosenfeld, editors. *Reconstructing the Academy: Women's Education and Women's Studies*. Chicago: University of Chicago Press, 1988.

Morris, Aldon D. *The Origins of the Civil Rights Movement: Black Communities Organizing for Change*. New York: Free Press, 1984.

Murray, Gail, editor. *Throwing Off the Cloak of Privilege: Southern White Women Activists in the Era of Civil Rights*. Tallahassee: University Press of Florida, forthcoming.

"My Beliefs and Associations Are None of the Business of This Committee." Southern Conference Educational Fund, n.d., pamphlet.

Nasstrom, Kathryn. *Everybody's Grandmother and Nobody's Fool: Frances Freeborn Pauley and the Struggle for Social Justice*. Ithaca: Cornell University Press, 2000.

Nekola, Charlotte, and Paula Rabinowitz. *Writing Red: An Anthology of American Women Writers, 1930–1940*. New York: Feminist Press, 1987.

Nelson, Steve, James R. Barrett, and Rob Ruck. *Steve Nelson, American Radical*. Pittsburgh: University of Pittsburgh Press, 1981.

Nold, James, Jr., and Julie Segal. *The Insiders' Guide to Greater Louisville*. Lexington: Lexington Herald-Leader Publications, 1985.

Nonnenmacher, Louise, and Carleton Lentz. *Years of Grace*. Anniston: Grace Church Publications, 1948.

Nuckols, S. V. "History of William Poage and His Wife, Ann Kennedy Wilson Poage Lindsay McGinty." *Register of the Kentucky Historical Society* 11, no. 1 (January 1913): 101–102.

Odum, Howard. *Race and Rumors of Race*. Chapel Hill: University of North Carolina Press, 1943.

O'Brien, Gail Williams. *The Color of the Law: Race, Violence, and Justice in the Post–World War Two South*. Chapel Hill: University of North Carolina, 1999.

O'Connor, Jessie Lloyd, Harvey O'Connor, and Susan M. Bowles. *Harvey and Jessie: A Couple of Radicals*. Philadelphia: Temple University Press, 1988.

"Old Fort Harrod State Park." Kentucky Department of Parks. 1995. Brochure in author's possession.

Olson, Lynne. *Freedom's Daughters: The Unsung Heroines of the Civil Rights Movement from 1830 to 1970*. New York: Scribner's, 2001.

Oppenheimer, Martin. *The Sit-In Movement of 1960*. Brooklyn: Carlson, 1989.

O'Reilly, Kenneth. "Liberal Values, the Cold War, and American Intellectuals: The Trauma of the Alger Hiss Case, 1950–1978." In *Beyond the Hiss Case: The FBI, the Congress, and the Cold War*, edited by Athan G. Theoharis. Philadelphia: Temple University Press, 1982.

———. *Hoover and the Un-Americans: The FBI, HUAC, and the Red Menace*. Philadelphia: Temple University Press, 1983.

———. *"Racial Matters": The FBI's Secret File on Black America*. New York: Free Press, 1989.

Orleck, Annelise. *Common Sense and a Little Fire : Women and Working-Class Politics in the United States, 1900–1965*. Chapel Hill: University of North Carolina Press, 1995.

Oshinsky, David. *A Conspiracy So Immense: The World of Joe McCarthy*. New York: Free Press, 1983.

Painter, Nell Irwin, with Hosea Hudson. *The Narrative of Hosea Hudson: His Life as a Negro Communist in the South*. Cambridge: Harvard University Press, 1979.

Patton, Randall. "The CIO and the Search for a Silent South." *Maryland Historian* 19, no. 2 (1988): 8–13.

Payne, Charles. *I've Got the Light of Freedom: The Organizing Tradition and the Mississippi Freedom Struggle*. Berkeley: University of California Press, 1995.

Pearce, John Ed. *Divide and Dissent: Kentucky Politics, 1930–1963*. Lexington: University Press of Kentucky, 1987.

———. *Memoirs: Fifty Years at the Courier-Journal and Other Places*. Louisville: Sulgrave, 1997.

Peebles, Jack. "Subversion and the Southern Conference Educational Fund." M. A. thesis, Louisiana State University at New Orleans, 1970.

Perry, Jennings. "Sedition in Louisville: The Braden Affair." *Nation*, 15 January 1955.

Philipson, Irene. *Ethel Rosenberg: Beyond the Myths*. New Brunswick, N.J.: Rutgers University Press, 1988.

Polenberg, Richard. "The Good War? A Reappraisal of How World War II Affected American Society." *Virginia Magazine of History and Biography* 100, no. 3 (July 1992): 295–322.

Protest the Jailing of Walter Collins. Louisville: SCEF leaflet, 1972.

Raines, Howell. *My Soul Is Rested: The Story of the Civil Rights Movement in the Deep South*. New York: Penguin, 1977.

Record, Wilson. *The Negro and the Communist Party*. Chapel Hill: University of North Carolina Press, 1951.

Redding, Louis. "Louisville Travesty." New York: Emergency Civil Liberties Committee, n.d. Pamphlet in author's possession.

Reed, Linda A. *Simple Decency and Common Sense: The Southern Conference Movement, 1938–1963.* Bloomington: Indiana University Press, 1991.

Rennick, Robert. *Kentucky Place Names.* Lexington: University Press of Kentucky, 1984.

Renov, Michael. *Hollywood's Wartime Woman: Representation and Ideology.* Ann Arbor, Mich.: University Microfilms International [UMI] Research Press, 1988.

Robinson, Jo Ann Gibson. *The Montgomery Bus Boycott and the Women Who Started It.* Knoxville: University of Tennessee Press, 1987.

Robnett, Belinda. *How Long? How Long? African American Women in the Civil Rights Movement.* New York: Oxford University Press, 1997.

Rogers, William Warren, Robert Ward, Leah Rawls Atkins, and Wayne Flynt. *Alabama: History of a Deep South State.* Tuscaloosa: University of Alabama Press, 1994.

Rosen, Ruth. *The World Split Open: How the Modern Women's Movement Changed America.* New York: Penguin, 2000.

Rosenberg, Rosalind. *Beyond Separate Spheres: Intellectual Roots of Modern Feminism.* New Haven, Conn.: Yale University Press, 1982.

Rosswurm, Steve, editor. *The CIO's Left-Led Unions.* New Brunswick, N.J.: Rutgers University Press, 1992.

Roydhouse, Marion W. "Bridging Chasms: Community and the Southern YWCA." In *Visible Women: New Essays on American Activism,* edited by Nancy Hewitt and Suzanne Lebsock. Urbana: University of Illinois Press, 1993.

Rupp, Leila, and Verda Taylor. *Survival in the Doldrums: The American Women's Rights Movement, 1945 to the 1960s.* Oxford: Oxford University Press, 1987.

Sabin, Arthur. *In Calmer Times: The Supreme Court and Red Monday.* Philadelphia: University of Pennsylvania Press, 1999.

Salmond, John. *A Southern Rebel: The Life and Times of Aubrey Willis Williams, 1890–1965.* Chapel Hill: University of North Carolina Press, 1983.

Schrecker, Ellen. *No Ivory Tower: McCarthyism and the Universities.* Oxford: Oxford University Press, 1986.

———. "Before the Rosenbergs: Espionage Scenarios in the Early Cold War." In *Secret Agents: The Rosenberg Case, McCarthyism, and Fifties America,* edited by Marjorie Garber and Rebecca L. Walkowitz. New York: Routledge, 1995.

———. *Many Are the Crimes: McCarthyism in America.* Boston: Little, Brown, and Co., 1998.

Schultz, Bud, and Ruth Schultz, editors. *It Did Happen Here: Recollections of Political Repression in America.* Berkeley: University of California Press, 1989.

Scott, Anne Firor. *The Southern Lady: From Pedestal to Politics, 1830–1930.* Chicago: University of Chicago Press, 1970.

Shaffer, Robert. "Women and the Communist Party, U.S.A., 1930–1940." *Socialist Review* 9, no. 3 (May–June 1979): 73–118.

Shoemaker, Ralph, editor. *Chronological List of Events in the* Courier-Journal *and* Times *History.* Louisville: Louisville Free Public Library, 1947.

Showalter, Elaine, editor. *These Modern Women: Autobiographical Essays from the Twenties,* revised edition. New York: Feminist Press, 1989.

Silver, James W. *Mississippi: The Closed Society.* New York: Harcourt, Brace, & World, 1963.

Simmons, Jerold. "The Origins of the Campaign to Abolish HUAC, 1956–1961, the California Connection." *Southern California Quarterly* 64, no. 2 (1982): 141–59.

Smith, Lillian. *Killers of the Dream.* New York: W.W. Norton, 1961 revised edition.

Smith-Rosenberg, Carroll. "The Female World of Love and Ritual: Relations between Women in Nineteenth-Century America." *Signs: A Journal of Women in Culture and Society* 1 (1975): 1–30.

Solomon, Barbara. *In the Company of Educated Women: A History of Women and Higher Education in America.* New Haven, Conn.: Yale University Press, 1985.

Sosna, Morton. *In Search of the Silent South: Southern Liberals and the Race Issue.* New York: Columbia University Press, 1977.

Starobin, Joseph. *American Communism in Crisis: 1943–1957.* Cambridge: Harvard University Press, 1972.

Sterne, Emma Gelders. "A House to Live In." In her *They Took Their Stand*. New York: Crowell-Collier, 1968.

Stone, I. F. *The Haunted Fifties*. New York: Random House, 1963.

Sullivan, Patricia. "Gideon's Southern Soldiers: New Deal Politics and Civil Rights Reform, 1933–1948." Ph.D. dissertation, Emory University, 1983.

———. "Southern Reformers, the New Deal, and the Movement's Foundation." *New Directions in Civil Rights Studies*, edited by Armstead Robinson and Patricia Sullivan. Charlottesville: University Press of Virginia, 1991.

———. *Days of Hope: Race and Democracy in the New Deal Era*. Chapel Hill: University of North Carolina Press, 1996.

Swerdlow, Amy. "The Congress of American Women: Left-Feminist Peace Politics in the Cold War." In *U.S. History as Women's History: New Feminist Essays*, edited by Linda Kerber, Alice Kessler-Harris, and Kathryn Kish Sklar. Chapel Hill: University of North Carolina Press, 1995.

Taylor, Beth. "Little Compton's Gentle Radicals." *Providence [R.I.] Sunday Journal*, 8 February 1981: 8–13.

Theoharis, Athan G., editor. *Beyond the Hiss Case: The FBI, The Congress, and the Cold War*. Philadelphia: Temple University Press, 1982.

Thompson, Becky. *A Promise and a Way of Life: White Antiracist Activism*. Minneapolis: University of Minnesota Press, 2001.

Thornbery, Jerry. "Operation Freedom and the Mississippi Movement." Unpublished paper read before the Organization of American Historians. Chicago. 29 March 1996.

———. "Amzie Moore and His Civil Rights Allies, 1951–1960." Unpublished paper read before the Southern Historical Association. Orlando, Florida. 12 November 1993.

Thrasher, Sue. "Oral History." *Southern Exposure* 12, no. 6 (November–December 1984): 80–81.

Tidball, M. Elizabeth. "Women's Colleges and Women Achievers Revisited." In *Reconstructing the Academy: Women's Education and Women's Studies*, edited by Elizabeth Minnich, Jean O'Barr, and Rachel Rosenfeld. Chicago: University of Chicago Press, 1988.

Trimberger, Ellen Kay. "Women in the Old and New Left: The Evolution of a Politics of Personal Life." *Feminist Studies* 5, no. 3 (fall 1979): 432–50.

Tyson, Timothy B. *Radio Free Dixie: Robert F. Williams and the Roots of Black Power*. Chapel Hill: University of North Carolina Press, 1999.

———. "Robert Williams, Black Power, and the Roots of the African American Freedom Struggle." *Journal of American History* 85, no. 2 (September 1998): 540–70.

U.S. Bureau of the Census. *County Data Book: Supplement to the Statistical Abstract of the United States*. Washington, D.C.: U. S. Government Printing Office, 1947.

Van Der Veer Hamilton, Vivian. *Looking for Clark Gable and Other Twentieth-Century Pursuits*. Tuscaloosa: University of Alabama Press, 1996.

Wald, Alan. "Communist Writers Fight Back in Cold War Amerika." In *Styles of Cultural Activism: From Theory and Pedagogy to Women, Indians, and Communism*, edited by Philip Goldstein. Newark: University of Delaware Press, 1994.

Walton, Richard J. *Henry Wallace, Harry Truman, and the Cold War*. New York: Viking, 1976.

Watters, Pat. *Down to Now: Reflections on the Southern Civil Rights Movement*. New York: Pantheon, 1971.

Webb, Ross A. *Kentucky in the Reconstruction Era*. Lexington: University Press of Kentucky, 1979.

Weigand, Kate. "The Red Menace, the Feminine Mystique, and the Ohio Un-American Activities Commission: Gender and Anticommunism in Ohio, 1951–1954." *Journal of Women's History* 3, no. 3 (1992): 70–94.

———. *Red Feminism: American Communism and the Making of Women's Liberation*. Baltimore: Johns Hopkins University Press, 2000.

Wheeler, Marjorie Spruill. *New Women of the New South: The Leaders of the Woman Suffrage Movement in the Southern States*. New York: Oxford University Press, 1993.

Whites, LeeAnn. "Rebecca Latimer Felton and the Problem of 'Protection' in the New South." In *Visible Women: New Essays on American Activism*, edited by Nancy Hewitt and Suzanne Lebsock. Urbana: University of Illinois Press, 1993.

Whitfield, Stephen J. *Culture of the Cold War*. Baltimore: Johns Hopkins University Press, 1991.

———. "Civil Liberties and the Culture of the Cold War, 1945–1965." In *Crucible of Liberty: 200 Years of the Bill of Rights*, edited by Raymond Arsenault. New York: Free Press, 1991.

Williamson, Andrew Woods, Henry Williamson, John Guy Bishop, and Robert Woodworth. *Descendants of Robert and John Poage*, Volume 1. Staunton, Va.: McClure Printing, 1954.

Williamson, Joel. *A Rage for Order: Black-White Relations in the American South since Emancipation*. New York: Oxford University Press, 1986.

Wolfe, Margaret Ripley. "Fallen Leaves and Missing Pages: Women in Kentucky History." *Register of the Kentucky Historical Society* 90, no. 1 (winter 1992): 64–89.

Wolfe, Thomas. *You Can't Go Home Again*. New York: Harper & Row, 1940; revised edition, 1998.

Woods, Barbara. "Black Woman Activist: Modjeska Montieth Simkins." Ph.D. dissertation, Emory University, 1978.

Woodward, C. Vann. *Origins of the New South*. Baton Rouge: Louisiana State University Press, 1951.

Wright, George C. "Desegregation of Public Accommodations in Louisville." In *Southern Businessmen and Desegregation*, edited by Elizabeth Jacoway and David R. Colburn. Baton Rouge: Louisiana State University Press, 1982.

———. *Life behind a Veil: Blacks in Louisville, Kentucky, 1865–1930*. Baton Rouge: Louisiana State University Press, 1985.

Yater, George H. *Two Hundred Years at the Falls of the Ohio: A History of Louisville and Jefferson County*. Louisville: Heritage Corporation, 1970.

Young. Charles. "American Inquisition Part One: The Trial of Alan and Margaret McSurely." *Southern Exposure* 11, no. 5 (September–October 1983): 15–19.

Zinn, Howard. *A People's History of the United States*. New York: Harper Perennial, 1990.

INDEX

Abernathy, Ralph, 274, 275
abolitionism, 4, 34, 161
Abzug, Bella, 319
African Americans:
    alienation from southern culture, 211
    armed self-defense by, 149, 247
    black nationalism among, 301, 314
    new generation of leadership in 1870s,
        210–211
    in nineteenth-century Kentucky, 7–9
    in post–civil rights era, 328, 329, 339
    in post–Civil War South, 52
    post-WWI exodus from South, 13
    in WWII, 53–54
Ahearn, Alberta, 123, 160, 172–173, 199,
    229, 232
Alabama Christian Movement for Human
    Rights, 208–209, 284
Allied Mills, 10, 15
Amatniek, Kathie: See Sarachild, Kathie
American Civil Liberties Union, 124, 144,
    169, 185–186, 187, 202, 230, 288, 325
    awards Roger Baldwin medal to Anne
        Braden, 328
    See also Kentucky Civil Liberties Union
American Federation of Labor, 25
American Peace Crusade, 123, 181
Anniston, Alabama:
    impact of Depression on, 16
    settlement and early history of, 15
Anniston Star, 16, 20, 28, 46, 47, 57, 61–62,
    63, 65, 68, 71, 190
anticommunism, southern:
    pre-WWII, 28
    See also Cold War, in South; civil rights
        movement
antifeminist literature, 70, 355 n.39
antinuclear movement, 1970s–1980s, 324
Appalachia:
    poverty of, 304
    SCEF program in, 303–304, 305, 306
Appalachian Volunteers, 306
Arens, Richard, 233
Arnall, Ellis, 54
Associated Press, 181, 219, 257

Atlanta Constitution, 52, 231, 233
Ayers, Col. Harry, 46, 61, 65
Ayers, Elise (Sanguinetti), 190

"Baby Boom," 44, 126
Baker, Bobby, 36, 41
Baker, Ella, xxiv, 131, 225, 241, 249, 250,
    255, 293, 316
    kinship with Anne Braden, 216–217, 256,
        260, 277, 280, 281, 286, 296
    on SCEF staff, 288, 294
Barnett, Albert, 235
Barnett, Mary Agnes, 121, 168, 190–191
Barnett, Walter, 120, 121, 156, 160, 168,
    190–191
Barry, Marion, 254
Beech, Gould, 76
Berkeley (CA) student movement, 266, 267
Bethune, Mary McLeod, 25
Bevel, Diane Nash: See Nash, Diane
Bilbo, Sen. Theodore, 182
Bingham, Barry, 71, 194–195
Bingham family, 80, 142, 164
Birmingham:
    1962 mass meeting held in, 284
    1963 church bombing in, 279, 293
    as bastion of segregation, x, 72–73, 219
    newspapers, 71–72
birth control, 42, 126
Black, Hugo, 236, 270
black nationalism:
    See African Americans; Black Panthers;
        Black Power movement
Black Panthers, 314, 320, 391 n.19
Black Power movement, 301–302, 304, 317,
    320
    Bradens' defense of, 314, 315–316
    in Louisville, 306
    repression of, 309, 314–317, 323, 324,
        327
Black Six, 315
Boone, Daniel, 4
Bond, Julian, 103, 256, 257, 265
Boswell Amendment, 64–65, 73–74
Boudin, Leonard, 186, 188, 235, 236, 265

Bown, Vernon, 149, 159, 160–161, 162, 168, 195, 199
Braden v. United States of America: See Braden, Carl
Braden, Anita McCarty, 127, 128, 149, 150, 162, 166, 177, 192, 213–215, 231, 272, 322
  illness and death of, 130, 294–297, 298, 300, 338
Braden, Anne Gambrell McCarty:
  ancestry and heritage of, 4–11
  asceticism of, 49, 329
  attends women's colleges, 33–35, 37–38, 40, 43, 44, 45, 47–48, 95
  awards bestowed on, 328, 391 n.40
  class identity of, 18, 69, 92–93, 96, 105, 112, 114, 338
  creates uproar at San Jose State University, 267–268
  and domestic ideal, 69–71, 104, 133, 149–150, 238
  elder years of, 327–331
  female friends and mentors in college, 37–38, 39–42
  and feminist consciousness, 42, 43, 45–46, 111–112, 114, 115–116, 117–118, 124, 132, 133, 260, 318–320
  fights marginalization in social justice activism, 228, 260, 262, 263–264, 267–268, 276, 286, 287, 289–290, 299
  impact of Carl's HUAC imprisonment on, 270, 271–272, 280, 281, 282–283
  impact of Folsom campaign upon, 66–68
  impact of WWII upon, 37, 45, 52, 56
  independence of, 104, 107–108, 133
  intellectual awakening of, 35–41, 45, 47, 49–52, 55–56
  long letters written by, 184, 253, 261
  love of journalism, xxiii, 29, 31, 37, 46–47, 49, 56, 217–218, 240
  love of literature and poetry, 23, 38, 49–50, 107
  and Marxism, 119, 189, 205, 235–236, 335, 338
  "McCarty drive" of, 35–36, 79, 209, 330
  memories of Great Depression, 16, 17
  and motherhood 112, 125–132, 155, 162, 167, 214–215, 246, 247, 249, 272, 296–297, 322, 334, 338
  as newspaper reporter, 46–48, 56, 57, 60–64, 67, 68, 71–74, 76–80, 86–89, 90–91, 95, 102, 105–106, 110, 112–113
  on lesbianism and love for Harriet Fitzgerald, 40–41, 50
  and the "other America," xxvi–xxvii, xxviii, 125, 187, 192, 210, 331, 340
  other romances of, 41–42, 43, 68–69, 78–80, 327
  as pariah in Louisville, 6, 167, 264, 296, 317, 323, 327–328

as part of transitional generation, xxi, 44–45, 133
politicization of, 50–51, 55, 56, 85–89, 91–93, 94–97, 100, 101–102, 104, 108
and Progressive Party, 93–95, 100–102, 118–120, 124
and "protectionism" of white women 42, 123–124, 319
and racism and racial identity, 11, 50–51, 86–87, 88, 95, 96, 121, 124, 198, 212, 238–239, 278–279, 300, 301, 304, 324, 327, 330–331, 336, 337, 345 n.7
relations with student activists, xxiii, 241, 242, 245–246, 248, 250–251, 252–253, 254, 255, 259–260, 265, 269, 281
relationship to CP, 119, 120, 171, 235–236, 268, 321, 334–335
relationship with biographer, xxv, 333, 335, 336, 337, 338, 341
relationship with Carl Braden, xxviii, 41, 84, 85, 89, 91, 95–96, 102, 103–112, 133, 180, 321–322, 327–328, 333, 336–337
relationship with parents, 15, 18–20, 23, 110–111, 129, 162, 166–167, 190, 212–215, 220, 296, 328–329, 337
religious views of, 20, 22–23, 49, 189, 238, 338
short-term employment of, 92–93, 113, 118, 202–203
and southern identity, xi, xxii, xxvii, 3–4, 5, 6, 10, 34, 51, 52, 205, 237–238, 278, 324, 330–331, 336, 337
as *Southern Patriot* editor, xxii, xxiv, 217–218, 240, 246, 255, 256, 295, 306, 321
tenacity as an activist, xi, xxvii, 327, 329, 330, 331, 333, 336–337, 340–341
in theater and dance, 36–37, 45, 49, 56
trade unionism of, 92–93, 114, 113–114
views on African American leadership and integration, xxi, 211, 223, 251, 301–302, 321, 324, 327, 339
vision of history, 6, 10, 77, 125, 210, 221–222, 290, 326
vision of social change, 303, 340–341
writings of, 19, 23, 37–38, 188–189, 237–240, 299
Braden, Anne and Carl:
  arrests for sedition (1954), xx, 162, 163, 164–165
  arrests for sedition (1967), 307–309
  compatibility of, 106–107, 109
  and financial stability, 111, 114, 202
  housing of young protesters, 130, 295–296, 303, 304
  HUAC subpoenas (1958), 231–232
  as mentors for younger activists, xxiii, 131–132, 303, 305, 306, 330
  in relation to Wade purchase, xx–xxii, 136, 137, 141, 142, 146, 147, 148, 149, 150,

154, 155, 156, 157, 158, 161, 162, 163, 164, 165, 166, 168
and SCEF, 201–202, 206, 208, 209, 211–212, 225, 226, 228, 229, 233, 240, 241, 270, 303, 306, 320–321
shared political commitment of, 103–104, 109, 131, 137
thought of jointly, xxii, 103
threats upon, 141, 149, 154, 161, 167, 170
use of press for civil rights cause, xxiii, 257–258
wedding of, 109–110
Braden, Carl:
1954 sedition arrest, trial, and conviction of, 161–173. (*See also* sedition case, Louisville [1954])
1958 testimony before HUAC, 230–233, 239
anticommunist drives against, xx, 128, 169, 177, 229, 230, 241, 260, 262–263, 276, 285–286, 287, 296, 299
biography of, 84–85
and *Braden v. United States of America*, 234–236, 241, 242, 265, 269–270
center commemorated for, 327
citations for contempt of Congress, 233
co-chairs National Alliance Against Racist and Political Repression, 317
critique of sexism, 111–112, 204
death of, xxiii, 321, 322, 327
and fatherhood, 125, 126, 127, 129–131, 168, 283, 296
first marriage of, 85, 105, 106, 111, 126
influence on Anne Braden, 80, 89, 91, 96, 102, 104, 105, 106, 108, 112, 133, 179–180, 336–337
investigation by southern state investigating committees, 241, 265
newspaper career of, 85, 113, 118, 168, 194–195
ouster from Louisville CIO meeting, 105–106
as pariah in Louisville, xxii, xxiv, 167, 170, 175, 199, 202, 203, 229, 265, 287, 296, 327
personality of, 85, 107–108, 111, 137, 327, 336–337
politics of, 85, 89, 113, 120, 121, 263
posthumous award to, 399 n.40
presidential clemency campaign for, 272–275, 281
prison experiences of, x, 133, 166, 168, 177, 178, 179, 180, 189, 191, 270–272, 275, 280, 282–283
romance with Anne McCarty, 105, 106, 109
seen as more threatening than Anne, 149, 168, 257
working-class identification of, 85, 89, 91, 113, 114–115

See also Braden, Anne and Carl; sedition case, Pike County (1967)
Braden, Elizabeth McCarty, 127, 129, 130, 131, 246, 252, 308, 321, 322, 323
Braden, James McCarty, 126, 128, 129, 131, 136, 149, 150, 156, 157, 162, 166, 168, 177, 192, 213–215, 223, 231, 270, 271, 272, 296–297, 308, 322
Braden, Mary Elizabeth, 84, 110, 127, 168, 190
Braden, Sonia, 85, 127, 165
Branton, Wiley, 285–286, 290
Braun, Theodore, 222–223
Brown v. Board of Education, xx, 63, 86, 135, 136, 139, 143, 145, 146, 147, 176–177, 196, 200, 201, 205, 206, 208, 222, 236, 265, 290
Browning, Joan, 131, 256, 259, 279
Brownmiller, Susan, 319, 391 n.17
Burns, Lester, 307
Butts, Charles, 286

Cable, George Washington, 228
Carroll, Alfred, 107, 100
Carmichael, Stokely, 303
Carter, Gladys, 287
Carver, Ilene, 322–323
Chaney, James, 298, 299
Channon, "Captain" Ralph, 21–22
Chavis, Ben, xi, 315, 316–317, 323
Children of the Confederacy, 19–20
Christian Nationalist Crusade, 101
CIO, 54–55, 61, 62, 65, 67, 68, 77, 85
African Americans in, 54
changed postwar climate for, 89–90, 93, 113
founding of, 25
and Marshall Plan, 98
split in, 114, 115
and Wallace campaign, 98, 105–106
See also labor movement
Citizens' Committee to Preserve American Freedoms, 204, 205
civil liberties, 26, 27, 67, 124, 178, 180, 185, 186, 193, 199–200, 203–204, 206, 208, 209–210, 232, 234, 235, 237, 240, 242, 252, 265, 267, 273, 283, 299
and academic freedom, 267–268, 277, 389 n.47
as battle against anticommunism, 280–281, 339
and "chilling effect" principle, 298, 307
as right of 1930s labor to organize, 339
in the 1960s South, 284–286, 287–288
civil rights:
for Communists, 132
federal policies and, 87–88, 101, 138, 228, 230, 246, 282
Civil Rights Act (1964), 293, 303
Civil Rights Congress, 122–123, 150, 154, 156, 160, 162, 171, 181

civil rights movement, 127, 130, 192, 193, 197, 199, 200, 205, 207
  addresses economic justice, 294, 299
  anticommunism within ranks of, xxiv, 144, 207, 216, 252, 254–255, 262–263, 264–265, 285–286, 299
  apex of, 303
  connection to anti-Vietnam activism, 302–303
  decline of, 313
  invigorated by WWII, 52–53
  as limited by anticommunism, xxviii, 287, 288–291
  nonviolence in, 246, 247–248, 265, 285, 286, 331
  press coverage of, 218–219, 257–258
  public accommodations, 293
  relationship to other 1960s movements, 280, 294, 300, 303–304, 315, 328
  repression against, xxi, xxiii, 309, 314–316
  and rise of Black Power, 299–302, 389 n.2
  role of ideology in, 260–261
  sit-ins, xxiii, 131, 143, 197, 198, 218 245–248, 249–250, 256, 280, 294, 302, 325
  students in, 241, 245, 246–249, 251, 252, 255, 268, 293, 339 (*See also* Student Nonviolent Coordinating Committee)
  whites in, xxi, xxv, 205, 209, 210, 211, 219–220, 224, 227–228, 242, 251–252, 274, 277, 280, 284, 300–302, 331, 344 n.12
  women's leadership in, xxv, 215–216, 290, 344 n.12
Clark, Septima, 223
Coe, John, 232, 235, 265
COINTELPRO, 314, 321
Cold War, xx, 83, 99–100, 116, 229, 286
  as curbed by Supreme Court decisions, 236
  decline in domestic anticommunism of, 203, 268, 316
  decline of anticommunism in South, 309, 313
  espionage cases of, 118, 144, 176
  and gender relations, 44, 102, 149–150, 180
  impact on American left, xxviii, 187, 264, 289–290, 330–331, 335
  impact on Braden children, 127–129
  onset of, 44, 58, 66, 74–75, 76, 87
  as opening for racial reforms, xxv, xxviii, 87, 207, 289
  Red Scare aspect of, xxi, 88, 90, 93, 97–96, 104, 113, 114, 118–119, 144–146, 154, 173, 176, 186, 204, 229, 275, 281, 289–290
  Red Scare in Louisville, xx, 120–121, 135, 143, 154, 156–157, 158, 159, 160, 161, 170, 171, 184, 190, 195, 198, 199

  in relation to liberalism, xxviii, 119, 120, 125, 144, 167, 169, 185, 187, 197, 206, 207, 228, 239, 260, 269, 288–289, 290, 291
  resistance to Red Scare of, 116–117, 175, 181, 186, 192, 193, 203–204, 242, 266, 273, 281 (*See also* civil liberties)
  in South, xxii, xxiv, 59, 60, 75, 77, 84, 89–90, 97, 100, 120, 144–145, 170, 171, 176, 186, 195–196, 198, 200, 204, 211, 220, 224, 227–228, 229–230, 233, 259, 265, 268, 270, 273, 274, 290–291
Collins, Walter, 315–316
Combs, Bert, 308
Combs, Dan Jack, 307
Commission on Interracial Cooperation, 26, 207
Communist Party (CP, CP-USA), 126, 164, 227
  African Americans and, xx, 16–17, 26, 59, 77, 123, 124, 137, 167, 170
  allegiance to Soviet Union, 75, 334
  association with as basis for persecution, 156–157, 161, 162, 169, 170–171, 172, 188, 189, 204, 206, 207, 230, 233, 240–241, 268, 316–317
  and Civil Rights Congress, 124, 171
  "CP Eleven," 119, 120
  and gender relations, 111–112
  impact for broader left of demonization, 75, 144, 235–236, 252, 290, 330–331, 335
  and New Left in 1970s, 321
  and Popular Front, 25–26, 27, 28, 74, 229, 264, 330–331, 334–335
  in post WWII era, 73, 74, 75, 93, 101, 170, 185, 187
  in South, 16–17, 75, 84, 97, 145, 147, 227, 229, 230
  and southern labor movement, 54, 73, 74, 75, 84, 89–90, 91
  role in Progressive Party, 99–100, 118–119, 171
  U.S. membership numbers, 17, 193, 99
Communist Workers Party, 325–326
Confederate "lost cause," 4, 8, 19, 52
Congress of Racial Equality, 144, 249–250, 264, 288
Connor, Eugene "Bull," 27, 72, 73
Corderay, George, 154
Cotton, Helen, 51
Council on Soviet-American Friendship, 189
Crabb, Mattie Owen, 4–5, 6, 7, 8
Crabb, William, 6, 7, 8
Crabbe, Agnes Thorne, 8, 18, 33
Crabbe, Lindsay, 8
Crumlin, Jim, 86–87, 203, 223
Curry, Connie, 259, 260
Curtis, Judge L. R., 156, 157, 159, 169, 177, 195

Dabbs, James MacBride, 239
Dady, Bill, 295, 296
Daily Worker, 156, 169, 227
Dalton, Rev. Albert, 122, 189
Danville Female College: *See* Stratford College
Daughters of the American Revolution, 19
Davis, Angela, 189, 322
    background of charges against, 316
    Bradens' defense of, 316–317
Davis, Sallye, 316
Day Law, 9, 86
    efforts to repeal, 139
DD Club, 30
DeBow's Review, 34
Democratic Party, 18, 288, 291
    1944 Convention and Wallace vice presidential ouster, 55
    1964 convention, 299–300, 302, 313
    1984 convention, 326
    post-WWII schism, 93, 94
Dennis, Peggy, 133
desegregation, rural Kentucky school, 222–223
Dies, Martin, 28
divorce, post-WWII era, 70
Dixiecrats, 100–101, 113
Doctorow, E. L., 175, 198
Dombrowksi, James, 182, 192, 206, 208, 210, 211, 212, 217, 221, 222, 226, 230, 232, 234, 235, 240, 254, 258, 262, 263, 266, 284, 285, 287 294, 295, 297, 298, 322, 327, 338
    ends association with SCEF, 320
    retirement from SCEF directorship, 305
Dombrowski v. Pfister, 297–298, 298
    and "chilling effect" principle, 298, 307
Donner, Frank, 191, 234, 281
draft resistance, 315–316, 317
Draper, Allen, 190
Drennon Springs Hotel, 8
DuBois, W. E. B., 13, 57, 102, 117
Durr, Clifford, 281
Durr, Virginia, 29, 119, 145, 182, 192, 205, 210, 212, 220, 221, 235, 247, 264

Eastland, Sen. John, 54, 145, 182, 207, 229
Edwards, Melvin, 177–178
"Eight of May," 15
Eisenhower, Dwight, 151
Elder, Lillian, 117
Emergency Civil Liberties Committee, 177, 185–186, 187, 232, 233
Eminence, Kentucky, 3–4, 8, 9, 10, 15, 18, 36, 110, 322
Episcopal Church, 102, 122, 338
Episcopal League for Social Action, 189
Episcopal Society for Racial and Cultural Unity, 263
Ethridge, Mark, 71, 80, 157, 158, 211

Evart, Chuck, 41
Evers, Medgar, 293, 294

Fair Employment Practices Commission, 71, 94
FE (United Farm Equipment Workers), 91–92, 100, 114, 115, 116, 118, 173, 212
FE Women's Auxiliary, 115–116
Federal Bureau of Investigation (FBI), 164, 169, 170, 172, 173, 184, 185, 191, 192, 203–204, 213, 229, 237, 275
    and COINTELPRO, 314, 321
    involvement in Pike County sedition charges, 307, 388 n.39
Federated Press, 118, 169, 181, 183, 227, 257
Feminine Mystique, The, cultural context for, 44, 45, 69, 70, 71
feminism, 42, 112, 117–118
    decline in organized, 43
    defined, 351 n.36
    left feminism, 112, 117, 123
    and maternalism, 45–46
    of National Woman's Party, 42–43
    and persistence of feminist thought, 43, 44–45
    See also women's rights movement
Fifth Amendment in relation to CP membership, 161–162, 171, 233, 267
Finlator, Rev. W. W., 241
First Amendment in relation to Congressional investigations, 233, 234, 236, 237
Fitzgerald, Harriet, 39–40, 50, 51, 58, 70, 71, 77, 92, 96, 102, 106, 110, 166, 167, 183, 267
Fitzgerald, Ida, 39, 40, 46, 50, 104, 183
Florida Legislative Investigation Commission, 265, 281
Folsom, James "Big Jim," 66–68, 71, 73, 74, 76
Fontaine Ferry Park, desegregation drive, 295
Ford, I. O., 161, 162, 168, 172, 183, 199
Foreman, Clark, 24, 26, 29, 98, 101, 183, 186, 200, 251
Forman, Jim, 265–266, 278, 286, 299, 300, 301, 304
Fort Harrod, 4, 5
Fort Knox, antiwar organizing at, 306
Fort McClellan, 41, 46, 47, 63
freedom rides, 241, 253, 266, 270, 289
Freedom Summer, Mississippi, 293, 297, 298, 299, 300
    Bradens' role in, 298, 299
Friedan, Betty, 44, 70, 355 n.39

Gandhi Corps, 295
Gazette and Daily, 257
Gelders, Joe, 26–27, 29, 97

GI Bill, 138
Gibson, Rev. Theodore, 281
Gilbert, Louise, 150, 161, 162, 183, 199
Goodman, Andrew, 298, 299
Grace Episcopal Church, 20–22, 167
   Young People's Service League of, 22
Grady, Henry, 15, 52
Great Depression:
   as catalyst for social reform, 20–21,
      24–25, 26, 267, 291
   impact on Anniston, 16
   impact on marriage rates, 36
   women's rights and, 42
Great Gatsby, The, 14
Greensboro Massacre, 325
   legal outcome of, 391 n.35
Grimke, Angelina, 228
GROW project, SCEF's, 314, 318
Grubbs, Millard, 151, 160, 196
Grzelak, Frank and Josephine, 120, 162, 166

Hall, Sam, 22
Hamer, Fannie Lou, 131
Hamilton, A. Scott, 155, 156–157, 158, 159,
      160, 161, 162, 163–164, 165, 167, 169,
      170, 171, 173, 180, 190, 194, 199, 228,
      229, 232, 237, 238
   death of, 195
Hamlett, Ed, 280, 299, 300
Hanisch, Carol, 317–318, 345 n.14
Hardman, Nina, 142
Hayden, "Casey," 131, 255, 281
Heustis, Carl, 154, 160
Higgins, James, 257
Higgins, Lawrence, 157, 169, 170, 173
Highlander Folk School, 25, 145, 192, 216,
      223, 237, 247, 276, 277, 289, 290, 299,
      303
Hill, Joe, 322
Hiss, Algier, 100, 176, 282
Hitler-Stalin Pact, 75, 359 n.50
Hitt, John, 147, 151, 152, 155, 160, 165
Hogan, Lenore, 324
Holt, Len, 249–250, 264
Horton, Myles, 145, 182, 192, 338
House Committee on Un-American
      Activities (HUAC), 84, 130, 169, 184,
      193, 232, 237, 239, 241
   Berkeley protests against, 266, 267
   creation of, 28, 59
   in Hollywood, 93, 176, 204
   investigates SCEF, xxii, 208, 230–231,
      232, 233
   investigates southern civil rights
      movement, 173, 265, 273, 285
   opposition to, 94, 183, 185, 199–200, 204,
      231, 234, 235, 240, 242, 274
   reinvigoration after WWII, 75–76
housing: See segregation, in housing
Hudson, Ben, 140, 141

Hudson, Hosea, 77, 97

Internal Security Act, 124, 144
International Harvester, 91, 115
International Labor Defense, 123, 185
Interracial Hospital Movement, 121–122

Jackson Daily News, 285–286
Jackson, Blyden, 13
Jackson, Jesse, 326
Jefferson County Grand Jury, investigation
      into Rone Court dynamiting, 156–157,
      158–159, 160, 161, 164
Jefferson County police, 147–148, 153, 154
John Birch Society, 270
Johnson, Dorothy, 270
Johnson, Lee Otis, 315
Johnson, Lyman, 86
Johnson, Lyndon, 302, 304
Johnson, Manning, 170
Johnson, Marshall, 69, 78, 79, 80, 107

Kelley, Thomas, 295
Kennedy, John F., presidential
      administration, 274–275, 288–289
Kennedy, Mabel, 33, 38–39, 183
Kentucky, settlement of, 4–6
   Civil War history of, 6–8
Kentucky Alliance (Against Racist and
      Political Repression), xi, 317, 323, 327
Kentucky Civil Liberties Union, 202, 308,
      325
Kentucky Fairness Alliance, 132
Kentucky v. Braden, 191
   outcome of, 194
Kentucky Human Rights Commission, 296
King, Coretta Scott, 216, 253, 260, 261
King, Ed, 255, 256, 258, 266
King, Rev. Martin Luther, Jr., 197, 211, 227,
      239, 246, 249, 268, 289, 297, 302, 325
   assassination of, 313, 315
   association with Bradens, 216, 253, 260,
      261–263, 271, 286, 287, 288
   and Carl Braden clemency campaign,
      272–274
King, Mary, 297
Kinoy, Arthur, 297–298
Kling, Arthur, 202, 209
Kolkin, Miriam, 183
Korean War, 118, 192
Krohne, Liz, 304
Ku Klux Klan, x, xi, 7, 9, 54, 80, 94, 151, 196,
      240, 304, 314, 323
   resurgence of in 1970s, 324–325
   and violence in Greensboro, 325
   See also racial violence
Kunstler, Bill, 297–298, 307, 308

Labor Information Center, 114, 115, 118
labor movement, 25, 26, 304

African Americans and, 54
leftists in, 59–60
and Operation Dixie, 65, 357 n.16
opposition to in post-WWII era, 61–62, 65, 68, 89–90
in South, 26–27, 61
See also CIO; FE
Labor's Voice, 114, 116
LaFollette, Robert, 27
Lamont, Corliss, 185
Lane, Barbara, 95, 110, 183
Lawrence, David, 228
League of Young Southerners, 355 n.46
Letter to White Southern Women, 319–320
Lewis, Fulton, 241
Lewis, John, 143, 382 n.61
liberalism:
alliances with left, 323
and embrace of anticommunism, 93, 97, 99–100, 144, 146, 357 n.11
impact of WWII on in South, 54–55, 65
southern New Deal era, 40, 46, 65
See also Popular Front and Cold War
Little Compton, 187, 231, 239, 253, 322
Lloyd, Jean, 30, 31
Logan, Beverly, 36
Logan, Sumpter, 222–223
Lorch, Grace, 377 n.84
Louisiana Joint Legislative Committee on Un-American Activities, 287, 297
Louisville:
border status of, 7, 13–14, 85–86
race relations in, 8–9
school busing crisis in, 323
Louisville Area Negro Labor Council, 120
Louisville Courier-Journal:
Anita McCarty's letter to, 190
Carl Braden's employment by, 118, 168, 181, 194–195
coverage of Bradens, 142, 146, 165, 239, 317, 327, 328, 334
coverage of race, 142, 143, 146, 196, 211
criticized by national press, 176
criticizes grand jury, 157–158
history of, 79, 80
liberal prestige of, 71
opposes anticommunism, 90, 115, 119, 120–121, 365 n.33
in relation to Wade house purchase, xx, 142, 146, 148, 152, 153
Louisville Defender, 86, 142, 147, 184
Louisville Times, 79, 80, 84, 86, 87, 90, 102, 105, 110, 113, 143, 155, 157, 164, 195
loyalty oaths, 83
in unions, 90
See also Taft-Hartley Act
Lubka, Lew, 162, 168, 199
Lucy, Autherine, 195, 221
Lusky, Louis, 169, 173, 178, 186, 193
Lynes, Carlos, 141

Marxist-Leninist groups, rise of in 1970s, 323–324, 325
massive resistance, 145, 146, 176, 196, 201, 219, 222
Maund, Al, 181, 192, 227
McCarran Internal Security Act: See Internal Security Act
McCarthy, Sen. Joseph, 144, 145, 156, 164, 173, 176, 177, 187, 196, 203, 237, 259, 389 n.4
McCarthyism: See Cold War, Red Scare aspect of
McCarty, Anita Crabbe, 4, 8, 10, 11, 14, 15, 18, 19, 20, 22, 23, 33, 34, 46, 48, 68, 111, 129, 166, 190, 212–214, 296, 321, 328
McCarty, Gambrell, 10, 11, 14, 15, 18, 20, 21, 46, 56, 64, 129, 166, 190, 212–214, 296, 328–329
McCarty, Lindsay, 14, 18, 19, 36, 213, 328
McCarty, Mai, 18
McClellan, John, 389 n.4
McCrackin, Maurice, 225
McDew, Chuck, 279
McFerren, John, 225–226
McGee, Willie, 123–124, 160, 179, 319
McGill, Ralph, 97, 233
McGinty, Anne Poage, 4, 5–6
McSurely, Al, 306–307
continued prosecution of, 389 n.4
McSurely, Margaret, 306–307
continued prosecution of, 389 n.4
Melish, Mary Jane, 189
Melish, William Howard, x, 189, 226–227, 258
Meredith, James, 278–279
Meredith, Jane, 253
Militant Church Movement, 122
Miller, Dorothy, 131, 279
joins SCEF staff, 304
Millis, Walter, 187
Minutemen, 270
Mississippi Freedom Democratic Party, 298, 299, 303
Mitchell, Charlene, x, 316
Monroe "kissing case," 240, 379 n.112
Monsky, Herb, 110
Montgomery bus boycott, xxiii, 201, 202, 215, 221, 227, 248
Moore, Amzie, 224–225
Morgan, Juliette, 220–221, 234
Morris, Aldon, 224
Morris, John, 263–264
Morrow, Gov. Edgar, 163
Moses, Bob, 262, 285, 286, 288, 299, 303
Mulloy, Joe, 306–307, 316
Mulloy, Karen, 306–307

NAACP, 9, 14, 25, 54, 73, 86, 97, 125, 144, 154, 203, 215, 223, 224, 225, 246, 250, 256, 281, 316
Alabama ban on, 209, 230

liberalism of, 59, 288, 293
Nash, Diane, 131, 289
National Alliance Against Racist and Political Repression, x, xi
    formation of, 316–317
National Anti-Klan Network, 325–326
National Book Award, 239
National Committee to Abolish HUAC, 227, 273
National Council of Churches, 299
National Guardian, 181, 183, 219–220, 222, 257
National Lawyers' Guild, 297, 299
National Student Association, 259, 260
National Women's Political Caucus, 319
Nazi Party, 325
Neal, Mildred, 116
Neal, Sterling, 91, 116, 173
New Deal:
    dismantling of in postwar era, 54, 58–59
    as impetus for southern reforms, 24–25, 28–29, 46, 77
    opposed by southern Democrats, 26, 52, 64
    and organized labor, 26, 89, 97, 101, 211, 290, 335
New Left, 132–133, 242, 267, 294, 303
    1970s dissension in, 320, 321
    fragmentation of, 323
"New South" ideology, 52, 56
Nixon, E. D, 215–216, 217
Nunn, Louie, 307

Oberlin, Richard, 164
O'Connor, Harvey, 185, 187, 203, 204, 205, 232, 233, 239, 322
O'Connor, Jessie Lloyd, 187, 239, 322
October League, 321, 326
Old Left, xxvi-xxvii, xxviii, 103, 120, 132–133, 206, 210, 242, 267, 291, 305, 330, 338–339
    composition of, 335
    internal dissension in, 187
    in South, 335
Olden, Rev. J. C., 122
open housing movement, in Louisville, 303, 306
Operation Freedom, 225–226
Oxnam, Bishop Bromley, 241

Palmer Raids, 163
Paschall, Eliza, 288
Patterson, William, 124, 125, 171, 201, 300
peace movement, xxiv, 117, 225, 247, 253, 324
    in 1980s, 324
    against Vietnam war, 280, 302, 306, 315, 316, 318
Pennsylvania v. Nelson, 163, 180, 191, 193–194, 229, 232, 236

Perdue, Rev. M. M. D., 122, 167, 250
Perry, Jennings, 187
Pfister, James, 297–298
Pickett, Clarence, 274
Pittsburgh Courier, 54, 239
Plessy v. Ferguson, 8–9
Poage, Anne: *See* McGinty, Anne Poage.
Poage, William, 5
Pogue, Mary, 5
Popular Front, 74, 75, 77, 80, 132–133, 182, 229, 264
    defined, 359 n.50
    destruction of by Cold War anticommunism, 88, 101–102, 118, 200, 330–331
    origins of, 25–26
    in South, 97, 206–207, 331, 335
    use of term, 339
    and Wallace presidential campaign, 93, 100
Prattis, P. L., 239
prisoners' rights movements, 316–317
Progress in Education, 323
Progressive Party, 94, 120, 124, 157, 171, 181
    and civil rights activism, 98, 100
    in Louisville, 99, 113, 118, 119, 121, 147, 154, 183
    in South, 101
    role of CP in, 358 n.44

racial violence, 9, 13, 25, 54, 62, 72, 87, 149, 152, 198, 208, 224, 227, 240, 258, 277–278, 298, 315, 324–33
    as defense of southern white women, 42, 123, 319
    in Wade purchase, xxi, 142, 143, 146, 148, 149, 152, 156, 159, 165, 197, 198
Rainbow Coalition, 326
Randolph-Macon Institute, 33, 39
    See also Stratford College
Randolph-Macon Woman's College, 39, 40, 46, 253
    cultural climate of, 48–49, 51
    gives award to Anne Braden, 328
    Louisville alumnae group, 184
    prestige of, 47
Rankin, John, 101
Ratliff, Thomas, 307, 308
Reagan, Ronald, 326
Reconstruction, 7, 26, 65
Red Scare:
    Post-WWI, 162
    Post-WWII: *See* Cold War
Report on Economic Conditions of the South, 26, 27, 28
restrictive covenants, 9, 136
Rinehardt, Lawrence 159, 160, 185
Roberts, Ellen, 263
Robeson, Paul, 83–84, 98, 102, 114, 120
Rockwell, Norman, 44

Rone, James, 140, 141, 152, 159, 196
Rone, James Jr. "Buster," 140, 141, 152, 159, 185
Roosevelt, Eleanor, 25, 27, 28, 29, 206, 225, 226–227, 239
Roosevelt, Franklin:
    election of, 16
    and New Deal, 24, 26, 28, 46, 52, 55, 58, 59, 75, 89, 98
    support for organized labor by, 25, 26
    red-baited, 151
Rosenberg, Ethel and Julius, 118, 144, 165, 176, 179, 192, 198
"Rosie the Riveter" image, 44
Rustin, Bayard, 252, 254

Sarachild, Kathie, 317–318
Schoolfield, Lucile, 37, 56, 70, 108, 341
Schwerner, Michael, 298, 299
Scottsboro case, 16, 25, 123, 154
    role of CP in, 17
Seawell, Malcolm, 240
sedition case, Louisville (1954):
    anticommunist atmosphere surrounding, 156–157, 160, 164–165, 167–168, 170
    arrests and indictments, 161–162, 163, 164, 168
    and Carl Braden appeal bond, 177, 179, 186, 190–191
    conviction overturned, 194
    grand jury leading to, 156–161
    lessons from, 180
    outcome of charges, 194, 195
    press coverage surrounding case, 187–188
    press reaction to Braden conviction, 176, 181
    postponements of subsequent trials, 180
    ripple effects of in Kentucky and South, 199, 203, 222, 228–229, 287,
    travels to publicize, xxii, 183–184, 187, 191, 192, 193, 202
    trial of Carl Braden, 169–173, 181
    See also Braden, Anne and Carl; Louisville Courier-Journal; sedition defendants; Wade, Andrew
sedition case, Pike County, Kentucky (1967), 306–309
    courtroom atmosphere of, 308
    defense invokes "chilling effect" principle, 307
sedition defendants (Louisville):
    fightback of, 180–182, 183
    final statement of, 197
    legal defense of, 368 n.98
    lives after case, 199
    unity of, 184
sedition law, Kentucky, 162, 191–192, 194, 307
    declared unconstitutional, 309
    text of, 163

sedition laws, state, 162–163, 191–192, 193–194, 231–232, 240, 377 n.84
Sedler, Robert, 308
Seeger, Pete, 109, 187, 216, 323
segregation:
    in Birmingham, 72–73, 219
    as bolstered by anticommunism, xxii, 139, 145, 147, 151, 158, 159, 165, 170, 171, 176–177, 180, 182, 185, 186, 195–196, 199, 201, 207, 209, 230, 233, 238, 265
    bombing in support of, 152–153, 208, 227, 268, 269, 273, 274, 287, 289–290
    challenges to, xx, 14, 24, 27, 100, 121–122, 124, 135, 136, 142, 143, 149, 150, 154, 195, 198, 207, 218, 222–223, 237–238, 248, 250, 258, 268, 278–279, 293, 295–296
    in education, 86, 121, 136, 196, 197, 201, 222 (See also Day Law; Brown v. Board of Education)
    in housing, 9, 135, 138–139, 152–153, 196, 198
    in late 1960s social movements, 315
    laws pertaining to, 8–9
    in Louisville, 9, 13–14, 85–86, 88, 121, 136, 142, 147, 154, 165, 238
    white southerners' defense of, 62 (See also massive resistance)
Seifert, Marshall, 21–22
Senate Internal Securities Sub-Committee, 76, 144, 145, 176, 185, 204, 207, 229, 230, 232, 235, 298
    Arkansas hearings of in relation to Bradens, 377 n.84
Sentner, Bill and Toni, 126
Seventh Street unions, 92, 94, 106, 114, 115
Shawnee Homeowners Association, 138
Sherrod, Charles, 269
Shirah, Sam, 279–280, 300
Shively, Kentucky, 139–140, 151, 159, 196, 197
Shively Newsweek, 147, 151, 152, 154, 155, 156, 159–160
Shuttlesworth, Fred, 208–209, 216, 217, 218–219, 260, 261, 262, 271, 273, 274, 278, 281, 286
    post-1967 work of, 317, 320, 322, 323
    in SCEF presidency, 283–284, 294, 300
Shuttlesworth, Ruby, 218
Silver, James, 339
Simkins, Modjeska, 230–231, 317, 320
Simonson, Kay and David, 198
Smith, Gerald L. K., 101
Smith, Lillian, 97, 102, 188, 237
Smith Act, 59, 100, 119, 120, 124, 163, 185, 193–194, 203
social gospel movement, 20–21, 189, 335, 338
Socialist Party, 54, 163, 188, 202
South End Savings and Loan, 140, 148, 151

Southern California Civil Liberties Union, 204
Southern Christian Leadership Conference, 209, 211, 216, 217, 249, 261–263, 288, 289, 297, 303
 Anne Braden gives keynote address to, 286
 anti-Klan work of 1970s, 314, 315
 opposition to Vietnam War, 387 n.27
Southern Conference Educational Fund (SCEF), x, xxii, 145, 181, 295, 308
 1963 raid on headquarters of, 297–298
 1970s dissension in, 320–321
 alliances with civil rights leaders, 211, 215–217, 226, 227, 231, 242, 288
 attacks on integrity of, 208, 233–234, 240–241, 285–286, 289, 297, 298
 board and advisory committee, 240
 Bradens, Dombrowski leave, 321
 Bradens join staff of, xxii, 201–202, 206, 208, 209
 and Carl Braden HUAC case, 234–235
 directed by Bradens, 305
 economic justice program of, 294, 303–304
 effectiveness of, 376 n.65
 founding of, 65
 "Freedom and the First Amendment" conference, 281
 "Friends of SCEF," 216
 fundraising for, 212, 215–216, 226–227
 growth of in late 1960s/70s, 304, 306, 317
 and HUAC southern hearings (1958), 230–234
 impact of Black Power upon, 304
 interracialism of, 212, 215, 251–252, 327
 move of headquarters to Louisville, 305–306
 as movement halfway house, 224–226
 nonexclusion policies of, xxii, 182, 226, 229–230
 and "Operation Open Debate," 303
 origins of, 182, 210
 Pikeville, Kentucky, program, 306 (See also sedition case, Pike County, Kentucky [1967])
 politics of, 207, 290–291
 position on Vietnam War, 387 n.27
 purchase of buildings, 305, 317
 relations with women's liberation movement, 317–318
 SCEF Conference on Voting Restrictions, 212, 224, 230
 taken over by October League faction, 321
 on whites organizing whites, 299, 300
Southern Conference for Human Welfare (SCHW), 73, 74, 77, 84, 90, 98, 183, 186, 206, 207, 208, 234, 262
 and anti-poll tax drive, 28, 29
 continuation of southern conference movement from, 145, 182, 294, 324, 327
 founding of, 24, 54, 64, 291
 and race politics, 60, 65, 73, 97, 210, 211, 234, 262, 291, 294
 voice for southern left-liberalism, 54–55, 65, 95
Southern Interagency Group, 285–286
Southern Manifesto, 177, 196
Southern Mountain Project, SCEF's, 304, 306, 314,
 obstacles faced in, 304–305
southern nationalism, 34
Southern Negro Youth Congress, 26, 57, 60, 73, 290
Southern Organizing Committee for Economic and Social Justice (SOC):
 anti-Klan work of, 324–325
 early campaigns of, 324
 mission of, 323–324
 origins of and relationship to SCEF, 323
 shift to nonwhite leadership, 327
Southern Patriot, x, xxii, 5, 65, 181–182, 183, 206, 208, 209, 217–218, 222–223, 237, 240, 246, 249, 252, 255, 256, 260, 264, 275, 295, 301, 334
Southern Regional Council, 207, 230, 260, 285, 288, 328, 387 n.20
Southern Student Organizing Committee, 290, 303
 ambivalence toward SCEF, 387 n.20
 as inheritor of SNCC white student project, 301, 355 n.46
 origins, 280, 300–301
Southern Tenant Farmers' Union, 25
Spiker, LaRue, 150, 161, 162, 199
Spock, Benjamin, 128, 129
St. Stephen's Episcopal Church, 122, 155
Stembridge, Jane, 252–253, 254–255, 256, 264
Sterne, Emma Gelders, 20
Stockholm Peace Appeal, 117, 120
Stone, I. F., 188, 219, 257, 270
Stoney, Bill, 167
Stoney, Jim, 20–22, 167, 189–190
Stovall, Rep. Thelma, 122
Stratford College, 33, 34, 35, 36, 37, 38, 39, 41, 45, 46, 47, 51, 95
Stratford Traveller, 35, 36, 37–38
Strickland, Shirley, 51
Student Nonviolent Coordinating Committee (SNCC), xxiii, 131, 132, 252, 293, 294, 297, 298, 303, 306
 alliances with other student organizations, 266, 279–280
 attacks on in liberal press, 300
 and "beloved community" vision, xxiii, 279, 300, 315, 339
 and turn to Black Consciousness, 301

Bradens' assistance to, 256–257, 258–259, 267
founding of, 249
and integration, 300
as inspiration for wider '60s activism, 266–267, 291, 294
repression of, 314
SCEF funding for, 258–259
relations with SCEF, 252, 254–255, 275, 277, 283, 288, 289, 297
warned away from Bradens and SCEF, 257, 259, 289
shift to all-black- leadership, 301
and Vietnam protest, 303
condemnation of Vietnam War, 387 n.27
white student project, 254–255, 275–280, 301
whites in, 249, 251–252, 253, 277, 279–280, 300–302
exodus of whites from, 304 (See also Southern Student Organizing Committee)
and whites' "reentry problem," 304
women in, xxiii, 131–132, 279
Students for a Democratic Society, 283, 294, 295, 303
suburbanization, post-WWII, 137–138
Subversive Activities Control Board, 144

Tachau, Eric, 148, 197
Taft-Hartley Act, 90, 91, 98
Talmadge, Herman, 54
Thorne, William P., 8
Thrasher, Sue, 260, 290, 300
Triplett, Henry, 268
Truman, Harry S., 117, 151
ascension into vice presidency, 55
origins of anticommunism in administration of, 74, 83, 93, 94, 98, 99, 365 n.28
civil rights actions of, 87, 101
and New Deal, 58–59
Tucker, C. Ewbank, 154, 232, 249, 250, 274
Tucker, Connie, 327
Tyson, Tim, 301

U.S. Civil Rights Commission, 241
U.S. Department of Housing and Urban Development, 138
United Auto Workers, 114, 115, 126, 183
United Black Protective Parents, 323
United Electrical, Radio, and Machine Workers of America (UE), 115
United Nations, 55–56, 58
Uphaus, Willard, 253

Vietnam, U.S. actions in, 302
See also peace movement
Vivian, C. T., 325, 329

Voluntary Civil Rights Commission, 217, 225, 241, 246, 261
voting rights, 7–8, 9, 54, 212, 225, 230, 285, 293, 298, 303, 313, 328, 329

Wade, Andrew, 200, 238, 301
biography, 137
and Braden sedition case, 171, 173, 178, 181, 184
and grand jury investigation, 157, 159, 164, 167, 196, 197, 198, 199
and Rone Court house, xx, 135, 136–137, 139, 140, 141, 147, 148, 149, 150, 151, 152, 153–154, 155
Wade, Charlotte, xx, 136, 141, 148, 149–150, 151, 152, 153, 155, 181, 196, 197, 198, 200, 238
Wade, Rosemary, 150, 152, 153, 160
Wade Defense Committee, 148, 149, 150, 151, 153, 154, 155, 159
Walker, Wyatt Tee, 262–263, 273, 274, 281, 288
Wall Between, The, x, xxiv, 50–51, 78, 188–189, 209, 213, 232, 237–240
Wallace, Carla, 132
Wallace, Gov. George, 287, 326
Wallace, Henry, 55, 58, 66, 74, 83, 93, 94, 97, 98, 99–100, 101, 102, 119, 181
War on Poverty, 304
Warren, Earl, 236
Washington Committee for the Louisville Cases, 183
Watergate, 324
"We Are Seven" Club, 29–30
We Shall Overcome, 216
Weber, Palmer, 183
Wednesday Study Club, 20
Weitzman, Danny, 191
Wells, Lyn, 326
West, Don, 192, 377 n.84
West End Community Council, 287, 303
See also open housing movement
West End, Louisville's, xxiv, 138–139, 150, 198, 223, 287, 315, 327
Wetherby, Gov. Lawrence, 122
White Citizens' Councils, 196, 206, 210, 220, 222, 225, 325
Montgomery Citizens' Council, 221
"white flight," 139, 223, 287
White, Walter, 25
Wilkinson, Frank, 203–204, 232, 233, 270, 272–273, 274, 275, 282, 283, 322
Williams, Aubrey, 76–77, 98, 145, 182, 192, 200, 205, 206, 207, 215, 234, 235, 274
on organizing white southerners, 208, 212
conflicts with SCEF direction, 226–227
Williams, Robert, 246, 247
Wilmington Ten, xi, 315, 316
Wilt, Stanley, 159, 185

Wofford, Harris, 274
Wolfe, Thomas, 49–50
Women for Peace, 116–117, 123, 247
women's colleges:
    and female romantic friendships, 40
    and persistence of feminist thought, 43
    ideology of women's higher education
        and, 39
    southern, 34–35, 47, 48
Women's International League for Peace
        and Freedom, 118, 150, 183, 247, 264,
        303
women's liberation movement, 315, 317–318
    Anne Braden and, 318–319, 320
    critiques of singular focus of, 318,
        319–320, 324
    emergence of, 317
    relationship to southern civil rights
        movement, 317, 328
women's rights movement, of early twentieth
        century, xxi, 19, 34, 112
    decline of, 42–43, 44
    reborn in second wave, 133
    in South, 42
    from suffrage to feminism, 42
    See also women's liberation movement
Wood, Jim, 262

World War II:
    and Allied victory in Europe, 56
    draft registration for, 35
    growth in marriage and birth rates
        during, 36, 44
    impact on Anne Braden's college choices,
        34
    impact on race relations and
        consciousness, 53, 101
    impact on southern economy, 52–53
    and popular culture, 37, 45–46
    prompts conservative reaction, 44, 54, 55,
        69–70, 71, 101
    U.S. entry into, 36
    women's college enrollments and, 44
    women's employment and, 39, 42, 43, 44

Yater, Marjorie and George, 169
Yates v. U.S., 203
Young, Andrew, 289
Young Women's Christian Association, 18, 51

Zellner, Bob, 275–279, 280, 285, 299, 314,
    joins SCEF staff, 304
Zellner, Dottie: See Miller, Dorothy
Zollinger, Robert, 161, 164, 168, 172, 173,
    178